Local communities in the Victorian census enumerators' books

The cover illustrations follow the career of one of the army of census enumerators recruited to produce the CEBs. The photographs show William Woollings, enumerator for part of the parish of Orsett, Essex, in 1861, together with the Mill house in which he lived. The map showing the village of Orsett is taken from the 1st edition of the Ordnance Survey six-inch series. The final piece of the jigsaw is an illustration of the Census Office in Craig's Court London, where the CEBs were eventually sent to be indexed and analysed in order to produce the official reports presented to Parliament.

The photographs of William Woollings and his home are reproduced with the kind permission of Barbara Woollings, the great-grand-daughter of William. The picture of the Census Office is taken from the *Illustrated Times*, 13 April, 1861.

Local communities in the Victorian census enumerators' books

Edited by

DENNIS MILLS
and
KEVIN SCHÜRER

A LOCAL POPULATION STUDIES SUPPLEMENT

Published in 1996 by
LEOPARD'S HEAD PRESS LIMITED
1–5 Broad Street, Oxford, OX1 3AW.

ISBN 0 904920 33 X

The publication of this volume has been assisted by an award fom the Marc Fitch Fund, which is gratefully acknowledged.

Printed in Great Britain by
Progressive Printing (UK) Limited, Leigh-on-Sea, Essex

Contents

List of Contributors

TOM ARKELL *Formerly Lecturer in Arts Education, University of Warwick*

MARK BRAYSHAY *Lecturer in Geography, University of Plymouth*

VALERIE BURTON *Associate Professor of Maritime History, Memorial University of Newfoundland, Canada*

JENNY DYER *Teacher of History at Cadbury Sixth Form College, Birmingham, and Open University Tutor*

CHRISTINE HALLAS *Director of the Leeds Centre for Victorian Studies and Head of the School of Humanities and Cultural Studies, Trinity and All Saints' College, Leeds*

ADRIAN HENSTOCK *County Archivist, Nottinghamshire*

EDWARD HIGGS *Wellcome Lecturer in the History of Medicine, University of Exeter*

P. R. ANDREW HINDE *Lecturer in Demography, University of Southampton*

NEIL M. HOWLETT *Formerly student of Jesus College, University of Cambridge*

MELVYN JONES *Lecturer in Geography, Sheffield Hallam University*

DENNIS MILLS *Staff Tutor in Social Sciences, Open University*

AUDREY PERKYNS *Retired teacher, former graduate and research student of Royal Holloway College, University of London*

CHARLES RAWDING *Head of Geography at Waltham Toll Bar School, South Humberside*

JOHN B. REDFERN *Retired Secondary School Teacher and former Open University student*

OSAMU SAITO *Lecturer in Economic History, Hitotsubashi University, Japan*

KEVIN SCHÜRER *Lecturer in History, University of Essex*

RUTH SCOTT *Formerly Lecturer in Geography, Roehampton College of Education*

ROGER SMITH *Formerly Professor at the Department of Surveying, Nottingham Trent University*

IAIN C. TAYLOR *Local Historian, also with interests in Family History*

DAVID THOMSON *Lecturer in History, Massey University, New Zealand*

WILLIAM TURNER *Formerly a mature student of the Open University*

NOREEN VICKERS *Librarian by profession, currently researching for a Ph.D.*

MARTIN B. WHITE *Formerly Research student, University of Edinburgh*

JOHN WHYMAN *Lecturer at the Centre for Economic History, University of Kent at Canterbury*

BOGUSIA WOJCIECHOWSKA *Formerly Research student, University of Kent at Canterbury*

MINORU YASUMOTO *Lecturer in Economic History, Komazawa University, Japan*

Foreword and acknowledgements

Most books of this kind are a communal effort, and this one is no exception. Over two dozen authors have been involved, as well as other helpers and advisers. However, my first acknowledgement must be to thank my co-editor, Dr Kevin Schürer, for the tremendous amount of work that he has devoted to ensure that this volume appears in print. Dr Schürer has not only contributed to the work of writing the editorial introductory chapters, but also ploughed his way through the tedious job of correcting earlier texts to conform with the current style. The house style of *Local Population Studies* has changed subtlely several times since No. 8 came out in Spring 1972, when John Whyman's article was published — the oldest piece of work in this volume. Dr Schürer has had to keep a sharp look-out for statements that the passage of time have made anachronistic, notably announcements such as 'the 1881 census enumerators' books will be open to the public in three years' time', and has made editorial additions drawing attention to subsequently-published material, where appropriate. The labour-intensive task of compiling the text of the accumulative bibliography has also fallen to Dr Schürer, as well as that of contacting authors and copyright holders, and of carrying out most of the negotiations with the Trustees of the Marc Fitch Fund.

The contributing authors must also be thanked for revising their work, many supplying illustrative material not originally published in *LPS*. My colleagues on the editorial board of *LPS* provided both practical support and helpful comments, especially Terry Gwynne and Geoffrey Stevenson who read through the entire text more than once. Matthew Woollard also read the entire typescript and offered much valuable comment. Ruth Bridgen of the Cambridge Group for the History of Population and Social Structure helped type some of the material, and Fiona Lewis carried-out copious editorial changes to the text. Dr E. Higgs also kindly made a proof copy of his book *A clearer sense of the census*, (HMSO, 1996) available to the editors. Thanks are also due to Gilly Maude who copy-edited the text and to Jane Van Tassel who provided the index. The Department of History at the University of Essex, in which the *LPS* General Office is located, is also acknowledged for its support.

The illustrative material reproduced in the volume has been taken from a number sources. All of the extracts from the census enumerators' books (Figures 1.1, 6.1, 27.4, 27.6, 27.8, 27.9, see text for PRO document references) are Crown copyright material and are reproduced with the permission of Her Majesty's Stationery Office. The extract from the Cardington listing of 1782 (Figure 16.1) is reproduced with the kind permission of the Bedfordshire Record Office, and that of the tithe map for Ashbourne (Figure 29.1) with the permission of the Derbyshire County Record Office. Figures 28.1 and 28.2 are both taken from R. J. Dennis, *English industrial cities of the nineteenth century* (1984, pp. 226–7), and we are grateful to Cambridge University Press for permission to reproduce them. We also acknowledge the Sutcliffe Gallery, Whitby, for granting permission to reproduce a photograph taken by Frank M. Sutcliffe (Figure 30.1) and Western Morning News Co. Ltd for the abstract from the *Western Morning News* (Figure 27.2).

Lastly, it should be noted that the publication of this volume has been assisted by an award from the Marc Fitch Fund, which is gratefully acknowledged. Equally, a debt is owed to Roy Stephens of Leopard's Head Press whose help has enabled this volume to appear in print.

Dennis Mills
October, 1996

1

Communities in the Victorian censuses: an introduction

D. R. MILLS AND K. SCHÜRER

Community and the censuses

Community is a word that is often used but whose meaning is not always clear. This is true when it is applied to the past as well as to the present. For most people, the word community conjures up an instant picture, but, given that the images will vary from person to person, and that many of these images are framed by a certain set of values, it is difficult to define 'community' in a few short words. And, if it is difficult to describe what we mean by community, it is almost impossible to define it coherently and agree to a set of criteria by which to measure it. It is a term with many uses. In a large number of cases it implies an intention to consider either the whole population of a particular place, or as near a representative cross-section as possible. The 'places' in question are usually discrete geographical entities – villages, towns, or specific areas within them – however, community history may also frequently involve the study of organisations within a particular place, such as friendly societies, denominational groups, schools, hospitals, and so forth. In all these situations the census enumerators' books (CEBs) provide either an unrivalled source, or at least a very valuable framework, depending on the task in hand. Certainly they make possible community history of a quality different from that of periods before and after their availability.[1]

The taking of a national census began in 1801 and has continued at decadal intervals ever since, with the exception of the wartime year of 1941, and with the addition of the 10 per cent sample census of 1966. The first four censuses were administered on the basis that enumerators were asked only for simple numerical information such as totals of males and females and rudimentary information on occupations and ages. Nevertheless, enumerators' working lists of names, usually of household heads, have survived in a small number of instances and resemble the *ad hoc* community listings of earlier and contemporary generations which are equally thin on the ground.[2]

1 Drake *et al. Getting into community history.*
2 Gibson and Medlycott, *Local census listings.*

The 1831 census saw an increase in the numbers of questions asked, and, after the setting up of the General Registry Office in 1837, a proposal for a further increase led to a fundamental debate about how the enumeration should be conducted. There was serious concern that enumerators might make up information if the system did not allow for the possibility of checking their work. The solution adopted was to require enumerators to record the names of all individuals enumerated, which made it possible for households to be revisited and the information checked.[3]

Thus, in 1841, for the first time, enumerators were given forms, termed householders' schedules, for issue to all the householders in their districts. Enumerators were expected to help household heads where necessary, this being at a time long before compulsory education – indeed the 1841 census must surely be the first occasion on which the government required information from every household in the country. After census night the enumerators collected the schedules and transferred the information in them to CEBs. With a few exceptions the schedules were destroyed, but the CEBs, after local checking, were sent to the Registrar General's Census Office, established on a temporary basis under the auspices of the General Registry Office in Somerset House, London. Here they were subjected to statistical analysis for the production of published census reports.[4]

Under a 100-year confidentiality rule, the CEBs, transferred to the Public Record Office (PRO), have gradually been made available for public scrutiny. As late as the 1960s, the PRO produced the original books themselves, but owing to heavy use, the public may now only use these in the form of microfilms or microfiches. However, this has the compensating advantage that copies have been acquired by many local archive offices and reference libraries, and even by family history societies.[5] Most libraries have print-out facilities allowing the researcher to take copies of CEB pages home for intensive study. Although this may seem expensive, a great deal of time is saved. Interpretation of handwriting does not have to be done on the spot and is made easier by placing pages side by side for purposes of comparison.

Partly because of the war and its aftermath, historians were slow to avail themselves of the 1841 CEBs when they were first open to inspection, and even those of 1851 were not as eagerly anticipated on the first day of 1952 as has since become the tradition. The earliest known academic article to make use of the CEBs appeared in the *British Medical Journal* in 1951, and Lawton's article of 1954 represents one of the very first research reports based substantially on the CEBs.[6] After

3 Drake, 'The census', 25.
4 These are listed in the appendix to chapter 8, below.
5 Gibson, *Census returns on microfilm*.
6 Taylor, 'The taking of the census'; Lawton, 'Economic geography of Craven'.

this there was an accelerating build-up of activity apparently reaching a peak in the second half of the 1970s.[7]

Research projects using the CEBs have tended to fall into two quite disparate groups. Large-scale studies by PhD students and university teams, from the late 1960s making use of mainframe computers, have usually been focused on Victorian cities and have frequently used a scientific sample of households across a city.[8] Small-scale studies by 'local historians' and local history classes have, conversely, been characterised by their interest in communities up to only the size of small market towns or industrial settlements, and have seldom used a sampling strategy. Relatively few studies have examined small sections of large towns. Ironically, the proliferation of personal computers has not led to an increase in the number of publications based on the CEBs, a state of affairs for which two reasons may be suggested. For the professional historian and the social scientist, both the source and the quantitative approach have had to compete with other 'fashions', whilst at the popular level, the continuing rise of family history has overshadowed the use of CEBs in local history projects. As against this, an encouraging recent development is the publication of the first of a series of substantial books based on a computerised study of the whole of Hertfordshire in 1851, carried out at the University of Hertfordshire.[9]

There has, however, been a steady stream of articles based on the CEBs in the pages of *Local Population Studies* since the appearance of its first number in the autumn of 1968, and its editorial board feels the time is ripe to bring many of these studies together in order to encourage the further exploitation of census material. After all, the surface of this great reservoir of data has so far hardly been disturbed by academic activities, even if we agree that, broadly speaking, reliable methodologies have been established.

Furthermore, there has been a disappointing reluctance among many census researchers to compare their results with other research addressing similar questions. We hope the present volume will provide many points of comparison in a convenient form, and would go so far as to suggest to 'beginners' that they deliberately set out to model their work on an existing publication so that direct comparisons can be made between at least two districts. In this way, the distinction between the unique and the general experience may begin to emerge more clearly. Yet equally, this need not, indeed should not, inhibit further innovations in the use of the CEBs.

7 Mills and Pearce, *People and places*, 7.
8 See, for example, the various cases cited in Dennis, *English industrial cities*.
9 Goose, *Hertfordshire in 1851*.

The undermentioned Houses are situate within the Boundaries of the [Page 1

Civil Parish [or Township] of	City or Municipal Borough of	Municipal Ward of	Parliamentary Borough of	Town or Village or Hamlet of	Urban Sanitary District of	Rural Sanitary District of	Ecclesiastical Parish or District of
St. Michael	Lincoln	Upper	Lincoln		Lincoln		St. Michael

No. of Schedule	ROAD, STREET, &c., and No. or NAME of HOUSE	HOUSES: Inhabited	HOUSES: Uninhabited (U.), or Building (B.)	NAME and Surname of each Person	RELATION to Head of Family	CONDITION as to Marriage	AGE last Birthday of Males	AGE last Birthday of Females	Rank, Profession, or OCCUPATION	WHERE BORN	If (1) Deaf-and-Dumb (2) Blind (3) Imbecile or Idiot (4) Lunatic
1	45. Steep Hill	1		George E. Dunkerton	Son	Unm	10		Scholar	Battersea, Surrey	
				Ernest A. do	Son	Unm	7		Scholar	S. Nicholas, Lincoln	
				Edward B. do	Son	Unm	3			S. Nicholas, Lincoln	
2	46. Steep Hill	1		Henry M. Brummitt	Head	Mar	[illegible]		~~Carver, Gilder,~~ Picture Frame maker	Lincoln	
				Elizabeth do	wife	Mar		38		Cammeringham, Lincolnsh.	
				Edith do	daur.	Unm		9	Scholar	Lincoln	
				Kate do	daur.	Unm		8	Scholar	Lincoln	
				Frank do	Son	Unm	7		Scholar	Lincoln	
				Henry do	Son	Unm	5		Scholar	Lincoln	
				Elizabeth do	daur.	Unm		4		Lincoln	
				Walter do	Son	Unm	2			Lincoln	
				Mary F. do	daur	Unm		6 mo		Lincoln	
3	47. Steep Hill	1		Robert Lee	Head	Mar	62		Tailor and News Agent	Alford, Lincolnshire	Deaf in one ear
				Susanna Lee	Wife	Mar		57		North Elmham, Norfolk	
				Frederick Chapman	Boarder	Unm	46		Tailor	Downham Market, Norfolk	Deaf in one ear
4	48. Steep Hill	1		Jacob Brown	Head	Mar	57		Shoemaker	Doncaster, Yorkshire	
				Jane do	Wife	Mar		73		Billinghay, Lincolnsh.	
5	49. Steep Hill	1		Frederick Day	Head	Mar	45		Joiner	Colchester, Essex	
				Emma do	Wife	Mar		38		Campsea Ashe, Suffolk	
				Caroline do	daur.	Unm		12		Lincoln	
				Elizabeth do	daur	Unm		9		Lincoln	
				Richard do	Son	Unm	7			Lincoln	
				Nancy do	daur	Unm		4		Lincoln	
6	50. Steep Hill	1		Jane Bingham	Head	W.		60		Lincoln	
				Charles do	Son	Unm	20		Cabinet maker	Lincoln	
	Total of Houses...	6		Total of Males and Females...			13	12			

NOTE.—*Draw the pen through such of the words of the headings as are inappropriate.*

* See the last Entry

Eng— Sheet B.

Caption for Figure 1.1

This is the first page of the enumerator's book for the parish and enumeration district (ED) of St Michael in the Upper Ward of the City of Lincoln in 1881. The enumerator is himself a figure of interest since, if identification is correct, he was only 17, below the statutory minimum of 18 for enumerators. His first name is a little difficult to read in his book, but he is almost certainly the John Chesterton Holmes, reporter, who was residing at the same date in his father's household at 16, Flaxengate, St Martin's Parish, a few hundred yards away from the ED in which he worked. His father was none other than Henry Holmes, Registrar of Births, Deaths, and Marriages for the Lincoln District!

Source: PRO RG 11/3243, f. 118.

Geographically, the articles reprinted in this volume reflect the concentration of those found generally in *LPS*. In any case, the censuses of Ireland and Scotland were administered in accordance with slightly different criteria from England and Wales, with the two countries each having their own Registrar General, independent of the GRO in London. Articles making use of the Irish and Scottish CEBs are usually to be found in the respective national history journals.[10]

Characteristics of the CEBs

Before moving on to the reprinted articles it is desirable to consider briefly the major characteristics of the CEBs as an historical source, whilst recognising that this is ground already well trodden.[11]

The first and most fundamental point is that the CEBs are not strictly speaking an original source in the same sense as land tax assessments or tithe and enclosure awards or parish registers. The enumerator may have influenced what a householder recorded on his or her schedule (the original document), and, in any case, this information was sometimes edited by an enumerator as it was transferred to the CEB. The latter ranks as a transcription of an original document, and therefore, strictly speaking, is not an original source itself.

A second point is that, although the census in principle contained the whole population of the country on a single night, this did not apply at the level of local communities, since there were always some individuals away from their places of normal residence. Whilst for the censuses of 1841–61 the numbers of absentees were generally recorded, little further information was set down. Thus the British census falls into the category of what is termed a *de jure* enumeration, as opposed to *de facto*. In other words, individuals were recorded *in situ* on census night rather than being allocated to the places where they 'normally'

10 Details of work on Irish and Scottish CEBs can be found in Mills and Pearce, *People and places*. See also Collins, 'Analysis of census returns'; Collins and Pryce, 'Census returns'; Flinn, *Scottish population*; Royle, 'Irish manuscript census records'.

11 Armstrong, 'Social structure'; Drake, 'The census'; Tillott, 'Sources of inaccuracy'; Lawton, *Census and social structure*; Mills, *Guide*; Mills and Pearce, *People and places*; Higgs, *Making sense* and *Clearer sense*; Lumas, *Making use*; and Mills and Drake, 'The census, 1801–1991'.

resided, if different. At a community level, this may sometimes have important consequences.[12]

A third basic point is to emphasise that a census is fundamentally different from the 'running record' of vital events such as those in parish registers. Even the study of consecutive censuses will miss many movements into and out of an enumeration district, whether by virtue of migration, or births and deaths. A striking example can be found in the churchyard at Canwick, Lincolnshire, where stand the headstones of Fanny, Annie, William and Eva, the children of farmer Sleightholme, none of whom survived their second birthday and none of whom appears in the 1871 or 1881 CEBs, although their parents appear in both.

What then do the CEBs tell us? Starting with that of 1881, whose format is illustrated in Figure 1.1 above, the page is headed by an area description.[13] Several slots have been filled in, as is often the case in an ancient city like Lincoln, with several parishes as well as electoral wards. In country areas the administrative geography might be a good deal simpler, especially where agricultural townships were coterminous with ecclesiastical parishes. Below the area descriptions come the 10 column headings indicating the personal details recorded:

1. *No. of Schedule.* In our example, notice the first address is 45, Steep Hill and the schedule number is 1, with house numbers descending as schedule numbers go up. This suggests, as is in fact the case, that the street was split between two ancient parishes, and, therefore, two enumeration districts. The asterisk in the margin was inserted by the enumerator to draw attention to additional information about this household which he had added at the end of his district – a glance at the first entry in Figure 1.1 reveals that the parents' details were missing.

2. *Road, Street, &c. and No. or Name of House.* In rural areas there is often little or no information here, for the simple reason that it did not exist. In urban areas, beware of subsequent changes of street name and the renumbering of houses. It should not be assumed that enumerators entered the information from their schedules in any specific geographical order, even though they were supposed to number schedules as they were delivered.[14]

3. *Houses.* Inhabited houses in the left-hand division of the column are a useful aid in distinguishing between households and so-called 'housefuls', the latter term being used when there was more than one

12 This point is taken up by Burton in chapter 6, below.
13 Mills and Drake, 'The census, 1801–1991', 37; Higgs, *Making sense*, 133–4; Higgs, *Clearer sense*, 198–200 all give fuller information.
14 Tillott, 'Sources of inaccuracy', 96.

separate household in the same dwelling.[15] Uninhabited houses and those being built were recorded in the right-hand division and helped in providing a rough check against population fluctuations.

4. *Name and Surname of each Person.* A straightforward entry as a rule, provided the handwriting is clear. Difficult handwriting is compounded by the common practice of putting ditto marks for surnames on lines below the household head.

5. *Relation to Head of Family.* Most entries present no difficulty. One of the commonest problems is the appearance of daughter-in-law and son-in-law in early censuses instead of the more modern stepdaughter and stepson. Confusion can usually be avoided by reference to names and ages. Whilst boarder and lodger were supposed to be distinguished by only the former taking meals with the family, in practice it is very doubtful if this was a consistent use. Therefore, these two relationships have to be treated as one. In Figure 1.1 notice in household 3 that Frederick Chapman, a single man fairly obviously working for the household head, is listed as boarder. In such circumstances, one can well imagine that he took his meals with his employer and the latter's wife, and had not negotiated separate cooking facilities for himself. The term visitor begs the question as to how long for, and some authors exclude visitors from further analysis. Finally, notice the archaic use of the term head of family, where head of household is now used, indicating that servants, boarders, etc were embraced, as well as non-conjugal kin.

6. *Condition as to Marriage.* Generally straightforward, although the entries usually appear in abbreviated form. Where no entry is made, as with many teenagers, it seems safe to assume the person had never been married. The enumerator in Figure 1.1 had gone to the unnecessary trouble of entering 'unm' against even the names of babes-in-arms!

7. *Age last birthday.* This is divided into two sub-columns, with the age of males being entered in the left hand side and females the right. Census Office checkers' marks and poor handwriting make some ages difficult to read, and very occasionally there is evidence that the age was entered in the wrong column. The accuracy of the stated age is

15 This termed was coined by Laslett, see 'Introduction', 23–8, 34–9. The identification of households in the CEBs is complicated by the fact that the GRO's definition of this term and their instructions to enumerators, were both ambiguous and inconsistent over time. This has frustrated historians' efforts to define common household units from census to census. See Anderson, 'Standard tabulation procedures', 142–3 and Tillott, 'Sources of inaccuracy', 104–5, as well as Higgs, 'The PRO', 103–5 and 'Structuring the past', who is dismissive of these attempts. An overview of the changing definitions is provided in chapter 23. See also Higgs, *Making sense*, 58–62; *Clearer sense*, 64–71.

another matter.[16] In Figure 1.1 Elizabeth Day's age (schedule 5) was omitted, probably by chance. There are two places where the enumerator nearly made the mistake of writing female ages in the male column – Elizabeth Brummitt (schedule 2) and Jane Brown (schedule 4). The checker's mark on the age of Henry Brummitt almost obscures the figure 38 entered.

8. *Rank, Profession, or Occupation.* This column is at the same time the most used in census analysis and contains the most conceptually complex entries. At the root of some of the difficulties lie the multiple intentions indicated by the title. Thus the insertion of a 'rank' such as 'lady' or 'gentleman' or 'magistrate' usually implied the absence of a gainful occupation, but some other ranks such as 'admiral' or 'colonel' are much more complicated, e.g., was he retired, on half-pay, or fully committed to the service? Sometimes these statuses are indicated. As to occupation, suffice it to note here the relative lack of information about part-time workers, notably married women and young people residing with their parents. The term 'scholar' was entered in the occupation column, but circumstantial evidence, especially in earlier censuses, of the way this term was used (e.g., for children under five), suggests that it is not necessarily a reliable variable. How many days of the week and how many weeks in the year the child attended, and whether it was a genuine school, rather than a disguised sweat-shop, were not recorded. In 1841, the inclusion of 'independent means' led to many people of very slender resources sharing this description with retired professionals, gentry, and the like, and this problem also occurs in later censuses. In Figure 1.1, Henry Brummitt's occupational entry of 'carver, gilder and picture frame maker', and more especially Robert Lee's (schedule 3) more straightforward duality of occupation as 'tailor and newsagent', are good examples of how conscientious householders and enumerators could give the historian a fuller picture than the minimum response.

9. *Where born.* This should include county and place in that order if the enumeration district and the place of birth were both in England and Wales. Otherwise the country of birth was sufficient, although more detail is often given especially for birthplaces in Ireland and Scotland. In Figure 1.1, the enumerator chose to write the information as for a postal address, and not in the prescribed form of county name first, followed by place. In the case of Lincoln-born people, he entered the parish for two children on the first schedule, but not for anyone further down. Many people in a large city may not have known the name of the native parish, nor in country districts left long ago were they always sure of the precise place of birth, e.g., like one of our

16 This issue is treated in chapters 9 and 12 by Thomson and Perkyns, respectively.

grandfathers, they may have confused the first village remembered with the true birthplace.

10. *If Deaf-and-Dumb, Blind, Imbecile or Idiot, Lunatic.* The exact wording of this column covering physical disabilities changed more than any other in the Victorian censuses, details of which are given in Table 1.1 below. Academic use of the information in this column has been very limited, in part as a result of the generally-held unreliabliability of the answers on account of the fact that they were not subject to medical oversight.[17] Notice in Figure 1.1 that the two tailors were said to be deaf in one ear – a good example of the ambiguity of entries in this column. Some of the descriptions appear occasionally in the occupation column, presumably as an explanation for the lack of an occupation.

There were minor variations in the headings through the period 1841–1901, summarised in Table 1.1. Of particular note are those of 1841 and 1891–1901. The 1841 census was the first to make use of householders' schedules and represented a transition between the very simple censuses of 1801–31 and the more fully developed model employed from 1851. Less information was sought in relation to birthplaces and ages, and the relationship column was absent.[18] Therefore, unless there are special circumstances suggesting otherwise, avoid using the 1841 census. In 1891 and 1901, extra questions were asked about employment status, but as these were inconsistently answered the occupational data afforded by that census is, on balance, no better than that of earlier censuses.[19] Of greater reliability and significance in 1891 was the beginning of the collection of information on housing, the numbers of rooms in houses with less than five rooms being recorded.

The CEBs in context

Specialised and intensive use of the CEBs will become evident from reading the chapters which follow, but the wider use of the source in the study of local communities also needs consideration. Now that so many census indexes have been published by family history societies, as well as transcriptions, it is much easier to link individuals mentioned in other sources with their entries in the CEBs. However, great care should be exercised to ensure that correct, or at least plausible, nominal

17 For an exception see, Benjamin, 'Human afflictions', plus a letter on the subject in *Local Population Studies*, 37 (1986), 55–6.

18 Higgs, *Making sense*, 109–13 and 120–6; and Higgs, *Clearer sense*, 175–87 have descriptions and facsimiles of all the formats used from 1841 to 1901. Armstrong, 'The CEBs: a commentary', 73–81, contains facsimiles of instructions to enumerators and of CEB page formats for 1841–1871.

19 See Schürer, 'The 1891 census'; Crompton, 'Changes in rural service occupations' and below.

Table 1.1 Structure of the nominal pages in CEBs: England and Wales, 1841–1891

Description of column	Variations
Number of schedule	Not in 1841.
Address information	In 1841 the term 'place' was used, but longer headings produced similar responses.
Houses, inhabited, uninhabited and building	Not in 1841 or 1851. In 1901 inhabited, in occupation, not in occupation and building.
Number of rooms occupied if less than five	Only in 1891 and 1901.
Name and surname	'Names' in 1841.
Relation to head of family	Not in 1841.
Condition (as to marriage)	Not in 1841.
Ages of males and females	In 1881–1901 'age last birthday', but this was not a real change.
Rank, profession or occupation	In 1841 'profession, trade, employment, or of independent means'. In 1891 and 1901 'rank' was dropped.
Employer, employed, neither employer nor employed (three columns)	In 1891 only.
Employer, worker, or own account	In 1901 only.
If working at home	In 1901 only.
Where born	In 1841 whether born in the same county as residence, or in Scotland, Ireland or Foreign Parts.
Whether deaf-and-dumb, blind, imbecile or idiot, lunatic	None required in 1841; limited to blind and deaf-and-dumb in 1851 and 1861. In 1901 'feeble-minded' instead of 'idiot'.
Language spoken	In Wales only in 1891 and 1901, the question being limited to English, Welsh, or both. Children under three excluded in 1901.

Source: Higgs, *Making sense*, 76–7, 109–13. Higgs also reprints examples of specimen pages of CEBs from 1841 to 1901 (pp. 120–6). There is similar material in his *Clearer sense*, 90–1, 175–87.

record linkage is achieved. Frequently there are several persons of the same name in the CEBs of even a small town or village, when there appears to be only one person of that name mentioned in other documents. Some can easily be eliminated on grounds of extreme age, or marital status, or occupational description, but success in eliminating all the remaining competing possibilities is not assured.[20] Conversely, specialist students of the census should be aware of the desirability of making links in the opposite direction, at least with more convenient sources such as directories, since these will fill out the picture of many individuals cryptically described in the census.

To return to the points made about community history at the beginning of this chapter, a case can be made out for using census material in a very wide range of studies of Victorian communities. In the first place, it is important to take account of the size of the chosen community relative to neighbouring places, and relative to the same place today. Whether or not the population was rising or falling in the study period is also relevant, since rapidly expanding communities would contain over-average proportions of children and in-migrants, whilst declining communities would be ageing and static. Comparisons with national or maybe regional trends will help to put local trends into perspective, but since national trends are an average of widely divergent circumstances, other comparisons, such as with county totals, or with a ring of neighbouring communities, are also desirable. The sex balance is also a fundamental criterion, since it is associated with local biases in employment: male-oriented in agricultural areas and where heavy industry existed, female-oriented in well-established towns and in textile areas. Such matters are perhaps better researched from the printed census reports, rather than the CEBs themselves.[21]

Any general history of a community which concentrates on the activities of an elite can be immeasurably improved by careful use of information found in the CEBs. The size and structure of a prominent individual's household is not generally available in other sources, and yet may be among the most revealing 'facts' about them. In a political study it will be interesting, possibly important, to discover the origins of the 'actors', whether they are natives, and if incomers, from how far. Their occupational description in the CEBs may establish the number of their employees and the information as to age may usefully confirm what is known or suspected from other sources. Equally, the exact or approximate place of residence may be pinned down at further points in the subject's career.

Whilst it is well to remember the limitations of one-night snapshots, the CEBs can afford the community historian useful insights into the life of institutions such as prisons, hospitals and workhouses; and quasi-institutions such as inns and lodging houses, and even ships.[22]

20 The technique of nominal record linkage has generated a large and, in parts, complex literature. See in particular the two special issues of the journal *History and Computing* devoted to record linkage; **4** 1, (1992) and **6** 3, (1994). See also Etherington, *Bonfire Boys* and the appendix to chapter 21, below.

21 See Part II, below.

22 See chapters 5, 6 and 7 in Part I, below.

They may be less useful in the case of educational institutions containing boarders, since, except in the case of the June enumeration of 1841, CEBs refer to dates which may have fallen during the Easter holiday period.

Many local studies focus on groups within the community, or particular aspects of life. Here again the CEBs have a valuable part to play, since those prominent in religious, cultural, educational and social-service type activities can be identified in their domiciliary contexts. Where membership lists are available or can be reconstructed, much deeper analysis is possible. For example, for the Sussex coastal town of Lewes, Etherington has linked his 'Known Bonfire Population' with directories and CEBs: these men were members of one of the six Bonfire Societies of the town which existed for a combination of reasons, the most important being to symbolise Protestant affiliations on 5 November each year.[23] The history of a school, which usually relies heavily on log-books and governors' minutes mentioning only a sprinkling of the names of pupils, can be transformed by the use of an admissions register in which all children's names are recorded. If this, in turn, can be linked to a CEB, so much the better for deeper social analysis, rather than the outline history of the building and a little bit about its occupants.

Finally, perhaps there are few more satisfying exercises than the reconstitution of communities on the basis of CEBs and some combination of directories, tithe surveys, town plans, rate-books, etc. Allocating the individuals recorded in the CEBs to the actual cottages, houses and homes in which they resided, many of which may survive making fieldwork easier, adds a geographical insight to the perspectives already mentioned. In such cases it may be desirable to use the 1841 CEBs[24] in order to capitalise on the link with a tithe survey or other closely contemporaneous document.[25]

Structure of the volume

This volume comprises six major parts, each of which is introduced by its own editorial comment, with reprinted chapters to follow. Part I concentrates on the enumeration process, a process fundamental to the reliability of the CEBs, yet remarkably neglected in the literature generally. Part II moves on to the contents and use of the printed census reports published by the Registrar General in the two or three years following each census. These comprise a statistical distillation of the data contained in the CEBs. This part of the book also considers the reliability of the basic data. Part III begins a consideration of the use of

23 Etherington, 'Community origin' and *Bonfire Boys*.
24 In conjunction with those of 1851.
25 See Part VI, below, especially chapter 29 by Henstock.

nominal data in the CEBs themselves, by looking at occupations, that being the most widely exploited of the different types of information available in the CEBs. In the Victorian economy, migration was an essential means of achieving the massive changes of the period, and is thus given a Part of its own. Part V discusses family and household structure and Part VI, which completes the main text, looks at residential patterns and house repopulation.

Part I

The enumeration process

2

The enumeration process

D. R. MILLS AND K. SCHÜRER

The process

It is important to remember that the aim of the census authorities was not to produce census enumerators' books, but to produce reports to parliament and for the educated public at large, about the demographic, occupational, and social condition of the country's population. The health of the nation was another matter of great concern to the government, being reported in the *Annual Reports of the Registrar General,* which could be read against the background provided by census reports.

These reports contain the aggregate material derived from the CEBs, the role of the latter being merely a means to an end. The survival of the CEBs depended on a good deal of luck, which in the case of the Irish documents only extended to a relatively small proportion.[1] The printed reports contain many tables which should be consulted by the community historian, more particularly those containing the totals and other summary data for the smallest administrative units, since these give an invaluable overview of the demographic situation in a district before the researcher plunges into the detail of the CEBs. Some of this information has been published in summary Tables of Population for 1801–1901 (and occasionally for longer periods) in the *Victoria Histories* of individual counties.[2] Students of particular aspects, such as migration, occupations, age pyramids, sex ratios, and so on, should seek in the printed reports some general tables on these subjects at national, county, or city levels. A listing of these reports appears as the appendix to chapter 8, below.[3]

The description of the enumeration process has already been broached in chapter 1, and has been described at some length in other publications,[4] but a summary at this point will put into context the discussion of the enumerators themselves, which follows in the next

1 Higgs, *Making sense,* 19–20; Royle, 'Irish manuscript census records' and 'Ecclesiastical census'.

2 Mills and Drake, 'The census, 1801–1991', 26–35.

3 In addition, Drake, 'The census', 32–41, lists the reports and the administrative levels at which specific data were made available. There is similar, but fuller information in Lawton, *Census and social structure,* 294–319.

4 Tillott, 'Sources of inaccuracy', 83–4; Armstrong 'The CEBs: a commentary', 30–2; Higgs, *Making sense,* 10–5 and *Clearer sense,* 11–6; and Lumas, 'Making Use', 6–9.

section of the chapter. The General Registry Office, which came under the Home Office, was responsible for the taking of censuses from 1841, and it administered the enumeration process through the geographical framework provided by the poor law unions. These had been set up by the Poor Law Amendment Act of 1834, and the registration district boundaries were drawn to coincide with union boundaries. This is one reason why registration district boundaries do not necessarily nest within the boundaries of ancient geographical counties, since union boundaries reflected market town catchment areas, and these often spread for commercial reasons over parts of two counties.

There were 624 registration districts in 1841, each in the charge of a superintendent registrar and divided into a total of 2,190 sub-districts, each with a registrar of births, deaths and marriages. The registrars were instructed to divide their sub-districts into enumeration districts (EDs), of which there were over 30,000 in 1841. One of the geographical quirks encountered by community historians is that, although the EDs, and even the sub-districts, were revised in some areas to take account of changes in population, in other areas change lagged well behind administrative changes and the growth of population, saddling some enumerators with several thousand people to enumerate. Any historian working over several censuses in an urban or industrial area must pay careful attention to this point, in order to be sure they are comparing like with like.

Each enumerator was issued with enough household schedules for their ED – more in urban areas than rural areas to counterbalance the lesser amount of walking in densely populated areas – an enumerator's book, and an instruction and memorandum book. Of the latter, none survives in the Public Record Office. As is still the practice, the enumerator provided each householder with a schedule to be completed for census night (always a Sunday night, 1841–1901), following instructions printed on the schedule. The schedules were collected by the enumerator on the following day, a process which was accompanied in many cases by the enumerator helping the householder to complete the schedule, or even filling it in for them. In 1871 the enumerators were asked to record in their enumeration books how many schedules they had filled in. The proportions varied considerably from one ED to another, even within a single sub-district: for example, the percentages varied between 5.3 and 64.7 in the Great Missenden (Buckinghamshire) sub-district.[5] Whichever way the schedules were completed, the historian has to rely essentially on information given by the householder, although enumerators were instructed to correct 'any manifestly false particulars'. There might be errors as to ages and birthplaces in particular, occupations might be distorted for reasons of

5 Drake and Mills, 'Census enumerators', 2.

self-importance or to hide shady activities and so on; but neither deliberate nor unwitting errors appear to call into question the general validity of the information in CEBs.

Then came the second main stage of the process – the transferral of information from schedules to CEBs. It is very clear to seasoned users of the CEBs that this process was accompanied by much editorial interference on the part of the enumerators. Some would consistently use 'farm lab.' instead of the officially approved abbreviation 'ag. lab.'. Some would reduce all second Christian names (or even every Christian name) to initials, whilst most wrote all Christian names in full. Some would use ditto marks or the abbreviation 'do.' at all opportunities, such as on the repetition of surnames and occupations; others would not. Some, as in Figure 1.1, reproduced in the previous chapter, put the answer to 'where born' in a form different from the model given in the instructions. Such examples are obvious from internal evidence – what we shall never know is the extent of more subtle and perhaps more important editing which cannot be checked systematically against other sources.[6]

There are also other idiosyncrasies relative to the use of pages. Some enumerators used every line on a page, as so enjoined, whilst others would leave a space at the end of a page in order to start the next page with a household head. There is even occasional evidence that an enumerator, as it were, shuffled their pack of schedules in an attempt to use every line, but also to start each new page with a new household! Such practices indicate that it cannot be assumed that schedules were entered in CEBs in some kind of geographical order. When full addresses are given, or a contemporaneous list of addresses and occupiers is available, this matter may be analysed in detail.

Often overlooked by students of the CEBs are the pages of 'common form' which precede the first main page onto which the enumerator began to transcribe the nominal information from the collected schedules. The preliminary pages contain, for example, copies of the directions to the enumerator and how the books should be filled in, as well as declarations by the enumerator, registrar, and superintendent registrar that the work had been completed satisfactorily.

On the very first page of the CEB the enumerator was invited to describe their district. In towns this description frequently comprises lists of streets and parts of streets. For example, in 1891 John Woodcock

6 Nervousness can, however, be overdone. Crompton, 'Changes in rural service occupations', reports general congruence between CEBs and directories in relation to tradesmen and craftsmen in Hertfordshire. One of the editors has been fortunate enough to view the original householders schedules for selected communities from the 1911 and 1921 censuses, for which there are no CEBs, their use being halted after the census of 1901. They are, as yet, closed to public inspection and were viewed in compliance with the Official Secrets Act. This exercise clearly demonstrated that much abbreviation of the original schedules was carried out, yet without necessarily changing the context of the information.

Wiggins, a solicitor's clerk described ED 13 in the Witney district in the following terms: 'Part of the township of Witney comprising the North and part of the South side of Corn Street [the principal street of the town], commencing [sic] and including Duck Alley. Croft Lane including Printers' houses and those adjoining Waggon and Horse Yard, Sylvester Row, Swingburn Row, Lowell's Yard (not to include 1 house and 1 cottage lately occupied by Jenkins)'.[7] The specification of rows and yards running off principal streets is especially useful as these are likely to have disappeared and may not have been marked on contemporary maps, or, if marked, have not been named.

In country areas all manner of variation can be found, much depending on the complexity of settlement and administrative geography. 'All the parish or township of X' was often thought sufficient, and is sometimes all the student actually needs. A more complex example from an area of hamlet settlement is that of Edward Calvert, the enumerator for EDs 7–11a in the Registrar's District of Wetheral, Cumberland, who in 1851 felt disposed to write: 'All that part of the Ecclesiastical district of St Pauls Holme Eden in the parish of Wetheral, comprising Holme Eden, Langthwaite, and the whole village of Warwick Bridge'. He then added 'the population of this district are mostly employed in a cotton mill or dyeworks, or are dependent thereon'.[8]

Returning to the common form pages, there are summary tables of the totals of houses, persons and schedules for each page of nominal information, which can be useful for checking the nominal pages themselves, as the arithmetic of enumerators was not always their strongest quality. In the 1841–61 censuses there is information on itinerants and temporary increases and decreases in population, the latter usually finding its way into the printed reports, and hence into the Tables of Population published in the *Victoria Histories*. For example, the population of Sunninghill in 1841 included 536 visitors at Ascot Heath Races.[9]

The enumerator was given a week for writing up their book, whereupon it was checked by first the registrar and then the superintendent registrar, both of whom had access to the schedules. It is now difficult to find out how effective this process was, but historians using the CEBs will occasionally come across amendments of either an arithmetical or a textual character which appear to be in a different hand from that of the enumerator. Upon the superintendent registrar being satisfied with the work of his team, the schedules and books were dispatched to the Census Office. Here clerks, engaged specially for the work carried out further checks, and performed the

7 Data supplied by Miss Judith Wildsmith.
8 Cumbria FHS, *Wetheral 1851*, 41.
9 Minchin, 'Table of population', 237.

Figure 2.1 Clerks in the Indexing Department of the Census Office, 1861

This picture shows clerks working in the Indexing Department of the Census Office. Their task was to collate information from the CEBs onto large abstracting sheets, examples of which can be found in the PRO (RG 27/3–6). These were then used for compiling the tables in the published reports. Taken from the *Illustrated Times*, 13 April, 1861.

Figure 2.2 A census playbill, 1861

ACT I.

LIBRARY AT FAIRDALE HALL,—EVENING.

ACTS II & III.

CHAPLAIN'S PARLOUR AT TOLMINSTER GAOL.

ACT IV.

Scene 1.—MORNING-ROOM AT FAIRDALE.

Scene 2.—Dr. BILLINGS PRIVATE ASYLUM.

ACT V.

LIBRARY AT FAIRDALE HALL,—MCRNING.

PRECEDED AT 7, BY THE LAUGHABLE FARCE,

THE CENSUS.

Name and Surname	Relation to Head of Family	Age last Birthday	Rank, Profession, or Occupation	Alias.
MR PETER FAMILIAS	*Head of Family*	51	*Fundholder*	Mr. ROBERT LYONS
MISS ROSE MAGENTA	*Niece*	19	*Heiress*	Miss MARIE LINDON
MR. ALBERT PUMPS	*Intruder*	24	*Lover*	Mr. WHEATCROFT
TATURS	*Servant*	40	*Gardener*	Mr. REDWOOD
JENNY MOBCAP	*Servant*	20	*Confidante*	Miss CHARLES
MRS PERKYSITES	*Housekeeper*	*Age unknown*	*Spinster*	Miss ASHFORD
G. WOA (*Badge* 2967)	*No Relation*	*Age doesn't matter*	*Cabman*	Mr. WALDEN
CRUSHER (27 Z)	*Servants' Follower*	*Age no consequence*	*Policeman*	Mr. BOUSFIELD

Treasurer..Mr. W. CHARMAN
Musical Director... Mr. ISIDORE DE SOLLA
Scenic Artist..Mr. W. B. SPONG

PRICES.—Private Boxes, £2 10s. Orchestra Stalls, 7s. 6d. Balcony Stalls, 4s. Family Circle, 2s. Pit Stalls, 2s Pit, 1s. Gallery, 6d.

Box Office open from 11 to 4.

No fees of any kind, nor restrictions as to Evening Dress except in Orchestra Stalls and Private Boxes. Places can be secured at all the Libraries.

Doors open at 6.30 Carriages can be ordered at 10.45

PROGRAMMES. ONE PENNY EACH

This illustration is part of a playbill advertising a play to be performed at *The Theatre Royal*, New Sadler's Wells, on Saturday, 16 April, 1861. *The Census* was a curtain raiser for the principal attraction of the evening, a play by H. A. Jones entitled *His Wife*.

laborious task of producing tables for the census reports from the many millions of 'facts' recorded in the CEBs (see Figure 2.1 above). With a few exceptions the schedules were destroyed.[10] The taking of the 1841 census was the first time government had conducted a fact-finding process requiring every householder in the country to complete what, in essence, we might term today a questionnaire. Due in part to this unique and quite novel position, all of the censuses of the mid-nineteenth century provoked satirical comment, such as that shown in the playbill illustrated in Figure 2.2 above.[11]

The enumerators

The enumerators were obviously key players in the process, yet, until recently, relatively little attention was paid to them and their social origins, their local knowledge and to their likely effectiveness. In appointing enumerators, the Census Office had a clear picture of what constituted a suitable candidate:

> The enumerator, in order to fulfil his duties properly, must be a person of intelligence and activity; he must read and write well, and have some knowledge of arithmetic: he must not be infirm or of such weak health as may render him unable to undergo the requisite exertion: he should not be younger than eighteen years of age, nor older than sixty-five: he must be temperate, orderly and respectable, and be such a person as is likely to conduct himself with strict propriety, and to deserve the good-will of the inhabitants of his district. He should also be well acquainted with the district in which he will be required to act; and it will be an additional recommendation if his occupations have been in any degree of a similar kind.[12]

It is perhaps remarkable, in an age when adult life started at 21, that the age of 18 should have been taken as an acceptable minimum. At the other extreme, 65 was not always observed as the maximum, since Daniel Matheson of Uxbridge served as an enumerator in 1851 at the age of 74 (see appendix below) and other examples have been found by Arkell in Cornwall (Table 4.2). Typical ages shown in the appendix were in the range 25–45. Many enumerators were resident in their own EDs, including the majority of the examples shown in the appendix. Women could be enumerators from 1891, and the appendix includes one example from Rochester.[13]

10 Benwell and Benwell, 'Llandyrnog', describes the survival of schedules for this sub-district of Denbighshire in 1851, the CEBs for which are missing. A few other scattered CEBs are missing elsewhere and at various dates.

11 See also Charlton, 'Bag in hand'; Turner, 'Two census songs'.

12 1851 Census Great Britain, *Population tables. Part I, vol. I*, BPP 1852–3 LXXXV, cxxxv.

13 Thirty-six other female enumerators have been listed by Mrs Lumas and her team at the PRO; several were related to registration officials. There was also one female registrar, standing in for her elderly father of 81: Lumas, 'Women enumerators', 3–5.

The number of schedules handled by enumerators varied considerably. For 1871, *The Times* reported that the average number was 131 houses and 696 people, but this embraced a range from 64 to at least 4,800 people.[14] The examples in the appendix range from 26 to 380 schedules, containing the particulars of 84 to 2,030 people, a range repeated in Arkell's Cornish examples. Allowance needs to be made, of course, for varying geographical circumstances, but the appendix lacks any examples from areas with very far-flung populations. Other factors were at work too, such as the rapid growth of industrial communities like Mexborough; the convenience of keeping small rural parishes separate from each other; and possibly even the personal contacts of the enumerator, demonstrated in the particulars of Miss Prothero at Rochester, who was given a small ED in a very 'polite' area.

Apart from being female, her social background was atypical of the enumerators appearing in the table, who were mostly 'lower middle class' – self-employed tradesmen and craftsmen and small farmers. Beatrice Prothero, aged 19, had slightly higher status and an important connection: she was a pupil teacher whose father and brother were solicitor's clerks, the brother also a Deputy Registrar of Births, Deaths and Marriages. Of those listed in the appendix, the enumerator with the highest social status was Dr Collins, a GP at Bourton-on-the-Water, Gloucestershire. At the other extreme was Thomas Masters, an agricultural labourer, but probably a key man in his small country parish, since he was the parish clerk.

Contents of Part I

Chapter 3 by Higgs uses the example of servants to illustrate the process of enumeration, and the subsequent process by which the CEBs were transformed into tables in the printed census reports. (See also the note under Table 13.5 on the special problems of the farm workforce.) Arkell's chapter 4 follows up the theme of the previous section, being much the most extensive study of enumerators yet published. It analyses the socio-economic background of the 89 men in considerable detail, with a summary of the population sizes of their districts.

Chapter 5 by Taylor gives the reader an opportunity to learn about the enumeration process outside normal households, specifically in Liverpool's institutions such as workhouses and infirmaries, which were treated as separate EDs; and quasi-institutions such as lodging houses, hotels, and even '32 persons in barns, sheds, etc.'. Taylor also found a few barge populations in Liverpool, a subject complemented by Burton's study of vessel enumeration returns (chapter 6). This demonstrates how fragile the census process could be at the margins, and brings to mind the enumerator's description of a vagrant in one

14 Quoted in Drake, 'A note on the enumerators', 15.

Lincolnshire parish as 'roaming around the parish on census night'. As a local example of the unpredictability of floating populations, one may also turn to a study of canal-boat families at Banbury, Oxon.[15] Part I is rounded off by Whyman's enquiry about visitors to Margate, their social standing, numbers of servants, where they were staying, and other characteristics, as revealed by the 1841 census, the only one in the nineteenth century to be taken in a summer month (chapter 7).

Appendix

Data relating to a selection of enumerators collected by the Local Population Studies Society enumerator project

Registration District: Doncaster, Yorkshire West Riding
Enumeration District: 12, part of township of Mexborough
If resident therein: Yes
Census year: 1891
Population: 2,030
Number of schedules: 380
Enumerator's details: John Bullock, 42, head, grocer.
Comments: Employer, one son (a grocer's assistant). Churchwarden of parish church.

Registration District: Doncaster, Yorkshire West Riding
Enumeration District: 13, part of township of Mexborough
If resident therein: No – in ED 15
Census year: 1891
Population: 1,262
Number of schedules: 246
Enumerator's details: Thomas Bland, 41, head, letterpress printer.
Comments: Employee, probably worked on *Mexborough Times*.

Registration District: Midhurst, Sussex
Enumeration District: 2B, part of Tillington parish
If resident therein: Yes
Census year: 1851
Population: 494
Number of schedules : 94
Enumerator's details: Charles Chalwin, 31, unmarried son, grocer.
Comments: Head of household was widowed mother aged 63, victualler of pub. Charles took over in 1852–5.

Registration District: Askrigg, Yorkshire North Riding
Enumeration District: 2, Township of Carperby cum Thoresby
If resident therein: Yes
Census year: 1851
Population: 342
Number of schedules: 72

15 Gibson, 'Canal boat families'.

Enumerator's details: William Sarginson, 52, head, farmer of 88 acres (tenant).
Comments: Enumerator in 1861, overseer 1865–6 for Aysgarth township.

Registration District: Stow-on-the-Wold, Gloucestershire
Enumeration District: 5, Bourton-on-the-Water parish
If resident therein: Yes
Census year: 1851
Population: 1,040
Number of schedules: 215
Enumerator's details: Henry Ramsey Collins, 28, head, general practitioner (MRCS).
Comments: Two servants, rateable value of property in 1850, £25.

Registration District: Highworth and Swindon, Wiltshire
Enumeration District: Part of 13, Inglesham parish
If resident therein: Yes
Census year: 1841
Population: 84
Number of schedules: 27
Enumerator's details: Thomas Masters, *c.* 30, head, agricultural labourer and parish clerk.
Comments: Father was a drover, later kept a pub at Inglesham. Enumerator for 1851 and 1861 censuses, in which his own description varies slightly. Still resident and parish clerk in 1871, see next entry.

Registration District: Highworth and Swindon, Wiltshire
Enumeration District: 11A, Inglesham parish
If resident therein: Yes
Census year: 1871
Population: 128
Number of schedules: 27
Enumerator's details: William Gerring Booker, 27, head, farmer of 75 acres.
Comments: Employed 3 men and 2 boys. Not resident in ED in 1861. Replaced Masters (see above).

Registration District: Woodstock, Oxfordshire
Enumeration District: 4, Steeple Barton parish
If resident therein: Yes
Census year: 1861
Population: 859
Number of schedules: 208
Enumerator's details: Caleb Nicholls, 45, head, tailor.
Comments: Employed 2 men and 1 boy. Wife a schoolmistress. One servant and two employees in household. Also enumerator in 1871 and 1881.

Registration District: Woodstock, Oxfordshire
Enumeration District: 5, village of Westcott Barton
If resident therein: Yes
Census year: 1891
Population: 215
Number of schedules: 52
Enumerator's details: George Money, 31, head, relieving officer.
Comments: One domestic servant.

Registration District:	Medway, Kent
Enumeration District:	5, Cathedral precincts, Rochester
If resident therein:	No – in ED 6
Census year:	1891
Population:	156
Number of schedules:	26
Enumerator's details:	Miss Beatrice Prothero, 19, daughter, candidate pupil teacher.
Comments:	Father and brother both solicitor's clerks; brother also Deputy Registrar.

Registration District:	Headington, Oxfordshire
Enumeration District:	Cuddesdon, including Denton and Chippinghurst
If resident therein:	No
Census year:	1881
Population:	493
Number of schedules:	103
Enumerator's details:	James Waterman, 22, head, carpenter.
Comments:	Living at Newington, about 5 miles away. Son of previous enumerator for district.

Registration District:	Howdenshire
Enumeration District:	9, Broomfleet civil parish
If resident therein:	Yes
Census year:	1891
Population:	243
Number of schedules:	53
Enumerator's details:	Richard Nicholls, 35, head, schoolmaster.
Comments:	Born Cornwall. Wife a schoolmistress, 3 children and 1 servant in household.

Registration District:	Uxbridge, Middlesex
Enumeration District:	1c, Eastcote parish
If resident therein:	Yes
Census year:	1851
Population:	503
Number of schedules:	105
Enumerator's details:	Daniel Matheson, 74, head, farmer of 40 acres.
Comments:	Born Buckinghamshire. Employed 2 labourers, finished at his own house.

Registration District:	Uxbridge, Middlesex
Enumeration District:	1c, Eastcote parish
If resident therein:	Yes
Census year:	1861
Population:	437
Number of schedules:	104
Enumerator's details:	Daniel Matheson, 47, head, farmer of 40 acres
Comments:	Son of 1851 enumerator, started at his own house.

3

The tabulation of occupations in the nineteenth-century census, with special reference to domestic servants

EDWARD HIGGS

The published returns

The statistical abstracts contained in the parliamentary census reports are our principal source for reconstructing the occupational structure of Victorian society. As such they have been widely used by historians, sociologists and economists, and are a vital component of all statistical models of the economy of that period. However, despite the obvious importance of the source, very little work has been done to gauge its accuracy. With notable exceptions,[1] most students of the period have been content to accept the figures contained in the census reports at face value. The present chapter is not an attempt to measure the overall discrepancies in the occupational totals quoted in the census reports. It can merely suggest some way in which such discrepancies may have occurred and encourage others to undertake the local census studies which may allow such an evaluation to be made. An example of the problems involved in the interpretation of such published occupational tables will be given with reference to the employment of domestic servants in one northern district in the period 1851–71.

When examining these statistics it is important to recognise that they are several stages removed from the reality of nineteenth-century society. They represent a series of interpretations of fact made in turn by the householders who filled in the original schedules, by the enumerators who collected these and copied them into their enumeration books, and by the clerks in the central Census Office who tabulated the results. Each would have interpreted the subtle distinctions between household relationships according to their own experience and values. When evaluating the reliability of these data it will therefore be necessary to look at the process of taking the census from the differing points of view of the individuals involved. It is also necessary to examine the assumptions underlying the interpretation of these statistics by modern historians.

1 Tillott, 'Sources of inaccuracy', 82–133. See also chapters 12 and 19 by Perkyns, below.

These strictures certainly apply when dealing with terms such as 'servant' and 'domestic employment'. 'Service' in the nineteenth century was a legal term rather than the description of an occupation. It related to a certain relationship between employer and employee, and could be applied equally to living-in farm labourers and to housemaids in aristocratic households. Thus in the nineteenth-century census schedules the term 'servant' could appear in the column reserved for information on an individual's relationship to the household head, as well as in the column giving occupations. On the other hand, 'domestic' occupations such as that of the housekeeper might not imply any contractual or legal relationship within the household, but rather a function carried out by a member of the family within the home. A housekeeper could merely be the keeper of the house, in other words, a housewife. But such a function could also be performed by a distant relative who in every social sense was regarded as outside the family unit, and who might even be paid on a contractual basis. Such subtle, but nevertheless important, distinctions would be difficult to communicate through a census form, and were easily lost in the process of transcription and interpretation which the compilation of the nineteenth-century census involved. In dealing with such matters it is necessary to distinguish between 'domestic service' as a description of a legal and social system, and the term 'housemaid' as a description of a person performing a set of duties in the home of their employer. In nineteenth-century usage, however, such distinctions were often blurred

The administration of the census

The taking of a Victorian census for the whole of England and Wales, and the derivation of statistics from the results was a considerable administrative task. After the passing of the necessary Census Act, the department in charge of taking the census (this was the General Registry Office (GRO) from 1841 onwards) established a temporary Census Office in London. This, staffed by temporary clerks, undertook the tabulation of the information compiled locally. Until 1841 the census was supervised in the field by the overseers of the parishes, but with the establishment of civil registration in 1837 and the transfer of responsibility for the census to the GRO following Rickman's sudden death in 1840, the district of the local Registrar of Births and Deaths became the local unit of administration. This official had to divide his district into enumeration districts, and to appoint an enumerator for each.

The latter, also employed on a temporary basis, distributed household schedules to each householder, who filled them out on the night of the census. The enumerator had to copy these into books which were then sent to London for tabulation under various headings.[2]

Such an administrative system could only produce consistent statistical results if there was a clear policy on tabulation at the centre, and if the staff involved were properly trained and supervised. Since the Census Office was only a temporary institution none of these conditions could be adequately fulfilled in the nineteenth century. The Registrar General and his predecessors appear to have been too preoccupied with the establishment of the Census Office, and its staffing, to give much time to the serious consideration of such policy. The temporary clerks employed were not of a high quality, and appear to have received little training in methods of tabulation.[3] It was admitted in 1890 that these clerks could not be adequately supervised,[4] and this must have applied to an even greater extent to the local enumerators and to the householders who filled in the original schedules.

Given this administrative system modern researchers must be alive to the numerous difficulties in interpreting the statistics presented in the official census reports. We have no means of gauging how far Victorian householders could understand the census schedules, or how far the enumerators standardised the entries they copied into their books for despatch to London. Nor do we know how the clerks working in the Census Office interpreted these schedules, or how they may have revised them. Such revisions certainly took place, as when multiple occupations were reduced to a single component for ease of tabulation. Thus in existent schedules the term 'farmer and butcher' is often reduced to 'farmer' or 'butcher' by the deletion of the other, complementary occupation.

The example of servants

More work needs to be done on the relationship between the enumerators' books and the tabulations in the published census reports, for which they formed the raw material. The example which follows examines domestic servants and their employers in the Registrar General's District of Rochdale in the period 1851–71. This work was based on one-in-four random samples of households containing domestic servants in the CEBs for this district in the censuses of 1851–71.[5] As has been suggested already, a 'domestic servant' could be defined in two ways, either by occupation or by relationship to the head of the household. In the analysis which follows a 'servant-

2 See Higgs, *Making sense*, 13–4; *Clearer sense*, 15–6, for fuller details.

3 *Report of the Committee appointed by the Treasury to inquire into certain Questions connected with the taking of the Census*..., BPP 1890 LVIII, viii.

4 *Report of the Committee appointed by the Treasury*, BPP 1890 LVIII, viii.

5 PRO HO 107/3032–3051; RG 10/4112–4132. The wider work of which this analysis forms part is presented in Higgs, *Domestic servants and households*. See also, Higgs, 'Domestic service and household production'.

Table 3.1 Servants, aged 20 years or over: Rochdale district sample, 1851

Servant types	Sample total	'True servants'	Census total (divided by 4)
General (F)	217	158	244.75
Butler	1	1	0.00
General (M)	21	9	17.25
Coachman	3	1	0.25
Groom	4	0	0.25
Gardener	16	2	0.00
Housekeeper	66	10	65.50
Cook	5	5	8.75
Housemaid	18	9	13.25
Nurse	9	6	5.75
Governess	3	2	0.00
Ladies maid	2	2	0.00
Laundrymaid	1	1	0.00
Kitchenmaid	1	1	0.00
Footman	0	0	0.00
Companion	0	0	0.00
Total	367	207	356.25

Notes: The published census totals are divided by four to make them compatible with one-in-four census sample. For the definition of 'true servants', see text.

Source: 1851 Census of Great Britain, *Population tables. Part II, vol. II*, BPP 1852–3 LXXXVIII, 636–47.

employing household' is defined by occupation, that is, it includes an individual designated as one of a variety of the terms 'servant' and 'maid', or as a 'butler', 'footman', 'groom', 'coachman', 'gardener', 'governess' or 'nurse'.

As can be seen from Table 3.1, above, the sample of such households from the 1851 CEBs produced totals of persons aged 20 and over in the various servant occupations which, in general terms, were comparable to those found in the published census report.[6] The match was very close in the case of housekeepers. This led to the conclusion that the clerks in the Census Office merely summed the occupational entries in the schedules to arrive at the total number of domestic servants in the district.

However, a large number of these individuals in the sample were not enumerated as servants in terms of the relationship to the head of household in which they lived. Out of the total sample of 367 persons in servant occupations aged 20 years or over, 160, or over 40 per cent, were not enumerated as such, the vast majority of these being related by kinship to the household head.[7] In Table 3.1 the number of persons

6 1851 Census of Great Britain, *Population tables. Part II, vol. II*, BPP 1852–3 LXXXVIII, 636–47.

7 The term 'kinship' being used here in its widest sense to indicate any relationship by marriage or birth.

in particular servant occupations in the sample who were also servants in relationship to the household head are given in the second column under the heading 'true servants', the remainder being either lodgers or relatives.

These figures can be interpreted in several different ways. Such servants resident with kin may have been normally employed as living-in domestics but may have been temporarily out of work. This would, however, have represented a very high level of unemployment. Conversely this might indicate a large population of day-servants, who worked in the homes of their employers by day and who returned to lodge with their relatives at night. A third possibility is that these 'domestics' not only lodged with their kin but also worked in their homes.

The Victorian Registrar Generals and modern historians have often tended to assume a dichotomy between life in the home and work in the outside world. Our conception of an occupation has tended to be conditioned by our expectation that 'work' is an activity carried on outside the home which can be measured by the money equivalents of wages or profits. Thus it has often been assumed that the number of persons in servant occupations in the nineteenth-century census tabulations represented the number of men and women working for board, lodging and wages in the homes of middle-class employers with whom they had some contractual arrangement.[8] There is some evidence, however, that many of the Rochdale householders who filled in their schedules on the night of the census saw 'service' as a set of functions which could be carried on within the family.

Thus, amongst the 66 'housekeepers' of all ages found in the 1851 sample only 10 were also servants in relationship to the head of the household in which they resided. Of the remaining 56 women, no fewer than 23 were the heads of the households in which they lived, and another 15 were the wives of the head of the household.

Similarly out of the 38 'nurses' living with kin enumerated in the Rochdale district sample of 1851, 18 were aged under 10 and only 3 were not members of the nuclear family. Such children were probably part of that vast army of child-minders so familiar in nineteenth-century textile towns, where so many married women worked. Amongst the 36 households containing such 'nurses', 27.8 per cent contained 3 or more children aged under 10, compared with 16.0 per cent amongst a control sample of 201 randomly selected Rochdale households. Since these figures are aggregate percentages drawn from samples one cannot be certain that they are a true reflection of the actual figures which would have been obtained from a study embracing

8 See, for example, Perkin, *Origins of modern English society*, 143; McLeod, *Class and religion*, 26.

all households or all servant employing households. However statistical theory allows us to estimate, at various levels of confidence, the degree to which sample proportions will deviate from the true figures in the underlying population. In this case we can be at least 80 per cent certain that this difference in the two proportions quoted was not caused by sampling error.[9]

Amongst the remaining 88 female 'kin servants', who were neither housekeepers, nurses, nor specifically 'working at home', some, if not all, may have been 'day-servants' or temporarily unemployed. However, certain aggregate characteristics of the households in which they lived suggest that many may have been working at home. Thus, in 1851, out of 69 households containing such servants 31, or 44.9 per cent, contained a head who was widowed, compared with 17.9 per cent amongst the control sample.[10] Similarly, amongst the former group of households, 57.1 per cent contained 5 or more persons, compared with 46.3 per cent amongst the control sample.[11] Many of the households containing such 'kin-servants' were headed by persons of relatively high social status. Thus 34.3 per cent of these households were either retailers or farmers, compared with only 16.5 per cent amongst the control sample.[12] These aggregate characteristics suggest that many of these women were probably working at home, often standing-in for absent wives, in fairly prosperous homes.

In addition, of these 88 women, 43.1 per cent were not members of the nuclear family, compared with a mere 7.0 per cent amongst the 478 females in the control sample.[13] This indicates that such 'servants' were a feature of relatively unusual extended families.

9 This is done by calculating the difference between the two percentages involved and then comparing this with the likely magnitude of the statistical error given by the following formula:

$$\textit{Sampling error} = t\ \textit{statistic} = \sqrt{\frac{Ps_1(1 - Ps_1)}{n_1 - 1} + \frac{Ps_2(1 - Ps_2)}{n_2 - 1}}$$

Where:
Ps_1 = first sample percentage treated as a proportion of one;
Ps_2 = second sample percentage treated as a proportion of one;
n_1 = number of cases in population from which first proportion derived;
n_2 = number of cases in population from which second proportion derived.
The t statistic is a computed value which can be reduced in size to correspond to certain confidence levels. Thus, if we wish to be 95 per cent certain that the difference between two proportions is statistically significant, we multiply the results of the equation to the right of the t statistic in the formula by the value of t at 95 per cent, that is 1.96. If the resulting sampling error is smaller than the difference actually observed between the sample proportions then we can be 95 per cent certain that this discrepancy was not solely due to sampling error but represents a true difference between the underlying populations. In the case quoted above the difference is not significant at 95 per cent, but by reducing the t statistic to the 80 per cent confidence level we get a positive result. In other samples from the 1861 and 1871 censuses the differences between the analogous percentages were significant at the 80 and 95 per cent levels respectively.

10 Difference statistically significant at the 95 per cent confidence level.

11 Difference statistically significant at the 80 per cent confidence level.

12 Difference statistically significant at the 95 per cent confidence level.

13 Difference statistically significant at the 95 per cent confidence level.

None of these individuals can automatically be said to be misenumerated. However, the position of many of them within the households of their kin, and the aggregate characteristics of such households, suggest that a significant number will have worked at home as 'home-helps'. As Anderson has pointed out, in nineteenth-century Lancashire there was a heightened propensity for relatives to provide each other with support within the home, especially at times of family crisis.[14] The extent to which widows remained at home as 'housekeepers' whilst their children were at work, or children acted as 'nurses' for the babies of the female factory wives during the widowhood of the household head, all reflect the importance of this tradition of 'huddling'. The fact that such relationships could be regarded as occupations reflects the recognition of their importance by such families.

This propensity of householders to interpret occupations in ways alien to our own preconceived notions can also be found amongst census enumerators. Thus, in 1861, out of 234 households in one enumeration district in the Castleton area of Rochdale, the enumerator described 49 housewives as 'housekeepers' in his copy of the original schedules. Similarly, in the same census, out of the 249 households in an enumeration district in Wardleworth, the enumerator described 141 housewives in the same manner. For these officials the term 'housewife' and 'housekeeper' appear to have been synonymous.[15]

How did the clerks in the central Census Office interpret the results of the census? The short answer is that we do not know. However, an examination of the census schedules for the Rochdale district and the census reports for the period 1851–71, suggests that some attempt was made to compensate for the type of misenumeration mentioned above. Although the match between the 1851 census sample and the tables in the 1851 census report shown in Table 3.1 is close, this is not the case for 1861. In that year the census sample gave a total of 628 persons[16] aged over 19 in servant occupations, whilst the census report gave a total of 1,533 for the same age group, or 383.25 when divided by four to bring the figure in line with the one-in-four census sample.[17] The same report recorded 253 housekeepers of that age, although the census sample would have led us to expect no fewer than 968 (±14). The

14 Anderson, *Family structure*.

15 PRO RG 9/3032–3051.

16 Plus or minus 2 to allow for sample error, calculated by the formula:

$$P \pm t\sqrt{\frac{P(1-P)}{n-1}}$$

Where: P = number of servants treated as a proportion of all servants;
n = number of cases in the population of all servants;
t = t statistic.

17 1861 Census of England and Wales, *Populations tables. Vol. II, pt II*, BPP 1863 LIII, 634–47.

inference to be drawn is that the clerks did not merely add together all the occupations to get the occupational totals. On the other hand they did not do so by adding up all those persons recorded as 'servant' in the column headed 'Relationship to the Head of the Household'. An examination of all households in the 1861 Rochdale census reveals that this figure would have been only 1,321 for all servants of all ages.

An examination of the census reports for other areas over the same period suggests that similar attempts were made to rectify the 'mis-specification' of servant occupations. Thus, in 1851, the Borough of Blackburn was recorded in the census report as having 733 persons employed as 'housekeepers', nearly 38 per cent of the entire servant population.[18] By 1861 the number of 'housekeepers' recorded had fallen to 51, or under 3 per cent of the servant total.[19] Over the same period the number of 'housekeepers' in the Borough of Oldham rose from 48 to 146.[20] It is evident that some alterations were being made to the raw statistics contained in the census schedules, but to what system and with what consistency cannot be determined.

Even assuming that the census reports accurately reflected the number of traditionally defined living-in domestic servants, it would still be unwise to use them uncritically to reconstruct changes in local occupational structures over time. Just as the term 'domestic servant' might represent the work of a woman in the home of her relatives, it might also cover other types of work which are today regarded as separate occupations. Thus, during the period 1851–71, between a third and a quarter of all living-in servants in Rochdale worked for retailers. Most of these servants would have worked in the shop, a supposition confirmed by other local sources. The distinction between the servant and the shop-assistant is therefore an artificial one. Those who attempt to explain the decline of domestic service in the late-nineteenth century by the rise of alternative employment, especially in shops, may be mistaking the cause for the effect. The decline of the domestic may not be linked to the 'rise' of the shop-assistant, rather to the change of nomenclature as the home-based, family shop was replaced by the lock-up shop and the chain store. As retailing ceased to be a domestic business, so workers in this section of the economy ceased to be called domestic servants.[21]

18 1851 Census of Great Britain, *Population tables. Part II, vol. II*, BPP 1852–3 LXXXVIII, 652.

19 1861 Census of England and Wales, *Population tables. Vol. II, pt II*, BPP 1863 LIII, 652.

20 1851 Census of Great Britain, *Population tables. Part II, vol. II*, BPP 1852–3 LXXXVIII, 652; 1861 Census of England and Wales, *Population tables. Vol. II, pt II*, BPP 1863 LIII, 652.

21 For a broader discussion of the GROs handling of census data see Higgs, *Clearer sense*, 154–68.

Conclusion

If such mis-specifications were a general feature of the nineteenth-century census it might lead us to revise our views on the economic and social role of women in Victorian England and Wales.[22] If we assume that all the 'servants' who lived with relatives in Rochdale worked at home, then out of 2,065 persons, described as working in servant occupations in 1851, only 1,113, or 53.9 per cent, were properly enumerated. If such a discrepancy was found over the whole country, then approximately a half million women may have been wrongly enumerated in the mid-nineteenth-century census reports. This may certainly be a gross overestimation, but the precise level of this discrepancy can only be gauged by detailed studies of the role of 'kin-servants' in industrial and agricultural communities. It is to be hoped that the present chapter has raised enough questions about the mechanics of the Victorian census to encourage others to undertake such studies.

At the heart of the matter lies the definition of an occupation and work, and the relationship between the economic world and the home. Confusion between 'domestic' and 'business' activities may have existed in the homes of retailers, farmers,[23] and in all small businesses where the help of the servant, wife, or children was indispensable. Victorian ideology attempted to keep the two spheres of home and work separate, but we must not fall into the trap of believing that all Victorians shared these beliefs, or that such a division always existed in practice.

22 See Higgs, 'Women, occupations and work' for an extension of this point.

23 For the problems of interpretation with the agricultural workforce, see Higgs, 'Occupational censuses'.

4

Identifying the census enumerators: Cornwall in 1851

TOM ARKELL

This chapter aims at investigating who the census enumerators were and what their background was, as well as evaluating their task in hand. It is substantially based on Ray Woodbine's Herculean labours on the Cornish census of 1851 which is available currently in the form of published transcripts with indexes for 91 contiguous enumeration districts (EDs) in central and south-east Cornwall.[1] These stretch from Wadebridge in the north to Fowey and Looe in the south and cover Bodmin and Lostwithiel as well as the surrounding countryside. They provide an ideal opportunity to track down all the census enumerators and to analyse the most accessible and salient data about them, although it must be remembered that for those EDs on the edge of the area all the adjacent parishes cannot be searched thoroughly.

At least 90 of the 91 enumerators were male because the forename of only one was recorded with an initial rather than the full name. Two-thirds of them lived in the district for which they were responsible and only 5 per cent outside the parish; the rest were recorded as living in other EDs within the same parish. The population of their EDs ranged from 116 to 1,154, normally in inverse proportion to their areas. Altogether one quarter of the EDs had fewer than 300 people, a half had between 300 and 600 inhabitants and another quarter had over 600.

The task of identifying the enumerator is easiest when the ED's first or last schedules contain a person with the enumerator's name. This occurred in 3 EDs in 10 in this sample and even when there were other men in the same district with the same name the possibility that they might have been the enumerator can be discounted. But uncertainty arises when he has no special place and more than one right name is traced in the census enumerators' books. Here this applied to nearly 1 case in 5 or a total of 16 instances. The instructions given to the local registrars on selecting their enumerators, quoted at length in chapter 2 above, provide some help in unravelling this problem.

In six instances the circumstances of one individual made them so much more likely to have been the enumerator than the others that one

1 They have been transcribed and published by R. Woodbine, 5 Priory Close, Par, Cornwall.

can accept them as such with few reservations. In one ED, for example, where three of the right name lived in the parish but not in the district, the claims of a mine labourer (aged 64) and an agricultural labourer (59) yield to those of a draper and grocer of 33. In another a 'tea and calico draper' (47) overrides his father, a retired commercial traveller (78), and a Greenwich pensioner (50). In three others a landed proprietor (56), a victualler (35) and a farmer's son (22) are preferred respectively to an agricultural labourer (28), a lodging bargeman (43) and a landed proprietor (80). A rather different problem occurred in one ED in Bodmin where the initial 'R' was substituted for the enumerator's forename and so extended the potential choice to five men from the town – three Roberts, a Richard and a Roger. Since only the Richard lived in the particular ED and he was also the town clerk (53), he is the prime contender from this group, but if it ever emerged that the 'R' did not stand for Richard, this decision would be invalid.

However, no similar selection can be made with any confidence in ten other EDs. In the most complex of these elimination exercises six adult males had the same name as one of the two enumerators in Blisland parish (of only 606 inhabitants), with four living in the relevant ED and two in the other half of the parish. The latter were a farmer (aged 84) and an annuitant (60) who was a lodger and so must be discounted along with two others – an agricultural labourer (47) and a farm servant (24). But either a farmer (aged 70) or his son of 20 could have been the enumerator. Four other EDs also had both a farmer (aged 67, 65, 57 and 39) and a farmer's son (aged 26, 29, 18 and 22) with the same name as the enumerator and, although the farmers' claims may appear to be stronger, one cannot choose between them and their sons without guessing. Elsewhere there are equally impossible choices between a farmer's son (32) or a schoolmaster (22), a fund holder (65) or a master blacksmith (30), a master carpenter (61) or a carpenter (38), a mason (28) or a master mason (51) and a labourer (52) or a farm servant (24). Although one of each pair may appear as the more likely candidate, none can be selected with any certainty as the district's enumerator and the last one pose particular problems because if there had been a third alternative, such as a farmer or grocer, the labourer and farm servant would have been eliminated with very few qualms.

In the ensuing analyses, therefore, this ED has been omitted together with one other in Menheniot where the enumerator was George Martin Pooley. No George Pooley appears in or around the parish in any of the transcripts completed so far by Mr Woodbine, although one of its other EDs does contain an unacceptably weak candidate in Martin Pooly, a shoemaker (28) who was merely a lodger in the household where he lived. Thus identifying all the enumerators

Table 4.1 Occupations of 89 enumerators: Cornwall, 1851

	n.	sub-totals	%
Agricultural (with mining)			
A1 Farmer		24.5	27.5
A2 Farmer's son		13	14.6
A3 Others		5	5.6
gardener	1		
land agent	1		
wood bailiff	1		
copper miner	1		
mine agent	1		
Total		42.5	47.8
Non-agricultural			
N1 Craftsmen		16.5	18.5
cordwainer	3		
mason	3		
carpenter	2		
joiner	2		
blacksmith	1.5		
bootmaker	1		
cabinetmaker	1		
miller	1		
saddler	1		
tailor	1		
N2 Traders & dealers		15	16.9
butcher	3		
grocer	3		
auctioneer	2		
draper	2		
flour dealer	1		
innkeeper	1		
ironmonger	1		
mercer	1		
victualler	1		
N3 Others		15	16.9
schoolmaster	5.5		
scholar	1		
parish clerk	2		
postmaster	1		
relieving clerk	1		
town clerk	1		
gentleman	2		
landed proprietor	1		
fund holder	0.5		
Total		46.5	52.2

is more difficult than one might anticipate and so the analysis which follows has been confined to 89 of the 91 districts. And for those nine EDs which have two plausible candidates for enumerator rather than

Table 4.2 Characteristics of 89 enumerators by occupation group: Cornwall, 1851

	All %	Ag. %	Non-Ag. %	A1 n.	A2 n.	A3 n.	N1 n.	N2 n.	N3 n.
Relationship to household head									
Head	77.0	65	88	23.5	–	4	14.5	14	12.5
Son	22.4	35	11	1	13	1	2	1	2
Nephew	0.6	–	1	–	–	–	–	–	0.5
Marital condition									
Unmarried	19.7	33	8	–	13	1	1	1	1.5
Married	75.8	62	88	22.5	–	4	14.5	13	13.5
Widowed	4.5	5	4	2	–	–	1	1	–
Age									
18–29	18.5	27	11	–	10.5	1	0.5	2	2.5
30–39	29.2	33	26	9.5	2.5	2	6	4	2
40–49	23.6	19	28	7	–	1	2	7	4
50–59	18.0	15	20	5.5	–	1	4.5	1	4
60–70	10.7	6	15	2.5	–	–	3.5	1	2.5
Household size									
1–4	30.3	5	54	1	1	–	10	8	7
5–8	44.4	52	38	10	8	4	5.5	7	5
9+	25.3	44	9	13.5	4	1	1	–	3
Female servants									
0	57.3	44	70	7	6.5	5	14.5	8	10
1	30.3	33	28	10	4	–	2	6	5
2	12.4	24	2	7.5	2.5	–	–	1	–
Residence									
in same ED	68.0	81	56	22.5	9	3	11.5	7	7.5
first in CEB	(11.2)	(21)	(2)	(7)	(1)	(1)	(1)	–	–
last in CEB	(19.1)	(26)	(13)	(8)	(3)	–	–	(3)	(3)
in rest parish	26.4	16	35	2	4	1	5	6	5.5
in other parish	5.6	2	9	–	–	1	–	2	2
Birthplace									
same parish	60.1	60	60	15	8.5	2	9.5	11	7.5
adjacent parish	15.7	19	13	5.5	1.5	1	2	–	4
rest Cornwall	18.5	16	20	3	3	1	4	3	2.5
outside Cornwall	5.6	5	6	1	–	1	1	1	1
Population of EDs									
0–199	10.1	9	11	3	1	–	5	–	–
200–399	32.6	51	16	12.5	8	1	–	3	4.5
400–599	32.6	26	39	5.5	2.5	3	5.5	5	7.5
600–799	13.5	12	15	2.5	1.5	1	4	3	–
800+	11.2	2	19	0.5	0.5	–	2	4	3

none, each is counted as 0.5. In these analyses, the rural and urban areas are not studied separately because only 13 EDs at most can be classified as urban and all but 4 of them derive from towns with no more than 1,200 inhabitants. In addition, mining was the predominant economic activity in substantial parts of the countryside.

Not surprisingly, by far the largest occupational group among the enumerators was farmers and their sons (42 per cent), while only two were employed in mining. Table 4.1 above shows how diverse the occupations of the other enumerators were, with only one group with 5.5 (schoolmasters) and four with three each (butchers, cordwainers, grocers and masons). The table also shows how, for the purpose of analysis, they have been grouped together into two virtually equal halves, with each split into three further sub-divisions. The one for agriculture (with mining) comprises farmers, farmers' sons and others and the non-agricultural one craftsmen, traders and dealers and a rather diverse rest with those of independent means and those working in administration and education. The only logic behind the two miscellaneous sub-groups is of course that they are the product of the other compelling four and of the convenience of avoiding additional groupings that would be meaninglessly small.

Many of the main characteristics of the enumerators and of the principal differences between the agricultural and non-agricultural groups are as one might anticipate (see Table 4.2 above). Three-quarters of the enumerators headed their own households and virtually all the rest were sons; their marital condition was distributed similarly with three-quarters married, one-fifth unmarried and nearly 1 in 20 widowed. Because most of the bachelors were farmers' sons, only 65 per cent of the agricultural group headed their own households (compared with 88 per cent for the others) and 33 per cent were unmarried rather than 8 per cent of the non-agricultural enumerators. The latter were also significantly older, with 63 per cent 40 and over in comparison with 40 per cent of the agricultural ones.

On the other hand, the agricultural enumerators lived in much larger households: 44 per cent had nine or more residents compared with 9 per cent for the others. The agricultural enumerators also had more resident female servants: the proportions with two, for example, were 24 per cent of the agricultural group and 2 per cent of the non-agricultural one. Sometimes the number of female domestic servants can be taken as a crude indicator of social standing, although widowers were more likely to have housekeepers, and wives might employ teenage general servants as substitutes for grown-up single daughters if they had none at home.

The agricultural enumerators were also more likely to enumerate the district in which they lived (81 per cent rather than 56 per cent for the non-agricultural) and to have smaller populations in their EDs. Sixty per cent of the agricultural enumerators had under 400 inhabitants, but only 27 per cent of the non-agricultural ones, while all but one of the 10 EDs with populations of over 800 were tackled by non-agricultural enumerators. But there was no marked difference between the two groups on one other important characteristic – the enumerators' birthplaces. Three-fifths of both were born in the parish which they enumerated.

As yet, this remains only a preliminary study of these Cornish enumerators. To understand better the significance of these data one needs to know how close their characteristics came to those of the other males aged 18 to 70 living in the same area.[2] It is also important to discover how many of them held office locally in the previous decade or so and in what capacity, and how many acted as enumerators 10 years later on. But perhaps most important of all one needs to know how much variation there was in the quality of the work between the different enumerators and whether any rational explanation can be offered for this.[3]

2 In this sample the enumerators' ages range from 18 to 70.

3 For two such examples see Woollings, 'An Orsett census enumerator' and Harwood, *Chaps and maps*, 9–13.

5

Liverpool's institutional and quasi-institutional populations in 1841 and 1851

IAIN C. TAYLOR

Unlike many national censuses, those of the United Kingdom have always enumerated population as it was located on census night: the so-called *de facto* population. In other words, persons were enumerated where they slept that night whether or not it was their usual place of abode. While the advantages of avoiding double counting can be seen, a disadvantage is that anyone not sleeping at home on census night is nearly impossible to find in the CEBs.

Some countries allocate this 'floating' non-resident population to its 'usual' place of residence: the *de jure* population. The significance of these two different practices for those interested in tracing individuals should be apparent.

While it would be well-nigh impossible to trace single visitors in private homes without tabulating the entire national census, it would be feasible to accumulate over time a listing of establishments which catered for the traveller, the homeless, orphaned, sick, poor, student and criminal classes as research on the CEBs proceeds. In addition, such listings would also provide a quantitative gauge of the broad dimensions of the 'non-household' or institutional population of the country – itself an important consideration when questions of preparing representative samples of the population as a whole are being asked. The material presented in this chapter represents an examination of the sizes and types of such institutional and 'quasi-institutional' populations for Liverpool in the mid-nineteenth century.

Liverpool, as a major seaport and point of embarkation for foreign migrants, had a large number of persons passing through the town, frozen like a single frame in a movie film, by the census enumeration on census night. Liverpool might be reasonably expected therefore to present something of an extreme case in the size and diversity of such typical populations. However, further research could provide some perspective on this matter.

The groups of transients and segregated persons in the city fell broadly into two classes. The first was officially recognised by the census as 'institutional', and a separate set of schedules was

Table 5.1 The official institutional population: Liverpool, 1851

Registration sub-district	Institution type	Population male	female	total
1. St Martins	–	–	–	–
2. Gt Howard	Gaol	599	355	954
3. Dale Street	–	–	–	–
4. St George	Bluecoat Hospital	242	117	359
5. St Thomas	–	–	–	–
6. Mt Pleasant	Workhouse	536	648	1,184
	Infirmary	133	114	247
7. Islington	Brickfield Barracks	279	32	311
8. Toxteth Park	–	–	–	–
9. Everton/Kirkdale	Industrial School	656	497	1,153
	Workhouse	318	430	748
	Barracks	333	34	367
	Gaol	339	83	422
10. West Derby	–	–	–	–
Totals		3,435	2,310	5,745

Notes: The parish of Liverpool in 1851 comprised Registration sub-districts 1–8. These, plus the out-townships recorded in Registration sub-districts 9 and 10, constituted the Borough of Liverpool.

distributed to the persons in charge of the institutions. As shown in Table 5.1 above, in Liverpool such places included: gaols, hospitals and asylums, schools, almshouses, refuges and institutes, barracks and military establishments. Persons on boaıd ships (not inland craft) were separately enumerated by ships' captains and the results forwarded directly to London.[1]

The second type were recorded in the normal household CEBs and although not officially designated as institutions, from their non-familial nature they are clearly closer in form to to institutions than to normal households. Some of these were obviously small 'institutions' considered too small for a separate enumeration;[2] others have been termed 'quasi-institutions' by researchers in that they lie on the borderline between 'normal' households and definite institutions. This research uses the, admittedly arbitrary, figure of more than 10 persons described as, lodgers, boarders, etc. in the household to designate such a group as 'quasi-institutional'.

1 See chapter 6 by Burton, below.

2 The official definition of what constituted an institution by the Census Office was problematic. For the census year 1851–81 institutions which numbered over 200 inmates should have been automatically enumerated in the separate institutional books. In 1891 this figure was reduced to 100 inmates. However, size was not the only criterion used. What might be seen as 'standard' types of institutions – workhouses, goals, schools, barracks, etc. – should have been recorded in the special institutional books regardless of the number of inmates and staff they housed. Consequently, a 'grey area' developed over the type of enumeration book in which institutions smaller than the official size were to be recorded. See Higgs, *Making sense*, 37–9; *Clearer sense*, 35–7.

Table 5.2 Institutional and quasi-institutional population: Liverpool, 1851

Registration sub-districts	Institutional population	Quasi-institutional population	Total population
1. St Martins	–	818	61,777
2. Gt Howard	954	206	27,942
3. Dale Street	–	328	31,763
4. St George	359	189	19,823
5. St Thomas	–	109	33,957
6. Mt Pleasant	1,431	654	41,990
7. Islington	311	462	40,970
Parish	3,055	2,766	258,222
Out-townships	2,690		
Borough	5,745		367,700

Notes: The quasi-institutional population of the out-townships is excluded

From an examination of the CEBs for the parish of Liverpool in 1851, which constituted 70 per cent of the borough population, many such households were encountered. A list of these households is presented as an appendix to this chapter. The total size of this quasi-institutional population, unrecorded by the official institutional returns, is impressive. A total of 2,766 persons was found, a figure which represents only some 10 per cent less than those listed in the parish of Liverpool's bulging official institutions, which held 3,055 persons.[3] In total the institutional population of the parish of Liverpool, more broadly defined, constituted 5,821 – in all about 2.3 per cent of the total population (Table 5.2 above).

The examination of institutional populations, both official and quasi, is a neglected area of research, and is one that warrants greater attention by community historians. Liverpool, although in some respects a special case, was clearly not unique in terms of its quasi-institutional populations.[4] Similar situations would have existed in most large towns and cities throughout the nineteenth century. Indeed, the comparative study of quasi-institutions may provide useful insights into the size and nature of the transient populations and workforce of the last century.

3 It should be added that the figure of 2,766 should be regarded as a minimum number, since some quasi-institutions in the CEBs might have been inadvertently missed in the search.

4 For a discussion of the institutional and quasi-institutional population of 13 communities spread throughout England and Wales in the period 1891–1921 see Garrett *et al. Like others do around us*, chapter 2.

Appendix

Location of the institutional and quasi-institutional population: Liverpool, 1851

The references on the left of institutions listed below indicate the respective call numbers for the enumerators' schedules at the Public Record Office. The final three figures designate the enumeration district code, written in the top right corner of the enumeration book cover. IS* denotes a separate institutional book.

1. *St Martins*

HO 107/2177/1tt	Irish lodging house, Regent St (57 lodgers) emigrants
HO 107/2177/1tt	Irish lodging house, Regent St (15 lodgers) emigrants
HO 107/2177/1tt	Irish lodging house, Regent St (25 lodgers) emigrants
HO 107/2177/1tt	Irish lodging house, Regent St (16 lodgers) emigrants
HO 107/2177/1uu	Irish lodging house, Clay St (11 lodgers) boarding house
HO 107/2177/1vv	'A large number of persons, not inhabitants, almost exclusively Irish emigrants to America, 163 persons'
	Boats and barges in canal 145 persons
HO 107/2177/1hh	'27 temporary residents'
HO 107/2177/1jj	66 'visitors from the country'
HO 107/2177/1nn	4 persons on a barge
HO 107/2177/1pp	283 'emigrating to America'
HO 107/2177/1rr	6 emigrants

2. *Great Howard*

HO 107/2178/1J	27 on a barge
HO 107/2178/1L	11 in an Irish lodging house
HO 107/2178/1P	19 on barges
HO 107/2178/1Q	42 on barges
HO 107/2178/1T	107 Cavalry (Polish) in barracks
HO 107/2178/1S	954 in Gaol, Great Howard Street

3. *Dale Street*

HO 107/2179/1E	32 persons in Irish lodging houses, Lace Street
HO 107/2178/1U	33 persons in an hotel
HO 107/2178/1U	25 Welsh emigrants in a Welsh emigrant house, Union Street
HO 107/2718/1U	17 emigrants in a licensed victuallers
HO 107/2178/1U	15 Lincolnshire emigrants in a boarding house
HO 107/2179/1V	20 emigrants in a licensed victuallers
HO 107/2179/188	55 persons in the 'Royal Hotel'
HO 107/2179/1CC	131 persons in the 'Crooked Billet', 'Wellington', and the 'George' hotels

4. *St George*

HO 107/2180/1A	34 persons in barns, sheds, etc.

HO 107/2180/1A	9 shop assistants, Haymarket
HO 107/2180/1l	11 shop assistants, in two shops. Colquit Street
HO 107/2180/1J	52 drapers' assistants in shops, Bold Street
HO 107/2180/1J	13 boarders at a commercial travellers hotel
HO 107/2180/1L	70 'Americans proceeding to Exhibition'
HO 107/2180/IS	359 persons in Bluecoat Hospital, including 334 scholars

5. *St Thomas*

HO 107/2181/1F	27 Scottish seamen in a boarding house
HO 107/2181/1U	82 persons in the Southern and Toxteth Hospitals

6. *Mount Pleasant*

HO 107/2182/1A	78 persons in the 'Waterloo Hotel'
HO 107/2182/1D	76 persons in the 'Adelphi Hotel'
HO 107/2182/1G	24 girls at school
HO 107/2182/1U	44 persons at the Lock Hospital
HO 107/2182/1U	68 persons at the Lunatic Asylum
HO 107/2182/1EE	160 female orphans
HO 107/2182/1EE	44 in deaf and dumb institute
HO 107/2182/1HH	57 females in penitentiary
HO 107/2182/1II	79 females in Almshouses
HO 107/2182/1JJ	24 persons in Asylum
HO 107/2183/IS	1184 persons in the Workhouse
HO 107/2183/IS	247 persons in the Infirmary

7. *Islington*

HO 107/2184/1A	47 persons in the 'Stork Hotel'
HO 107/2184/1B	124 persons in a drapers training school
HO 107/2184/1C	137 persons in five hotels
HO 107/2184/1D	102 inmates at the Blind Asylum
HO 107/2184/1J	11 females at the Catholic Lying in Hospital
HO 107/2184/1GG	22 persons in the Catholic Blind Asylum
HO 107/2184/1ll	19 assistants in a grocer's store
HO 107/2185/IS	279 military in Brickfield Barracks and 32 females

8. *Toxteth Park*

HO 107/2188/1AD	3 persons living in a 'boat on the beach last three years'
HO 107/2188/1AO	24 females in the Beneficial Female Institute

9. *Everton*

HO 107/2190/1C	46 men (and women) in a military hospital
HO 107/2190/1D	36 children in the Soho Ragged School
HO 107/2190/IS	1153 at Kirkdale Industrial School
HO 107/2190/IS	748 in the Workhouse
HO 107/2190/IS	367 in Barracks
HO 107/2190/IS	422 in Gaol

10. *West Derby*

HO 107/2192/1A	39 persons in hospital
HO 107/2192/1H	64 nuns at the Mount Vernon Convent

6

A floating population: vessel enumeration returns, 1851–1921

V. C. BURTON

Demographic and community historians are very familiar with the scope of the census household enumerations, but less so with the enumeration of vessels. Moreover, historians are not always fully aware of the use which the Registrar General's Census Office made of the data extracted from vessel schedules; yet these data could appreciably affect the demographic and other characteristics of communities as represented in the official census reports. The scope of, and procedures for, vessel enumeration will be outlined, and this will be followed by an examination of some of the methodological errors introduced by the Census Office when processing vessel data for publication. Since these errors arose from the attempt to find standardised, if oversimple, administrative procedures, they are best demonstrated through specific examples which will serve to alert the local historian to potential fallibilities in the census wherever a floating population is concerned.

Procedures for vessel enumeration

Vessel enumeration applied to persons aboard craft in home waters or on inland rivers and waterways at the time of a census.[1] As shown in Table 6.1 below, these nominal residents of Great Britain numbered 50,664 in 1851, when vessel enumeration was first introduced, rising to 109,603 in 1911. Table 6.2 below depicts the distribution of persons on vessels by county: the greatest concentrations of floating residents were, predictably, in major commercial and naval ports, in the counties of Devon, Dorset, Lancashire and Hampshire, for example. However, the crew of a ship or river vessel could be returned in any part of the country and this, on occasion, had some remarkable consequences.

1 T. H. Lister, the first Registrar General, suggested that persons afloat in British waters should be 'properly described as residents'; Memorandum on the Census of 1841, PRO RG 27/1, 5. The standard definition of home waters was 'within the limits of the United Kingdom, the Isle of Man, the Channel Islands and of the Continent of Europe extending inclusive from the river Elbe to Brest'; 1851 Census Great Britain, *Population tables. Part I, vol. I*, BPP 1852–3 LXXXV, xvi. Returns of seafarers in foreign waters outside these limits were made by the Registrar General of Shipping and Seamen. See also Higgs, *Making sense*, 39–45; *Clearer sense*, 38–45.

Table 6.1 Numbers of persons enumerated on census vessel schedules: Great Britain, 1851–1921

Census date	Royal Navy	Category of vessel enumerated: Merchant Navy	Foreign & colonial	Barges & boats	Total
1851	6,440	28,536	7,714	7,974	50,664
1861	15,174	29,393	18,263	6,990	69,820
1871	14,141	39,824	12,545	17,617	84,127
1881	10,574	54,325	9,728	10,190	84,817
1891[a]	18,598	35,546	11,938	12,277	78,395
1901	24,766	36,503	12,166	8,130	81,565
1911[b]	46,375		63,228		109,603
1921[b]	26,445		58,229		84,674

Notes: *a* = Figures for the Royal Navy in 1891 include men in naval barracks.
b = There were no separate returns for the three categories merchant navy, foreign and colonial and barges and boats in the census reports of 1911 and 1921.

Source: 1851 Census Great Britain, *Population tables. Part I, vol. I*, BPP 1852–3 LXXXV, cxxx; 1861 Census England and Wales, *Population tables and report, vol. I*, BPP 1862 L, xxx; 1871 Census England and Wales, *Population tables: Areas, houses and inhabitants, vol. I*, BPP 1872 LXVI, xl; 1881 Census England and Wales, *General report and tables. Area houses and population*, BPP 1883 LXXIX, xix; 1891 Census England and Wales, *Vol. II Area, houses and population*, BPP 1893–4 CV, xxxiii–xxxiv; 1901 Census England and Wales, *Summary Tables*, BPP 1903 LXXXIV, 136–8; 1911 Census England and Wales, *Summary Tables*, BPP 1914–16 LXXXI, 73; 1921 Census England and Wales, *General Tables*, (HMSO, London, 1925), 12; 1861 Census Scotland, *Population tables and report, vol. I*, BPP 1862 L, xxxvi; 1871 Census Scotland, *Eighth decennial census of population, vol. II with report*, BPP 1873, LXXIII, xi; 1881 Census Scotland, *Ninth decennial census, vol. I*, BPP 1882 LXXXVI, 188; 1891 Census Scotland, *Tenth decennial census, vol. I*, BPP 1892 XCVI, 203–4; 1901 Census Scotland, *Population of Scotland with Report, vol. I*, BPP 1902 CXXIX, 309; 1911 Census Scotland, *Reports and Tables, vol. II*, BPP 1913 LXXX, 90; 1921 Census Scotland, *Reports and Tables, vol. I City and County Parts*, (HMSO, London, 1922–4).

The categories of data recorded on vessel schedules were similar to those of the household schedules with modifications to take account of the vessel as a unit of enumeration: the craft's tonnage, type and (where applicable) port of registry were noted; the inappropriate designation 'relationship to head of household' was replaced by a description of the individual's capacity on board the vessel – Mate or AB (Able Bodied Seaman), for instance (Figure 6.1). However, one potentially useful piece of information about this itinerant population, usual place of residence, was not required.[2] Enumeration was done by ships' captains, naval officers and others in command of craft. Completed forms were collected by customs personnel in UK ports,

2 Even had this information been gathered it is unlikely that the census could have undertaken the massive task of re-assigning individuals to their home towns and villages.

Table 6.2 British counties where persons enumerated on vessel schedules in the census of 1911 exceeded 3,000

County	Number enumerated on vessel schedules	% of total entered aboard Royal Navy vessels
Hampshire	12,490	81.7
Devon	10,819	90.9
Kent	9,807	65.7
Dorset	6,925	94.9
Essex	6,914	44.3
Lancashire	6,328	4.8
Glamorgan	4,925	–
London	4,219	0.1
Ross & Cromarty	4,195	95.3
Cornwall	3,501	29.4
Cheshire	3,126	7.2
Total[a]	73,249	

Notes: a = The total number of persons cnumerated on board vessels in Great Britain was 109,603.

Source: 1911 Census England and Wales, *Area, Families and Population, vol. I*, BPP 1912–13 CXI, 604–14; 1911 Census Scotland, *Reports and Tables, vol. I*, BPP 1912–13 CXIX.

or by the ordinary local enumerators if returned outside the limits of a port, and forwarded to the Census Office.[3] Officials then processed the data for publication by amalgamating them with data from household schedules for the enumeration districts contiguous to the recorded location of the vessels.[4] This procedure was carried out regardless of evidence that, for the most part, persons aboard vessels had none but the most tenuous connections with the population on *terra firma* close to which their vessels floated on census night. It was an ill-judged expedient, too unquestioningly adopted by the Census Office, with consequences which are demonstrated below.

The floating population

It should first be emphasised that the floating population was highly atypical of the population at large in terms of gender, age, birthplace and occupation. Unfortunately, for the researcher dependent on published census returns alone, the data are intractable: the age, birthplace and occupational profile of the floating population was nowhere given separately from that of the resident population. Indeed the local historian might remain unaware even of the existence of

3 Memorandum on the Census of 1841, PRO RG 27/1, 5; Registrar General's Letterbooks, PRO RG 29/2, letter dated 27 September 1890 to the Registrar General of Shipping and Seamen; Forms and Instructions for taking the census, 1861 to 1921, PRO RG 27/2–9.

4 Vessel schedules are preserved at the PRO and are available for consultation subject to the 100–year rule. Those for 1851 were, apparently, destroyed.

floating 'residents' in their chosen community but for a table indicating the numbers of persons enumerated on vessel-schedules (by parish) which was appended to the published population returns for each county. The only characteristic of the floating population to be systematically recorded was gender. These data, aggregated for England and Wales from the census volumes of 1891 and 1901, indicate that over 97 per cent of the persons enumerated on vessel schedules were male.[5] This was perhaps, to be anticipated, given that the majority of persons aboard vessels were seafarers, either of the Royal or Merchant Navy. Furthermore, extrapolation from other sources suggests that the floating population was predominantly composed of young men between the ages of 20 and 35 years who were disproportionately of Welsh, Scottish, or Irish extraction. It was a characteristic of seafaring that men went to sea in their youth, quitting for a job ashore in middle age.[6] Vessel schedules related to a unit of employment not to a unit of residence as did household schedules.[7] When the Census Office treated vessel schedules as comparable with household schedules, the result was to introduce distortions of varying degrees into the published census returns of communities.

A mobile population

It might be questioned whether the distortions were overly significant given that every port was bereft of some of its customarily resident seafarers on census night; was the addition of the floating population offshore merely compensation for absentees, the characteristic of the two groups being in some way interchangeable? This possibility can be dismissed, for it fails to take account of the itinerant nature of seafaring employment and the variability of shipping movements. The national and international flux of shipping meant that at any one time (i.e. at the time of a census) a motley assortment of British and foreign crews were to be found in most ports. Thus, for instance, the floating population of a port was liable to include greater proportions of foreigners than the population ashore. Cardiff, a cosmopolitan port, was an extreme example: two-fifths or more of the seafarers enumerated on board ship at each census between 1861 and 1901 were foreigners.[8] In England and Wales at large, as many as one in four of the ships enumerated at the

5 1891 Census England and Wales, *Vol. IV, General Report*, BPP 1893–4 CVI, xxiv; 1901 Census England and Wales, *Summary Tables*, BPP 1903 LXXXIV, 138.

6 Burton, 'Counting seafarers', 316.

7 Vessel enumeration poses some of the same methodological problems as institutional enumeration, but there were no institutions quite so mobile as vessels.

8 Census England and Wales, population returns for Cardiff 1861 to 1901 inclusive.

Figure 6.1 An example of a vessel schedule for 1871

CENSUS
OF
THE POPULATION,
1871.

SCHEDULE FOR VESSELS.

NAME of VESSEL: Challenger
Official Number if any: 11708
PORT or Place to which she belongs: Waterford
Her Tonnage: 132
Schooner
Coasting
NAME of MASTER: William Hughes

Place at which the Schedule is delivered to the Master and the Date of Delivery:
Southampton 29th March 1871

Position of the Vessel ... Laying in the ... at Southampton

To the **MASTER or PERSON in CHARGE of the VESSEL.**

1. You are requested to insert the particulars specified on the other side respecting all the persons who slept or abode on board the Vessel **ON THE NIGHT OF APRIL 2nd,** in compliance with an Act which passed the House of Commons and the House of Lords in the last Session of Parliament, and received the assent of Her Majesty The Queen on the 10th of August, 1870.

2. This Paper must be properly filled up **ON THE MORNING OF APRIL 3rd,** signed by yourself and delivered to the appointed Officer, who will apply to you for it.

[3. Should you be the **MASTER** of a **BRITISH VESSEL** and be out on the *night of April 2nd,* on a Coasting or short foreign voyage, you must fill up the Form on *April 3rd* and deliver it with the *LEAST POSSIBLE DELAY either at the Custom House of the British Port of arrival, or to the Officer who may apply for it.*]

4. Persons who refuse to give correct information incur a penalty of Five Pounds.

5. The Return is required to enable the Secretary of State to complete the Eighth Census, which is to show the exact numbers, ages, and conditions of the people—their arrangement in different ranks, professions, and trades—their distribution over sea and land—their increase and progress during the last ten years.

Approved,

H. A. BRUCE, *Home Office, Whitehall, Dec. 9th, 1870.*

GEORGE GRAHAM, *Registrar General.*

NUMBER of PERSONS belonging to the Vessel **ON SHORE** on the night of Sunday, **APRIL 2nd:—**

	ABSENT ON SHORE. (Names not entered in the Schedule on the other side.) Males	Females	Total
Crew			
Passengers			
Total			

NAME and SURNAME	CONDITION	AGE [Last Birthday] of Males	AGE of Females	RANK or OCCUPATION	WHERE BORN		Whether Deaf-and-Dumb, Blind, Imbecile or Idiot, Lunatic
William Hughes	Widower	56		Master	Pembroke	S. Wales	Nil
John Thomas	Married	38		Mate	Llanelly	S. Wales	Nil
David Charles	Married	34		A. B.	do	do	do	Nil
Hugh Skilley	Married	24		A. B.	Bellavelle	Ireland	Nil
Julian Le Jaume	Married	33		A. B.	Bingledue	France	Nil
John Bays	Single	16		Boy	Brixham	Devon	Nil

I declare the foregoing to be a true Return, according to the best of my knowledge and belief.

6 — Witness my Hand. (Signature) William Hughes

Source: PRO RG10/1194, Southampton.

censuses of 1891 and 1901 were foreign.[9] This explains why the most common occupation of foreigners recorded in censuses was seafaring. However, taking 1891 as an example, three-quarters of foreign seafarers were not enumerated on shore but in coastal waters, and few of them were truly residents of the country.[10]

Remarkably, the Registrar General professed to believe that seafarers in home waters at the time of a census were located in the very ports where they had 'wives, children and homes'.[11] However, even the most cursory examination of shipping movements would have revealed the error of this assumption. Interpretation of vessel schedules should be informed by insight into the longer-term pattern and type of a port's shipping.[12] A specific example may be made of the vessel schedule reproduced as Figure 6.1 above. The vessel *Challenger* was engaged on regular coal-carrying runs between South Wales and Southampton and, although her crew were enumerated in Southampton, the strong probability is that their homes and families were in the port of Llanelly, to which their vessel returned.[13] This schedule is evidence of a general trend; that strangers to a port remained on board ship, thus avoiding expenditure on lodgings, particularly if their voyage was uncompleted and their wages unpaid. Conversely, local seafarers went ashore to the company of family and friends and were, therefore, subject to household enumeration.

With few exceptions, vessels were not localised around home ports in the way which the Registrar General supposed. The fishing port of Grimsby had a staple trade which involved many local men and yet census returns reveal that the predominance of fishing boats owned and crewed from Grimsby did not preclude the craft of other UK and foreign ports. In 1881, 1,403 of the 2,292 persons enumerated on vessel schedules for Grimsby were aboard local fishing boats; with some justification were they regarded as residents of the port.[14] Nevertheless trawling fleets from further afield were drawn by the rich fishing grounds off Grimsby with the result that vessel enumeration also included 441 fishermen from such places as Hull, Lowestoft and Yarmouth and from ports in Scandinavia; they were likewise returned as 'residents' of Grimsby though, in this case, with little justification.[15]

9 1891 Census England and Wales, *Vol. IV General report*, BPP 1893–4 CV, xxxiv; 1901 Census England and Wales, *Summary Tables*, BPP 1903 LXXXIV, 138.

10 1891 Census England and Wales, *Vol. IV General report*, BPP 1893–4 CV, 67.

11 1871 Census England and Wales, *Preliminary Report*, BPP 1871 LIX, xxii.

12 Sources which might be consulted for their regular reports of shipping movements are *Lloyds Weekly Shipping Index* and *Shipping Gazette Weekly Summary*.

13 Crew agreement of the Challenger, Southampton City Record Office 11708/1871.

14 Census vessel enumeration schedules, 1881 Grimsby, PRO RG 11/3276–7. The 2,292 persons enumerated on vessel schedules constituted 8.1 per cent of the population of the parish of Great Grimsby (total population 28,503). 1881 Census England and Wales, *Area, houses and population*, BPP 1883 LXXIX, 409.

15 The remaining floating 'residents' were aboard a variety of British and foreign home trade and foreign going vessels.

The errors of the Registrar General's supposition are further illustrated by the example of Falmouth. The small-scale local traffic of this port was overshadowed by North Atlantic liners which made a port of call at Falmouth and by the vessels of the Royal Navy base. Thus at the census of 1881, a total of 2,301 persons were enumerated on vessel schedules, of whom 1,142 were naval personnel (aboard three ships) and 421 were foreign seafarers. Only 51 individuals in these returns could be legitimately connected with the Falmouth community. Conspicuous by their more distant origins were the crews of vessels on the North Atlantic passage registered at Liverpool, Dublin, Hamburg and Le Havre.[16] Any ship in harbour at the time of a census, however temporarily, was liable to the enumeration of its crew and passengers.[17] It was, though, a travesty to enumerate birds of passage as if they were customary residents. The objections were particularly strong in the case of Falmouth, where the floating population constituted over one-third of the borough's total population as returned in the census of 1881.[18]

The example of Falmouth highlights the importance of taking note of Royal Navy vessels, which added considerably to the floating population of some counties (see Table 6.2). Most, but by no means all, of these ships' crews were incorporated in the returns of settlements conspicuous for their naval establishments. Several such exceptions may be detected in the population returns for Cornwall and Kent where vessels technically based at naval ports were enumerated off the shore of small rural parishes. Thus, in 1901, the crews of Royal Navy ships off the parish of Maker (across the Tamar estuary from Devonport) effectively doubled its enumerated population to 2,274 persons.[19] The parish of Hoo in Kent with 301 residents in 1911, gained a floating population of 154 by virtue of one naval vessel off its shores.[20] Civilian ports were occasionally turned to military use, as was the case with Southampton in 1901 when troop movements connected with the Boer War probably accounted for most of the 1,090 persons returned on vessel schedules.[21] By no means could it be supposed that these troops were resident in the town, yet their inclusion on the total of population for the contiguous enumeration district gives an exaggerated impression of crowded housing conditions in the dock area of Southampton.

16 Census vessel enumeration schedules, 1881 Falmouth, PRO RG 11/2318.

17 Officials responsible for a vessel census at another international port, Southampton, complained of the practical difficulties of accurately enumerating persons aboard German liners because of their very brief call at the port; PRO RG 29/2, letter dated 21 March 1891.

18 The total population of Falmouth borough was 5,973; 1881 Census England and Wales, *Area, houses and population*, BPP 1883 LXXIX, 273.

19 1901 Census England and Wales, *County Reports. Cornwall*, BPP 1902 CXVIII, 170. Included in the population figure of 2,274 were 1,014 persons on board ship.

20 1911 Census England and Wales, *Area, Families and Population, vol. I*, BPP 1912–13 CXI, 170.

21 1901 Census England and Wales, *County Reports. Hampshire*, BPP 1902 CXIX, 51; *Southampton Daily Echo*, 30 March and 1 April 1901. At the previous census only 202 persons were enumerated on vessel schedules in the same parish.

The amalgamation of data from vessel schedules with data from household schedules for contiguous enumeration districts was not, therefore, justified by the rationale which the Registrar General suggested. The over-burdened officials of the Census Office were content with any expedient which made easier the complex job of processing data.[22] Moreover, further errors were perpetrated.

A population at sea

Captains of ships at sea, but supposedly in home waters at the time of a census, were required to complete vessel schedules, noting their position at midnight. Subsequently the census officials used this reference to 're-allocate' the floating population to what was judged to be the nearest enumeration district, however arbitrary their decision. The Registrar General himself confessed 'it has been a matter of guesswork to allocate a considerable proportion of the shipping population'.[23] Amongst the 1881 manuscript census returns for Cardiff, Swansea and Sunderland are schedules of vessels which were as far from those ports on census night as Rotterdam, Antwerp, Bilbao and Bordeaux.[24] The crews had no evident connection with these three British ports, yet their enumeration details were incorporated with those of the inhabitants of Cardiff, Swansea and Sunderland.[25] The implications of this practice may disconcert local historians, especially those who are dependent on published rather than manuscript returns, when it is appreciated that at the time of a census ships were, inevitably, randomly located around the British Isles. On census night 1901, a liner in transit to East India Dock dropped anchor in the Downs. Her crew, consisting of men from Poplar and Canning Town were, therefore, enumerated as residents of St Margaret-at-Cliffe, Kent and constituted as much as 15 per cent of the population of this small rural parish.[26] Similar anomalies in the published census returns for 1901 were noted by the Registrar General. These included the addition of 242 persons to the Isle of Grain's resident population of 532; remarkably, 164 of the floating population were aboard foreign vessels at the mouth of the river Scheldt.[27] It is not surprising, therefore, that in

22 The limitations of the Census Office are made glaringly apparent in out-letters to the Treasury between the 1880s and the 1900s, see PRO RG 29/2 and the *Report of the Committee appointed by the Treasury to inquire into certain questions connected with the taking of the Census*, BPP 1890 LVIII.

23 Memorandum on the Census of 1911, PRO RG 19/45.

24 Census vessel enumeration schedules, 1881, PRO RG 11/15001, Sunderland; PRO RG 11/5286 & 11/5291, Cardiff; PRO RG 11/5364, Swansea.

25 Some of the vessels made their first UK call at Cardiff, Swansea or Sunderland, hence the schedules were collected at those ports, but the fact that the ships were not re-located to their locations on census night indicates that the census officials were inconsistent in following their own stipulated procedures.

26 Memorandum on the Census of 1911, PRO RG 19/45, 54–5. The vessel schedule is unavailable under the 100–year rule, but the crew agreement of the *Galician* for this voyage can be consulted, PRO BT 100/139.

27 Memorandum on the Census of 1911, PRO RG 19/45.

1911 the Registrar General commented that 'for many reasons it appears undesirable to include [the shipping population] in the age, occupation and birthplace tables [of the published census]'.[28] Yet despite this observation, the practice was not altered until 1931.

In several of the examples cited in this chapter, 10 per cent or more of the population of a parish was constituted by persons aboard vessels either in port or at sea off the parish at the time of a census. Their connection with the resident community was often no more substantive that the geographical accident of their vessel's location on census night. Furthermore, the demographic and other characteristics of the floating population as recorded on vessel schedules were quite unlike those of the resident population enumerated on household schedules. The conflation of data from vessel schedules and from household schedules respectively was an administrative expedient adopted by the Census Office with little regard to the resulting distortions in the published census returns. The cases given here are but limited exemplification of the anomalies to which the community historian should be alert when using the published census statistics of maritime and riverine settlements.

28 Memorandum on the Census of 1911, PRO RG 19/45.

7

Visitors to Margate in the 1841 census: an attempt to look at the age and social structure of Victorian holidaymaking

JOHN WHYMAN

Margate, having originated in the eighteenth century as a major coastal watering place, enjoyed particular renown during the 1830s and 1840s as a well developed and popular steamboat resort.[1] The number of passengers arriving at and departing from Margate by water communications amounted to 2,219,364 over 35 years between 1812–13 and 1846–7, giving an annual average of 63,410 passengers. The number of passengers coming and going annually during the three years prior to the arrival of the South Eastern Railway in December 1846 averaged 86,802.[2]

Since 1801 there have been three summer censuses, 30 May 1831, 7 June 1841 and 20 June 1921; and, particularly in the case of seaside resort towns, the exact date of the census can be of vital importance to the information obtained from the census returns. We know this from the census of 1921, undoubtedly the best recent example of a summer census. This shows for Margate a total resident population of 46,480, but the Registrar General, taking into consideration the fact that the season was sufficiently far advanced by then to produce a large number of visitors in the population, subsequently reduced the 1921 resident population of Margate to 27,740. Following the 1831 census, it was reported that 'Margate and Ramsgate have increased in Population (2,496 and 1,954 Persons respectively) which is attributable to their being resorted to as Watering Places'.[3] What, therefore, can we conclude from the 1841 census?

Finding visitors in the CEBs

The 1841 count was only two weeks earlier in the year than that of 1921. It was recorded that 'the Return for Margate includes 245 Persons in the Royal Sea Bathing Infirmary, 68 Seamen, etc., in vessels and

1 For a more extended treatment of this article and further information on Margate see Whyman, *Aspects of holidaymaking*, vol. II, 674–99, 720–4.

2 Calculated from the *Report of the Select Committee on Ramsgate and Margate Harbours*, BPP 1850, 660.

3 1831 Census Great Britain, *Abstract of the population returns*, BPP 1833 XXXVI, 206n.

steam packets in the harbour and 1,586 visitors'.[4] This figure of 1,586 visitors on 7 June 1841 is quoted in Pimlott's, *The Englishman's holiday: a social history*, along with 590 visitors at Blackpool, 89 at Shanklin, 186 at Cleethorpes, 65 at Seaton, 49 at Budleigh Salterton, 50 at Cromer, 44 at Skegness, and 60 at Bridlington.[5] Of these returns, 1,586 is clearly the most impressive figure, but it does not tally with information obtained from the Margate CEBs. It is estimated that there were 1,297 visitors within Margate over the census night of 7 June 1841. 1,265 can be specifically identified in 22 of the CEBs for Margate. All told, there were 23 CEBs, the last of which mentions the presence of 'Gentlefolk Visitors 32'[6] and 1,265 plus 32 gives 1,297. In the other enumeration districts, however, visitors were usually recorded as such by means of a tick, cross or small 'v' or 'L' entered against their names, or they were bracketed in groups in lodgings, boarding houses, or hotels as visitors.

This distinguishing of visitors by a tick, cross, or small 'v' or 'L' appears to be an unorthodox local variation, and certainly no instructions were specifically given as to whether such people should be distinguished, or how. Nor did the Margate householders always follow the guidance on the householder's schedule concerning the rounding of ages to the nearest quinquennium below the true age.[7]

The CEBs confirm an important characteristic of Victorian holiday-making, namely that few mid-nineteenth-century holidaymakers stayed in hotels or boarding houses. Hotel occupancy was invariably temporary while alternative lodgings were sought. Most visitors resided with a lodging-house keeper, there being 97 to choose from in Margate in June 1841, or quite frequently occupied spare rooms or parts of a tradesman's house or business premises.

The presence of visitors within the 23 CEBs for Margate in 1841 is indicated in at least two other ways. Firstly, the enumerators were asked to state the cause of any increase in population since the 1831 census and their comments provide clear-cut evidence of the presence of holidaymakers; for instance, 'Chiefly Visitors from London'[8] or 'Visitors from London principally for Sea Bathing or Pleasure'[9] Secondly, and yet another clear indication that the season had commenced in Thanet, was the enumeration of 72 people (68 males and 4 females) on board seven vessels, four of which were steam packets

4 1841 Census Great Britain, *Abstract of the answers*, BPP 1843 XXII, 128n .
5 Pimlott, *Englishman's holiday*, 77.
6 PRO HO 107/468/2.
7 On the instructions given to the 1841 enumerators see 1841 Census Great Britain, *Abstract of the answers*, BPP 1843 XXII, and Higgs, *Making sense*, 68; *Clearer sense*, 78. However, it should be noted that the instructions also noted that 'the *exact age* may be stated if the person prefers it'.
8 PRO HO 107/468/3.
9 PRO HO 107/468/5.

Table 7.1 Numbers of males and females: Margate, 1841

	Males	Females	Total
Visitors	496	769	1,265
Residents[a]	4,429	5,356	9,785
Total	4,925	6,125	11,050

Notes: a = includes staff and patients in the Infirmary.

Table 7.2 Age structure: Margate, 1841

	Total population					Visitors			
Age	Males		Females		Age	Males		Females	
group	n.	%	n.	%	group	n.	%	n.	%
0–4	640	13.0	611	10.0	0–5	94	19.0	83	10.8
5–9	661	13.4	633	10.3	6–10	51	10.3	66	8.6
10–14	673	13.7	610	9.9	11–15	47	9.5	93	12.1
15–19	411	8.3	648	10.6	16–20	30	6.0	99	12.9
20–24	401	8.1	698	11.4	21–25	40	8.1	91	11.8
25–29	336	6.8	540	8.8	26–30	38	7.7	77	10.0
30–34	322	6.5	472	7.7	31–35	29	5.8	50	6.5
35–39	265	5.4	353	5.8	36–40	33	6.7	64	8.3
40–44	263	5.3	340	5.5	41–45	32	6.5	45	5.9
45–49	206	4.2	289	4.7	46–50	38	7.7	43	5.6
50–54	212	4.3	284	4.6	51–55	20	4.0	18	2.3
55–59	134	2.7	164	2.7	56–60	18	3.6	16	2.1
60–64	128	2.6	157	2.6	61–65	7	1.4	11	1.4
65–69	101	2.0	126	2.0	66–70	11	2.2	10	1.3
70–74	73	1.5	93	1.5	71–75	6	1.2	2	0.3
75–79	31	0.6	47	0.7	76–80	2	0.4	0	0.0
80+	32	0.6	42	0.7	81+	0	0.0	1	0.1
Unk.	36	0.7	18	0.3					
Totals	4,925	100	6,125	100		496	100	769	100

Source: 1841 Census Great Britain, *Abstract of the answers*, BPP 1843 XXII, 124–5.

within Margate Harbour.[10] The London to Thanet steamboats proceeded to Margate or Ramsgate and returned to London, apart from day excursions, on alternative days. Three of the steam packets had on board crews numbering respectively 19, 18 and 15, making 52 in all.

There is clearly no reason to doubt the residence of 1,297 visitors within Margate over the census night of 7 June, 1841. In total they represented a high figure for so early in the season, added to which 214 patients were receiving seasonal treatment in the Royal Sea Bathing Infirmary. The 1851 Census, by contrast, was conducted on 31 March when the holiday season had not commenced, and there were no patients in Margate's Royal Sea Bathing Infirmary.

10 PRO HO 107/468/3.

Age and social composition of Margate's holidaymakers and their geographical origins

Tables 7.1 and 7.2 above detail the age and sex structure of the 1,265 visitors who are known to have been staying at Margate on 7 June, 1841 compared to the total resident population. The first of these shows that 61 per cent of the visitors to Margate were female, compared with only 55 per cent of the resident population. The preponderance of female over male visitors at all ages between 11 and 40 is very noticeable. Visitors tended to be rather younger than the resident population as a whole; children under 15 comprised 39 per cent of the male visitors and 31 per cent of the female visitors. Almost 37 per cent of the female visitors were aged between 11 and 25 compared with under 24 per cent for males. Apart from relatively lower female mortality, female servants and governesses helped to swell the female age groups 11–15, 16–20, 21–25 and 26–30. Eighty-nine servants and governesses had been brought down to supervise the domestic arrangements of the lodging.

The opportunity to take holidays, which were invariably unpaid holidays, varied with age and family circumstances. The expenses of running a home (rent, rates, servants' wages) continued while paying for a holiday elsewhere. Relative affluence when young, single, or newly married (without children) was reduced or negated while raising a family (depending on the number of children, income or alternative source of wealth). When parents were middle-aged and the family had grown up, relative affluence could return again, the grown-up children contributing perhaps to the running expenses of the home. The real crux was the family holiday, as Elizabeth Brunner's study of holiday-making in 1945 pointed out.[11]

Single people or brothers and sisters staying together were numerous among the Margate visitors of 7 June 1841. There were in addition the following combinations of visitors:

Whole families (husband, wife and children) or families indicating the presence of a father.	90
Husbands and wives with no children.	63
Mothers and family, no fathers being present.	71

The latter two categories are of interest. The husband and wife combinations were mainly either middle aged and elderly in their 50s and 60s, or they were still comparatively young, in their 20s. Fathers without guaranteed holidays would, if they could afford it, send their families away to the seaside, preferably not too far from London where they could visit them at weekends. Margate, linked by steamboats with

11 Brunner, *Holiday making*, 18.

Figure 7.1 Steamboats leaving Margate

Source: Oulton, *Picture of Margate*, 104.

London, was ideally located for this sort of family arrangement, which gave rise to a late Saturday steamboat 'called in the language of the place, "The Hats' Boat" or "The Husbands' Boat"'[12] (see Figure 7.1 above).

Initially, in the eighteenth century, the demand for holidays came nominally from the aristocracy, gentry, clergy and a few among the professional and mercantile classes. The increasing wealth of the middle classes and tradesmen, particularly during the first half of the nineteenth century, increased the demand for holidaymaking, and the existence of cheap means of water communication between London and Thanet caused this process to develop relatively early in the case of Margate. In the 1840s the adjectives 'genteel' and 'vulgar' were used to describe in very general terms the company frequenting the Isle of Thanet.

> Ten people land at Margate for one that lands at any other part of the island... That part of society which is called 'Fashionable', and which once frequented the place have long since deserted it almost entirely... The place is annually visited by tradespeople, varying degrees of prosperity, or... 'respectability', by professional men and their families, and by not a few retired independent gentlefolk... At

12 Anon, 'The Isle of Thanet', 147, 152.

> Ramsgate we are much dearer, duller and more genteel than at Margate... Margate is 'shocking vulgar' in our sight. Margate comes to us, and we stare at her: but Ramsgate goes not to Margate.[13]

Contemporary observations of mid-nineteenth-century holidaymaking which stress gentility and vulgarity must inevitably confuse the social historian to some extent. Who saw who as vulgar or genteel is not an easy question to answer.

Table 7.3 below, derived from the 1841 CEBs, shows the occupations of 601 Margate visitors, 98 different occupations being represented among them. The social trends of holidaymaking as revealed by occupations suggest that the middle-classes were strongly entrenched in Margate by 1841. Aristocratic and titled visitors, or the old categories of nobility, gentry, and clergy, were few in number, though gentry, no doubt, were probably well represented among the 352 visitors of independent means. This is the hardest category to break down. While it is disappointing to find so many in this vague category, the instruction to enumerators in 1841 as to 'Profession, Trade, Employment, or of Independent Means', stated:

> Men, or widows, or single women, having no profession or calling, but living on their means may be inserted as independent, which may be written shortly thus, Ind.[14]

Independent means can be taken to include an unearned income from inherited wealth, from urban or agricultural rents, and/or from investments. Industrialisation, the growth of towns and the constructions of canals, harbours, railways, and public utilities, particularly gas and waterworks undertakings, had greatly widened the opportunities of middle-class investment income.

Of the 352 visitors of independent means, no fewer than 222, or 63 per cent were women who had a strong tendency to so record themselves. Some had only rather indirect links with the expanding middle classes and the investing public generally. Some were spinsters or widows of independent means. Some were wives and mothers whose husbands were left behind in London, perhaps only to come down at weekends, as noted above. There is no means of knowing the occupational title which was appropriate to a married woman of independent means, but it may be presumed to have been middle class, professional, or commercial in the vast majority of cases. The 130 male visitors of independent means, a proportion of whom were elderly of retired, compares therefore with 70 tradespeople, 32 merchant or manufacturers and 27 drawn from the professions. Titled visitors numbered no more than three viz.: Sir W. White, aged 50, Independent,

13 Anon, 'The Isle of Thanet', 150, 157.
14 PRO RG 27/1 56–7.

Table 7.3 Occupational structure of Margate visitors, 1841

Given occupation	n. of individuals with occupation
Independent	351
Servant (female)	79
Merchant	12
Clerk	7
Solicitor	7
Servant (male)	7
Mechanic	5

Occupations recorded four times: Engineer, Farmer, Wine merchant

Occupations recorded three times: Boiler maker, Clergyman, Governess, Grocer, Law stationer, Tailor

Occupations recorded twice: Army, Bookseller, Confectioner, Cooper, Draper, Dressmaker, Goldsmith, Innkeeper, Lawyer, Licensed Vitualler, Navy (half pay), Painter, Plasterer, Schoolmaster, Shipowner, Stockbroker, Surgeon, Surveyor, Tobacconist, Warehouseman

Occupations recorded once: Accountant, Agricultural labourer, Artist, Auctioneer, Barrister-at-law, Bill broker, Brassfounder, Broker, Builder, Butcher, Chemist, Cloth factor, Coachman, Coal merchant, Collector, Compositor, Conveyancer, Coppersmith, Cordwainer, Cork cutter, Decorator, Dentist, Embosser, Engraver, Florist, Furnishing undertaker, Furrier, Gas engineer, Hat maker, Independent Bart., India rubber merchant, Ironmonger, Joiner, Linen draper, Mariner, Manufacturer, Milliner, Missionary, Nurseryman, Nursery seedsman, Optician, Outfitter, Paper stainer, Pattern drawer, Pianoforte maker, Picture dealer, Plumber, Publisher, Railway Officer, Saddler, Shell merchant, Ship surveyor, Silk mercer, Stationer, Tea dealer, Timber merchant, Upholsterer, Vice Admiral, Victualler, Wax chandler, Woollen factor

Major occupational categories	n.
Independent	352
Servant or governess	89
Trade	70
Merchant, dealer or factor	25
Professional, other than legal	16
Legal profession	11
Engineer or mechanic	10
Manufacturer or maker	7
Clerk	7
Military or Naval	5
Farming	5
Clerical	4
Total	601

staying near the Duke's Head,[15] Lady Bathurst, aged 40, Independent, residing with her daughter and servants,[16] and Sir Thomas Apreed,

15 PRO HO 107/468/3.
16 PRO HO 107/468/4.

Figure 7.2 Margate Front, 1820

Source: Oulton, *Picture of Margate*, 83.

aged 45, Independent Bart,[17] both staying in Fort Crescent. The Church and farming were also noticeably well down in the list.

The third major occupational group, coming after people of independent means and domestic servants and governesses, comprised tradespeople. They, along with merchants, dealers and factors as a combined group of 95, exceeded the number of servants and governesses. Tradespeople, merchants, dealers, factors, the professions, engineers, mechanics, manufacturers, and clerks, numbering 146, exceeded in total the 130 male visitors of independent means. The professions, including the church and armed services, were outnumbered by tradespeople by about 2:1. Shopkeepers and tradesmen multiplied in number and wealth during the first half of the nineteenth century, most noticeably in London, the resident population of which doubled between 1801 and 1851.[18] Nineteenth-century England may have remained an aristocratic country[19] but confronted by the commercial and industrial changes of the period, the aristocracy were unable to retain an eighteenth-century monopoly hold over the resorts and spas of England when faced with the growing economic strength

17 PRO HO 107/468/4.

18 On the expanding prosperity of shopkeepers see Davis, *History of shopping*, 252, 256–7; Adburgham, *Shops and shopping*, 42; and Alexander, *Retailing in England*, 89–109, 239–41.

19 Thompson, *English landed society*, 1.

of the middle classes. Margate had become, by 1841, one of the holiday resorts of an extensive and diverse middle-class.

The 1841 CEBs also provide some indication of the geographical preference and distribution of visitors in the town according to street or district. The cost of taking lodgings varied according to the period of the season and according to location, lodgings with a sea-view being preferred but always being the dearer. By far the largest proportion of well-to-do visitors favoured lodgings with a close proximity to the sea-front, as pictured in Figure 7.2 above.

Visitors to Margate in June 1841 were staying in 76 districts, streets, squares, terraces, crescents, rows, places, and lanes, with a decided preference for sea-front lodgings or lodgings in close proximity to shops, libraries, baths, the theatre, etc., in the more fashionable streets or squares. 504 visitors were residing in lodgings or hotels with direct access to the sea-front viz.:

Buenos Ayres	31
Upper and Lower Marine Terraces	240
The Parade	37
The Fort Area including Fort Crescent	135
Cliff Terrace	30
Zion Place	31
Total	504

Of the 504 visitors, 348 were concentrated in the Upper and Lower Marine Terraces and in Fort Crescent. The Parade contained two of the leading hotels of Margate, the White Hart and the York Hotel, having between them 14 visitors. They were sizeable establishments, the White Hart employing a clerk, three female servants, and two male servants, and the York Hotel six female servants and two male servants.[20] Eighteenth- and nineteenth-century seaside towns developed as terraces of tall houses and hotels strung out along the sea-front.[21] Behind the sea-front there was a mixture of areas and properties: some fashionable squares and streets; a High Street or an area or areas of shops selling necessities and good quality wares; residential parts containing some lodging houses, some of which would be for poorer visitors, and rows of meaner streets, housing the working population, whose employment depended in large measure upon the money spent by visitors on the sea-front.[22] On the outskirts or periphery of the town settlement became increasingly agrarian. The residence of Margate visitors by street and district in 1841 exactly reflects this pattern. Slightly inland from the sea-front there were 31 in lodging houses in Danehill Row, 49 residing in

20 PRO HO 107/468/2.
21 Williamson, *The English channel*, 327.
22 Williamson, *The English channel*, 327.

Table 7.4 Birthplaces of Margate visitors, 1841

Birthplace	n.
Kent	128
Other county	1,081
Scotland	8
Ireland	23
Overseas	20
Unknown	5
Total	1,265

the main thoroughfare of the High Street, which was in close proximity to the circulating libraries, bathing rooms, the Theatre Royal, the assembly rooms etc., as was the fairly fashionable district bounded by and incorporating Hawley Square, Union Crescent, Cecil Square, Cecil Street, Hawley Street, Churchfields Place, Churchfield Place, Princes Street, and Vicarage Place, housing altogether at least 100 visitors.

Lying west of Margate, and indeed west of the Margate Sea Bathing Infirmary, were 27 visitors in Garlinge, 75 in Westbrook, and 19 in Rancorn, that is, a total of 121, most of whom it must be supposed were out-patients of the Infirmary, containing among their number a high proportion of children. In Garlinge there were 13 children under the age of 10 who were residing in lodging or boarding houses independently of any other relatives.[23] In Westbrook there were 26 children similarly placed.[24] Garlinge, Westbrook and Rancorn were settlements detached from Margate in 1841, very much on the periphery of urban settlement. Westbrook contained among its inhabitants 12 coastguards,[25] while the area known as Rancorn, Mutrix, Marsh Bay, Street and Street Green, Dandelion, Garlinge, Crowhill, and Hartsdown, had 48 agricultural labourers as one of the 25 occupations represented among 121 persons.[26]

The birthplaces of Margate's visitors in June 1841 is summarised in Table 7.4 above. Just about 10 per cent of visitors spending holidays in Margate had been born in Kent. However, the vast majority almost certainly came from London, which in Table 7.4 is included in the 'other county' category. Indeed the census enumerators' statements in 1841 attributing the increase in population since 1831 in great measure to visitors from the capital. In the 1840s Margate attracted a few foreign visitors, and a few others who had been born in foreign parts having apparently returned to settle in England.

23 PRO HO 107/468/6.
24 PRO HO 107/468/3.
25 PRO HO 107/468/3.
26 PRO HO 107/468/6.

Figure 7.3 The Royal Sea Bathing Infirmary, 1820

Source: Oulton, *Picture of Margate*, 62.

The Royal Sea Bathing Infirmary

Quite apart from the 1,297 visitors in Margate over the census night of 1841, there were also 214 patients who were receiving seasonal treatment in the Royal Sea Bathing Infirmary, illustrated in Figure 7.3 above. This was founded by the pioneering eighteenth-century Quaker physician, John Coakley Lettsom (1744–1815), who had come to believe that fresh air, sea water, sunlight and regular habits were essential to the treatment of many diseases, especially those of the chest and all tubercular troubles.[27] The Infirmary, intended for poor people suffering from scrofula or tuberculosis, coming mainly from London, was founded in 1791 and opened its doors in 1796 at Westbrook, as 'the oldest orthopaedic hospital in the world'.[28] The Infirmary had treated 3,756 patients up to January 1816,[29] and by December 1850 it was reckoned that 'no less than 22,000 persons have obtained relief through this charity'.[30]

27 Raistrick, *Quakers in science and industry*, 311; Dainton, *England's hospitals*, 93.
28 Strange, *Royal Sea Bathing hospital*, 13.
29 *The Gentleman's Magazine*, January 1816, 17.
30 *The Gentleman's Magazine*, December 1850, 632.

Table 7.5 Age structure of the Royal Sea Bathing Infirmary: staff and in-patients

Age	Males	Females	Total
Staff			
Under 20	1	2	3
21–30	1	6	7
31–40	1	4	5
41–50	1	6	7
51–60	1	1	2
Over 61	0	1	1
Total	5	20	25
In-patients			
5	7	2	9
6	3	4	7
7	10	9	19
8	10	5	15
9	14	3	17
10	10	6	16
11	8	4	12
12	3	2	5
13	4	9	13
14	10	3	13
15	15	13	28
Sub-total	94	60	154
20–24	15	8	23
25–29	4	12	16
30–34	4	3	7
35–39	8	1	9
40–44	3	0	3
45–49	0	1	1
Over 50	0	1	1
Totals	128	86	214

The Infirmary was enumerated separately in one of the special enumeration books designed for institutional establishments.[31] This shows that on census night the Infirmary was home to a total of 245 individuals, of whom 214 were in-patients (128 males and 86 females); 25 were officers and staff of the Infirmary, mainly female nurses and maids; and the rest personal guests staying with the Infirmary's resident surgeon, William Oliver Chalk. In enumerating the patients, the steward entered year by year all the ages of the child patients from 5 to 15 years (see Table 7.5 above), and it is clear from these figures that children aged 15 years and under constituted the bulk of the in-patients of the Infirmary; 73 per cent in the case of males and just on 70 per cent in the case of females. The in-patients were cared for by staff, over 50 per cent of whom were aged 35 years and over. The Infirmary

31 See chapter 5 by Taylor, and Higgs, *Making sense*, 37–9; *Clearer sense*, 35–7.

Table 7.6 Occupational structure of male in-patients in the Royal Sea Bathing Infirmary

Occupations mentioned three times: Agricultural labourer, Printer, Shoemaker, Tailor

Occupations mentioned twice: Footman, Lighterman, Plumber, Porter

Occupations mentioned once: Artist, Banker's clerk, Bricklayer, Bricklayer's labourer, Cabinet maker, Carpenter, Compositor, Counting office clerk, Druggist, Gardener, Servant, Medical student, Nurseryman, Ostler, Painter, Ploughman, Schoolmaster, Tea dealer, Waiter, Watch gilder, Wheelwright, Whipmaker, Wine porter

also treated out-patients, the presence of whom, including a high proportion of young children from Garlinge, Westbrook and Rancorn has been noted above.

The occupations of the male patients recorded in the institutional CEB are detailed in Table 7.6 above. As distinct from the visitors to Margate, the in-patients of the Royal Sea Bathing Hospital were largely working class. Only 6 of the 49 male in-patients aged 15 years and over were entered without occupations, and since 30 out of the 49 were given as aged either 15 or 20, it seems reasonable to conclude that the vast majority of these in-patients were journeymen or labourers. The following rough classification suggests that the in-patients of the Infirmary were of a much lower income and social strata than the average 1841 holidaymaker to Margate. The ability of these people to benefit by way of sea air and sea-bathing or convalescence depended solely on the existence of a charitable institution such as the Royal Sea Bathing Hospital.

The overwhelming majority of the staff and patients of the Infirmary were returned as having been born outside Kent. Only 8 of the 31 individuals enumerated as officers, staff or residents in the surgeon's household were born in the county (25 per cent), while for the in-patients the figure was even lower, the Kent-born accounting for just 9 out of a total of 214 (4 per cent).

Conclusion

Because the census of 1841 was an early summer census, the presence within Margate of 1,297 visitors and 214 patients in the Royal Sea Bathing Infirmary becomes crucial in interpreting the trends in the resident population of the town in the early-eighteenth century. As shown in Table 7.7 below, the effect of excluding visitors and patients from the 1841 total removes the impression of a marked sustained increase of population in Margate up to 1841.[32] The population of Margate having grown markedly up to 1831 then entered a period of

32 The figure for 1841, uncorrected for the presence of visitors has been taken at its face value by Morgan, 'Development of settlement', 54, 57–8.

Table 7.7 Growth of population: Margate, 1801–1871

Year	According to census	Standardised census population
1801	4,766	4,766
1811	6,126	6,126
1821	7,843	7,843
1831	10,339	10,339
1841	*11,050*	*9,539*
1851	10,099	10,099
1861	10,019	10,019
1871	13,903	13,903

decline and stability which lasted for three decades. 1831, it should be noted, was also a census held fairly late in the year (30 May) so that while the 1841 population figure for Margate is obviously inflated, that for 1831 might be too. In 1851, the resident population was still lower than for 1831, and was to fall further to 10,019 in 1861, thereafter reversing this decline with an increase of the order of 38.7 per cent between 1861 and 1871.

The calculations derived from the 1841 CEBs concerning visitors to Margate are perhaps unique. The position as regards neighbouring Thanet resorts of Broadstairs and Ramsgate is unfortunately less satisfactory. The most relevant Broadstairs return covering the High Street, Charlotte Street, York Place, Chandos Place, and Nuckell's Place,[33] where visitors are known to have resided during the nineteenth century, makes no attempt to identify visitors from inhabitants and merely attributes the computed increase of population amounting to 72 persons since 1831, to 'Gentry visiting Broadstairs during the summer season'. In the case of Ramsgate, visitors can be found in the leading hotels of the town, or in positions fronting the sea,[34] and although it might be possible to make some approximate calculations of visitors to Ramsgate and Broadstairs, by scrutinising lodgings and hotels for wealthy and professional people, born outside Kent, such as counting of possible visitors would represent no more than a vague estimate of holidaymakers to these two resorts in June 1841.

Census material exists as one of the most valuable quantifiable sources for studying local economic and social history, yet the details which emerge from the 1841 CEBs provide only a static picture at one point in time. There is, however, much detailed material existing in other sources, which can be used to corroborate the evidence drawn from the 1841 CEBs. The 1841 returns, considered in conjunction with other contemporary sources, provide a good insight into the patterns and extent of early Victorian holidaymaking.

33 PRO HO 107/468/18.
34 Whyman, *Aspects of holidaymaking*, vol. II, 696–9.

Part II

Population and demography

8

Population and demography

K. SCHÜRER AND D. R. MILLS

Given the work undertaken subsequently, it is easy to overlook the fact that the primary purpose of the censuses was to provide basic information on the size of the country's population. This is no more evident than in full title of the Act of Parliament that gave rise to the first census enumeration of 1801 – *An Act for taking an Account of the Population of Great Britain, and of the Increase or Diminution thereof.*[1] This first census was taken when the country was experiencing some of the highest growth rates in population ever recorded (see Table 8.1 below),[2] and in retrospect it is hard for us to believe that contemporaries were uncertain if the size of the population was actually going up or down.[3]

The published reports of the censuses have always provided tabulations on the overall size of the population, sometimes broken down by age and sex, for all of the major administrative areas – parishes, hundreds, counties, registration districts, and so on.[4] Indeed, since 1851 the census authorities have adopted a specific policy of publishing an abstract of the population totals of the principal administrative areas as soon as possible after census day, the so-called *Preliminary Report*.[5] These, and the other more detailed reports, a full listing of which are given as an appendix to this chapter, contain a wealth of information on basic population trends. Despite this, they remain relatively under-used by the local community historian whose inclination has been to turn directly to the CEBs. An exception to this is chapter 11 by Smith which brings together information from both the published census returns and the annual reports of the Registrar General – giving details on the numbers of births, deaths and marriages for key administrative areas – to analyse the movement of migrants into the town of Nottingham, paying special attention to the

1 The Act, perhaps ironically, was passed on the last day of the eighteenth century, 31 December, 1800. 41 Geo. III c. 15.

2 Wrigley and Schofield estimate that, in the case of England, gross reproduction rates reached a figure of 2.931 in 1806, the highest rate since 1541. Wrigley and Schofield, *Population history*, Appendix A3.1, 528–9.

3 See, Glass, *Numbering the people*.

4 In addition, Drake, 'The census', 32–41, lists the reports and the administrative levels at which specific data were made available. There is similar, but fuller information in Lawton, *Census and social structure*, 294–319.

5 However, the actual term 'preliminary report' was not used until 1871.

Table 8.1 Population size, growth rates and sex ratio: England and Wales, 1801–1911

	Total population (000s)	Increase since last census (000s)	Percentage increase	Females per 1,000 males
1801	8,893			1,057
1811	10,164	1,272	14.3	1,054
1821	12,000	1,836	18.1	1,040
1831	13,897	1,897	15.8	1,036
1841	15,914	2,017	14.5	1,046
1851	17,928	2,013	12.6	1,042
1861	20,066	2,139	11.9	1,053
1871	22,712	2,646	13.2	1,054
1881	25,974	3,262	14.4	1,055
1891	29,003	3,028	11.7	1,063
1901	32,528	3,525	12.2	1,068
1911	36,070	3,543	10.9	1,068

Source: Mitchell, *British historical statistics*, 9.

development of the new suburb of Radford.[6]

The need to provide accurate population statistics at a local level in certain respects became even more pressing after the Local Government Act of 1888 which, in addition to other changes, created county boroughs. The formation of this new tier of local government made the county boroughs administratively and financially independent of the county council in which they were geographically situated, and as such they were free from payment of the county rate. Moreover, their status was defined principally by size, the requirement being a population of at least 50,000 inhabitants.[7] Thus an accurate measure of population totals was of key importance. This fact is clearly demonstrated in the remarkable story of Eastbourne. This south coast town was clearly growing quite rapidly in the late-nineteenth and early-twentieth century, and in 1901 recorded a census population of 43,337. Thinking that by 1907 the population had passed the magic figure of 50,000 the Town Council made representation to the Local Government Board (LGB) applying to become a Borough, a status which would give it control over the spending of its rates which currently went to the parent East Sussex County Council. To prove its size, the LGB required Eastbourne to undertake an informal census, which it duly did on 8 October, 1907, returning a population of 50,696. The LGB, however, refused to accept this, concerned that the extra 696 could easily be accounted for by non-resident visitors to the town, and so ordered an

6 For other examples of the use of information from the published census reports in combination with the Registrar General's *Annual Reports* at a national and regional level see Woods, *Population of Britain*, and Lawton, 'Population' and 'Population and society'.

7 The first County Boroughs of 1888 were defined by the population sizes attained at the time of the 1881 census.

independent enumeration to be conducted. Consequently the Town Council and the LGB contacted the Registrar General who advised that the parties wait until the 1911 census. The Town Council, however, wished to push ahead and contracted the General Registry Office to undertake an *ad hoc* census. After due preparation this was carried out on the 24/25 January, 1909, recording a total population of 49,286 with which the application to the LGB for Borough status was dismissed.[8]

Age data

Next in line from overall population size the ages of individuals as recorded in the census are of central significance to much analysis based on the CEBs. However, it is relatively well-known that the census enumerations often suffer from age mis-reporting as a result of both deliberate falsification and unintentional inaccuracy. In her study linking the inhabitants of Colyton (Devonshire) between the censuses of 1851 and 1861, Robin found that only 51.5 per cent of the men and 52.4 per cent of the women had an age gap of exactly 10 years, while 6.9 per cent and 9.5 per cent respectively recorded a discrepancy of 1 or 2 years either way.[9]

Similarly, comparing data from the same census years for the parish of Hathersage (Derbyshire), Tillott found that 60.6 per cent of the population (males and females combined) had a gap of exactly 10 years, a further 28.0 per cent a discrepancy of 1 year, with the remaining 11.4 per cent having a discrepancy of 2 years or more. In comparison, the Yorkshire parish of Braithwell recorded figures, respectively, of 67.5, 22.4 and 10.1 per cent.[10] Lastly, in his study of Preston, Anderson found that for 475 persons living in the Lancashire town between 1851 and 1861 only 53.0 per cent had an exact gap of ten years, but that the discrepancy was greater than 2 years for only 4.0 per cent of the population, greater than 5 years for less than 1.0 per cent.[11] Similar findings to these have been reported by those comparing instead the entries in the census returns with the appropriate parish baptism registers. In particular, Razzell's pioneering study of 45 parishes (taking only natives over 17 years of age in 1851 and excluding married women due to the problems of surname change) found an exact match for only 46.5 per cent of the sample population, 31.8 per cent having a discrepancy of 1 year, 10.5 per cent a 2 year discrepancy,

8 PRO RG 44/A and RG 44/B.

9 Quoted in Higgs, *Making sense*, 67; *Clearer sense*, 79–80. It is, of course, the case that due to the changes in the actual date of the census from decade to decade some individuals may not have experienced a real age difference of exactly 10 years if their birthday fell within the band of days between the date chosen for one census and the next.

10 Tillott, 'Sources of inaccuracy', 107–8.

11 Anderson, 'The study of family structure', 75.

and 12.5 per cent with a discrepancy greater than this.[12] Although the similar exercise undertaken by Yasumoto, reproduced in this part of the volume as chapter 10, in which he compares the 1851 CEBs and the baptism register for the Yorkshire parish of Methley, finds a much higher degree of correspondence, with 88 per cent of the population recording a precise match, it is clear that the ages recorded in the Victorian censuses can only be taken as an approximation of the 'real' situation. Because of this, the local community historian will often find it preferable to present age distributions in grouped age-spans, usually in five year age groups. Lastly, despite the fact that much remains uncertain about the precise recording of ages, one important point for the community historian emerges: as Higgs has put it, 'the standard of age reporting plainly varied from place to place'.[13] Thus, scope remains for further local-based research. In particular, little is yet known about how the accuracy of age reporting varied regionally, or between town and country.

From the analysis to date, it seems fair to assume that women, for whatever reasons, were worse at recording their 'true' ages than men (both in terms of volume and degree of variance), and that the tendency toward misreporting was itself clearly age-specific. This pattern is confirmed by Perkyns' detailed local study of six Kentish parishes reproduced in chapter 12. Although the elderly are generally believed to have been especially remiss in their reporting of ages, with a tendency for rounding up or down to a number ending in zero or five, chapter 9 by Thomson argues that, for the late-nineteenth century at least, the elderly 'appear to have had a fair idea of their ages and not to have reported them capriciously'. It is certainly the case that the misreporting of ages by the elderly did not reach the alarming proportions evident in the Irish census of 1911 brought on by the 1908 Pensions Act which instituted means-tested, non-contributory pensions for those aged 70 and over.[14] As one might expect, the recording of ages improved gradually over time, with a marked improvement coming in 1921 when the census schedule was amended to allow for the recording of ages in terms of both years and months.[15] In her chapter, Perkyns shows that over the period 1851–81 there was a slight improvement in accuracy, however, the fact that in some parishes the improvement was not strictly chronological again points to the need for further research in

12 Razzell, 'Evaluation of baptism', 123–7. For a similar example see Wrigley, 'Baptism coverage'.

13 Higgs, *Making sense*, 68; *Clearer sense*, 80.

14 Work on the Irish census of 1911 has shown that many exaggerated their ages in the hope of qualifying for a pension under the provisions of the Act. See Budd and Guinnane, 'Intentional age-misreporting'.

15 The published reports of 1911 included an analysis of age distribution for the whole country by single year which highlighted the extent of age mis-statement and prompted the compilation of a special report on the subject. This in turn lead to the revision of the question on age asked in 1921. See 1911 Census England and Wales, *Ages and Condition as to Marriage*, BPP 1912–3 CXIII, xxxix–xlviii.

this area.[16]

Most of the attempts to check the accuracy of age statements mentioned above do so by comparing two or more sources and noting the differences, for example, matching census with census, or census with parish register. Although effective, it is invariably a long and complex procedure because of the linking of personal information required.[17] An alternative that has been employed by demographers using just one single census, but which has been little employed by local population historians, is the so-called Whipple index. In effect, this is a summary measure of digit preference, as discussed in chapter 9 by Thomson, which calculates the propensity of ages ending in a particular number to be recorded in favour of others. By convention, it is used to provide a measure of the preference for ages ending in zero's or five's since demographers have observed a general tendency for populations to round their ages up or down to the nearest quinquennial figure. Indeed, it should be remembered that for the census of 1841 individuals aged 15 and over needed, if they wished, only to state their age in 5-year bands, rounding their age down. The index is calculated as follows:

1) count the number of individuals with ages recorded as either 25, 30, 35, 40, 45, 50, 55, or 60;
2) multiply this total by five;
3) count the number of individuals (inclusive) aged 23 to 62;
4) divide the first total by the second and multiply the answer by 100.

The result is an index number where a value of 100 indicates that no preference is shown for ages ending in either 0 or 5. A figure higher than 100 shows that 0 and 5 ages were more 'popular' than others, and a figure lower than 100 the converse.[18] In this example, reproduced in its original form, the index is for those aged 23–62. Obviously, the method could be widened to include other ages, or narrowed to a more specific age-range. In his study of mid-nineteenth-century York,

16 In their study using aggregate census data, comparing the relative sizes of age cohorts recorded in the censuses of 1821 to 1931, adjusting appropriately for migration and using model life-table mortality schedules, Lee and Lam concluded that there was a general and steady improvement in the reporting of ages throughout the period. See Lee and Lam, 'Age distribution'.

17 The matching of CEBs across different years together with registration material is generally termed 'nominal record linkage'. Much literature has been produced on this topic, especially in relation to the application of computer techniques in order to quicken the process and make it more efficient. The early work by Wrigley, *Identifying people in the past*, still remains a classic, but readers should also note the articles and references in a special issue of the journal *Historical Methods* **25** 1 (1992) and two issues of the journal *History and Computing*; **4** 1 (1992) and **6** 3 (1994).

18 The calculation of the Whipple index is discussed in Willigan and Lynch, *Sources and methods*, 84–5.

Armstrong calculated values of 120.4 for male heads of household in his sample of the 1851 CEBs and 129.0 for their wives, while Dupree found similar results for a sample of the CEBs of Stoke-on-Trent for 1861, being 125.8 and 113.2, respectively.[19] These contrast with figures of 112.6 and 116.9 (males and females, respectively) which have been calculated for the entire populations recorded in seven CEBs for the City of York for 1891. Equally, a group of 12 rural parishes fringing the market town of Saffron Walden at the same date produce figures of 104.9 and 102.7.[20]

The accuracy of ages is clearly of importance in employing another standard demographic measure, in this case the Singulate Mean Age at Marriage (SMAM) which uses census data to estimate the average marriage age experienced by the census population in question. This measure is used by Hinde in chapter 26, Part V, to help explain variations in household structure in the two areas which he examines. However, with this exception, it remains a method seldom used by local population historians. The SMAM was first developed by Hajnal in his pioneering work on comparative European marriage patterns, and worked examples have subsequently been produced in accessible publications elsewhere, including the pages of *LPS*.[21] Consequently, it is neither necessary nor appropriate to reiterate the details of the technique again in this volume. In essence, the calculation hinges around the comparison of the age-specific percentages of the population (divided by sex) who are as yet unmarried with those who are married, or have previously been married. In so doing, it is possible to calculate the mean age at which the transition from one state to the other occurred. It is, of course, only a surrogate measure for age at marriage and suffers from a number of problems,[22] yet, despite these SMAMs still provide a powerful tool for exploring the marital experiences of populations in a comparative framework.

19 Armstrong, *Stability and change*, 36–7; Dupree, *Family structure*, 354–5.

20 The 1891 York sample includes six EDs from the Warmgate sub-Registration District (RG 516:4, EDs 3, 5, 14, 23, 24, 28) and two from the Micklegate sub-Registration district (RG 516:3 EDs 3 and 7). The 'Saffron Walden' sample includes EDs covering the entire parishes of Chrishall, Elmdon, Strethall, Littlebury, Wendons Ambo (all RG 201:2), and Arkesdon, Clavering, Langley, Newport, Quendon, Rickling, Wicken Bonhunt (all RG 201:1).

21 Hajnal, 'Age at marriage'; Schürer, 'A note concerning'; Drake and Finnegan, *Sources and methods*, 185.

22 There are three principal problems, all related to the basic cross-sectional nature of the CEBs. First, it mixes together the experience of those who married at some point in the past, on the one hand, and those who will marry at some point in the future on the other. Thus, the technique assumes that the age structure of marriage is the same for all those enumerated in the census, which may not be the case if age at marriage is changing. Second, it may be affected by age- and period-specific migration. Third, it does not take into account the possibility of mortality differences between the married and non-married. See Schürer, 'A note concerning' for details.

Child/woman ratio

Lastly, it is worth mentioning another demographic measure which can be calculated directly from CEBs and which is also used in the chapter by Hinde, namely the child/woman ratio (CWR) which can be used to estimate fertility levels. In its crudest form the CWR takes the number of children enumerated aged less than five and divides this by the number of married women aged 15 to 44.[23] The figure is then normally expressed as a rate per 1,000 married women aged 15–44. Thus, a population with 500 married women of the appropriate age and 600 children aged under five would produce a CWR of 1200 (600/500=1.2; 1.2x1000=1200). This basic formula can be elaborated to form age specific fertility rates by breaking down the numbers of married women into five year age groups and comparing these totals with the numbers of mothers with children aged less than five. Although a useful tool in providing summary information on the ages at which childbearing started, reached its peak and began to decline, the method assumes that all infants and young children were enumerated with their mothers on census night, which might not have been the case. A further problem is that the method neglects the potential impact of mortality on infants as well as mothers. For example, a mother may have given birth to three children during the course of the five years prior to the census, but if only two of these survived and were enumerated in the census, the CWR in this individual case would be under-estimated by a third. This can be seen in the case of the Sleightholme family of Canwick, Lincolnshire, mentioned in chapter 1, four of whose children died under the age of two years between 1871 and 1881. As a consequence of this problem demographers have devised various methods of adjustment to take account of the mortality factor and to produce more accurate estimates.[24] In the absence of full and detailed information on the numbers of births, marriages and deaths, used carefully the CWR and its more sophisticated variants can be, and have been used to great effect to compare fertility levels across nineteenth-century communities. Such measures have been used to investigate the decline in fertility levels and the impact of the greater 'spacing' of births to reduce fertility as opposed to the earlier 'stopping' of childbirth.[25] Still more could be

23 For an early example of the use of CWR see Hareven and Vinovskis, 'Patterns of childrearing'.

24 Details are given in Shryock and Siegel, *Methods and materials*, 500–5 and Woods and Smith, 'The decline of marital fertility', 219–22.

25 For examples using CEBs see Garrett, 'The trials of labour' and Reay, 'Before the transition'. Both of these studies employ the use of another set of fertility measures, *M* (big M) and *m* (little m). These are similar to the CWR in concept but additionally employ standardised model fertility schedules. See Coale and Trussell 'Model fertility schedules'; Coale and Trussell, 'Technical note'; Grabill and Cho, 'Measurement of current fertility'; and the comments made in Hinde and Woods, 'Natural fertility patterns'. For more general literature on the fertility transition see, Garrett *et al.* *As others do around us*; Woods, 'Approaches'; Teitelbaum, *The British fertility decline*; Gillis et al. *The European experience*; Szreter, *Fertility, class and gender*.

known about the details of the late-nineteenth-century decline in fertility, especially in relation to the behaviour of different occupational groups within communities. As such, the CEB-using community historian has much to offer.

Contents of Part II

The accuracy of age reporting in the CEBs is a central theme in this Part of the volume. It provides a key focus to three of the four chapters – those by Thomson, Yasumoto and Perkyns, chapters 9, 10 and 12 respectively. Perkyns' study of 6 parishes in Kent examines nearly 20,000 person-entries across the 4 censuses of 1851–81. In contrast, Thomson's chapter concentrates on the elderly section of the population in two contrasting communities, Puddletown and Ealing. Both, however, examine the accuracy of age reporting by matching successive CEB information and noting the inconsistencies. In contrast, the chapter by Yasumoto links the CEB data with parish register information, and again, examines the extent and nature of consistency or inconsistency between the two sources.

The remaining contribution, that by Smith (chapter 11), is one of the few chapters in the volume to concentrate on the wealth of information published in the census reports – details of which are listed in the appendix which follows. Using these in combination with statistical material from the Registrar General's *Annual Reports*, the author is able to construct a detailed picture of the patterns of migration into two of Nottingham's nineteenth-century suburbs.

Appendix

A list of the published census reports, 1801–1901

1801 England, Wales, Scotland

Abstract of answers and returns, pursuant to Act 41 Geo. III, for taking an account of the population of Great Britain in 1801, and the increase and diminution thereof, BPP 1801 VI, 813–; BPP 1801–2 VI–VII, 1–.

1811 England, Wales, Scotland

Abstract of answers and returns, pursuant to Act 51 Geo. III, for taking an account of the population of Great Britain in 1811:

Preliminary Observations, BPP 1812 XI.

Enumeration Abstract, BPP 1812 XI.

Parish-Register Abstract, BPP 1812 XI.

Comparative statement of the population of Great Britain in 1801 and 1811, BPP 1812 X, 171–.

1821 England, Wales, Scotland

Abstract of answers and returns, pursuant to Act 1 Geo. IV, for taking an account of the population of Great Britain in 1821:

Preliminary Observation, BPP 1822 XV.

Enumeration Abstract, BPP 1822 XV.

Parish-Register Abstract, BPP 1822 XV.

Comparative statement of the population of Great Britain in 1801, 1811 and 1821, BPP 1822 XXI 631–.

1831 England, Wales, Scotland

Comparative account of the population of Great Britain in 1801, 1811,1821, 1831, with annual value of real property, 1815, also, statement of the progress of the inquiry regarding the occupations of families and persons and duration of life, as required by population act 1830, BPP 1831 XVIII, 1–.

Abstract of the population returns of Great Britain, 1831:

Enumeration. Vols I & II with Index to the Names of Places at the end of Vol. II, BPP 1833 XXXVI–XXXVII.

Parish Registers, BPP 1833 XXXVIII.

Number of inhabited houses, uninhabited and building; number of families residing in such as are inhabited; occupation of families; number of males and females in each county in England, 1801, 1811, 1821, 1831, BPP 1833 V, 638–.

1841 England, Wales, Scotland

Accounts of the Total Population in 1841, of each county of Great Britain; distinguishing males and females, and showing the rate per cent. increase or decrease in each county as compared with population, 1831; also the number of houses inhabited, uninhabited, and building, according to the Census, 1841; similar returns for Channel Islands, Isle of Man; also, comparative statements of the population and number of houses, 1801, 1811, 1821, 1831, for each county in Gt. Britain; also, population of each city and Royal and Parliamentary burgh in Scotland, BPP 1841 Session 2 II, 277–.

Abstract of the answers and returns made pursuant to Act 3 and 4 Vict. c. 99 and 4 Vict. C. 7 (Enumeration Abstract, 1841):

Part I, England and Wales, and Islands in the British Seas, BPP 1843 XXII, 1–.

Part II, Scotland with Index to Names of Places at end of each Part, BPP 1843 XXII, 1–.

Index of names of places in the enumeration abstract of England and Wales, BPP 1843 XXII, 515–.

Index of names of places in the enumeration abstract of Scotland, BPP 1843 XXII, 587–, 679–.

Abstract of the answers and returns made pursuant to Acts 3 and 4 Vict. c. 99, and 4 Vict. c. 7, for taking an account of the population of Great Britain; age abstract, 1841:

Part I, England and Wales, and islands in the British Seas, BPP 1843 XXIII, 2–.

Part II, Scotland, BPP 1843 XXIII, 25–.

Abstract of the answers and returns made pursuant to Acts 3 and 4 Vict. c. 99, and 4 Vict. c. 7, for taking an account of the population of Great Britain; occupation abstract, 1841:

Part I, England and Wales, and islands in the British Seas, BPP 1844 XXVII, 1–.

Part II, Scotland, BPP 1844 XXVII, 385–.

1851 England, Wales, Scotland

Forms and Instructions prepared for the use of the persons employed in taking an account of the population of Great Britain by virtue of the Act 13 and 14 Vict. c. 53, BPP 1851 XLIII, 1–.

Tables of Population and houses in the divisions, registration counties, and districts of England and Wales; in the counties, cities, and burghs of Scotland; and in the islands in the British seas, BPP 1851 XLIII, 73–.

Population and houses, according to the census of 1851, in the counties and divisions of counties, and in the cities, boroughs, and towns returning members to Parliament in Great Britain, BPP 1852 XLII, 475–.

Population and number of houses, according to the census of 1851, in every county and division of a county, and in all cities and boroughs returning members to Parliament in Great Britain, with the number of members returned; also in towns containing upwards of 2,000 inhabitants not returning members to Parliament, BPP 1852 XLII, 491–.

Population tables. Part I. Numbers of the inhabitants in the years 1801,1811,1821,1831, 1841 and 1851:

Vol. I. Report; objects of census and machinery employed; results and observations; appendix of tabular results and summary tables of England and Wales, Divisions I to VII; area, houses, 1841 and 1851; population, 1801, 1811, 1821, 1831, 1841 and 1851, BPP 1852–3, LXXXV, 1–.

Vol. II. England and Wales continued, Divisions VII to XI; Scotland; islands in the British seas; appendix; ecclesiastical divisions of England and Wales, BPP 1852–3 LXXXVI, 1–.

Population tables. Part II. Ages, civil condition etc., and inmates of workhouses, prisons etc.:

Vol. I. Report; results and observations; appendix of tabular results and summary tables; England and Wales, Divisions I to VI, BPP 1852–3 LXXXVIII, pt. I, 1–.

Vol. II. England and Wales continued, Divisions VII to XI; Scotland; islands in the British seas, BPP 1852–3 LXXXVIII, pt. II, 1–.

Index to parishes, townships and places in Population tables of Great Britain, BPP 1852–3 LXXXVII, 1–.

Religious worship (England and Wales). Report; history and description of the various churches; spiritual provision and destitution; appendix containing summary tables and tabular results, BPP 1852–3 LXXXIX 1–.

Education. Report; summary tables etc., BPP 1852–3 XC, 1–.

Religious worship and education (Scotland). Report and tables, BPP 1854 LIX, 301–.

1861 England and Wales

Tables of population and houses enumerated in England and Wales and in islands in British seas on 8 April, 1861, BPP 1861 L, 855–.

Population tables. Vol. I. Numbers and distribution of the People, with index to Names of Places, BPP 1862 L, 1–.

Population tables. Vol. II. Ages, civil condition, occupations and birthplaces; and inmates of workhouses etc. (in two parts), BPP 1863 LIII, pt. I, 265–, pt. II, 1–.

Vol. III. General Report; with appendix of tables, BPP 1863 LIII, 1–.

1861 Scotland

Tables of population etc., of houses, and rooms with windows, in Scotland and its islands, on 8 April 1861, BPP 1861 L, 911–.

Population tables and report:

Vol. I. Numbers of inhabitants, families etc. in civil counties and parishes, registration counties and districts etc., and islands; also classification of families according to size etc., BPP 1862 L, 945–.

Vol. II. Ages, civil or conjugal condition, occupations, birthplaces, and inmates of poorhouses etc., BPP 1864 LI, 49–.

1871 England and Wales

Census of England and Wales 1871, preliminary report, and tables of population and houses enumerated in England and Wales, and in islands in British seas on 3 April 1871, BPP 1871 LIX, 659–.

Population tables: Areas, houses and inhabitants:

Vol. I. Ancient Counties, BPP 1872 LXVI, pt. I, 1–.

Vol. II. Registration or Union Counties; with an index to the Names of Places in population tables, BPP 1872 LXVI, pt. II, 1–.

Population abstracts:

Ages, civil condition, occupations and birthplaces of people (Vol. III), BPP 1873 LXXI, pt. I, 1–.

General report (Vol. IV), BPP 1873 LXXI, pt. II, 1–.

1871. Scotland

Tables of population, of families, of children receiving education, of houses, and rooms with windows in Scotland and its islands on 3 April 1871, BPP 1871 LIX, 813–.

Eighth decennial census of population, taken 3 April 1871:

Vol. I. Population of various types of areas, Houses, with report, BPP 1872 LXVIII, 1–.

Vol. II. Ages, Education, Civil condition, Birthplaces, Occupations, with report, BPP 1873 LXXIII, 1–.

1881 England and Wales

Preliminary report and tables of population and. houses for England and Wales, and in islands in British seas on 4 April 1881, BPP 1881 XCVI, 1–.

Vol. I. Area, houses and population: Ancient Counties, BPP 1883 LXXVIII, 1–.

Vol. II. Area, houses and population: Registration counties, BPP 1883 LXXIX, 1–.

Vol. III. Ages, condition as to marriage; occupations and birthplaces of people, BPP 1883 LXXX, 1–.

Vol. IV. General report and tables, BPP 1883 LXXX, 583–.

Islands in British seas; Isle of Man, Jersey, Guernsey and adjacent islands, BPP 1883 LXXX, 707–.

1881 Scotland

Tables of population, houses, rooms with windows in Scotland and its islands on 4 April 1881, BPP 1881 XCVI, 143–.

Ninth decennial census, taken 4 April 1881, with report:

Vol. I. Population of various types of areas, public institutions, etc., BPP 1882 LXXVI, 1–.

Vol. II. Ages, Education, Civil condition, Birthplaces, Occupations, General Index, BPP 1883 LXXX, 1–.

1891. England and Wales

Preliminary report and tables of population and houses enumerated in England and Wales and in islands in British seas on 6 April 1891, BPP 1890–1 XCIV, 1–.

Vol. I. Area, houses and population: administrative and ancient counties, BPP 1893–4 CIV, 1–.

Vol. II. Area, houses and population: registration areas and sanitary districts, BPP 1893–4 CV, 1–.

Vol. III. Ages, conditions as to marriage, occupations, birthplaces, and infirmities, BPP 1893–4 CVI, 1–.

Vol. IV. General report, with summary, tables and appendixes, BPP 1893-4 CVI, 629–.

Index to population tables, BPP 1893–4 CIV, 519–.

Islands in British seas; Isle of Man, Jersey, Guernsey etc.,w PP 1893–4 CVII, 1–.

1891 Scotland

Tables of population, of families, of houses and of rooms and windows in Scotland and its islands on 5 April 1891, BPP 1890–1 XCIV, 153–.

Tenth decennial census, taken 5 April 1891, with Report:

Vol. I. Report with Appendices, Population of various types of areas, Houses, BPP 1892 XCIV, 1–.

Supplement to Vol. I., BPP 1893–4 CVII, 65–.

Vol. II., Part I. Ages, Education, Civil condition, Working status, Indices, BPP 1893–4 CVII, 215–.

Vol. II., Part II. Ages, Education, Civil condition, Working status, Indices, BPP 1893–4 CVIII, 1–.

1901 England and Wales

Preliminary report and tables of population and houses enumerated in England and Wales and in islands in British seas on 31 March 1901, BPP 1901 XC, 1–.

Series of County Parts, BPP 1902–3 (series of 53 parts, all separately numbered).

Index to population tables in the county volumes, BPP 1903 CVIII, 335–.

Islands in British seas; Isle of Man, Jersey, Guernsey etc., BPP 1903 LXXXIV, 313–.

Summary Tables, BPP 1903 LXXXIV, 1–.

General Report, with Appendices, BPP 1904 CVIII, 1–.

1901 Scotland

Preliminary Report, BPP 1901 XC, 203–

Parliamentary Burghs, Counties, Population, etc. 1901 and 1891, BPP 1902 CXXIX, 1133–.

Eleventh decennial census, taken 31 March 1901, with Report:

Vol. I. Population of various types of areas, Houses, BPP 1902 CXXIX, 687–.

Vol. II., Ages, Marital Civil, Education and Birthplaces, BPP 1903 LXXXVI, 205–.

Vol. III., Report, Occupations, BPP 1904 CVIII, 625–.

Other reports relating to the censuses

Minutes of evidence taken (session 1830) before the select committee on the Population Bill, BPP 1840 XV, 469–.

Tables of the rates of increase, and of the population, deaths, and rates of mortality at different ages, in the divisions, registration counties, and districts of England; of the male and female population at the several censuses 1801 to 1841; of the ages of the male and female population, 1841; and of the male and female population of the parliamentary counties as constituted in the years 1801 to 1841, BPP 1849 XXI.

Comparative statement of the expenses of the census of Great Britain in 1841 and 1851, number of persons enumerated, heads of information comprised in enquiry, and cost per 1,000 of population, BPP 1854 XXXIX, 333-.

Return of expenses of Census of England and Wales in 1861, number of persons enumerated, heads of information comprised in enquiry and cost per 1,000 of the population; with comparisons of former charges in 1841 and 1851, BPP 1863 XXIX, 249–.

Population of England and Wales, and of Scotland in 1831 and 1861 with percentage of increase, BPP 1866 LVII, 605–.

Suggestions offered to Home Department by members of Statistical Society in relation to ensuing census, BPP 1870 LVI, 585–.

Table of allowances to be made to superintendent registrars etc. employed in execution of Act for taking census of England and Wales, 1871, BPP 1871XXXVII, 143–.

Expenses incurred in taking census in 1871 for England and Wales, Scotland and for Ireland: with comparisons of former charges in 1841, 1851, and 1861, BPP 1875 XLII, 155–.

Number of male persons, of ages 18 to 25, in United Kingdom according to census of 1851, and of 1871, BPP 1876 LX, 239–.

Return relating to areas, inhabited houses, and male population of United Kingdom, BPP 1876 LX, 275–.

Return of the population at each decennial period from 1801 to 1881, increase or decrease at 1841 as compared with 1801, and in 1881 compared with 1841: (1) For the whole kingdom; (2) For each county; (3) For each parish; (4) List giving above particulars for each Royal and Parliamentary burgh places etc., BPP 1883 LIV, 315–.

Return of number of Gaelic speaking people by counties, parishes, and registration districts, under census of 1881, BPP 1882 L, 855–.

Letter of Registrar-General, relative to a complaint against remarks of his (on question of Welsh speaking population) in Census Report, 1891, BPP 1894 LXIX, 1–

Report of the committee appointed by the Treasury to enquire into certain questions connected with the taking of the census with evidence and appendices, and the Treasury minute appointing the committee, BPP 1890 LVIII, 13–.

9

Age reporting by the elderly and the nineteenth-century census

DAVID THOMSON

Information on age was first sought from all the inhabitants of England and Wales in the census of 1821, and the question has been repeated in various forms in all subsequent enumerations. The quality of the replies received has troubled both the census takers and social historians using these materials ever since. Was the question being asked really understood by the respondents – or the enumerators? Was it 'age now' or 'age next birthday' that was being sought? How well were the ages of young children recorded? What of those of the female population: could the 'known veracity of English women', as one early census report charmingly put it, be relied upon?[1]

The census takers of 1851 and 1861 were surprisingly sanguine in reviewing their newly-founded procedures and the results obtained, reflecting perhaps the unbounded faith in figures of the Utilitarians in government service, Dickens' men of Fact and Calculation. After reviewing some of the possible sources of error in the reporting of age, the 1851 census takers concluded that:

> taking all these circumstances into account, we are convinced that the results of the returns of ages, after slight corrections, are available for nearly every practical purpose to which they are likely to be applied.[2]

A similar faith continues throughout the reports of 1861 and 1871, with brief pauses to query records of extreme old age. In 1881, however, a note of real uncertainty enters the reports, paradoxically at the very time at which the accuracy of the census-taking was judged, by assessments made at the time and subsequently, to have improved considerably. While evincing a strong politic desire not to appear critical of earlier reports – 'These causes [of inaccuracy], we should say, were fully recognised by our predecessors in earlier reports'[3] – the reporters in 1881 concluded on a cautious note:

1 1851 Census Great Britain, *Population tables. Part I, vol. II*, BPP 1852–3 LXXXVIII, xxxiii.

2 1851 Census Great Britain, *Population tables. Part I, vol. II*, BPP 1852–3 LXXXVIII, xxxiii.

3 1881 Census England and Wales, *General report and tables*, BPP 1883 LXXX, 17–8.

> As regards ages, there can be no doubt that the returns made by individuals are in a very considerable proportion of cases more or less accurate.[4]

And even more circumspectly:

> The age-figures and especially those of the female sex, must be looked upon as being at best simply approximative.[5]

Subsequent reports continued in this guarded vein. In the 1891 report we read, for example, that

> A very large proportion of persons, not improbably indeed the greater number of adults, do not know their precise ages and can only report it (sic) approximately.[6]

Increasingly elaborate attempts to calculate corrective factors have been made since 1901, but the results remained inconclusive and guarded with cautionary notes. In 1951 a new approach was devised, using the matching of a random selection of census schedules against the birth registers of the same individuals. Thus, definite assessment of the veracity of self-reporting could at last be made.

Age reporting and the elderly

Since the earliest census of age the self-reporting of the elderly population has been strongly questioned. It has been held as self-evident that the old will be vague or evasive, and wild overstatement in the more extreme ages has been taken as axiomatic. The tendency to such, notes the 1891 report, is a 'well-known habit'.[7] This uncertainty, in turn, leaves in some doubt estimates of the total aged population of pre-twentieth century Britain. Attempted corrections by late-nineteenth- and early-twentieth-century census reporters have availed little here, for, as they themselves readily admitted, their reassessments incorporated too many estimates of estimates.

The use of the CEBs as a source for the writing of social and community history has raised once again the question of veracity. Most students of the materials have skirted the issue as not particularly germane to their research. Armstrong, for example, in an early 'manual' on the handling and potential of these sources, comments that:

> The basic accuracy of some of the information is open to some degree of error, for example in the recording of ages. No allowance can be made for this, although the critical student ought to be aware that the problem is there.[8]

4 1881 Census England and Wales, *General report and tables*, BPP 1883 LXXX, 19.
5 1881 Census England and Wales, *General report and tables*, BPP 1883 LXXX, 19.
6 1891 Census England and Wales, *Vol. IV General report*, BPP 1893–4 CVI, 27.
7 1891 Census England and Wales, *Vol. IV General report.*, BPP 1893–4 CVI, 29.
8 Armstrong, 'The CEBs: a commentary', 76.

Similarly, in his guide to the sources for a study of nineteenth-century history, Rogers writes:

> Of course, not all of these [reports of ages recorded in the 1851, 1861 and 1871 census enumerators' books] were accurate, especially amongst the older (through forgetfulness).[9]

But is this all that can be said? Or needs to be said, especially if specific age-groups within the population are to be considered? The consistency of age reporting by the elderly is here assessed in a couple of ways from within the census materials themselves. This chapter is based on an analysis of the CEBs for two English communities. One is the village of Puddletown in Dorset, dominated by agriculture and its service industries, and with a population of 1,297 in 1851; the second, the parish of Ealing in extra-metropolitan Middlesex, with a population of 9,828 in 1851 which reflected both the continuing agricultural character of the rural town, and its new-found role as one of London's first 'middle-class' residential suburbs. The first was a settlement with a declining population, the latter one of rapid expansion. Puddletown evidence is used to suggest some changes over a 40-year period, while Ealing affords glimpses of the effects of social complexity.

'Digital preference', the tendency of persons when asked their age to give a round figure such as 50 or 60, and to a lesser extent figures ending in an 8, has long been suspected and tested for by census takers. The general conclusion has been that the phenomenon did occur, and that most movement has been downwards, reporting 60 instead of 61, and 50 instead of 51.[10] Amongst the Puddletown and Ealing elderly this phenomenon was manifested to varying degrees – the results are summarised in Table 9.1 below.

Hypothetically we would expect that approximately 10 per cent of those aged, for example, 55–64, would be aged 60, which is near the midpoint of the 10–year age category. In practice, for a variety of reasons, real-life populations and censuses do not achieve this result: nor is the age ending in zero (60) the exact counterpoint of the range 55–64. For example, in 1911, the first census year for which age by single year was published for all persons, 11.5 per cent of the group aged 55–64 gave their ages as 60, while 10.4 per cent and 9.3. per cent of the following two 10–year age ranges gave their ages as 70 and 80 respectively. Any large deviation from the expected proportion of 10 per cent would be evidence of a preference for reporting an age ending

9 Rogers, *This was their world*, 40.

10 See, for example, 1901 Census England and Wales, *General Report, with Appendices*, BPP 1904 CVIII, 63–4. The test and assumptions noted there can be strongly questioned.

Table 9.1 Age-rounding by persons aged 55 to 84: Puddletown and Ealing, 1851

	Puddletown				Ealing			
	male		female		male		female	
	%	n.	%	n.	%	n.	%	n.
Persons aged 55–64 giving age of 60	21	44	21	42	16	263	14	296
Persons aged 65–74 giving age of 70	15	20	0	20	21	148	14	175
Persons aged 75–84 giving age of 80	(17)	6	(0)	9	12	42	16	63

Notes: In this and subsequent tables, figures are placed in brackets when they are based on less than 20 cases. The n. figures refer to the total number of persons aged 55–64, 65–74 and 75–84 respectively.

in a zero.[11] Given the smallness of the samples used here, especially that of Puddletown, we should expect some deviations from random fluctuation, but though there is some evidence of age-heaping it does not seen to have been pronounced, with the exception of those claiming to be age 60 in Puddletown, and males claiming to be age 70 in Ealing. Interestingly, little difference between the two communities emerges. Females in both communities appeared to round out their ages slightly less often than did males: twentieth-century results suggest this also.[12]

A couple of further analyses involving age-rounding can be made. For the small Puddletown community it was possible to compare the phenomenon over four consecutive censuses, from 1851 to 1881. The results appear in Table 9.2 below. Little definite emerges from this table. Perhaps the reporting by those in their sixties did improve by the end of the period, although the progress was not at all smooth. The samples of the older groups were too small to be of much use: statistical oddities were almost bound to occur. Overall, the apparent randomness of the results, reflected in wild fluctuations in levels of giving figures ending in zero, suggest little systematic distortion. The fact that several totals in 1871 and 1881 fell below what might have been expected from twentieth-century evidence further suggests randomness rather than deliberate distortion or evasiveness.

11 1911 Census England and Wales, *Ages and condition as to marriage*, BPP 1912–14 CXIII, 1–2. Testing for digit preference is discussed in the editorial introduction to this section of the volume. For the more mathematically inclined, a discussion of the various tests and models which demographers have devised in dealing with this topic can be found in Shryock and Siegel, *Methods and materials*, 114–19. More simply, a chi-squared test could also be made to test the significance of the results: see Bradley, *Glossary for local population studies*, 34–5.

12 By using smaller age-ranges, centred upon the zero figure, the analysis suggested here could be elaborated to explore more closely just where the 'age-rounders' might be coming from. It is clear, for instance, that the groups aged 59 and 61 were depleted in this sample. Where 60 year-olds should have formed about one third of those in the range 59 to 61, we find that in Puddletown the proportions of 60 year-olds were 41 to 53 per cent respectively for males and females: in Ealing the proportions were 53 and 56 per cent.

Table 9.2 Age rounding by persons aged 55 to 84: Puddletown, 1851–1881

Males	1851		1861		1871		1881	
	%	n.	%	n.	%	n.	%	n.
Persons aged 55–64 giving age of 60	21	44	20	44	25	36	6	33
Persons aged 65–74 giving age of 70	15	20	17	29	7	30	17	23
Persons aged 75–84 giving age of 80	(17)	6	(11)	9	(6)	18	(14)	7

Females	1851		1861		1871		1881	
	%	n.	%	n.	%	n.	%	n.
Persons aged 55–64 giving age of 60	21	42	17	52	9	32	11	27
Persons aged 65–74 giving age of 70	0	20	17	29	12	33	9	33
Persons aged 75–84 giving age of 80	(0)	9	(0)	5	(20)	15	(13)	8

Notes: See notes to Table 9.1.

With the Ealing sample a differentiation by social class was attempted. Such ventures are of course fraught with traps for the unwary. The scaling used here, based upon the occupation information contained on the census schedules, follows the lines suggested by Armstrong.[13] If this five-class scale is viewed as a rough continuum from wealthiest to poorest, rather than as a set of five distinct (and defensible) categories, the results should have some validity. The summaries appear in Table 9.3 below.

Little that is conclusive emerges here, and the irregular results at both ends of the scale probably stem from weaknesses in the classifications used. The phenomenon looks as though it might possibly be class-related for males, with the very rich and the very poor more likely to return a rounded age. The female results present no pattern: the rich seemed just as likely or unlikely as the poor to give ages ending in zero.

Age matching over consecutive censuses

This second and more significant test provides another view of the age-reporting, by matching information recorded at successive censuses

13 Armstrong, 'Information about occupation', 191–225.

Table 9.3 Percentages giving age in figures ending in zero, all persons aged 55 to 84 by sex and social class: Ealing, 1851

Social class	male		female	
	%	n.	%	n.
I) wealthiest	22	32	15	33
II)	15	85	13	129
III)	15	149	15	113
IV)	19	165	15	186
V) poorest	31	22	17	53

Notes: The social class categories given in this and subsequent tables is based on Armstrong, 'Use of information about occupation'.

concerning specific identifiable individuals. Of course many move, die, change names, or for a variety of other reasons remain unidentifiable from one census to the next, so that the 'trace rate' was not always high, and it remains an open question whether those who were traced fully represent all their fellows. It seems at least arguable that they did not, that the traced 'stable' population would be more consistent in their replies to census takers than the untraced 'floating' population. Nevertheless the exercise seems worthwhile: in Puddletown at least the trace rate was high enough to suggest that, after allowing for deaths, only a minority were escaping detection.

Puddletown

From Puddletown a total of 92 persons aged 60 or more in 1861 were traced as having been present 10 years earlier: in the following years the trace rate dropped, suggesting perhaps that mobility, even amongst the elderly, was increasing. The results are summed in Table 9.4 below.

Table 9.5 below records the consistency of the reports given by the traced portion of the Puddletown elderly. There is no way, from within the census materials themselves, of checking the veracity of the first recorded age for each individual; what is actually being checked is the consistency of successive reports of age in the decennial censuses.

The aged have popularly been accorded little knowledge of, or regard for, their true ages. Mayhew's Londoners, for example, invariably have but little notion of their own ages, and the Puddletown elderly agricultural labourers can have been little more educated or literate than the poor of the metropolis. Yet 80 per cent or more of the males here were found correct to within a year, and at least some of the errors could have ensued from legitimate confusion as to the question being asked. Of note, too, were the number of 'self-correcting' adjustments by individuals who were traced over 20 years. Often such persons gave ages short or long by a year or two at one census but 'compensated' the next time round, so that at the end of 20 years and

Table 9.4 Trace rate of persons aged 60 and more: Puddletown, 1861–1881

	1861		1871		1881	
	%	n.	%	n.	%	n.
Persons present 10 years earlier	72	127	57	147	51	101

Notes: A few long-lived individuals appeared in two, even three totals.

Table 9.5 Consistency of age-reporting, all persons aged 60 and more: Puddletown, 1861–1881

Males	1861	1871	1881
Percentage reporting consistently	60	60	63
Percentage out by one year only	26	20	19
Percentage out by two years	7	12	11
Percentage out by three & more years	7	8	7
Total number	45	44	27
Females	**1861**	**1871**	**1881**
Percentage reporting consistently	38	43	64
Percentage out by one year only	34	27	16
Percentage out by two years	11	12	12
Percentage out by three & more years	17	18	8
Total number	47	40	25

Notes: Because of the smallness of the sample, a differentiation by age within the total elderly population was not possible. This omission undoubtedly confuses the figures somewhat: the improvement in female reporting noted in 1881, for example, may well have resulted from changes within the age structure of the sample, but the analysis to follow will show that the extent and direction of such possible errors is difficult to predict.

3 censuses their ages were consistent once again. Finally, it was observed in passing that inconsistencies very often went in twos, that married couples would both so indulge, invariably in the direction of eliminating large discrepancies between their ages. In some senses, of course, such behaviour indicates a scant regard for the figures, but it does perhaps suggest more knowledge and calculation than ignorance and fancy behind the answers given.

In short, the Puddletown elderly appear to have had a fair idea of their own ages, and not to have reported them capriciously. There appears also to have been an improvement in the quality of female reporting over the period studied, although it must be noted that, throughout, from one-fifth to nearly one-third of women were inconsistent by at least two years. Reporting by the aged males remained remarkably unchanged. That female consistency fell below

Table 9.6 Number and direction of inconsistencies in age-reporting: Puddletown, 1851–1881

Period of age change by age group	Age lowered by (years)			Age correct	Age raised by (years)			
	3+	2	1	0	1	2	3+	n.
Males								
50s to 60s	2		1	41	9	6	3	62
60s to 70s	2	1	4	21	11	2	1	42
70s to 80s				9		3		12
Females								
50s to 60s	7	1	5	24	11	7	2	57
60s to 70s	3		6	20	6	3	3	41
70s to 80s	1	1		6	3	1	1	13

that for males suggests at first a contradiction of the earlier finding with regard to the use of ages ending in zero. The contradiction is not too serious however: it may indicate only that females were more sophisticated in their deception than males. The latter test should be given more credence since the tracing of specific individuals provides a more precise picture of age adjustment. While both sets of results should be read together, for they test slightly different phenomena, the first was included in part to point up its limitations.

A follow-up analysis supports this finding of consistency and knowledge rather than randomness and guesswork in the results. The cases were studied by redividing upon the basis of age-grouping and the direction of the inconsistencies was charted. Because the numbers involved were small, the three different periods (1851–61, 1861–71 and 1871–81) were treated all together. Since the consistency of the reporting in general was not found to change markedly over these years, the procedure should not be too distorting. The results appear in Table 9.6 above.

Clearly, age-reporting inconsistencies were not randomly spread. Most movement was in the direction of an upward easing of age by a year or two. Extreme inconsistencies were very rare, and sometimes undoubtedly the result of recording slips. Interestingly, the small sample here showed a few signs of differential age-distortion by the various age-groups. Individuals moving into their seventies and eighties were no more inclined – if anything, were less inclined – to distort their ages than those moving into their sixties. Men, for the most part, eased their ages up. Female responses were more complex, suggesting ambiguous feelings and pressures surrounding old age. The same is hinted at when it is noted that downward movement of ages, contrary

Table 9.7 Direction of age-distortions as percentage in each case of the total in each age/sex group: Puddletown, 1851–1881

Period of age change by age group	Age eased down	No distortion	Age eased up
Males			
50s to 60s	5	66	29
60s to 70s	17	50	33
70s to 80s	0	75	25
Females			
50s to 60s	23	42	35
60s to 70s	22	49	29
70s to 80s	16	46	38

to expectations, remained as common amongst the very old as amongst the 'young-old'. Table 9.7, above, summarises these results.

Ealing

A similar matching was made for the larger Ealing population, although the listings of 1851 and 1861 only were searched. The trace rate here, somewhat lower than that for Puddletown (see Table 9.4), is shown in Table 9.8 below. Successful matching rose progressively with the lower social groups, witness to the recent arrival of 'middle-class' residents in an older rural community. The patterns revealed by these traced cases are recorded in Tables 9.9 and 9.10 below, both worked following the Puddletown model.

What emerges from these tables is that age-reporting does bear some relationship to social class. The most consistent ages, as might have been expected, were recorded by the wealthier sections of the community, but the overall social-class patterns were complex and the possible social forces behind them can only be hinted at. Males in classes I and II preferred to ease their ages downwards, while those in groups III and IV eased theirs upwards. Females in groups I, II and IV chose to age themselves, for the most part, while those in group III clearly preferred the opposite. The substantial portion of both sexes of all groups who were inconsistent by a wide margin should also be noted: such proportions were not found in Puddletown. The group V results perhaps approach Mayhew's poor who had but little idea of their ages.

Amongst monied and professional men there was perhaps a tendency to play down the advance of one's years and the enforced retirement from the civil service for example, which, a standard feature

Table 9.8 Trace rates for persons aged 60 and more, as a percentage of each sex/social group: Ealing, 1851–1861

Social class	Male	Female	Both sexes
I	20	27	24
II	43	36	39
III	53	46	49
IV	56	46	51
V	50	50	50
All	49	42	46

Notes: The total number aged 60+ in 1861 = 853.

Table 9.9 Consistency of age-reporting of persons aged 60 and more: Ealing, 1851–1861

Social class	n.	Age lowered by (years)			Age correct	Age raised by (years)		
		3+	2	1	0	1	2	3+
Males								
I	7	1		1	4			1
II	29	2	3	4	14	3	1	2
III	64	2	2	9	25	7	9	10
IV	87	9	3	5	28	17	8	17
V	4			1	2		1	
Females								
I	13	2			6	1	1	3
II	33	7	2	5	11	1	3	4
III	60	2	2	4	21	14	3	14
IV	76	5	2	7	27	5	10	20
V	16	3	1	4	3	1	2	2

of twentieth-century life, was beginning to face the Victorian middle-classes.[14]

The pressures of ageing upon poorer persons, who formed the great bulk of the population and whose behaviour consequently represents the basic pattern for the community, could well have been in the opposite direction. This would help explain the decisive break between groups I and II and groups III and IV in terms of age lowering and raising. The nineteenth-century poor law, it has often been noted, made more favourable provision for the aged than for younger persons, for example in the granting of out-door relief instead of forcing entry into the workhouse, and in the matter of diet within the institutions

14 It emerged from both the Puddletown and Ealing studies that the term 'retired' was reserved almost exclusively for professional men in 1851, but by 1871 and 1881 it was increasingly used to describe the position of aged males generally.

Table 9.10 Direction of age distortions as percentage of total in each sex-social group: Ealing, 1851–1861

Social class	Age lowered	Age correct	Age raised
Males			
I	(28)	(58)	(14)
II	31	48	21
III	22	39	39
IV	19	32	49
V	(25)	(50)	(25)
Females			
I	(15)	(46)	(39)
II	42	34	24
III	13	35	52
IV	18	36	46
V	(50)	(18)	(32)

of relief. This may have caused the poorer groups to emphasise their mounting years. Not all of groups III and IV, of course, would come within the ambit of the Poor Law Guardians. Nevertheless, Booth's studies of the widespread recourse to the poor law amongst the aged in the 1890s, coupled with the known uncertainties of nineteenth-century life, regarding for instance the security of savings in financial institutions or the employment prospects of the young upon whom the elderly might increasingly depend, strongly suggest that fear of an enforced dependence upon the resented poor law might well afflict the ageing craftsmen and shopkeepers of social class III along with the labourers of group IV. The female pattern, with its aberration in group II, remains unexplained.

Tables 9.11 and 9.12 below, with their division of the Ealing elderly by age rather than social groups, bring out a number of further points. As in Puddletown, those in their fifties and sixties were found the group most likely to inflate their ages, and to do so wildly. Their elders by contrast, with the exception of the very small group of oldest men, inflated their reports less often, less wildly, and were more likely to deflate them, to play down the advance of their years. Nearly all the gross distortions detected (those of 5 or more years over the 10-year period) were in the direction of adding years to real age: 3 men and 8 women in moving from their fifties to their sixties, disguised the true advance of their years by 5 or more, but 11 men and 15 women aged themselves by as much. Allowing that a few of these may have been the result of copying errors, the balance in favour of significant ageing seems undeniable. Substantial social pressures were clearly causing men and women nearing the end of their working lives to inflate their ages. Different pressures caused a more mixed reaction amongst

Table 9.11 Age reporting consistency by sex and age groups: Ealing, 1851–1861

Period of age change by age group	n.	Age lowered by (years)			Age correct	Age raised by (years)		
		3+	2	1		1	2	3+
Males								
50s to 60s	127	6	4	7	41	13	11	18
60s to 70s	46	8	4	20	33	20	6	9
70s to 80s	15	13		13	40	13	8	13
Females								
50s to 60s	129	9	3	6	36	13	9	24
60s to 70s	57	12	5	16	35	7	9	16
70s to 80s	13	8		23	31	8	15	15

Table 9.12 Age reporting consistency by sex and age groups (summary of Table 9.11): Ealing, 1851–1861

Period of age change by age group	Age lowered	Age raised	Inconsistent by 3+ years	Inconsistent by 5+ years
Males				
50s to 60s	17	42	24	11
60s to 70s	32	35	17	4
70s to 80s	(26)	(34)	(26)	(20)
Females				
50s to 60s	18	46	33	18
60s to 70s	33	32	28	12
70s to 80s	(31)	(38)	(23)	(8)

their elders. The male and female figures both followed very similar patterns, although females in the first two age groups were more inclined to be wildly inconsistent. In the higher age groups the numbers involved were too small to allow much to be read into the results: no attempt has been made to assess the ages reported above 85.

There can be little doubt that some social class factors are being confused with age factors here. The sample, even when drawn from a sizeable community, proved insufficient for meaningful age, sex and social group analyses to be made concurrently. In this survey there is obviously some overlap in that each of the variables is not being carefully controlled. Thus, social classes III and IV are disproportionately represented in the fifties and sixties age bracket, while class V persons tended on average to be a few years older than those of other classes.

But other significant imbalances were not detected. The social groupings, for the most part, did not vary greatly in their age composition: the range for the average ages of the five social groups was less than five years. More pertinently, persons from, for example, groups III and IV who were in their late sixties or older, behaved more like their age-mates from the other social groups than like younger members of their own.

Puddletown and Ealing: a comparison

Both similarities and contrasts have emerged. In Puddletown the consistency of reporting from one census to the next was found to be significantly higher than in Ealing. No social group in Ealing, not even the most wealthy and educated, approached the record of the Dorset labourers and small town craftsmen. This was true, further, at all ages tested here. The assumed connection between literacy and knowledge of age is in turn brought into question. Community habits and pressures would seem of greater importance. The smallness and closeness of the Dorset community may, for example, have militated against extravagant claims such as could more easily be made in a community marked by mobility. The census enumerators were possibly known personally to the respondents in the smaller settlement.

The analysis of age reporting by different age groups in the two communities produced parallel results. In both, the 'young-old' rather than the 'old-old' were found most likely to inflate their ages, and to do so in an extreme manner: the oldest respondents were to a surprising degree willing to play down and hide the advance of their years. Females in both instances provided more of the substantial inaccuracies encountered, but in all other aspects the patterns of the two sexes were remarkably similar.

Few studies similar to these have appeared in print so that there is little check upon them available at present. Anderson and Tillott have both commented briefly upon the inconsistency found in the age reporting of all age groups in the mid-nineteenth-century censuses, but not upon the elderly in particular.[15] Anderson found that, of the 475 persons he was able to trace in the censuses of Preston in 1851 and 1861, 53 per cent had reported consistently. In Hathersage (Derbyshire) and Braithwell (Yorkshire) Tillott found consistency ratings of 61 and 68 per cent respectively amongst traced populations of 353 and 157. The Puddletown and Ealing results ranged from about the levels noted by Tillott to well below those detected by Anderson. The elderly studied here were also considerably more likely to report very erratically. Anderson writes that only 4 per cent of the Preston sample were wrong by more than two years, while 5 per cent were inconsistent to this

15 Anderson, 'Study of family structure'; Tillott, 'Sources of inaccuracy', 108.

extent in both of Tillott's samples. But that is about as far as the comparisons can be taken for the time being.

The consistency found in this study, it should be noted in conclusion, does not approach twentieth-century standards, as might well have been expected. In 1951, when sample population ages given in the census were matched against the birth certificates of the same individuals, 94 per cent of the males and 87 per cent of the females aged 60 or more were found to have reported correctly.[16] That is, on a much more demanding test of accuracy over 60 or 70 years, as compared with the test of consistency over just 10 years, the twentieth-century elderly scored more highly.

Comment

The main purpose of this exercise has been to show that analysis of the ages recorded in the nineteenth-century censuses can lead to interesting questions about the communities under study. The columns of figures of ages in the CEBs, a largely neglected factor in these social documents, deserve greater attention. Few definite conclusions have been drawn here – a point of significance in itself, for what has emerged is that a seemingly individual process such as reporting age is a social event, subject to social pressures and community conventions. No 'standard correction' of the nineteenth-century figures, such as numerous census takers have sought to devise, can be suggested because different communities clearly followed different practices. The Puddletown evidence, for instance, would tend to support the optimism of the reports of 1851 and 1861; the Ealing findings by contrast reinforce the caution of later reports, though for reasons other than those suspected by their authors.

Throughout, it has been suggested that the elderly were not so much unknowing, uncaring or forgetful concerning their ages as consciously or unconsciously adjusting them in accordance with a host of pressures peculiar to their social position. What those pressures were must remain the focus of local studies, but they would include poor law and charity policies and facilities for particular age groups; employment prospects for young and old, male and female; local traditions of family and kin support; conventions as to marriage ages, family sizes and many more. Asking questions about age can lead to a new look at many aspects of life in the past.

16 1951 Census England and Wales, *General Report*, (HMSO, London, 1958), 36–9.

10

How accurate is the Methley baptismal registration?

MINORU YASUMOTO

The chief concern underlying the research of which this chapter forms a part has been to investigate the relationship between industrialisation and population change. An examination of the demographic implications of industrialisation for a village on the fringe of an industrial town in the old West Riding of Yorkshire has been made elsewhere.[1] The demographic data for this were derived from a family reconstitution exercise on the parish registers. The extent to which the registers of the parish accurately recorded vital events was, therefore, crucial. This chapter provides some material for a discussion of the deficiencies in coverage of the parish registers, by taking, as a case study, baptismal registration in the same parish (Methley), during the late-eighteenth and early-nineteenth centuries when, it has been argued, English parochial registration was at its worst.[2]

The accuracy of parish registration has been assessed in the following ways. First of all, to measure the completeness of the baptism coverage, the method developed by Razzell, and later refined by the Cambridge Group, has been applied.[3] This involves checking the completeness of baptism coverage for people surviving to the census of 1851, by comparing the entries in the enumerators' books of the census, which provide information on the name, age and birthplace of an individual in the parish, with those in the baptism registers. The assumption that the statements of name, age, and birthplace as seen in the 1851 census would themselves be perfect, may be checked to some extent by comparing them with those of the people who survived to be recorded in the 1861 census.

As shown in Table 10.1 below, of a total of 816 Methley residents identified in both the 1851 and 1861 censuses, 565 stated in 1851 that Methley was their birthplace.[4] Some 45 of these (8.0 per cent), however, claimed in the 1861 census to have been born elsewhere, whereas 6.8 per cent of the people (17 out of 251) who stated other parishes as their birthplace in 1851 named Methley as their birthplace ten years later. For

1 See Yasumoto, *Industrialisation*, 1–51.
2 See, for example, Krause, 'English registration, 1690–1837', 386.
3 Razzell, 'Evaluation of baptism', 123–34; Wrigley, 'Baptism coverage', 303–13.
4 Calculated from the CEBs for Methley 1851 and 1861, PRO HO 107/2329, RG9/3432.

Table 10.1 Consistency in stating birthplace: Methley, 1851–1861

Birthplace 1851	Birthplace 1861 Methley	Other	Total
Methley	520	45	565
Other	17	234[a]	251
Total	537	279	816

Notes: *a* = Of these, 29 individuals recorded different birthplaces in the two censuses.

Table 10.2 Consistency in stating age: Methley, 1851–1861

	Age disagreements (in years) Under 2	2 – 3	4 – 5	6+
n. born in Methley in 1851	515	41	5	5
Percentage	91.2	7.3	0.9	0.9
n. born elsewhere in 1851	193	42	8	3
Percentage	78.5	17.1	3.3	1.2

the same 816 people, 791 (96.9 per cent) may be considered as more or less consistent in their age statements; the disagreement in stated age between the two censuses being within three years, as Table 10.2 above shows. Although the 1851 census has been regarded as much more complete than previous ones,[5] the above consistency in birthplace and age statements in the census indicates that it cannot be assumed to be perfectly accurate, especially in the birthplace statements, and that we should, therefore, be careful in using the information in the census to assess parish register reliability.

Comparison of the census of 1851 with baptism registers reveals the following facts. The second column of Table 10.3 below gives the number of people, divided into age groups according to their stated age in the 1851 census, who claimed Methley as their birthplace. As is shown in the third column, as many as 87.8 per cent (947 out of 1,078) of those who stated in 1851 that Methley was their birthplace have been found in the Methley baptism registers. Of 131 people who named Methley as their birthplace but who were not recorded in the baptism registers, 37 have been found baptised in the 11 other parishes around Methley (shown in Table 10.4 below); the percentage of those who might have failed to register their baptisms is thus reduced from 12.2 to 8.7. In fact this overall figure of 91.3 per cent might be improved upon were the registers of other neighbouring parishes to be checked.

5 See, for example, Tillott, 'Sources of inaccuracy', 83.

Table 10.3 Entries in the baptismal registers and the CEBs compared

Age	[1]	[2]	[3]	[4]
0–1	67	56	1	10
2–4	185	160	1	24
5–9	189	167	2	20
10–14	153	143		10
15–19	100	89	2	9
20–24	76	71	4	1
25–29	61	54	2	5
30–34	40	36	4	
35–39	49	42	2	5
40–44	43	37	4	2
45–49	34	30	3	1
50–54	19	17	1	1
55–59	18	13	4	1
60–64	12	8	2	2
65–69	15	12	1	2
70–74	8	7	1	
75–79	3	2	1	
80–84	5	2	2	1
85–89	1	1		
Total (n.)	1078	947	37	94
Percentage	100.0	87.8	3.5	8.7

Notes: [1] = Methley-born population in 1851, excluding 91 married or widowed women whose maiden names are unknown, and 2 infants buried before baptism; [2] = found in the Methley registers; [3] = found in the registers of neighbouring parishes; [4] = not found in any registers.

Source: Baptismal entries are taken from Lumb, *The registers of Methley*, and for 1813–51 the original parish registers (now in Leeds District Archives).

For the people born between 1782 and 1831 (who correspond to the 20–69 age groups in Table 10.3 above, the era with which we are primarily concerned), the proportion of those whose baptisms are not recorded in the registers is as low as 5.4 per cent, whilst the figures for the birth cohorts (1762–81) and (1832–51) are 5.9 and 10.5 per cent respectively. If we turn to other aspects of the changing adequacy of registration, especially the discrepancies in age between the census statements and the registers for those whose baptisms are found in the latter, we also find confirmation that the degree of deficiency in the baptism registration of this parish is much lower than that observed for other parishes.[6] Furthermore there seems to be no sign of an increasing delay in baptising between 1780 and 1829; the percentage of the age agreement up to and including 1 year and 11 months between the census statements and baptism dates in registers being 92.0 (301 in 327) for 1780–1829, whereas for 1760–79, and 1830–51, the figures are 80.0 (12 in 15) and 97.0 (623 in 642) respectively (Table 10.5 below).

6 For discrepancies in age between census statement and baptism data in registers for 47 parishes, see Razzell, 'Evaluation of baptism', 126.

Table 10.4 Methley residents in 1851 whose baptism was traced in the registers of other parishes

Parish	n. of baptisms
Leeds township	11
Armley	1
Hunslet	3
Wortley	1
Rothwell	12
Garforth	2
Kippax	2
Ledsham	2
Brotherton	1
Normanton	1
Swillington	1
Total	37

Table 10.5 Discrepancies in age between census and parish registers

	Years														
Cohort	<1		1		2		3		4		5		6		Total
	n.	%	n.	%	n.	%	n.	%	n.	%	n.	%	n.	%	n.
1760–9	1	25.0	2	50.0	1	25.0									4
1770–9	9	72.7			1	9.0	1	9.0							11
1780–9	13	68.4	2	10.5	3	15.8							1	5.3	19
1790–9	25	75.8	3	9.1	2	6.1	1	3.0			2	6.1			33
1800–9	54	79.4	10	14.7	2	2.9	1	1.5	1	1.5					68
1810–9	68	78.2	10	11.5	5	5.7	1	1.1	2	2.3	1	1.1			87
1820–9	111	92.5	5	4.2			2	1.7	1	0.8	1	0.8			120
1830–9	196	89.9	17	7.8	2	0.9	1	0.5	2	0.9	1	0.5			218
1840–9	340	92.9	13	3.6	5	1.4	5	1.4	2	0.5			1	0.3	366
1850–1	51	87.9	6	10.3			1	1.7							58
Total	868	88.2	68	6.9	21	2.2	13	1.3	8	0.8	4	0.4	2	0.2	984

The interval between the date of birth and baptism, calculated from the Methley registers that record both, also suggests that the average interval between the two during the late-eighteenth and early-nineteenth centuries was generally fairly short by English standards (Table 10.6 below).[7] Half the children had been baptised within a month or so and three-quarters within 50 days. It is also likely that behaviour in respect to the registration of baptisms during the period was more consistent than that seen in other parishes, as semi-interquartile ranges testify. Rather more important is the fact that the figures both for the interval and the range imply general improvement in regis-

7 Berry and Schofield, 'Age at baptism', 435. As for the exceptionally short intervals between the dates of birth and baptism, which have been found in the registers of north Shropshire parishes, see Jones, 'Infant mortality in Shropshire', 315.

Table 10.6 Birth–baptism interval data from the Methley registers recording date of birth

Period	n. of baptisms	% of incomplete entries	Intervals in days by which stated percentage had been baptised 25%	50%	75%	Semi-interquartile range
1790–9	447	3.6	25	35	52	13
1800–9	603	0.3	25	31	48	11
1810–9	573	2.4	23	29	43	10
1820–9	563	9.0	23	28	41	9
1790–1809	1,050	1.7	25	33	49	12
1790s–1800s[a]	–	1.5	18	34	95	38

Source: a = mean of the data for 27 parishes derived from Berry and Schofield, 'Age at baptism', 457.

Table 10.7 Birth–baptism interval data from Methley registers, 1790–1850

	n. of baptisms	Interval in days by which stated percentage had been baptised 25%	50%	75%	Semi-interquartile range
Children who died before the age of one year	153	3	21	34	15
Others	2148	25	31	48	11

tration in this parish from the 1790s. In general, then, it can be said that the accuracy of parish registration in Methley is fairly high so far as the coverage of baptisms is concerned. There also seems to be no reason to think that the registration carried out by the parish authorities noticeably deteriorated during the period under review.

Lastly, let us examine Table 10.7 above, which compares the interval between the date of birth and baptism for those children who are found to have died before the age of one year with that for those who survived. The purpose is to check whether there is any association between early baptism and early death.[8] If a tendency is found for the baptism of those who died early to have taken place early, it would suggest that the parents tended to secure the early baptisms of those of their offspring who looked weak and seemed likely to die. The figures in Table 10.7 above show the interval for those dying before the age of one year to be shorter than that for those who survived. This would

8 For further details regarding the implications for birth–baptism short-fall of the association between early baptism and early death in registers see Wrigley, 'Births and baptisms', 283, 296.

have the effect of further reducing the birth/baptism shortfall and is yet further evidence to support the proposition that the registration of baptism in this parish may be regarded as an efficient form of birth registration.

11

Population movements and the development of working-class suburbs in 1801–1851: the case of Nottingham

ROGER SMITH

Introduction

It is generally accepted that the demographic growth of the industrialising towns and cities during the first half of the nineteenth century was dependent upon an inflow of population from the surrounding rural areas. During the second half of the nineteenth century, the inhabitants of those, by then, maturing industrial settlements began to be grouped into socially segregated residential areas.[1] An earlier school of urban historians explained this in terms of the middle classes moving out to newly-built suburbs.[2] This was not quite the case in Nottingham.

Until 1845, with the passing of the General Enclosure Act, the growth of the town's population was contained because the commons and commonable lands, which all but surrounded the built-up area of the old town, were not available for development. This is a well-known aspect of Nottingham's history and need not be dwelt upon further.[3] However, partly because of the land famine, a number of industrialised villages situated beyond the municipal boundaries, such as Radford, Lenton, Hyson Green and Sneinton, began to form and grow during the first half of the nineteenth century. Effectively they can be seen as working-class 'overspill' suburbs of the old town. The basic argument of this chapter, therefore, is that the first stage of suburbanisation in Nottingham was essentially a working-class one.

Although the point will not be explored in any detail here, it is worth noting that Nottingham's upper-class suburbanisation did not take place until the second half of the nineteenth century. The first stage of that movement (apart from limited activities in the Park) had to wait until after the enclosures when the Arboretum was laid out and the upper classes began to move into what had previously been the Sandfield and what was to become the All Saints' parish.[4] This was

1 For discussion of this see Carter, *Urban geography*, especially chapters 2 and 9.
2 Mumford, *The city in history*, 554–61.
3 For example, Butler, 'Common lands'; Chambers, *Making of modern Nottingham*, chapter 2; Church, *Economic and social change*, 162–92.
4 See Smith, *The process of inner city housing regeneration*, 15–20

followed in the 1870s by extensive upper-class residential development in the Park.[5] Such house-building activities took place between the old town and the industrialised suburban villages. So it was that the social ecology of Nottingham by the end of the nineteenth century had taken the form of distinct pockets of working-class and upper-class residential development, with some of the working-class parts lying further out from the town centre than the upper-class parts.

This latter aspect of Nottingham's history has been outlined here only to stress the point, that if we are fully to understand the growth patterns and structure of the mature industrial town, we have to understand what was happening during the first half of the nineteenth century.

By drawing on data available in the Registrar General's *Annual Reports of Births, Deaths and Marriages in England* for the years 1841–51, the printed volumes of the decennial censuses for 1801–51 and the CEBs for 1851, the aim of this chapter is to explore the relationship between migration into Nottingham during the first half of the nineteenth century and the growth of these industrialised suburban villages in the Registration District of Radford (i.e. Radford, Lenton, Hyson Green and Sneinton). Three points should be made here. First, unless otherwise stated Nottingham and Radford are defined according to registration district boundaries. Second, the data from the CEBs are based on a sample taken from every tenth household in Nottingham and every fifth household in Radford. Third, little quantitative data from that source, or the printed volumes, directly answers the questions we would like to be answered. The statistics, therefore, are guides to trends, rather than quantitative measurements.

Population growth in Nottingham

Let us turn initially to the overall population growth of Nottingham and Radford between 1801 and 1841. During these 40 years the population total of Nottingham increased from 28,861 persons to 53,091, whilst that of Radford went from 3,831 to 22,473.[6] Thus in 1841, although Radford contained less than half of the population of Nottingham, the district had grown at a considerably faster rate (by 487 per cent compared to 84 per cent). We do not have the information to apportion the causes of these two rates of growth between in-migration and natural increase (that is the increase of births over deaths). But we do know by how much each population grew between 1801–11, 1811–21, 1821–31 and 1831–41. This information is displayed in Table 11.1 below. If we assume that the percentage growth of population in England and Wales between each census represents the rate of natural

5 Brand, *Park estate*, especially 25–9.

6 1851 Census Great Britain, *Population tables, Part I, vol. I*, BPP 1852–3 LXXXV, 32–3.

Table 11.1 Population growth, Nottingham and Radford, 1801–1841

	Population	% increase England & Wales	Population increase if at same rate as England and Wales	Presumed migration
Nottingham				
1801	28,861	–	–	–
1811	34,253	14.0 (1801–11)	32,901	+1,352
1821	40,415	18.1 (1811–21)	40,453	–38
1831	50,680	15.3 (1821–31)	46,801	+3,879
1841	53,091	14.3 (1831–41)	57,927	–4,836
Radford				
1801	3,831	–	–	–
1811	5,704	14.0 (1801–11)	4,367	+1,337
1821	7,348	18.1 (1811–21)	6,736	–612
1831	16,568	15.8 (1821–31)	8,509	+8,059
1841	22,473	14.3 (1831–41)	18,937	+3,536

Source: 1851 Census Great Britain, *Population tables. Part II, vol. I*, BPP 1852–3 LXXXV, 603.

increase in the country as a whole, and, if we further assume that rates of natural increase between the census in Nottingham and Radford were the same as those for England and Wales, we can make some estimates of the breakdown of growth by natural increase, and net migration in the two areas.[7] We can illustrate the technique with an example. Between 1801 and 1811 the overall population of Radford grew by 1,873 to 5,704. The population of England and Wales grew during the same period by 14 per cent. Had Radford's population grown at the rate experienced by England and Wales as a whole (i.e. its assumed rate of natural increase) then by 1811 it would have reached a population of 4,367. But in reality it did not. It had a population of 5,704. The difference of 1,337 is assumed to be the result of net in-migration during the decade. By applying the technique to each inter-censal period between 1801 and 1841, we find that Radford's total growth of 18,642 contained 13,544 net migrants (or 73 per cent of its overall growth). Nottingham's overall growth of 24,230, in contrast, contained, on a net basis, only 357 migrants (or only 1.5 per cent of its overall growth).

The Nottingham result is a surprising one. We would have expected a much higher proportion of in-migrants. To an extent we can use the more refined data available from the Registrar General's Reports for the 1841–51 decade to gauge the reliability of the assumptions we made for the 1801–41 period. During the decade 1841–51 the population of England and Wales grew by 12.6 per cent. The Registrar General's Reports provide us with the total figures of births and deaths in Nottingham and Radford between 1841 and 1850. On the basis of these

7 This was a technique employed by Sigsworth, 'The City of York', 225.

figures Radford's population grew through natural increase by 13.8 per cent, during this period. But for Nottingham it was only 5.4 per cent. In other words, between 1841 and 1851 the rate of natural increase in Radford was similar to the rate of population increase in the country as a whole. That gives us confidence in the soundness of our assumptions used in the 1801–41 period and so for our conclusions. We can have much less confidence in our assumptions during that period for Nottingham. During the decade 1841–51 Nottingham has a much lower rate of natural increase than the growth rate of the country as a whole. If that pattern held good for the years between 1801–41, then the volume of migration into Nottingham will have been underestimated quite considerably. None the less the estimated discrepancy between the net rates of population moving into Nottingham and Radford is so great that we are forced to admit that migration was a much more powerful factor accounting for the growth of Radford than for Nottingham. To an extent, the 1841–51 data bear out this point: during this decade Radford's population grew by 5.3 per cent through net migration compared to Nottingham's 4.6 per cent.

Origin of migrants

We now turn to ask about the birthplaces of those migrating into Nottingham and Radford. The printed data from the 1851 census provide some help as well as presenting a major problem. According to the census, 58.4 per cent of the population of the Borough of Nottingham (an area somewhat smaller than that of the Registration District) aged 20 and over had not been born there.[8] Although this was a relatively low figure compared with say Liverpool (77.4 per cent of the adult population was migrant in 1851) or Manchester (72.2 per cent) it is still none the less higher than might have been expected from the discussion in the previous section.[9] We have already accepted that our estimates of migration into Nottingham are understated. But we have also stressed that our figures are *net* not *gross*. In 1851, the adult population of Nottingham could have contained both a relatively low population of *net* migrants and a high proportion of resident adult migrants, provided that during the first half of the nineteenth century there had been a substantial *gross* exodus of population from Nottingham of those born in the town. We shall subsequently go on to argue that that was indeed the case and that there was a substantial movement of Nottingham born people into Radford.

Unfortunately, the printed volumes of the 1851 census do not provide us with information about the numbers of adults living in

8 1851 Census Great Britain, *Population tables. Part II, vol. II*, BPP 1852–3 LXXXVIII, 605.

9 1851 Census Great Britain, *Population tables. Part II, vol. II*, BPP 1852–3 LXXXVIII, 664.

Table 11.2 Birthplaces of inhabitants, aged 20 and over: Nottingham and Radford, 1851

Place of birth	Nottingham %	Radford %
Nottinghamshire	65.0	68.9
Leicestershire and Derbyshire	14.6	17.4
Rest of England and Wales	15.5	11.5
Scotland	0.7	0.5
Ireland	3.3	1.2
Elsewhere	0.9	0.5

Source: 1851 Census Great Britain, *Population tables. Part II, vol. II,* BPP 1852–3 LXXXVIII, 603.

Radford who were born there, so that no direct comparison can be made with Nottingham *vis-à-vis* the proportion of migrants residing in both areas. What we can do, however, is to draw up a table based on the counties of birth of the adults in the two Registration Districts provided in the printed volumes.

We can see from Table 11.2 above that nearly 80 per cent of the adults in Nottingham and over 85 per cent of the adults in Radford were born in Nottinghamshire, Leicestershire and Derbyshire.[10] As the boundaries of Leicestershire and Derbyshire are in close proximity to Nottingham, it can be argued that the migrants generally travelled only relatively short distances. It can also be argued that there were proportionately more of these short distance migrants in Radford than Nottingham.

By turning now to the enumerators' schedules and examining the places of birth of the household heads, we are for the first time able to compare the proportion of migrants in Nottingham directly with those in Radford.[11] In Nottingham 58.8 per cent of heads were migrants compared to 84.5 per cent in Radford. This provides us with supporting evidence of the greater impact, at least proportionately, of migration in Radford than Nottingham. We can also appreciate the scale of movement of population from Nottingham to Radford. Of all the migrant household heads in Radford, 29.4 per cent came from Nottingham.

If we assume that between 1801 and 1851 Radford received on a net basis 14,729 migrants,[12] and also assume (on the basis of the birthplace of household heads) that some 30 per cent of them were born in Nottingham, then between 1801 and 1851 at least 4,400 were Nottingham born, 15 per cent of the town's population.

10 These figures, of course, include those born in Nottingham and Radford. For convenience we shall refer to all persons aged 20+ as adults.

11 For a more detailed study of household and family structures in Nottingham in 1851, see Smith, 'Early Victorian household structure', 69–84.

12 13,544 in the period 1801–41 plus 1,185 in the period 1841–51.

Table 11.3 Population increases by age cohort: Nottingham and Radford, 1841–1851

Nottingham						
Age range in 1841	0–4	5–9	10–14	15–19	20–24	25–29
n. in 1841	6,195	5,954	5,745	5,443	5,235	4,453
Age range in 1851	10–14	15–19	20–24	25–29	30–34	35–39
n. in 1851	5,896	6,513	6,134	5,026	4,026	3,694
Difference 1841/51	–299	+559	+389	–417	–1,193	–759
Radford						
Age range in 1841	0–4	5–9	10–14	15–19	20–24	25–29
n. in 1841	3,214	2,878	2,581	2,112	1,892	1,757
Age range in 1851	10–14	15–19	20–24	25–29	30–34	35–39
n. in 1851	3,008	2,908	2,609	2,019	1,764	1,649
Difference 1841/51	–206	+30	+28	–93	–128	–108

Source: Registrar General, *Eighth Annual Report,* (1849), 228; 1851 Census Great Britain, *Population tables. Part II, vol. II,* BPP 1852–3 LXXXVIII, 533.

Such a figure fits in well with the argument advanced earlier that a substantial number of Nottingham born people left the town and their places were taken by those born outside. That a majority of adults in the town were migrants in 1851 is thus compatible with low *net* in-migration.

Age profile of migrants

We need to say something about the age of migrants when they moved into Nottingham or Radford. There is nothing we can say about that for the period before 1841, but we can say a little for the period 1841–51. The argument is, however, somewhat tortuous. It is based on a comparison of the population of the two areas broken down by age groups and presented in the Registrar General's *Report* of 1849 and the 1851 printed census volumes. Thus we have for Nottingham and Radford the populations for 1841 and 1851 given in 5–yearly age bands (0–4, 5–9, 10–15, etc.): see Table 11.3 above.

Those in the under five age band would have graduated to the 10–14 age band by 1851; those from the 5–9 age band would have graduated into the 15–19 age band by 1851; etc. For convenience we shall call these 'graduating age bands'. Where there is no migration, each graduating age band would be expected to be smaller in 1851 than 1841. The loss would be accounted for by mortality. But, if there is an *increase* in the graduating age bands (that is to say of the numbers of 20–24 year olds in 1851 is *greater* than the numbers of 10–14 year olds in 1841), then the increase can only be accounted for by net in-migration.

In applying this approach to Nottingham we find that in 1841, there were 5,954 persons aged under five in the town. In 1851 there were 6,513 persons aged 10–14. This must mean that on a net basis between the censuses at least 559 persons who had moved into Nottingham were aged under 14. Furthermore there were 5,443 inhabitants aged 10–14 in 1841 in the town; in 1851 there were 6,134 persons aged 20–24. This must mean that between the censuses at least 389 persons aged between 10–14 moved into Nottingham. By adding these two figures of net migration together we can argue that between 1841 and 1851 at least 948 of the town's in-migrants were aged under 25. As earlier calculations have indicated that, on a net basis, 2,465 people came into Nottingham during the decade, we may estimate that perhaps 39 per cent of them were under 25.

If we undertake a similar exercise for Radford we find that the 1851 age group of 15–19 (2,908) was only 30 more than for 1841 5–9 age groups; and that the 1851 20–24 age group (2,609) was only 28 more than the 1841 10–14 age group. Thus we can assume that at least 58 of the migrants into Radford between 1841 and 1851 were aged under 25. On the basis that Radford received on a net basis some 1,185 migrants during the decades, we can assume that at a minimum only 2.5 per cent were aged under 25.

Too much reliance should not be placed on these figures, but the discrepancy between Nottingham and Radford estimates of the proportion of migrants aged under 25 are so great that we must be compelled to admit that generally migrants into Nottingham were younger, on the whole, than those into Radford.

In this section we attempt to relate the migration patterns into Nottingham with those into Radford, drawing on data from the 1851 enumerators' schedules. If we take those household heads in Nottingham in 1851 born outside the town, and with at least one offspring living in the household, we find that in 63 per cent of cases the only or eldest child was born in Nottingham. On the assumption – clearly not valid in every case – that the eldest child in residence on the night of the census was the only or first born child, we can argue that the majority of migrants into Nottingham either came in an unmarried state or before having a child.

If we examine comparable figures for Radford we find that only 41.7 per cent of migrant heads with at least one child in 1851 had a presumed eldest child born in Radford. The assumption to be made from this is that migrants into Radford were much more likely to have moved in as part of a nuclear family than was the case of those moving into Nottingham. Such a view correlates well with our earlier findings that migrants into Nottingham tended to be younger than those moving into Radford.

We have already demonstrated that a high proportion of Radford immigrants came from Nottingham. Radford was an overspill area for the town. Yet 48.5 per cent of Nottingham born heads in Radford, with at least one child within the family unit, had their only or eldest children born in Radford. In other words, Nottingham born immigrants were *more* likely to have their first child born in Radford than all migrants into Radford generally. Here we can detect a pattern of Nottingham born adults seeking accommodation in Radford before their first child was born.

If we take non-Nottingham born migrants with at least one child at home living in Radford, we find only 39 per cent had their only or first child born in Radford, i.e. a much higher proportion of such migrants moved into Radford as part of a family unit than was the case with Nottingham born heads. Of these non-Nottingham born migrant heads in Radford, 21 per cent had their only or first child born in Nottingham. This suggests a pattern of migrants moving into Nottingham before starting a family (whether or not they moved into Nottingham in an unmarried state, we do not know) having at least one child born in the town and then 'overspilling' into Radford.

But 40 per cent of non-Nottingham born migrant heads in Radford had their only or first child born outside of Nottingham or Radford. Twenty-seven per cent of such children were born in the same locality as the head. We do not know whether they came directly to Radford from their original birthplace or via some other locality.

Conclusion

From this barrage of statistics certain trends appear. It would seem that Nottingham's growth in population during the first half of the nineteenth century – rapid though it was in terms of its earlier history – gained relatively little from net migration. Having said that, there are grounds for thinking that in Nottingham's case gross migration was considerably in excess of net. There was a substantial out-migration from the town, including a substantial proportion of Nottingham born persons, moving to areas like Radford, to find accommodation and start their families. Such an out-migration was somewhat more than offset, however, by an inflow into Nottingham of presumably younger single persons largely from the surrounding countryside.

Many of those moving into Nottingham came to seek work in the town, especially in the lace industry. Whereas 59 per cent of all household heads in Nottingham in 1851 were born outside the town, 63 per cent of heads who were lacemakers were born outside. Lacemaking was an expanding trade. Framework knitting by the 1830s was not. This may explain why in 1851 only 48 per cent of framework knitting heads had been born outside the town.

If there was an influx of young single migrants into Nottingham, this possibly accounts for the fact that in 1851 there were 0.41 lodgers per household in Nottingham compared to 0.25 lodgers per household in Radford. Sixty-two per cent of lodgers in Nottingham in 1851 had not been born in the town.[13]

Whereas 14 per cent of Nottingham households can be designated as upper class, only 7 per cent of Radford households could have been so classified in 1851.[14] Furthermore, whereas 19 per cent of Radford's heads were lacemakers, this compares with only 7 per cent in Nottingham. These figures are consistent with the argument that there was a significant movement of married couples with or without children belonging to the working classes moving into Radford.

We should, perhaps, note here that Chapman had argued that superior working-class houses were built in the Radford area, although Hawkesley – the nineteenth-century Nottingham engineer, social enquirer and reformer – stressed that many of the houses in Radford were little better than some of the worst slums in the old town.[15]

One of the characteristics of the maturing industrialised towns of the nineteenth century was the development of suburbia. In Nottingham the first manifestation of this was, as we have argued here, the development of working class rather than upper class suburbs. There was an attempt in the 1830s to develop the Park as an upper class suburb, but this largely failed.[16] The working-class overspill suburbs were essentially the result of the land shortages in the old town brought about by the failure to enclose the commons and commonable lands. The subsequent enclosure of those lands resulted in some working class suburban development in the Meadows and St Ann's. But the upper-class development on the old Sandfield (between Parliament Street and the Forest) took place between the old town and Hyson Green, Lenton and the industrial village of Radford. When the upper-class development of the Park took place in the 1870s, that too took place between the old town and Lenton and Radford. So it was that the social geography of Nottingham at the end of the nineteenth century took the form of pockets of residential development based on class, rather than in the form of bands with the highest social groupings living further from the town centre than the lowest. The nineteenth-century geographical distribution of social structure in Nottingham was thus more complex than some of the simpler models of nineteenth-century urban growth provided by geographers would suggest.

13 Smith, 'Early Victorian household structure', 73.
14 For the definition of social class used see Smith, 'Early Victorian household structure', 72.
15 Chapman, 'Housing in Nottingham', 67–92.
16 Brand, *Park estate*, 9–13.

12

Age checkability and accuracy in the censuses of six Kentish parishes, 1851–1881

AUDREY PERKYNS

Many of the calculations made in demographic studies are related to age-specific data. Consequently the accuracy with which age was recorded in the past is of obvious importance. Yet there have been comparatively few studies which investigate this. These are reported in the editorial introduction to this section of the volume.[1] Most of these studies involve some form of sampling and compare two censuses, usually consecutive ones and, as Armstrong comments, referring to Tillott's figures, 'essentially this method tests consistency, and, since it to some extent compounds the errors of both censuses, the true errors in any one census will be considerably less than those given above.'[2]

Some recent studies have correlated data from both censuses and baptism registers, the first by Razzell in 1972. Over 45 parishes, taking natives over 17 and excluding married women, he found 46.5 per cent of those matched with a baptism record to be correct, 31.8 per cent to be wrong by one year, 10.5 per cent to be wrong by two years and fewer with greater discrepancies; he also found that the discrepancies were substantially higher in the 81–90 age group.[3] Yasumoto's lists of decadal cohorts matched between the 1851 census and baptism registers for Methley (Yorkshire), reported in chapter 10 of this volume, show 88 per cent correct.

The present study

This chapter, like that of chapter 19, investigates the total census populations of six adjacent Kentish parishes, Hartlip, Newington, Rainham, Stockbury, Upchurch and Lower Halstow, over the five censuses 1841–81, in relation to the data from the parish registers of the six. The six parishes (see Figure 12.1 below) differ in character: Hartlip and Stockbury remained agricultural backwaters, while Rainham grew quite fast and Upchurch and Halstow very fast over the period, as the brickmaking industry developed and their occupational patterns

1 See Tillott, 'Sources of inaccuracy', 107–8; Anderson, 'Study of family structure', 75; Higgs, *Making sense*, 67–8; *Clearer sense*, 78–80.
2 Armstrong, 'The CEBs: a commentary', 36.
3 Razzell, 'Evaluation of baptism', 123–7.

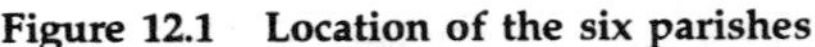

Figure 12.1 Location of the six parishes

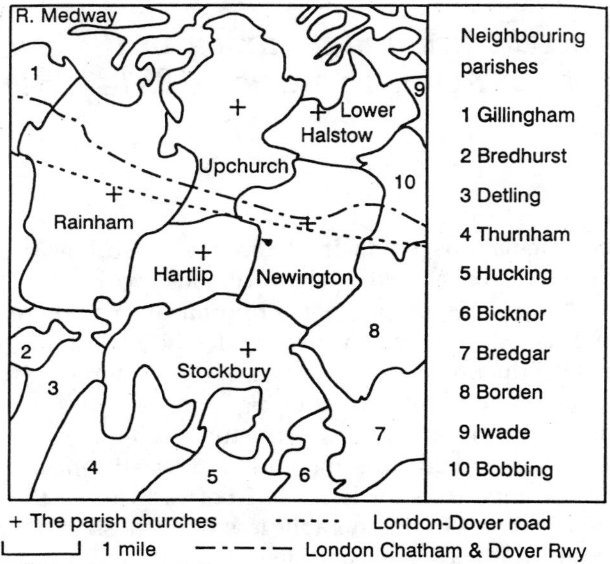

changed accordingly; Newington fell between the two types.[4]

For this study two different methods of calculation were used. The first was a technique similar to one described above: a straight check on the given age of all who could be identified as appearing in two consecutive censuses. The results of this will be compared below to those of a quite different technique. This other method was designed to ascribe a probable age to each person whose age was checkable. The given age was entered in an AGE field; the probable age was entered in an AGECALC field (where the age was not checkable the AGECALC was entered as 0; this made it easy to identify the checkable population for all calculations); a third field, AGEUSE, consists of the AGECALC age where this is not 0, otherwise the AGE age. The advantages and disadvantages of this method will be considered below. Such a technique achieves findings beyond mere consistency, though consistency between census entries was one factor in the process of checking. The relative sizes of the six parishes under study in the period 1851–81 and the proportions checkable are given in Table 12.1 below.

4 In this area the civil and ecclesiastical parishes coincided. All were 'open' parishes. Microfilm copies were used for the censuses: the PRO references to the CEBs are sometimes missing from the microfilm and are sometimes very badly faded. The references seem to be as follows: 1851: Stockbury HO 107/1618; the other five parishes HO 107/1627. 1861: Hartlip and Halstow RG 9/528; Newington, Rainham and Upchurch RG 9/529; Stockbury RG 9/504. 1871: Stockbury not available; the other five RG 10/983 or 10/984. 1881: Hartlip and Halstow RG 11/972; Newington and Rainham RG 11/974; Upchurch RG 11/977; Stockbury RG 11/933.

Table 12.1 Checkability[a] and accuracy of ages in the six parishes

Parish	[1] Total population	[2] Number checkable	[3] Percentage checkable	[4] % of [2] correct	[5] % of [2] within 2 yrs[b]
Hartlip					
1851	342	302	88.3	86.1	96.4
1861	319	271	85.0	82.7	95.2
1871	355	282	79.4	83.0	95.7
1881	378	229	60.6	79.9	94.8
Newington					
1851	731	598	81.8	77.8	95.0
1861	854	668	78.2	75.9	92.8
1871	1013	729	72.0	75.3	94.4
1881	1,038	635	61.2	74.7	93.2
Rainham					
1851	1,155	980	84.8	80.2	94.9
1861	1,422	1,171	82.3	76.6	93.2
1871	2,082	1,550	74.4	77.1	93.6
1881	2,696	1,670	61.9	78.5	94.6
Stockbury					
1851	589	494	83.9	73.9	91.1
1861	613	497	81.1	74.5	92.8
1871	590	442	74.9	72.6	93.9
1881	621	388	62.5	79.6	94.6
Upchurch					
1851	407	366	89.9	76.5	92.6
1861[c]	314	284	90.4	76.1	93.3
1871	777	636	81.9	78.6	95.0
1881	1,112	662	59.5	79.3	93.4
Lower Halstow					
1851	344	316	91.9	80.1	93.4
1861	373	340	91.2	77.1	94.1
1871	504	388	77.0	79.6	95.6
1881	701	454	64.8	75.3	93.6
Total 1851–81	19,330	14,352	74.2	77.6	94.0

Notes: *a* = by criteria listed in Table 12.2; *b* = correct or with a discrepancy of less than 2 years; *c* = 154 of the 468 records are missing, destroyed.

Table 12.2 Criteria for checking ages: all parishes

	1851	1861	1871	1881	All
Birthdate	2.2	1.9	0.8	0.8	1.4
Baptism + census[a]	39.3	50.3	45.3	37.5	43.0
Census[a], no baptism	25.1	35.6	41.8	33.9	34.4
Baptism, no census[a]	21.8	9.6	8.6	25.8	16.5
Marriage + burial age	0.2	0.3	0.1	0.0	0.1
Marriage or burial	7.5	1.9	2.9	2.5	3.5
Workhouse census	0.1	0.1	0.1	0.0	0.1
Census 1841[b]	3.8	0.2	0.1	0.0	0.9
Total number	3,056	3,231	4,027	4,038	14,352

Notes: *a* = an additional entry in a census 1851 to 1881; *b* = supporting evidence only from an entry in the 1841 census.

Criteria for checkability

The criteria used for ascribing an AGECALC are listed in Table 12.2 above which shows the percentage of the checkable population 1851–81 falling into each category. The criteria are listed in order of usefulness and the figures were arrived at by a process of elimination, those in each category being deleted after being counted. The order of usefulness decided upon was as follows:

1) date of birth;
2) baptism record plus an entry in at least one other census 1851–81;
3) another census entry 1851–81 but no baptism record;
4) a baptism record but no other census entry 1851–81;
5) age at marriage plus age at burial;
6) age at marriage or age at burial;
7) a workhouse census entry;
8) supporting evidence from the 1841 census only.

The bare figures need to be supplemented by some discussion about the nature and reliability of each criterion. Obviously the first, date of birth, is unique as unequivocal evidence of age. The proportion of the checkable population for whom this evidence is available varies considerably between years and parishes, as is clear from Tables 12.3a and 12.3b below. These show that birthdates have been found for 125 individuals who appear in the censuses on 254 occasions. Birthdates were recorded in the baptism registers haphazardly and capriciously, except for a detectable tendency to record the better off and those baptised aged two or more. The two major exceptions, when over half of those baptised had birthdates recorded, were in Stockbury between January 1834 and February 1836 and in Halstow between March 1849 and February 1852. Tables 12.3a and 12.3b reflect these concentrations.

The value of birthdates obviously depends on the accuracy with which these dates themselves were recorded. A reference to birth certificates, the only irrefutable check, would be impracticable. But a review of the given ages of those with birthdates suggests a high degree of accuracy. Of the 68 individuals with more than one entry 1841–81, all but 5 have at least 1 entry that tallies with the birthdate, most more. Of the five who are always wrong, four give ages which are too high on one occasion and too low on another, leaving only one who gives a consistent minus one on each of the two occasions when he appears. This strongly suggests that errors are more likely to be in the census ages than in the birthdates.

Because birthdate evidence is of unique importance, it has been discussed in greater detail than is necessary for the other checking

Table 12.3a Census entries 1841–1881 checkable by birthdate data

	Hartlip	Newington	Rainham	Stockbury	Upchurch	Halstow	Total
Pre–1820	2	23	14	3	4	5	51
1820–29	1	2	5	0	8	2	18
1830–39	10	10	6	37	7	8	78
1840–49	0	3	3	1	2	22	31
1850–59	0	4	2	8	3	39	56
1860–69	0	1	1	0	7	0	9
1870–79	0	1	4	5	1	0	11
Total	13	44	35	54	32	76	254

Table 12.3b Census individuals 1841–1881 having birthdate data

	Hartlip	Newington	Rainham	Stockbury	Upchurch	Halstow	Total
Pre–1820	1	8	5	1	1	2	18
1820–29	1	1	3	0	3	2	11
1830–39	6	4	3	20	3	3	38
1840–49	0	2	1	1	1	10	15
1850–59	0	4	1	4	2	18	29
1860–69	0	1	1	0	3	0	5
1870–79	0	1	2	5	1	0	9
Total	8	21	16	31	14	35	125

criteria. Table 12.2 above shows that in every year a fair percentage could be checked by both baptism and another census entry.[5] Generally the reason for the order of usefulness is self-evident but one or two explanations are appropriate. A baptism record was used only if it was not obviously late, unless age at baptism was recorded. A late baptism might be detected from the baptism together of two or more siblings who were given different ages in the census(es) or from consistent ages for an individual over multiple census entries that disagree with the baptism. Since baptism can occur at any age, a given census age which seems too high by baptism criteria alone may be evidence either of a late baptism or of age inaccuracy. But since baptism is unlikely to precede birth a given census age which is too low must be wrong. The only caveat here is the possibility that a second child of the same name was born but not baptised after the one with the recorded baptism died leaving no burial record; this in unlikely to occur often, and the spacing of siblings' ages often furnishes additional evidence. However, the result is that a bias is built into the assignment of AGECALC ages, in that ages patently too low have been corrected while those which might

5 This table is calculated for the six parishes combined. However, differences between parishes are minimal except for a few birthdates.

have been too high have not been corrected unless there is evidence other than the baptism date to support the AGECALC.

Age at marriage and age at burial are less useful. The former is not given very often and is not always correct according to other criteria: in particular very young girls sometimes inflate their ages at marriage and husbands seem reluctant to be recorded as younger than their wives. Burial ages are sometimes inflated, especially for the old. Comparatively few checks were dependent on these criteria, except for 1851.

An individual workhouse record is intrinsically as valuable as any other census record but there are so few of them that this category has been placed low in the order of priority.

Finally, again usually for 1851, in a few cases the only supporting evidence is from the 1841 census, when ages, for those over 14, were required only to the nearest 5 below. In spite of this, a high proportion of those recorded are checkable and a surprisingly high percentage are correct. For the 131 cases where this criterion has been used for assigning an AGECALC, 54 per cent recorded an exactly consistent age in 1841, another 15 per cent are within one year and 20 per cent seem correct by the requirement of the nearest five below; the few others were assigned an AGECALC for a variety of reasons, including sibling spacing.

An AGECALC was not assigned at all if the available evidence was irreconcilable. On the other hand, in twenty cases altogether, out of the total of 14,352 checkable, where two or more entries differ by little more than one year (above or below ten), AGECALCS have been assigned more or less arbitrarily. Other criteria were used too rarely to quantify, often indeed uniquely.

Representativeness of birthdate and checkable populations

The value of birthdates (for precise assessments of accuracy) and checkability (for fairly reliable assessments) seems clear, but the validity of findings based on these for extrapolation to the total population must depend on the extent to which the birthdate and the checkable populations respectively are representative of the total population. In order to discover this various aspects of correlation were considered between total, checkable and birthdate populations, namely age groups, social class, birthplace, sex ratio and status in household.

The results of a survey relating to birthdates as compared to the total and checkable populations 1851–81 are to be found in Tables 12.4a and 12.4b below. The big variations between parishes and between years reflect the data in Tables 12.3a and 12.3b. Age-group ratios match fairly closely, though there are comparatively few birthdates in the over 59 age groups. The social class ratios show higher proportions in the

Table 12.4a Birthdate population: 1851–1881 (all parishes)

Category ratios of checkable population

Parishes	Checkable	Birthdate	%	Years	Checkable	Birthdate	%
Hartlip	1,084	11	1.0	1851	3,056	67	2.2
Newington	2,630	27	1.0	1861	3,231	62	1.9
Rainham	5,371	47	0.9	1871	4,027	31	0.8
Stockbury	1,821	23	1.3	1881	4,038	34	0.8
Upchurch	1,948	28	1.4				
Halstow	1,498	58	3.9				
Totals	14,352	194	1.4		14,352	194	1.4

By age group	Checkable	Birthdate	%	By social class	Checkable	Birthdate	%
Under 10	4,022	53	1.3	I	198	17	8.6
10–14	1,688	24	1.4	II	1,444	39	2.7
15–19	1,235	16	1.3	III	2,615	37	1.4
20–29	1,963	36	1.8	IV	7,992	82	1.0
30–39	1,710	19	1.1	V	1,947	19	1.0
40–49	1,418	20	1.4	UK	156	0	0.0
50–59	1,102	16	1.5				
Over 59	1,214	10	0.8				
Totals	14,352	194	1.4		14,352	194	1.4

By status in household	Checkable	Birthdate	%	Status in household Ratio of total population Total	%
Head	3,369	48	1.4	4,119	1.2
Wife	2,593	16	0.6	3,327	0.5
Son/daughter[a]	7,228	116	1.6	9,493	1.2
Parent	107	0	0.0	160	0.0
Other relation	624	8	1.3	936	0.9
Servant[b]	500	9	1.8	984	0.9
Lodger[c]	381	4	1.0	794	0.5
Visitor	35	0	0.0	159	0.0
Totals[d]	14,837	201	1.4	19,972	1.0

Notes: *a* = Including in laws; *b* = Domestic, farm and trade servants; *c* = Lodgers and boarders; = Numbers are greater because some individuals come into two categories.
The social class groups are based on those given in Armstrong, 'Information about occupation', summarised as follows: I = Professional; II = Intermediate; III = Skilled; IV = Partly skilled; V = Unskilled; UK = Unknown.

higher classes. Social class has been categorised according to Armstrong's recommendations.[6] It has been ascribed to all the employed according to their recorded occupations and to those without

6 Armstrong, 'Information about occupation'.

Table 12.4b Birthdate population: errors 1851–1881 (all parishes)

	By age group Total	Errors	%		By social class Total	Errors	%
Under 10	53	10	18.9	I	17	3	17.6
10–14	24	7	29.2	II	39	4	10.3
15–19	16	2	12.5	III	37	4	10.8
20–29	36	12	33.3	IV	82	32	39.0
30–39	19	4	21.1	V	19	3	15.8
40–49	20	5	25.0	UK	0	0	0.0
50–59	16	5	31.3				
Over 59	10	1	10.0				
Totals	194	46	23.7		194	46	23.7

	By status in household Total	Errors	%		By sex Total	Errors	%
Head	48	15	31.3	Males	106	30	28.3
Wife	16	6	37.5	Females	88	16	18.5
Son/daughter	116	23	19.8				
Parent	0	0	0.0				
Other relation	8	0	0.0				
Servant	9	1	11.1				
Lodger	4	2	50.0				
Visitor	0	0	0.0				
Totals	201	47	23.4		194	46	23.7

Notes: See notes to Table 12.4a.

occupations according to the head of the household. It should be noted that the 'unknown' class (UK) includes a large proportion of visitors, while classes IV and V should be considered together since enumerators were inconsistent in allocating workers to general labouring or more specific occupations.

The sex ratio (f=100) for the total population 1851–81 is 107; for the birthdate population it is 120; there were more men than women in all parishes except Hartlip; an even higher proportion of males had a birthdate recorded. It is not surprising to find that 91.2 per cent of those with birthdates were born in one of the six parishes and another 6.2 per cent within five miles; in this respect the birthdate population is very unlike the total population. The proportions for status in household are shown against both the total and the checkable populations. No parents or visitors and few wives or lodgers have birthdates; there is a high proportion of other relations and servants compared with the checkable population but a smaller proportion of these compared with the total population; heads and their children are most likely to have a birthdate. In this respect birthdates are not similar to the total or checkable populations.

Table 12.5a Checkability[a]: characteristics 1851–1881 and 1851–1871

	1851–81 Total Population	1851–81 Checkable %	1851–71 Total Population	1851–71 Checkable %	1851–71 1851–81 % Difference
By parishes					
Hartlip	1,394	77.8	1,016	84.2	6.4
Newington	3,636	72.3	2,598	76.8	4.5
Rainham	7,355	73.0	4,659	79.4	6.4
Stockbury	2,413	75.5	1,792	80.0	4.5
Upchurch	2,610	74.6	1,498	85.9	11.3
Halstow	1,922	77.9	1,221	85.5	7.6
By age groups					
Under 10	5,695	70.6	3,768	80.0	9.4
10–14	2,182	77.4	1,438	81.9	4.5
15–19	1,740	71.0	1,124	74.0	3.0
20–29	2,856	68.7	1,877	74.5	5.8
30–39	2,339	73.1	1,602	79.7	6.6
40–49	1,777	79.8	1,159	85.7	5.9
50–59	1,325	83.2	871	87.8	4.6
60–69	863	85.8	563	90.8	5.0
70–79	438	85.2	302	89.7	4.5
Over 79	115	87.8	80	93.7	5.9
By social status					
I	292	67.8	209	74.6	6.8
II	1,879	76.9	1,332	81.8	4.9
III	3,702	70.6	2,347	75.5	4.9
IV	10,610	75.3	6,755	82.5	7.2
V	2,556	76.2	1,923	82.9	6.7
UK	291	53.6	218	58.7	5.1
By birthplace[b]					
Census parish	8,941	89.9	6,129	94.5	4.6
The other 5	2,453	93.5	1,659	95.1	1.6
Within 5 miles	2,959	58.3	1,974	65.5	7.2
Within 20 miles	2,838	52.4	1,812	60.4	8.0
Elsewhere	2,109	38.3	1,196	46.7	8.4
Not known	30	0.0	14	0.0	0.0
Totals[c]	19,330	74.3	12,784	80.7	6.4
By status of household					
Head	4,119	81.8	2,752	86.4	4.6
Wife	3,327	77.9	2,198	84.7	6.8
Son/daughter	9,493	76.1	6,227	83.5	7.4
Parent	160	66.9	95	74.7	7.8
Other relation	936	66.7	621	72.5	5.8
Servant	984	50.8	767	54.1	3.3
Lodger	794	48.0	460	60.9	12.9
Visitor	159	22.0	104	23.1	1.1
Totals[d]	19,972	74.3	13,224	80.7	6.4

Notes: *a* = by criteria listed in Table 12.2; *b* = see notes to Tables 12.4a and 12.8c; *c* = totals of each of above groups; *d* = totals bigger because some people fall into two categories.

Table 12.5b Statistics relating to age checkability 1851–1881 (all parishes)

	1851	51–61	1861	61–71	1871	71–81	1881
Total population	3568		3895		5321		6546
% checkable	85.7		83.0		75.7		61.7
% difference		2.7		7.3		14.0	
Not native[a]	34.0		37.1		44.0		44.9
% difference		3.1		6.9		0.9	
No baptism	45.7		48.8		58.5		60.3
% difference		3.1		9.7		1.8	
Previous census[b]	20.6		23.9		30.4		29.4
% difference		3.3		6.5		–1.0	
Next census[c]	46.6		49.1		49.2		No figures available
% difference		2.5		0.1			

Notes: *a* = birthplace outside the 6 parishes; *b* = age 10 or more but not in previous census; *c* = not in next census (for reasons of death or migration).

The characteristics of the checkable population can indicate both how far it is representative of the whole and also how effective the methodology is. The checkable percentage decreases gradually from 1851–71 but markedly 1871–81 (the checkable percentages being 86, 83, 76 and 62 respectively). Table 12.5b above shows some correlation between the 1851–71 decline and select criteria of checkability relating to migration. There is no such correlation for 1871–81, indeed the reverse, probably because increasing employment opportunities (in some parishes) were attracting migrants who stayed. The major explanation for the fall in checkability in this last decade is the lack of any means of checking the under ten age group of 1881 (a high proportion of the total population) except for those with a baptism record.

Table 12.5a above, by listing analogous calculations for 1851–71 and 1851–81 shows the difference made to checkability by the availability of both previous and next censuses. (The 1841 data, though less specific, are useful for 1851.) The main difference, unsurprisingly, is in the under ten age group. The lower checkability of the 15–39 age groups is explained by their greater mobility.[7]

The sex ratio for the checkable population is 110, as against 107 for the total population, which is not a big difference. The slightly higher checkability of males is related to the fact that women (especially wives) are less likely to have been born in the census parish, and of those who claim to have been so fewer are likely to have an identifiable baptism, possibly because they are unrecognisable by their married names. The fact that a higher proportion of those born in the

7 The decadal cohort aged 10–19 has been separated into two categories because there is much evidence to show important variations between lower and upper teens.

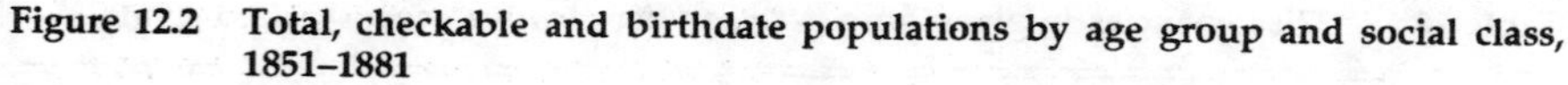

Figure 12.2 Total, checkable and birthdate populations by age group and social class, 1851–1881

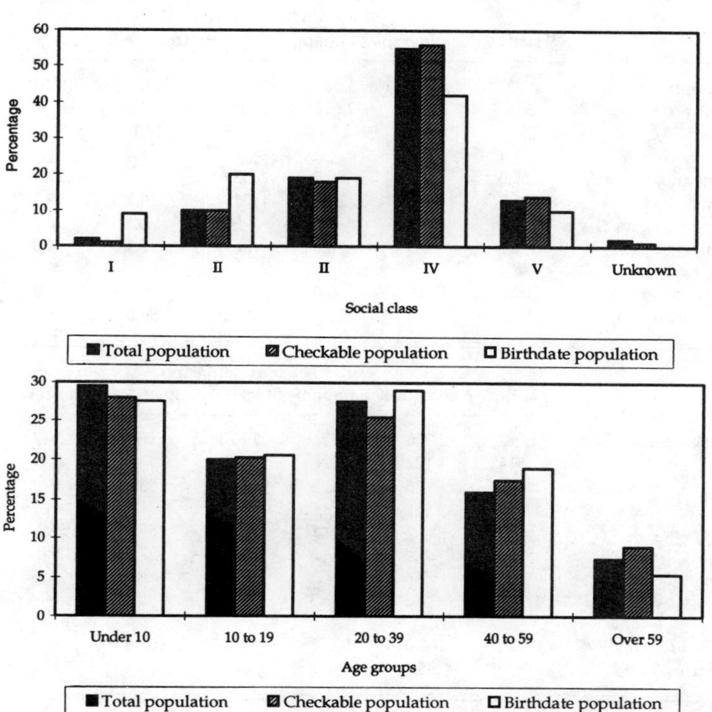

neighbouring five parishes is checkable than of those born in the census parish itself supports the theory of considerable local mobility and/or the erroneous recording of birthplaces in the census parish. Otherwise checkability declines with the distance of the birthplace. This is confirmed by a comparison of the 1851–71 and 1851–81 figures for Upchurch and Halstow where there was a big in migration of labour from outside the area during this last decade.

This also explains the increase in the number and decrease in the checkability of lodgers between 1871 and 1881. Heads are most checkable, also children who can be checked in two censuses. There is little overall difference between total and checkable populations as far as social class is concerned, though Hartlip had more in the top class and Upchurch and Halstow more in the bottom two.

The above analysis, because it has sought explanations for anomalies, has inevitably tended to emphasise them, but Table 12.5a suggests a high overall level of correlation between the total and checkable populations. The graph (Figure 12.2 above) illustrates this for social classes and age groups for total, checkable and birthdate

Table 12.6 Discrepancies in given ages between consecutive censuses 1851–1881

	Males (all years)						
	Hartlip	Newington	Rainham	Stockbury	Upchurch	Halstow	All
Total in observation[a]	985	2,791	5,509	1,927	1,997	1,470	14,737
Identified[b] no.	544	1,248	2,612	942	952	698	6,996
Identified %	55.2	44.7	47.4	48.9	47.7	47.5	47.5
No discrepancy[c] %	67.5	58.3	60.1	53.6	60.4	59.9	59.5
Discrepancy 1 year %	25.7	28.0	27.6	31.4	26.2	29.5	28.0
Discrepancy 2 years %	4.8	7.8	6.4	9.0	6.3	6.3	6.9
Discrepancy >2 years %	2.0	5.9	5.9	6.0	7.1	4.3	5.6
Total % of identified	100.0	100.0	100.0	100.0	100.0	100.0	100.0
Discrepancies 0 or 1	93.2	86.3	87.7	85.0	86.6	89.4	87.5

	Females (all years)						
	Hartlip	Newington	Rainham	Stockbury	Upchurch	Halstow	All
Total in observation[a]	1,081	2,706	5,326	1,678	1,699	1,317	13,807
Identified[b] no.	514	1,122	2,278	695	741	608	5,958
Identified %	47.5	41.5	42.8	41.4	43.6	46.2	43.2
No discrepancy[c] %	67.1	55.7	59.1	59.0	59.5	59.2	59.2
Discrepancy 1 year %	23.1	29.4	27.3	27.8	27.4	25.0	27.2
Discrepancy 2 years %	4.9	8.6	7.3	7.6	8.6	9.2	7.7
Discrepancy >2 years %	4.9	6.3	6.3	5.6	4.5	6.6	5.9
Total % of identified	100.0	100.0	100.0	100.0	100.0	100.0	100.0
Discrepancies 0 or 1	90.2	85.1	86.4	86.8	86.9	84.2	86.4

Notes: *a* = Each individual in each census is compared with the previous and next census. Thus 1851 and 1881 were compared once, 1861 and 1871 twice. As a consequence the numbers on which these calculations are based are higher than the sum of the population in the 4 census years. *b* = Individuals identified as appearing in consecutive censuses. *c* = The number of years of discrepancies is the number above or below 10.

populations. The least checkable groups are those born at a distance, lodgers and servants. Special considerations apply to those under ten and, to a lesser extent, to married women. The disadvantage of using a final available census which cannot be checked against a subsequent one seems to be minimal, except in the case of the under tens (inevitably) and any group which changes incidentally at this moment, as is the case with lodgers in this exercise.

Comparison between the two techniques of checking

Tables 12.6 above and 12.7(a/b) below allow a comparison between the two techniques of checking. Table 12.6 shows the results of a comparison of given ages between two consecutive censuses (previous and/or next) for the people identified as appearing in both. The figures

Table 12.7a Age discrepancies of those checkable by multiple criteria: parishes

	Males (all years)					
	Hartlip	Newington	Rainham	Stockbury	Upchurch	Halstow
Total population	665	1,846	3,744	1,295	1,434	1,017
Checkable %	80.0	73.1	74.6	76.6	73.6	78.9
No discrepancy %	83.3	75.8	77.6	73.4	78.6	79.3
Discrepancy 1 year %	12.8	18.3	16.3	18.9	14.7	16.0
Discrepancy 2 years %	2.6	3.4	3.2	4.0	3.0	2.6
Discrepancy >2 years %	1.3	2.5	2.9	3.7	3.7	2.1
Total % of checkable	100.0	100.0	100.0	100.0	100.0	100.0
Discrepancies 0 or 1	96.1	94.1	93.9	92.3	93.3	95.3

	Females (all years)					
	Hartlip	Newington	Rainham	Stockbury	Upchurch	Halstow
Total population	729	1,790	3,611	1,118	1,176	905
Checkable %	75.7	71.6	71.4	74.2	75.9	76.9
No discrepancy %	83.0	75.9	78.4	76.8	77.5	76.2
Discrepancy 1 year %	12.1	17.6	15.8	17.0	16.8	16.8
Discrepancy 2 years %	2.7	3.6	3.3	2.8	3.5	3.7
Discrepancy >2 years %	2.2	2.9	2.5	3.3	2.2	3.3
Total % of checkable	100.0	100.0	100.0	100.0	100.0	100.0
Discrepancies 0 or 1	95.1	93.5	94.2	93.8	94.3	93.0

Table 12.7b Age discrepancies of those checkable by multiple criteria: years

	Males (all parishes)				
	1851	1861	1871	1881	All
Total population	1,827	2,023	2,715	3,436	10,001
Checkable %	86.5	84.1	77.4	62.3	75.2
No discrepancy %	77.3	76.3	78.1	77.8	77.4
Discrepancy 1 year %	16.0	17.2	16.5	16.3	16.5
Discrepancy 2 years %	3.9	3.5	2.7	3.0	3.2
Discrepancy >2 years %	2.9	3.1	2.7	2.9	2.9
Total % of checkable	100.0	100.0	100.0	99.9	100.0
Discrepancies 0 or 1	93.3	93.5	94.6	94.1	93.9

	Females (all parishes)				
	1851	1861	1871	1881	All
Total population	1,741	1,872	2,606	3,110	9,329
Checkable %	84.8	81.7	73.9	61.0	73.2
No discrepancy %	80.4	77.0	76.2	77.9	77.8
Discrepancy 1 year %	14.4	16.2	17.8	16.1	16.2
Discrepancy 2 years %	2.6	3.5	3.2	3.9	3.3
Discrepancy >2 years %	2.6	3.3	2.9	2.1	2.7
Total % of checkable	100.0	100.0	100.0	100.0	100.0
Discrepancies 0 or 1	94.8	93.2	94.0	94.0	94.0

are an aggregate of all these calculations. Tables 12.7a (for parishes) and 12.7b (for years) follow a similar pattern but list those checkable by multiple criteria, counting discrepancies between given age and probable age. Separate statistics are given for males and females. (Table 12.1 gives the basic figures for each parish and year separately, for both sexes.)

The first and most obvious difference between the figures of Tables 12.6 and 12.7(a/b) is between the percentage of the total population identified in consecutive censuses and the far higher percentage of the total population found to be checkable by multiple criteria. This alone recommends the more laborious technique.

The latter method also produces a far higher percentage with no discrepancy at all and a slightly higher percentage with no discrepancy greater than one year. The former difference can be partially explained by the policy adopted in ascribing AGECALCS to those differing from an adjacent census by 9 or 11 years; in the absence of additional evidence, the assumption was made that the given age, though apparently discrepant by one year, was correct, since birthday might coincide with census date. As this applied to 15 per cent of the checkable population it is a serious consideration and the assumption might seem unjustified on the grounds that the coincidence could not have been that frequent. However, evidence from the birthdate population shows that 63 out of the 254 entries (1841–81) (25 per cent) and 17 out of the 46 errors (37 per cent) (53 per cent of the 32 errors of under 2 years) had birthdays within 1 month of the census. If similar proportions apply to the total population it seems likely that many of the 15 per cent in question could be either correct or within one month of the correct age. They would not have been included as errors in Table 12.7 but would in Table 12.6. This must furnish part of the explanation for the difference between the percentages found to be correct by the two methods, but the major factor seems clearly to be that stated above: that the simple comparison of given ages between consecutive censuses compounds the errors of both. This seems to indicate the advantages of multiple checking.

The extent and nature of inaccuracy in age reporting

It is now possible to consider more fully the extent and nature of age discrepancies detected by multiple checking. In the birthdate population, of all 194 census entries 1851–81, 148 (76.3 per cent) are correct and 180 (92.8 per cent) have no error greater than one year. This result is closer to the figures calculated from multiple checking than by comparison of consecutive censuses alone. Table 12.4b shows no explicable pattern for the characteristics of those with errors among the

Table 12.8a Age discrepancies by age group: 1851–1881 (all parishes)

Age group	Checkable population	Category ratios of checkable population All errors n.	%	Errors >1 year n.	%	Errors >2 years n.	%
Under ten	4,022	300	7.5	25	0.6	9	0.2
10–14	1,688	247	14.6	17	1.0	1	0.1
15–19	1,235	256	20.7	31	2.5	8	0.6
20–29	1,963	491	25.0	117	6.0	42	2.1
30–39	1,710	582	34.0	180	10.5	74	4.3
40–49	1,418	491	34.6	158	11.1	82	5.8
50–59	1,102	415	37.7	166	15.1	86	7.8
60–69	740	263	35.5	108	14.6	57	7.7
70–79	373	141	37.8	57	15.3	33	8.8
Over 79	101	29	28.7	10	9.9	7	6.9
Totals	14,352	3215	22.4	869	6.1	399	2.8

Table 12.8b Age discrepancies by social class: 1851–1881 (all parishes)

Social class	Checkable population	Category ratios of checkable population All errors n.	%	Errors >1 year n.	%	Errors >2 years n.	%
I	198	23	11.6	5	2.5	4	2.0
II	1,444	266	18.4	70	4.8	32	2.2
III	2,615	469	17.9	119	4.6	50	1.9
IV	7,992	1,924	24.1	511	6.4	226	2.8
V	1,947	481	24.7	143	7.3	75	3.9
UK	156	52	33.3	21	13.5	12	7.7
Totals	14,352	3,215	22.4	869	6.1	399	2.8

Table 12.8c Age discrepancies by birthplace 1851–1881 (all parishes)

Birthplace	Checkable population	Category ratios of checkable population All errors n.	%	Errors >1 year n.	%	Errors >2 years n.	%
Census parish	8,041	1,462	18.2	334	4.2	139	1.7
Other 5	2,293	667	29.1	228	9.9	109	4.8
Within 5 miles[a]	1,724	462	26.8	111	6.4	49	2.8
Within 20 miles[b]	1,487	416	28.0	131	8.8	69	4.6
Elsewhere	8,07	208	25.8	65	8.1	33	4.1
Totals	14,352	3,215	22.4	869	6.1	399	2.8

Notes: *a* = outside the 6 parishes but within a radius of 5 miles from Rainham; *b* = more than 5 but less than 20 miles.

birthdate population, presumably because numbers were too small. Males account for 70 per cent of such errors.

Table 12.8d Age discrepancies by status in household 1851–1881 (all parishes)

Status	Checkable population	Category ratios of checkable population All errors n.	%	Errors >1 year n.	%	Errors >2 years n.	%
Head	3,369	1,130	33.5	395	11.7	185	5.5
Wife	2,593	859	33.1	263	10.1	117	4.5
Son/daughter[a]	7,228	886	12.3	115	1.6	44	0.6
Parent[b]	107	36	33.6	17	15.9	9	8.4
Other relation	624	148	23.7	37	5.9	20	3.2
Servant[b]	500	142	28.4	36	7.2	17	3.4
Lodger[c]	381	127	33.3	53	13.9	32	8.4
Visitor	35	9	25.7	5	14.3	2	5.7
Totals[d]	14,837	3,337	22.5	921	6.2	426	2.9

Notes: *a* = including in laws; *b* = domestic, farm and trade servants; *c* = including boarders; *d* = numbers are greater because some individuals come into two categories.

The characteristics of those in the checkable population with age discrepancies are listed in Tables 12.8(a–d) below, which deal respectively with age groups, social class, birthplaces and status in household. Each table distinguishes between total errors, those of over one year and those of over two years, and each states the percentage of the checkable population falling into the appropriate category. The nature of the errors of over two years differs somewhat, so these will be considered later and the following remarks apply to errors of less than that.

Table 12.8a above shows a generally greater tendency to error with greater age. The General Reports for the censuses of 1851, 1881 and 1891,[8] on the evidence of expected survival rates between censuses, point to recurrent excesses or deficiencies in particular age groups, especially an excess among the oldest who tend to exaggerate their ages, possibly with outdoor relief in mind, and also an excess in the female 20–29 group, which is attributed to the wilful inaccuracy of teenage domestic servants and the vanity of older women.

Thomson, in chapter 9 of this volume, studying the elderly in Puddletown and Ealing, finds greater accuracy in the rural area, where the circumstances of a small community would have militated against extravagant claims. He reports that men tended to ease their ages up, women to follow a more complex pattern. A survey of the quinquennial age groups of all age errors in the present study shows that of the over seventies 44 men reported a higher age and 39 a lower age; the equivalent figures for women were 46 and 41. All groups up to

[8] 1851 Census Great Britain, *Population tables. Part I, vol. I*, BPP 1852–3 LXXXV; 1881 Census England and Wales, *General report and tables*, BPP 1883 LXXIX; 1891 Census England and Wales, *Vol. II. Area, house and population*, BPP 1893–4 CV.

Table 12.9 | Age group size correspondence from census to census

Males	1841/1851		1851/1861		1861/1871		1871/1881	
Age in *y*	*x*	*y*	*x*	*y*	*x*	*y*	*x*	*y*
10–14	165	97.6	170	99.4	197	99.5	267	98.9
15–19	136	100.0	130	99.7	133	99.3	218	99.1
20–24	101	100.0	94	106.4	100	103.0	150	101.3
25–29	72	106.9	84	96.4	68	92.7	96	99.0
30–34	70	98.6	79	96.2	68	110.3	95	105.3
35–39	79	93.7	71	95.8	79	94.9	87	97.7
40–44	67	91.0	65	115.4	73	100.0	106	102.8
45–49	59	105.1	67	89.6	64	98.4	93	95.7
50–54	59	81.4	51	103.9	71	93.0	80	105.0
55–59	49	112.2	48	95.8	57	108.8	80	88.8
60–64	47	97.9	37	105.4	53	90.6	65	110.8
65–69	26	103.9	38	92.1	28	128.6	58	93.1
70–79	35	117.1	48	104.2	40	92.5	51	100.0
>79	10	100.0	10	120.0	17	105.9	12	108.3
Mean deviation[a]		6.1		6.6		6.9		4.4

Females	1841/1851		1851/1861		1861/1871		1871/1881	
Age in *y*	*x*	*y*	*x*	*y*	*x*	*y*	*x*	*y*
10–14	159	103.1	138	97.8	168	101.2	213	100.5
15–19	117	92.3	88	95.5	116	94.0	171	97.1
20–24	80	98.8	77	111.7	72	113.9	120	102.5
25–29	60	121.7	52	96.2	44	104.6	71	108.5
30–34	63	77.8	63	96.8	72	95.8	84	89.3
35–39	63	114.3	61	95.1	73	94.5	83	103 6
40–44	70	82.9	63	104.8	81	95.1	108	101.9
45–49	54	98.2	60	98.3	52	111.5	82	103.7
50–54	70	91.4	49	110.2	59	91.5	89	96.6
55–59	40	112.5	40	90.0	55	96.4	58	106.9
60–64	34	105.9	45	108.9	43	100.0	59	96.6
65–69	27	111.1	33	93.9	28	114.3	46	93.5
70–79	35	94.3	40	100.0	48	95.8	43	97.7
>79	8	150.0	8	112.5	11	109.1	11	109.1
Mean deviation[a]		13.1		6.0		6.5		4.7

Notes: *a* = from 100 per cent correspondence; *x* = size of group ten years younger in previous census; *y* = size of group in next census as percentage of *x*.

the age of 19 (male) and 24 (female) were more likely to put their ages up. From there up to the age of 70, each group was more likely to put ages down.

The question of recurrent excess or deficiency in particular groups was investigated by Lee and Lam in a study comparing national cohorts from census to census and calculating adjustment factors based on life table survival ratios (after taking account of migration).[9] They confirm the tendency of the oldest to exaggerate and the excess in the female 20–24 group, also detecting a deficiency in the 55–59 group.

[9] Lee and Lam, 'Age distribution', 445.

They found that accuracy improved as the century advanced. A calculation of quinquennial cohorts was made for the present study, solely from the population identified in two consecutive censuses. Complete accuracy of reporting would produce an exact correspondence in such a population between each age group in the later census of each pair and the group 10 years younger in the earlier. The deviation from such equality can be seen in Table 12.9 above. The overall results of this survey show an improvement by 1881, when the mean deviation from 100 per cent accuracy was less than 5 per cent for both men and women, though 1871 is less accurate than 1861. The inaccuracy of the 1841–51 figures must be partially ascribed to the three months difference in census dates. Any such comparison tends to compound the errors of both censuses; and Lee and Lam explained that errors are magnified for groups as distinct from individuals.

As far as particular groups are concerned, no consistent pattern could be detected for the over 65s, but most groups over 79 are too large. The 15–19 group is almost always too small and the 20–24 group too large. Since attention has been focused on the 20–24 group this was investigated more fully. Of the 143 women with an age error and reporting an age 20–24, 89 have a probable age within the same group; of the remaining 54, 27 should be 15–19 and 72 should be 25 or more, but of this group 15 should be only 1 year more and 6 only 2. The biggest discrepancy is a 31 who gives 21, probably because she had recently married a much younger man. Thus there is no evidence of large-scale misrepresentation down to the 20–24 group by older women motivated by vanity. As to the domestic servant hypothesis, this study has found that of the 42 servants under 21 who have an age error, 37 (88 per cent) put their ages up, but only 7 of these move into a higher quinquennium, 6 being errors of only 1 year, so this does not seem to provide the main explanation for the size of the 20–24 group here.

The 1881 Report also notes a deficiency in the under five group, but in this study 5 per cent of the checkable population in this group were found to be in error, as against 10 per cent of the 5–9 group.

The other characteristics of the error population can be dealt with more quickly. Generally speaking, the higher the social class (Table 12.8b), the less likelihood of error, though class II has a slightly higher percentage than class III.

It is interesting that the highest incidence of error falls among those born in one of the five parishes other than the census parish itself (Table 12.8c), though the variations are not very great. Comparatively few of those born at a distance were checkable.

Table 12.8d shows that sons and daughters are much less likely to have an error, as might be expected, since most were in the youngest age group. Parents are most likely to record an error, and the reverse applies to them. Otherwise there is surprisingly little variation in the percentages of the different categories of status in household except for the higher proportions of lodgers.

The sex ratio (f=100) of all errors is 112 per cent; of errors over 1 year, 112; and of errors over 2 years 117. Thus there is a slightly higher ratio of males among those with errors than in the checkable population (110) and the total population (107). Table 12.7a/b shows that the ratio is not quite consistent between different parishes and different years.

The fact that the worst errors (those over two years) often show different trends from the lesser errors probably results from a different reason for the error. The lesser errors might be ascribed to carelessness or ignorance, but the larger errors seem sometimes to have different causes. There are 399 such errors accounting for 352 individuals, 44 of whom have an error of more than 2 years on more than 1 occasion. 135 of them also make a lesser error (of 1 or 2 years) more than once, but 55 have a unique error among otherwise correct entries. Eighty-eight report an age with a unit of 0 and 34 with a unit of 5. Twenty-eight are wrong by a multiple of 10 and this could be the consequence of poor handwriting which could also account for the confusion of 6 with 0 and 3 with 8, also the 1 child who is recorded as 10 instead of 1, hardly an error due to ignorance. The apparently high incidence of large error in social class I is explained by the low total numbers in this category together with the fact that 3 of the 4 were probably clerical errors, 2 wrong by exactly 10 years and 1 by 20.

The general tendency to report ages where the unit figure is 0 or, to a lesser extent, 5 is noted in each General Report and by Thomson who points out that an exact 10 per cent for each unit is unlikely, larger deviations being expected in smaller samples.[10] A calculation of the numbers of reported ages for each unit figure 0–9 made for this study shows that over the whole checkable population with a given age 15–74 there was a mean deviation from the theoretical 10 per cent of 1.0 per cent for males and 0.7 per cent for females. (The equivalent figures for the corrected ages are 0.8 and 0.7 per cent.) A separate calculation for each decennial cohort from unit 5 to unit 4 in the total population (chosen so that 0 would be at the centre) shows increasing deviation from the 10 per cent mean with age, especially for females where the 65–74 group has a mean deviation of 2.4 per cent. Among males the 0 unit accounts for 12–14 per cent of each decennium from 25 upwards, but among females only the decennia centred on 50 and 60 reach comparable figures. The 5 unit accounts for about 11 per cent of males in each decennium and 9–10 per cent of females. The smallest percentages are usually found in units 1–4, confirming Thomson's

10 See chapter 9 by Thomson, above.

finding that ages were usually rounded down, as does the fact that 63 per cent of the 0 units were rounded down. The error population has a higher proportion of 0 units than the total population, but not of 5 units. A higher proportion of lodgers than of any other group reports a 0 unit age, both in the total and in the error populations.

Conclusions

The conclusions of this exercise point first to the advantages of checking by multiple criteria, though the use of such criteria where numbers are very small seems of limited value. Secondly they support the more optimistic view of overall age accuracy, rather than the view of the General Report of 1881 which finds 'the returns made by individuals ... more or less inaccurate', or the repeated accusations 1851–81 of ignorance and wilful misrepresentation, especially by women. The findings from these six parishes in Kent more generally support the view of Wrigley, that census 'ages were very well recorded in the main'[11] or of Thomson, that even the elderly 'appear to have had a fair idea of their ages and not to have reported them capriciously'.[12] While it seems advisable to exercise some caution in the use of age data for the categories that are intrinsically less likely to be checkable, it appears that a high proportion of the population in this part of the country knew their ages and recorded them carefully.

11 Wrigley, 'Baptism coverage', 299.
12 See chapter 9, above.

Part III

Employment and occupations

13

Employment and occupations

D. R. MILLS AND K. SCHÜRER

Without doubt, the information in the CEBs most used by historians is that appearing in the column headed 'Rank, Profession, or Occupation'.[1] An analysis of over 400 publications based on the CEBs discovered that occupation was studied by 257 authors, migration coming next with 218.[2] One reason for this is that occupations give a good idea as to both the economic and the social structure of past communities, another is that occupation has often been related to other attributes given in the census, such as birthplace, or address. The fundamental interest in occupations is also reflected in the chapters included in this book, since in addition to the five chapters comprising the selection for this Part, several chapters in other Parts of the book also devote attention to the subject. These are discussed at the end of this chapter. The bulk of the chapter, however, is devoted to a lengthy, but we believe, necessary, discussion of occupational classification for this is a problem which invariably, at some stage or other, confronts the community historian. First, though, we should consider the nature of the information being recorded in this column of the CEBs.

Meanings of occupational descriptions

Part of the fascination of the topic for the community historian comes from trying to imagine, on the basis of a usually one- or two-word description, the precise nature of the working lives of those enumerated. Even the familiar 'railway engine-driver' or 'agricultural labourer' or 'general domestic servant' may not be straightforward, demarcated occupations, nor is their social standing necessarily a simple matter. Moreover, in some cases descriptions have continued in use for a very long time whilst the nature of the occupation has changed considerably, for example, clerk, nurse or estate agent. In other cases the reverse has happened, where new descriptions have been

1 For the period 1851–81 the census schedule remained largely unchanged in regard to the occupation question. However, following the Treasury Inquiry of 1890 the census of 1891 was expanded to include a question that required individuals to indicate whether they were either an employer, an employee or worked on their own account. This was repeated in 1901 and enriched by the addition of a question requesting individuals to state their place of work either at home or not at home. For details see chapter 2, above; Higgs, *Making sense*, 90–1, 109–13; *Clearer sense*, 109–10, 175-80.

2 Mills and Pearce, *People and places*, 8.

adopted with little relative change in the job, for example, rodent operative for rat catcher, dining assistant for kitchenmaid.

On top of this, old occupations have disappeared and with them the intimate knowledge of nineteenth-century trades, crafts and industrial processes, which researchers must do their best to recover. For example, how many users of the census have mistaken cake merchants for confectioners, when in fact they were purveyors of cattle food? In his recent study of Wigston (Leicestershire) from the 1891 census, Elliott lists 23 railway-related descriptions. Most are relatively easy to understand, at least superficially, but what exactly were the 'carriage examiners' and the 'bar nippers'? Moving onto local industries, what were the 'rough stuff cutters' doing in their clicking room? (Answer – they cut out the soles and heels from tanned leather). Is it necessary to have married into the hosiery trade (as one of the editors did) in order to find out what the Griswold operatives and circular machine hands were about?[3]

Those who have used a number of sources for the same community at closely related dates will have noticed the inconsistency of occupational descriptions from one source to another. Morris has reported inconsistencies in Leeds around 1834: descriptions in wills and poll books appear to have been influenced by social status considerations, whilst those in directories were affected by the desire to advertise services, for example, a solicitor adding in the directory that he was agent for the Sun Insurance Company.[4] It seems likely that directory entries will be fuller than census entries. Perhaps, as the latter were not made public, they may have been less prone to emphasise social standing, but it is difficult to generalise without the opportunity to go back and ask the respondents further searching questions. For example, the enumerator of Canwick (Lincolnshire) in 1851 put himself down as poet and blacksmith, but no trace of poems has so far been found, and in following censuses Richard Ellis appears simply as blacksmith.

Examples from Durham City in 1851 amplify the difficulties of comparison between census and directory. A managing solicitor's clerk in the census appears perhaps more importantly as a sharebroker in the directory, and a man described as 'half pay in the Army' is a Captain in the directory. A master coachmaker in the census adds whitesmith in the directory to attract more custom; and an innkeeper adds brickmaker. An LSA (Licentiate of the Society of Apothecaries) and gen. practitioner prefers plain, old-fashioned surgeon in the directory, as perhaps better understood. The printer compositor who appears in the directory as a beerhouse keeper and the coachman as a greengrocer set

3 Elliott, *Wigston*, 15, 21 and 25.

4 Morris, 'Fuller values, questions and contexts', 11–6; see also Morris, *Class, sect and party*.

us a different problem. Have they changed their jobs, or are the directory entries really their wives earning pin money?[5]

Last, but not least by any means, is the basic point that the researcher is very much in the hands of householders and enumerators, perhaps the latter quite as much as the former. In particular, the Cambridge Group's work on the 1911 and 1921 censuses, by which time the process of copying entries from householders' schedules into enumerators' books had been halted, has brought to light clear evidence that the enumerators at earlier censuses did considerable amounts of editing through standardising occupational descriptions. The contrast between the 1891–1901 enumerators' entries and the 1911–21 householders' entries indicates that the latter were willing to give more information than the enumerators had been willing to copy out.[6] There is also much circumstantial evidence that enumerators were not of equal diligence in recording any occupational descriptions, especially in regard to married women, and boys and girls residing with their families but apparently not still at school, especially girls. In other words, all CEBs do not record all persons in employment and this is particularly evident in the case of the 1841 census.[7]

Occupational analysis

Many smaller-scale studies, often those carried out by local history classes, make only what might at first sight appear to be a descriptive use of information on occupation. For example, Horn and Horn limited themselves mainly to an appendix in which the occupations of the residents of their two Buckinghamshire villages were listed and the numbers following them were given, males and females being separated.[8] However, the chief purpose of doing this emerges as a means of comparing Ivinghoe, the main subject of the chapter, with a contrasting community, Great Horwood, which lacked the straw plaiters found in such large numbers in Ivinghoe.

From the simple listing, the reader is able to make two other kinds of comparison frequently at the root of local studies of occupations. First, there is the contrast with the present day occupational character of the same place, well enough known in broad terms to a local history class, even if seldom recorded in detail.[9] Second, local studies often show that the village or small town of the Victorian period was far

5 Butler, *Durham, 1851*, references 11866, 12171, 3794, 4146, 5028, 3953 and 3845 respectively.

6 Schürer, 'Understanding and coding occupations', 106.

7 See below, Table 13.5. Higgs, *Making sense*, 81–5; *Clearer sense*, 97–103 and 158–9 discusses in some detail the problems of women's and children's occupations, including the use of the term 'scholar'.

8 Horn and Horn, 'An "industrial" community'.

9 For an example of a recent private census compared with CEBs see, Steel, *Lincolnshire village*, especially 19, 84, 168–9; and for a modern village census of occupations see Haydon, 'Widworthy in 1992'.

more self-sufficient than the same or similar places today. Additionally, it is possible to extend such an analysis to determine the central place hierarchy of an area. The greater the range of occupations in the service trades, the higher the settlement may be said to be within the hierarchy.[10] Most central place studies have been carried out by using information available in trade directories and rate books, but the use of the CEBs makes possible more sophisticated analyses, in the sense that they record all persons in employment, rather than merely householders and the heads of enterprises.[11]

A large-scale evaluation of CEBs and corresponding directories has been conducted by Crompton in 31 north Hertfordshire parishes, matching the names of master tradesmen and craftsmen in the 1851 CEBs with Kelly's 1851 directory and those in the 1891 CEBs with Kelly's 1890 directory. The overall result for the first pair of sources is that, using 474 entries in the census and 492 in the directories, she matched 329 pairs on the basis of very strict criteria.[12] Allowing for the high probability of a real match in many such cases, as well as for the turnover between the dates of the two sources, the latter show a high degree of consistency one with another. In particular, the closeness of match between the totals (474 and 492) was also found at the level of individual settlements, so that an assessment of service provision and the settlement hierarchy based on either source gives the same result. Thus, inconsistencies are of the kind that rightly worry family historians, but should not call into question either source for the purposes of occupational analysis on a significant scale.[13]

Occupational classification

There is, therefore, much that can be done by analysing occupations, looking at the presence or absence of each individual occupation without attempting, or before attempting any systematic grouping of occupations. Most large-scale studies and many small ones, however, have used one type of grouping or another (and sometimes more than one), if only because of the welter of different occupations that existed in the past.[14] Grouping occupations simplifies the picture, making it

10 In such analyses dual occupations should be included under both occupations, in order to assess the range of central place functions as fully as possible. Introductions to central place theory and urban hierarchies can be found in many student texts on human geography, and even in dictionaries and encyclopaedias of geography. Possibly the most comprehensive treatment is in Carter, *Urban geography*, chapters 4, 5 and 6. Also very useful is Pacione, *Rural geography* 27–45. For a discussion of central place theory in relation to local and community history, see Schürer, 'The future for local history'.

11 Shaw, *British directories*, 31–6; Shaw, 'Reliability of directories', 13; Page, 'Market towns', 85–8.

12 For example, Wilfred Jones, joiner was not regarded as a match with William Jones, carpenter.

13 Crompton, 'Changes in rural service occupations', 201.

14 For example, Durham City in 1851 recorded nearly 700 different descriptions in a population of about 13,200; Butler, *Durham 1851*, viii.

easier to comprehend, especially through comparisons between the same place at different censuses, or different places at the same census.

There are three basic types of occupational classification in use: those based on economic criteria, usually referred to as industrial classifications; those intended to determine social status; and those which are a mixture of the industrial and social types. In some respects, the industrial classifications are simpler and nearer to the intentions of the General Registry Office during the mid-Victorian period. Under William Farr's leadership as Superintendent of Statistics between 1838–80, the census was designed to assist the movement for the improvement of public health, one element being overcrowding, another the supposed chemical relationship between materials used in workplaces and the spread of diseases. This is why householders were to record the materials on which their household members worked, as well as the names of occupations.[15] Frequently householders and enumerators did not do that and for this reason one often sees words such as wool, cotton, wood, metal, etc., added in different hands, presumably by sub-registrars and registrars, although also conceivably by checkers at Somerset House, working from local intelligence.

The industrial groupings adopted by researchers have usually taken as a starting point the groupings used in census reports, in which, although there may be many divisions and sub-divisions, the underlying concept is that of primary, secondary, and tertiary occupations. To the primary group belong all activities such as farming, fishing, mining and quarrying which extract resources from the earth. The secondary group comprise manufacturing activities which turn raw materials into finished end-products; to this group building and construction workers are often somewhat tentatively attached. The tertiary group are occupied in providing services which for the most part do not have a tangible end-product.

Such a sub-division of human activity calls into question the possibility that many people in the Victorian period belonged, either by virtue of dual occupations, or simply by definition to more than one group. Moreover, although some of the sub-divisions are intended to separate entrepreneurs and managers from workpeople, the basic industrial groups, such as, for example, farming, mining, cotton manufacture, construction and so on, include men and women of widely differing income, life styles, and social standing. For certain purposes it is important to distinguish between, say, railway porters and station masters, and to formulate occupational groupings which

15 Higgs, *Making sense* 15–6; *Clearer sense*, 17–8. William Farr, 'saw disease as being caused by the intake of various chemicals into the blood, causing a process of chemical change which poisoned the system'. One source of the chemicals lay in the occupations of the people. This zymotic germ theory was progressively replaced by modern biological germ theory from the 1870s, and gradually the GRO came to see occupations as primarily important in the census for economic and social reasons.

reflect social stratification and the common ground shared by specific income groups, regardless of where and how that income was earned.

In the process of devising social status groupings it is necessary to face two basic questions. The sociologist distinguishes between social class and social status, the one associated with the name of Marx, the other with Weber. Marx was interested in the conflict between classes differently placed in the processes of production, whilst Weber was more interested in status and life styles. Although historians using the census frequently use the term social class, this is seldom meant in the Marxian sense, and has become a synonym for a group of people whose economic standing, and therefore their life styles, are thought to have been similar, i.e., a social status group in the Weberian sense. Of course, from a simple entry in the CEB, such as farmer, teacher, dealer, vicar, or even property owner, it is difficult to make any detailed deductions about life style, and the historian is usually confined to working on the basis of assumed income, making particular life styles possible or impossible.

The other basic question relates to the extent to which mid-Victorian society was already stratified along social status lines which have become more clearly defined and acknowledged in the present century. In agricultural villages, as well as in some single-industry settlements and even certain districts of cities, there is also the practical point that very few people, if any, belonged to the highest social status groups. In the quest for a suitable scheme of social stratification, it is also a matter of controversy that the usually adopted classification is based on the Registrar General's scheme of 1950, and not even that of 1911.

Having considered some general points about occupational groupings, the remainder of the chapter comprises sections which discuss in turn each of the main classification schemes used by students of the CEBs.

The simple tripartite industrial classification

Over the last two hundred years there has been a movement out of extractive industries, especially agriculture, into manufacturing, and subsequently out of both groups into service industries. By using this simple three-fold division, students of the CEBs can hope to chart some aspects of this broad historical change, as well as to demonstrate major economic differences between communities at a particular census date.

As noted above, a significant objection in principle to this simple division is that in the mid-nineteenth century occupational specialisation was not so far advanced, especially in rural areas, as to make it tenable in practice. Many Victorian tradesmen and women were producer-retailers whose day-to-day activities ranged over secondary and tertiary functions. The publican who brewed his beer, the shoemaker who sold new footwear to retail customers and mended their old boots, bakers who took their own bread out to their customers, and wheelwrights who repaired as well as made vehicles are but four examples. Farmers might also be retail dairymen, and the market gardener was by definition carrying out two functions. In most cases, it will probably be acceptable to put such people in the primary or secondary categories, merely noting that this arbitrarily reduces the size of the Victorian tertiary sector and exaggerates the shift towards it in subsequent decades as retailing becomes a separate occupation in all but a few cases.

The use of this simple categorisation is well illustrated in Royle's work on three Leicestershire towns in 1851, where it clearly showed up their strongly contrasting economies. At Melton Mowbray, a traditional market town, 53 per cent of employed persons were in the tertiary sector; at Hinckley, a market town with a highly developed textile industry, 76 per cent were employed in manufacturing; and at Coalville, a new mining town, 67 per cent were in the primary sector.[16]

A more recent example of the use of a simple three-fold economic grouping can be found in the work of Goodger in the Darent Valley parishes of north-west Kent in 1841.[17] He shows that of an occupied population of 8,760, 40.0 per cent, were engaged in primary occupations mostly in agriculture, 24.4 per cent in secondary occupations and 34.4 per cent in tertiary occupations. Goodger then goes on to use a more refined industrial classification, with six categories: extractive and transformative industries; and distributive, producer, social and personal services. As Goodger points out, this more refined classification brings out, for example, the point that, of the occupied population working in tertiary employment, no less than 72.7 per cent were concentrated in personal services. However, it has to be said that much the same can be done by employing one of the other well-used industrial classifications discussed below.

Tillott's classification scheme

One such scheme is that of Tillott, who was an early worker on CEBs, especially with extra-mural classes in Yorkshire and Lincolnshire in the 1960s. It can be described as basically an industrial scheme, but with undertones of a social status approach. While to some extent overtaken by later schemes, Tillott's has continued to be used in rural areas for which it was originally designed, defining rural to take in small country towns whose economic and social structure differed relatively little from that of large agricultural villages. Table 13.1 below shows a range of 13 groups, all except one being based on gainful employment

16 Royle, 'Small town society', 52.
17 Goodger, 'Social science models'.

Table 13.1 Tillott's occupational and social groupings for urban analysis

Group		Occupations included
1	Agricultural self-employed or Managers	Farmer, farmer's son, farm bailiff, market gardener, seedsman (with land), cowkeeper, cottage farmer
2a	Skilled Agricultural Workers	Drill machine labourer, foreman agricultural labourer, horse breaker, stable man, self-employed gardener, shepherd, hedger
2b	Agricultural Labourers	Farm labourer (or 'Ag. Lab.'), farm servant, field-worker, cottager (but not cottage farmer).
3	Shopkeepers, Traders, Petty Entrepreneurs (not employing more than 5 persons)	Foodstuffs, retail e.g. baker, and wholesale e.g. flourdealer Clothing, e.g. draper Victuallers, wine and tobacco Carriers and boat proprietors, coal merchants Miscellaneous, includes ironmongers, glass and china dealers
4	Skilled Craftsmen, non-industrial (i.e. not in factories, see group 5b)	Metal working and machinery, e.g. blacksmith, nail maker, brazier Building, e.g. mason, carpenter Clothing, e.g. clogger, dressmaker, tailor Leather, e.g. harness maker, cordwainer (shoemaker) Miscellaneous, includes wheelwright, clockmaker
5a	Manufacturers, Industrialists, Wholesalers or Managers of Large Enterprises	e.g. cotton manufacturer, timber merchant, steel manufacturer
5b	Skilled Industrial Craftsmen	Cotton, e.g. carder, piecer, rover, stripper, tatler Wool, e.g. comber, steam loom weaver, siser Iron, e.g. moulder, puddler Miscellaneous, includes mill hand, operative, engine tender, mechanic
6	Extractive Industries	Mining, quarrying, forestry, fishing
7a	Upper Professional	e.g. doctor, banker, lawyer, all clergy, surveyor
7b	Lower Professional	e.g. auctioneer, preacher, teacher, veterinary surgeon
8	Clerical (not supervisory)	e.g. solicitor's clerk, parish clerk
9a	Upper Servants	e.g. butler, gardener, gamekeeper, lady's maid, cook
9b	General Domestic Servants	e.g. coachman, under-gardener, general servant, footman
9c	Lower Servants	e.g. charwoman, servant boy
10a	Private Income Recipient	e.g. fundholder, gentleman
10b	Rentiers	Proprietors of land/houses
10c	Annuitants	
11	Semi-Skilled and Service Workers	e.g. cab driver, mariner, postman, canal lock keeper, ostler, waiter, midwife, castrator, chimney sweep, private soldier and NCO
12	Labourers and Unskilled Workers	e.g. labourers, road labourer, railway porter, errand boy
13	Supervisory Workers	Includes shopkeepers and traders not in either groups 3 or 5, e.g. workhouse master, postmistress, rail inspector

Source: Adapted from an unpublished document issued by P. Tillott (23/11/1966).

Table 13.2 Tillott's consolidated classes

	Consolidated Classes	Primary Groups
I	Upper class	Groups 5a, 7a, 10a, 10b
II	Intermediate – non-agricultural	Groups 7b, 10c, 13
III	Intermediate – agricultural	Group 1
IV	Skilled workers and similar	Groups 2a, 3, 4, 5b, 6, 8, 9a
V	Semi-skilled workers	Groups 2b, 11
VI	Domestic servants, semi-skilled	Group 9b
VII	Labourers and unskilled workers	Groups 9c, 12

Source: Based on an unpublished document issued by P. Tillott (23/11/1966).

employment. The appearance in group 10 of gentlemen, fundholders, annuitants and rentiers raises practical problems, especially in regard to the annuitants who appear to have lived in widely differing circumstances, as well as the conceptual question as to whether these descriptions relate to 'occupation' at all, as opposed to social standing.

Otherwise elements of the tripartite industrial approach can be seen: groups 1, 2 and 6 belonging to the extractive sector; groups 4 and 5 to manufacturing; and all remaining groups to the tertiary sector. The distinction between group 4, with its non-industrial crafts, including building, and group 5, the industrial, is interesting. Especially in the mid-Victorian censuses of 1841, 1851, 1861, which were the only ones available in manuscript form when Tillott wrote, the researcher is made well aware of the mixture of traditional and 'modern' economies which still prevailed, despite textbook implications that the industrial revolution was 'over' by *c.* 1830.

However, Tillott's scheme has attributes of social classification as well as industrial. For example, all agricultural employers and managers are in group 1 and all agricultural employees in group 2, and the latter are sub-divided on the basis of income and skill. Similarly in group 5, the employers and managers of large industrial enterprises are kept separate from their skilled craftsmen. It is therefore possible to reshuffle and collapse Tillott's sub-divisions into a system of five or seven social classes. Table 13.2 above is set out in the form of seven 'consolidated' classes, from which the five-class version can be derived by joining class II to class III and class V to class VI.

One of the largest populations studied by Tillott's students was that of 8,748 in north-west Lindsey (Lincolnshire), an area now including much of Scunthorpe and the villages between that town, the Trent and the Humber. Although its use of groups 11 and 13 does not appear to correspond to Table 13.1, Table 13.3 below shows how the working population was distributed between the main groups and is included here for purposes of comparison. The numerical dominance of agricultural workers in an area lacking significant domestic industries

Table 13.3 The occupations of north-west Lindsey, Lincolnshire, 1851 according to the Tillott scheme

Group	Description	Total	%
1	Farmers	424	11.0
2	Agricultural workers	1,591	41.4
3	Tradesmen	153	4.0
4	Craftsmen	668	17.4
7	Professions	75	2.0
8	Clerical	56	1.5
9	Servants	690	18.0
10	Independent	113	2.9
11	Victuallers	27	0.7
12	Labourers	41	1.1

Source: Tillott and Stevenson, *North-west Lindsey*, 3.

should be noted, over 50 per cent appearing in extractive industries compared with 40 per cent in the Darent Valley. Also notable are the large numbers of servants and the small numbers in the professional and independent groups. As similar distributions are likely to be found in many areas of the country, they signal the difficulties of using social classifications in rural areas on practical grounds, owing to the large numbers of farm labourers and such small numbers of 'middle-class' people. Moreover, as the table suggests, the most numerous employers in north-west Lindsey were farmers, at 11.0 per cent of the working population, and relating these people to an essentially urban scheme is fraught with difficulty both conceptually (were any farmers 'middle-class'?) and practically (which farmers, above which acreages, and so on?).

Booth–Armstrong industrial classification

Towards the end of the century, the social reformer Charles Booth, dissatisfied with the Registrar General's industrial classification, produced his own system which, reworked by Armstrong, has become the basis for many studies using the CEBs or the census reports. It can, however, still be described as an occupational scheme biased towards the study of mortality based on environmental causes, especially in the sub-sections where material handled became a prominent feature. It contains the following 10 major categories:

Agriculture
Mining
Building
Manufacture
Transport
Dealing
Industrial service
Public service and professional sector
Domestic service
The residual population

Table 13.4 Charles Booth's economic groupings

Code	Description
AG	*Agriculture*
AG1	Farming, includes farmers, labourers, etc., forestry
AG2	Land service, e.g. agricultural machine proprietors
AG3	Breeding, includes breeders, vets, drovers, farriers
AG4	Fishing
M	*Mining*
M1	Mining
M2	Quarrying
M3	Brickmaking, but includes sand, flint and gravel workers
M4	Salt and water works
B	*Building*
B1	Management, e.g. architects, builders
B2	Operatives, e.g. bricklayers, thatchers, carpenters
B3	Roadmaking, inc. railway navvies
MF	*Manufacture*
MF1	Machinery
MF2	Tools, includes gemsmiths, pin and steel pen makers
MF3	Shipbuilding, includes sailmakers
MF4	Iron and steel, includes blacksmiths
MF5	Copper, tin, lead, inc. whitesmiths
MF6	Gold, silver, jewellery
MF7	Earthenware, includes glass, plaster and cement
MF8	Coals and gas
MF9	Chemical, includes ink and matches
MF10	Furs and leather
MF11	Glue, tallow, etc., includes soap, manure
MF12	Hair, includes brushes, quills, combs, bone workers
MF13	Woodworkers (excludes MF14)
MF14	Furniture, includes French polishers and undertakers
MF15	Harness and carriage, both road and rail
MF16	Paper
MF17	Floorcloth and waterproof
MF18	Woollen, includes knitters of wool
MF19	Cotton and silk
MF20	Flax, hemp, etc., includes rope and net workers
MF21	Lace
MF22	Dyeing
MF23	Dress, includes hosiery, hat, glove, footwear
T	*Transport*
T1	Warehouses and docks (excludes Manchester warehousemen)
T2	Ocean navigation, includes ship's cooks and stewards
T3	Inland navigation
T4	Railways
T5	Roads, includes toll collectors
D	*Dealing*
D1	Coals
D2	Raw materials, e.g. timber, corn, wool
D3	Clothing materials, e.g. cloth merchants, Manchester warehousemen
D4	Dress (both wholesale and retail)
D5	Food (ditto)
D6	Tobacco (ditto)
D7	Wines, spirits and hotels (ditto)
D8	Lodging and coffee houses
D9	Furniture (apparently wholesalers), but inc. pawnbrokers
D10	Stationery and publications
D11	Household utensils and ornaments, e.g. ironmongers
D12	General dealers
D13	Unspecified, e.g. merchants, brokers, valuers, salesmen
IS	*Industrial Service*
IS1	Banking, insurance and accounts
IS2	General labourers
PP	*Public Service and Professional*
PP1	Administration (central)
PP2	Administration (local)
PP3	Administration (sanitary) i.e. town drainage and scavenging
PP4	Army, officers and men, act. and ret.
PP5	Navy (ditto)
PP6	Police and prison officers
PP7	Law
PP8	Medicine, includes dentists, chemists
PP9	Painting, i.e. art, includes animal preservers
PP10	Music and amusements, e.g. performers, games and sportsmen
PP11	Literature, i.e. authors, editors, journalists, etc.
PP12	Science
PP13	Education
PP14	Religion
DS	*Domestic Service*
DS1	Indoor service, includes institutional servants

Table 13.4 continued

Code	Description	Code	Description
MF24	Sundries connected with dress, e.g. umbrellas, buttons	DS2	Outdoor service
		DS3	Extra service, appears to be self-employed, e.g. chimney sweeps
MF25	Food preparation, inc. cattle food		
MF26	Baking		
MF27	Drink preparation, includes maltsters		
MF28	Smoking, includes pipes		*Residual Population*
MF29	Watches, instruments and toys	I	Property owning
MF30	Printing and bookbinding	II	Indefinite, inc. vagrants, lunatics, etc.
MF31	Unspecified manufacturers, artisans, apprentices, factory labourers	III	Dependent classes, e.g. children, housewives

Source: Based on Armstrong, 'Information about occupation', 255–93.

The first two correspond to the extractive industries, since agriculture includes forestry and fishing; and mining includes quarrying and brickmaking as sub-divisions. The five categories from transport to domestic service correspond to the tertiary or service sector. As the oddly-named industrial service group includes (1) banking, insurance and accounts and (2) general labourers, it is usually desirable to keep these disparate occupations apart by using two totally separate categories. The residual population, subdivided into property-owning, dependent classes such as children and housewives, and 'indefinite' might be abandoned in some situations as persons 'not gainfully employed' or 'economically inactive'.

All groups are divided and sub-divided and Booth followed the census authorities in using raw materials as the basis for sub-dividing manufacture into 31 basic divisions (Table 13.4 above). The bias towards manufacturing has been noted by Clark, but the Booth–Armstrong scheme has nevertheless been adopted by the English Small Towns project which he directs.[18] Indeed, considering that manufacturing was much the biggest sector and engaged about a third of the occupied population, a considerable sub-division is necessary. In this scheme, it would probably not be practicable to separate the 'traditional' from the 'modern' manufacturing, although Armstrong appears to have done this approximately for York on the basis of supporting information from directories.[19] The basis of the problem lies in the fact that, for example, men who were blacksmiths and wheelwrights could equally have been employed in a large foundry or

18 Clark, 'English Small Towns project', 25.

19 Armstrong, *Stability and change*, 28 and 45. The same criticism can be levelled to some extent at the study of the Berkhamsted district, where although the local specialisation in straw-plaiting is picked out, use of the Booth–Armstrong classification has 'lost' all other traditional trades and crafts, so that they do not get the attention they deserve in the text. However, by way of compensation, this includes the close analysis of female and child labour-force participation: Goose, *Hertfordshire in 1851*, 30–46.

Table 13.5 Summary of occupational sectors in England and Wales, 1841–1891

	Occupational sector					
	1841 n. %	1851 n. %	1861 n. %	1871 n. %	1881 n. %	1891 n. %
Agriculture and Fishing	1,308 22.4	1,777 21.9	1,718 18.7	1,525 14.8	1,371 12.3	1,296 10.2
Mining	210 3.6	335 4.1	425 4.6	475 4.6	562 5.0	677 5.4
Building and construction	353 6.0	461 5.7	549 6.0	664 6.5	796 7.1	836 6.6
Manufacturing	1,798 30.8	2,755 33.9	3,117 33.9	3,359 32.7	3,599 32.2	4,139 32.7
Transport	148 2.5	345 4.3	436 4.7	524 5.1	654 5.8	826 6.5
Dealing	351 6.0	547 6.7	674 7.3	838 8.2	924 8.3	1,149 9.1
Industrial service, financial	41 0.7	45 0.6	68 0.7	119 1.2	225 2.0	310 2.5
Industrial service, general lab's	319 5.5	332 4.1	310 3.4	517 5.0	560 5.0	596 4.7
Public service and professional	240 4.1	400 4.9	505 5.5	578 5.6	659 5.9	828 6.5
Domestic service	1,078 18.4	1,121 13.8	1,384 15.1	1,684 16.4	1,838 16.4	1,991 15.7
Total occupied population (%)	5,846 100.0	8,117 100.0	9,185 99.9	10,281 100.1	11,188 100.0	12,649 99.9
Entire population	15,914	17,928	20,066	22,712	25,974	29,003
Activity rate (%)	36.7	45.3	45.8	45.3	43.1	43.6

Notes: Each cell in the table contains the numbers of persons (1,000s) engaged in a sector, followed by the corresponding percentage of the total occupied population. In the penultimate row of cells the entire population of England and Wales is given, followed by the percentage of that population who were enumerated as occupied (the economic activity rate). On the special problems of the agricultural workforce, see Wrigley, 'Men on the land' and Higgs, 'Agricultural workforce'. The latter (709–11) suggests adjustments along the following lines for agriculture only, omitting the fishermen included in the table above: 1851 – from 1,625 thousands to 2,151 and from 20 to 25 per cent of the total employed population; 1861 – 1,546 to 2,055, and 17 to 22 per cent; 1871 – 1,323 to 1,860 thousands, and 13 to 18 per cent.

Source: Armstrong, 'Information about occupation', 253–83; entire population based on Mitchell, *British historical statistics*, 8.

in a traditional setting, although some enumerators did put in information such as 'blacksmith in foundry'. No attempt was made to distinguish between 'modern' and 'traditional' in Table 13.5 above, in which the figures were calculated by Booth and amended by Armstrong from the published census reports.

The first point to be made about Table 13.5 is that it issues a warning about the reliability of the 1841 census, which, with an economic activity rate of only 36.7 per cent compared with an average of about 44 per cent at the following censuses, clearly did not do such a thorough job of recording occupations, probably in most cases of women and young persons. It is remarkable how consistent the census data for 1851 to 1891 are in this respect. Minor variations in particular occupations, changes in the age structure of the population, changes due to the onset of schooling, and probably some changes in the attitude towards women's occupations, appear to have combined to all but cancel one another out. The fall of more than two percentage points between 1871 and 1881 might provisionally be ascribed to a fall in juvenile employment because of increased numbers in school.

Table 13.5 also demonstrates the steep fall from 1841 to 1891 in the percentage of those engaged in agriculture and fishing, which is not matched by a corresponding increase in those engaged in manufacturing. Even allowing for some re-categorisation from manufacture to retailing, as producer-retailers supposedly declined in numbers, the proportion remains remarkably steady at about 33 per cent from 1851 to 1891. Building and construction rose modestly and then fell back again between 1881 and 1891. With relative declines in domestic service and the nebulous category of general labourers, as well as in the much more substantial agricultural sector, the growth areas were in mining and the remaining service sectors. Sectors which experienced more than a doubling in their relative size were transport and financial service; whilst increases of between 50 and 100 per cent occurred in mining, dealing, and public and professional service. The local researcher will find it useful to refer to this table to gauge the occupational structure of his community, since local comparisons between sectors need to be supplemented by comparisons with the national picture. In particular, there had to be steady growth of the whole population in order for the community not to fall back from the national norm of constant expansion.

Cambridge classification

Strictly speaking this is not a classification at all but rather a device to link together the various classificatory schemes implemented by the GRO.[20] It is principally orientated towards computer-using historians in that it exists not in the form of a straight-forward one-way classification but as a multi-dimensional 'look-up' table, enabling the researcher to move between different classification schemes. In effect, the scheme harmonises the various classifications of occupation used in the published census reports from 1851 to 1921. It does this by taking the

20 The scheme is described in Schürer, 'Understanding and coding occupations'.

official classification scheme used in each census report in turn and in comparing the details of each new classification with those of previous years, breaks down the various schemes into what may be termed 'minimum occupation groupings'. These groupings can then be used a little like building blocks, so that the particular set of census data being analysed can be 'reconstructed' to mirror anyone of the official classifications in use between 1891 and 1921. Given that the Registrar General's classifications for both 1911 and 1921 have been included in this exercise, it can also be seen as moving away from the bias towards the study of occupation-specific mortality, which is the hallmark of the Register General's industrial scheme of the Victorian period (and other schemes based on it). In this respect the employment classifications of 1911 and 1921 are intellectually radically different from those of previous decades, being devised by a Census Office which was fully aware of the need 'to produce statistics which were more representative of the economic performance of the nation'.[21] The extension of the scheme to the twentieth century is also interesting in that provision is made to allow occupation information to be re-classified according to the Registrar General's social groups first introduced in 1911, as well as the modified social classification of 1921, both of which have been claimed as superior to the 1950 scheme when used in conjunction with nineteenth-century CEB data. It is to social-class groupings, rather than industrial-economic groupings, that we now turn.

Social classification: Anderson

It must be recognised that schemes based on economic criteria suffer from the defect that they place thousand-acre farmers with the poorest agricultural labourers, admirals with seamen, cotton masters employing hundreds of operatives with the operatives themselves, and so on. Therefore, there is a need to base some studies at least partly on a classification rooted in social, rather than industrial criteria, recognising the common interest of people on similar incomes, even though these may have been derived from quite different kinds of work.

One of the earliest schemes to be used was that employed by Anderson in his study of Preston (Table 13.6 below). This is a more complex scheme than can be constructed on the basis of census information on its own, taking into account actual income levels and regularity of income, based on literary information in other local sources. Nevertheless, it is important for showing what might be possible in other areas where such information is available, coupled with sufficient time to collect and analyse it. Moreover, the scheme can also be used to underpin the validity of simpler schemes based on

21 Schürer, 'Understanding and coding occupations', 102. In particular, the distinction between occupation and industry is much more fully appreciated.

Table 13.6 Socio-economic group distribution: male sample, Preston, 1851

Socio-economic group		Income (full work)[a]	Regularity of income[b]	Employ-ment status[c]	All aged 10 and over %	All aged 20 and over %
I	Professional and managerial[d]	vh/h	r	E/SE	2	2
II	Clerical	m/l	r	Ed	3	4
III	Trade	most m	rd	E/SE	8	11
IV	Higher factory	m	rd	Ed	10	13
V	Artisan	m	sir	Ed/SE(E)	18	20
VI	Lower factory	l	rd	Ed	21	13
VII	Labourer, etc.[e]	l/vl	ir	Ed/(SE)	14	18
VIII	Hand-loom weaver	vl	ir	SE(Ed)	4	5
IX	Unclassified	mixed	mixed	mixed	8	10
X	Not employed[f]	–	–	–	12	4
	All	–	–	–	100 (n = 2,346)	100 (n = 1,607)

Notes: *a* vh = very high; h = high; m = medium; l = low; vl = very low. Medium is above 20s. per week; low 10s. to 20s.; very low under 10s.
b r = regular; rd = regular except in depressions; sir = somewhat irregular; ir = irregular.
c E = employer; SE = self-employed; Ed = employed. Symbols in brackets indicate that this is a small minority only. SE includes those employing family members only.
d Including all tradesmen with more than one domestic servant.
e Including hawkers and other itinerant traders.
f This group consists largely of children not yet in employment.
Source: Anderson, *Family structure*, Table 1, 26.

census data only, since similar wage rates and conditions of employment are likely to be found in some other areas. The social structure of a large textile town is also a useful broad comparison for other workers, even though they may be using a different scheme. For example, only 2 per cent of the male population could be classified as professional or managerial, whilst those on medium rates of pay stood at about 48 per cent of men over 20 years of age, those on low rates 36 per cent, leaving 14 per cent as unclassified or not employed.

Social classification: Armstrong

One of the weaknesses of Anderson's scheme is that it cannot be universal, and cannot, therefore, be used for making comparisons across the country. The scheme adopted by Armstrong in his study of York, by contrast, has the potential of universality, and has been used in the study of many other localities. It has to be admitted that these are nearly all urban areas, often other large towns, though whether this situation has come about because rural historians are inclined to think that the scheme was inappropriate for rural areas, or whether they are less sociologically inclined is an open question.

Armstrong selected the Registrar General's scheme of 1950, rather than the earlier scheme of 1911, as the basis for his study of York in 1841 and 1851, arguing that population may have moved between the 1950 classes since 1841, but that the socially-accepted hierarchy of individual occupations has remained stable. It may be the case that there have been bigger changes in the proportions in individual occupations, and therefore classes, than in the social hierarchy, but changes in the latter need to be considered very carefully when attributing occupations to classes. For instance, has there not been a relative decline in the social standing of clerks and others who enjoyed a comparatively high standing in Victorian times simply because of their literacy at a time long before compulsory schooling? Shifts in the opposite direction have probably occurred where professional training has altered standards out of all recognition. For example, a degree or equivalent is now necessary for entry into the teaching profession, a sharp contrast to the situation *c.* 1850 when many teachers had not even passed through a period as pupil teachers. Similar questions should be asked about such callings as accountant, independent minister, museum curator, reporter, and sharebroker, all attributed to class I by Armstrong, and bookkeeper, commercial teacher, factor (unspecified) and relieving officer, attributed to class II.

Nevertheless, Armstrong's use of the Registrar General's 1950 scheme of social classification has won substantial support from students of the census, and any serious study of social stratification should make use of it, at least for purposes of comparison. However, it would be a mistake to think that comparisons can be precise, since few authors have published an attribution list, and Armstrong's is only illustrative, being confined to the occupations found in the York sample.[22] An attribution list has to be used by a researcher in order to ensure consistent allocation of individual occupations to one of the five social classes in the scheme. Since occupations vary greatly over the country, the York illustration leaves open many questions about occupations which do not occur within it.

The following extract comes from the York study and sets out Armstrong's main principles and argument. It is given in full since careful attention must be paid to the precise wording adopted by Armstrong. Whilst the five-class scheme is described in the Registrar General's terms and Armstrong used the latter's attribution lists as a basis for his own, some important general modifications are set out in the numbered paragraphs 1–4. In respect of paragraph 4, it should be stressed that terms such as annuitant or independent means, on cross

22 Armstrong, 'Information about occupation', 215–23, reprinted in Mills and Drake, 'The census, 1801–1901', 48–9.

reference to other sources (or even evidence within the census schedule), can sometimes be seen to refer to people of extremely modest means, perhaps only just avoiding parish relief and in no way suitable candidates for inclusion in class II. In respect of the economically inactive, the answer seems to be to use only clear cases of high social status for inclusion anywhere in the classification scheme. Such a strategy helps to increase the small classes I and II, whilst consigning annuitants and similar to a residual class, will not deprive classes III–V of large proportions of their members. The comments made by Armstrong on the 1841 census underline the difficulties in using that census and make it appropriate to suggest that, now so many later censuses are available, it should not be used unless there are particular local reasons for persevering with it.

> Few of the difficulties facing the local, regional or urban historian are as critical as those stemming from the need to classify census occupational data. From one point of view, the reduction of occupations into broad categories is bound to occasion some loss of detail, whilst on the other hand, historians simply cannot work without some degree of classification.
>
> In this study, census occupational data has been arranged according to two principles – the industrial, which throws light on the economic contours of the society under consideration; and secondly, by social ranking or class. On the first, there is little which needs to be said here. The basis of the scheme of allocation used to arrange *printed* census data on a broadly industrial principle is to be found in an article written by Charles Booth, and elaborated by myself elsewhere. In this study it has been used only in connection with a few tables . . . but, I hope, to useful effect. Since the development of this method of analysis followed my work on the material in the census enumerators' books, it was not applied to that data, although there is no reason, in principle, why it should not be.
>
> All households in the census samples were, however, given a social classification. . . . This rested on the Registrar General's scheme, which refers to five classes, 'homogeneous in relation to the basic criterion of the general standing within the community of the occupations concerned', viz.,
>
> Class I — Professional, etc., occupations
> Class II — Intermediate occupations
> Class III — Skilled occupations
> Class IV — Partly skilled occupations
> Class V — Unskilled occupations

The 1951 attribution lists published by the Registrar General were used to give a classification for each household head, with the following modifications in 1851:

1) All employers of 25 or more were raised to Class I, whatever their classification in the Registrar General's lists.

2) All 'dealers', 'merchants' (except those distinctly described as brokers or agents (class II) or hawkers (class V)), and all persons engaged in retail board, lodging and catering were initially classed as III, despite the fact that the Registrar General's lists place them variously.

3) From class III (or in a few cases IV), *upon consideration of individual cases*, those who employed at least one person (rather than members of their own families), were then raised to class II. In boarding, catering, etc., the employment of one or more servants was taken to count for this purpose, and the general effect was to raise into class II all those whose undertakings were at all substantial; for, at a minimum, the employment even of an apprentice is an obvious indication of self-employed status.

4) House and land proprietors, whose 'living off interests' or 'of independent means', annuitants and paupers were placed in classes I, I, I, I, II and V respectively. A few very uninformative entries ('Husband away', 'spinster', etc.) were placed in a residual class X. Retired persons were classified on the basis of previous occupations.

For the 1841 sample, it was necessary to proceed on a somewhat different basis, since individuals were not asked to state whether or not they were employers, nor the number of their employees. Accordingly, the maintenance of servants was brought into play as a criterion of class at various points, and the social classification scheme, again using the 1951 attributions as the point of departure, was as follows:

Class I. Professional, etc. (as in 1851), less the handful of large entrepreneurs, not identifiable.

Class II. Individuals who would have been classed as II or III on the 1851 procedure, provided they employed at least one servant.

Class III. The same, where no servants were employed.

Classes IV and V. According to the initial attribution lists.[23]

23 Armstrong, *Stability and change*, 13–4.

Table 13.7a Social class of household heads, using the Armstrong version of the Registrar General's 1950 scheme, for selected districts in 1851

District n.	York 753 (sample)	Sleaford 778	Wakefield 3,246	Nottingham Sample of whole city	Chalcots 117
Class I	7.8	5.3	6.8	3.4	35.0
Class II	14.2	21.1	11.5	11.6	47.9
Class III	51.3	35.0	49.3	61.9	14.5
Class IV	13.7	26.8	12.8	13.8	0.9
Class V	13.0	9.1	14.0	9.5	1.7

Source: York: Armstrong, *Stability and change* 189. York had a total population of 36,303 in 1851.
Sleaford: personal communication, Wendy Atkins.
Wakefield: Cowlard, 'Identification of social areas', 241. Unclassified households amounted to 5.6%. His figures for 1861 are similar except that only 5.6% appear in class II, but 52.9% in class III.
Nottingham: Smith, 'The social structure of Nottingham'. The population of Nottingham was 57,407 in 1851.
Chalcots: Rau, 'Who chose Chalcots?' 16. Chalcots was part of Hampstead.

Table 13.7b Social class of household heads, using the Armstrong version of the Registrar General's 1950 scheme, for selected districts in 1871

District n.	Hastings 4,330	Lincoln 5,492	Coventry 8,535	Windsor 3,420	Farnworth 6,151
Class I	11.5	4.4	1.5	7.1	3.2
Class II	22.0	13.0	12.2	14.2	9.8
Class III	39.9	53.0	67.8	35.5	59.3
Class IV	16.1	16.2	10.3	27.2	18.2
Class V	10.5	13.5	8.1	16.0	9.6

Notes: Values of n. represent the numbers of inhabited houses, less institutions, from which a 10 per cent sample was taken. Farnworth is near Bolton.
Source: Ebery and Preston, *Domestic service*, 57 and 63. The authors also give comparable data for Reading and other smaller Berkshire towns, Bolton and other nearby textile areas.

Tables 13.7a and 13.7b above include data presented by the Armstrong methodology for a selection of areas in England and provide a basis of comparison for further studies. In particular, there is a wide variety of circumstances relating to class I, with 11.5 per cent of household heads in Hastings ranging down to only 1.5 per cent in working-class Coventry. Well outside this range with 35 per cent was the small study area of Chalcots, an upper class suburb of London, indicating how much more variation could be found in small areas within cities. The range in other classes, whilst more muted, is still considerable, Armstrong's swollen class III, for instance, ranging from about 35 per cent to almost 70 per cent, with the exceptional Chalcots outside this range.

It should be noted that all these examples follow the York study in classifying household heads only, or, putting it another way, whole households have been classified on the basis of heads' occupations. Clearly this distorts reality, since many households contain servants and apprentices, as well as younger unmarried men and a few women at the outset of careers, for example, journeymen later to become masters, farmers' sons later to be farmers. Therefore there is a bias towards the older age groups.

Armstrong's social classification has found less favour than his industrial classification, even with researchers who have accepted the usefulness of social classification, but it seems they have frequently used the five-class scheme as some kind of starting point. In some studies of small areas classes I–II and IV–V appear together in order to balance out the large class III. Others of differing scales have worked on the basis of three broad categories of upper-middle class, skilled workers, and semi- and unskilled workers. A further variation has been to adopt something more modern, like the following six socio-economic groups: professional, intermediate, skilled non-manual, skilled manual, semi-skilled, and unskilled.[24] There has also been a debate about the possibility of modifying the Armstrong social classification scheme, as discussed in the next two sections.

Social classification: Royle

During 1977–8 a debate occurred between Royle on the one hand, and Armstrong and Holmes on the other.[25] Royle wished to alter Armstrong's social classification scheme in three ways, firstly by abandoning class IV, the semi-skilled, on the grounds that in 1950 this represented the semi-skilled assembly-line worker who had no place in Victorian society.[26] Whilst this has some merit, Royle displaced agricultural workers into class V, where they perhaps belonged in terms of income, but not in terms of skill, being so much more skilful than men such as errand boys, news vendors, porters, rag and paper collectors, and scavengers, whom Armstrong attributed to class V.

Secondly, Royle used the 'space' so created to accommodate skilled manual workers in his class IV, leaving routine non-manual in class III, much as the same two categories are often separated in classes IIIa and IIIb in modern schemes. Royle thus recognised the point made above about clerks, and also removed the problem of the 'over-large' class III,

24 Pooley, 'Residential mobility', 270.
25 Royle, 'Social stratification'; Royle, 'Reply'; and Holmes and Armstrong, 'Social stratification'.
26 Royle, 'Reply', 128.

Table 13.8 **The social structure of Lutterworth and Melton Mowbray, Leicestershire, in 1851, using the Registrar General's and Royle's schemes**

Class	Lutterworth		Melton Mowbray	
	RG %	R %	RG %	R %
I	5.1	4.8	5.0	4.5
II	14.7	14.7	15.2	16.8
III	42.9	12.1	41.9	14.5
IV	22.3	30.8	23.2	24.6
V	15.0	37.7	14.7	39.6

Notes: RG = Registrar General's scheme; R = Royle's scheme.
Source: Royle, 'Social stratification', 128.

which Armstrong freely admitted.[27] However, Royle's amendment merely transferred 'over-size' from class III to class V, as shown in Table 13.8 above. Indeed, the result is sometimes worse than that shown in Table 13.7, since Royle's social classification of household heads in the new Leicestershire mining town of Coalville in 1851 produced a class V of 77.4 per cent.[28]

Lastly, Royle wished to refine classes I and II by using the presence of co-residential servants as a criterion additional to occupation and status as an employer. This raised the greatest criticisms since it was thought to confuse class with life style. Perhaps, more importantly, it prevents servant-keeping from being related to social status, since it introduces a circularity of argument. In that later investigators have preferred Armstrong's scheme to Royle's, it can be said that the former won the debate, despite the importance of Royle's criticisms.

Social classification: Mills and Mills

More recently, a question has been asked concerning employment status arising from Armstrong's rule in paragraph 3 in the extract above, that persons with at least one employee in appropriate occupations could be raised from class III to class II. Mills and Mills argued that in the Victorian period the status of being in business on one's own account was sufficient to justify a self-employed man such as a wheelwright or blacksmith being attributed to class II regardless of whether he also employed other people.[29] Further, they drew attention to the inconsistency amongst householders and enumerators in their recording in the CEBs of master or journeyman status, and of the number of persons employed. They recommended that the CEBs should be supplemented by trades directories to ascertain which tradesmen

27 In paragraph 3 of the extract above and in Armstrong, 'The CEBs: a commentary', 56. If one class contains 50 per cent or so of the total population studied, it is very difficult to differentiate its characteristics from those of the whole population.
28 Royle, 'Small town society', 52.
29 Mills and Mills, 'Stratification revisited'.

Table 13.9 Classification by the Registrar General's scheme: household heads, Sleaford, Lincolnshire, 1851

Class	Armstrong criteria		Mills' criteria	
	n.	%	n.	%
I	42	5.3	42	5.3
II	169	21.1	245	30.6
III	280	35.0	206	25.8
IV	214	26.8	212	26.5
V	73	9.1	73	9.1
Unknown	22	2.8	22	2.8

Source: CEBs for Sleaford, 1851, with supplementary information from county trade directories of 1842, 1849, 1851 and 1856; data worked and supplied by W. Atkin.

and craftsmen were running enterprises of their own. This procedure has the incidental merit of moving a significant number of men and a few women to class II from Armstrong's overburdened class III (see Table 13.9 above).

Social classification: Banks

Banks' work is not strictly comparable to the other work reviewed here, since it is based entirely on data contained in the printed census reports, rather than manuscript data. However, although the figures are also only estimates, they are valuable in giving some insight into the national pattern for England and Wales, first of all over the period 1841–81. Banks' table using a version of the five-class scheme for all males aged 20 and over (and not household heads) shows remarkable consistency over the five censuses. Class I ranges over the narrow band from 8.5 to 10.9 per cent of the total. Comparable figures for class II are 12.3 to 14.0 per cent; class III, 20.0 to 21.5 per cent; class IV, 36.3 to 44.1 per cent; and class V, 14.2 to 18.4 per cent. The only discernible trends are a fall of 7.8 percentage points in class IV, balanced partly by a rise of 4.2 points in class V.[30]

Banks also made a comparison of the results obtained by using the 1911 and 1950 systems of classification for males over the age of 15. The figures for the 1881 and 1891 censuses are shown in Table 13.10 below, showing similar levels for the sizes of classes II, IV and V, but wide and worrying variations in classes I and III.

The debate continues, particularly in the work of the Cambridge Group relating to the 1891–1921 censuses reported above, the need to use both an industrial or economic scheme and a social-class scheme is still accepted. One object of their coding is to make it possible to

30 Banks, 'Social structure', 194.

Table 13.10 **Social class composition of males over 15, England and Wales, percentages**

Social class	I	II	III	IV	V
1881 (1911)	11.6	14.5	27.7	29.2	17.0
1881 (1950)	2.1	14.6	39.8	30.5	13.1
1891 (1911)	12.1	14.9	27.2	28.6	17.2
1891 (1950)	2.3	14.4	40.6	29.6	13.1

Source: Banks, 'Social structure', 197.

put occupations into social or economic groups from the same basic table. However, the attributions of the 1911 scheme have been preferred to those of 1950.[31]

We think it is good advice to suggest that at the outset of their work students of the CEBs should look carefully through the literature to find pieces of research on similar lines to those contemplated.[32] Having identified some points of comparison, the classification schemes used in the relevant studies should be replicated, at least for comparative purposes, if not throughout the entire study. This chapter indirectly demonstrates the relative lack of comparative work on occupations, as in many aspects of work on the CEBs. Without comparisons, we are still, after 40 years of endeavour, looking at a patchwork quilt of studies which contains more holes than continuous material.

Contents of Part III

Chapter 14 by Scott is a study of an agricultural population who were pioneers on Exmoor after its enclosure in 1819. A distinctive feature is the preponderance of males in the 1841 census, including ten all-male households, followed by a gradual balancing of the sex ratio, until in 1871 there was a majority of females. Scott is complemented by Hallas' chapter 15 on rural tradesmen and craftsmen. Although many rural studies have used the CEBs, it is surprising how few have focused sharply on the core rural occupations, as do these two chapters, in particular the tradesmen and craftsmen. Hallas' study is also unusual in having made use of the five censuses from 1841 to 1881.

In chapter 16, Saito looks at another neglected topic – women's work – comparing CEBs with evidence for the late-eighteenth century taken from the community listings for Corfe Castle and Cardington. A further illustration of combining CEBs with other sources comes in chapter 17, where Jones has used estate records in his study of some West Riding coal miners and ironstone miners. Generally speaking,

31 Schürer, 'Understanding and coding occupations', 105.
32 Perhaps using Mills and Pearce, *People and places.*

aristocratic landowners did not encourage the growth of industrial populations on their estates, but the Earls Fitzwilliam made the usual exception for the exploitation of mineral resources. This was seen in much the same light as farming and forestry, with the added bonus of royalty payments on coal brought up.

Elsewhere in the volume, occupations figure significantly, as in chapter 3 by Higgs on servants, and chapter 20 by Turner, concerned with textile workers in a migration context. In Part V, family and household structure provides the context for studies of agricultural workers (in the case of chapter 26 by Hinde) and miners (chapter 27 by Brayshay). In the last Part of the book, in which residential patterns are discussed, there are contrasting studies on jet workers in Whitby and agricultural workers, chapters 30 and 32 by Vickers and Rawding, respectively.

14

Population and enclosure in the mid-nineteenth century: the example of Exmoor

RUTH G. SCOTT

The nineteenth-century CEBs make it possible to examine at micro-level the composition and to some extent the mobility of population during the second half of the nineteenth century, a period which for many communities was one when considerable demographic change was taking place. This chapter analyses the rural community of Exmoor over three decades using the CEBs of 1841–71.[1] Exmoor is a rewarding area for a study of this kind, enclosed as it was almost entirely from the waste in 1819. Roughly 1,000 hectares were newly enclosed at this date; the 'old enclosures' in existence being approximately 43 hectares around Simonsbath House in the centre of the parish.[2] The enclosure and reclamation of Exmoor are very well documented, and little can be added to Orwin's work on the subject,[3] but scant attention has been paid to the population of the area during what must have been a period of revolutionary change on the moor.

In 1819, Exmoor ceased to exist as a royal forest. Until that date it had been administered for the crown by a warden, the last one being Sir Thomas Dyke Acland, who, when his lease as warden expired in 1814, suggested that the crown might find it advantageous to dispose of the freehold of the forest, hoping, in fact, to become its purchaser.[4] His hope foundered, however, when he was outbid by John Knight, an ironmaster from Wolverley in Worcestershire, intent upon the aggrandisement of his estates and exhibiting the speculative flair so common in land transactions at the time. Knight was already a pioneer farmer with a lifelong interest in the revival of agricultural practice consequent upon the high prices being paid for farm produce in the late-eighteenth and early-nineteenth centuries. His main aim was to reclaim Exmoor and use it for rotation farming under a demesne system.

1 PRO HO107/965, HO107/1890, RG9/1606–7, RG9/2180

2 The old enclosure surrounded Simonsbath House, built in about 1654 by James Boevy and occupied until 1819 by the Deputy Forester.

3 Orwin and Sellick, *Reclamation of Exmoor Forest*. This book brings up to date an earlier work of the same title by Orwin, published in 1928, in the light of freshly available source material.

4 Acland, *Memoir and letters*.

His first schemes involved the building of roadways and a boundary wall, 46 kilometres long. This was completed in 1824, and he was able to turn his attention to breaking the ground at Cornham and Honeymead, both on south facing slopes in the Barle valley, and sheltered from the very worst of the weather. Here he carried out spading, burning, liming and 'halving'.[5] He attempted a four-course rotation which, according to family correspondence in the 1840s, produced 'fine' crops of wheat, barley, oats and turnips, and began to stock the land with highly-bred Hereford and Highland cattle which he travelled considerable distances to obtain.[6] However, his efforts and substantial success as a pioneer farmer do not concern us in detail here.

In one respect, Knight's enterprise fell short of the mark. He seemed to have little idea of how to set about colonising the forest, and this proved, perhaps, his most serious shortcoming. He always favoured unmarried men as labourers, and the area, being extra-parochial, was, by the time he took over, already noted for its lawlessness, isolation and complete lack of social amenities.

However, 1841, the year of the first available census schedules, marked a turning-point in the management of the Knight Exmoor estates, because John handed over to his son Frederic, a firm believer in the advantages of tenant farming and the importance of attracting families, rather than single men, to the moor. To family men he offered accommodation, high wages and, in time, social amenities. Advertisements were placed in the press, both locally and further afield, offering 6d. per day for boys, 2s. for men and 2s. 6d. for craftsmen. He succeeded in attracting a number of tenants to the moor, but they were more often than not short stayers, and there were considerable gaps during which the farms lay untenanted.

The 1841 census lists 163 persons, a dramatic increase of the order of 313 per cent from the 1831 figure. In 1841 there were 116 males and only 47 females, but the imbalance in sex structure was even greater than this in actuality, since 100 labourers, presumably male, were absent on census night 'having left the parish on Saturday evening according to their custom, to sleep in the adjoining parishes and return on Monday morning'.

A closer look at the schedules for 1841 reveals that the policy of letting farms adopted by Frederic Knight was not affecting the population structure of the moor; indeed, John Knight's demesne farming experiment is reflected in the large number of single men living in communities. Of a total of 80 labourers and male servants, only 10 have wives and families with them on the moor: these in

5 'Halving'; the first ploughing, in which bullock teams ploughed every alternate furrow-width, the furrow-slice being turned over onto the unploughed strip beside it.

6 Knight Manuscript, Kidderminster Public Library.

Figure 14.1 Population pyramids: Exmoor, 1841–1871

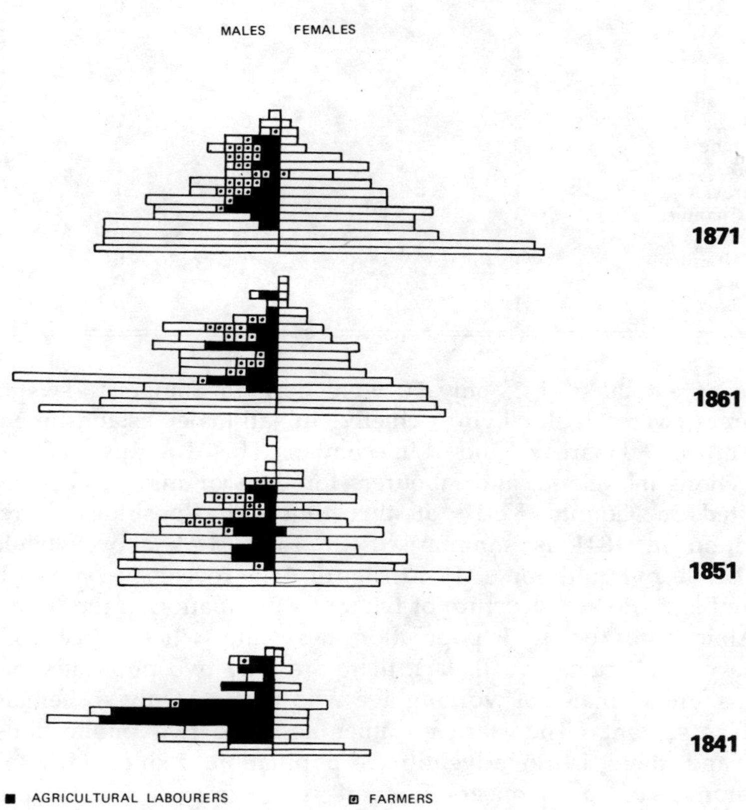

cottages at Simonsbath, Cornham, Honeymead, Limecombe and Ferny Ball. The remaining 70 lived either in all-male households – there were 10 of these, ranging in size from 9 at Bale Water to 3 at Simonsbath – or with nuclear families as at Warren cottage, later renamed Warren Farm, where a 20-year-old unmarried labourer lived with another labourer and his family. Only 22 of the labourers were Somerset men, and this situation reflects closely that revealed in the total population,

Table 14.1 Habitation: Exmoor, 1841

Settlement	n. of buildings	n. of nuclear families	n. of labourers in lodgings	n. of all-male communities	Total n. of labourers
Simonsbath village	5	2	2	3	11
Gallon House	1	1	0	0	1
Slate Rock	1	1	0	0	1
Warren Cottage	1	1	1	0	2
Cornham	3	2	0	1	8
Honeymead	3	1	0	2	11
Bale Water	2	0	0	2	12
Limecombe	3	3	11	0	14
Hoaroak	1	0	0	1	4
Clovenrocks	1	0	0	1	7
Moles Chamber	1	1	3	0	3
Ferny Ball	2	2	1	0	1
Holes Allotment	1	1	3	0	3
Burcombe	1	1	1	0	1
Green Barrow	1	1	0	0	1

where of a total of 163, only 50 were born in Somerset. Twenty-two labourers were Irish, living chiefly in all-male establishments at Clovenrocks, Hoaroak and Limecombe. The Knights had family connections in Ireland, and labourers for Exmoor may well have been recruited in County Kerry at this time. The position as regards habitation in 1841 is summarised in Table 14.1 above, while the population pyramid for 1841 in Figure 14.1 reveals very clearly the unusual age and sex structure of Exmoor's population at the time.

Almost all the 1841 population falls into what Vince calls the 'primary rural' category.[7] In fact, there are only two publicans and two masons among males of working age who do not. Only six females are listed as servants. There are no amenities save two public houses in 1841, and there is no adventitious population. Exmoor has all the appearance of a 'pioneer frontier' in terms of its population composition and this is perhaps most clearly demonstrated in its sex ratio of only 42 females per 100 males.

Table 14.2 below attempts to give the constitution of nuclear families in 1841. It would appear that in general families with large numbers of children did not take lodgers. There is, however, one instance, at Limecombe, where a family with three children boarded eleven (male) lodgers. All-male households are analysed in Table 14.3 below. There is little evidence to suggest that people in all-male

7 Vince, 'Rural population of England and Wales'. Vince defined 'primary rural' as that part of the rural population depending directly on the land, including foresters but excluding miners; 'secondary rural' as that part of the population serving the needs of the primary, and 'adventitious' as those not dependent on the land or serving those who are so dependent.

Table 14.2 Nuclear families: Exmoor, 1841

Settlement	Parent(s) present	Child(ren) present	Lodgers in nuclear families All	Male	Female
Simonsbath Village	1	1	5	2	3
Simonsbath Village	2	2	0	0	0
Slate Rock	2	1	1	0	1
Warren Cottage	2	5	1	1	0
Cornham	2	4	0	0	0
Cornham	2	3	0	0	0
Honeymead	2	1	1	1	0
Limecombe	2	5	0	0	0
Limecombe	2	2	1	0	1
Limecombe	2	3	11	11	0
Moles Chamber	2	0	5	4	1
Ferny Ball	2	2	1	1	0
Ferny Ball	1	1	0	0	0
Holes Allotment	2	2	5	4	1
Burcombe	2	1	4	3	1
Green Barrow	2	0	4	2	2

Notes: A definition of nuclear families is given in chapter 23, Part V.

Table 14.3 All-male households: Exmoor, 1841

Settlement	Total male population	With same surname	Aged <20	Aged 20–30	Aged 30+	Born Somerset
Simonsbath	3	0	1	2	0	0
Simonsbath	5	0	1	4	0	2
Simonsbath	3	0	0	2	1	0
Cornham	8	2	3	2	3	3
Honeymead	4	0	0	4	0	3
Honeymead	7	2	3	4	0	6
Bale Water	4	0	0	3	1	1
Bale Water	9	4	1	5	3	3
Hoaroak	4	0	0	3	4	0
Clovenrocks	7	0	0	6	1	0

households were related – if surname is used as the criterion there exist four Huxtables, two Courts and two Goughs. Otherwise all surnames are different. The Huxtable family is interesting, though, in its long association with the moor.

By 1842, however, Frederic Knight's policy of attracting tenants was well under way, and he aimed at farmers from afar rather than from local Devon and Somerset parishes. His reasons were sound: the locals saw Exmoor as summer grazing and not as potential farmland; furthermore the local farms were traditionally small family-run affairs.[8] The appointment of a Lincolnshire man as agent was no accident, and

[8] Fussell, 'Farming systems', 179–204.

Knight hoped that he might attract through him farmers from areas where large-scale improved farming was already flourishing.

Judging by the CEBs for 1851, the agent, Robert Smith, must have been successful, especially in the east Midlands. All farms over 120 hectares were, by 1851, being farmed by men from Dorset, Leicestershire, Northamptonshire or Lincolnshire, with the one exception of Cornham, where a Somerset man was tenant.[9] Of the smaller farms, six were farmed by Somerset men, one of whom, at Tom's Hill, confessed to the enumerator to being 'out of business', and the remaining six by Devonians. Undoubtedly some run-down farmers were attracted by Knight's low rents, but were unable to survive, as frequent changes of tenancy testify. Larkbarrow, for example, built in 1846 and let in the same year, quickly changed hands, once in 1849 and again twice in 1852.

The 1851 CEBs show that the number of houses inhabited had doubled in the intercensal period since 1841 and the total population had risen from 163 to 275. Males did not out-number females to the same extent though, the 'pioneer fringe' character of the area having been modified to one of family settlement.

This is clearly borne out by the 1851 population pyramid displayed in Figure 14.1 above. Occupational structure also points up a contrast: in 1851 agricultural labourers make up only 15 per cent of the population as against 49 per cent in 1841, and occupations overall among working males are not so utterly dominated by the 'primary rural' category. Sixteen persons fall into the 'secondary rural' group, though there is still no adventitious population. Thirteen labourers had established their families on the moor, and a school, founded in 1845, had 28 pupils in 1851. The all-male household had almost disappeared, with only four remaining, and three of these containing only one or two men. Only 3 of the 42 men listed as labourers had been on the moor 10 years earlier. Two of them already had families with them then, while the third, Anthony Huxtable, is seen to have married and had four children since 1841, the two youngest being Exmoor born. Turnover in the labouring force appears therefore considerable, most of the newcomers being drawn from nearby Devon and Somerset parishes. In 1851 not one Irish-born man remains, according to the census. The obvious, however, should perhaps be pointed out, that place of birth is not necessarily that of habitation immediately prior to settlement on Exmoor, and this is one of the limitations of using the CEBs in this way.

9 Orwin and Sellick, *Reclamation of Exmoor Forest* contains an interesting account of Hannam's first-hand description of life on the moor.

Between the census years of 1851 and 1861 Exmoor became a parish,[10] and the 1861 population was 323, with the number of inhabited buildings rising from 54 to 62. It is striking that only two farms are being tenanted by non-local farmers, and that of the remaining holdings only three are farmed by Somerset men, the vast majority being tenanted by north Devonians from parishes adjoining the moor. This Devon bias is perhaps attributable to the fact that the cold clays of north Devon, on the windward side of the moor presented much more similar farming conditions than did the parishes on the mellower, Somerset side. It was from the farming stock of Devon that most of Exmoor's farmers finally came.

Labourers and farm servants in 1861 make up 15 per cent of the total population, numbering 49. Twenty-two males fall into the 'secondary rural' category, and there is no dramatic contrast with 1851; instead the 1861 figures show a small increase in both primary and secondary occupations, with the establishment of more amenities and the steady growth of Simonsbath village where, by 1861, most of the secondary group is to be found. Among female workers there are eight servants, five housekeepers, a cook, a teacher and a dressmaker, occupations here too beginning to diversify.

Among 49 labourers, 24 now have established their wives and families, a substantially higher proportion than in 1851. It is of interest to note that Anthony Huxtable, a labourer in 1851, has now moved into the category of farmer, and his children number two more, both born on the moor. Apart from Huxtable, however, evidence can be found for only two other labourers remaining from 1851 to 1861, and none save him had remained over the 20-year period.

Among the men working on the land, turnover is again considerable and the vast majority are local born. Only two non-locals appear, in fact, both from Dorset, and the last vestiges of Exmoor as a pioneer community have disappeared. The growth of the village of Simonsbath, now with its parish church and school, as a focal point for the moorland surrounding it, is again noticeable as far as the distribution of people engaged in secondary occupations is concerned.

By the late 1860s, earlier attempts to cultivate stretches of the moor under a four-course rotation were to some extent modified by the introduction of rape-seed in place of turnips. This innovation turned out to be an important one, for rape takes only six weeks to mature and provides excellent winter feed for sheep. The rape-seed/sheep

10 Exmoor became a parish in 1856. The first application for parochialisation was made in 1845 by tenants of Knight's farms. Knight himself opposed it, however, as he hoped that the absence of rates would attract more settlers. He felt able to support a new application in 1852. The Knight connection continued until 1963 when the British Museum Act abolished family trustees, the last of whom was Richard Ayshford Knight.

Table 14.4 Turnover of Exmoor farmers in the mid-nineteenth century

Name	Present 1851	Present 1861	Present 1871	Name	Present 1851	Present 1861	Present 1871
Hannam	X	–	–	Mills	–	X	–
Chapple	X	–	–	Comer	–	X	X
Hedditch	X	–	–	Carter	–	X	X
Harold	X	–	–	Carter	–	X	X
Meadows	X	–	–	Shapland	–	X	X
Biggin	X	–	–	Richards	–	X	X
Searson	X	–	–	Huxtable[a]	–	X	X
Coombes	X	–	–	Holcombe	–	X	X
Balmond	X	–	–	Fry	–	X	X
Sebley	X	–	–	Steer	–	X	X
Collins	X	–	–	Elworthy	–	X	X
Buckingham	X	–	–	Rudd	–	X	X
Williams	X	–	–	Fry	–	–	X
Smith (Robert)	X	X	–	Comer	–	–	X
Poole	X	X	X	Scott	–	–	X
Skinner	X	X	X	Reed	–	–	X
Blake	X	X	X	Fry	–	–	X
Gillard	X	X	X	Smyth	–	–	X
Norman	–	X	–	Fry	–	–	X
Vellacott	–	X	–	Tucker	–	–	X
Baker	–	X	–	Buckingham	–	–	X
Gould	–	X	–	Baker	–	–	X
Creek	–	X	–	Rudd	–	–	X
Dixon	–	X	–	Thorne[a]	–	X	X

Notes: [a] = Huxtable was recorded as a farmer in 1861 and a labourer in 1871, while for Thorne the situation was reversed.

combination proved to be a good one and, in fact, remained established on Exmoor for many decades. Production of lamb and mutton increased, with wool prices gradually giving ground as meat prices went up. The animals were either butchered in Simonsbath or sent to the railhead at South Molton on the hoof. Land was systematically improved, with dressings of lime and natural ashes being used on soil which had already undergone paring, burning and ploughing in order to break up the intractable clay-iron hard-pan. By the late 1870s, over 10,000 ewes and lambs were counted on Exmoor, most of them Scottish blackface and Cheviots, which could be overwintered on the moor more successfully than the local Exmoor Horn.

The 1871 census enumerated a total population of 339, only a slight overall increase on 1861. On this occasion the labouring force makes up 17 per cent of the total population, numbering 58. Only 18 males fall into the 'secondary' group, but among females the number has risen considerably to 38, including 24 servants, 8 housekeepers, 3 nurses, a teacher, a governess and a cook. The fertility ratio is 102, whereas in 1861 it had been only 79. All farm workers, except four Dorset men and

Table 14.5 Succession to farms: Exmoor, 1851–1871

Name of farmer 1851	Name of farmer 1861	Name of farmer 1871
George Gillard	(George Gillard) son	(George Gillard) son
John Blake	John Blake	John Blake
William Poole	William Poole	William Poole
James Skinner	James Skinner	(Grace Skinner) widow
	Fred Comer[a]	(Francis Comer) father
	John Carter	John Carter
	William Carter	William Carter
	Samuel Shapland	Samuel Shapland
	George Richards	George Richards
	Antony Huxtable	Antony Huxtable (lab.)
	Robert Holcombe	Robert Holcombe
	William Fry	William Fry
	Joseph Steer	Joseph Steer
	Thomas Elworthy	Thomas Elworthy
	William Rudd[a]	(George Rudd) Brother

Notes: a = In both these cases, although the farms had changed hands, the 1861 farmers are still on Exmoor, in charge of other holdings.

one Scottish shepherd, were local born, with, for the first time, a group of Exmoor-born men, numbering eight in all. In both 1851 and 1861 only one labourer had been born on the moor. Ten of the 1871 labourers had been on Exmoor already in 1861, giving the lowest turnover to date, but still nevertheless a considerable one.

Of the 26 farmers listed in 1871, 19 were Devonians, and it is of interest to find 2 Rudds from the parish of Charles and 3 Frys from Kentisbury, both cold upland parishes on the windward side of the moor. Six farmers come from Somerset, including, for the first time, an Exmoor-born man and two Comers from the parish of Withypool. Huxtable is not, this time, listed as a farmer, but he is still on Exmoor as a labourer. Perhaps his eight hectare holding proved too small to be profitable and to support a growing family. An attempt to summarise the position with regard to turnover among farmers, a far less mobile group than labourers, is made in Tables 14.4 and 14.5 above.

As far as the parish of Exmoor is concerned, the CEBs covering the mid-nineteenth century clearly shed light on the enclosures of 1819 and the changing policies of subsequent managers of the Knight estates. The vast area enclosed, and the size of many of the holdings thus formed – Honeymead, for example, covered 840 hectares, and there were several more over 400 hectares – make Exmoor an exception to most other areas of waste enclosure in south-west England. Added to this, the establishment of so many new farms in the 1840s and after makes it an ideal area in which to examine population composition and change *ab initio* in the light of the extremely detailed information available from the CEBs. The general thesis on the growth and structure of population as a result of the colonisation of a new frontier is borne out by the example of Exmoor. As settlement becomes more permanently established the effects of enclosure on population composition are noticeably diminished. Local labour and local farm tenantry become more common and the ratio of females to males and the numbers engaged in secondary occupations rise.

Though there are limitations to be considered by anyone using the CEBs as a major source, their usefulness remains unquestioned; indeed, they offer such a variety and sophistication of information that they demand sophisticated techniques of analysis if they are to be used over a wide area.

15

Craft occupations in the late-nineteenth century: some local considerations

CHRISTINE HALLAS

Introduction

One of the distinctive features of traditional English rural society is the diversity of occupations to be found within the community.[1] The primary activity of agriculture, sometimes in association with extractive industry, required the support of a wide range of crafts and services. The country craftsmen included both those, such as blacksmith and wheelwright, who serviced the primary industries of the countryside, and those, such as tailor and shoemaker, who supplied the rural population with their basic needs. The rural craftsman was, therefore, integrally associated with the relatively self-sufficient rural economy which persisted in England and Wales well into the nineteenth century.[2] Continuing rural population growth to the mid-nineteenth century stimulated demand for the products and services of the rural craftsman in both local and regional markets.[3] Further, the concentration of specialist crafts in some places influenced the local population trends. The number and prosperity of rural craftsmen, therefore, increased broadly in line with the growth of rural population. It has been observed that total numbers employed in virtually all crafts dropped consistently from either 1861 or 1871, and that in many areas employment in country crafts per thousand of population fell from 1851.[4] The causes of this decline have been the subject of much debate.[5] The link with declining rural population is inescapable, but of

1 Chartres, 'Country trades', 416–7.

2 Chartres and Turnbull, 'Country craftsmen', 314–28. Chartres and Turnbull comment that rural crafts reached their peak during Victoria's reign although at different times depending on technical innovations in the various industries and the ability to mass-produce articles, 317.

3 Everitt, 'Country carriers', 179. Chartres and Turnbull, 'Country craftsmen', 317. Chartres, 'County trades', 417–8; Mitchell and Deane, *Abstract of British historical statistics*, 60, 366.

4 For example, in the North Riding of Yorkshire, Chartres and Turnbull, 'Country craftsmen', 319–20.

5 Anderson Graham, *Rural exodus*; Longstaff, 'Rural depopulation'; Saville, *Rural depopulation*, 20–30; Chartres and Turnbull, 'Country craftsmen', 320–1; Crompton, 'Changes in rural service occupations', 193–203.

Figure 15.1 The regional setting of the study area

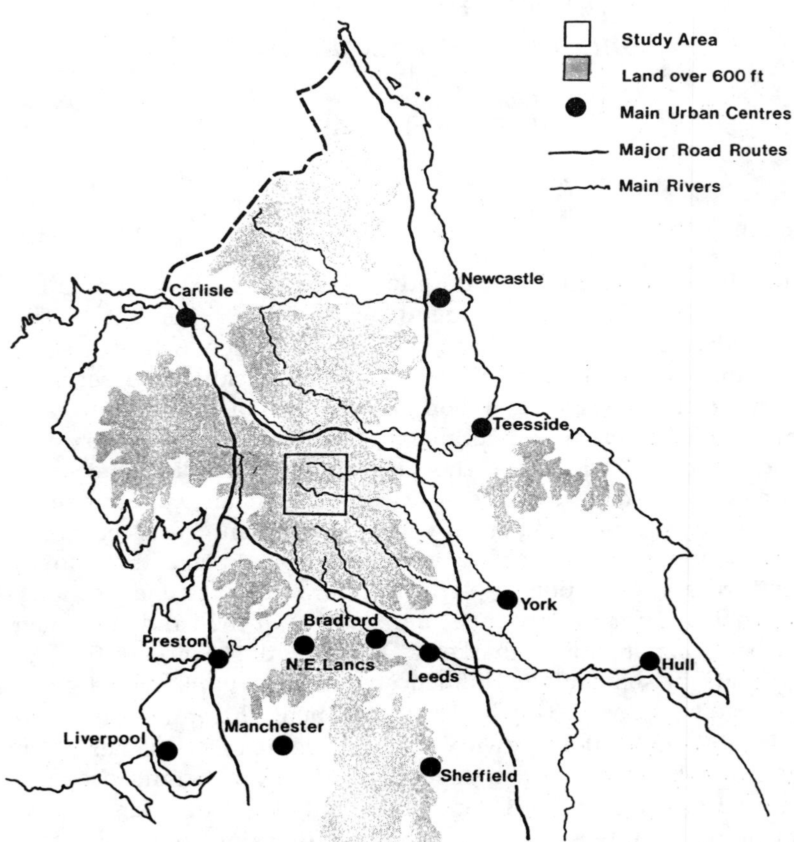

comparable importance was the impact of industrialisation and the competition from factory-made goods which improved transport facilitated. Contemporaries noted the connection between the decline of rural crafts and industrialisation and commented that it was a period of rapid change.[6] However, as is demonstrated in this chapter, industrialisation did not cause a uniform decline in rural crafts either in terms of spatial distribution or within specific crafts. Also, albeit to a limited extent, many country craftsmen were able to adapt and take

6 Anderson Graham, *Rural exodus*, 30–2; Longstaff, 'Rural depopulation', 414.

Figure 15.2 The study area

advantage of some of the changes brought about by industrialisation. Recent research has shown that the contraction of the rural craft industry was generally gradual, and, even at the end of the nineteenth century, the rural craftsman remained an important figure in the life of the countryside.[7]

A Yorkshire case study

Wensleydale and Swaledale provide a useful case study for an analysis of the craft industry in the late-nineteenth century. They are two of the most northerly of the Yorkshire dales, and are situated in a relatively remote upland region, which lies between the industrial towns of the West Riding and Lancashire to the south and the estuaries of the Tees, Wear and Tyne to the north-east (see Figure 15.1 above). Upper Wensleydale (81,000 acres) includes all the townships in that dale from Carperby westwards; lower Wensleydale (18,000 acres) includes all the townships from Leyburn westwards to West Witton; Swaledale (74,000 acres) includes all the townships in that dale from Marrick westwards (see Figure 15.2 above).

7 Chartres and Turnbull, 'County craftsmen', 314–5.

The economy of Wensleydale and Swaledale in the nineteenth century was based on the primary industries of agriculture and lead, supported by crafts and services. The agriculture of the area was largely pastoral. However, while all elements of livestock farming remained important, towards the end of the century in Wensleydale emphasis was placed increasingly on dairy farming. Although there was some lead mining in Wensleydale, the industry was predominantly in Swaledale. Lead mining in the area probably enjoyed its heyday in the early 1800s, but there were other buoyant periods during the nineteenth century. It was only after the 1870s that the lead mining industry entered its final decline. Despite the adjacent position of the two dales and their apparent geographical unity, close examination reveals that there were three distinct economic areas; (upper Wensleydale, i.e. Aysgarth Rural District; lower Wensleydale, i.e. part of Leyburn Rural District; and Swaledale, i.e. Reeth Rural District) which exhibited marked differences in the development of both primary and secondary industries. A detailed analysis of selected crafts in the three areas provides an indication of the extent to which the rural craft industry survived in the late-nineteenth century, and illustrates the degree to which the fortunes of the industry varied even within a small area. This chapter, in highlighting the diversity of experience within the two dales, demonstrates the importance of testing at local level generalisations concerning the development and decline of the craft industry in the nineteenth century.

Crafts and the Dale's economy

The place of crafts in the economic structure of a nineteenth-century rural society provides a useful guide to the degree of self-sufficiency and vitality of the community. Table 15.1 below shows, in simplified form, the occupational structure of upper and lower Wensleydale and Swaledale in the period 1841–81.[8] The occupational structure of upper Wensleydale was that of an area with a broadly typical rural economy, that is of agriculture being closely supported by crafts and services.[9] In contrast, a much lower proportion of the occupied population of lower Wensleydale was employed in agriculture, and a much higher proportion was employed in the extractive industries and in crafts. In Swaledale nearly half the workforce was employed in extractive industry in 1851. The proportion declined progressively to a little under

8 For a detailed occupational classification see Hallas, 'Economic and social change', 605–7. The occupations have been categorised primarily on the basis of Booth's classifications presented in Armstrong, 'Information about occupation', 228–310. The CEBs for 1891 are in the process of being analysed and the findings will be published in the near future.

9 Vince notes that in rural areas secondary occupations (i.e. those which involve serving the needs of a primary rural population) form a ratio of about 2:1 to primary occupations. See Vince, 'Rural population of England and Wales', 504–13.

Table 15.1 Structure of occupied population: upper and lower Wensleydale and Swaledale, 1841–1881

	1841		1851		1861		1871		1881	
	n	%	n	%	n	%	n	%	n	%
Upper Wensleydale										
Agricultural	990	48.2	1,095	42.5	1,218	46.0	1,235	47.1	1,213	49.1
Extraction	65	3.2	100	3.9	131	4.9	128	4.9	102	4.1
Craft	281	13.7	353	13.7	347	13.1	329	12.5	304	12.3
Others	719	35.0	1,090	42.3	1,054	39.8	1,046	39.9	962	38.9
Total occupied[a]	2,055		2,579		2,647		2,624		2,471	
Total population	5,725		5,635		5,649		5,473		5,482	
Lower Wensleydale										
Agricultural	365	40.9	323	27.0	259	21.3	258	22.0	304	26.7
Extraction	58	6.5	207	17.3	239	19.7	128	10.9	103	9.0
Craft	181	20.3	246	20.6	252	20.8	257	21.9	222	19.5
Others	290	32.5	441	36.9	496	40.9	567	48.3	554	48.6
Total occupied[a]	892		1195		1214		1173		1140	
Total population	2,463		2,655		2,999		2,703		2,722	
Swaledale										
Agricultural	429	19.5	531	19.5	669	25.3	762	32.8	795	38.4
Extraction	1,052	47.7	1,343	49.4	1,203	45.6	959	41.3	671	32.4
Craft	238	10.8	263	9.7	277	10.5	204	8.8	201	9.7
Others	489	22.2	676	24.9	629	23.8	602	25.9	554	26.8
Total occupied[a]	2,205		2,718		2,641		2,323		2,068	
Total population	6,758		6,820		6,196		5,370		4,717	

Notes: *a* = In the count of total occupied, dual occupations have been assigned to both categories, consequently the total number of occupations is greater than the total occupied populations. Since the percentage figures in this table relate the number in each occupation group to the total occupied, due to the double-counting caused by dual occupations the percentage columns will not total to 100 per cent, the discrepancy being proportional to the number of dual occupations recorded in a particular year.

Agricultural = workers in agriculture including adult members of the farmer's family, farmer's children where they are returned as working on the farm but excluding the farmer's wife; Extraction = workers in the lead, coal and quarrying industries; Craft = workers in the craft industries; Others = workers in the textile and service industries, professional people, manufacturers and managers, workers in miscellaneous occupations including servants, non-agricultural and unspecified labourers, clerical workers, railway employees and jockeys. The proportion of occupied population to total population over the period varied from 32.6 per cent in Swaledale in 1841 to 47.9 per cent in upper Wensleydale in 1871. Where children (14 years and under) were returned as working, they have been included in the relevant category. Women are included in the table but they did not constitute a high percentage of craft workers and their work was usually in dressmaking or related crafts. For example, in 1881 in upper and lower Wensleydale and Swaledale women constituted 26.3 per cent, 22.1 per cent and 32.8 per cent respectively of the total employed in craft work.

a third in 1881, by which date agriculture had become the principal

Table 15.2 Numbers employed in selected crafts: upper and lower Wensleydale and Swaledale, 1841 and 1881

	Upper Wensleydale		Lower Wensleydale		Swaledale	
	1841	1881	1841	1881	1841	1881
Blacksmiths	32	20	16	14	31	22
Stonemasons	39	53	15	31	36	23
Shoemakers	63	43	36	21	34	30
Total population	5,725	5,482	2,463	2,722	6,758	4,717

Notes: Includes masters, journeymen and apprentices.

employer. The proportion of craft employment in Swaledale was consistently lower than in Wensleydale with its agricultural predominance and two important market towns.

Predictably, craft employment was most highly developed in the relatively diverse economy of lower Wensleydale. Expressed as a proportion of the economically active population, it was substantially more important than in primarily agricultural upper Wensleydale and twice as important as in Swaledale, which was dominated by the lead mining industry. In all three areas the peaking of craft employment accords with the national pattern and closely follows the population peaks.[10] However, the statistics disguise the extent to which the three areas were interdependent. The population of upper Swaledale made use of craftsmen in upper Wensleydale. For example, there were several carrier routes connecting the two dales. The Garth family who lived in upper Swaledale record frequently using the facilities of Wensleydale.[11] So, although crafts provided an important support to agriculture and the rural population, this did not necessarily result in an even distribution throughout the area and some communities enjoyed a greater concentration of crafts than others.

The timing of decline

Employment in the different crafts did not necessarily follow the same trends, as Table 15.2 above shows by reference to the three specific craft groups of blacksmiths, stonemasons and shoemakers. The three craft groups have been selected as representative of the craft types found in the countryside, that is, those dealing with animals and transport, those concentrating on stone and building and those providing footwear and clothing for the local population.

Although nationally there was not an absolute decrease in the number of blacksmiths until the end of the century, both in the North

10 Chartres and Turnbull, 'Country craftsmen', 319–20.

11 Barker MSS (Documents in private hands), 2/5/1–6, Garth Day Books, 1795–1936, *passim*. The carrier network in the two dales is discussed in detail in Hallas, 'Economic and social change', 457–61. See also Everitt, 'Country carriers', 179–202.

Table 15.3 Blacksmiths and shoemakers per thousand total population: upper and lower Wensleydale and Swaledale, 1841 and 1881

	Upper Wensleydale	Lower Wensleydale	Swaledale
Blacksmiths			
1841	5.6	6.5	4.6
1881	3.6	5.1	4.7
Shoemakers			
1841	11.0	14.6	5.0
1881	7.8	7.7	6.4

Riding of Yorkshire, where numbers peaked in 1851, and in the two dales, there was a decrease in numbers from the mid-nineteenth century.[12] Numbers of shoemakers also declined as the local population fell and as mass-produced articles became more widely available. Stonemasons, however, although suffering a decrease in Swaledale, enjoyed an increase in Wensleydale. This reflects the changing needs of the population in each dale and the facility in Wensleydale to export stone.

The significance of the figures in Table 15.2 can be more fully understood when the number of workers in selected crafts per thousand population are identified (see Table 15.3 above). In upper Wensleydale and lower Wensleydale the number of blacksmiths per thousand population declined between 1841 and 1881, but in Swaledale, which lost almost one-third of its blacksmiths over this period, there was a small increase in numbers per thousand. This small increase was probably the result of Swaledale reverting to a predominantly agricultural economy which required the support of blacksmiths. As with crafts generally, the more diverse economy of lower Wensleydale is reflected in the fact that it had the highest number of blacksmiths per thousand. The proportion of blacksmiths in all three areas was consistently lower than in the North Riding. The 1881 North Riding figure of 6.2 compares with rates of 3.6 to 5.1 in the three areas.[13] The incidence of shoemakers follows a similar pattern. The number of shoemakers per thousand population fell in both upper and lower Wensleydale between 1841 and 1881 whereas in Swaledale, although numbers declined, there was an increase in numbers per thousand. The number of shoemakers per thousand in the North Riding exceeded numbers in the three areas until 1881, when at a rate of 6.4 to 7.8 the local level overtook the North Riding figure of 6.3.[14] The comparatively high proportion of shoemakers per thousand in the two dales in 1881 was due to the relative isolation of the area and, consequently, its

12 Chartres and Turnbull, 'Country craftsmen', 314–9.
13 Chartres and Turnbull, 'Country craftsmen', 317–9.
14 Chartres and Turnbull, 'Country craftsmen', 318–9.

greater reliance on local craftsmen even after the coming of the railway.

In contrast to the trend with blacksmiths and shoemakers, as demonstrated by Tables 15.2 and 15.3, the number of stonemasons, although declining in Swaledale increases in both upper and lower Wensleydale between 1841 and 1881. While the increase in the number of stonemasons may conceal some incorrect recording of quarrymen, the growing export of dressed stone from several large quarries and a rise in building activity within Wensleydale account for most of the increase.[15] For example, 8 of the 15 stonemasons recorded in Hawes in 1851 were born in Gilling, near Richmond.[16] They may have been employed by a firm building the new parish church in 1850 or the new Independent church which was completed in 1851.[17]

An indication of the incidence of different craft businesses, as distinct from the numbers of employers and employees, may be obtained from the local trade directories.[18] The numbers of blacksmiths', stonemasons', and shoemakers' businesses per thousand population are set out in Table 15.4 below. The number of blacksmiths' businesses per thousand was highest in lower Wensleydale, reflecting the importance of crafts in the area's mixed economy. The lower numbers of blacksmiths per thousand recorded in upper Wensleydale may point to the increasing reliance placed on the lower dale facilities, particularly in the latter part of the century. In Swaledale the directory information for 1893 would seem to corroborate the evidence presented earlier in Table 15.3 and to imply an increasing demand for blacksmiths as dependence on agriculture superseded reliance on the lead industry. The number of shoemakers' businesses per thousand in Swaledale was consistently lower than in either of the two Wensleydale areas, possibly reflecting differences in standard of living and also the reliance of parts of Swaledale on Wensleydale craftsmen. As with blacksmiths and shoemakers, the number of stonemasons' businesses per thousand was highest in lower Wensleydale for most of the period, but in 1872 and 1893 lower Wensleydale was second to upper Wensleydale and Swaledale respectively.

Some indication of the size of blacksmiths' and shoemakers' businesses may be obtained by combining elements of Tables 15.3 and 15.4, as shown in Table 15.5 below.[19] Between 1841 and 1881 the size of blacksmiths' and shoemakers' businesses in upper and lower Wensleydale fell, matching the fall in the number of blacksmiths and shoemakers per thousand of population. In Swaledale, although the

15 Hallas, 'Economic and social change', 350–90.

16 CEBs Hawes 1851, PRO HO107/2380.

17 Whellan, *History and topography of York*, 410–1.

18 Directories usually record only the name of the owner/manager of the business concerned and not names of employees.

19 Stonemasons have not been included in this table since some of those enumerated in the CEBs as stonemasons may have been quarry men.

Table 15.4 Selected craft businesses per thousand population: upper and lower Wensleydale and Swaledale, 1823–1893

	Upper Wensleydale	Lower Wensleydale	Swaledale
Blacksmiths			
1823	2.8	3.7	1.7
1840	2.6	3.2	2.2
1857	2.8	3.7	1.6
1872	2.9	3.3	1.9
1893	2.1	3.9	3.1
Stonemasons			
1823	2.0	4.4	0.4
1840	3.3	5.3	2.1
1857	2.7	5.0	1.9
1872	4.0	3.7	2.0
1893	3.8	3.9	4.4
Shoemakers			
1823	4.8	8.5	2.3
1840	5.6	10.6	4.0
1857	6.5	4.7	4.4
1872	5.5	5.9	3.0
1893	4.2	5.6	3.7

Source: Baines, *History of the county of York*; White, *History of East and North Ridings*; Kelly, *Directory of the North and East Ridings*, (1857, 1872, 1893).

Table 15.5 Size of blacksmith and shoemaker businesses: upper and lower Wensleydale and Swaledale, 1841 and 1881

	Number of employers and businesses per thousand population								
	Upper Wensleydale			Lower Wensleydale			Swaledale		
	Emp	Bus	E/B	Emp	Bus	E/B	Emp	Bus	E/B
Blacksmiths									
1841	5.6	2.6	2.2	6.5	3.2	2.0	4.6	2.2	2.1
1881	3.6	2.5	1.4	5.1	3.6	1.4	4.7	2.5	1.9
Shoemakers									
1841	11.0	5.6	2.0	14.6	10.6	1.4	5.0	4.0	1.3
1881	7.8	4.9	1.6	7.7	5.8	1.3	6.4	3.4	1.9

Notes: The 1881 figure for businesses is derived from an average of 1872 and 1893, see Table 15.4.
Emp = Employees; Bus = Businesses; E/B = Number of employees divided by number of businesses.

number of blacksmiths per thousand increased slightly, the size of blacksmiths' businesses fell marginally whereas a marked increase in the number of shoemakers per thousand was translated into a significant increase in the size of shoemakers' businesses.

The general pattern which emerges is one of the size of craft businesses falling in line with the fall in population. The increase in the size of shoemakers' businesses in Swaledale is an unexpected deviation from this pattern.

Table 15.6 Threshold of population at which shoemakers appear: Aysgarth, and upper and lower Wensleydale and Swaledale, 1841, 1871, 1881

	Population per shoemaker			
	Aysgarth	Upper Wensleydale	Lower Wensleydale	Swaledale
1841	30	91	68	199
1871	38	93	169	298
1881	93	128	130	157

The emergence of shoemakers

The spatial distribution of shoemakers illustrates the concentration of some craft occupations in specific townships. Both Aysgarth and, to a lesser extent, Thoralby, specialised in shoemaking. In Thoralby the craft declined from four shoemakers in 1823 to three in 1840 and to one in 1893.[20] The number of shoemakers in Aysgarth declined also, from nine in 1841 to six in 1871 and to four in 1881. In Aysgarth, as Table 15.6 above shows, the population threshold for shoemakers was much lower than in the three areas generally, indicating the extent of specialisation in this craft in Aysgarth.

An Aysgarth shoemaker's account book for the years 1857 to 1873 provides an indication of the amount of business undertaken, and confirms that local shoemakers served a wider area than their immediate village.[21] As with many other craftsmen, the shoemaker, Francis Thompson, followed more than one occupation and was returned as 'farmer and shoemaker' in a contemporary directory.[22] He does not appear to have been an employer of outside labour, but ran his business alone. The account book indicates that Thompson made all types of footwear. The business covered most of Wensleydale and substantial orders were taken from adjacent Coverdale and nearby Richmond. Occasional orders came from Wharfedale. to the south and from places further afield.

In 1861 Thompson achieved a peak of 237 orders and received payments of £296 11s. 6d. The following year his receipts of £308 14s. 2d from 231 orders were the highest of the period. In this year some 50 orders came from Aysgarth, 137 from elsewhere in Wensleydale, 33 from Coverdale (about 6 miles distant), 2 from Swaledale (about 10 miles away), 3 from dales to the south (about 9 miles away) and 6 from

20 Baines, *History of the county of York*, 564; White, *History of East and North Ridings*, 612; Kelly, *Directory of North and East Ridings*, 27. Aysgarth village acted as a mid-dale service centre and throughout the century had a relatively high proportion of its occupied population in crafts and services. The tendency for crafts to cluster in specific areas has been identified elsewhere, Hall, 'Occupation and population structure', 69.

21 Hall MS (Document in private hands), Francis Thompson, Shoemaker's Account Book, 1857–71.

22 Kelly, *Post Office Directory of Yorkshire*, 1164.

Richmond (about 15 miles away). The shoemaker, therefore, was serving an area of up to 20 miles radius from his home. The mileage, however, does not give an indication of the difficult terrain which needed to be traversed to reach all the places outside Wensleydale. The shoemaker received some of his payment in kind, which suggests the continuing existence of a partial barter economy. Several of the individual accounts in each year were for sums in excess of five pounds, indicating that some of Thompson's customers were people of substance.

The business of another shoemaker, Robert Hunter of Askrigg, was neither as large nor covered such an extensive area as that of Francis Thompson.[23] Hunter's business rose to a peak in the mid-nineteenth century when in 1852 he took orders worth £103 11s. 10d. from 128 people. The business quickly declined and throughout the 1860s and 1870s he made shoes for less than 10 people per annum. In 1883 business revived slightly to a peak of 13 people, but then declined and after 1884 he had fewer than 10 customers a year. As with Thompson and in common with craftsmen and tradesmen elsewhere, Hunter also took some of his payments in kind.[24] Most of Hunter's customers were local, but a significant proportion were from Swaledale. Of 128 customers in 1852, at least 24 came from Swaledale, 1 lived in Northallerton, 30 miles away and 1 came from Catterick Bridge, 20 miles away. All the others were from upper Wensleydale. Hunter made large quantities of clogs and, like Thompson, his main market was the local working man. Apart from the relatively buoyant 1850s, unlike Thompson, his customers rarely placed orders amounting to more than one pound.

The rise and fall of the fortunes of the local shoemakers was predictable. Although the footwear industry in Britain was developing into a large wholesale industry in specific locations from the early-nineteenth century, concentration was not pronounced before the middle of the century. The increase in output was due to the expansion of the home market, to export demand and to the requirements of the military for men fighting in the Crimea.[25] Even in 1851 only 6 per cent of the master manufacturers of footwear employed more than 10 men, so the industry remained mainly in the hands of craftsmen.[26] However, an increasing population, coupled with the rise in the standard of living and the influence of fashion, led to a growing demand for footwear and

23 Upper Dales Folk Museum MS, R. Hunter, Shoemaker's Day Books, Askrigg, 1845–96.

24 Chartres, 'County trades', 310; Chartres and Turnbull, 'Country craftsmen', 324–5.

25 Church, 'Labour supply and innovation', 39.

26 Church, 'Labour supply and innovation', 25–6.

encouraged the adoption of technical innovations.[27] This quickened the move into mass-production which eventually led to the demise of the craft of shoemaker. Hunter and Thompson eventually reached their peak of output in the 1850s and 1860s, and, although their decline may have been influenced by personal factors, it coincided with the mass-production of footwear and the arrival of the local railway, first to Leyburn in 1856 and then throughout the dale in 1878.[28] Perhaps the inevitable demise of the local craft industry was foreseen by the shoemaker who placed the following advertisement in a local paper in 1860:

> to be disposed of, the old established business of a clog and shoemaker in a lead mining district which has been carried on with success by one family for fifty years, at present in full operation employing an average of four men.[29]

Conclusion

The census returns and the directories indicate that craft employment in Wensleydale and Swaledale followed the same broad trend that was evident regionally and nationally. Although craft employment may have delayed the consequence of industrialisation and urbanisation for much of rural England, it is widely accepted that by 1900 country crafts were everywhere in decline.[30] This was the case in Wensleydale and Swaledale, although overall decline appears to have been deferred until the last quarter of the nineteenth century, somewhat later than in the country as a whole.[31] Lawton ascribed the rural exodus in the second half of the nineteenth century to the loss of rural industry, much of it in crafts, due to the impact of mechanisation.[32] A general exodus from crafts in the two dales in the second half of the nineteenth century is not discernible and, although in decline, craft employment remained an integral and important element in the economy throughout the century. As a rule, if a craft was in evidence in a township in 1823, it was likely to be present in 1872 and, most probably, still there in 1893, although in decreased numbers.[33] As Saville so appositely comments:

27 Church, 'Labour supply and innovation', 26, 42. Church notes that technical innovation was also encouraged by a short supply of skilled labour in the localities which specialised in footwear manufacture, Church, 'Labour supply and innovation', 29–30.

28 Church, 'Labour supply and innovation', and Hallas, *The Wensleydale railway*.

29 *Richmond and Ripon Chronicle*, 14 July, 1860.

30 Chartres and Turnbull, 'Country craftsmen', 327.

31 Lawton, 'Rural depopulation', 215; Mingay, *Rural life*, 177; Chartres and Turnbull, 'Country craftsmen', 319–20.

32 Lawton, 'Rural depopulation in England', 215.

33 Baines, *History of the county of York*; Kelly, *Post Office Directory of Yorkshire*.

> So long as village and parish populations did not fall markedly, and while the local and regional markets were still intact and under no serious pressure from national competition, the outlook for the rural craftsman was a secure one.[34]

In addition to the impact of mechanisation, improved transport has been regarded generally as one of the principal causal factors in the decline of rural crafts.[35] In Wensleydale and Swaledale this relationship is inconclusive. The isolation of the area, and the consequent high cost of importing factory products, enabled craftsmen in the two dales to continue business long after their counterparts in more accessible parts of the countryside had succumbed to competition from mass-produced goods. It is worth noting that the number of craftsmen in lower Wensleydale increased, both absolutely and per thousand of population, after the arrival of the railway at Leyburn in 1856. However, the fact that the railway was not opened beyond Leyburn until 1878 and failed to penetrate Swaledale beyond Richmond, may account, in some measure, for the relatively later decline of crafts in the two dales.[36] Even after the arrival of the railway it would appear that the potential for receiving large quantities of mass-produced goods was not realised immediately, and the rural craftsman was able to survive in the dales into the twentieth century.

34 Saville, *Rural depopulation*, 209.

35 Saville, *Rural depopulation*, 22; Longstaff, 'Rural depopulation', 414–5; Anderson Graham, *Rural exodus*, 30.

36 Hallas, 'Impact of a rural railway', 31, 43.

16

Who worked when? Lifetime profiles of labour-force participation in Cardington and Corfe Castle in the late-eighteenth and mid-nineteenth centuries

OSAMU SAITO

Introduction

At what age did people enter the labour force in the past? When did individuals stop working? These are straightforward questions, yet nevertheless little systematic investigation has so far been made to answer them.[1] One simple method of exploring these issues is to examine the percentage of males or females in each age group who were employed. For this the CEBs are well-suited as a source. In order to gain a chronological perspective, pre-census listings of inhabitants are also analysed for Cardington, Bedfordshire, in 1782 and Corfe Castle, Dorset, in 1790, both of which are exceptionally detailed and of CEB-like quality.[2] A sample page from each of these two listings is reproduced below (Figures 16.1 and 16.2). Using these sources, this chapter will analyse age- and sex-specific patterns of participation in the labour force. Emphasis will also be laid on the position of the individual in the family with respect to labour supply and the effects of cottage industry on the wife and children of the family.

The communities of Cardington and Corfe Castle

Cardington and Corfe Castle were both located in a rural setting and had some similarities and some differences in economic structure. Neither Bedfordshire nor Dorset were rich counties at the turn of the century. In 1803, for example, poor-relief expenditure per head in the two counties was at about the same level, well above the average for England and Wales of about 9s., whilst the figures for the two parishes themselves, at 22s. for Cardington and 19s. for Corfe Castle, were even higher than the county averages for Bedfordshire and Dorset

1 Exceptions include Conrad, 'Emergence of modern retirement'; Laslett, *Fresh map of life*, 122–39; Thomas, 'Age and authority'; Plakans, 'Stepping down'.

2 Baker, *Inhabitants of Cardington* and Hutchins, *History and antiquities of Dorset*.

Figure 16.1 An example of the list of inhabitants, Cardington, 1782

1st Jany 1782. CARDINGTON. 1.

Cottage No 1.

		Age. Y.	M.	D.
Occupier	Essex Hartop Lab.r Born at Keysor	43	–	–
Wife	Elizabeth, Maiden-name Billen. Born at Cardington And late Wid.w of William Urine. S.L.	46	–	–
Children.	By first Husband viz.			
	1st. Elizabeth, Married at Warden	27	–	–
	2d. Hannah, Married at Meppershall	24	–	–
Children	By her Present Husband: viz.			
	3d. Thomas. Works for Mr. Whitbread	17	–	–
	4th. Mary.	16	–	–
	5th. Phebe S.L.	14	–	–
	6th. Joseph-billen. at School by Mr. Howard.	10	–	–

Note, That S.L. means Spins Linen: S.J. Spins Jersey. S.L.&J. Spins Linen & Jersey; and M.L. makes Lace.

Source: *A general account of the number of persons in each house. January 1st 1782.* Bedfordshire County Record Office, P38/28/1.

Figure 16.2 An example of the list of inhabitants, Corfe Castle, 1790

Housekeepers. Males. Name.	Age	Condition.	Occupation.	Housekeepers. Females. Name.	Age	Condition.	Occupation.	Residence.	Children and Grandchildren resident with their Parents. Males. Name.	Age	Occupation.	Children and Grandchildren. Females. Name.	Age	Occupation.	Name.
—		—	—	Sarah Jenkins	66	Widow	Knits	Mark[t].-pl.	—		—	—		—	—
—		—	—	Ann Rolles	38	Spinster	Baker	Ditto	—		—	—		—	—
Wm. Langtree	38	Married	Butcher	Martha Langtree	38	Married	—	Ditto	Wm. Langtree Tho. Langtree Mary Langtree	13 12 1	Breechesmaker — —	Mary Langtree Eliz. Langtree —	9 4	— — —	— — —
Robert Whitcher	25	Bachelor	Claycutter	—		—	—	—	—		—	—		—	John Trent
William Smith	32	Married	Fisherman	Susanna Smith	29	Married	—	High-str.	William Smith John Smith	5 2	— —	Susanna Smith —	4	— —	— —
—		—	—	Miriam House	45	Widow	Schoolmistress	Ditto	—		—	Elizabeth House Miriam House Susannah House	24 22 18	Plain work, &c Plain work, &c Plain work, &c	— — —
James Chaffey	36	Married	Baker	Frances Chaffey	32	Married	—	Ditto	James Chaffey William Chaffey John Chaffey Henry Chaffey	7 4 1½ ½	— — — —	Sarah Chaffey — — —	9	— — — —	Joseph Chaffey — — —
—		—	—	—		—	—	—	—		—	—		—	—
Rev. John Gent	49	Married	Curate	Mary Gent	29	Married	—	Ditto	John Gent	3	—	Elizabeth Gent Mary Gent Jane Gent	9 7 1	— — —	— — —
—		—	—	Elizabeth Damon	60	Spinster	Knits	Ditto	—		—	—		—	—
Robert Jenkins	38	Married	Shoemaker	Ann Jenkins	28	Married	—	Ditto	Joseph Jenkins	1	—	Mary Jenkins	2	—	Henry Brown
William Butler	60	Married	Blacksmith	Elizabeth Butler	54	Married	—	Ditto	—		—	—		—	—
—		—	—	Julian Webber	67	Widow	Knits, &c.	Ditto	—		—	—		—	—
John Chipp	39	Married	Blacksmith	Honor Chipp	31	Married	—	Ditto	—		—	Mary Chipp, his bast[d] daughter	13	Knits	—
—		—	—	Mary Dennis	70	Widow	Midwife	Ditto	—		—	—		—	Thomas Ridout Tho.Ridout, jun. John Ridout
James Keats	58	Married	Quarrier	Alice Keats	62	Married	—	Ditto	John Keats Joseph Keats	18 11	Quarrier Quarrier	Mary Keats —	15	Knits —	— —
—		—	—	Mary Hibbs	74	Widow	—	Quaker's M. House	—		—	—		—	Barth. Welsh

Lodgers and Inmates. Males. Name.	Age	Condition.	Occupation.	Lodgers and Inmates. Females. Name.	Age	Condition.	Occupation.	Servants and Apprentices. Males. Name.	Age	Servants and Apprentices. Females. Name.	Age	Total per House.	Probable Weekly Earnings	Remarks.
—		—	—	—		—	—	—		—		1	S. Jenkins, 1s.	On Parish Pay.
—		—	—	—		—	—	—		—		1	A. Rolles, 1s. 6d.	
— — —		—	—	— — —		—	—	—		—		7		
John Trent	1	—	—	Hannah Trent Jane Trent	28 2	Married —	Washes, &c. —	—		—		4	R. Whitcher, 10s. H. Trent, 2s. 6d.	Han. Trent's Husband run away.
— —		—	—	Ruth Toop —	21	Spinster —	Knits, &c. —	—		—		6	W. Smith, 7s. R. Toop, 1s. 6d.	H. Trent on Par. Pay.
— — —		—	—	Hetty Murphy — —	13	—	Boarder	—		—		5		
Joseph Chaffey — — —	21	Bachelor	Claycutter	— — — —		—	—	—		—		8	Jos. Chaffey, 10s.	
—		—	—	—		—	—	—		—		0	—	Empty House
— — —		—	—	— — —		—	—	—		Elizabeth Sheers Ann Senneck —	19 18	8		
—		—	—	—		—	—	—		—		1	E. Damon, 1s.	On Parish Pay.
Henry Brown	28	Bachelor	Thatcher	—		—	—	—		—		5	H. Brown, 8s.	
—		—	—	—		—	—	—		—		2		
—		—	—	—		—	—	—		—		1	Julian Webber, 1s.	On Parish Pay.
—		—	—	Mary Chipp, his Mother	66	Widow	Knits	—		—		4	M. Chipp, 1s. M. Chipp, jun. 1s. 6d.	M. Chipp, jun. on Parish Pay.
Thomas Ridout Tho.Ridout, jun. John Ridout	40 16 8	Married — —	Blacksmith Blacksmith —	Jane Ridout, da[r] to Mary Dennis Mary Ridout Ann Ridout Jane Ridout Elizabeth Ridout	40 12 6 3 1	Married — — — —	— Knits — — —	— — — —		— — — —		9		
— —		— —	— —	— —		— —	— —	— —		— —		5	James Keats, 15s. John Keats, 10s. Jos. Keats, 6s. Mary Keats, 1s. 6d.	

Notes: The figure is reproduced in two sections with the first of the columns relating to lodgers repeated for easy reference.

Source: Hutchins, *The history and antiquities of Dorset*, vol. I, xc.

Table 16.1 Occupations of male household heads

	Cardington				Corfe Castle			
	1782[a]		1851		1790		1851	
	n.	%	n.	%	n.	%	n.	%
Agricultural								
Farmer, fisherman	26	17.3	29	11.8	45	21.2	29	8.4
Labourer	89	59.3	146	59.3	42	19.7	84	24.3
Non-agricultural								
Tradesman, craftsman	31	20.7	64	26.0	94	44.1	106	30.7
Clay cutter					28	13.1	93	27.0
Labourer							24	7.0
Not gainfully occupied	4	2.7	7	2.8	4	1.9	9	2.6
Total	150	100.0	246	100.0	213	100.0	345	100.0

Notes: *a* = Unlike other tables in this chapter, this covers all households. Unspecified labourers have been assigned to the agricultural labourers category; the figures for clay cutters in Corfe Castle include quarriers in 1790 and labourers in clay pits in 1851.

respectively.[3] But, as these figures suggest, Cardington may have suffered from economic difficulties at the turn of the century more than Corfe Castle. For the former parish, agriculture was the only means of occupation for men, which meant it was difficult for them to be in constant employment throughout the year.[4] As a result the majority of male children were sent out to work in service in neighbouring parishes.[5] In comparison, Corfe Castle had a small market town within the parish and based its economy not only on farming and trade, but also on other activities such as clay-cutting. This basic difference in occupation structures can be seen in Table 16.1 above. For the women and children of both parishes, textiles and clothing industries of the domestic type offered employment opportunities. In Cardington, lace making and spinning were carried out by women and female children, while spinning and knitting were found in Corfe Castle, although Corfe women, especially married women, were much less involved in industrial activity than the Cardington women.

Changes in local economic structure over the first half of the nineteenth century also affected the two parishes differently. It seems

3 *Abstract of the Answers and Returns made pursuant to the Act 43 Geo. 3, relative to the Expense and Maintenance of the Poor*, BPP 1803–4. Population figures are taken from the 1801 census. Studies of both Bedfordshire and Dorset poor law administration and practice indicate that increases in poor expenditure in this period were not the results of maladministration but responses to growing economic distress; therefore, we may rely on per capita expenditure as a rough guide to the poverty problem in each parish. See Grey, 'Pauper problem in Bedfordshire', and Body, 'Administration of the poor laws'.

4 Stone, *Agriculture of the County of Bedford, 1794*, as cited by Marshall, *Reports to the Board of Agriculture*, 561.

5 Schofield, 'Age-specific mobility' and Wall, 'Age at leaving home'. For more general information on age-specific mobility see Wall, 'Leaving home' and Schürer, 'The role of the family'.

clear from Table 16.1 that there were no significant shifts in occupational structure of male household heads, which was the core of the whole economic structure. Lace making, too, which does not appear in the table, is likely to have recovered from the recession after the French wars, despite the severe competition from the machine-based counterpart, and still occupied a lot of Bedfordshire women in the 1850s.[6] However, some important changes were taking place behind the seeming stability. In Bedfordshire, agriculture, which was described by Thomas Stone in his *Report* to the Board of Agriculture in 1794 as in 'a deplorable state',[7] had improved by the mid-nineteenth century. This improvement, especially in the clay lands in the northern part of the county where Cardington is located, was attributed to successful underdraining, which was often combined with enclosure and engrossing. Thus, in 1857, William Bennett wrote:

> At the commencement of the present century no county in England, probably, stood in need of underdraining more than Bedfordshire, and within that period few counties have made greater progress in this department of good husbandry.[8]

In Dorset, on the other hand, while the clay industry was still prosperous in the 1850s, cottage industries, such as stocking-knitting which was found in Corfe Castle in 1790, had disappeared as a result of competition from the east Midlands.[9] Spinning, the other industrial activity that occupied the Corfe females in 1790, and which had been introduced originally to provide jobs for the poor, was already in the mid–1790s described by a contemporary as a failure.[10]

Thus the analysis which follows is of two communities with different economic circumstances. These can be summarised as follows. In Cardington in 1782, the problem of poverty arising from the instability of employment in farming must have been very serious, although the cottage industries offered ample employment opportunities to women and children. In 1851, however, agriculture could employ more men than in 1782, while a large number of females were still engaged in industrial activities. In Corfe Castle in 1790, males had a wider occupational choice than in Cardington and employment opportunities for females also were not lacking. However, in 1851, whilst the major industry which employed males was still thriving, the industrial employment for females had all but completely disappeared.

6 Horn, 'Child workers', 781–2. In this, however, she does not touch on adult women workers.

7 Marshall, *Reports to the Board of Agriculture*, 561.

8 Bennett, 'Farming of Bedfordshire', 4. Moreover, it seems that the judgement expressed in various forms that land was under-utilised had already disappeared by the 1840s, personal communication from Mr Peter Grey formerly of Bedford College of Education.

9 Body, 'Administration of the poor laws', 45.

10 Hutchins, *History and antiquities of Dorset*, 276.

It is against this economic background that the patterns of labour-force participation will be discussed.

The sources

Before the analysis is presented, the main sources used should be evaluated, especially in terms of the extent to which they recorded occupations accurately. First, it must be realised that the CEBs do not provide a total picture of employment. The main concern of the General Registry Office was to collect information on the numbers in gainful employment. Thus, adult males in full-time paid employment tend to be recorded quite accurately. Equally, those *usually* in full-time work but otherwise temporarily out of work should also have been recorded as such by the enumerators. Yet for others in more marginal forms of employment, those employed part-time or on a casual basis for example, the situation is less certain.[11] The 1851 census for Corfe Castle lists a small number of individuals as 'occasionally works on farm', 'weeding' or 'stone picking', yet this is the exception rather than the rule. As a result, the enumeration of the work undertaken by women and children is especially problematic. In the case of farmers, the census of 1851 explicitly instructed sons or daughters employed at home or on the farm to be returned as 'Farmer's son', etc., and the example page on how to complete the census schedule gave an example of a 'Farmer's wife' on the assumption that the family of the householder would be actively involved in the work of the farm.[12] Despite the fact that the 1851 census, like those of 1861–81, instructed that 'the occupations of women who are regularly employed from home, or at home, in any but domestic duties, [are] to be distinctly recorded', evidence points to the fact that the employment of women was prone to under-enumeration, especially in cases where work was of an infrequent or informal basis.[13] The same is also true of children.[14] In short, in instructing their enumerators and processing the information on employment, the officials of the General Registry Office clung rather too rigidly to the oversimplistic and idealised notion of an adult male 'breadwinner' head of household providing for his dependent family.[15]

11 The enumeration of employment is discussed in Higgs, *Making sense*, 78–85; *Clearer sense*, 95–112. For a more general discussion on the problems of interpreting occupation information see chapter 13; Schürer, 'Understanding and coding occupations'; Morris, 'Fuller values, questions and contexts'.

12 Due to the vagaries of the recording of farmers and other agricultural occupations the overall numbers working in agriculture presented in the published Census Reports has been questioned. See Higgs, 'Occupational censuses' and Wrigley, 'Men on the land'.

13 See Higgs, 'Women, occupations and work'; Garrett, 'Women's work'.

14 See Davin, 'Working or helping?'.

15 See Horrell and Humphries, 'Transition to the male-breadwinner family'.

Table 16.2 Labour-force participation rates by sex and age group

Age group	Males								Females							
	Cardington				Corfe Castle				Cardington				Corfe Castle			
	1782		1851		1790		1851		1782		1851		1790		1851	
	%	n.	%	n.	%	n.	%	n.	%	n.	%	n.	%	n.	%	n.
5–9	0.0	39	9.8	112	10.8	83	0.0	124	23.3	43	39.0	77	13.3	83	0.7	137
10–14	2.4	42	66.3	98	55.3	76	36.4	129	66.7	39	64.9	74	69.7	76	10.7	92
15–19	80.0	5	94.7	76	96.5	57	98.2	110	80.8	26	77.9	77	79.2	53	40.5	111
20–24	80.0	10	92.6	54	92.7	41	93.9	66	79.3	29	76.3	59	67.4	43	38.7	62
25–29	95.0	20	93.0	57	100.0	36	100.0	71	89.5	19	72.1	61	42.1	57	21.4	70
30–34	94.1	17	97.7	43	100.0	38	96.4	55	87.0	23	67.3	49	34.3	35	8.7	46
35–39	100.0	12	100.0	34	100.0	46	100.0	47	73.7	19	62.5	48	24.3	37	13.2	53
40–44	100.0	15	96.8	31	100.0	23	98.3	59	61.9	21	52.9	34	34.6	26	13.0	54
45–49	100.0	16	100.0	28	100.0	24	97.9	48	72.2	18	59.4	32	22.2	27	2.9	34
50–54	100.0	15	96.6	29	100.0	22	100.0	28	35.7	14	50.0	24	39.3	28	17.6	34
55–59	90.0	11	96.2	26	100.0	18	95.2	21	50.0	10	60.0	25	26.3	19	19.2	26
60+	81.0	21	87.5	40	88.5	61	84.7	72	46.7	15	67.3	49	36.7	60	8.2	85

Notes: This table excludes all cases where age is unknown, and for Cardington, 1782, farmers, clergymen and persons of independent means, and their families and servants.

Since both the listing of inhabitants for Cardington and Corfe Castle were 'one-off' enumerations lacking the formal procedures and administration of the CEBs, it is not so easy to comment on the completeness with which employment was recorded. Generally, like the CEBs, adult males seem to be reasonably fully recorded, yet in the case of Cardington there are two notable and unfortunate omissions. Unlike the CEBs, the families of farmers, including sons, are not designated by an occupation description. Also, although the Cardington survey provides unique information on the occupation of children of families who were resident in the village, but for those who were employed as servants outside of the parish, this information is not reciprocal. In other words, information is lacking on servants employed in Cardington who had come to the parish to work from the surrounding villages. Consequently, in the analysis that follows, the children of farmers are excluded from the Cardington figures, as are all living-in servants. Other minor adjustments are noted in the subsequent tables.

Age- and sex-specific participation rates

The proportion of men and women in each group employed in Cardington and Corfe Castle at the end of the eighteenth century and in 1851 is shown in Table 16.2 above and diagrammatically in Figures 16.3 and 16.4 below. It is clear from the two graphs that the profile for males does not vary a great deal. In all cases, except in Cardington in 1782, the rate of participation rises sharply to the age of 15, remains on a plateau during the prime working ages and falls in the age group 60 plus. This pattern suggests that the age of 15 saw boys rush into the labour force in the form of either going into service away from the

Figure 16.3 Age-specific profiles of labour-force participation: males

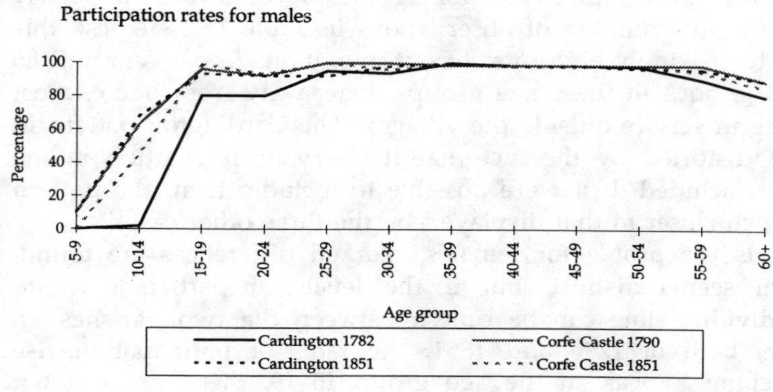

Figure 16.4 Age-specific profiles of labour-force participation: females

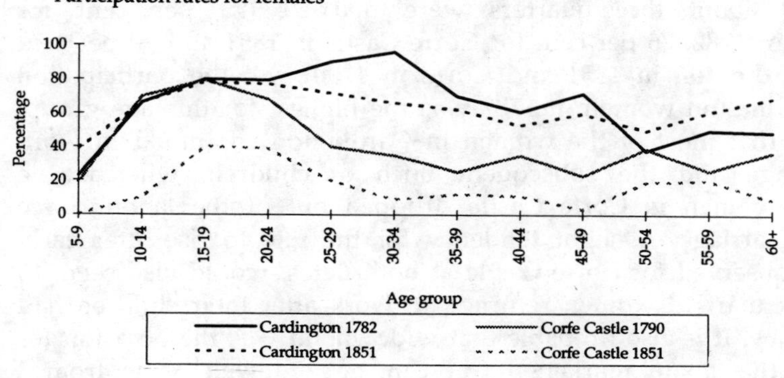

parental home or taking employment at home; that almost all males in ages between 15 and 59 had a gainful occupation; and that some of them began to stop working after the age of 60. For Cardington in 1782, the labour-force participation rates for ages 15–19 and 20–24 are fairly low, but as the low number of observations in Table 16.2 suggest, this may be due to strikingly high rates of out-migration: 78 per cent and 85 per cent of the boys in these age groups were away from home, most of them being in service outside the village.[16] The Cardington pattern in 1782 is also distorted by the fact that the servant population in the village is not included. If it were possible to include them, the pattern would be much closer to that displayed by the three other cases.

As regards the profile for females, marked differences are found. Each pattern seems distinct, but if the levels of participation are ignored, a dividing line can be drawn between the two parishes. In Corfe Castle, both in 1790 and 1851, the rates of participation rise rapidly, reaching a peak in the age group 15–19, then comes down quickly to a low level, and then shows a slight upward turn (although it has been admitted the latter is almost obscured by fluctuations in the rate between age groups). In Cardington in 1782, on the other hand, the rate continues to rise until the age group 25–29, and the lowest point does not occur in early adulthood but in the age group 50–54. In 1851, although a peak is apparent in the age group 15–19, as in Corfe Castle, the rate shows a more gradual decline after this peak than Corfe and a shallower trough in the age group 50–54 compared with the 1782 data.

It is evident that the differences between the patterns of the two parishes were mainly due to behaviour of married women. Of those aged 25–29 about three-quarters were married (79 per cent for Cardington in 1782, 76 per cent for Corfe Castle in 1851 and 70 per cent both for Cardington in 1851 and Corfe in 1790), yet the participation rate for Cardington women in 1782 was the highest for this age group. This means that most of the women in Cardington continued to work after marriage and the subsequent birth of children, whereas the majority of women in Corfe Castle dropped out of the labour force soon after marriage. A slight tendency for the rate to rise after early adulthood, observed for Corfe Castle at both dates, would also seem to indicate that married women returned to work after their children had passed infancy. It is also probable that widowhood was the occasion for a return to the labour market: the percentage widowed rising from 3 per cent for ages 20–39 to 20 per cent for 40–59 in 1790, and from 2 per cent to 15 per cent in 1851. Indeed, as is shown in Table 16.3 below, more widowed than married women were employed under the age

16 Schofield, 'Age-specific mobility', 265; Wall, 'Age at leaving home', Table 2.

Table 16.3 Labour force participation rates for married and widowed women by age group

	Married				Widowed			
	1782/90		1851		1782/90		1851	
	%	tot. n.	%	tot. n.	%	tot. n.	%	tot. n.
Cardington								
20–39	82.0	61	66.7	114	80.9	21	70.0	20
40–59	51.1	47	61.0	77	–	–	–	–
60+	60.0	5	55.0	20	40.0	10	72.0	25
Overall	67.5	114	63.7	211	67.7	31	71.1	45
Corfe Castle								
20–39	8.0	87	2.7	147	86.4	22	48.1	27
40–59	6.5	62	3.7	109	–	–	–	–
60+	21.8	23	0.0	40	76.5	17	11.4	35
Overall	8.7	172	2.7	296	82.1	39	27.4	62

Notes: The table excludes wives or widows of farmers. The figure for Cardington, 1782, includes wives under the age of 20.

of 60.[17] Evidence for such a return to the labour market is less prominent among the Cardington women. This, however, is perhaps largely due to the fact that a much greater proportion of women tended to remain in work throughout the early post-marriage and child-rearing periods.[18]

Finally, although one might have expected that women, whether widowed or not, would stop working after the age of 60, this was not always true. In Corfe Castle in 1790, for example, the percentage increases after age 60. As can be seen from Table 16.3, the employment situation of elderly women is far from clear-cut.

Turning attention to the situation of children and young adults, Tables 16.4 and 16.5 below confirm what has already been said concerning the economic conditions in the two communities in the late-eighteenth century. Three facts suggest that the Cardington boys were suffering from a lack of local employment. A very low proportion of the boys under the age of 15 were in the labour force; a very small number of those aged 15 and over were employed at home; and only a

17 However, this does not mean that the number of young children to be cared for had no bearing in the decision of women to enter the labour force. A similar situation to that described by Garrett for the textile town of Keighley, Yorkshire, in which early marriage and child bearing facilitated the return to work, may have prevailed. See Garrett, 'Trials of labour'.

18 The tendency for married women to re-enter the labour force after their children grew up was not observed in the Lancashire textile factory town of Preston in 1851; Anderson, *Family structure*, 72. However, among Irish married women in London and framework knitters' wives in Shepshed, Leicestershire, in the same year, the percentage employed rose slightly from the middle to later stages of the life-cycle: Lees, 'Mid-Victorian migration', 34; Levine, *Family formation*, 29. The more detailed work of Garrett points to the fact that for low-status textile workers the combined factors of early marriage and low and early fertility enabled women to rejoin the work force. The wives of higher-status families tended not to return to the factories, while a return to work for widows was relatively common place. Garrett, 'Trials of labour'.

Table 16.4 Labour-force participation rates for children by sex and age group

	Males				Females			
	1782/90		1851		1782/90		1851	
	%	n.	%	n.	%	n.	%	n.
Cardington								
5–14	1.2	81	37.0	189	43.9	82	60.3	121
15+	75.0	8	92.2	103	83.3	48	83.5	91
Corfe Castle								
5–14	32.1	140	18.3	241	42.5	134	1.4	208
15+	94.4	54	94.5	145	75.9	58	34.6	127

Notes: Married children resident with parent/s; servants; and the children of farmers, clergymen and persons of independent means are all excluded from this table. In the case of Corfe Castle, children of dairymen/women, however, are included, for some are supposed to have been agricultural labourers and it is hard to distinguish them from graziers.

Table 16.5 Occupations of children

	Cardington				Corfe Castle			
	1782		1851		1790		1851	
	n.	%	n.	%	n.	%	n.	%
Male Children								
Craftsman/tradesman	5	71.4	14	8.5	28	29.1	39	21.9
Labourers								
Agricultural	–	–	144	87.8	30	32.3	74	41.6
Clay cutting	–	–	–	–	14	14.6	32	18.0
Other	–	–	–	–	4	4.2	12	6.7
Rope making	–	–	–	–	10	10.4	–	–
Other	2	28.6	6	3.7	10	10.4	21	11.8
Totals	7	100.0	164	100.0	96	100.0	178	100.0
Female children								
Agriculture	–	–	–	–	–	–	9	20.0
Textiles/clothing								
Spinning	11	15.1	–	–	26	26.3	–	–
Knitting	–	–	–	–	68	68.7	–	–
Lace making	61	83.9	119	79.9	–	–	–	–
Straw plaiting	–	–	12	8.1	–	–	5	11.1
Other	–	–	11	7.3	2	2.0	19	42.2
Other	1	1.4	7	4.7	3	3.0	12	26.7
Totals	73	100.0	149	100.0	99	100.0	45	100.0

Notes: Children of farmers are excluded from this table.

few occupations were available for them in the village. For the Corfe boys, on the contrary, almost the reverse was true, while girls in both parishes seem to have been in a similar situation. Two-thirds of girls in the age group 5–14 and more than three fourths in the 15–plus group

Table 16.6 Occupations of married and widowed women

	Cardington				Corfe Castle			
	1782		1851		1790		1851	
	n.	%	n.	%	n.	%	n.	%
Agriculture	–	–	–	–	–	–	6	25.0
Textiles/clothing								
Spinning	48	49.5	–	–	8	17.0	–	–
Knitting	–	–	–	–	25	53.2	1	4.2
Lace making	37	38.1	135	81.3	–	–	–	–
Straw plaiting	–	–	13	7.8	–	–	1	4.2
Other	3	3.1	4	2.4	2	4.3	2	8.3
Other	9	9.3	14	8.4	12	25.5	14	58.3
Totals	97	100.0	166	100.0	47	100.0	24	100.0

had an occupation, most of them being employed in cottage industries. By 1851, as shown in Table 16.4, some changes had occurred in the levels of participation in the labour force. Many more sons of the Cardington cottagers stayed in the village as agricultural labourers than had done so in 1782. For the Corfe girls, as spinning and knitting had disappeared, the percentage employed at ages 15 and above was half the earlier level, and the number of 5–15 year-olds in the labour force had become negligible. In contrast, the Corfe boys had not been seriously affected, thanks to the thriving clay industry, except that they were no longer involved in rope making, which had given employment to younger children. While lace making in Cardington occupied roughly the same proportion of girls in 1851 as it had in 1782, spinning had disappeared, with its place being taken by the spread of straw-plaiting and other miscellaneous forms of employment.

Turning to the question of the labour-force participation of women, it is clear that the disappearance of the cottage industries in Corfe Castle affected adult women more than female children. Among adult women, some contrasts are found when marital status is controlled for. About two-thirds of married women were working in Cardington, whereas less than one-tenth were recorded as employed in Corfe Castle. But the figures for widows are much less divergent and, hence, the difference between married and widowed women is wide in Corfe Castle but quite small in Cardington (Table 16.6 above). In 1851 only 8 out of 296 married women were given an occupation, and the percentage for widows, who presumably had a greater need for cash income, also declined from 82 per cent to 27 per cent. On the other hand, the proportion of Cardington women in the labour force hardly changed. Looking at the figures for all age groups, slightly fewer married women and slightly more widows were employed. However, a discernible shift had occurred in the age structure of the employed female population. Fewer women at an earlier stage of married life and more at a later stage had employment in 1851 than in 1782, although the percentage for ages 20–39 was still as high as 67 per cent in 1851. This shift may be interpreted as greater care being devoted to young children than in the late-eighteenth century, and it is likely that this new situation, together with the higher proportion of male children employed at home, reflected an improvement in economic conditions which took place during the 70 years after 1782.

Economic considerations and family work

Due to the relative stability of the labour participation rates it is possible to conclude that the duration of the working live's of adult males was quite insensitive to changes over the period in economic circumstances. The same is also true, to some extent, of male children aged 15–19, although it seems that they did have to face a choice between going into service and staying at home in underemployment when no industrial employment was available in the parish. Indeed, if employment opportunities outside Cardington had not been available for the Cardington boys in 1782, the only work available to them would have been seasonal work in the fields. On the other hand, the figures for females, both adults and children, and male children under the age of 15, showed variability according to the prevailing economic conditions of the parish. Among females, the proportion of widows and girls aged 15 and over in the labour force exceeded that of married women and girls under 15. The difference between married and widowed women (except for those aged 60 and over) probably arises from the fact that widowhood forced them to re-enter the labour market to support their families.

In families where both parents were present, it appears that it was children who first had to take employment to supplement their father's earnings when the family was under pressure of poverty. Since boys over 15 were supposed to start working whatever the circumstances, it was girls, especially those over 15, who entered the labour market in response to the family's needs. Obviously, the difference between boys and girls at the point of entry into the labour force was dependent on what kind, as well as what amount, of demand for labour existed in or around the village, and hence, dependent on what amount of money could be earned, for the range of occupations for boys and their earning powers was different from girls.[19] Yet it is interesting to see that the wife was probably in a more marginal position with respect to

19 The 1790 Corfe Castle listing gives, though not in all cases (n=31), 'probable' weekly earnings of individuals, which show that, given the differences in occupations available, a boy under the age of 15 could on average earn 2s. 7d., twice as much as a girl of the same age.

Table 16.7 Working wives with at least one daughter of working age

	Daughter/s Working	Daughter/s Not working	Total
Daughter's age 15+			
Cardington			
1782	6	1	7
1851	32	2[a]	34
Corfe Castle			
1790	4	0	4
1851	1	0	1
Daughter's age 10–14			
Cardington			
1782	5	6	11
1851	26	4	30
Corfe Castle			
1790	4	0	4
1851	1	0	1

Notes: All cases where husbands had no recorded occupation are excluded.
a = Includes one case where one of the daughters in the relevant age group was working.

labour supply than daughters over fifteen, despite very little differences in the range of occupations available and wages earned among females in various age groups.[20]

This proposition can be tested by breaking down the cases of working wives with at least one daughter of working age according to whether the daughter or daughters worked or not (Table 16.7 above). If all or nearly all the daughters worked, this can be taken to mean that the wife only had to work when the family income had to be supplemented, even though the daughters had already begun to earn.[21] As far as the age group 15+ is concerned, Table 16.7 gives support to the hypothesis, for three cases in the 'not working' column turn out to be exceptions. One is the case of a daughter aged 16 with her working sister aged 14 – the 16-year-old must have been unable to work for some reason. A second is a similar case, where one of the two daughters, both over 20, did not work. A third is the case of a craftsman's wife who owned a shop, which suggests that some factors other than necessity may have played a part in determining the participation rate of the female members of that family. For the

20 The weekly earnings of females (all marital statuses combined) from spinning and knitting in Corfe in 1790 were as follows: under 14, 1s. 3d.; 15–19, 1s. 4d.; 20–29, 1s. 7d.; 30–39, 1s. 4d.; 40–49, 1s. 2d.; 60+, 1s. 1d.

21 Table 16.7 does not include wives who were not working. Rather more of these had daughters who were also non-workers. In this category, there were more tradesmen and craftsmen than is the case of families with working wives. However, it is interesting that there were a significant number of families with non-working mothers but working daughters.

daughters aged 10–14, the results are much less conclusive. An interpretation might be that their position in the family was as marginal as that of the wife.

Conclusion

Since information about wage rates and other factors which determine the supply of labour is scanty and indirect, it is not possible to explain the findings in precise terms. Nor is it wise to draw a general picture of the profile of labour-force participation in the past from the evidence presented in this chapter. Not only is the analysis based on only two parish examples, but also the documents used provide very little information about part-time or seasonal work. Consequently, it remains unknown if productive but unpaid work was undertaken by family members. This type of work, together with seasonal work, clearly constituted an important part of the world of work in the past.

However, one thing is clear. The effect of cottage industry on the labour-force participation profiles of females was remarkable and perhaps even unique. This claim is based on the fact that none of the twentieth-century industrialised countries, where an upward trend in activity rates of married women is almost universal, shows such a high figure (82 per cent) as Cardington in 1782 produced for married women aged 20–39. The 1971 census for England and Wales, for example, records an activity rate of 58 per cent for married women aged 45–54, but this is for married women whose child-rearing period is over and the figure also includes part-time employment and those temporarily out of work.[22] If the pattern found for the Cardington women in 1782 should turn out to be unique, it was probably a consequence of the combined effect of poverty and opportunity provided by cottage industry, given the fact that the wife was in a marginal position in the family in relation to the supply of labour.[23] Some of the occupations available for women in the industrialised world can let women combine work and home so easily. As the availability of part-time jobs at office or factory has grown, child-care and household work have become less of a barrier to women re-entering the labour market, but even so, this

22 For the English experience in the twentieth century, see Gales and Marks, 'The work of women', 67.

23 It is interesting that the Cardington figures for married women in employment, both in 1782 and 1851, are far greater than those for Shepshed in 1851, which has been called 'the most intensively industrialised village in Leicestershire' – 67.5 per cent and 63.7 per cent of married women in Cardington were employed, as against 39.6 per cent in Shepshed (all figures exclude the wives of farmers; Shepshed percentage calculated from Levine, *Family formation*, 51). We do not know, however, what accounts for this. It might be because Cardington families were poorer than those of Shepshed, although Shepshed, too, provides a good example of coexistence of poverty and cottage industry, or it could be that framework knitting, in which most of the working wives in Shepshed were employed, required relatively less female labour. Indeed, even if we take just the wives of framework knitters, whose wages were lower than those of agricultural labourers, only 49.3 per cent were working (Levine, *Family formation*, 22, 29–30, 51).

trend has not produced a pattern similar to the Cardington one. It would be too early to speculate at this stage if the victory of the factory over the domestic system has increased or decreased the aggregate demand for female labour,[24] but the decline of cottage industry must certainly have had a great impact on the life-time profile of female labour-force participation. How great this could be may be judged from the striking differences in the age pattern and participation levels between Cardington in 1782 and Corfe Castle in 1851.

24 For contrasting views, see McKendrick, 'Home demand and economic growth' and Richards, 'Women in the British economy'.

17

Combining estate records with census enumerators' books to study nineteenth-century communities: the case of the Tankersley ironstone miners, c. 1850

MELVYN JONES

Introduction

Although the use of the CEBs has been quite extensive, with the notable exception of the house repopulation technique, their use in conjunction with other contemporary sources, particularly when they are in a supporting role, has been less widely reported.[1] This chapter is concerned with demonstrating some of the ways in which CEBs[2] can be used alongside the records of a landed estate to shed light on certain aspects of the social and economic structure of industrial communities in a semi-rural setting.

The estate in question was, in the mid-nineteenth century, the south Yorkshire property of the fifth Earl Fitzwilliam (1736–1857). It occupied an extensive area between the towns of Barnsley and Rotherham, with outlying parts in Sheffield. Altogether it covered more than 17,000 acres. The main estate, which extended over large parts of the extensive Wath and Rotherham parishes and one third of the parish of Tankersley, was centred on Wentworth Woodhouse, a large Palladian mansion in Wentworth township in the parish of Wath (Figure 17.1 below).

Outcropping within the estate were several important coal and ironstone seams which were worked from at least the mid-eighteenth century. The most important of these were the Barnsley coal seam, which was nine feet thick in this area, and the Tankersley ironstone seam. The Tankersley ironstone seam, as shown in Figure 17.1, outcrops to the west of Tankersley Park, a medieval deer park, and then swings eastwards through Wentworth township to the south of Wentworth Woodhouse and its park. The seam dips away beneath Tankersley parish and Wentworth township, towards the north-east. Obviously minerals are first exploited at their outcrop where they can be reached

1 Examples of this technique may be found in Henstock's chapter 29 in this volume and Mills, 'House repopulation', 86–97.

2 Using the 1851 CEBs for the Tankersley area: HO 107/2333, HO 107/2334, HO 107/2345.

Figure 17.1 The study area

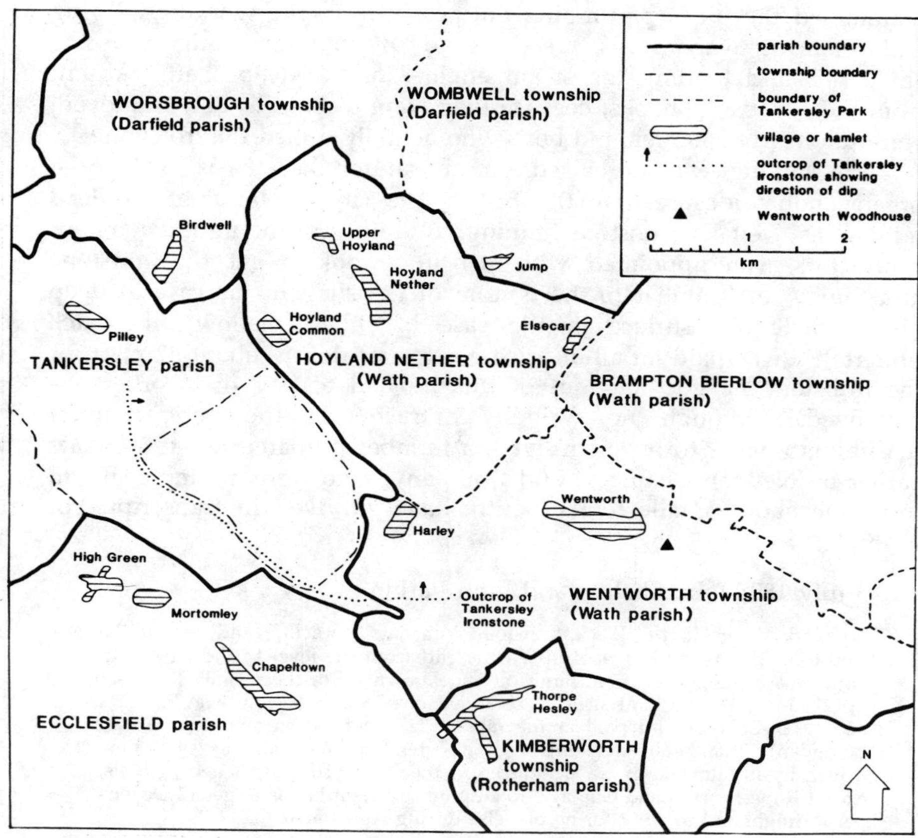

without undue difficulty, but later, deeper pits have to be sunk to reach the dipping seams. In the case of the Tankersley ironstone, mining first took place on the western and south-western edges of the park, then moved to the north of the park, then into its central and eastern parts, and finally beyond the park to a deep pit in Hoyland Nether township. From the early-nineteenth century until *c.* 1880 the ironstone supplied the Elsecar and Milton ironworks in Hoyland Nether township.

A casual browser among the Wentworth Woodhouse Muniments in Sheffield Archives[3] could be forgiven for believing that ironstone mining on Earl Fitzwilliam's estate in south Yorkshire in the mid-nineteenth century was a very small industry indeed. The 1853 wage books, for example, list only about 40 men and boys at the ironstone

3 Wentworth Woodhouse Muniments in Sheffield Archives. Referred to hereafter as WWM/SA.

grounds.[4] For the most part, the persons named in the wage books were members of a small staff, headed by a mineral agent, who maintained the pits by pumping out water from the workings, laying and repairing wagonways, erecting and dismantling headgear at the small pits and tending the steam engines at the deep shafts. Absent from the 1853 wage books, because they were technically self-employed, were the nearly 300 men and boys who actually mined the ironstone.

The mining was organised on an 'undertaker' basis, a type of organisation widespread in the British Isles in coal mining and lead mining as well as ironstone mining. In this system, undertakers, or contractors, were appointed, who then undertook to 'get' the ironstone and 'hurry' or 'tram' it to the bottom of the shaft in the case of deep pits, and to the surface in the case of small, shallow pits. Each undertaker was paid an all-in price per ton or dozen (about 42 cwt) for the ironstone he got, and out of this he had to pay the workers he employed. Although no written contracts for the period under discussion appear to have survived, a number prepared about 50 years earlier by Newton Chambers and Company, who were mining coal and ironstone about a mile to the south, have survived in transcript. For example:

5 July 1805 John Shelton and John Parkin.[5]

To work 2 pits in the Black Ironstone Mine at Thorncliffe and get all the Ironstone 31 yds more or less up on the end from the level to the Bassett in both pits, to be got, hurried, hung on and Drawn on to the pit hill, to be set up 22" high, 18' x 3' and shall be reckoned one Doz to be led away in carts and D/D C Ft 81 and paid at the rate of 22/- per Dozen, and to allow to L(ongden) C(hambers) N(ewton) & Co 6/- per Dozen for all the levels new driven by instalments of 1/- per dozen of the stone. To find their own tools, except Ropes, corves and Gin, also to employ sufficient hands to get 12 Dozens per fortnight and to work for no one else during Agreement.

			His	
Witness	John Hollings	John		Shelton
	5/- Ernest	John		Parkin
			Mark	

Given the organisation of the industry, its rural setting and its location in a largely unpopulated part of the Wentworth estate away from established settlements, a number of interesting questions spring to mind: did the ironstone miners live in isolation or were they drawn from the established villages and hamlets in the area? From where did the miners commute to work? Did kinship play an important role in recruitment into undertakers' teams? To what extent did incomers find employment in the small tightly knit work units?

4 WWM/SA A1557.

5 Miscellaneous Documents in Sheffield Archives, MD/SCL 3590(d). Comparison with other agreements show that the abbreviation D/D means delivered, and C ft 81 means 81 cubic feet.

Two lists of estate employees in the Wentworth Woodhouse Muniments, when used in conjunction with the enumerators' books of the 1851 census, enable us to address these questions in some detail and with some confidence.

The nature of the estate records

The first list is an enumeration of the 100 men and boys who were employed at the ironstone grounds in September 1849.[6] The workforce is divided into 14 undertakers' teams, 12 working in small bell pits and 2 at a deep pit, with the undertakers (10) or partnerships of undertakers (4) clearly indicated at the head of each team. For each miner the full name and place of residence are given and, in the case of those under 20 years of age, their ages.

In 1849, only one of the two ironworks in Hoyland Nether was in blast, but two months later both works were leased to a Staffordshire ironmaster. The demand for ironstone grew quickly and the number of ironstone miners increased accordingly. The relatively small and fluctuating numbers of ironstone miners in the 1840s, and the rapid expansion in the early 1850s, were recorded with great accuracy in detailed lists, compiled by the various heads of department on the Fitzwilliam south Yorkshire estate, for the purpose of distributing the St Thomas' Day charity donation on 21 December each year and the Collop Monday charity in March each year.[7] It is not clear when these two charities began, or when they ceased, and this is the subject of further research. Detailed lists have been located for 1768, 1811–28 and 1841–56.[8] The charities are mentioned in the account books for other years, but no other detailed lists appear to have survived. At the back of the 1849 list there is a 'Rule of Admissability' to a claim for the St Thomas' Day donation: 'Any person regularly employed in the Service of Earl Fitzwilliam and employed at that time. Persons employed at that time at a merely occasional job are not entitled.'[9] The note also instructed each head of department to attend 'to identify his men'. A quantity of meat and a sum of money were given on St Thomas' Day and meat only on Collop Monday.

It is the St Thomas' Day list for 1850 that has been analysed for the purposes of this study.[10] The complete list names 1,242 persons grouped according to occupation and, in some cases, principally miners, by place of work. The list included 606 men and boys employed at collieries, 271

6 WWM/SA G-45.

7 In the supplement to his *Sheffield Glossary* 1891, Sidney Oldall Addy stated that on Collop Monday, the day before Shrove Tuesday, 'poor people go to their richer neighbours to beg a collop or slice of bacon, to supply the fat in which pancakes are baked on the following day', 13.

8 WWM/SA R2A–42; WWM/SA A1543; WWM/SA A1412–A1424.

9 WWM/SA A1412.

10 WWM/SA A1419.

men and boys employed at the ironstone pits, 77 employees at the estate workshops and on a railway, 41 farm workers at the home farm, 28 carpenters, 26 woodmen, 16 grooms, and sundry gatekeepers, masons, slaters, quarrymen, bricklayers, painters and glaziers, millers, saddlers, smiths and former employees and widows of former employees in almshouses. A few names among the lists of male workers were of women, denoting widows on estate pensions.

The 1850 St Thomas' Day list was compiled on 16 December, just three and a half months before the 1851 census (which was conducted on the night of 30/31 March) and then adjusted for the Collop Monday charity three weeks before the census (Collop Monday was on 10 March in 1851). Seventy-nine of the one hundred ironstone miners named in the 1849 list, and 251 of the 271 named in the 1850 list, have been identified in the 1851 census.

Ironstone miners' places of residence and extent of residential segregation

Figure 17.2 below shows the distribution of the places of residence of the 251 ironstone miners who were identified from the December 1850 St Thomas' Day list (D), compared with the distribution of the places of residence of coal miners working in three collieries in the same area also owned by Earl Fitzwilliam (A, B and C), In the December 1850 St Thomas' Day list there were 87 men and boys employed at Elsecar High Colliery, 121 at Elsecar Mid-Colliery and 88 at the recently opened Elsecar Low Colliery. Of these, 83 employed at Elsecar High, 115 at Elsecar Mid and 82 at Elsecar Low have been located in the 1851 census returns. The search in the census returns for both the ironstone and coal miners covered all those townships and/or parishes named in Figure 17.2 (A), together with Wortley township to the west of Tankersley. What needs to be emphasised is that in Hoyland and the surrounding townships and parishes there were miners of coal and ironstone who were employed in collieries and ironstone pits other than those owned by Earl Fitzwilliam. The combined use of the charity list and the enumerators' returns results in the identification of miners working at specific places rather than coal miners and ironstone miners in general.

In one sense, Figure 17.2 contains few surprises in that, as expected, there is generally a close relationship between place of work and place of residence, but a close inspection of the maps reveals some interesting minor spatial patterns. The existence of an estate-built mining village at Elsecar explains the concentration of coal miners in the eastern corner of Hoyland township in close proximity to two of the collieries. Outside Elsecar there are some interesting variations over short distances. For example, the village of Hoyland Nether at the centre of Hoyland, with

Figure 17.2 Distribution of the places of residence of Elsecar coal miners and Tankersley ironstone miners, December 1850

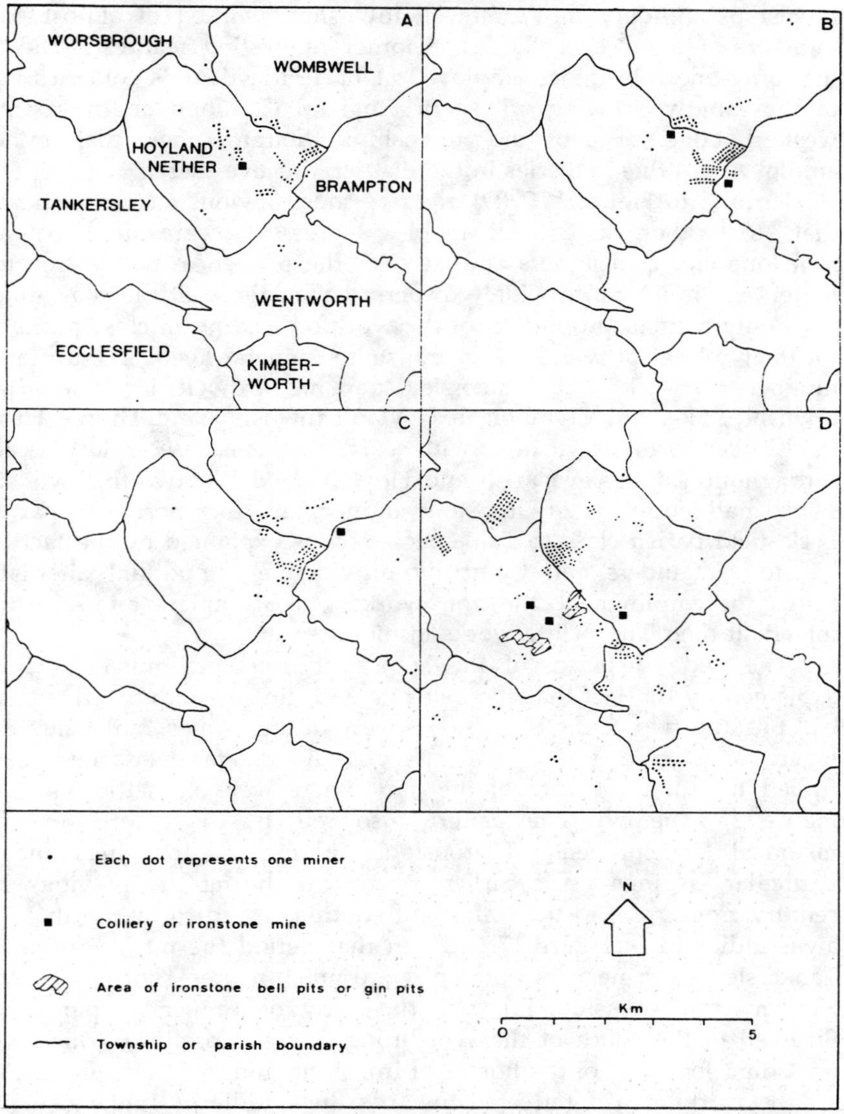

A
B
C
D
WORSBROUGH
WOMBWELL
HOYLAND NETHER
TANKERSLEY
BRAMPTON
WENTWORTH
ECCLESFIELD
KIMBER-WORTH

- Each dot represents one miner
- Colliery or ironstone mine
- Area of ironstone bell pits or gin pits
- Township or parish boundary

N
Km
0 5

Notes: Map A shows the places of residence of miners employed at Elsecar High Colliery, the location of which is shown by the black square. Map B shows the places of residence of miners at Elsecar Mid Colliery which had two pits, one at Elsecar and another at Jump, again shown by black squares. Map C shows the places of residence of miners at Elsecar Low Colliery. Map D shows the places of residence of ironstone miners. By 1850 the two shafts in Tankersley parish were used for drainage and ventilation only. The shaft in Hoyland (called Skiers Spring) is the engine pit referred to in the estate records after that date. Three ironstone miners lived beyond the area shown on the map.

three exceptions, only housed miners at the nearby Elsecar High Colliery. On the other hand, miners living in Jump, across the Hoyland township boundary in Wombwell township, worked in almost equal numbers at all three collieries. Another interesting feature is the fact that only one coal miner employed at Earl Fitzwilliam's collieries lived in the rapidly growing village of Hoyland Common on the extreme western edge of Hoyland township, though other coal miners, employed at other collieries in the district, did live there.

Turning to Figure 17.2 (D), the two most obvious characteristics are that, first, there is a remarkable degree of segregation between ironstone and coal miners and, second, the residences of the ironstone miners are much more widely dispersed than those of the coal miners, with only a small proportion of the workforce living in close proximity to their place of work. The ironstone miners lived in substantial numbers at Pilley in Tankersley parish, Birdwell in Worsbrough township, Hoyland Common in Hoyland township and Thorpe Hesley in Kimberworth township, with a fairly dense secondary scatter throughout Tankersley parish and Hoyland and Wentworth townships. The small number of ironstone miners in the northern part of Ecclesfield parish close to Tankersley Park is explained by the fact that Newton Chambers and Company provided an important alternative source of employment for iron workers, coal miners and ironstone miners at their Thorncliffe works in that area.

The wide dispersal of the homes of ironstone miners is partly explained by the fact that the bell pits and gin pits (advanced types of bell pit) and two of the three shafts were in the former Tankersley Park where, apart from one or two cottages and the farm attached to the ruined hall in the centre of the park, there were no settlements (see Figure 17.3 below). The pattern also reflects, to some extent, the historical development of ironstone mining in the area and in particular, as mentioned earlier, its retreat during the previous half century from areas to the south and south-east and to the north of the areas indicated in Figure 17.2 (D). In that period the pits, working the Tankersley seam near its outcrop, were much nearer Thorpe Hesley in Kimberworth township, Pilley in the north of Tankersley parish and Birdwell in the south of the Worsbrough township, all of which were important locations of the homes of ironstone miners in December 1850. As the working had retreated towards the middle of Tankersley Park and to Skiers Spring (the deep shaft mine in Hoyland township in Figure 17.2 (D)), so the workforce had lengthened its journey to work, so that villages such as Birdwell, Pilley and Thorpe Hesley retained their importance as centres where Tankersley ironstone miners lived, even though journeys to work had doubled during the first half of the nineteenth century. Of those coal and ironstone miners whose places of

Figure 17.3 Ironstone bell pits and shaft mines (bottom left) in Tankersley Park in 1840–1841

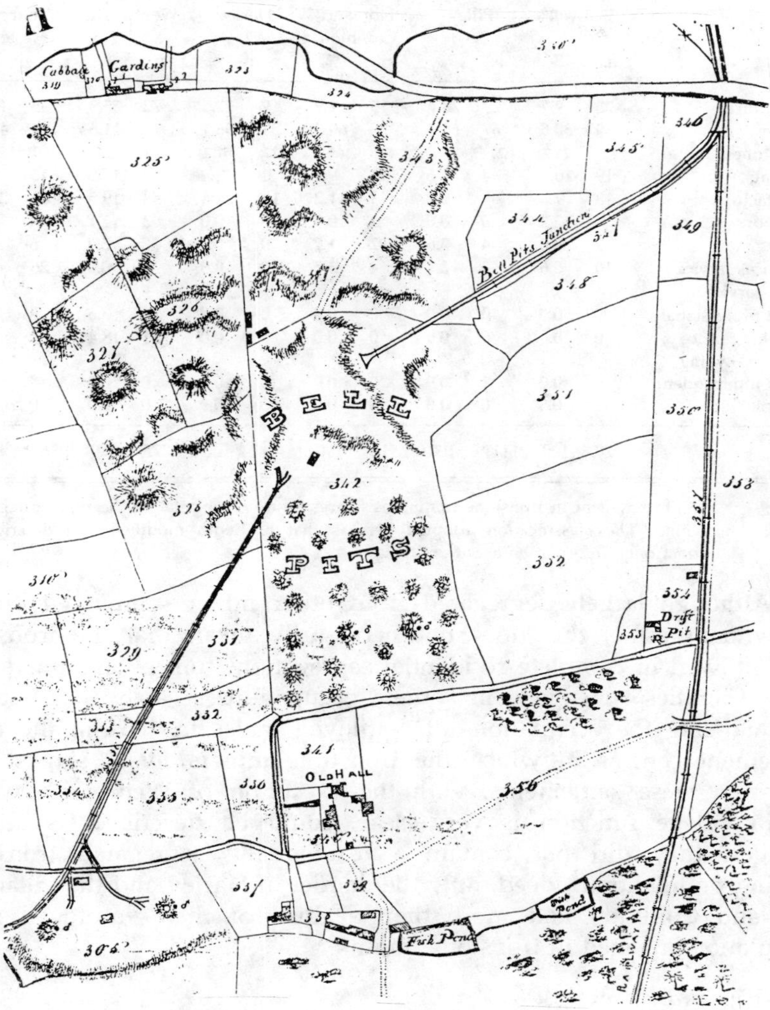

Source: WWM/SA A1647–14.

residence have been located in Figure 17.2, only 4 per cent of the coal miners lived more than two kilometres from their place of work, the vast majority living no more than a few minutes' walk from the colliery at which they worked. By contrast, over 45 per cent of the ironstone miners walked between 3 and 4 kilometres to work, with as many as 95 per cent walking at least 1 kilometre.

Table 17.1 Occupations of employed males: selected settlements in the Tankersley area, 1851

	Birdwell		Pilley		Hoyland Common		Harley		Wentworth		Thorpe Hesley	
	n.	%	n.	%	n.	%	n.	%	n.	%	n.	%
Agriculture	35	19.7	23	20.7	15	12.9	7	17.1	72	25.9	45	12.5
Mining	89	50.0	67	60.4	70	60.3	23	56.1	32	11.6	154	42.8
ironstone mining[a]	*42*	*23.7*	*21*	*18.4*	*53*	*45.7*	*21*	*51.2*	*7*	*2.5*	*100*	*27.8*
Building	19	10.7	4	3.6	11	9.5	1	2.4	47	17.0	15	4.2
Manufacture	13	7.3	9	8.1	13	11.2	10	24.4	54	19.5	103	28.6
Transport	4	2.2	0	0.0	1	0.9	0	0.0	3	1.1	4	1.1
Dealing	7	4.0	4	3.6	2	1.7	0	0.0	8	2.9	6	1.7
Industrial service	10	5.6	3	2.7	4	3.5	0	0.0	0	0.0	26	7.2
Public service and professional	0	0.0	0	0.0	0	0.0	0	0.0	10	3.6	2	0.5
Domestic service	0	0.0	0	0.0	0	0.0	0	0.0	51	18.4	1	0.3
Property owning and independent	0	0.0	1	0.9	0	0.0	0	0.0	0	0.0	4	1.1
Indefinite	1	0.5	0	0.0	0	0.0	0	0.0	0	0.0	0	0.0
Totals	178	100	111	100	116	100	41	100	277	100	360	100

Notes: *a* = Employment in ironstone mining as expressed as a sub-total of the main category of Mining. The classification adopted here is that of Booth modified and described in Armstrong, 'Information about occupation'.

Although largely segregated from other miners employed on the Fitzwilliam estae, this does not necessarily mean that the ironstone miners lived in complete residential segregation from other miners and from families engaged in other occupations. Table 17.1 above, summarising the occupations of employed males in 1851 in the main settlement centres in which the ironstone miners lived, shows that, although these settlements, with the exception of Wentworth whose estate village function is very clear, could be described as mining villages, they did not contain a residentially segregated ironstone mining population. Indeed, only the hamlet of Harley and the village of Hoyland Common had more than a third of their employed male population engaged in ironstone mining.

Kinship and teamwork

Though not segregated residentially from other miners, agricultural workers, self-employed metalworkers and workers in iron manufacturing, there was, nevertheless, a certain closeness among the ironstone miners. Every working day, unlike most of their neighbours, they left their villages to walk a fair distance to their workplace, often in another parish, and when they arrived they spent their day working in isolation in a close-knit team under an undertaker. On the other hand, the overwhelming majority of local miners worked in their home

Figure 17.4 Horse gin and gin boy

village, in bigger teams. Moreover, the boys who worked in the coal pits as trappers and horseboys were employed and controlled by the pit manager rather than by an undertaker.

In putting together his team, an ironstone undertaker would try to ensure the greatest efficiency and therefore the greatest profit. This meant having a getter or getters to mine the ironstone, hurriers or trammers to take it in corves (wagons) from the working place to the pit bottom and, in the case of small, shallow pits, coupling the corves onto ropes or chains (called hanging-on) to be wound up the shaft by a gin boy who operated a pulley system by leading a horse or pony round a circle at the pit top (Figure 17.4 above). It was then taken away from the pithead to be banked prior to being taken to the furnaces. Getting was normally done by experienced miners in their prime. According to the evidence collected in south Yorkshire by the sub-commissioner of the Children's Employment Commission (Mines) in 1842[11] some getters were as young as 17 or 18, but typically they were in their twenties, thirties and forties. Older men helped to fill the corves and were employed as hangers-on and banksmen. Teenagers were used as hurriers and the youngest of all – including 9–year-olds in 1851 – were employed as gin boys.

11 *Children's Employment Commission (Mines)*, vol. XVI, report of J. C. Symons, the Sub-Commissioner for the Yorkshire Coalfield, 1842.

Figure 17.5 **The structure of the ironstone mining labour force at the Tankersley ironstone grounds in 1850–1851**

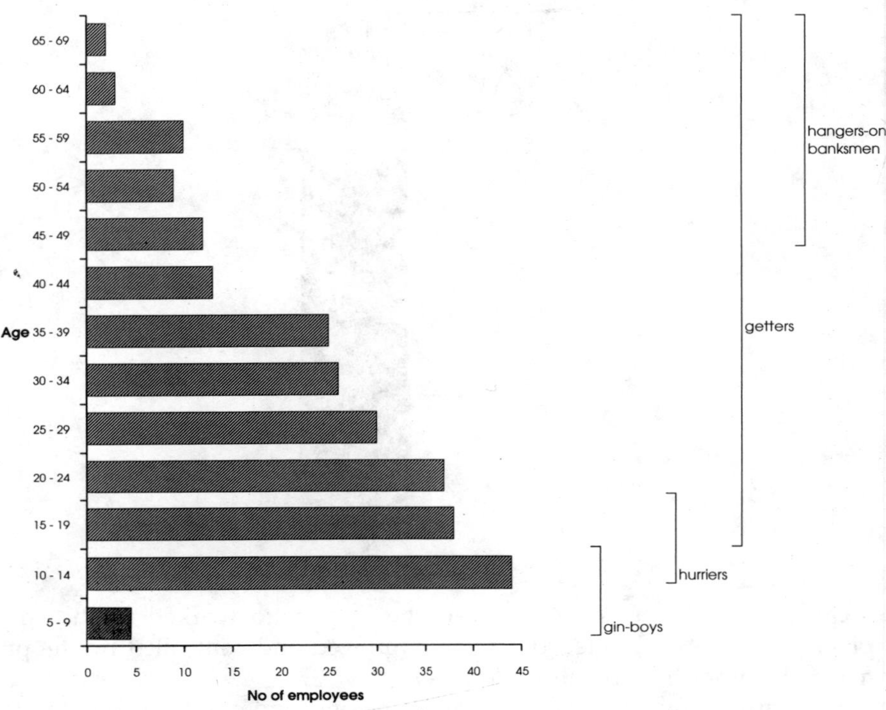

Notes: Undertakers and their teams only: members of the maintenance staff at the ironstone grounds are excluded.

The ironstone miners would obviously go through an occupational life-cycle, starting as gin boys, progressing to be hurriers, becoming getters in their prime, and then, as their health and strength declined, taking on the less arduous roles of hangers-on or banksmen. Figure 17.5 above shows the structure of the Tankersley ironstone mining labour force in 1850–51 arrived at by combining the names given in the December 1850 St Thomas' Day list with the ages and occupations stated in the March 1851 census returns.

Teams were likely to be made up on the basis of a number of criteria: skill, work rate, reliability, availability, sentiment and profit would all have played a part. Because of the heavy nature of the work and the ageing process, teams must have been constantly changing as miners fell ill, died or moved into other teams as lighter or heavier work became available, or moved into other occupations. The appointment of new undertakers from the mining population would also have caused the disintegration of existing teams, as would the formation of their new companies of workmen.

In a deep pit there was less need for young boys than in a small pit. Corves here were trammed over larger distances, but only to the bottom of the shaft, so that gin boys were not required. Nor were boys employed as trappers, to open and close airtight doors, as they were in the deep coal pits where gaseous explosions were a constant threat. There were more opportunities in the small pits for youths and boys. In such pits, teams were small, consisting of between four and eight members, and as many as half of them were young boys employed as trammers and gin boys.

There were certain advantages for undertakers in employing members of their own families. The main advantage was that earnings were kept within the family. If they were young, they could also be more easily controlled and directed than other employees; they could possibly also be worked harder at no extra, or even less, expense. Evidence in government enquiries at the time suggest considerable abuse in situations where undertakers employed their own children, with an insistence on very long hours and unrealistic output targets. The mineral agent at Thorncliffe only a mile or so from Tankersley told the sub-commissioner of the Children's Employment Commission (Mines) at the beginning of the 1840s that:

> Those [undertakers] who have got their own children at work with them use them worse than the others. I am quite sure of this. Where the lads are hired by the undertaker, they will stick up for themselves and will not work more than the time agreed on, but where the undertakers employ their own children, they can make them do as they like.[12]

In the same report, a boy of 17, who worked for his undertaker father as a getter, the most demanding job in a pit, said:

> I get and have been getting for two years. I find it very hard work indeed; it tires me very much; I can hardly get washed of a night till 9 o'clock, I am so tired. My father always tells me what to get. I and another boy have to get 35 corves a day; each corve holds nearly 4 cwt . . . . we work from five in the morning till nearly five in the evening and have about ten minutes for dinner.[13]

Whether an enlightened manager and a caring father or a bullying tyrant, an undertaker's ability to recruit family members varied according to personal circumstances. Obviously, undertakers in their forties or fifties with large families, and perhaps a large number of

12 *Children's Employment Commission (Mines)*, witness no. 60, 237.
13 *Children's Employment Commission (Mines)*, witness no. 67, 240.

Table 17.2 Selected structural characteristics of the undertakers' teams working at the Tankersley ironstone grounds in September 1849

Team	Size of team	Age of undertaker	Make-up of team: men	Make-up of team: boys	Number related to undertaker
Bell pits/gin pits					
Pit 1	5	42,44[a]	4	1	3
Pit 2	5	45	3	2	2
Pit 3	5	27	3	2	0
Pit 4	6	29	5	1	1
Pit 5	8	30	5	3	0
Pit 6	7	56	4	3	3
Pit 7	8	44	6	2	5
Pit 8	4	44	3	1	1
Pit 9	6	24	3	3	1
Pit 10	4	37	3	1	0
Pit 11	8	23,23[a]	5	3	0
Pit 12	6	30	3	3	1
Engine pit (deep shaft pit)					
Team 1	20	33,30[a]	18	2	1
Team 2	8	56	8	0	3

Notes: *a* = Two undertakers in partnership; in these cases the figure in the last column shows those persons related to one or the other or both of the undertakers.

nephews, were in a much better position to introduce their kin into their work teams than relatively young undertakers whose brothers were probably already established in other teams or occupations and whose own children were too young to be recruited.

Attention may now be turned to the undertakers' teams working at the Tankersley ironstone grounds in September 1849. Selected characteristics of the teams are summarised in Table 17.2 above. Bearing in mind what has already been said about the differences in the undertakers' responsibilities between the deep pits and the small pits, it is interesting to note the virtual absence of boys (under 15 years old) from the two undertakers' teams at the deep pit. Indeed, there were only 5 miners under 21 in team 1, and only 1 under 21 in team 2 at that pit. In the case of team 2, where 4 of the 8 team members were related, they were a father of 56 (the undertaker) and his grown up sons aged 35, 28 and 26.

It is clear from the table that in the small bell pits and gin pits there was a relationship between the age of an undertaker and the number of kin in his team. In 3 of the 4 instances where there were no relatives of the undertaker in a team, the undertakers were aged 30 or under. Conversely, in all 4 cases where between 2 and 5 subordinate team-members were relatives, the undertakers were in their forties and fifties.

Table 17.3 Examples of undertakers' teams in the bell pits and gin pits at Tankersley in September 1849

Name	Age	Assumed role	Known relationship to undertaker
A – Pit 1			
James Burgon (undertaker)	42	getter	brother-in-law of WS
William Smith (undertaker)	44	getter	brother-in-law of JB
Thomas Smith	51	banksman	brother of WS, brother-in-law of JB
Ezra Smith	15	hurrier	WS's son; JB's nephew
William Smith	9	gin boy	TS's son; JB's and WS's nephew
B – Pit 2			
James Trippett (undertaker)	45	getter	
Thomas Sylvester	54	getter	none
George Smith	15	hurrier	none
Edward Trippett	11	hurrier	son
Henry Trippett	10	gin boy	son
C – Pit 6			
William Bennett (undertaker)	56	getter	
George Bennett	24	getter	son
Thomas Bennett	21	getter	son
James Bennett	19	getter	son
Henry Smith	14	hurrier	none
William Bell	13	hurrier	none
Samuel Platts	9	gin boy	none
D – Pit 3			
William Bennett Jnr (undertaker)	27	getter	
Henry Wroe[a]		getter	none
David Holden	15	hurrier	none
Charles Ward	13	hurrier	none
Samuel Ward	11	gin boy	none
E – Pit 10			
William Jubb (undertaker)	37	getter	
William Hunter	43	getter	none
Charles Smith	16	hurrier	none
John Senior	14	gin boy	none

Notes: *a* = Individual not located in the 1851 census returns.

Table 17.3 above gives further details of a representative sample of 5 of the 12 teams operating in September 1849. The team in pit one was the only one in which all members were related. The team was headed by two brothers-in-law. The nephew of one (William South) was the gin boy (Figure 17.6 below); James Burgon, the other undertaker, was childless according to the census of 1851. The other members of the team were the brother of one of the undertakers and his son.

In pit two, the middle-aged undertaker was accompanied by his two young sons; the elder of the two probably hurrying and the younger acting as gin boy. The other two members of the team were another

Figure 17.6 William Smith and his wife Millicent

William Smith was a gin boy at Tankersley in 1849

Source: Chapeltown and High Green Archive.

middle-aged getter and a teenager, George Smith, who probably acted as his hurrier. George Smith was a near neighbour of the undertaker.

William Bennett, the undertaker who headed the team in pit six, was also accompanied by his sons, but in this case two were in their twenties and undoubtedly getters. The structure of the undertaker's family in 1849 (he then had 4 sons aged 27, 21 and 19 and a daughter aged 16) meant that he had to look outside his immediate family for two hurriers and a gin boy. William Bennett junior, the undertaker in pit three and the eldest known son of William Bennett of pit six, was only 27 years old, unmarried and still living with his father. He had almost certainly learned his trade as a member of his father's team and only left it relatively recently. None of the other three members of his team who have been located in the census were his relatives.

The team in pit ten also comprised unrelated members. Although 37 years old, William Jubb, the undertaker, still had a very young family (his five children were aged 9, 6, 4, 2 and 1) and the eldest two were girls. In Jubb's case he made up his team by employing two near neighbours, William Hunter and John Senior, and 16–year-old Charles Smith, who could not be accommodated in the team in which his father worked. His father was Thomas Smith in pit one, and the place Charles might have filled was already taken by his cousin Ezra Smith whose father was one of the undertakers in that pit.

Birthplaces of ironstone miners

In a study of nineteenth-century Ivinghoe, a Buckinghamshire straw-plaiting community, a distinction was drawn between Ivinghoe and 'its manufacturing counterparts in the north and midlands'. While Ivinghoe's labour force was overwhelmingly home grown, those of industrial communities in the north and midlands, the authors imply, were not.[14]

Figure 17.7 below, showing the birthplaces of ironstone miners working at Tankersley in December 1850, suggests that such a general statement may be quite misleading. Local patterns of migration are likely to be related to the balance between demand for, and supply of, labour, rather than some inherently regional characteristic of the centre of in-migration. The Tankersley ironstone miners, were overwhelmingly locally born, a not surprising circumstance in view of what has already been revealed about the organisation of the industry. More than 97 per cent of the 251 men and boys employed at the ironstone grounds in December 1850 and who have been located in the 1851 census were born in the West Riding, of whom 236 (94 per cent) were born in south Yorkshire within 15 kilometres of the ironstone grounds, and 195 (78 per cent) were born in Tankersley parish and the adjacent townships of Worsbrough, Hoyland Nether, Wentworth and Kimberworth within 6 kilometres of the ironstone grounds. All 16 (out of 18) of the undertakers leading teams at the ironstone grounds in September 1849, who have been found in the 1851 CEBs, were born in the same narrow area. Of the 7 ironstone miners born outside the West Riding of Yorkshire, 6 had originated less than 55 kilometres from Tankersley. Two of these, from Nottinghamshire, were young nephews of undertakers who may have been specially brought to south Yorkshire to fill gaps in teams. They were aged 11 and 13, were probably gin boys, and worked in teams headed by young undertakers with no boys of their own of those ages.

14 Horn and Horn, 'An "industrial" community', 9–20.

Figure 17.7 **Birthplaces of the ironstone miners working at Skiers Spring (the engine pit just outside Tankersley parish) and Tankersley Park, December 1850**

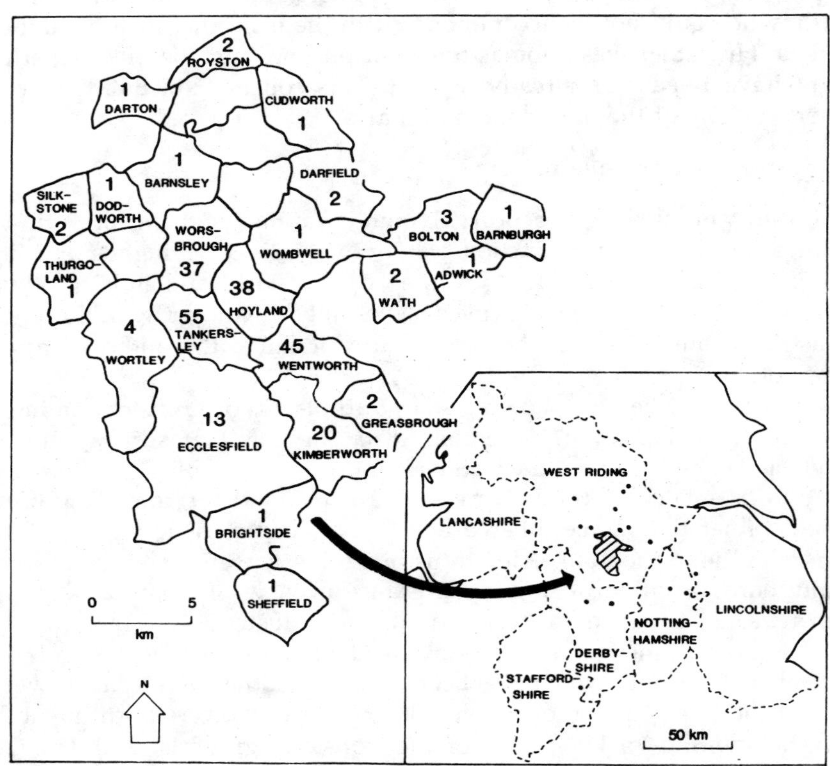

Conclusion

Brief, selective and, in places, speculative as this analysis has been, it shows the potential of the combined use of census enumerators' returns and estate and other local records. The evidence presented here shows that this approach may throw light on such matters as labour recruitment, family allegiance to particular occupations, the structure of labour forces, labour migration and residential segregation by occupation.

Part IV

Migration and population turnover

18

Migration and population turnover

D. R. MILLS AND K. SCHÜRER

The 'laws' of migration

The use of occupational data has been largely descriptive and for purposes of combinations with other variables. Work on birthplace data, by contrast, has shown a considerable interest in testing hypotheses of general application. The extent to which the towns grew by migration, as opposed to high birth rates, was an early topic of interest studied largely by the use of aggregate data. In rural areas a general interest has centred round the extent to which the population could be seen as static, apart from the out-migration to the towns and overseas. Birthplace data in the CEBs make it possible to establish the direction and distances involved in life-time migration, a term which refers to the fact that hardly anything is known other than the place of birth and the place of current residence. For some individuals it is possible to add 'migration traces' which can be sketched out for parents (or at least mothers) by using the birthplaces of co-resident children. The proportion of the population for which this is possible often turns out to be disappointingly small, since it depends on catching couples during the child-rearing period in the life cycle, and on their having migrated during that period. Returning to the basic point about distance, overwhelmingly, internal migration was over short distances, such as from a village to a town within a 10- or 20-mile radius, or within an area which shared a labour market for particular skills. As to direction, speaking in very general terms, a large amount of rural–urban migration is captured by the CEBs, but migration from town to town is also discernible at the higher skill levels or where there were changes within a specialised labour market. Many students have been surprised by the substantial amount of 'circulatory' migration within the countryside, much of it apparently associated with the institutions of service and tied cottages, or movements made in order to gain varied experience within an occupation.

In addition to being used on their own, birthplace data, as suggested already, have frequently been used in combination with other variables such as age, gender, occupation, and marital status. This has enabled students to answer some of the questions posed by Ravenstein over a century ago as a series of 'laws', more properly hypotheses to be tested. His laws can be presented in simplified form as follows:

1) The major causes of migration are economic, i.e., determined by the labour market.

2) The majority of migration is over short distances, but migrants with higher skills move over much longer distances.

3) The major direction of migration is from agricultural to industrial areas.

4) Females are more likely to leave their birthplaces than males, but those males who do move away on average move longer distances than females.

5) Most migrants are young unmarried adults.

6) Migrants proceed to their ultimate destinations by a series of steps.

7) Areas of heavy out-migration also exhibit counter currents of inward migration.

8) Migration increases as industries develop and the transport system improves.

9) The natives of towns are less migratory than those of rural areas.

10) Large towns grow more by migration than by natural increase.[1]

Some of these hypotheses are more easily tested than others by using the CEBs, some are more satisfactorily approached through the aggregative tables, and yet others are too diffuse to be tested in their original form, yet can still stimulate our thinking.[2] A good example of a hypothesis too diffuse to test, at least directly, is the first one. Undoubtedly many people did move for better job opportunities, but the impetus and direction of movement were also clearly influenced by having contacts in particular areas, even family or friends they could go to in the receiving area. There were many factors at work, and identifying and isolating particular economic factors is far from easy.

In the case of the second hypothesis, it has been shown many times over, using both printed tables at the county level and straight-line distances in association with CEB data, that the flow of migrants to a

1 Based on Grigg, 'Ravenstein'; Ravenstein, 'Laws, (1885)' and 'Laws (1889)'.

2 The remainder of this section owes a great deal to the discussion in Mageean and Pryce, *Patterns and processes*; Lawton 'Peopling the past', 264–7. Scores of Open University students have also chosen migration as a project topic. In this context the Open University has recently published a CD-Rom disc containing student research reports for 1994: *Studying family and community history, 19th and 20th centuries: Project reports in family and community history*, (1996), reference no DA301, CD R0008: enquiries to Prof. R Finnegan, Faculty of Social Sciences, Open University, Milton Keynes, MK7 6AA.

particular point decayed (i.e., lessened) with increasing distance from that point.[3] There have also been many instances where professional men and those with specialised skills such as those associated with the railways, are known to have migrated over large distances compared with servants and labourers. However, the important exceptions of the unskilled Irish settlers in many English and some Scottish towns show that circumstances varied considerably.

For the greater part of the century, the industrial and urban areas were gaining population rapidly, and most of this appears to have been due to migration from the nearby countryside – just how much is discussed in the next section. However, a point to be noted here is that towards the end of the Victorian period suburbanisation of the countryside had become well-established around the biggest centres of population, that is, commuting had begun. This process amounted to a counterflow such as that mentioned in hypothesis 7, and, as the use of the CEBs extends into those of 1891 and 1901, this counterflow will become increasingly a feature of local community studies. Counterflows of other kinds, such as returning migrants, or replacement migration can also be discerned.

The greater propensity of women to migrate has been very largely borne out by detailed work by many scholars. Women lacked sufficient job opportunities in country areas, whereas towns had many more openings in factories, shops and more especially in domestic service. On top of these factors, women more often moved on marriage than did men, whose own jobs were usually better paid than any their brides might have clung on to where they had been living. Many modern studies have likewise confirmed hypothesis 5, that families were less likely to move than young unmarried adults (this point is taken up again in the next section but one).

Step migration is still not very clearly established as a general feature of the process, although many family historians have come across individual examples of ancestors reaching their ultimate destinations by a progression of steps. A good example of a test of the hypothesis is to be found in Anderson's study of Preston. Another example of step migration is that reported by Gwynne and Sill in relation to Middlesbrough, where particular skills of the iron-workers encouraged them to move between iron districts as these prospered and declined.[4]

3 An important point to bear in mind is that rings of equal width around a receiving point, such as 0–4, 5–9 miles and so on from the centre, do not contain equal areas. The areas of the rings get bigger with increasing distance, and in an evenly distributed population this means that the potential contributions to the migrant flow get bigger with increasing distance. Despite this, the flow generally diminishes in absolute numbers and tails off even more quickly if seen in relative terms.

4 Anderson, 'Urban migration'; Gwynne and Sill, 'Mid-century immigration'; and Mageean and Pryce, *Patterns and processes*, 70–5.

Hypothesis 8 presents difficulties at the local level, first of all because the calculation of out-migration from, say, a place newly connected to the railway system, involves the use of the Registrar General's Annual Reports as a means of estimating natural changes in the population (the balance between births and deaths). Only when these are known can the balance of inter-censal change be attributed to migration. So far as the CEBs and in-migration are concerned, there is the practically insoluble difficulty of disentangling a range of factors concerning the growth of particular industries, as well as developments in the transport system.

The possibility that townspeople might be less migratory than those in the countryside has attracted little attention. It might be thought 'obvious' that in the Victorian period the growth of industry was the main engine of migration, hence once migrants had reached the economic 'haven' of an urban job, they would proceed no further. It will be shown in the penultimate section of this chapter that there was much 'circulatory' migration within the countryside, as well as a large volume of rural–urban migration. Hence rural folk may have been more migratory than urban, but there are no studies known to us which have directly tested the hypothesis with CEBs data, (although mobility within cities has been the subject of several studies).

Last, but by no means least, is the hypothesis that the increase in the population of urban and industrial areas was due more to migration than it was to natural increase: this is discussed in the next section.

Migration to the towns

The growth of population is summarised in Table 8.1 (chapter 8, above), which shows that the population of England and Wales doubled between 1801 and 1851 and again between 1851 and 1911. In addition, this country was the first in the world in which over 50 per cent of the population was enumerated in urban areas. There is, of course, some disagreement between authorities as to the definition of 'urban' – for example, does it include mining villages, which can be described as industrial but not urban? For the present purpose the matter was resolved 30 years ago by Law, who showed that whichever of the usual definitions was taken, England and Wales passed the 50 per cent threshold in the 1840s, i.e., by the 1851 census (Table 18.1 below). According to Law's calculations the growth of the whole population between 1801 and 1911 was 27.2 millions, of which 25.4 millions, or 93.3 per cent occurred in urban areas.[5]

5 Law, 'Growth of urban population', 126–32.

Table 18.1 Growth of the Urban Population of England and Wales, 1801–1911

Census year	Urban population (millions)	Per cent of total
1801	3.00	33.8
1811	3.72	36.6
1821	4.80	40.0
1831	6.15	44.3
1841	7.69	48.3
1851	9.69	54.0
1861	11.78	58.7
1871	14.80	65.2
1881	18.18	70.0
1891	21.60	74.5
1901	25.37	78.0
1911	28.47	78.9

Source: Law, 'Growth of urban population', Table V, 130.

What proportion of this massive increase of over 25 millions was derived from migration, as opposed to natural increase? It is not possible to answer the question for the period as a whole, but Cairncross established a generally accepted figure for the period from 1841 to 1911. Surprisingly, for the urban and colliery registration districts (as defined by Welton) where the increase was 182 per cent over the 70-year period, 151 per cent was due to natural increase and only 31 per cent to migration. However, it was still possible for Lawton to say that the major determinant of fluctuations in the rate of change was migration. This is presumably because the bulk of migrants were young adults moving ahead of their reproductive years – they soon set off baby booms, rapid natural increases of which the rural areas were correspondingly deprived. Many urban areas had relatively short periods of intense migration as new industries expanded rapidly, but were adequately sustained thereafter by natural increase.[6] Similarly, even rural areas could display distinctive demographic characteristics as a result of sudden spurts of in-migration. This is illustrated in the male preponderance on Exmoor in the decades after enclosure, followed by a rapid broadening out of the age–sex pyramid (chapter 14).

Migration in the countryside

Migration from the countryside absorbed the intellectual energy of many contemporaries, as is the case with later scholars. Undoubtedly, this is a feature of rural life which should never be forgotten when migration within the countryside is being studied. The rural figures

[6] Cairncross, 'Internal migration'; Lawton 'Population changes' especially 60, 62, 65 and 70–1; and Woods, *Population of Britain*, 36. See also Lawton, 'Population' and 'Population and society'.

Table 18.2 Percentage native born in selected villages and towns in Leicestershire, 1851

Settlements	Population	% native
Loughborough – hosiery & engineering	10,977	60.7
Hinckley – hosiery	5,974	70.7
Coalville – new mining town	620	18.3
Four large agricultural villages	3,875	55.3
Four hosiery villages, with farming	7,764	70.0
Four mining villages, with farming	5,279	47.5

Source: Smith, 'Population', 151.

corresponding to the urban figures quoted in the previous paragraph sum up the trend over the period 1841–1911. A natural increment of 5.3 million (a gain of 86 per cent) was almost entirely counter-balanced by net out-migration of 4.5 million (minus 73.2 per cent).[7] Nevertheless, this section concentrates on migration within the countryside, since this study has been relatively neglected and contains distinctive interests and insights into migratory behaviour. Moreover, historians of rural communities working on CEBs have access to plentiful data on migration into their villages, in contrast to the relative paucity of easily collected data on out-migration. The section is focused still further by concentrating on four of the few studies that have analysed large rural populations by the simple method of examining the proportions of the population resident on census night in the places of their birth. Whilst this method has severe limitations, it has the advantage that it can quickly produce data for populations large enough for the drawing of general inferences.

One of the very earliest uses of the CEBs is to be found in Smith's contribution to a volume of the Leicestershire *Victoria County History* published in 1955,[8] his figures on the proportions native and non-native being summarised in Table 18.2 above. The hosiery industry had been in decline for several decades, with the result that in-migration to both hosiery villages and towns had been discouraged, 60–70 per cent of the population being natives of their current places of residence. By contrast, the expanding mining settlements were more attractive at 47.5 per cent native and a much lower figure still, as expected, for the new settlement of Coalville. Farming villages fell between the extremes, even in a period of much surplus agricultural labour, and one may suspect here the effect of 'circulatory migration' of indoor farm servants and labourers living in tied cottages.

7 Lawton, 'Rural depopulation', 208.
8 Smith, 'Leicestershire population', 151.

Bryant's work was based on an 1851 population of about 14,000 in the Dart valley of Devon, taking in the three small towns of Totnes, Ashburton and Buckfastleigh, as well as eight rural parishes.[9] Resident natives constituted 58.5 per cent of the total, with slightly higher proportions of natives in the towns, which at this date were of declining importance, therefore not attracting large numbers of in-migrants. The native proportion varied more widely at the level of individual settlements, from only 40 per cent in Woodland parish (with 188 inhabitants) to 72 per cent in Buckfastleigh Town (2,170) and 74 per cent in Dean Prior (507). Observing these variations, Bryant put forward the hypothesis that larger populations were more stable. The larger settlements could absorb a larger proportion of moves between jobs and homes within their boundaries. One can add the choice of marriage partners to these two factors, perhaps reducing the number of brides leaving their birthplaces to join their husbands.

Bryant also assembled evidence largely from outside the CEBs to the effect that many people moved short distances across the Devon countryside in search of work. In order to maximise the use of the CEBs in showing intermediate moves, he developed 'the birth-confinement-residence-trace'. Where a family had made several moves, the trace would start at the mother's place of birth, move on to the birthplaces of the children (confinements) and finish at the place of residence current on census night. Such traces often show patterns which can be described as 'circulatory migration', not necessarily coming back to the mother's birthplace, but not describing clear movements in steps to a town, or other 'obvious' magnet. The trace has its limitations, one of which is lack of proof that the children were born at the mothers' places of residence – for example, some mothers may have gone to their own mothers or other relatives for their confinements. However, the most severe limitation is that of quantity, many parents apparently being less migratory than they had been as footloose young adults.

A third large study of rural migration was also based on the 1851 census, with more than 18,000 people in the database.[10] Although this population cannot be seen as a random sample, it has been collected from widely separated parts of England, mainly in the East Midlands and the South East, and may, therefore, have a significant value for comparative purposes. Fifty-five per cent of this population were living in the places where they had been born, rather more men than women, supporting Ravenstein's hypothesis about gender differences. Almost 20

9 Bryant, 'South Devon', especially 132–3 and 137–41.

10 The database has been constructed by Dennis Mills and acknowledgement for the considerable help given to him should also be paid to Michael Anderson, Philip Aslett, Susan Davies, Tom Doig, Michael Edgar, Wyn Grimette, Joan Grundy, Beryl Hazelwood, and Joan and John Mills.

Table 18.3 Birthplace status in a rural population, 1851

Villages	[1]	[2]	[3]	[4]	[5]	[6]
(a) All	18,490	55.3	19.1	25.4	58.8	51.7
(b) Small Lincs limestone	1,113	37.0	21.9	40.2	38.4	35.5
(c) Large Lincs limestone	2,118	50.2	13.8	35.8	53.3	46.8
(d) Deeping Fen, S. Lincs	1,063	26.7	24.6	48.3	24.4	30.0
(e) Collingham, E. Notts	1,743	52.7	13.3	34.0	56.9	48.5
(f) Small N. Bucks	1,919	47.2	27.8	24.5	55.3	38.7
(g) Large N. Bucks	1,871	67.1	15.9	17.0	75.5	58.5
(h) Cambs/Herts border	2,427	71.1	14.5	14.3	75.7	66.5
(i) Dorset	3,770	61.4	20.9	17.4	63.6	59.2
(j) Bentley, N. Hants	753	58.6	24.2	16.6	65.6	51.5
(k) Shorne, N. Kent	944	53.6	21.9	24.4	55.5	51.6
(l) Canon Pyon, Hereford	699	52.5	16.9	29.9	52.5	52.5

Notes: Of the total, 56 persons were omitted because of lack of birthplace information.

[1] = Population; [2] = Percentage native; [3] = Percentage born within 5 miles; [4] = Percentage born beyond 5 miles; [5] = Male percentage native; [6] = Female percentage native.

(b) = Aisthorpe, Brattleby, Burton, Cammeringham, North and South Carlton, Scampton, near to and north of Lincoln;
(c) = Ingham, Nettleham, near to and north of Lincoln;
(f) = Addington, Beachampton, Chackmore, Chetwode, Middle Claydon, Foscott, Hillesden, Lillingstone Dayrell, Radclive, Shalstone, Thornton;
(g) = Great and Little Horwood, Thornborough;
(h) = Melbourn, Cambs and Barkway, Herts;
(i) = Worth and Langton Matravers and Studland in Purbeck; Hinton St. Mary, Okeford Fitzpaine, Childe Okeforde and Stourton Caundle in Vale of Blackmore.

Table 18.4 Percentage native born by age, in a rural population, 1851

Age group	% native	Age group	% native
0–4	86.7	35–39	38.1
5–9	78.3	40–44	38.1
10–14	71.0	45–49	37.6
15–19	54.9	50–54	32.7
20–24	46.7	55–59	36.2
25–29	41.8	60–64	35.8
30–34	37.5	65+	37.1

Notes: Villages as in Table 18.3 – total population with ages and birthplaces both recorded = 18,430.

per cent more were living within five miles of their birthplaces. The native element fell steadily down to the age-group 25–29 and then flattened out. Thus for the whole population rather more than a half were living in their birthplaces, but for the age groups thirty and over the figure was only rather more than a third (Tables 18.3 and 18.4

above). This general age-specific trend in proportions native-born is also noted by Anderson in his analysis of a sample of CEB data for 1851 drawn from the whole country. In his discussion of rural migration he splits the figures for larger rural parishes (those with a population greater than 2,000) from those for small parishes (population less than 2,000). While both display the same basic age-specific pattern, interestingly, the larger rural parishes recorded slightly higher proportions of non-native born at all ages.[11]

Table 18.3 takes the analysis down to the level of individual districts. As the smallest of these had a population of 699, and most fell in the range 1,000–2,000, the figures are generally valid in statistical terms and the picture of broad differences between the South East and the East Midlands is reliable. Thus the proportions of native-born varied in the latter high-wage area from *c.* 26 to 53 per cent, compared with *c.* 47 to 71 per cent in the low wage area of south-east England. There were only two departures from the rule that females were more migratory (on the single criterion of being non-native to their places of residence). One exception was Canon Pyon (Herefordshire) where the figures for males and females were exactly equal. The other exception was Deeping Fen in south Lincolnshire, like Exmoor, an area of new settlement, in which there was a significant preponderance of males (58 per cent), many of whom were living-in farm servants. In Lincolnshire and Buckinghamshire wide differences between large and small villages are discernible, with large villages having relatively higher proportions of natives.

Breakdown figures by major occupational groups are also available. The least migratory group were those engaged in a wide range of occupations representing local specialisations, perhaps because these were declining specialities with little demand for new labour from outside even the parish of birth (68 per cent native). Farmworkers (53 per cent) and tradesmen and craftsmen (48 per cent) came next, not showing as sharp a difference as the skill differences between them might have led one to expect. Variation around the mean was greater in the case of the farmworkers, and this seems to be due to differences in the incidence of living-in farm service and tied-cottage provision. Those with higher skills and/or capital, the farmers (36 per cent) and professionals (22 per cent), had smaller proportions of natives within their ranks. However, this interpretation is disturbed by the position of servants, predominantly women, of whom only 24 per cent were in service in the places of their birth.[12]

Goose's work on the Berkhamsted district of Hertfordshire constitutes the last of the large rural studies summarised here, taking in

11 Anderson, 'Problem of assimilation?', 87.

12 Further discussion of the figures for the Buckinghamshire and Lincolnshire parishes is available in Mills and Mills, 'Rural mobility'.

about 11,000 people, again from the 1851 census.[13] The proportion who were natives was 54.6, a figure remarkably close to the studies already mentioned. This proportion varied from 45.3 to 66.3 per cent, but the number of settlements is too small to draw any conclusions on the relationship of the variation to settlement size. Females predominated over males in the migrant population. There was a strong relationship between occupation and mobility: farm workers were nearly twice as likely as farmers to be natives of their places of residence, and those who had moved seldom came from outside the county. However, straw plaiters were even less mobile than farm workers: 75 per cent as compared with 61 per cent, another echo of the Mills study.

Conversely, the domestic servants of the small town of Berkhamsted were only 20 per cent native, and as three-quarters of them fell into the age group 10–29, this points again to the life-cycle nature of migration. Taking the whole population, there was a steady fall in the proportion of natives from 85.2 per cent of the 0–4 age group to 42.1 per cent of the 25–29 age group. Thereafter the proportion fluctuated minimally on a plateau falling to a minimum of 32.6 per cent in the 65-plus age group. These figures bear a close resemblance to those in Table 18.4. Goose makes the interesting point that about two people in three had eventually left their places of birth, making this the norm for the whole population.

Migration and family histories

Finally, it is useful to note a new approach that has recently been made to migration through the large-scale use of individual residential histories. At the centre of many of these life histories lies nominal-level CEB data linked from decade to decade, but augmented by drawing upon a large amount of family history and genealogical evidence gathered from such sources at the GRO's civil registers and parish register information. Such evidence counterbalances the snapshot views of the census and some other migration sources, and opens up the subject to a wider cross section of the population than the particular groups, such as paupers and apprentices, who are the subject of some commonly used sources on migration. Equally, not being reliant upon the evidence of CEB data, given appropriate documentary sources life histories can also be constructed for pre- and post-CEB periods. Preliminary results indicate support for Ravenstein's hypothesis that most migration was over short distances: mean distances up to about 1880 were only 35 km (22 miles). However, the evidence challenges assumptions that stepwise moves to bigger settlements were

13 Goose, *Hertfordshire in 1851*, 56–60. The figures quoted here exclude the 622 people living in Frithsden, a hamlet straddling the parishes of Berkhamsted and Northchurch, a fact that probably confused residents when filling in the birthplace column on their schedules.

preponderant, and plays down the importance of rural-to-urban migration. Family migration appears to have been more important than previously thought, but young single migrants were conspicuous in long-distance moves to bigger centres of population. Gender differences in distances were insignificant, but women were more likely to move for marriage and less for employment. 'Occupation and associated skills, education and income were more important factors affecting migration'.[14]

Contents of Part IV

Part IV contains four very different kinds of study, beginning with Perkyns' consideration of the accuracy of birthplace evidence in the CEBs (chapter 19). This was based on comparisons between CEBs (discrepancies recorded as errors) and between CEBs and baptismal registers (discrepancies recorded as anomalies). The results were on the whole reassuring, with greater proportions of discrepancies among non-natives; and among servants, lodgers and visitors. Turner's contribution in chapter 20 is far more conventional, representing a popular genre, in which the in-migration of an occupational group has been studied: the calico workers of Accrington. Interestingly, he employed Bryant's birthplace-trace technique to pinpoint circulatory migration around Accrington; migration due to the closure of works was also noticed.

In chapter 21 Wojciechowska displays a different dimension, that of persistence in the population of a Kentish Wealden parish, as between the 1851 and 1861 censuses and between the 1861 and 1871 censuses. There is an appendix of wider interest, where she discusses the rules she adopted for nominal record linkage. Finally in Part IV, chapter 22 is a study of family migration to Grantham and Scunthorpe, in which White has challenged the orthodox view that the typical migrant was a young, single adult. In breaking new ground the author was obliged to use a complex methodology, involving assumptions that need to be carefully considered. However, his conclusions interestingly anticipated some of those arrived at by Pooley and Turnball using a totally different route (see previous section).[15]

Elsewhere in the book, other chapters contain material of interest to specialists in migration, including chapter 11 by Smith on Greater Nottingham; 14 by Scott on the pioneer population of Exmoor; 17 by Jones on migration of ironworkers in the West Riding; and 27 by Brayshay on some of the effects of out-migration on the remaining population in a Cornish mining area.

14 Pooley and Turnbull, 'Migration and mobility'.
15 Pooley and Turnbull, 'Migration and mobility'.

19

Birthplace accuracy in the censuses of six Kentish parishes, 1851–1881

AUDREY PERKYNS

Introduction

'The information relating to birthplaces in the census is of considerable importance... Despite its importance very little work has been done on the accuracy of this information, especially since there are few other sources to check it against.'[1] Higgs cites a few examples of such work: Anderson's work on the population of Preston in two successive CEBs showed a 14 per cent discrepancy among the 475 traced;[2] Wrigley's analysis of birthplaces of household heads in Colyton showed a 15.7 per cent discrepancy for male heads and 6 per cent for females.[3] Yasumoto in chapter 10 cross-references data from the CEBs and baptism registers for Methley and finds birthplace discrepancies of 8.0 and 6.8 per cent, respectively, for those found in both the 1851 and 1861 CEBs.[4] Anderson points out that many of these discrepancies are minor; some so minor that they represent only a spelling variation and not a change of birthplace at all. Tillott suggests that the birthplace is subject to clerical error rather than anything more serious, pointing especially to inaccuracies arising from the use of dittos.[5] Armstrong cites Anderson's data as the sum total of our knowledge about the reliability of the returns and describes the task of checking against parochial data as possible but laborious.[6]

A study of the total populations of six adjacent Kentish parishes in five successive censuses, 1841–81, has made possible just such an analysis, through cross-referencing, though the 1841 data are omitted from this topic because specific birthplaces were not recorded then. The six parishes are Hartlip, Newington, Rainham, Stockbury, Upchurch and Lower Halstow, and have been described earlier in chapter 12.[7]

1 Higgs, *Making sense*, 71–4. In *Clearer sense*, 83, the quote is slightly reworded.
2 Anderson, 'The study of family structure', 75. Cited in Higgs, *Making sense*, 72; *Clearer sense*, 85.
3 Wrigley, 'Baptism coverage', 299–306. Cited in Higgs, *Making sense*, 73; *Clearer sense*, 86.
4 See chapter 10, above.
5 Tillott, 'Sources of inaccuracy', 108–9.
6 Armstrong, 'The CEBs: a commentary', 37.
7 The CEB references are the same as given in chapter 12. A map showing the location of the six parishes also appears in chapter 12.

Table 19.1 Three occupational classes 1851 and 1881

Parish	[1] Working population[a]	[2] Agri-cultural	[3] 2 as % of 1	[4] Mining	[5] 4 as % of 1	[6] Labouring	[7] 6 as % of 1
Hartlip							
1851	125	81	64.8	0	0.0	0	0.0
1881	151	85	56.3	1	0.7	0	0.0
Newington							
1851	291	181	62.2	0	0.0	1	0.3
1881	396	213	53.8	39	9.9	3	0.8
Rainham							
1851	459	285	62.1	6	1.3	16	3.5
1881	994	325	32.7	197	19.8	71	7.1
Stockbury							
1851	225	173	76.9	1	0.4	1	0.4
1881	223	164	73.5	0	0.0	3	1.4
Upchurch							
1851	181	131	72.4	10	5.5	0	0.0
1881	449	114	25.4	134	29.8	131	29.2
Halstow							
1851	119	41	34.5	9	7.6	39	32.8
1881	274	50	18.3	145	52.9	12	4.4
Totals							
1851	1,400	892	63.7	26	1.9	57	4.1
1881	2,487	951	38.2	516	20.8	220	8.9

Notes: a = All groups of workers include employers and employees, male and female, all ages. The occupation groups are based on those of Booth modified by Armstrong in 'Information about occupation'. Those in the mining classification are mostly brickmakers.

It is difficult to gauge how far these parishes can be regarded as typical. There are certain significant variations among the six. Hartlip and Stockbury remained agricultural backwaters, their percentage population growth 1851–81 being 10 and 5 respectively. On the other hand Rainham, Upchurch and Halstow grew by 133, 173 and 104 per cent respectively, largely because of the development, in response to demand from London, of the brickmaking industry and the transport and service trades which accompanied it.[8] Table 19.1 above shows the percentages of the working population classified respectively as agricultural workers, mining workers and general labourers in each parish in 1851 and 1881. This gives some indication of the effect of the growth of the brickmaking industry. Newington, with a population growth of 42 per cent, is seen to fall between the places of rapid growth and change and those which remained stagnant.

8 The population increases over the 30 years 1851–81 represent average annual percentage growth rates as follows: Hartlip 0.4; Newington 1.4; Rainham 4.5; Stockbury 0.2; Upchurch 5.8; Lower Halstow 3.5. The decade 1861–71 was the decade of greatest growth.

Table 19.2 Proportions of populations with baptism records in the six parishes

Parish	[1] Total population	[2] n. born in the area	[3] n. with baptism record in the area[a]	[4] 3 as % of 1	[5] 3 as % of 2
Hartlip					
1851	342	236	187	54.7	79.2
1861	319	205	155	48.6	75.6
1871	355	214	148	41.7	69.2
1881	378	185	144	38.1	77.8
Newington					
1851	731	461	361	49.4	78.3
1861	854	500	391	45.8	78.2
1871	1,013	521	362	35.7	69.5
1881	1,038	543	360	34.7	66.3
Rainham					
1851	1,155	752	592	51.3	78.7
1861	1,422	890	680	47.8	76.4
1871	2,082	1,185	774	37.2	65.3
1881	2,696	1,560	1,003	37.2	64.3
Stockbury					
1851	589	387	291	49.4	75.2
1861	613	402	315	51.4	78.4
1871	590	331	254	43.1	76.7
1881	621	326	260	41.9	79.8
Upchurch					
1851	407	289	252	61.9	87.2
1861[b]	314	205	184	58.6	89.8
1871	777	456	376	48.4	82.5
1881	1,112	586	448	40.3	76.5
Lower Halstow					
1851	344	231	202	58.7	87.5
1861	373	250	223	59.8	89.2
1871	504	273	235	46.6	86.1
1881	701	406	308	43.9	75.9
Totals	19,330	11,394	8,505	44.0	74.6

Notes: *a* = late baptisms excluded; *b* = 154 of the 468 records are missing, destroyed. This applies to all subsequent tables in this chapter.

Method

The two basic means of checking birthplaces by cross-referencing were (a) within the census data themselves and (b) with baptism records where they exist in the six parishes for the census populations.[9] There are two important criteria for the use of baptism records for this purpose: first the baptism must be soon after birth and secondly the crucial datum is not the place where the baptism was registered but the place of residence at the time.

9 The Centre for Kentish Studies references for the parish registers are: Hartlip P175; Newington P265; Rainham P296; Stockbury P348; Upchurch P377; Lower Halstow P168.

Baptisms have been used as supplementary evidence only if they took place within six to eight months of birth. This interval can sometimes be calculated with certainty because a date of birth or age at baptism is given, though this occurs only in a minority of cases; it can sometimes be inferred from ages recorded through successive censuses or the age sequence of siblings, for instance. The number of late baptisms varies between parishes. Late baptisms have been excluded from the figures for baptisms given in Table 19.2 above. This shows that the percentage of the total populations found to have a useable baptism record in one of the six parishes is quite high, while the percentage of those born in one of the six and having a baptism record there is very high.[10] Indeed, it is probably even higher than this table suggests, since some wives whose maiden names are unknown might have been baptised there.[11]

While baptisms can be useful additional evidence for those whose birthplace can be checked by multiple appearances in the censuses, they are crucial for those who appear there only once (single entries). Table 19.3 below shows the number of baptismal records available for cross-checking birthplace accuracy for single entries. A record of the place of residence at the time of baptism was not required until after 1812, so no earlier baptisms have been included in these figures for single entries if there is a discrepancy between birthplace and place of baptism (there are only 7 such). In all but 79 (3.3 per cent) of the 2,404 single entries with baptisms the baptism residence coincides with the census birthplace. A careful scrutiny was made of these 79 exceptions. Thirty-three showed evidence of a move at about the time of birth/baptism; 21 were in families which moved very frequently or showed evidence of a short stay in another parish; 8 were in families of yeomen farmers with lands in several adjacent parishes; 6 were orphans or illegitimate children (3 of these with birthplaces in Milton might well have been born in the workhouse); three others had birthplaces carefully distinguished from the preceding and following entries. All of these (71) may well have recorded a correct census birthplace, even

10 Levine, in an exercise cross-matching parish registers and samples from the 1851 census populations of Shepshed (an industrial village) and Bottesford (a closed rural village) (both in Leicestershire) showed higher and more consistent rates of baptism in the latter than the former, and also evidence of localised mobility: Levine, 'Reliability of parochial registration', 107–22. He, like Yasumoto in chapter 10, also shows how often 'missing' baptisms can be found in neighbouring parishes. The same point is made in a paper by Wall, 'Reconstitution and census', 73–90.

11 Of wives whose maiden names are identifiable only through the presence of a relation in the household, quite a few were baptised in one of the six but must have married elsewhere; this could well apply to others with no additional means of identification. The extensive reconstituting of families has made possible many identifications which might otherwise have gone unknown, most particularly the identification as kin of a number of people returned only as lodgers; and the identification of the maiden names of wives whose marriages are not recorded in the six parishes, often either through the identification of her kin in her household or through the realisation that the eldest child, previously thought to be without a baptism record, was illegitimate and baptised under the mother's maiden name.

Table 19.3 Single census entries and baptism records in the six parishes

Parish	[1] Total population	[2] Singles with baptism	[3] Singles no baptism	[4] Checkable pop. (1–3)	[5] 4 as % of 1
Hartlip					
1851	342	70	69	273	79.8
1861	319	34	49	270	84.6
1871	355	20	75	280	78.9
1881	378	44	152	226	59.8
Newington					
1851	731	149	221	510	69.8
1861	854	72	212	642	75.2
1871	1,013	75	314	699	69.0
1881	1,038	3,114	431	607	58.5
Rainham					
1851	1,155	200	280	875	75.8
1861	1,422	106	286	1,136	79.9
1871	2,082	129	600	1,482	71.2
1881	2,696	452	1,083	1,613	59.8
Stockbury					
1851	589	99	169	420	71.3
1861	613	56	131	482	78.6
1871	590	26	157	433	73.4
1881	621	124	244	377	60.7
Upchurch					
1851	407	97	84	323	79.4
1861	314	20	35	279	88.9
1871	777	56	163	614	79.0
1881	1,112	176	483	629	56.6
Lower Halstow					
1851	344	77	55	289	84.0
1861	373	30	42	331	88.7
1871	504	43	127	377	74.8
1881	701	135	264	437	62.3
Totals	19,330	2,404	5,726	13,604	70.4

though it differs from the baptism place of residence. That leaves only eight cases: five of these may have incorrect census birthplaces (four are in long lists of dittos and one is a servant). The remaining three cases are interesting. Two are a brother and sister aged six and four who alone of their family are ascribed birthplaces in Bobbing, while all the siblings were baptised and the others were born in Newington; for the younger the baptism register records for place of residence 'Newington but belonging to Bobbing.' The meaning of 'belonging to' in this context is open to speculation. The last of the eight exceptions was a six year old living in Rainham with her grandparents, presumably temporarily, since her family in Upchurch includes a three-day-old baby. Her grandparents gave her birthplace as Rainham, carefully distinguishing her from their own children, so this may well have been

Table 19.4 Discrepancies in birthplaces

Parish	[1] Total population	[2] n. of E	[3] 2 as % of 1	[4] n. of A	[5] 2+4 as % of 1	[6] Checkable population[a]	[7] 2 as % of 6	[8] 2+4 as % of 6
Hartlip								
1851	342	4	1.2	1	1.5	273	1.5	1.9
1861	319	5	1.6	3	2.5	270	1.9	3.0
1871	355	3	0.9	6	2.5	280	1.1	3.2
1881	378	2	0.5	4	1.6	226	0.9	2.7
Newington								
1851	731	12	1.6	8	2.7	510	2.4	3.9
1861	854	10	1.2	16	3.0	642	1.6	4.1
1871	1,013	18	1.8	29	4.6	699	2.6	6.7
1881	1,038	19	1.8	22	4.0	607	3.1	6.8
Rainham								
1851	1,155	15	1.3	20	3.0	875	1.7	4.0
1861	1,422	33	2.3	26	4.2	1,136	2.9	5.2
1871	2,082	40	1.9	36	3.7	1,482	2.7	5.1
1881	2,696	50	1.9	34	3.1	1,613	3.1	5.2
Stockbury								
1851	589	9	1.5	12	3.6	420	2.1	5.0
1861	613	22	3.6	17	6.4	482	4.6	8.1
1871	590	19	3.2	13	5.4	433	4.4	7.4
1881	621	10	1.6	11	3.4	377	2.7	5.6
Upchurch								
1851	407	5	1.2	4	2.2	323	1.6	2.8
1861	314	11	3.5	5	5.1	279	3.9	5.7
1871	777	12	1.5	19	4.0	614	2.0	5.1
1881	1,112	28	2.5	16	4.0	629	4.5	7.0
Halstow								
1851	344	7	2.0	7	4.1	289	2.4	4.8
1861	373	11	3.0	7	4.8	331	3.3	5.4
1871	504	7	1.4	19	5.2	377	1.9	6.9
1881	701	16	2.3	16	4.6	437	3.7	7.3
Totals	19,330	368	1.90	351	3.7	13,604	2.7	5.3

Notes: E = Error: this year's version of birthplace certainly or probably wrong.
A = Anomaly: one discrepancy among many; right version not known.
a = See column 4 of Table 19.2 for calculation of checkable population.

correct, though her baptism and residence at the time were in Upchurch. So all but a handful of baptism records support, or at least fail to contradict, the census birthplaces. This analysis seems to show that baptismal records are a very useful source for checking birthplaces. Baptism records have also been used as an extra check for multiple census entries. The last column of Table 19.3 shows that the percentage of the population which is checkable is very high in all parishes until 1871, though it falls in 1881, mainly because those aged under 10 (a significant proportion of the population) cannot be checked against another census.

In the case of multiple census appearances any birthplaces found to be definitely or probably wrong have been coded E (for error) ; multiple differences where the correct version is uncertain have been coded A (for anomaly). Table 19.4 above lists the numbers and percentages of errors and anomalies in each parish 1851–81. A calculation of the total numbers over all 24 censuses shows 368 errors and 351 anomalies in 19,330 observations. Errors amount to 1.9 per cent of this total and errors and anomalies together (719) amount to 3.7 per cent. These 719 represent, not individuals, but occasions on which an error, certain or possible, occurred. The 368 errors account for 338 individuals (30 have 2) and the 351 anomalies for 158 individuals. (Eight of them have a mixture of Es and As, so there are in all 488 different individuals with at least one birthplace discrepancy.) As the 158 individuals coded A appear on 2, 3 or 4 occasions, it is likely that they have given a correct birthplace on at least one occasion. It is therefore reasonable to deduct these 158 from the total of 719, and this reduces the number of certain or possible errors to 561, or 2.9 per cent of the total population.

However, since there is no means of knowing the proportion of errors among the single entries with no baptism records, the numbers of these should be deducted from the total population in order to find the percentage of discrepancies in the total checkable population. The numbers and percentages for the checkable population in each census are to be found in the last 2 columns of Table 19.3. The total checkable population over all 24 censuses is 13,604. The 368 errors represent 2.7 per cent of this number and the 719 errors and anomalies together represent 5.3 per cent. The 561, the nearest obtainable figure of certain and possible errors, represents 4.1 per cent of the checkable total. This last figure seems to be the most satisfactory overall estimate.

In addition to those coded E or A, there are 58 records that were entered as blank or not known, but these birthplaces are, in fact, known from other years. These have not been included in the Es and As, since they are not discrepancies of the same sort. If they are added to the 719, the total of 777 represents 4.0 per cent of the total population and 5.7 per cent of the checkable population.

Birthplace discrepancy

It is difficult to account for such variations as exist in birthplace accuracy between individual parishes and years as shown in Table 19.4. Hartlip has the best record and Stockbury the worst. All are better in 1851 than subsequently. The very high figures for Stockbury in 1861 and 1871 might be attributable to the fact that its enumerators were somewhat less literate than those elsewhere. John Jennings in 1861 was a publican and Daniel Goodhew in 1871 was a victualler and farmer.

Both had good clear hands, but also impressively idiosyncratic spelling and a tendency to carelessness. However, John Jennings was also the enumerator in Stockbury in 1851 where the figure for discrepancies is far lower. Perhaps familiarity with the job had bred a certain contempt for detail. And the enumerator in Halstow in 1881, which also has a high percentage of discrepancies, was a pernickety young schoolmaster with a penchant for irrelevant details subsequently crossed out by his superiors.

It seems unjust to blame the enumerator for some of the errors, and some mistakes seem to suggest that he had difficulty in reading illegible handwriting or perhaps on occasion he misheard what was said. Possible examples of the former are Chilham/Chatham, Dymchurch/Newchurch, Eastbourne/Littlebourne, Uffington/Orpington (both of these given as in Berkshire and as an alternative to Reading which appears on a third occasion). Harriet Andrews, twice given as Boughton (pronounced Bawton) and once as Borden, perhaps misled the enumerator by the way she spoke. Another case of this surely is that of Emily Philpott, recorded as Guildford, Surrey in 1871 and Kent, Sturry in 1881. And the enumerator of Upchurch in 1881 must be forgiven for crossing out and overwriting the data for the Jacobs family: Amelia, wife of George, and her eldest child were born in Queenboro', but the family lived on the island of Greenboro' in Upchurch and the next two children were born there.

However, the enumerator was not always so anxious to be accurate. Among the 368 errors there are 116 dittos (over 31 per cent). He probably should have known that Manchester and Newmarket were not in Kent, though he could hardly have been expected to recognise some of the small places named by migrants from other counties. Finally, John Longley, the schoolmaster in Rainham continuously from 1851–81 and the enumerator of one part of Rainham 1861–81, who seems to be meticulous as well as neat and literate, gives his own birthplace twice as Chatham and twice as Rochester.

Some apparent discrepancies pointed out by computer checking turn out not to be real discrepancies at all, and have not been counted as such for the purposes of this exercise. Sometimes a seeming discrepancy is merely a matter of added detail, for example specifying one of the several Boughtons in Kent. Sheppey might be more exactly entered as Queenborough, or Australia as Melbourne. On the other hand detail can sometimes cause confusion, for example the person who gives Malling as her birthplace in one census, specifying East Malling in another, and Town (West) Malling in a third.

Quite often the name of a farm or of a smaller district within a parish is given instead of the parish name itself, and in this case, as

Tillott recommends, local knowledge is essential,[12] and a standard work of reference is important, such as exists for Kent in the form of Wallenberg.[13] So one can ascribe Darling (Darland) to Gillingham, Beacon Hill and Luton to Chatham, Troy Town to Rochester, Yelsted to Stockbury and Maresbarrow (Meresborough) to Rainham. St Margaret's always seems to mean Rochester and St Mary's Hoo. An individual who gives Yelsted in one year and Stockbury in another has not been counted as a case of birthplace error; he knew he was born in Stockbury and tells us so on both occasions, if in different words. Some of these variations can be difficult to interpret, especially where a phonetic spelling of a mispronounced name is used, though the places named in the description of the enumeration district which appears at the beginning of the census record are helpful indicators.[14] There was also some confusion about parish boundaries; hence an entry such as 'Key Street, Newington, Bobbing'. Key Street is on the Dover Road which forms part of the boundary between Bobbing and Borden and is listed by Wallenburg in Borden; Newington is adjacent to both.

The opposite situation arises in the 40 instances when people have nominated the nearest large place to their probable birthplace on one occasion but are more exact on another, for example Chard-Taunton, Uffington-Reading, Stock-Chelmsford, Brook-Canterbury, Buckland-Dover.

Where Hollingbourne or Milton is given on one occasion, and a parish within its hundred on another, it is possible that the person concerned was born in the workhouse but was thought of as belonging to the parish named.[15] This explanation is likely to be relevant in the case of 7 errors and 8 anomalies. A reference to workhouse censuses can often supplement a vague entry in a parish in another year.

In a very few cases, it looks as if a child (especially a first child) was born at the mother's home but in later years was thought of as born in the same parish as the rest of the family. Family reconstitution can throw light on such problems.[16]

Among the real discrepancies, over 51 per cent of the errors also have a correct entry on more than one occasion. Over 27 per cent of these can be checked against a baptism record. Baptism registers

12 Tillott, 'Sources of inaccuracy', 109.

13 Wallenberg, *The place-names of Kent*.

14 For example, Boar's Ear as the sole given birthplace is not immediately identifiable as Beaux Aires farm in Stockbury, but the Stockbury enumerators in their description of the parish produce such ingenious versions as Bousears and Bowshare as well as a more nearly correct Bozair.

15 At the time of the 1851 census, Grace Bronger, alias Godden, was in Hollingbourne workhouse, aged 1, with her mother; her birthplace was given as Hollingbourne. In 1861 when she is with her mother and step(?) father in Stockbury and in 1871 when she is a servant in Newington her birthplace is given as Stockbury.

16 Jane Smith, wife of William, was recorded as Rainham in 1851 but Galway in the next three censuses. Marriage records identify her as the daughter of a woman who appears in the Rainham census of 1851 with a Tipperary birthplace.

combined with census data can indicate when a family migrated to the area and help to point to the approximate date at which the birthplaces of the children of these families can correctly be assigned to the six parishes and thus to detect mistakes in later censuses.

If parents appear to be punctilious about getting their children baptised, even the absence of a baptism can sometimes be useful negative evidence especially if combined with an absence from one census of a family who appear in the preceding and subsequent ones. The care with which parents distinguish the birthplaces of siblings is another indication of accuracy. It quite often happens that an individual has a correct birthplace as long as his parent is responsible for his schedule but when he becomes head of a household he associates himself with the place he lived in as a child, wrongly believing himself to have been born there. Heads responsible for wives' entries sometimes made similar mistakes about them.

There are some insoluble muddles. Michael Fitzgerald, a tailor of Newington, gives Aspley as his birthplace in 1861, Woburn in 1871 and Sandy in 1881 (all in Bedfordshire). Jesse Attwood, an agricultural labourer of Stockbury, gives Hollingbourne in 1851, Thurnham in 1861 and Hucking in 1871. Elizabeth Dennis gives Minster (Sheppey) and Canterbury respectively when she is head of her household in Halstow in 1851 and 1861; in 1871 and 1881 when she is living in her son-in-law's household in Upchurch her birthplace is given first as Strood and later as Canterbury. Sometimes the explanation is obviously that a husband's and wife's birthplaces have been transposed. The worst muddles about birthplace seem to occur in the same families with uncertainties about ages. In all, about one third of those with birthplace errors or anomalies also have an age error.

Some apparent muddles may have an explanation. The yeoman farmer recorded in Newington 1861–81 who gave his own birthplace as Halstow, Borden and Milton respectively, his wife's as Milton, Upchurch, Milton and his daughter's as Borden, Bobbing and Borden may well have held land in several parishes. The same applies to William Walter, a substantial farmer and a J.P. by 1881, who sometimes gives Bobbing and sometimes Upchurch. Baptism records seem to confirm this point for these yeomen farmers, who held their land under the Kentish custom of gavelkind by which it was divided between heirs.

Many of the cases illustrated above suggest a very considerable mobility, but mobility within a small area. Some families moved so often that they seem hardly to be able to remember which of their numerous brood was born where. There are as many as 53 examples of this problem among errors and 34 among anomalies. There were quite

Table 19.5a Status in household of people with birthplace discrepancies

Status	[1] Total population	[2] %	[3] Checkable population	[4] %	[5] n. in E	[6] %	[7] n. of A + E	[8] %
Head	4,119	20.6	3,136	22.3	130	33.9	289	38.8
Wife	3,327	16.7	2,350	16.7	110	28.7	201	27.0
Son/daughter[a]	9,493	47.5	7,039	50.1	82	21.4	155	20.8
Parent[a]	160	0.8	97	0.7	3	0.8	11	1.5
Other relation	936	4.7	597	4.3	19	5.0	24	3.2
Servant	984	4.9	469	3.3	21	5.5	29	3.9
Lodger	794	4.0	345	2.5	18	4.7	33	4.4
Visitor	159	0.8	29	0.2	1	0.3	2	0.3
Total[b]	19,972	100.0	14,062	100.0	384	100.0	744	100.0

Notes: E = Error: this year's given birthplace certainly or probably wrong.
A = Anomaly: one discrepancy among many; right version not known.
a = including in-laws; *b* = total numbers exceed those on other tables because some individuals fall into more than one category.

Table 19.5b Category ratios for status in household

	[1] Proportions checkable	[2] Proportion in Error	[3] Proportions in Error+Anomaly	[4] Proportions in Error	[5] Proportions in Error+Anomaly
Head	76.1	3.2	7.0	4.2	9.2
Wife	70.6	3.3	6.0	4.7	8.6
Son/daughter[a]	74.2	0.9	1.6	1.2	2.2
Parent[a]	60.6	1.9	6.9	3.1	11.3
Other relation	63.8	2.0	2.6	3.2	4.0
Servant	47.7	2.1	3.0	4.5	6.2
Lodger	43.5	2.3	4.2	5.2	9.6
Visitor	18.2	0.6	1.3	3.5	6.9
All	70.4	1.9	3.7	2.7	5.3

Notes: Column 1 = Column 3 as % of Column 1 in Table 19.5a.
Column 2 = Column 5 as % of Column 1 in Table 19.5a.
Column 3 = Column 7 as % of Column 1 in Table 19.5a.
Column 4 = Column 5 as % of Column 3 in Table 19.5a.
Column 5 = Column 7 as % of Column 3 in Table 19.5a.
a = including in-laws.

a few military and naval families, as well as bargemen, whose occupation made them mobile.[17] Even more striking is the fact that 536 (over 74 per cent) of all errors and anomalies are within 5 miles of the alternative version of the birthplace; and 399 (over 55 per cent) are within 2 miles, or in an adjacent parish.

17 Elizabeth Baker, present in Rainham 1841–71 as wife, widow and remarried, gave Woolwich and Sheerness as alternative birthplaces.

Table 19.5c Status in household: servants and lodgers by parishes and years

Parish	Numbers and category ratios (total population = 100) Total n.	Servants n.	Servants Ratio	Lodgers n.	Lodgers Ratio
Hartlip	1,429	105	7.4	36	2.5
Newington	3,762	209	5.6	149	4.0
Rainham	7,652	354	4.6	300	3.9
Stockbury	2,458	179	7.3	43	1.8
Upchurch	2,677	104	3.9	161	6.0
Halstow	1,994	33	1.7	105	5.3
Total[a]	19,972	984	4.9	794	4.0
Year	**Numbers and category ratios (total population = 100) Total n.**	**Servants n.**	**Servants Ratio**	**Lodgers n.**	**Lodgers Ratio**
1851	3,682	288	7.8	122	3.3
1861	4,061	221	5.4	158	3.9
1871	5,481	258	4.7	180	3.3
1881	6,748	217	3.2	334	5.0
Total[a]	19,972	984	4.9	794	4.0

Notes: *a* = Total numbers match those on Table 19.5a.

The characteristics of birthplace misreporting

It is useful to trace some of the characteristics of those with birthplace discrepancies, particularly sex ratio, status in household, age group, social class and the birthplace itself. The first of these can be briefly stated: the sex ratio (f=100) for the total population over all parishes and all years is 107.2; that for errors, 119.6, and that for errors plus anomalies, 116.9. There was a majority of males in all parishes except Hartlip and in most years, and it seems that males were even more likely to record a birthplace error.

Tables 19.5 above, and Tables 19.6, 19.7 and 19.8 below, respectively, are concerned with the other four characteristics. The numbers of errors in each category are given, also the percentage which these numbers represent as a proportion of total errors, but it is more important and interesting to look at each category as a percentage of the same category in the total or checkable population, and this is what the category ratios do. These columns show which categories seem most or least likely to record birthplace errors. In the case of age groups Table 19.6 shows clearly that errors (and anomalies) become increasingly likely with age. For instance, for every 100 under the age of 10 in the

Table 19.5d Status in household: servants and lodgers by parishes and years

Parish	Numbers and category ratios (checkable population = 100) Checkable n.	Servants n.	Servants Ratio	Lodgers n.	Lodgers Ratio
Hartlip	1,076	47	4.4	23	2.1
Newington	2,545	88	3.5	69	2.7
Rainham	5,316	176	3.3	128	2.4
Stockbury	1,742	77	4.4	26	1.5
Upchurch	1,895	62	3.3	46	2.4
Halstow	1,488	19	1.3	53	3.6
Total[a]	14,062	469	3.3	345	2.5

Parish	Numbers and category ratios (checkable population = 100) Checkable n.	Servants n.	Servants Ratio	Lodgers n.	Lodgers Ratio
1851	2,783	153	5.5	74	2.7
1861	3,262	121	3.7	75	2.3
1871	4,012	111	2.8	104	2.6
1881	4,005	84	2.1	92	2.3
Total[a]	14,062	469	3.3	345	2.5

Notes: *a* = Total numbers match those on Table 19.5a.

checkable population, there are 0.8 with a birthplace error; in the 10–19 age group this increases to 2.2. If errors and anomalies are considered together, the number per hundred of the checkable population increases steadily from 1.4 for the under tens to 10.5 for the over fifty-nines. The similar columns in Table 19.7 suggest that social classes IV and V are more likely to have birthplace errors and class I least likely.[18]

Table 19.5b shows errors classified by household status in proportion to both total and checkable populations. In view of the age group findings it is not surprising to see that sons and daughters are least likely to record an error and parents much more likely (parents particularly likely to record an anomaly rather than an error) but it is perhaps more surprising to find heads, who were responsible for their own and others' details, so high on the list. Errors among servants, lodgers and visitors form a higher proportion of the checkable than of the total population which reflects the fact that a smaller percentage of these three categories is checkable, this being clear from Table 19.5a.

Over all parishes and all years together, there is a high degree of correlation in respect of household status between total and checkable populations (a correlation coefficient of +0.99), but some variation

18 The social classification used is that suggested by Armstrong, 'Information about occupation'. Social class has been ascribed to all the employed according to their jobs, to others according to the head of the household. 'UK' means class unknown and this includes a large proportion of visitors.

Table 19.6 Age groups of people with birthplace discrepancies

Age group	Checkable population	%	n. in E	E %	Ratio	n. of E + A	E + A %	Ratio
	Numbers and percentages of errors and anomalies plus category ratios for each age group (checkable population for each age group = 100)							
Under 10	3,924	28.8	30	8.2	0.8	56	7.8	1.4
10 – 19	2,835	20.8	63	17.1	2.2	110	15.3	3.9
20 – 39	3,400	25.0	124	33.7	3.7	234	32.6	6.9
40 – 59	2,375	17.5	104	28.3	4.4	207	28.8	8.7
Over 59	1,070	7.9	47	12.8	4.4	112	15.6	10.5
Total	13,604	100.0	368	100.0	2.7	719	100.0	5.3

Notes: E = Error: this year's given birthplace certainly or probably wrong.
A = Anomaly: one discrepancy among many; right version not known.

Table 19.7 Social classes of people with birthplace discrepancies

Social class	Checkable population	%	n. in E	E %	Ratio	n. of E + A	E + A %	Ratio
	Numbers and percentages of errors and anomalies plus category ratios for each class (checkable population for each class = 100)							
I	182	1.3	1	0.3	0.6	1	0.1	0.6
II	1,363	10.0	20	5.4	1.5	57	7.9	4.2
III	2,471	18.2	39	10.6	1.6	96	13.4	3.9
IV	7,592	55.8	255	69.3	3.4	442	61.5	5.8
V	1,854	13.6	47	12.8	2.5	110	15.3	5.9
UK	142	1.0	6	1.6	4.2	13	1.8	9.2
Total	13,604	100.0	368	100.0	2.7	719	100.0	5.3

Notes: E = Error: this year's given birthplace certainly or probably wrong.
A = Anomaly: one discrepancy among many; right version not known.
The social classification is based on that suggested by Armstrong, 'Information about occupation'; UK = class not known.

between parishes and between years, as is evident from Tables 19.5c and 19.5d, which give a breakdown for just two categories, servants and lodgers.[19] Table 19.5c shows that there were proportionately more lodgers in the total population in Upchurch and Halstow, and, in 1881 (where and by when the brickmaking industry had developed), there were more servants in Hartlip and Stockbury (which remained agricultural parishes). The proportion of servants over all parishes decreases gradually from 1851 to 1881. A comparison of Tables 19.5c and 5d shows that the proportions of these categories in the checkable population are always smaller than their proportions in the total population. This is especially noticeable where their percentages in

19 Servants include domestic, trade and agricultural; lodgers include boarders.

Table 19.8a Birthplaces of total and checkable populations

Birthplace	[1] Total population	[2] %	[3] Checkable population	[4] %	[5] Category ratio 3 as % of 1
Home parish	8,941	46.3	7,883	58.0	88.2
Neighbour[a]	2,453	12.7	2,221	16.3	90.5
5 miles[b]	2,959	15.3	1,537	11.3	51.9
20 miles[c]	2,838	14.7	1,298	9.5	45.7
Outer Kent[d]	688	3.6	224	1.7	32.6
London[e]	351	1.8	108	0.8	30.8
Elsewhere	1,070	5.5	333	2.5	31.1
Not known	30	0.2	0	0.0	0.0
Total	19,330	100.0	13,604	100.0	70.4

Notes: *a* = one of the other 5 parishes of this exercise;
b = within a radius of 5 miles from the centre of Rainham excluding the above;
c = within a radius of more than 5 but less than 20 miles;
d = elsewhere in Kent and Sussex;
e = the former LCC area.

Table 19.8b Birthplaces of errors and anomalies (Es and As)

Birthplace	[1] n. in E	[2] %	[3] n. of E + A	[4] %	[5] Category ratios[f] E	[6] E + A
Home parish	46	12.5	73	10.2	0.6	0.9
Neighbour[a]	114	31.0	128	17.8	5.1	5.8
5 miles[b]	107	29.1	224	31.2	7.0	14.6
20 miles[c]	71	19.3	186	25.9	5.5	14.3
Outer Kent[d]	9	2.5	43	6.0	4.0	19.2
London[e]	6	1.6	19	2.6	5.6	17.6
Elsewhere	15	4.1	46	6.4	4.5	13.8
Not known	0	0.0	0	0.0	0.0	0.0
Total	368	100.0	719	100.0	2.7	5.3

Notes: *a–e* as for Table 19.8a; *f* = each equivalent category of checkable population = 100.

the total population are highest, suggesting a high level of in-migration. The fact that fewer servants, lodgers and visitors than other categories are checkable and that more of these show errors suggests the need for special caution in the use of their birthplace data.

This is particularly so since lodgers written off as 'not known' were not included in these figures. In 1841, in Newington, the enumerator was the son of a victualler living in his father's household who provided no names, no occupations and no birthplace counties for five lodgers in his father's inn. There is no later case as bad as this, but there are altogether 23 inn lodgers in the CEBs of 1851–81 with no birthplace given. Some employers seem to have been meticulous about supplying correct birthplaces for their domestic and farm servants living in; others just listed them all as the census parish.

A further line of enquiry was prompted by findings made by Razzell in a pilot study of cross-matching register and census data (1851 and 1861): that there were more discrepancies in urban than rural areas, that migration was an important factor in causing birthplace errors and that birthplace evidence was significantly more reliable for natives than for those not born in the census parish.[20] The data in Tables 19.8a and 19.8b above support these findings.[21] It is clear from Table 19.8a that there are far more errors among non-natives than natives, the latter accounting for only 12.5 per cent of errors and 10.2 per cent of errors plus anomalies. But the table also seems to show that 60.1 per cent of Es and 49.9 per cent of As plus Es belong to those born within 5 miles, and 79.4 per cent and 74.8 per cent respectively to those born within 20 miles, which appears to confirm the earlier presumption of a high degree of localised mobility. However, Table 19.8b suggests that caution is advisable in drawing inferences from these conclusions, since calculations can be made only on the checkable part of the population and this, unsurprisingly, is biased in favour of those born in or near the census parishes. The checkable population categories shown in Table 19.8a as ratios of the total population categories indicate this clearly: for every one hundred in the total population born in the census parish 88.2 are checkable, but the ratio steadily decreases to 31.1 for those born 'elsewhere'. The single, apparently surprising, exception, that those born in the neighbouring five parishes are more likely to be checkable than natives, may be explicable by the tendency to often incorrectly record the census parish as the birthplace, for example by the use of dittos or by some employers for their servants. In this respect one might regard native birthplaces as less reliable.

When the category ratios for errors and anomalies are considered (Table 19.8b) it is clear that natives still represent a very small proportion, but other ratios are more evenly divided over the various distances from the census parish. For instance, the London figure given as a percentage of all errors and anomalies (2.6 per cent) does not look as impressive as the category ratio, which shows that for every one hundred native Londoners in the checkable population there were 17.6 errors or anomalies.

20 Razzell, 'Evaluation of baptism', 121–46.

21 Where there are known errors, the correct version of the birthplace has been used for this calculation.

Conclusion

The conclusions of this exercise are generally reassuring. The percentages of errors seem to be a good deal lower than those cited in the first paragraph of this chapter. This is perhaps partly due to the fact that variations of spelling or description have not been counted as discrepancies if they were clearly intended to indicate the same place. The effectiveness of cross-referencing and checking is in proportion to the number of baptism and census data used. It is encouraging to know that, when sufficient time and data have been available for the necessary processing, this has demonstrated, first, that a large percentage of the population is checkable, especially up to 1871, second, that quite a small percentage of the checkable population shows any birthplace discrepancy, and third, that many of the discrepancies that do exist prove not to be very serious. The findings point to the need for two caveats: that the birthplaces of servants, lodgers and visitors might justify a modicum of suspicion; and that caution is advisable in using birthplace data as the sole basis for calculating mobility, in view of the degree of localised mobility implicit in this analysis. Nevertheless, the fact that about three quarters of alternative versions are within five miles of each other and over half within two miles supports the proposition that fear of inaccuracy should not constitute a major impediment to researchers using this evidence.

20

Patterns of migration of textile workers into Accrington in the early-nineteenth century

WILLIAM TURNER

Introduction

The inclusion of detailed information on place of birth in the CEBs has enabled the study of general patterns of migration towards expanding industrial centres during the first half of the nineteenth century. However, to date, there have been few attempts to look at the patterns for specific occupational groups. A study of the cotton manufacturing and calico printing industry in Accrington in 1851 reflects not only the attractive power of the growing town for unskilled workers, within a relatively restricted locality, but also the wider catchment area for skilled and professional groups, (particularly within calico printing) many of whom came from other places associated with the industry.

Calico printing was established in Accrington before 1807. By 1851 there were five works in the town employing approximately 1,200 hands. There were also 12 integrated cotton-spinning and weaving mills employing 1,380 hands.[1] These mills produced the calico cloth which was used in the calico printing industry. In the early 1850s there began a period of more rapid expansion in the town's industry, as witnessed by the construction of new cotton mills and engineering works whose employees later in the decade far exceeded the numbers engaged in calico printing. Nevertheless, in 1851 the industrial structure of Accrington was largely dominated by calico weaving and printing.

The town is covered by the 1851 CEBs for the townships of Old Accrington and New Accrington.[2] The townships were adjacent and, for most non-local government matters, were considered by the inhabitants simply as 'Accrington'. Therefore, for the purpose of analysis, the various CEBs were combined.

Data

In attempting to examine migratory movements of heads of household, the information on birthplace has been used extensively, taking birthplace as a surrogate measure for place of origin. It is realised that

1 Rothwell, *Industrial heritage*, 2–6.
2 CEBs 1851, Accrington, PRO HO 107/2250.

Table 20.1 Definition of socio-economic groups (SEGs)

Anderson's definitions	SEG	Accrington cotton workers	SEG
Professional & managerial	I		
Clerical	II	Professional, managerial, supervisory	I
Trade	III		
Higher factory	IV	Skilled	II
Artisan	V		
Lower factory	VI	Unskilled	III
Labourer	VII		
Hand-loom weaver	VIII		
Unclassified	IX	excluded	
Not employed	X		

Notes: On the assumption that wages paid were appropriate to skills, lists of occupations and wage rates for 1849 and 1852 were used as a guide to place occupation with socio-economic groups.

Source: Based on Anderson, *Family structure*, 26. Occupations and wage rates for 1849 were taken from Turnbull, *Calico printing in Great Britain*, 215. Average hours per day and wages paid at Broad Oak Paintworks, Accrington in 1852 were taken from Hargreaves, *Recollections of Broad Oak*, 20.

this assumption will not always be true, but it is justified in the absence of more precise data. In some cases the progress of families towards the town can be plotted by noting the birthplaces of children. But in no case is it possible to determine the total number, or duration of, intermediate residences. Also, where heads of household were single men or where there were no children in a household either because of childless married couples or because of elderly married couples whose children had left home, it was not possible to identify any movements between place of birth and place of residence in 1851.

Information from the CEBs on occupations is very detailed and indicates the vast range of skills and specialisations that comprised the cotton industry. A total of 127 different occupational descriptions were identified. This information also emphasises the diversity of occupational status within the industry, ranging in this example from unskilled labourers to large employers.

Because of the desire to ascertain differences, if any, in the migration patterns of professional, skilled and unskilled workers, the occupations were arranged into three appropriate socio-economic groups (SEG). These are a modification of Anderson's ten SEG definitions and are shown in Table 20.1 above.[3] The group designated 'professional, managerial and supervisory' includes occupations such as 'master engraver', 'print works superintendent' and 'designer to calico printer'. Manufacturers were also included in this group, one of whom

3 Anderson, *Family structure*, 26.

Table 20.2 Heads of household employed in cotton industry by socio-economic groups: Accrington, 1851

	Total	%	n. of occupations
Profession etc.	52	6.3	26
Skilled	402	48.8	38
Unskilled	369	44.8	63
Total	823	100.0	127

described himself as a 'Turkey red dyer'. Occupations in the group composed of skilled workers in the industry include 'block printers', 'block cutters', 'mule spinners' and 'power loom overlookers'. Mechanics and millwrights are also included. The unskilled workers are mostly described as 'labourer at colour shop', 'labourer to engraver', 'labourer at madder breaking' (a dye used in calico printing), or are employed as specialist machinery attendants such as beamers, rovers or twisters, etc.

In 1851 Accrington had a population of 10,376 with 2,057 heads of household. A total of 823 heads of household (40 per cent) were employed in the cotton industry. Of these 823 heads of household, 44.7 per cent were in calico printing. The allocation of the 823 heads of household into socio-economic groups is shown in Table 20.2 above. The specialisation within the industry may be considered an influencing factor on migration, and particularly on the choice of destination. The complexity of this specialisation indicates that even unskilled occupations (albeit lower paid than skilled occupations) were still highly specific and could influence an individual's choice of destination.

Migration

The birthplace of the groups are mostly within the region of England comprising Lancashire south of the river Lune, the West Riding of Yorkshire and north-east Cheshire. This is shown in Table 20.3 below. Of the 40 persons, of all groups, who were born elsewhere, 2 of the professional group came from Carlisle and 2 (a 'manufacturing chemist' and 'a Turkey red dyer') came from France. Sixteen of the skilled workers came from other parts of England, from places as far apart as Carlisle and Mitcham, Surrey. (These two places were, incidentally, calico-printing towns.) Four came from Ireland, one from Scotland and one from Gibralter. Nine of the unskilled workers came from towns and villages in the North and East Ridings of Yorkshire, four came from Ireland and one was born in Wales.

Table 20.3 **Birthplaces of heads of household by socio-economic groups: Accrington, 1851**

	Born Lancs., West Riding and NE Cheshire		Born elsewhere		Total	
	n.	%	n.	%	n.	%
Professional etc.	48	92.3	4	7.7	52	100
Skilled	380	94.5	22	5.5	402	100
Unskilled	355	96.2	14	3.8	369	100
Total	783	95.1	40	4.9	823	100

Table 20.4 **Distribution of heads of household employed in calico printing in Accrington, born in calico printing towns**

Group	[1] calico printing workers[a]	[2] born in calico printing towns	[2] as a % of [1]
Professional	13	10	76.9
Skilled	191	115	60.2
Unskilled	164	80	48.8

Notes: *a* = does not include calico printing workers born in Accrington.

Examining Table 20.4 (above)in conjunction with Figure 20.1 (below), it can be seen that the distribution of professional and skilled workers are mainly to the north-east and south-east of Accrington (up to 15 miles), with a less distinct distribution to the north-west (up to 30 miles). The distribution of unskilled workers is weaker in that birthplaces are clustered within a 10 mile radius, with the north-east and south-east pattern much less clearly defined. Investigation into the reasons for the north-east and south-east distribution indicated that it followed a pattern similar to the distribution of calico printing and cotton mill sites throughout Lancashire and north-east Cheshire.

Of the 80 unskilled workers in calico printing born in calico-printing towns, 59 (73.7 per cent) were born within 10 miles of Accrington. They tended to migrate around Accrington in a circulatory manner. For example, a labourer born in Church had his first child born in Accrington, then one born in Bradshaw (near Bolton), one in Accrington again, two in Haslingden, then a sixth and final child in Accrington. The remaining 21 unskilled workers were mostly from calico-printing towns further afield to the south and east. Those calico-printing workers born in non-calico-printing towns and villages (84 in total) were, with few exceptions such as individuals from Dublin, Liverpool and Norfolk, migrants from the rural areas lying to the north and east of Accrington. Of these, most were likely to have been economically

Figure 20.1 Distribution of calico printing towns and villages and places of origin of calico-printing workers: Accrington, 1851

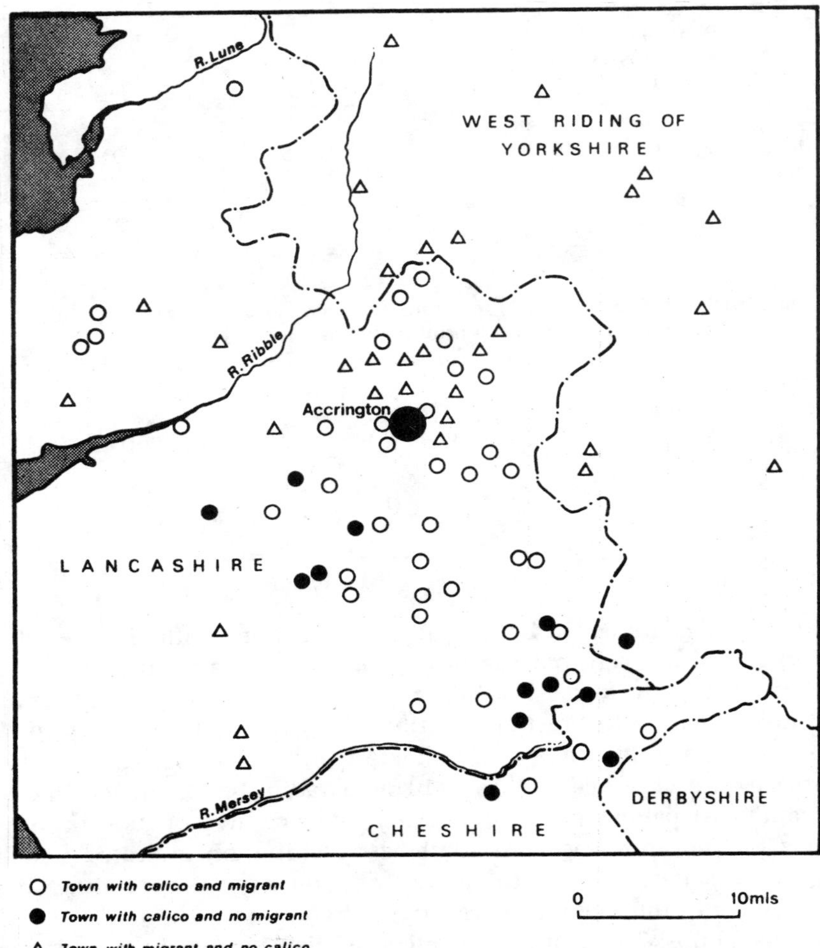

distressed, former handloom weavers becoming absorbed into other mechanised cotton occupations. This is a feature noted by Redford in his pioneering work on migration: 'From these districts many weavers went into the calico print trades as dyers, washers and labourers.'[4] It is significant that many unskilled migrants were from Lancashire and rural villages in the West Riding of Yorkshire and were present in Accrington in 1851 as 'dyers, washers and labourers'.

For the professional and skilled workers there is a distinctly different trend. During this period the calico-printing industry was adjusting itself to many technological changes. Most important were the

4 Redford, *Labour migration in England*, 41.

changes from block printing to machine printing and from natural dyes to synthetic aniline dyes. It was also subject to constant changes in fashion for the materials, designs, colours etc. The industry also suffered much from financial speculators and imprudent investors.[5] These adjustments and changes resulted in many financial failures of firms, which, by using hand-block printing techniques were being rendered uneconomic and non-viable by the competition of modernised firms using machine printing. These failures often precipitated movement of the workforce. These, particularly the skilled men, moved to other similar places of work so that they could continue in the occupations for which they had developed their skills. Examples of this are shown by the movement of a block printer, born in Salford, with four children born in Tottington, two born in Ramsbottom and one born in Accrington. The manager of a print works had one child born in Manchester, two in Stockport and one in Stubbins before moving to Accrington. All these towns had distinct calico-printing industries during that period. Lengths of stay at one place varied, with up to five children born at one place. There is also documentary evidence that industrial action by block printers resisting the introduction of new techniques sometimes ended in wholesale lock-out and the subsequent movement of groups of workers.[6]

Discussion

The picture is one of many skilled workers migrating in an effort to preserve their old skills in the face of competition from mechanised industry. The migration to Accrington could not always have been for higher wages. Accrington at that time was virtually ruled by the Hargeaves family of Board Oak print works. 'The Master is owner of all the property and reigns like a king – gives very low wages', was one contemporary opinion.[7]

The association between closures and subsequent moves to Accrington is illustrated by two examples. Firstly at Catterall, in the Fylde, a small calico printing works 'failed' in 1830. In 1851 there were 11 heads of household from Catterall living in Accrington and still employed in calico printing. The 11 were scattered throughout the town indicating an eventual dispersion over time. Secondly, at Ramsbottom, a calico-printing works employing 49 hands 'failed' in 1850. In 1851 six heads of household from Ramsbottom were employed in calico printing in Accrington. With them were a further eight heads of household, born in Carlisle, but with children born in Ramsbotton. (It was from Carlisle, a calico printing town, from which the previous owner of the

5 Turnbull, *Calico printing in Great Britain*, 70.

6 Graham, *A history of the print works*. First published 1850, reprinted as a series of articles in the *Manchester Guardian*, 1894.

7 Turnbull, *Calico printing in Great Britain*, 71.

Ramsbotton works had originally migrated in 1846, accompanied by a group of skilled calico printing workers).[8] This group of 14 families were housed relatively close together and were mainly skilled workers.

Long-distance migration to Accrington only amounted to a small proportion of total moves (7.7 per cent or four persons in the professional group). However, those professional workers who moved to Accrington had a strong influence on the industry. Of the four persons, two were in the Carlisle/Ramsbottom group, the remaining two came from France. These highly skilled migrants were responsible for introducing innovations into the calico-printing industry, and much of the development of the modern industry in Accrington may be linked to their influence. This suggests that developments in an industry were not always spread by the diffusion of ideas in a contagious fashion, but that innovations could be transmitted over considerable distances by a single migratory move.

If one equates calico-printing towns and villages with 'more advanced' communities, the results of the study indicate some confirmation of the view, put forward by Anderson, that migrants born in more advanced communities were more likely to enter into the more secure and better paid jobs in a town.[9] But it is equally likely that calico printing workers did not always migrate for higher wages. This study suggests that there was a strong current of migrants who were seeking to retain their old skills, at whatever cost, in the face of technological change. They chose not to oppose change, nor to adapt to change, but sought to employ their abilities and skills elsewhere. It is clear that the nature of migration for all groups was affected by, and also influenced, the economic and industrial structure of Accrington and its dominance in the calico printing and cotton industry during a period of economic and technological change.

In conclusion, each of the three groups of workers was affected differently, which in turn produced differences in migration patterns. For professional workers, migration was closely linked to the technological development of the industry, with some individuals being adversely affected by the changes occurring throughout the industry. For skilled workers, the challenge to their skills and traditions by the changes and unrest in the industrial towns served them to seek opportunities elsewhere within the industry. Finally, unskilled workers tended to migrate to Accrington as a result of the economic distress in the rural areas of Lancashire and the West Riding of Yorkshire, and were drawn into the town seeking work within the developing calico-printing and cotton industries.

8 Graham, *A history of the print works*.
9 Anderson, 'Urban migration', 131–43.

21

Brenchley: a study of migratory movements in a mid-nineteenth-century rural parish

BOGUSIA WOJCIECHOWSKA

Introduction

The movement of rural labour and the workings of the rural labour market have all too often been neglected by social historians in favour of the study of the effect of industrialisation on urban society.[1] Yet the condition of the southern agricultural labourer, and, in particular, his reluctance to move to the manufacturing areas of the north, were subjects for frequent comment in the nineteenth century:

> though of all classes . . . agricultural labourers are under the greatest necessity to leave their birthplaces, and have the greatest inducement to do so, no class is so hard to move away.[2]

For example, the workforce in the Weald of Kent was discussed in this context, the Weald being an area virtually devoid of industrial employment and noted for the presence of 'surplus' labour. T. L. Hodges reported to the Select Committee of the House of Commons on Emigration that:

> there is in almost every parish, and has for several years past been, a considerably larger number of people than the agricultural demands require . . . the parishes are in considerable distress.[3]

It was also an area with a high expenditure on poor relief. In the years 1841–71, Poor Law Unions in north/north-eastern Kent tended to have the lowest expenditure levels, while Unions with the highest levels were in the Weald. For example, in the periods 1841–71, and 1865–71, Gravesend Union had a per capita real expenditure level of 3s. 11d. and

1 Anderson, *Family structure;* indeed, Anderson admits to a need for economic/demographic research based on rural areas, p.170. Drake, 'Ashford 1840–1870'; Armstrong, *Stability and change;* Lawton, 'Population of Liverpool', 89–120; Anderson, 'Urban migration', 13–26; Clark, 'Kentish towns', 117–63. For some census-based exceptions see Schürer, 'The role of the family' and the contributions to Aslett *et al. Victorians on the move.*

2 Clifford, 'Labour bill', 125.

3 Evidence of T. L. Hodges (27 April, 1826) before the *Select Committee of the House of Commons on Emigration,* BPP 1826 IV, 133.

2s. 4d., while Hollingbourne Union had expenditure of 13s. 8d. and 10s. 2d. respectively.[4]

Migration studies at county and national level preclude a range of questions which together constitute a more detailed probe into labour mobility. From a county study we cannot, for example, confirm or deny the observations of those writers who, on the one hand, hold that agricultural labourers were in fact particularly immobile, or, on the other hand, the contrary view that they were very mobile, pulled by the attractions of industrial work and urban life. In order to discover whether or not this was the case, a closer examination of the composition of the 'movers' is essential. The task can be fulfilled most effectively by the study and linkage of the CEBs, an arduous task, even for the student of one parish. Brenchley, a parish lying in the heart of the Weald of Kent was found to be representative of the area and was selected for a study which would illuminate some factors influencing population mobility in a mid-nineteenth-century agricultural settlement in this region.[5]

The study parish

Brenchley was a parish whose population in mid-century numbered 2,704 people, and which continued to grow by as much as 17.3 per cent in the decade 1861–71.[6] The majority of its workforce was engaged in agriculture, nearly half of the adult males declaring themselves to be agricultural labourers (47.0, 46.6, and 46.8 per cent at the three censuses of 1841, 1851, and 1861).[7] At that time, when the absolute numbers of agricultural labourers were increasing (if we take workforce at the censuses of 1841, 1851, 1861 and 1871, the figures are 308, 392, 383 and 451 respectively), the numbers of small (20–100 acre) farmers were decreasing, in fact they fell from 53 to 41 per cent of all landholders in the years 1851–71.[8] The principal type of farming as given in the Tithe Award was that of arable, including the growing of hops. The reliance on corn meant that the district was likely to be much depressed in times of low corn prices, with resultant unemployment. In times of

4 'Real' expenditure was calculated using the Rousseaux Price indices, 1800–1913, cited in Mitchell and Deane, *Abstract of British historical statistics*, 471–2. The formula used to calculate real relief was: real relief = expenditure on relief (shillings and pence) + agricultural price index. See Poor Law Commissioners, Poor Law Board and Local Government Board Annual Reports, 1841–71, for expenditure on relief.

5 The representativeness of Brenchley was gauged by a detailed study of its occupational and demographic characteristics, namely, sex and age composition, and birth, death, marriage and population growth rates, and the subsequent comparison of those figures to those calculated for all the Wealden Union.

6 For a full discussion of Brenchley's economy see Wojciechowska-Kibble, 'Migration and the rural labour market'.

7 Adult is defined as synonymous with the workforce. A study of the CEBs for Brenchley revealed that those aged under 16 and over 70 represented an insignificant proportion of those gainfully employed. Consequently the age group 16–70 has been used to denote the adult population, or the workforce.

8 See Wojciechowska-Kibble, 'Migration and the rural labour market', 187–91.

crisis, the labourers had little alternative means of support as the percentage of household heads who held no land was high, and increasing (between 1851 and 1871 the figure rose from 87.5 to 93.8 per cent). However, as living-in was declining, the agricultural worker no longer had the security provided by this system of employment; in bad times he would now have to face the effects of increased food prices.[9] However, as living-in was usually a life-cycle phenomenon ending upon marriage, labourers always had to contend with making this adjustment. Furthermore, there was little alternative employment in an agricultural parish such as Brenchley, even the coming of the railway in the 1840s brought a minimal expansion in jobs.[10] The narrowness of opportunity is confirmed by a comparison of the occupational similarities/differences between fathers and sons; in 1851 and 1871, 96 and 95 per cent of sons with labouring fathers followed their father's occupations.[11] The sons who were least likely to follow in their father's footsteps were farmer's sons. In the two censal years of 1851 and 1871, 50 and 92 per cent respectively of those who left farming attained lower occupational status. Particularly striking is the fact that the fathers of these apparently downwardly mobile youths (as observed in the census of 1851) all had holdings under 75 acres.

However, it would be misleading to depict Brenchley as a pauperised parish. While agricultural labourers lacked any means of self-support or betterment, other than these jobs, their average wage of 12s. a week was on par with that for the county as a whole, and Kent was not considered to be a low-wage county. In fact, real wages did

9 Traditionally, a substantial proportion of farm servants (the bailiff, housekeeper, carter, ploughman, cowman, shepherd, dairy and kitchen maids) lived and ate with the farmer in the farmhouse. They thus had more security than labourers who lived outside the farm, as they were unlikely to be dismissed and turned out of the farm house in times of depression. There was the possibility that the farmer would continue to provide them not only with lodgings, but also board in times of unemployment. Upon marriage, the farm servant left his employer's house and became a labourer. However, this is not to imply that all those working in agriculture had once 'lived-in'. This was not the case, though as late as 1851, in Brenchley, 48.5 per cent of the farmers had employees living-in, a figure which dropped to 16.4 per cent by 1871. Tradesmen, though fewer in number, also practised this form of employment, and here the drop was from 23.1 to 8.8 per cent respectively. See also Kussmaul, *Servants in husbandry*, for a discussion of the decrease of the custom of 'living-in' from the late-eighteenth century onwards.

10 C. Tufnell, the assistant Poor Law Commissioner for Kent, 1835–42, estimated that nine-tenths of all railway employees in Kent were from outside the county. The South-Eastern Railway had a branch linking Brenchley parish (or more specifically the hamlet of Paddock Wood) with London built in 1842, but the Brenchley census shows that the percentage of the adult male labour force employed by the railway only grew from 1.6 per cent of the workforce in 1851 to 2.9 per cent in 1871.

11 The extent to which sons pursued their fathers' callings is in part a reflection of the restricted opportunities available for the younger generation. However, the study of inter-generational occupational change as an indicator of the rigidity of the social structure is undertaken with the following reservations: we can only trace co-resident fathers and sons, and not sons residing elsewhere. Unless we know the pursuits of all the sons, we cannot establish the precise degrees of occupational inheritance. Furthermore, a non-resident son could be working as a labourer for another employer, and yet in some later stage in his life-cycle, succeed to his father's holding. See Wojciechowska-Kibble, 'Migration and the rural labour market', 250–2.

not diverge markedly either in level or trend from those for the county or nation; in the early 1850s there was a rise in sustained real wages, though it was not as great as that which came about after 1870.[12] We can also infer the existence of unemployment from an examination of expenditure on poor relief. Local information is hard to gather, but from a few surviving relief ledgers and journals there is evidence to suggest that the early 1830s were very bad years indeed. At the time, approximately a quarter of Brenchley's household heads were claiming relief. Indeed, the Parish Overseer in 1832 was obliged to pressurise farmers into employing more labour. Brenchley's expenditure on poor relief was permanently above average for its Union, the county and England. However, after the mid-1850s, expenditure fell and the discussion of bad winters, bad harvests, and large-scale unemployment disappear from the Poor Law authorities' correspondence. Jones, when examining the agricultural labour market in England as a whole, presented a similar pattern of unemployment. He saw the 1840s as the turning-point in labour demand, a time after which there were continuous shortages of hands in the 1850s and 1860s. Indeed, he argued that the growth of Arch's Union in the 1870s was a response to a check in the upward course of the standard of living, as opposed to a desperate response to appalling conditions.[13]

Methodology

Reference was made at the beginning of this chapter to the census being an important source for the study of population mobility. There are two methods which can be adopted: firstly, an analysis of birthplace statistics, and, secondly, the linking of successive censuses. Birthplace statistics, or any single-year analysis of the CEBs present a generally static picture of the workforce or population. While such statistics identify the origins of the population at a specific moment in time, they do not indicate the subsequent persistence/mobility of the 'outsiders' or of the Brenchley-born, and it is not so much the origin of the workforce which is the measure of its response to socio-economic change as the

12 There is no unbroken series of statistics for the cost of living which would enable us to establish real wages in Brenchley during this period. Nevertheless, inferences can be drawn about the level and trend of wages in Brenchley from movements in the cost of living and real wages at the national and county levels, there being nothing in the Brenchley data to suggest that this would be inappropriate. The levels and trends in real wages were calculated using the Rousseaux Price indices (see footnote 4), and Bowley's agricultural wages: Real wages = Bowley's agricultural earnings + agricultural prices. If the value of real wages in the period 1830–35 (=64) is taken to equal 100, then the trend in real wages was: 1835–40 = 97, 1850–54 = 117, and 1870–74 = 141. See Mitchell and Deane, *Abstracts of British historical statistics*, 349–50 and 471–2.

13 Jones, 'Agricultural labour market in England', 322–38. For a more pessimistic assessment of the workers' employment prospects see Snell, 'Agricultural seasonal unemployment', 407–37. Snell identified the decrease in female employment and seasonality of male employment in the nineteenth century as serving to depress the family income.

transiency. Single-year analyses therefore disguise the rather brisk turnover of the population. The movement of labour is most effectively studied by the linking of successive censuses. This allows a fuller picture to be drawn of the rates of turnover and persistence (despite the fact that census linkage does not capture inter-censal change). These rates of turnover and persistence can be related in turn to contemporary environmental and economic stimuli.

The 1841 census did not record birthplace in detail; respondents were only asked whether or not they were born in the county of enumeration. Some 90 per cent of all 16–70-year-olds in Brenchley replied 'yes', the remainder replied 'no'. Successive censuses which specify the precise place of birth of each individual, reveal how the Kentish-born, and those from neighbouring counties, consistently formed the largest groupings in the parish. The almost exclusively local nature of Brenchley's catchment area within Kent, and some nearby Sussex parishes, is confirmed by the statistics referring to the parish of birth of the workforce. Approximately half of the 16-70-year-olds had been born in Brenchley, the others originating from a distance of only a few miles. The percentage of Brenchley-born declined from 51.8 to 43.8 per cent during the course of 20 years (1851–71), though they continued by far to be the largest contingent.

Population turnover

Three sets of census linkage were undertaken from the 1851 to the 1861 census, the 1861 to the 1871, and finally the 1851 to the 1861 to the 1871 census. Tables 21.1 and 21.2 below display the results of the 1851 to 1861, and 1861 to 1871 linkage.

In the three-way link, 927 persons had already been linked from 1851 to 1861. When these pairs were then linked to the 1871 census, 349 persons could be identified as having lived in Brenchley from 1851 to 1871. To summarise, in the decade 1851–61, 38 per cent of the 'truly linkable population' persisted; by 1861–71, the percentage had fallen to 31, and when the three-way link was conducted, 14 per cent of the truly linkable population were found to have remained in Brenchley for the 20 year period.[14] This considerable rate of turnover in Brenchley was not unexpected and had long been a feature of English rural life. In seventeenth-century Clayworth and Cogenhoe, Laslett and Harrison found that of the 401 persons present in 1676, after the subtraction of 91 deaths, 50.8 per cent persisted to 1688.[15] Clearly, although migration in mid-nineteenth-century rural communities was commonplace, it also

14 By 'truly linkable' is meant the population remaining after those who were registered in the parish registers as having been born or died between the two censuses are subtracted from the population, as the inclusion of such persons in the linking would artificially inflate the number of migrants.

15 Laslett and Harrison, 'Clayworth and Cogenhoe', 183.

Table 21.1 Linkage of the 1851 to the 1861 census

Persons available for linking (from both censuses)		5,572
Inter-censal deaths (from parish registers)		–146
Inter-censal births (from parish registers)		–488
Sub-total		4,938
Persons who could not be linked, the 'migrants'		3,084
Of these, numbers leaving after the 1851 census		1,632
Persons arriving in the inter-censal period		1,452
Difference	4,938–3,084 =	1,854
Total of persisters divided by 2 (as there were two census entries per person)		927
Total of matched pairs, 'persisters'		927

Table 21.2 Linkage of the 1861 to the 1871 census

Persons available for linking (from both censuses)		6,233
Inter-censal deaths (from parish registers)		–134
Inter-censal births (from parish registers)		–568
Sub-total		5,531
Persons who could not be linked, the 'migrants'		3,799
Of these, numbers leaving after the 1861 census		1,868
Persons arriving in the inter-censal period		1,931
Difference	5,531–3,799 =	1,732
Total of persisters divided by 2 (as there were two census entries per person)		866
Total of matched pairs, 'persisters'		866

varied in level from parish to parish. In her study of a nineteenth-century Essex village, taking into consideration non-persistence through death and the subtraction of temporary residents, Robin found that 64.5 per cent of the population of Elmdon stayed in the decade 1851–61.[16] In contrast, Schürer reports rates of 53 and 42 per cent for males and females, respectively, for a group of three Essex parishes centred around Hatfield Broad Oak in the west of the county, 1861–71, and rates of 42 and 39 per cent for a group of four parishes located on the Dengie Peninsula in the extreme east of the county, the latter being

16 Robin, *Elmdon*, 190. In fact that gap between Elmdon and Brenchley is even greater since Robin's migration figures are inflated by the inclusion amongst her migrants of women who could not be traced to the 1861 census as a result of name change through marriage.

much closer to the persistency levels displayed in Brenchley.[17]

When the census information concerning each individual was first coded, 20 separate pieces of information were recorded, including: birthplace, age, sex, marital condition, type of family, relationship to the head of the household, number of offspring, number of kin, occupation, area of land occupied by farmers.[18]

The birthplace statistics for Brenchley's workforce had shown the very local nature of Brenchley's catchment area. When the mobility of these persons was reviewed with reference to the county of birth, it was again evident that very few persons came from distant counties, and the few that did were unlikely to be in Brenchley on the occasion of the next census. The parish of birth data also demonstrated that the more distant the individual's birthplace was from Brenchley, the more likely it was that they would not be present at the time of the next census.[19] Two hundred and eighty-three Brenchley-born, or 36.2 per cent of the 1851 workforce, persisted from 1851–61, in comparison to 235 or 31.4 per cent, in the next decade. Fifty-four persons born in neighbouring parishes or those up to 6 miles away (or 23.6 per cent of the 1851 workforce) were still in Brenchley a decade later, the comparative figures for 1861 to 1871 being 50, or 21.8 per cent. It is evident that mobility was increasing, not only amongst the Brenchley-born, but amongst the workforce as a whole: 70.3 to 75.1 per cent. While persistence rates showed a positive relationship with birthplace, it is nevertheless likely that birthplace itself exerted no independent influence on persistence and further features of the persisters need to be explored.

The lack of either horizontal or vertical social mobility discussed earlier could have driven out the younger and more ambitious members of Brenchley's workforce. There was also a slight surplus of males in 1851 which may have been primarily related to migration. Obviously age is a useful variable for the study of migration. We know that for most persons marriage would have occurred in their early twenties, and that child rearing would have continued until the forties. In general terms, the responsibility and ties of individuals would increase with age, and we can hypothesise that these may have

17 Schürer, 'The role of the family', 113. This article includes a summary of other studies linking CEBs to study population turnover.

18 The information recorded was: surname, first name, age, parish of birth, union of birth, county of birth, sex, occupation, class, marital condition, place of residence in the parish, area of land occupied, type of household (see footnote 22 below), relation to head of household, the number of offspring, kin, staff, visitors, lodgers and boarders in the household. Surname, first name and the number of visitors were not used, since the name variable would tell us nothing about the reasons for persistence/migration, visitors were only temporary residents.

19 Looking at the Brenchley workforce, of all those born in Brenchley, 36.2 per cent persisted from 1851–1861, in comparison to 23.6 per cent from neighbouring parishes and parishes up to 6 miles away, and 20 per cent from parishes of 6–12 miles distance.

hindered mobility. This was found to be the case in Brenchley where persistency was found to increase with age, with the exception of those aged 51 and over in 1851–61, and those aged 16–20 and 51 and over in 1851–71, when this pattern was reversed.[20] However, even the most persistent of groups increased their mobility in the decade 1861–71, the one surprising exception being the very slight increase of 1.3 per cent in persistency amongst the 16–20 year-olds. The mobility of those over 55 may at first appear surprising, yet it was no doubt due to a greater likelihood of the break-up of the home involved in widowhood. The marginal increase in persistency amongst 16–25 year-olds was attributable to the increased persistency of young agricultural labourers.[21]

Overall, women and men had very similar persistency rates, although, as we shall discuss shortly, these rates differed markedly with age. A surplus of males in 1851 (the sex composition of Brenchley was 54 per cent male to 46 per cent female) would suggest a higher persistency rate amongst men in the previous decade. By 1871 the male 'surplus' was lower, due perhaps to males being slightly less persistent.

Given that persistency was affected by age, the mobility of Brenchley's eldest inhabitants could be related to their marital status. A breakdown of the marital condition of both migrants and persisters supports the suggestion that responsibility hinders mobility, for married persons were the least mobile. Indeed, of all workforce members described as married in the 1851 census, as many as 38.7 per cent were still present in Brenchley ten years later. Additionally, the widowed were very mobile. Thus unattached people, whether young or old, were liable to be mobile. The importance of the fact of being 'unattached' becomes evident when we compare the mobility of married and widowed older persons – the married revealed higher persistency rates. For the years 1851–61 and 1861–71, the unmarried exhibited persistency rates of 17.7 and 16.8 per cent, the married 38.7 and 30.0 per cent, and the widowed 15.2 and 17.1 pr cent respectively. Further analysis of migrant persons who were both old and widowed in 1851 showed that 'women with no stated occupation' to have been the dominant group (21.9 per cent), followed by the unemployed (18.8 per cent) and agricultural labourers (17.2 per cent). Perhaps these persons, affected by unemployment, retirement, sickness or poverty were obliged to return to their parish of settlement, enter the workhouse, or go and live with family or friends.

In our examination of life-cycle and labour mobility, we need also to examine the behaviour of different members of the family unit. As the

20 See Schürer, 'The role of the family', 118–9 for comparable findings.

21 Agricultural labourers aged 16–25 increased their persistence from 27.7 per cent in the period 1851–61 to 31.4 per cent between 1861 and 1871. Also the persistency of those aged 25–35 increased from 39.2 per cent to 45.3 per cent between 1851 and 1861 and 1861 and 1871.

majority of Brenchleyites lived in 'simple' households, it is not surprising that the greatest number of relatives were sons, daughters, wives and heads of households themselves.[22] Outside these immediate relatives the only other substantial groups were lodgers and servants (including assistants and governesses).

If lack of opportunities served to encourage the out-migration of the young, we would expect adult co-resident sons and daughters to be less persistent than their parents. In fact, while persistency amongst the former remained stable, persistent heads and their wives declined. Daughters were less persistent than sons, perhaps because they left home to marry or enter into service. Furthermore evidence supplied by the 20-year linkage showed that the wives, followed by the husbands, were the most persistent (16.5 per cent and 12.3 per cent respectively), their children less so (sons 9.4 per cent, daughters 6.7 per cent), while no servants and only three (5.2 per cent) of the assistants of 1851 could be found in Brenchley in 1871. Meanwhile, closer scrutiny of the sons revealed that of those who persisted either from 1851 to 1861, or from 1861 to 1871, 55 per cent and 75 per cent, respectively, were agricultural labourers. Once more members of the agricultural labouring class showed the strong influence of occupation on their mobility.

The effect of offspring on the mobility of family heads was for persistency to increase with the number of resident offspring. However, the numbers of heads of household with more than seven children were very small, and so too the numbers of persistent heads of household with such a number of children were small and therefore their persistency needs to be treated with caution. In fact, over the 20-year period, there were no such heads of family persistent in Brenchley. Meanwhile, the childless family type, the 'solitary', had a high level of migration, only 15.9 per cent persisted from 1851 to 1861. While childless family units had a tendency to be young, and so the additional factor of the effect of age on mobility has to be borne in mind, nevertheless it is clear that the presence of dependent offspring affected mobility. Yet the persistency rates between 1851 and 1861 of persons heading 'single', 'extended' and 'multiple' household types were 37.2, 29.9 and 12.5 per cent respectively. If heads of 'solitary' and 'multiple' family types had similar persistency levels, the relationship between mobility and household type is clearly not a straightforward one.

As persons of the 'no family' or 'extended' family types had kin residing with them, the relationship between the number of kin and mobility was examined. In fact, less than a fifth of all households had any resident kin, and of those only a quarter had more than one

22. Classifications of household types are those used by Laslett, 'Introduction', 28–32. These are discussed in chapter 23 (Part V).

relative. The number of kin was thus too limited to enable us to establish whether or not it exercised an impact on mobility.

From a study of the persistency of differing occupational groups, it is evident that persistency was consistently highest amongst agricultural workers, farmers and tradesmen, and lowest amongst professional, domestic and commercial persons. 32.1 per cent of Brenchley's agricultural labourers persisted from 1851–61, and 33.2 per cent from 1861–71. The respective figures for farmers were 35.4 and 30.9 per cent, for craftsmen/tradesmen, 31.9 and 23.9 per cent, for professional persons, 22.2 and 6.1 per cent, for domestics, 9.2 and 7.9 per cent, and finally for persons involved in commerce, 14.7 and 8.3 per cent.

While we must not forget that persistency was low for all occupational groups, the reasons for the low rate of persistency amongst professional persons, as opposed to the rate itself, are open to speculation; perhaps professionals such as clergymen and solicitors could not further their ambitions by remaining in as isolated place such as Brenchley, or perhaps they had short-term assignments.

Those engaged in commercial pursuits, such as railway servants and coachmen, were mobile by the very nature of their occupations, while those in service were well aware of the demand for servants in towns such as Tunbridge Wells.[23] Meanwhile craftsmen and any tradesmen were more likely to be tied by their businesses to Brenchley. Indeed, the nature of craftsmen's and tradesmen's businesses encouraged persistency, as familiarity with the local inhabitants stimulated trade. It is interesting to note that master craftsmen exhibited high rates of persistency: of all master craftsmen present in Brenchley in 1851, 46.2 per cent were still resident in 1861, while the comparative figure for grocers, millers and butchers was 43 per cent. It is unlikely that the few craftsmen resident in Brenchley felt any great need to leave the parish. Indeed, the high degree of occupational inheritance may have been a result of the fact that the sons were offered a secure livelihood. In contrast, journeymen craftsmen were mobile: of those resident in Brenchley in 1851, 37.5 per cent were present ten years later, while no journeymen tradesmen could be identified. Perhaps, having some work experience behind them, they sought greater opportunities in London. Apprentices on the other hand, were supposed (in theory) to stay to complete their terms of apprenticeship and obtain some work experience. They were therefore more likely to be traced from one census to the next over a ten-year interval than journeymen, indeed,

23 Evidence for the whereabouts of Brenchley's out-migrants is hard to obtain. A search of the census for neighbouring parishes and the town of Tunbridge Wells revealed these places to be popular destinations, in keeping with the belief that most migration was over short distances. Alternative sources of information are the Poor Law Union records, namely, those pertaining to the non-resident poor. A study of these revealed that 29.4 per cent of the heads of household who were recipients of relief were resident in Kentish Unions, 41.2 per cent in Sussex Unions, 14.7 per cent in London and 14.7 per cent elsewhere in the years 1845–66.

37.5 per cent of apprentice craftsmen persisted for the ten-year period 1851–61, though no apprentice tradesmen remained.

Like tradesmen and craftsmen, farmers, both owners and tenants, by the nature of their business, may have been more tied to the parish, or more specifically, the land, and consequently were not a very mobile occupational group. Furthermore, persistency levels were clearly associated with the acreage of land occupied. Persistency increased with the size of holding occupied. Yet, in conformity with the general pattern, persistency declined in the decade 1861–71, especially amongst the very small (under 20 acres) farmers, 8 of whom were present in the 1861 census and none in the 1871 census. Although the numbers involved were very small, from the 1851–71 linkage we learn that of the 12 heads of household who held land in 1851, none holding under 20 acres persisted to 1871. The consolidation of land was squeezing out the small farmer, though there was a revival of the 20 to 60 acre holder in the decade 1861–71. As cited earlier, agricultural labourers were regarded by contemporaries as the least mobile of all occupational groups. Clifford's view was somewhat exaggerated, taking little account of the extent to which labourers were prepared to move locally, from one parish to another. Nevertheless, they must be counted among the less mobile social groups. When supposedly better working conditions in other parts of the country were brought to their attention, either by the authorities or as a result of their increased literacy, they were reluctant to leave their locality.[24] Indeed, even when the Poor Law Commissioners financed the move, few applied, and of those who went, many returned.[25] No Brenchleyites were found in these lists of assisted migrants. The cost of any such move may have been prohibitive, especially as only a move to a northern agricultural area or town would appear to entail financial benefits. The constant threat of removal should they become chargeable upon the parish may also have acted as a disincentive. Clearly these options had limited appeal. Agricultural labourers may also have been reluctant to relinquish cottages received from their employers.

Summary of findings

Persons from long-distance birthplaces were more likely to make a further move than persons from short-distance birthplaces. Professional persons had higher rates of mobility than labourers, farmers or

24 Evidence of literacy is to be found in the parish's marriage registers which show the signatures of couples being married and therefore enable us to calculate the percentage signing with an *'x'*. In the years 1841–46 and 1867–71, 50 and 18 per cent, respectively, of the couples both signed with an *'x'*, 33 and 26 per cent had one partner signing with an *'x'* and 17 and 57 per cent had neither partner signing with an *'x'*.

25 PRO MH/32/71, records of E. Tufnell, the assistant Poor Law Commissioner for Kent, 1st March, 1842.

tradespeople. When the relationship between the two variables 'birthplace' and 'occupation' was explored, it emerged that the majority of professional persons had been born outside Kent (55.2 per cent in 1851), while almost all agricultural labourers (89.3 per cent in 1851), were living in their county of birth. In order to evaluate the comparative influence of distance and occupation, we examined the behaviour of the least mobile group, agricultural labourers, and the most mobile group, professionals, originating from Kent. It was found that, even when born in the same place, professionals were more mobile than labourers: 23 per cent persisted to 1861, in comparison to 37 per cent of agricultural labourers.

What becomes evident then is a clear geographical demarcation line for the respective labour markets. Labourers, farmers and tradesmen originated from and moved very locally, while professionals originated from and moved from further afield. The mobility of professionals could have been the product of a variety of factors, such as knowledge of opportunities elsewhere gained in transit and the ultimate lack of opportunity for professional persons in Brenchley.

This chapter sought to identify the movement of Brenchley's workforce in response to the continuing change in Brenchley's social relations and the labour market. The response focused on persistence/migration as indicators of the flows of labour, using the census as our source material. Other sources, such as Poor Law records, marriage registers and poll books were used in the original study, and the findings based on these sources complemented that of the census; however, their discussion is outside the scope of this chapter.

From the birthplace statistics, we discovered that, in general, Brenchley drew upon very local sources of labour, the majority of residents originating from the parish or its environs. There was a greater degree of turnover than expected, with the most mobile adults coming from distant places. Not only was there a clear division between migrants and non-migrants in terms of origin, but divisions also emerged along occupational lines. The migrants who originated from longer distances, and who displayed little tendency to remain in Brenchley, were overwhelmingly professional, commercial and domestic persons, while those from closer to Brenchley, who showed a greater reluctance to move, were labourers, farmers and tradesmen. It therefore became apparent that several distinctive labour markets were in operation. Even increased literacy did not produce a significant change in the labourer's behaviour. Indeed, while there was an overall increase in migration in the period studied, the labourers were one occupational group to increase their persistence, albeit fractionally.

The reasons for the reluctance of the agricultural labourers to move have already been suggested. Their increased persistency in the decade

1861–71 should not be exaggerated, though it is nevertheless of interest, especially since it was most pronounced amongst the younger members of the occupational group. Conditions in Brenchley underwent no sudden change in the 1860s, and there are no data to indicate that the 1860s were worse than the 1850s and that therefore the 'push' factors on labourers were stronger. Indeed, perhaps out-migration in earlier decades had resulted in improved conditions for those left behind, though agricultural labourers as a percentage of the workforce were steady throughout the period 1841–71. However, it is not the numbers *per se*, but the condition of the labourers which is of most importance.

An alternative explanation for their marginally changed behaviour in the decades 1851–61 and 1861–71 lies in the decrease of 'pull' factors. Perhaps there was a reduction in the pulling power of the towns which now supplied much of their workforce by natural increase.[26] Indeed, immigration from the south-eastern counties to London fell in the 1860s, and Brenchley itself started gaining population from net migration, though the turnover of the population was greater than in the previous decade.[27] However, neither the 'push' nor the 'pull' factors showed any substantial change in the 1860s, and since the increase in persistency on the part of labourers was only fractional, what is of greater importance is the comparative persistency levels of the different occupational groups. Bearing this in mind, although we have no evidence for worsening conditions in the 1860s, it seems that the high persistency levels of agricultural labourers were at once a reflection and a cause of their low standing and disadvantage within rural society.

26 See Cairncross, *Home and foreign investment*, 78. This is not to suggest that in the first half of the nineteenth century the towns relied primarily on immigration for their workforce by natural increase. See Pollard, 'Labour in Great Britain', 141–2.

27 See Shannon, 'Migration and growth of London' 79–86. In terms of net migration Brenchley was at first a loser of population, in the decades 1841–51 and 1851–61 its net loss by migration was 78 and 256, but then it experienced a net gain of 58 persons in the decade 1861–71.

Appendix

Rules for determining links between CEBs

In order to determine whether or not a pair of records were 'truly linked', the following conditions had to be met (and written in the form of a Fortran programme):

Stage 1: Essential conditions for a match

(1) Source must be different on the two records being matched (i.e. 2 different censuses):
(2) Sex must be identical on both records:
(3) Age must be one, two or three categories higher on the second record (each category consisted of five years):
(4) Marital condition must only change from single to married, married to widowed, or widowed to married:
(5) Names (surname compressed by Soundex[28] and initial of first name) must be identical on both records:
(6) County of birth must be identical on both records.

Potentially matched pairs having successfully passed the first stage were then tested further. They were tested using four variations which were not essential in order for a pair to be deemed truly matched. The only requirement was that a potential match must achieve a certain score on the basis of these variables to be truly a match.

Stage 2: Non-essential conditions for a match.

		agree	disagree	missing
(1)	Place of residence in parish on both records:	+3	–4	0
(2)	Adult's trade on both records:	+4	–3	0
(3)	Persons aged 15 and under, trade on records:	+4	+4	0
(4)	Parish of birth on both records:	+3	–3	0
(5)	Union of birth on both records:	+3	–3	0

A score of +2 had to be obtained on the non-essential variables for a pair of records to be deemed 'truly linked'.

An instruction was also written into the linkage programme which ensured that women who changed their name through marriage would not be counted as 'migrants' but as 'persisters' if they remained in Brenchley.

28 For an early description of the Russell Soundex system for coding surnames see, Phillips, 'Record linkage'. For a summary of other coding systems see Schürer and Pryce, 'Nominal lists'. For a worked example of the Soundex method see Katz, *The people of Hamilton*. Katz found that surnames compressed by the Soundex method matched exactly for 91.9 per cent of his truly linked pairs, while the initial matched exactly for 89.1 per cent. The surnames of all Brenchleyites had been coded using Soundex, to which a code was added to represent the initial of the first name. The reliability of the initial was never in doubt, as the enumerators always wrote out the first name of any individual in full. The only pitfall lay in the possibility of individuals reporting their first name differently from census to census, for example, William John could well become John William. Those attempting record linkage are advised to refer to some of the specialist literature on the topic: see, for example, the journals, *Historical Methods*, **25** 2 (1992) and *History and Computing*, **4** 1 (1992) and **6** 3 (1994).

22

Family migration in Victorian Britain: the case of Grantham and Scunthorpe

MARTIN B. WHITE

Introduction

While many scholars have noted the presence of single people, married couples and families among migrants, little or no systematic attempt has been made to assess the relative importance of these various groups within any particular migration stream. It seems to be generally assumed that most migrants were young and presumably single.[1] Yet, from a rather different perspective, much recent work, including that on Victorian Britain, has stressed the need to place migration within the wider context of the family.[2] This would seem to imply that, at least in certain places, the movement of families may have been of considerable importance. Studies of the more detailed Swedish evidence have reached contradictory conclusions over this question. Ohngren found that 80 per cent of incomers to the central Swedish town of Eskilstuna in the later-nineteenth century were 'lone' migrants who arrived without any family.[3] However, Akerman's study of other nineteenth-century Swedish material has led him to conclude that family migration was more important than has hitherto been realised.[4] This chapter attempts to cast some light on this issue by exploring the components of the migrant streams into the two Lincolnshire destinations of Grantham and Scunthorpe using the CEBs of 1881.

The study area

Until the middle of the nineteenth century, Grantham was a typical market town, largely untouched by the industrial revolution, possessing a wide range of traditional crafts and functioning as a service centre within a mainly agrarian economy. From then on, however, the town became one of the foremost industrial centres of Lincolnshire. This transformation was the result of two developments: the coming of the

1 Grigg, 'Ravenstein'.
2 See, Anderson, *Family structure*; Collins, 'Irish migration'; Schürer, 'Role of the family'. For a review of the literature, see Darroch, 'Fugitives or families?'.
3 Ohngren, *Folk i rorelse*, 376.
4 Akerman, 'Internal migration'.

Great Northern Railway and the rise of the agricultural engineering industry. From the 1850s the town grew rapidly in size and by 1881 the population had reached almost 17,000.[5] This population has been sampled using the CEBs.[6]

Scunthorpe was a very different kind of place in 1881. Indeed, it could hardly be called a town at all, but was, rather, a newly-formed and growing urban area based upon just one industry, iron, and depending heavily upon newcomers for its initial growth. At this time the five townships, which later merged to form the town of Scunthorpe, were still geographically separate. Until recently they had all been remote agricultural villages, but the discovery and subsequent exploitation of extensive iron ore deposits from the 1860s had transformed them into a thriving centre of the iron industry.[7] Migration into four of these five townships is explored here using the 1881 CEBs.[8]

Method

The census is a crude instrument with which to establish the familial components of migration. Broadly speaking, there are four related technical shortcomings. First, in many cases the information given is simply insufficient. For example, a migrant couple with co-resident migrant children most probably moved in as a family unit. Yet take away the children and the picture becomes unclear: did they arrive together or as single migrants who subsequently met and married? Second, the census may have been taken some considerable time after in-migration occurred and may no longer accurately reflect an individual's familial position at the time of his or her arrival. For example, all co-resident migrant offspring may have since left home, placing a truly migrant couple in an ambiguous category. Third, the census only shows those who moved in and have remained. Thus, while there may have been a greater inwards movement of single migrants than of whole families in preceding years, many of the single people may have subsequently departed in similarly greater numbers. The census would only capture the net effect of this turnover, understating single in-migration. Lastly, there is no guarantee that all members of a family unit actually moved at the same time. For example, a father may have been joined by the other members of his family at a later date.

5 For the development of Grantham in the nineteenth century see Honeybone, *The book of Grantham*; Wright, *Lincolnshire towns and industry*.

6 A one-in-three systematic sample was taken of households in Grantham Municipal Borough in the 1881 census.

7 For the development of the Scunthorpe district see Armstrong, *An industrial island*; Daff, 'Iron making at Scunthorpe'; Wardley, 'The Lincolnshire iron industry'.

8 Ashby, Brumby, Frodingham and Scunthorpe townships. The fifth township, Crosby, saw little development until the turn of the century.

Table 22.1 Marital status of migrant males, 1881

	Grantham %	Scunthorpe %
Single	24.9	24.2
Married	67.9	71.6
Widowed	7.2	4.0
Not known	–	0.2
Total n.	860	1,116

Table 22.2 Migrant category of married migrant males with co-resident wives, 1881

	Grantham %	Scunthorpe %
Native wife (i.e. husband assumed to have arrived alone)	20.3	9.1
'Intermediate' (migrant wife with no co-resident migrant children)	42.3	39.9
'Family mover' (migrant wife, migrant co-resident children)	33.3	48.3
Not known (birthplace(s) unclear: could be 'intermediate' or 'family mover')	4.1	2.7
Total n.	508	702

Yet, despite all these problems, the census can be made to yield crude estimates of the relative size of two components within the migrant stream. The intention here is to obtain a rough indication of how many individuals arrived:

1) as 'single' migrants without a spouse and family, or;
2) as 'family' migrants who did possess a spouse and family.

Tables 22.1 and 22.12, above, contain the raw census information from which we will obtain estimates of the size of these two groups. Table 22.1 gives the marital status of all migrant males in the two study locations, excluding those enumerated as dependent children. The 'married' category is broken down into various components in Table 22.2 using information on the birthplace of co-resident spouses and children (where present). If we ignore widowers; men who originally moved in as dependent children; and married men who arrived unaccompanied by their wives and/or dependent children, then the male migrants could have arrived in one of three possible states: as single men; as married men with a spouse but no children; or as married men with accompanying children.[9] The size of these three groups needs to be estimated using the data in the two tables. There are two problems in this regard.

First, the 'Intermediate' category in Table 22.2 contains those married couples where both partners were migrants but which either had no co-resident children or where all such children were born in the study area. This category includes, therefore, those who moved in as:

1) childless married couples;
2) couples with children but whose migrant offspring had all since left home;
3) unmarried migrants (arriving either independently or with their parent(s)) who had subsequently married another migrant.

There is no way these three strands can be delineated, and so this category has been excluded from the following analysis. This seems especially wise given the additional interpretative problem of whether the migration of childless married couples is best conceptualised as 'single' or 'family' movement .[10]

Second, many migrants recorded as 'single' or as 'married to native females' may have originally moved in as dependent children and had either since left home or been orphaned. These two groups must accordingly be reduced by an appropriate amount in order to obtain a more accurate estimate of the number of independent single in-migrants. The calculation of this amount can be illustrated using Grantham males as an example. The relevant figures are shown in Table 23.3, below.

The method assumes that dependent migrant children were as likely to leave home, or to be left behind by their out-migrating parents, as were their native counterparts. This assumption is made to facilitate the calculation of the appropriate adjustment ratios. Unfortunately, little information is available on the migratory behaviour of natives versus non-native. Of the turnover studies that have contrasted the migratory experiences of natives in relation to non-natives, Lawton and Pooley

9 The problem of separating ever-married migrant males who were resident in the census with their spouse from those who were not is greater in Grantham where 7.2 per cent of migrant males were widowed compared with just 4.0 per cent in Scunthorpe. Of those migrant males who were resident with their spouse, given the census is a static cross-sectional document, it is impossible to tell how many moved to the town as a child in their parents' family, or alternatively, moved unaccompanied by their wife and children.

10 Excluding married persons in the 'Intermediate' category of Table 22.2 and ever-married persons without a resident spouse results in a much reduced number of migrants, upon which the subsequent calculations are based. In the case of males the pool of migrants is reduced by 41 per cent in the case of Grantham and 38 per cent in the case of Scunthorpe. Unfortunately, it is impossible to suggest whether the excluded migrants exhibited significantly different migratory behaviour to those included in the analysis.

Table 22.3 **Worked example of the calculation of estimated 'single' migration: Grantham males, 1881**

	Unmarried males					
Age	a	b	c	d	e	f
0–9	457	24	145	8	25	17
10–14	141	5	87	3	13	10
15–19	100	17	61	10	49	39
20–24	47	11	31	7	54	47
25–29	20	5	6	2	30	28
>=30	12	18	10	n/a	43	43
Total	777	80	340	30	214	184

	Migrant males with native wives		
Age	g	h	i
20–24	8	1	7
25–29	18	1	17
>=30	77	n/a	77
Total	103	2	101

Notes: a = single natives living with parent(s)
b = single natives not living with parent(s)
c = single migrants living with parent(s)
d = 'false' independent single migrants (b/a × c)
e = single migrants not living with parent(s)
f = corrected estimate of single migrants (e – d)
g = married male migrants with native wives
h = 'false' independent single migrants (d/e × g)
i = corrected estimate of single migrants (g – h)

suggest that in the case of mid-nineteenth-century Liverpool, non-natives were less persistent than native born residents.[11] This feature is also displayed in the rural parish of Brenchley, Kent.[12] However, despite the fact that non-natives appear more migratory than the native born population, it is doubtful if birthplace alone serves as an independent influence upon migration, additional characteristics of the non-native population such as age and socio-economic status also influencing their migratory behaviour. The first step is to calculate the ratio of those who were not living with either parent to those who were so living for unmarried natives in each age group. For example, taking natives aged 20–24 in Table 22.3, there were 11 single men not living with either parent and 47 who were so co-residing (columns a and b). Applying the same ratio to the 31 migrants living with either parent (column c) suggests there were 7 men aged 20–24 in the town who had originally in-migrated as dependants but who had since left or lost their parental home (column d). This amount is subtracted from the 54

11 Lawton and Pooley, *The social geography of Merseyside*, 98.
12 See the previous chapter by Wojciechowska, (chapter 21).

Table 22.4 Relative size of the estimated 'single' and 'family' migrant groups, 1881

		Grantham	Scunthorpe
		%	%
Males:	'Single' migrants	62.8	45.5
	'Family' migrants	37.2	54.5
Total n.		454	622
Females:	'Single' migrants	68.5	31.2
	'Family' migrants	31.5	68.8
Total n.		537	493

enumerated migrants not living with their parents (column e) to arrive at an estimate of the 'true' extent of independent single in-migration among those aged 20–24, namely 47 (column f). Repeating the exercise for the other age-groups results in an overall estimate of 184 such migrants. Of course, this procedure only has a major impact among younger persons. There is no way of estimating how many older migrants had originally moved in as dependent children. Most older natives had left their parental home, thus denying us any real 'correction factor' to apply to the older single migrants. For this reason only those age groups under 30 are 'corrected' in this way. This is probably not too problematic given that, (all else being equal), older 'single' migrants would be less likely to have originally moved in with their parents than would their younger counterparts. This probably applies to the Scunthorpe district cases rather more than the Grantham ones, given that the former area's expansion was more recent.

Attention now turns to those married migrants with native spouses. The proportionate reduction already made to the single migrants in each age group is now applied to the corresponding age-group in this population. For example, we made a reduction in the 20–24 age-group from 54 to 47. Applying an equivalent reduction to the eight cases aged 20–24 in the second part of Table 22.3 results in a revised figure of seven cases. This is done for the other age groups and finally the sub-total in each part of the table is summed to give an overall approximation of the total number of single men who arrived independently of their parents (184+101=285).

Finally, having obtained an estimate of the number of migrants who arrived in an independent, unmarried state, this can be compared with the numbers who moved in with their spouse and offspring. The former are termed 'single' migrants, the latter 'family' migrants. The relative importance of these two types of movement among males and females is expressed in percentage form in Table 22.4 above. While male migration into Grantham largely followed an 'expected' pattern, the single movement predominant, the male stream into the Scunthorpe area was skewed markedly in the other direction, with family movement predominant. This difference was even more apparent when the whole exercise was repeated for females (Table 22.4).

Discussion

The key to this difference probably lies in the economic structure of the two locations. This is evident from the age-structure of the 'single migrant' stream. Excluding those who had subsequently married native spouses, 35.9 per cent of Grantham's ('corrected') single migrant males were aged under twenty, compared with only 17.6 per cent of the Scunthorpe district cases. The figures for females were 49.0 per cent and 38.2 per cent respectively. Boys in their teens moved into Grantham to take up appenticeships, or positions with tradesmen or at one of the many coaching inns. For girls, domestic service was the main attraction. A whole host of opportunities existed for young, single migrants. In comparison, the Scunthorpe district had few such openings. Jobs in domestic service, and trade and craft assistantships, were scarce. The iron industry traditionally favoured the employment of strong, mature men, and no system of apprenticeship existed.

The existence of such employment can, however, be seen from another perspective. Work on the family economy has shown that the movement of families to a particular destination is often encouraged by opportunities for wives and children to contribute, to the household budget. Such a phenomenon has been clearly observed among certain groups of textile workers in the nineteenth century.[13] Yet this does not seem to apply here. According to the estimates produced in this chapter, the destination with the least to offer in terms of family employment nevertheless experienced the greatest amount of family migration. In Grantham, 29.9 per cent of females aged ten and above worked; in Scunthorpe only 13.5 per cent did so.[14] The economic activity rate among co-resident children was also higher in Grantham (Table 22.5 below). These two case studies suggest that job opportunities for those in their teens worked to encourage single in-migration more than they did the movement of families within any 'family economy' framework. In part this surely reflects the introduction of compulsory schooling in the 1870s, together with other legislation which took younger children out of the labour market. It may also reflect the absence of any major domestic industry in either location in which younger children could be employed at home.

13 Anderson, *Family structure*; Collins, 'Irish migration'.

14 However, a figure of some 20 per cent for working females aged 10 and over is calculated for the parish of Frodingham in 1851. See, Tillott and Stevenson, *North-west Lindsey in 1851*. Frodingham is the ancient parish within which the townships of Scunthorpe were situated.

Table 22.5 Labour force participation rates of young people, 1881

		Grantham		Scunthorpe	
		%	n.	%	n.
Aged 10–14					
Males:	A	20.5	234	10.0	260
	B	26.3	19	47.1	17
Females:	A	4.1	246	2.0	245
	B	33.9	56	41.4	29
Aged 15–19					
Males:	A	89.9	169	70.5	112
	B	88.8	75	94.7	57
Females:	A	52.6	133	38.3	81
	B	76.3	156	65.2	66

Notes: A = co-resident with parent(s); B = not co-resident with parent(s).

Table 22.6 Relative size of estimated 'single' and 'family' male migrant groups within selected occupations: Scunthorpe, 1881

	Iron industry %	Non-iron industry %
'Single' migrants	41.1	55.4
'Family' migrants	58.9	44.6
Total n.	338	148

Table 22.6 above, breaks down the Scunthorpe area data into selected occupational groups.[15] The skew towards 'family' migration is more evident among those engaged in the iron industry than among those in other occupations.

Several factors may have worked to encourage a high level of 'family' movement among the Scunthorpe iron workers. In these early years of the north Lincolnshire iron industry, the demand for labour far outstripped the local supply. The iron companies had to venture far beyond the immediate countryside to fill even their least skilled vacancies. The growing port of Grimsby to the east and industrial south Yorkshire to the west were both competing destinations for the young single men of the north Lincolnshire countryside. So too was nearby

15 This table has been constructed in the same manner as was Table 22.4. The raw number of 'single' migrants within the two occupational groups are 'corrected' using the ratios obtained from the total native population. Using the terminology of Table 22.3, columns (a) and (b) remain the same in every case (differing only by sex and location) but the figures in columns (c), (e) and (g) are replaced by those pertaining to the particular population sub-group being examined. The calculation then proceeds as explained in the example given earlier.

Gainsborough, with its expanding engineering works.[16] The relative importance of families within local migration streams may partly reflect a deficient pool of single men.

Turning to those from longer distances,[17] and in particular those from other centres of the iron industry, other factors may have prevailed. First, the movement of families is sometimes taken to indicate a less favourable economic climate in the place of origin than that which attends single migration. Thus Jackson has observed of the early Victorian glass industry:

> The overall movement pattern between 1830 and 1851 was very much a one-way flow of glass makers of all ages from declining to new, expanding regions of glass-making: so-called established, stable areas of production did not exist to provide a surplus pool of skilled unmarried men who might move in search of better job opportunities, as appears to be the case in the iron-making and coal industries.[18]

Whether the iron industry had previously operated in this manner is debatable. What is clear, however, is that by the 1870s such 'stable areas of production' were less widespread. The shift of the main centres of the industry to Cleveland and north Lancashire was accompanied by a decline elsewhere. The Black Country, in particular, experienced a period of contraction at this time.[19] There is some evidence to suggest that 'family' migration was relatively more common from the Black Country than it was from other longer-distance sources. Of the male migrants to Scunthorpe born in the counties of Staffordshire and Worcestershire, 65.5 per cent were 'family' migrants. This compares with a figure of 52.8 per cent for male migrants from other long-distance (50 kilometres or more) locations.[20]

Second, mobility was almost a cultural trait among many iron workers in the nineteenth century.[21] For many men in the industry, family mobility was probably regarded less favourably than among other groups of workers. Indeed, the absence of employment opportunities for females and children in most areas of heavy industry[22] may well have made such movement more easy. The family was not having to surrender two, three or even more sources of income in the hope of a better deal elsewhere. Within the confines of the family budget, the only economic consideration was the relative employment

16 Wright, *Lincolnshire towns and industry*, chapter 10.

17 This crude distance distinction is admittedly arbitrary but is a useful means of organising this description of possible forces at work.

18 Jackson, 'Long-distance migrant workers'.

19 Birch, *British iron and steel industry*, 133–4.

20 However, this difference is not statistically significant: chi-square = 1.59 with one degree of freedom.

21 Birch, *British iron and steel industry*, 246; Gwynne and Sill, 'Census enumerators' books'; Harrison, 'Iron masters and iron workers'.

22 Bell, *At the works*.

prospects of the breadwinner in his present situation compared with those somewhere else. The very absence of any broadly-based family economy in many of these districts sending migrants may well have been as much a spur to family migration as its presence seems to have been in other places.

Third, a low age at marriage was a national characteristic of iron workers.[23] This means that the pool of potential migrants in an iron district probably contained proportionately more families and correspondingly fewer single adults than did other areas. From a different perspective, the tendency to earlier marriage reflected the important role played by the wives of iron workers. The nature of the work was such that domestic duties were even more arduous than in some other working-class households. The job was extremely dirty; wash day would be harder work than in other households. The long, unsociable shifts worked by the men enhanced the importance of a good domestic manager in the home. On the one hand, this meant that iron workers would be keen to find a good wife as soon as possible. Equally, for most girls in iron working families, marriage was the easiest means available for achieving some degree of independence from home. On the other hand, the high fertility of heavy industrial workers (in part a result of the low age at marriage) meant that many families would experience a succession of older sons taking up employment in the industry. Although these sons contributed to the family coffers, the domestic strain must nevertheless have become immense. Within the space of a few years, the work-load of many wives and mothers suddenly increased markedly, just as they themselves were ageing. The daily routine was even more irksome if father and sons did not all share the same shift. Given such pressures, it would not be surprising if many young men were obliged and expected to relieve their mother by finding a wife as soon as possible. A report from early this century commented that:

> This young man of the iron-working class usually has no misgivings about embarking upon matrimony early and without a sufficient income. He marries very young, often because he wants a home of his own. Either he is in his parents' home, where he is of course not the principal person to be considered, and is set on one side perhaps and has to undergo the discomfort and crowding entailed by being one of a family living in a small cottage; or he is a lodger, under much the same conditions.[24]

The importance of having a wife (and thus usually a family) was, perhaps, enough to outweigh the hindrance to mobility which

23 This is shown from ecological data in Anderson, 'Marriage patterns in Victorian Britain'. See also, Bell, *At the works*, 178–9.

24 Bell, *At the works*, 180.

dependants might have presented. Indeed, many iron workers might well have been reluctant to move very far without one.[25]

More generally, the movement of families over long distances may well have been more prevalent within the context of Redford's 'special industrial migration'.[26] All else being equal, the links between areas sharing a common form of industrial activity were likely to be stronger than those between contrasting communities. The network of information which serviced migration was probably better developed; the body of knowledge concerning the conditions at a certain destination all that more comprehensive. A man with a family would be less keen to uproot on the basis of mere hearsay.

The evidence presented here suggests that the composition of migrant streams could differ quite considerably between one destination and another, and that in certain circumstances married couples with children may well have outnumbered independent single in-migrants. Furthermore, the extent of family migration could be high even into those areas with poor employment prospects for wives and children. In sum, it would seem that the movement of families was indeed of major significance in some areas of nineteenth-century Britain, but, also, that this was not always a function of the 'family economy' conceived in the narrow sense of the employment of family members beyond the head.

25 A high incidence of lodging among married couples in the Scunthorpe district suggests a spouse was more valued than a house.

26 Redford, *Labour migration in England*, 35–160.

Part V

Family and household structure

23

Family and household structure

K. SCHÜRER AND D. R. MILLS

Community

As the most fundamental form of social organisation, it is only logical to expect the family to fulfil a major role in the development and structures of communities. One striking example of this can be found in the work of Marilyn Strathern in her classic anthropological study of community life in the rural village of Elmdon, situated in the extreme north-west corner of Essex. In attempting to explain how the community perceives itself and how it functions, Strathern focuses on the relationship between those families with a long association with the village and the migrant newcomers newly-settled in the parish. Her conclusion, as one might expect, was that there was not one community in the village but two, yet the characteristics each displayed were not entirely predictable. Although the 'insider community', consisting of those families with established roots in the village, was viewed as an essential part of the community, it played only a minor role in the institutional activities that for many gave the community life and meaning: village fêtes, coffee mornings, bring-and-buy sales, and so on. Not only was the organisation of such events chiefly the preserve of the newcomer families, the 'outsider community', but it was somewhat looked down upon by the 'insider community'. Consequently, a rather ironic situation existed in that, whilst involvement in such so-called community activities was seen by the 'outsiders' as an important step on the path to becoming 'insiders', by definition their very participation set them apart from the group they were so desperate to assimilate into.[1]

In a companion volume to the work of Strathern which examines the same village in a historical context, Robin used the CEBs to suggest that such dichotomies within rural parishes – communities within communities so to speak – are not new and may have existed in the nineteenth century, if not earlier, with separate sub-groups of families displaying different experiences in terms of patterns of employment, migration and maybe even household structure.[2] Although it is possible to cite other authors who have explored such themes, it is clear that

1 Strathern, *Kinship at the core.*
2 Robin, *Elmdon.* See also Richards and Robin, *Some Elmdon families.*

much more research is needed, particularly at the local level, to aid our understanding of the internal mechanisms and structures of community life in the past.

Identifying households

Analyses of CEBs have provided a back-bone to the study of historical family and household forms. When first investigating mean household size (MHS) Laslett was surprised at the overall consistency in size through time, and consequently suggested that a mean size of 4.75 could be justified for the period from the late-sixteenth century to the first decade of the twentieth century.[3] Recalculating the official census data from the published reports, Laslett illustrated that MHS was broadly level throughout the nineteenth century, until 1891 when a declining trend was started that continued through most of the twentieth century. Yet still, it was not until 1911, recording a figure of 4.36, that MHS fell below that reached in 1861 (4.38), after which point the national MHS fell more sharply.[4]

However, there are dangers in relying too closely on the figures presented by the published census reports. Much of the change, it could be argued, could be due to differences in the way in which households were defined by the census authorities rather than any real change *per se*. For the community historian working on the CEBs it is tempting simply to accept that each household starts with an individual described as 'household head' and continues until the next so designated person. However, the relationship descriptions provided in any given census are, of course, in part, determined by how households were defined by the census authorities and how census schedules were accordingly distributed. In the case of the Victorian census, the GRO's interests in this regard lay not with households, but rather with the identification of physical 'houses'. This was so that the size of the housing stock could be measured and thus enable the calculation of housing density to be linked to differential sanitary conditions and mortality levels. In theory this was relatively unproblematic and, although individual enumerators, particularly those in central urban areas, may have at times experienced difficulty in interpreting their instructions, the census office was clear in its notion of what constituted a house. Indeed, the definition of a physical house remained basically unchanged for the censuses of 1851 to and including 1901, being 'all the space within the external and party walls of a building'.[5] This

3 Laslett, 'Mean household size'. However, it is important to note that subsequent work has revised Laslett's impressions of the earlier pre-CEB period, stressing the need to use bands of 'multipliers' rather than a single figure. See, Arkell, 'Method for estimating' and 'Multiplying factors'.

4 Laslett, 'Mean household size', 140.

5 For the definition of census 'houses' during these years see Higgs, *Making sense*, 45–6; *Clearer sense*, 53–6.

rudimentary definition had been adopted by the International Statistical Congress of 1860 and was already rather out-of-date then. Throughout most of the Victorian period it clearly caused confusion among both householder and enumerator alike as to what constituted a structurally distinct dwelling, and, as a consequence, was substantially revised in 1911.[6]

Confusing though it was, this definition of what constituted a physical house is of critical importance to our use of census households, since it clearly impacted on the distribution of census schedules, and it is the schedules which act as the corner-stone in the definition of households. Critical to the allocation of schedules was the concept of 'occupation'. This was so for each of the censuses from the mid-nineteenth century through to 1921. Working to a principle of occupation that was very much governed by the ownership of property or the payment of rent, the instructions to the enumerators for the 1851 census stated that a schedule was to be left:

> for a family consisting of a man, his wife, and children; or of parents, children, servants and visitors;
> for a family consisting of parents and children, with boarders at the same table, and the servants of the family, if any;
> for a lodger alone, or two or more lodgers boarding together.[7]

This definition suggests that the conjugal family, as discussed in the following section, was central to the GRO's notion of what constituted a 'normal' set of domestic living arrangements, but the reference to boarders and lodgers illustrates awareness that the norm was certainly not universal. In a rather clumsy fashion, an attempt was made to distinguish between different types of lodging: principally between those who lodged either individually or in groups and were 'independent' of the main occupier; and those who were more integrated with the primary household, for example through the sharing of meals. The problem with this is that the division between independence and dependency was far from clear cut, especially since independence was measured both in terms of physical and social separation. This instruction of 1851 was repeated in 1861 and with minor word changes in 1871 and 1881 also.[8]

However, because of the inherent ambiguity, it was certainly the case that in distributing the schedules and retrospectively completing their books the enumerators interpreted the instruction in an inconsistent manner. The situation was further confused by the fact that the definition of occupation appeared to overlap with those of household and family. This is most clearly demonstrated by the

6 1911 Census England and Wales, *General Report with Appendices*, BPP 1917-18 XXXV, 24.
7 PRO HO 45/3579.
8 Higgs, *Making sense*, 59; *Clearer sense*, 66.

example pages of the *pro forma* enumeration books. For each of the censuses from 1861 to 1881 these illustrate two examples of multiple schedules being distributed to the same address or house. One lists a small family group with the first person identified as 'head' in the relationship column and the other family members assigned accordingly, yet the second enumerates a solitary lodger listed as such under the relationship column. In addition, the example provided on the schedule form showed a person identified as a boarder in terms of relationship and enumerated on the same schedule as the head of household. Consequently there was a double confusion: first, in regard to what constituted a separate 'occupation' and thus warranted a separate schedule form; and second, as to whether those enumerated on a second schedule form should be described independently of the primary household with a new household head being assigned, or as an extension of the primary household being described in relationship terms as lodger or inmate, for example.

This ambiguity on behalf of the GRO not only caused confusion for the enumerators, but has subsequently frustrated historians in their attempts to define common household units, standard across different censuses. In attempts to overcome the inconsistency with which the householders' schedules were distributed, recommendations have been made to ignore the allocation of schedules altogether and to concentrate on the relationship to household head column, treating as a household all those individuals listed between one head and the next.[9]

An attempt to find a way out of this confusion was made in 1891 when the instructions providing the definition of an occupier and to whom schedules should be distributed was streamlined. The term 'occupier' was to apply to the 'resident owner, or to a person who pays rent, whether for the whole of a house, or for a tenement consisting of one or more rooms', while schedules were to be left with 'the occupier of a tenement living alone, or for two or more lodgers living together in one tenement'.[10] However, lodgers and boarders, returned on the same schedule as the Head, were still listed on the example page provided to the enumerators. It was clear that each new schedule should have its own Head, but the distribution of schedules was still ambiguous. This was clarified in 1901 when the term 'lodger' was expunged altogether from the various illustrations to enumerator and householder alike, and enumerators were instructed to leave schedules:

> for the head of the family occupying the whole or part of a house. NOTE: A "family" is held to include a man, and his wife and children (if any), also any relatives, visitors, servants,

9 See Anderson, 'Standard tabulation procedures', 142–3 and Tillott, 'Sources of inaccuracy', 104–5. See also Higgs, 'The PRO', 103–5 and 'Structuring the past' who is dismissive of these attempts.

10 Higgs, *Making sense*, 60; *Clearer sense*, 67.

> and persons boarding with the family, and residing together under one roof.
>
> for a lodger (with or without family) separately occupying a room or rooms, and not boarding with any family in the house.[11]

With this, the intention was clear that independent lodgers, as opposed to boarders, should be regarded as separate households in their own right. The overall outcome of this is that the period between the censuses of 1891 and 1901 can be seen as a watershed in that after this point the institute of lodging in which a room or set of rooms was sub-let from a primary household, regardless of the number of lodging individuals involved, ceased to be viewed as an extension of the primary household, but instead was elevated to household status in its own right. Indeed, lodgers, so described, should have ceased to exist from the census of 1901. As a consequence, the drop in MHS after 1891, described by Laslett, might be viewed as little more than expected given that, from this date, single lodgers were not only provided with their own schedule but were counted as separate households and designated lone household heads accordingly. The clear message for the community historian in all of this is that great attention must be paid, especially when comparing information from the CEBs over time or from place to place, to the way in which the householders' schedules were distributed and the associated designation of relationships to heads of household. Irrespective of the official dictate from the GRO it is likely that, at the local level, enumerators may have taken matters into their own hands!

Household structure

In what is often seen as a manifesto for the study of family and household structures, Laslett, in his Introduction to *Household and family in past time*, set out a methodology for the interpretation and use of census-type documents.[12] Of particular importance is a classification scheme of co-resident kinship which assigns households to one of five broad categories, each in turn further sub-divided, plus a sixth 'Indeterminate' category (see Table 23.1 below). Since its inception, the scheme has become a *de facto* standard for the comparative study of family and household forms, across both time and space.[13] A variant of the scheme is used in chapters 26 and 27 by Hinde and Brayshay, respectively, and a worked example has appeared in *LPS*, which provides a useful guide for all those new to the scheme.[14]

11 Higgs, *Making sense*, 60; *Clearer sense*, 67.
12 Laslett, 'Introduction'.
13 See, Hammel and Laslett, 'Comparing household structure'.
14 Knodel, 'An exercise in household composition'.

Table 23.1 Structure of households: the classification of co-resident kinship

Categories
1. Solitaries
(a) Widowed
(b) Single, or of unknown marital status
2. No Conjugal Family
(a) Co-resident siblings
(b) Co-resident relatives of other kinds
3. Simple Family Households
(a) Married couple alone
(b) Married couple with never-married child(ren)
(c) Widowers with never-married child(ren)
(d) Widows with never-married child(ren)
4. Extended Family Households
(a) Extended upwards from head
(b) Extended downwards from head
(c) Extended laterally from head
(d) Combinations of types 4a–4c
5. Multiple Family Households
(a) Secondary unit(s) disposed upwards from head
(b) Secondary unit(s) disposed downwards from head
(c) Units all on one level
(d) Units all on one level, but with no member of the parental generation present[a]
(e) Combinations of types 5a–5d
6. Indeterminate

Notes: *a* = This category in which married siblings share a household without the parental generation present is also referred to as a *frérèche*.
Source: Based on Laslett, 'Introduction', 28–34.

The key to understanding the scheme is what is termed the 'conjugal family unit' (CFU). This, as the name implies, identifies a domestic group bound together by a marital unit, and as such can take one of three forms:

1) a married couple without never-married offspring;
2) a married couple with one or more never-married offspring;
3) a lone parent with one or more never-married offspring.

The term 'never-married' is used to distinguish those who have not as yet married from those who are either currently married, or who have been married previously and are currently widowed, or maybe separated. Thus, its meaning is rather more specific than simply unmarried. Equally, the term 'offspring' is used to mean any never-married children or step-children, regardless of age.

Applying this definition to the individuals listed in the census extracts given in Table 23.2 below one can begin to see how the scheme

Table 23.2 (A) Abbreviated extracts from the CEBs for Canwick, Lincolnshire, 1881

No. of Schedule	ROAD, STREET &c., and No. or NAME of HOUSE	HOUSES		NAME and Surname of each Person	RELATION to Head of Family	CONDITION as to Marriage	AGES last Birthday		Rank, Profession or OCCUPATION	WHERE BORN
80	Dower House	1		Montague Sibthorp	Head	M	33		Justice of the Peace	Lincoln
				Mabel Sibthorp	Wife	M		26		Noots, Wiseton
				Mabel Sibthorp	Daur.			3		Lincs, Scawby
				Esther Sibthorp	Daur.			1		Lincs, Canwick
				Coningsby Sibthorp	Brother	M	34		Justice of the Peace	Lincs, Hackthorn
				Mary Sibthorp	Sister-in-law	M		33		Notts, Averham
				Jane Robinson	Servant	U		24	Ladies maid	Yorks, Gilling
				Millicent Ward	Servant	U		24	Cook	Lincs, Blankney
				Harriett Friskney	Servant	U		26	House maid	Lincs, Fillingham
				Ann Scarcliffe	Servant	U		18	Nurse	Lincs, Coleby
				Elizabeth Heathcote	Servant	U		18	Scullery maid	Derbys, Sutton
				Mary Allen	Servant	U		33	Ladies maid	Rxborough, Kelso
				Thomas Quipp	Servant	U	15		Footman	Lincs, Branston
55	Canwick	1		George Robinson	Head	M	61		Wheelwright	Lincs, Langtofy
				Harriet Robinson	Wife	M		62		Northants, Helpstone
				George Willows	Servt	U	14		Wheelwright app.	Lincoln
				William Robinson	Son	M	36		Joiner	Lincs, Crowland
				Jane Robinson	Wife	M		35		Lincs, Branston
				Gerty Robinson	Daur.			4		Lincs, Canwick
				Walter Robinson	Son		2			Lincs, Canwick
				John Robinson	Son		1			Lincs, Canwick

Source: PRO RG 11/3238

Table 23.2 (B) Abbreviated extracts from the CEBs for Melbourn, Cambridgeshire, 1851

No. of House-holder's Schedule	Name of Street, Place, or Road, and Name or No. of House	Name and Surname of each Person who abode in the house on the night of 30th March, 1851	Relation to Head of Family	Condition	Age of		Rank, Profession, or Occupation	Where Born
23	High Street	Edmund Metcalfe	Head	M	33		Surgeon & L. A. C.	Cambs, Fowlmere
		Mary Metcalfe	Wife	M		43		Cambs, Foxton
		Elizabeth Hurrell	Wife's sister	U		50	Landed proprietor	Do.
		William B. Clapham	Lodger	U	24		Surgeon & L. A. C.	Essex, Writtle
		Elizabeth Grey	Servant	U		23	Cook	Cams, Stowe
		Cornette Barnard	Do.	U		23	Housemaid	Do., Haslingfield
45	High Street	James Webb	Head	M	35		Tailor (journeyman)	Cambs, Melbourn
		Sarah Webb	Wife	M		33		Do.
		Eliza Webb	Daur.			10	Scholar	Do.
		William Webb	Son		2			Do.
		Joseph Webb	Brother	U	32		Groom	Do.
		Elizabeth Baker	Niece			14	Scholar	Do.
51	High Street	William Taylor	Head	Wid	83		Farmer, 10 acres of land	Cambs, Melbourn
		Sarah Ann Dearman	Gd Daur.	U		31	Housekeeper	Do.
		Benjamin Porter	Gd Son	M	34		Retired publican	Lincolnshire, Lutton
22	High Street	George French	Head	U	37		Proprietor of houses	Cambs, Melbourn
		Sarah Ann French	Sister	U		33	Proprietor of houses	Do.
		Frances Huggen	Servt	U		19		Do.

Source: PRO HO 107/1708 (Eds 11a and 11b).
Note: L. A. C. is an abbreviation for Licentiate of the Apothecories Company

works. The first household, that of Montague Sibthorp, the son of the local squire in Canwick, Lincolnshire in 1881, contains two CFUs and is, therefore, a multiple household. The first is formed by Montague, his wife Mabel and two young daughters, the second by his married brother, Coningsby, and sister-in-law. Given that the Hammel–Laslett scheme only classifies the co-resident kin of the household head, the host of seven domestic servants attending to the Sibthorp brothers and their families has no bearing on the designated classification. Since the two CFUs in this household are related laterally, in other words they are of the same generation, and because no member from the parental generation is present, the household is assigned to the 5d category. In the English case it is actually quite rare to find married siblings living together, however, such family arrangements are believed to have been a distinguishing feature of pre-industrial household structure in southern Europe.[15] The second household in the example, that of George Robinson, is also a multiple household consisting of two CFUs. In this case, however, it is rather more normal in terms of its structure, consisting of George and his wife Harriett (the first CFU) and his married son William, daughter-in-law Jane and their three children (the second CFU). Since the second CFU is generationally downward from the first, the household is classified as being 5b. Notice, however, that the enumerator gave William a separate census schedule despite the fact that he and his family were clearly residing in the same house as his father.[16] Also note that the enumerator has adopted a 'shifting headship', referring to Jane the daughter-in-law as 'wife' and assigning the grandchildren accordingly.

The examples in Table 23.2 from Melbourn, Cambridgeshire in 1851, all feature co-resident siblings, yet none forms a multiple family household. The household of Edmund Metcalfe is a 4c, it having just one CFU, formed by Edmund and Mary, and one lateral relation, Mary's unmarried sister who is not a member of any CFU. The next household, that of James Webb and family, is classified as a 4d. Again it contains a single CFU consisting of James, his wife and young family, yet they are augmented by a co-resident brother and niece. This creates both a lateral and downward kin extension, hence the 4d designation. The household of William Taylor is also a 4d, yet in this case the CFU is not formed by the head of household, but instead by a married grandson, Benjamin Porter, wife and child. The head and a second grandchild create an upward and lateral extension to this CFU. Note also that 'shifting headship' is again employed by the enumerator, and that the CFU building block does not need to include the head of household.

15 Laslett, 'Introduction', 30–1.

16 As indicated by the single oblique stroke next to the address column and a new schedule number. See Higgs, *Making sense*, 59; *Clearer sense*, 66.

The final household containing brother and sister George and Sarah French does not include a CFU. Although the two are obviously related, no CFU is formed since neither are married (and have a spouse present) and there is no parental generation present. As there is no CFU the household cannot possibly be in either of the 3, 4 or 5 (simple, extended or multiple) categories and is instead assigned to 2a class.

It should be pointed out that the household examples just discussed, while being useful for illustrative purposes, are relatively uncommon. In the nineteenth-century CEBs the most common household type is invariably type 3b – a stereotypic family consisting of husband, wife and unmarried children only. Households containing co-resident kin such as those depicted in Table 23.2, in the Hammel–Laslett categories 2, 4 and 5, rarely form anything other than a small minority of cases. In chapter 27 by Brayshay, an analysis of various communities in 1851 shows that the proportion of households containing co-resident kin rarely rises above 20 per cent (Table 27.3). In a sample of pre-census listings of inhabitants for 100 communities, dated between 1574 and 1821, Laslett found that only 10.1 per cent of households contained kin, with relatives accounting for just 3.4 per cent of the population.[17]

Picturing households

In addition to producing a tabular classification scheme, Laslett also devised a standard form of visually representing the households recorded in census documents. This is usually referred to as the ideographic scheme. Again, it is most clearly explained by reference to the example households in Table 23.2. Comparing the information in this table with the ideographs in Figure 23.1 below, it can be seen that it is possible to represent any form of family arrangement via the genealogically-based diagrams of circles (females) and triangles (males). The membership of CFUs can be shown by encircling all the composite members, and the boundaries of households can also be indicated by a surrounding rectangle. This can then contain household members who are not part of the head's kin group, such as servants and lodgers.[18] At first such a scheme may appear unnecessary, but its main advantage lies in the fact that it easily conveys the exact membership of each household in a standard form, allowing for and 'correcting' the non-standard terminology of the census enumerator. As such, it is a useful tool for those investigating the household structure of communities in a comparative context.

17 Laslett, 'Introduction', 81.

18 In devising the scheme, Laslett also provided for the case in which two or more households might share the same house, a houseful. In such cases, the boundary of the houseful is represented by two broad lines, above and below. See, Laslett, 'Introduction', 41–2.

Figure 23.1 The ideograph system for representing households in the CEBs

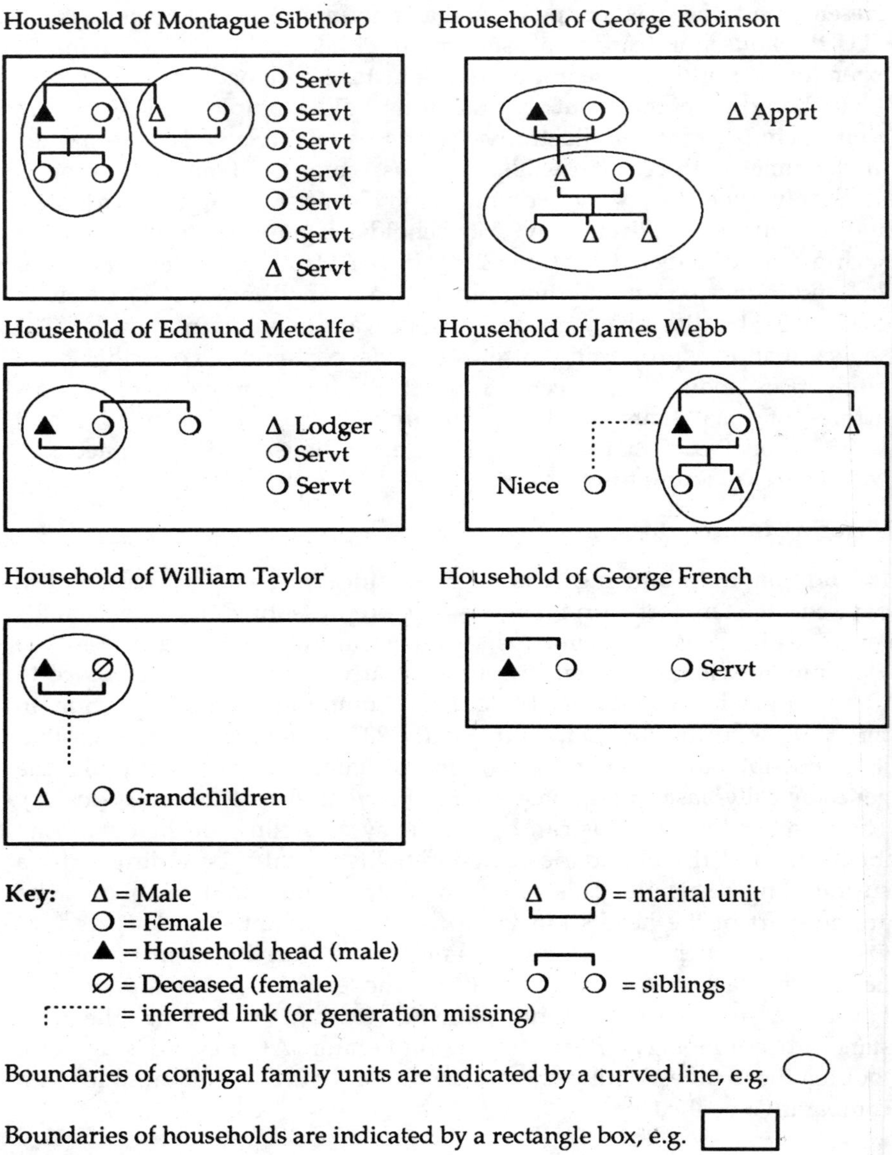

Household of Montague Sibthorp

Household of George Robinson

Household of Edmund Metcalfe

Household of James Webb

Household of William Taylor

Household of George French

Key: Δ = Male
O = Female
▲ = Household head (male)
Ø = Deceased (female)
⋯ = inferred link (or generation missing)

Δ O = marital unit

O O = siblings

Boundaries of conjugal family units are indicated by a curved line, e.g.

Boundaries of households are indicated by a rectangle box, e.g.

Notes: Refer to Table 23.2 for respective CEB entries. Adapted from Laslett, 'Introduction', 41–2.

Producing ideograms and classifying households is not, however, without its problems and it is important to realise a number of points. First, the classification scheme is only concerned with the co-resident kin of the household head. Consequently, various individuals are excluded from the classification all together, such as servants and lodgers, even if forming their own family groups. However, if either a servant or lodger is known to be also a relative of the household head then this kinship link takes precedence. Second, when assigning individuals to CFUs, it is the case that no individual can simultaneously belong to more than one CFU – children who marry, for example, leave their parent's CFU to form one of their own, and having left, they cannot return. Third, in addition to servants and lodgers, some individuals may not currently belong to a CFU at all, in effect having been removed, either permanently or temporarily, from their parents, spouse or children. Fourth, due to the ambiguity of kinship terminology used in the CEBs it may sometimes be the case that it is impossible to be certain about potential CFUs. For example, if a household contains both a widowed sister of the household head and a nephew it may be tempting to conclude that the child is that of the widowed sister, the two forming their own CFU. However, the nephew may equally be the child of a different sister or brother, in which case no CFU would be formed between them. One is left having to make best use of the evidence available, such as the respective names, ages, birthplaces, position in list and so on. A more common problem arises if a young grandchild is recorded in the same household as a mature daughter. Is this grandchild her child? If so, a CFU would be formed between them regardless of illegitimacy.[19]

Households in the CEBs

Although Laslett's pioneering work was focused essentially on the structure and form of the pre-industrial family, in other words the pre-CEB family, there is still much to be learnt from the study of household structure in the era of the CEBs. In part, this is because throughout the nineteenth century the published census volumes were remarkably silent on households and families. Certainly, overall numbers of both households and families are given for a myriad of administrative areas for each census year, and, from these, mean sizes can be calculated, yet hardly any analysis is presented on the form and structure of families. In 1851 the Registrar General presented a brief and, it must be said, somewhat confusing examination of household composition for a small sample of 14 Registration sub-districts, but following this initial attempt, the subject of family and household structure was not analysed

19 For a general criticism of the scheme see Lee and Gjerde, 'Comparative household morphology' and Wall, 'Introduction' 5–6. For a defence see Laslett, 'The character of familial history'.

again in detail until the census returns of 1951.[20] Most of our knowledge of family composition in the nineteenth century is therefore based on a re-examination of the available CEBs.

Much early work was focused on the impact of industrialisation on the organisation of the domestic group. The extent to which the so-called 'modern nuclear family' was a product of industrial capitalism has been an issue which not only occupied Marx and Engels, and in their wake various post-war sociologists, but was also the focal point of the pioneering study of Preston by Anderson. One of the first major census-based urban studies, this work demonstrated that the nuclear family was far from being a product of the industrial town. Indeed, the rapid urbanisation of Preston resulted in households having a greater residential kin component and wider kin recognition as families sought to provide both 'safety nets' against the insecurities of urban living as well as reception centres for newly-arrived migrants from the surrounding Lancastrian villages.[21] Yet Preston is not all England, let alone Wales or Scotland, and, as such, what is true for one town may not be true for another. Unfortunately few census-based studies on the scale of that of Anderson have been completed, yet that of Dupree for Stoke-on-Trent, indicates that a number of other additional forces, such as institutional support within the community, may have been in place in the nineteenth-century town, each of which helped shape the domestic group.[22] Certainly it is the case that there is plenty of scope for much more comparative research on these issues.

Both Anderson's study of Preston and Dupree's study of Stoke found the communities involved to have higher levels of co-resident kinship than the norm for Laslett's 'pre-industrial' sample of census-listings. In other words, there were more households assigned to the type 4 (extended) and 5 (multiple) categories using the classification scheme outlined in Table 28.1, for mid-nineteenth-century Stoke and Preston than for pre-industrial England. Extending this general finding, Ruggles has argued that 1851 marked the zenith of co-residential kinship in England and Wales, with households displaying a greater degree of complexity at this date than at any time before or since, at least in the post-reformation period. This, he suggests, was not just an urban phenomenon, but was true of rural communities as well. The factors that gave rise to this situation fall into three broad categories. One important factor was the underlying demographic regime of the period, in terms of the levels of mortality and fertility, and its influence on the size and shape of the kin component. In essence, the balance

20 1851 Census Great Britain, *Population Tables. Part I, vol. I*, BPP 1852–3 LXXXVIII, xl, c–ci. For a re-analysis and interpretation of this information see Armstrong, 'Mid-nineteenth-century York', 212–4.

21 Anderson, *Family structure.*

22 Dupree, *Family structure.*

between fertility and mortality at that time meant that individuals had on average more relatives alive than previously (and more than today) – this was particularly true of lateral kin, especially cousins. Other factors include economic forces and underlying Victorian values and perceptions of the 'ideal' family.[23] What is certain is the need for further evidence from local studies, especially for the later-nineteenth century about which little is known, since most studies have tended to concentrate their research efforts on the CEBs of 1851.

Household evolution

One of the underlying features of the census is that it is a cross-sectional source bounded in time. The CEBs may provide us with a picture of a particular household in terms of who lived with whom, but it is exactly that, a static picture providing an image of family life frozen at a particular point in time. Households and families are, however, dynamic, passing through a number of distinct so-called life-cycle phases. Censuses, therefore, although a most useful tool with which to explore patterns of family life in the past are not a perfect one. In an attempt to overcome this basic problem, historians have employed a variety of techniques. One approach adopted in the pioneering work of Anderson is to analyse the census data according to a number of stereotypic life-cycle stages. Thus, in the case of those families containing a married couple, the following classification of six key family stages was used in the Preston study:[24]

1) wife under 45; no children at home;
2) wife under 45; one child only at home, child aged under one year;
3) others with children at home but none in employment;
4) children at home and some, but under half, in employment;
5) children at home and half, or more than half, in employment;
6) wife over 45, no children, or one only aged over 20, at home.

A similar approach is to focus attention on a particular stage or aspect of the life-cycle. This is used with effect in the contribution of Dyer (chapter 25) in which she contrasts the experience of childhood in two Birmingham communities: Ladywood and Edgbaston. One important aspect of this study is that the child population is not looked at in isolation, but is viewed in the context of the households and families of which the children were an integral part.

23 Ruggles, *Prolonged connections*.

24 Anderson, *Family structure*, 202; 'The study of family structure', 60. The family life-cycle approach has been particularly championed by Hareven using US census material: see 'Cycles, courses and cohorts'; *Family time and industrial time*; and 'Family history at the crossroads'.

Figure 23.2 Population by age, sex and relationship to household head: Hatfield and Dengie, 1861

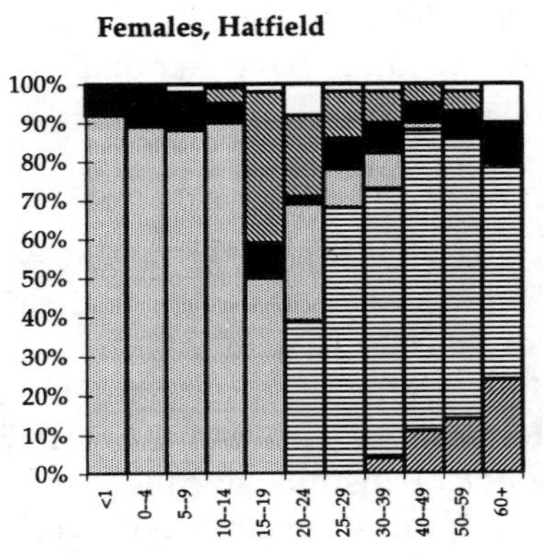

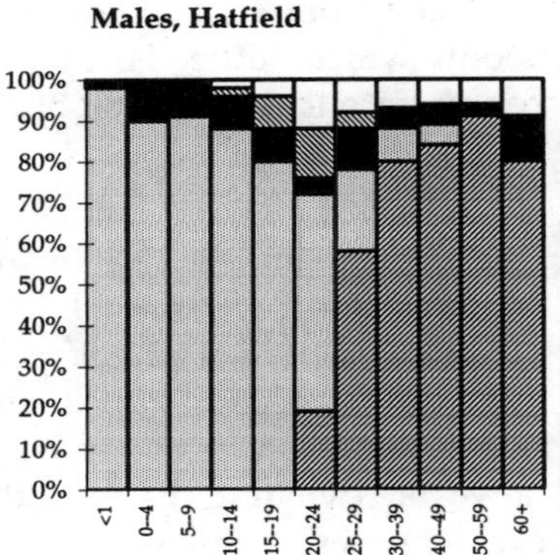

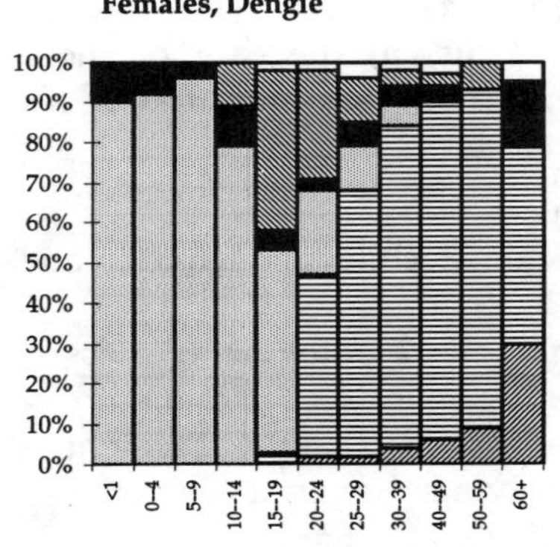

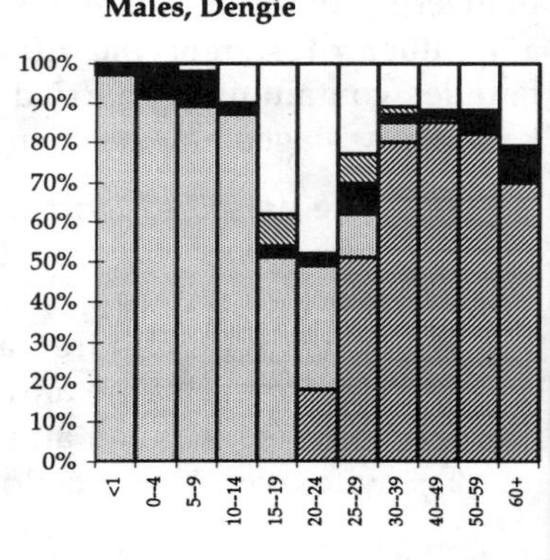

Head Spouse Offspring Relative Servant Inmate

Notes: These diagrams are based on those produced for Colyton in Wall, 'Work, welfare and the family', 271.

In a similar vein, a more simplistic, yet highly effective approach is to break the census data down by age and by household membership categories according to the relationship to household head information. Both the chapters by Brayshay and Howlett provide examples of such an approach, while another model is provided by Figure 23.2. This provides a vivid visual summary of some of the key characteristics of household composition in two areas of Essex as portrayed in the CEBs of 1861. Both are rural areas dominated by agriculture, but in the Dengie group of parishes in the east of the county, children appear to have left home earlier and the achievement of headship status, or household formation, was slightly delayed in comparison with the Hatfield group of parishes in the west of the county.[25] The importance of life-cycle service for young women in both of the areas is equally striking. It was much more common in the Dengie for males, especially between the ages of 15–29, to live as inmates, in other words as a lodger or boarder. This reflects the nature of farming in the Dengie marshlands, in which large isolated farms were not uncommon, with agricultural labourers often boarding in the farm outbuildings rather than living in the villages. As is normal in an English context, co-resident kin ('relatives') are relatively few in number throughout the life-cycle, but were generally more common in Hatfield than Dengie. However, it can be seen that for women in the later stages of the life-cycle the reverse was true, with Dengie recording more relatives, more heads of household and fewer wives in the 60 and over age group. This may point to a number of possibilities, including increased opportunities for elderly women to maintain their own households in Dengie, a higher rate of remarriage, or differential mortality rates causing women to be widowed earlier in Dengie in comparison with Hatfield. This example also demonstrates that whilst such diagrams are useful for exploring census data, and can pose a number of questions, especially in comparing CEBs for different places or dates, they cannot necessarily answer the questions they pose. Rather they point to the need to explore certain themes in greater depth.

Household formation and the incidence of service are both issues central to Hajnal's influential work on European marriage patterns in the past. This puts forward the notion of a stereotype model in which Europe is split into two by a hypothetical line running between St Petersburg in Russia to Trieste, Italy. To the east of this line, marriage was virtually universal and conducted at early ages, to the west, marriage was undertaken later and substantial numbers of the

[25] The Hatfield group includes the parishes of Hatfield Broad Oak, Great and Little Hallingbury, while the Dengie group is comprised of Southminster, Steeple, Asheldham and St Lawrence. CEBs 1861, PRO RG 9/807, 1087, 1118.

population remained unmarried throughout their lives.[26] For western Europe late age at marriage is linked to the tradition of a relatively long period in service immediately prior to marriage and the formation of a new independent household at the point of marriage.[27] This contrasts with the model for eastern Europe in which life-cycle service is absent and children (usually sons and their wives) remain in the parental household following marriage. Following this line of investigation, chapter 26 by Hinde examines the timing of marriage and the extent of service as recorded in the CEBs for two groups of parishes, one in Norfolk, the other in Shropshire. This study points to the existence of a link between household structure, marriage and service in an English regional context. In the case of the Norfolk parishes, male farm service had ceased to be the norm at quite an early date, certainly by the mid-nineteenth century. In contrast, service was still in place in the Shropshire parishes until at least 1881. Linked to this, marriage in Shropshire was later for both men and women and household formation was delayed.

This example demonstrates, quite forcefully, the bond between differing forms of household structure and life-cycle events of which marriage was undoubtedly the most fundamental. Indeed it could be argued that all of the themes covered in this volume – fertility, marriage and death; work and employment; migration and mobility – are essentially familial in character and, as such, impact on the structural composition and organisation of households since all are pieces of the larger and more complex jigsaw of the family life-cycle.

Contents of Part V

The themes of marriage, household formation and life-cycle service are central to chapter 26 by Hinde. In this he contrasts the experience of two groups of rural communities, one in Norfolk, the other in Shropshire. Following the pioneering work of Hajnal on marriage patterns, Hinde concludes that service was not only more prevalent in Shropshire and was still in evidence in the late-nineteenth century, it had a significant impact on the timing of marriage and subsequent family formation. The contribution by Dyer (chapter 25) concentrates on the position of children within families. Like the chapter by Hinde, Dyer's study explores its central theme through the investigation of two constrasting communities, in this case the areas of Edgbaston and

26 Hajnal, 'European marriage patterns' and 'Two kinds of pre-industrial household'. Hajnal's work was principally based on the analysis of census data at the aggregate level. In order to estimate the age at marriage from census data he devised the 'singulate mean age at marriage' which is discussed in Part II, chapter 8.

27 For a discussion of the relationship between marriage, service and household formation, see Smith, 'Fertility, economy and household formation'. For an examination of life-cycle service, see Laslett, 'The institution of service' and Kussmaul, *Servants in husbandry*.

Ladywood in Birmingham.

Prior to this comes Howlett's study of the Devonshire village of Appledore, chapter 24. Being a coastal community in which adult males earning a livelihood from the sea would be absent from the village and from their homes for long periods of times, and also like many a maritime community, a place which experienced relatively high male mortality rates in mid-life, the study provides a useful insight into the ways in which family life was both disrupted by the unpredictability of maritime employment and adapted to cope with the problems it created. Chapter 27 by Brayshay, although focusing on mining rather than fishing communities, bears some parallels to the chapter by Howlett in that the communities being studied are subject to disruption and change. In Brayshay's case, however, the disruption to family life is caused by depression in the west Cornwall mining industry. Given that many miners responded to this problem by searching for work abroad, often leaving their families for long periods at a time, the similaritites to Appledore are apparent.

24

Family and household in a nineteenth-century Devonshire village

NEIL M. HOWLETT

Introduction

The CEBs are, of course, the primary source of data about individuals and communities in the nineteenth century. They are, however, subject to limitations which can only be overcome by reference to additional sources. First, in common with all structured data-collection methods, the census relies upon categorisation to achieve simplicity and limit ambiguity. This can only succeed where the categorisations used correspond with those understood by the persons filling in the forms. An example of this is the use of the terms 'boarder', 'lodger' or 'visitor', or in the specification of relationships to the head of the household. A second problem, which arises from the use of the CEBs without any supplementation, is that they portray the household at a single moment in time.[1] Where there is much temporary absence, this can present a misleading picture of the nature of households. It is hoped to demonstrate the relevance of these points by presenting a case study of the village of Appledore in north Devon, based on a sample of 410 households out of a total of 463 enumerated in 1851, and of 488 households out of the 568 enumerated in 1871. Information obtained from the CEBs was amplified by a study of the parish registers, more particularly as to relationships between household members.

Appledore is situated at the confluence of the Taw and Torridge estuaries. In the nineteenth century, building or sailing ships provided the main source of occupation, employing half of all household heads. Men working the sea obviously could not avoid prolonged periods of absence from Appledore. To a lesser extent shipwrights were also periodically absent. Ships carpenters from Appledore sailed out to Prince Edward Island in the St Lawrence estuary early in the year, where they took advantage of plentiful supplies of timber to build small vessels on the beach. Before the St Lawrence froze up these would be jerry-rigged and sailed back across the North Atlantic to be fitted out in one of Appledore's dry docks.[2]

1 See the discussion in chapter 23.
2 See, Greenhill and Giffard, *Westcountrymen*.

Table 24.1 **Types of co-resident kin outside nuclear family by marital status of household head**

	Unmarried	Married, both spouses present	Married husband absent	widowed	Total n.	%
Appledore 1851						
Father	–	3	–	2	5	4.3
Mother	1	6	5	3	15	13.0
Brother	2	1	–	–	3	2.6
Sister	6	–	4	4	14	12.0
Nephew	3	3	1	1	8	6.9
Niece	1	3	4	13	21	18.3
Son-in-law	–	1	–	–	1	0.9
Daughter-in-law	–	1	–	1	2	1.7
Grandchild	–	13	–	22	35	30.4
Other kin	–	3	6	2	11	9.6
					115	99.7
Married daughters without husbands		8		6	14	
Appledore 1871						
Father	1	5	5	1	12	5.6
Mother	–	12	4	6	22	10.2
Brother	2	1	–	2	5	2.3
Sister	7	–	2	5	14	6.5
Nephew	3	–	3	7	13	6.0
Niece	3	5	2	6	16	7.4
Son-in-law	–	2	–	2	4	1.9
Daughter-in-law	–	5	2	7	14	6.5
Grandchild	2	47	1	41	91	42.3
Other kin	3	7	5	9	24	11.2
					215	99.9
Married daughters without husbands		5		5	10	
Preston 1851						
Father					17	3.3
Mother					29	5.7
Brother					97	18.9
Sister					–	–
Nephew					99	19.3
Niece					–	–
Son-in-law					120	23.4
Daughter-in-law					–	–
Grandchild					138	27.0
Other kin					13	2.6
					513	100.2

Source: Preston, 1851 from Anderson, *Family structure*, 45.

Table 24.2 Household situation of widowed people: Appledore and English parishes

	Appledore 1851				Appledore 1871				61 places in England before 1821			
	Widowers		Widows		Widowers		Widows		Widowers		Widows	
	n.	%	n.	%	n.	%	n.	%	n.	%	n.	%
Heading households containing:												
Unmarried offspring	4	24	43	44	12	44	52	48	120	57	243	47
Married or wid. son	0	0	1	1	0	0	2	2	9	4	7	1
Married or wid. dau.	2	12	6	6	0	0	5	5	5	2	5	1
No offspring	0	0	8	8	0	0	3	3	24	11	50	0
Sub-total	6	36	58	59	12	44	62	58	158	74	305	61
In households containing:												
Son or daughter	7	48	15	15	10	39	18	17	12	6	48	10
Son or daughter-in-law	1	7	1	1	0	0	0	0	2	1	17	3
Other kin	0	0	3	3	1	4	2	2	9	4	19	4
Other persons	2	14	14	14	3	11	18	17	12	6	65	13
Institutions	0	0	0	0	0	0	0	0	0	0	6	1
Grand total	17	100	98	99	27	100	106	100	211	100	510	100

Source: Household position of widowed persons by sex in 61 places in England before 1821, taken from Laslett, *Family life and illicit love*, 198.

Absentees from the CEBs and household structure

In 1871, 10.8 per cent of the population of Appledore was resident in households with relatives other than their spouses and unmarried children, and 29.7 per cent of households contained such relatives.[3] That this co-residence was a response to problems confronting these people or the families they were living with, can be shown by a more detailed analysis of the relationships between them. It seems people were living together in extended and multiple family households not because this was the ideal household structure which they sought, but because by living together they could mutually overcome the problems which faced all families and individuals. The ways in which they combined reflected the different problems which faced them.

In Table 24.1 above the presence of various types of relative is considered according to marital status of the household head, while the household position of all widowed persons is considered in Table 24.2 above.

First, it is clear that not all widowed people remained heads of their own households. Secondly, where they could not they normally lived as

3 The equivalent figures for 1851, 6.9 per cent and 23.4 per cent, are lower. However, this difference is accounted for by the larger number of kinship relationships unspecified in the census which can be reconstructed from the eight years of vital records which precede the 1851 sample.

subordinate members of their children's households, where they could also be child-minders. However, the difference between widowed people living in households headed by their children and the widowed headed households containing their married children is one of definition, not of function. In both cases, domestic and child-minding duties could be shared. The efficacy of kin-links and their primacy over other types of social interaction for widowed people can be seen from Table 24.2. In both 1851 and 1871, 79 per cent of widowed people were resident with kin, including those in households headed by married offspring; of those who were not living with kin, two-thirds were living alone. Most of the 21 per cent of those who were not living with kin probably had no surviving kin with whom they could live.

There is a structural similarity between unmarried and widowed household heads. Both were without a partner of their own generation within the household and were generally old. The probability of widowhood increased with age, and young unmarried people were unlikely to be heads of households for economic reasons. Old age was not normally expected to be attained, and the position of old people was anomalous. Although theoretically they held great social power by virtue of their experience, their effective power in the simple matter of looking after themselves was limited. They normally had to combine with other people to form a household, but the people with whom they combined differed. By definition, unmarried people had fewer kinds of relatives with whom they could combine, and most formed households with siblings. Widowed people too combined with siblings, but they also had a larger number and wider variety of other kin whose households they could join. Table 24.2 also shows that the proportion of widows heading such households was much higher than the proportion of widowers. One possible interpretation is that men, in the absence of their spouses, were much less capable of managing a household than women, who were domestic managers, and who could also obtain domestic employment which allowed them to supplement their income without leaving home. Of these widowed people who did head their own households, most lived with their children, both married and unmarried. This was the simplest combination. However, a very large number of widowed persons had their grandchildren, nephews and nieces living with them. Unmarried nephews and nieces could contribute much the same economic and domestic help that children could, but grandchildren, many of whom were very young, could not. These households represent a more extensive use of the traditional practice of grandparents caring for young children while their parents worked. It was common for young wives to accompany their husbands on vessels employed in trade in the Bristol Channel, leaving their children in the care of grandparents. This prolonged 'baby-sitting' could last for months if the parents were at sea, and was most easily operated by taking the children into the household as residents.

Households where the head was absent were effectively in a state of widowhood, which in most cases was only temporary, and was probably perceived to be so. This suggests that, although the functions of co-residents were the same in these households as in the household where the head was single, the perspective differed. Some types of kin were only resident in denuded households, that is, those in which one spouse was absent, through death or employment. This applies especially to young unmarried women, whose contribution to domestic management needs no elaboration. Their absence in complete households suggests that they were temporary residents, moving in only when the head was at sea (see Table 24.1). Another example of temporary residence is found in the category of married daughters resident with their parents, together with their children but not with their husbands. Although, it was not uncommon for newly-wed couples to reside with the brides' parents in the first years of marriage, these women, with children, were obviously not newly-wed.[4]

These households were not true multiple family households, but another type of temporary solution to the difficulties raised by the absence of the husband at sea. Instead of grandparents moving into the denuded household, the children moved to their grandparents to function as a household. That co-residence was only temporary is supported by the fact that only a relatively small number of fully nuclear families were co-resident with parents. The data cannot provide conclusive evidence of this interpretation, but there are two arguments which strongly support it. The first is the value of the strategy noted above. The second is the evidence that inhabitants of Appledore were not averse to leaving their normal residences. Mariners, when at sea, obviously always had to do so, and their wives also when they accompanied their husbands. Further evidence bearing on this comes from the fact that there were a large number of empty houses recorded in the CEBs, 40 in 1851, 50 in 1871, about one tenth of all the houses in the sample. Because of the nature of the recording not all can be accurately located. It is perhaps significant that of the 38 which can be located for 1871, half were in the 3 streets which had a proportion of mariners to all employed persons which exceeded the mean for the whole village by more than one standard deviation.

4 In an analysis of the residence patterns of married couples from the CEBs it was found that of 28 couples married less than 2 years who could be traced, 12 were living in the households of the brides' parents. Of these, five 'couples' actually comprised only the wife without her husband. Analysis of couples married between 5 and 7 years showed that, of 31 which could be traced, only 3 were living with the brides' parents, and all of these 'couples' were women without their husbands. These results strongly suggest that true multiple families were the consequence of the inability of newly married couples to set up their own households.

In 1851, there were 135, and in 1871, 96 people resident in households within which they had no kin relationships.[5] Some of these were lodgers and domestic servants as normally understood. However, as the identification of the relationships between these non-kin residents and the households in which they resided shows, many of them were performing the same functions as the co-resident kin discussed above.

This is not surprising. Not all people who needed aid may have had surviving kin who were able to give assistance. One may assume that the abilities and the requirements of individuals are related to their social position as defined by their sex and the state in their life-cycle. On this basis a typology was created which could be used to sort these resident non-kin from the information given about them in the CEBs.

The first category comprised children below the age of 15 years, of both sexes. There were 32 of these in 1851 and 10 in 1871, all recorded as 'scholars'. Of these 13 in 1851 and only 1 in 1871 are known to have had relatives in Appledore.[6] It seems likely that these children were taking advantage of Appledore's very good charity schools. Several were living with schoolteachers, and most came from other villages round the estuary, which suggests that they may have been children of sea-faring parents.

The second category is of unmarried women aged between 15 and 30 years. There were 61 of these in 1851 and 50 in 1871, nearly all recorded as 'domestic servants'. This is a complex category, and the role of individuals within it can only be understood in the context of the households in which they resided. Women whose occupation was given as 'domestic servant' were not necessarily financially rewarded. Domestic servants, in the stereotypic sense, resided in the various houses for an extended period and received wages. Most of these will be found in households headed by members of socio-economic groups I and II, (professional and white collar occupations). These households, although they did not comprise more than one quarter of all households, included more than 60 per cent of domestic servants both in 1851 and 1871.

In other cases, however, the relationship would seem not to have been so simple. Many domestic servants were recorded in households which would have had great difficulty in paying for their services. In

5 The difference in the proportions of the total population is a consequence of the number of persons who can be identified as kin in 1871, and who have therefore been assigned to the category of resident kin.

6 This conclusion is based on a reconstruction of the kin linkages between households in Appledore in 1851 and 1871, using information on relationships derived from references to the same families in the parish registers. Of the 13 children in 1851 with kin in Appledore, 12 were living with these kin. They were all living with their mothers, in five families, without their fathers, in households headed by other women with their children absent. Because of clarifying instructions issued by the General Registry Office such cases were classified as separate households in later censuses (see discussion in chapter 23). The one case in 1871 of a child with relatives in Appledore living with non-kin is of a two-year-old girl living in the household of a medical practitioner, presumably under treatment.

many of these it is possible to identify special reasons why the household would have benefited from additional help. Examples are, the infirmity through disease or old age of the household head,[7] or the presence of a child less than a year old. In many cases the family of origin of the young woman servant was found to have been resident in the same street, which suggests that these young women may have been acting out of affective rather than pecuniary interest. These young women were acting as kin for households who did not have kin, and many of them were possibly only temporary residents. In 1851 seven were present in households with children under a year old, in five of which the male head of the household was absent.

The next category consists of unmarried or widowed women over the age of 30; 9 in 1851 and 10 in 1871. Some were older women who either had never married, or were widowed before they had children and were forced to return to domestic service to support themselves. Others were probably only temporary residents in a particular household, giving their occupations as 'nurse' or 'midwife'. The distinction between permanent and temporary residents does not correspond with that between paid and unpaid servants. Midwives were temporary residents and were paid, as were dressmakers, of whom there were four in 1851 and two in 1871.

The fourth category includes all people, of both sexes, over the age of 65; there were 8 in 1851 and 16 in 1871. All were unmarried or widowed, with the exception of one couple who were living together. These persons were in the same position as co-resident grandparents, but were living with people who were not their kin, presumably because they had none with whom they could reside. In return for their keep they probably offered child-minding services, and in some cases payment out of income from annuities.

The final category is of men in employment over the age of 15, of which there are remarkably few, only 16 in 1851 and 17 in 1871. This seems surprising at first, in view of the transient nature of maritime employment. However, although Appledore was quite an important port, most of its shipping needs were provided by indigenous enterprise – vessels sailed by Appledore men who had families with whom they could stay. There was also a tendency for mariners to sleep on their vessels when moored in a 'foreign' port. Of those men who were resident with non-kin it is possible to identify two types. The first of these, five men in 1851 and two in 1871, had occupations related to that of the head of the household in which they were resident; they were presumably assistants or apprentices. The second type is made up of lodgers in the strict sense, and includes two itinerant musicians from

7 Cases of illness were based on the last column in the census (relating to disability, mental or physical) and to manuscript notes added to the census schedules by the local registrar, also the village medical practitioner.

London who were mostly resident in public houses and lodging houses.

Conclusion

Although this study is necessarily limited in its scope, it demonstrates, in the specific context of a Devonshire fishing village, how evidence on household composition may be used to infer how relatives and non-relatives combined in households, and may have helped each other over the difficulties which they encountered in the course of their lives. It also shows to what extent the roles of individuals within the household can be identified, simply from information on the age, sex and marital status of its members. Such an analysis must be the foundation for any research into the life of people in historical communities.

25

The child populations of Ladywood and Edgbaston in 1851

JENNY DYER

Introduction

In past western societies, children rarely formed less than a quarter of the population. Despite receiving greater attention in recent years, the study of the experience of children in past societies remains a much neglected subject. The process of rescuing children of the past from oblivion may be said to have begun with the work of Ariès, which, as he had wished and intended, inspired further investigation.[1] He can hardly have anticipated the range of disciplines which would be involved, nor the many directions in which research would proceed: sociologists, psychologists, anthropologists and art-historians with many others besides, have all contributed to the debate.[2]

The most contentious areas in the debate on the history of childhood centre on the relationship of children to the rest of society. Some historians, notably de Mause and Shorter, have presented the experience of children in earlier societies as an extended nightmare in which little progress in attitudes towards children may be discerned before the mid-nineteenth century when modern and 'enlightened' attitudes begin to emerge.[3] The 'whiggish' nature of this approach has been challenged by, amongst others, anthropologists and zoologists drawing on their studies of primitive societies and primates. Pollock's extensive study of parental attitudes to children indicates that the reality was altogether more untidy and complex. She rejects this 'unduly geological' approach (Schama's phrase) in favour of the notion that at any one time there was 'a great deal of individual variation'.[4] Orme's study of the language and toys of childhood in the Middle Ages provides some tentative support for Pollock in that he finds certain 'constants' in the lives of children in the Middle Ages and today – certain similarities in play, pre-occupations and the restraints imposed

1 Ariès, *Centuries of childhood*.

2 For a discussion of the direction of research since 1960 see Burton, 'Looking forward' and Morel, 'Reflections'. Burton advises caution in the interpretation of works of art and other pictorial representations of children. Morel identifies the variety of contributions from different disciplines and draws attention to the limitations of work to date.

3 de Mause, *History of childhood*; Shorter, *Making of the modern family*.

4 Schama, *The embarrassment of riches*, 496; Pollock, *Forgotten children*, 270.

by physical weakness.[5] Both approaches nevertheless leave scope for investigation into the particular social, economic and cultural circumstances which determined attitudes in specific societies. Pollock has drawn upon a range of personal sources, not previously used for this purpose, and suggests that the overwhelmingly dismal interpretation of the lives of pre-twentieth-century children has arisen because the sources most readily available tell us more about the history of child abuse than about the everyday experiences of the young.[6]

Feminist history has also drawn attention to new sources and approaches for the study of childhood. In much early work the emphasis on the ways in which the lives of women and children have been inextricably linked has, perhaps, obscured the importance of children in their own right. Such recent contributions as the essays edited by Steedman, Urwin and Walkerdine examine perceptions of childhood in the past through a study of the formative influence of words, language and text and help to refocus attention on the separate sphere of childhood.[7] Children now feature more prominently in school textbooks designed to meet the needs of the more student-centred approach of the schools' curriculum.

Historians of the family have responded with the greatest zeal to Ariès' challenge, perhaps in recognition of his own appreciation of demographic research. Levine and Wall have linked the function of children to changing household structures amongst communities at different stages of proto-industrial and industrial development, and to the different occupational groups within communities.[8] These changes find expression in fertility patterns and the number of children retained at home. Studying less-well documented sources for fourteenth-century Halesowen, Razi has shown that prosperous peasants were distinguished from their poorer neighbours less by superior houses or material possessions than by the number of living-in servants drawn mainly from the children of the poorer peasantry.[9] Thus the distinct role of children in the past has begun to emerge, no longer subsumed in the broad surveys of the family. Their contribution to the economy of both the family and the nation has been recognised, and they are no longer studied simply as a facet of the quality of life debate. Children may, indeed, have played a more active role than was previously believed. Social historians have tended to ask what impact

5 Orme, 'The culture of children in medieval England'.

6 Pollock, *Forgotten children*.

7 Steedman, Urwin and Walkerdine, *Language, gender and childhood*. It is refreshing to see contributions from primary school teachers whose discussions are informed by everyday contact with young children.

8 Levine, *Family formation* and 'Industrialisation and the proletarian family'; Wall, 'Work, welfare and the family'.

9 Razi, *Life, marriage and death*.

industrialisation had on the family; now it seems that the family itself may have influenced industrial developments. It is pertinent, therefore, to ask if children had a particular impact of their own on these developments.[10] But, despite this new emphasis, it remains true that sources which provide an insight into the inner world of the child are rare, and studies which make the child the focus of the investigation are the exception.[11]

The present study compares the household structure and family experience of children in two adjacent districts of mid-nineteenth-century Birmingham. The direction of the investigation was prompted by Laslett's observation that in pre-industrial communities large numbers of children had been deprived as a result of the loss of one or more parent. Laslett tentatively questions the commonplace assumption that the twentieth-century child is, to an unprecedented degree, deprived of an upbringing by at least one of its 'natural' parents as a result of separation or divorce. Laslett supposes that in pre-industrial society high adult mortality rates would just as frequently deprive a child of at least one parent, usually the father. The subsequent high incidence of second or even third marriages (or common-law unions) produced a significant number of step-parents as well as children brought up by their grandparents or kin.[12]

Anderson's extrapolations from the national returns of the 1851 census pursue many of the questions raised by Laslett. The significance of high adult male mortality is indicated by the fact that one in every nine family groups had a widow at its head. Lone parents were also likely to appear as secondary families. Only 45 per cent of those lone parents with a child under the age of 10 were living as heads of their own households – 36 per cent of this category lived with relatives while 9 per cent lived as lodgers.[13] A separate set of findings by Anderson indicates that marital break-up rates (albeit for different reasons) closely parallel modern figures.[14]

It is not simply the parentless or one-parent families which are worth investigating, but also the range and variety of household situations which the Victorian child might have experienced. Anderson's findings for Preston indicate that elderly kin were taken into the household to care for small children whose parents both worked in textile mills. This taking-in of kin is linked to housing

10 See discussion of this interaction in Anderson, 'What is new about the modern family?' (reprinted in Drake, *Time, family and community*).

11 Morel, 'Reflections'. For a discussion of the general problems and shortcomings of the history of childhood, see also Hendrick, 'The history of childhood and youth'. Much additional work on children has been produced since this article, but its observations remain pertinent.

12 Laslett, *Family life and illicit love*, 161–4.

13 Anderson, 'Households, families and individuals'.

14 Anderson, 'What is new about the modern family?' (reprinted in Drake, *Time, family and community*), 71.

shortages, which in turn resulted in some children growing-up in the households of their grandparents from which their own parents never managed to escape.[15] Furthermore, the literature of the period (but most particularly the nineteenth-century novel) is full of examples of children growing up outside the conventional nuclear family: Jane Eyre was brought up in the household of her socially superior aunt; Little Nell with her grandfather, and Pip of *Great Expectations* by his elder sister. Eppie in *Silas Marner* and Oliver Twist become quite separated from their kin, reared in the first case by a lone weaver somewhere between the social status of her two parents, and in the second reared in a fraternity of thieves. Children without the security of conventional family life were perceived by Victorians to face special problems and to act as vehicles of moral teaching: their lives often exposed the iniquities of the adult world. To what extent did this preoccupation reflect a reality of Victorian life?[16] To what extent did Ladywood and Edgbaston in the mid-nineteenth century conform to the general patterns which have emerged for other communities in this period?

Ladywood and Edgbaston in 1851

The 1851 CEBs provide the earliest information which allow us to be precise about an individual's position within a household. Many of the problems encountered by family research for earlier periods are avoided; it is possible to distinguish those of childhood years (defined as 14 and under) from those who are the offspring of their parents but may be adults and from those who were often included under the general category of servants. The 1851 returns were also chosen because Levine has suggested that this is a significant time at which to study working-class family life. In various parts of the country industrial households coexisted with the much larger number of 'proto-industrial' families who had adapted to the rise in demand without experiencing mechanisation.[17]

An initial survey of the 1851 CEB for Ladywood, a district to the north-west of Birmingham town centre, confirmed that the majority of households were those of skilled and semi-skilled workers in traditional workshops.[18] The wide variety of occupations included glass making and cutting, steel pen manufacture, iron moulding, button making and finishing, paper-box making, carpentry and employment in trades such as boat making associated with the nearby canal. A small number of

15 Anderson, *Family structure*. Conclusions concerning kinship reciprocation and the care of children are discussed on p. 171.

16 Here I have been influenced by Wall, 'Mean household size in England', which includes a discussion of fictional literature and shows the degree of correlation which exists between statistical and printed sources. This link with literature suggests an avenue to the 'sentiments' approach, see Flandrin, *Families*.

17 Levine, 'Industrialisation and the proletarian family'.

18 CEBs Ladywood, PRO HO 107/2051.

clerks employed in retail firms were living alongside skilled and semi-skilled workers, but there was little to indicate a more elevated life style than their neighbours: for example, they did not employ servants. It is not possible to ascertain from the census information whether or not heads of household were employed in workshops owned by others, or worked at home as their own masters. A builder, of 11 Cambridge Street, with two servants, and another, at King Alfred Place, employing three workers, were exceptions and reinforce the impression of Ladywood as a district where incomes were low, but work was widely available.[19] Birmingham was, of course, well known at this time for the large numbers of trades involving home-based workers.

The residential district of Edgbaston lay adjacent to Ladywood, but further from the centre of industrial Birmingham.[20] It was distinguished by a significant number of business and professional households considerably more prosperous than their Ladywood contemporaries, yet modest by the standards of élites in other manufacturing towns.[21]

The coverage of the survey

The investigation of Ladywood and Edgbaston reported in this chapter sought, in the first place, to discover the extent to which children lived in household environments other than the conventional nuclear family, defined as a two-generational household of children with their natural parents. The decision to match the Ladywood survey with one in Edgbaston was influenced partly by the observation that the fictional examples range across the social classes. The streets chosen for the Ladywood survey were Sheepcote Street and parts of Islington Place, Nile Street and Cumberland Street in the area known as Christchurch. The chosen streets in Edgbaston were Calthorpe Street, Calthorpe Fields, George Street, Frederick Street, Grandigan Terrace, Church Road and Ampton Road which extends from approximately one mile from the centre of Birmingham to two miles beyond. In both cases the route chosen by the census enumerator was followed. No method of sampling was chosen; as the research was designed to explore the significance of children as workers and consumers, it seemed important to establish their numerical strength in the two fairly homogeneous communities, and also to see how representative were certain types of household containing children. The total number of households surveyed in each community was 177, yielding a total of 911 persons in Ladywood and 1,022 in Edgbaston, a combined total of 1,933.

19 On the basis of the occupation of the head of household, most inhabitants of Ladywood may be classified as members of social Class IV, using Armstrong's classification of social groups for York in 1841 and 1851. See Armstrong, *Stability and change*, especially 13–5.

20 CEBs Edgbaston, PRO HO 107/2049 2B–2C.

21 For an analysis of the social character of Edgbaston in a slightly earlier period, see Davidoff and Hall, *Family fortunes*, 36–69.

The following information was collected for each household:

1) the number of children of 14 years and under;
2) their relationship to the head of household;
3) whether or not the head of household had a spouse present;
4) the number of adults who were related to the head of household;
5) the number of adults who were not kin;
6) the age of all occupants.

The information contained in the CEBs is, of course, liable to the deficiencies and inaccuracies discussed by Higgs[22] and elsewhere in this volume. In part these arose from the inadequate training of the recorders; for example, there were many mis-spellings and amendments, especially in the Ladywood returns. Where there is uncertainty about secondary families within the households identified by the enumerators, lodgers consisting of a man and wife (or woman identified as his wife) with or without children and not apparently related to the head of household, have been deemed to form a separate household. Single lodgers, whether or not kin, have been included in the family of the head of the household.

Results of the survey

The child population of the streets surveyed in Ladywood was 339, representing 37.2 per cent of the total. In the Edgbaston survey the child population was 252 representing 24.7 per cent, giving a combined child population of 591 or 30.6 per cent of the total. They suggest that Laslett's picture of the rural past, where children might be found 'thronging the churches, for ever clinging to the skirts of women in the house and wherever they went and above all crowding round the cottage fires',[23] had an urban and industrial counterpart in mid-nineteenth-century England. The much lower percentage of children in Edgbaston is accounted for by the presence of servants; all but two households contained at least one servant. Taking both communities together, 225 families representing 63.6 per cent of all households contained one or more children. The mean household size for families with children was 5.21 for Ladywood and 7.92 for Edgbaston. The larger households in Edgbaston are once again explained by the considerable number of servants.

The number of households below the mean household size is negligible; the several one-parent families in Ladywood most often contain lodgers or kin. In Edgbaston servants remain in residence in

22 See Higgs, *Making sense; Clearer sense.*
23 Laslett, *World we have lost*, 104.

Table 25.1a Household experience of children: Ladywood, 1851

Children living in or with	n. of households in category	% of households	n. of children	% of children
Two 'natural' parents with or without siblings	59	44.7	180	53.1
Two 'natural' parents plus servants	9	6.8	22	6.5
'Apparent' nuclear family with step-parents	4	3.0	10	3.0
Household of grand-parents	3	2.2	5	1.5
Household of uncle and aunt	6	4.3	6	1.8
Household of brother or sister	2	1.5	2	0.6
Two-parent household plus adult kin	14	10.1	25	7.3
Two-parent household plus lodgers with or without adult kin	17	12.3	46	13.6
One-parent household no additional kin	10 } 17[a]	12.3	32	9.4
One-parent household plus lodgers or kin	7			
Living in household as servant	2	1.5	2	0.6
Living in household as scholar	–	–	–	2.6
Other experiences	5	3.6	9	2.6
Totals	138	102.3	339	100.0

Notes: a = 11 females and 6 males.
The number of 'experiences' is rather higher than the number of households because some contained more than one childhood experience. The percentage expressed is the percentage of experiences.

one-parent families, leaving those households well over the mean 4.74.

The results of the attempt to classify the family experience of children in the mid-nineteenth century are contained in Tables 25.1a and 25.1b. Ten different childhood experiences have been identified besides that of living in a conventional nuclear family.

Comment and interpretation

In the case of Ladywood, the conventional nuclear family is fairly well established as the norm, especially since children in households with single lodgers (as well as with both parents) may not indeed have

Table 25.1b Household experience of children: Edgbaston, 1851

Children living in or with	n. of households in category	% of households	n. of children	% of children
Two 'natural' parents with or without siblings	2	2.2	5	2.0
Two 'natural' parents plus servants	53	57.0	149	59.1
Apparent nuclear family with step-parents	–	–	–	–
Households of grand-parents	2	2.2	4	1.6
Household of uncle and aunt	3	3.2	5	2.0
Household of brother or sister	2	2.2	5	2.0
Two-parent household plus adult kin	16	17.2	45	17.9
Two-parent household plus lodgers with or without kin	–	–	–	–
One-parent household no additional kin	6 } 9[a]	9.7	18	7.1
One-parent household plus lodgers or kin	3 }			
Living in household as servant	5	5.4	5	2.0
Living in household as scholar	2	2.2	12	4.7
Other experiences	2	2.2	4	1.6
Totals	96	103.5	252	100.0

Notes: [a] = Three females and six males. See notes to Table 25.1a.

experienced a childhood which was significantly different from those in households without lodgers. Yet the fact that 7 of the 17 one-parent households included lodgers or kin suggests that economic pressures led poorer families to make space for those who might contribute to the household budget or perhaps care for children while the remaining parent worked.

Different qualifications must be made in the case of Edgbaston. The majority of children lived in households with servants, but where both parents were present this closely resembled the conventional family. The range and variety of childhood experience within such a small community is nevertheless impressive. To obtain the number of parentless children (defined as those who have lost at least one parent) we should add to the 32 Ladywood children in one-parent households the children living with kin with no more than one parent. One such family group (included under 'other') lived with their widowed mother in the household of their great aunt. With the addition of step-children there were 60 parentless children (17.7 per cent) in Ladywood and 38 (15.1 per cent) in Edgbaston, giving an overall percentage of 16.6. The number of widowed householders with children under the age of 14 was 17 and 9 for Ladywood and Edgbaston respectively, giving some indication of the extent to which Victorian children's lives were affected by adult mortality rates. Anderson found a much higher number of lone parents living within other households in his national survey.[24] However, in the case of Ladywood the availability of work which could be done by women within the household may explain this difference.

The possibility of taking in a lodger who would contribute to the household income might also have made it possible for a widow to retain her own household. Ladywood seems to have been an area to which many young workers came to obtain work. However, we should note, too, that the figures given for widowed include widowers who would have found it easier to retain their own households. The figures for parentless children are, of course, unreliable since we cannot be sure that the children living in the households of kin were in every case parentless. We have already mentioned the possibility that grandchildren might be taken in to relieve the pressure on the parental household. On the other hand, the overall figure is almost certainly an underestimate. It is not possible, for example, to identify step-children with any certainty as there is no indication in the census returns of whether or not the head of household or his/her spouse had been married before. Where the wife of the household has children with a different surname or discrepancies of age are evident (a very young wife/husband married to a spouse with children who could not have been their biological parent) this was the most likely interpretation. In addition there were three 'nurse-children' in Ladywood, assigned to the 'other' category of Table 25.1a, about whose parents we have no information. Only one child, Jobs (Job?) Wall in an all-male household is positively identified as an orphan. It is possible that one or more of the six scholar-boarders in William Lead's school in Edgbaston was orphaned, but they have not been included in the 'parentless' category. There is some evidence here to lend support to Anderson's view that the most marked contrast between Victorian and modern childhood was the relatively large number of children who, while not orphaned, did not live with either natural parent.[25]

Households with children who had siblings over the age of 20 may include a 'concealed' illegitimate child. It is possible that some of these

24 Anderson, 'Households, families and individuals', 249. These figures are not strictly comparable, Anderson's lone parents being those with children under the age of 10 rather than 14.

25 Anderson, 'Households, families and individuals'.

unmarried adult offspring may have had offspring of their own who were designated as the children of their grandparents, rather than their true parent, in order to protect the family from any stigma of illegitimacy. Whatever the realities of Victorian morality, concepts of respectability may have been strong in all classes, and there is no reason to suppose that the families concerned should have admitted to the enumerator what they sought to conceal from the rest of the community. Certainly, the child reared in a family with a wide age-range amongst the offspring is likely to have been supervised by three or more adults for much of its infancy, or perhaps given over to the special care of one adult sibling (usually a sister) and to have experienced an infancy and childhood significantly different from that of a child where the age range amongst siblings was less marked. The unfortunate Jobs Wall and the three nurse-children appear to be severed from any kin, but it is likely in the latter case that the separation was a temporary one. There is little evidence to suggest (as in Preston) a serious housing shortage – which would put pressure on a family to take in kin or place children in the homes of elderly or childless kin. Several houses were unoccupied. The occupations of the women in Ladywood are all those which might have been carried out in the home, which may explain why there is no substantial evidence of kin living in to care for small children.

The tables display something of the variety of household experience, but not the complexity. Joseph and Martha Robinson of 208 Nile Street in Ladywood lived with their widowed mother in the household of their grandparents which, in addition, contained their cousin, Samuel Reader, one servant and five lodgers. The latter, all described as 'boatmen', would presumably have been employed in their grandfather's boat-making business. This household contained one of the two child servants in Ladywood.

Clearly, no very satisfactory conclusions may be reached on the basis of so small and limited a survey. Hareven has discussed the deficiencies of the 'snap-shot' approach of investigation based on census returns: the absence of any knowledge of the impact of life-cycles or of the fluidity of household structure; the difficulties of abstracting the role of the individual within the family as a result of the process of time and change.[26] Equally, it is impossible to catalogue the household of the past without being curious to find out more about the lives of children in the past than the glimpse which is presented by the census information. What is one to make of five-year-old Jobs Wall, the only certain orphan in an all-male household, none of whom were related to him? If we are right in supposing that the family imposed significant

[26] Hareven, 'Recent research on the history of the family', (reprinted in Drake, *Time, family and community*, 20–3.

restrictions on individual aspirations in mid-nineteenth-century urban society, then he may have come to enjoy an enviable freedom. Statistically, however, and if we can place any reliance on the impressionistic message of Victorian fiction, he is also less likely to have survived. In similar vein, why were the six scholars sent to board with William Lead? Further research using record linkage, school records and personal accounts (much more likely for Edgbaston than Ladywood) might help to provide some of the statistics with personalities and enable us to be more precise about childhood experiences. But, for the most part, the children of the past remain, as Pollock has concluded, 'indecipherable figures'.[27] Even where we can be more aware of their presence, the 'something mysterious' about children of the past remains.[28]

27 Pollock, *Forgotten children*, 264.
28 Laslett, *The world we have lost*, 104.

26

Household structure, marriage and the institution of service in nineteenth-century rural England

P. R. A. HINDE

The aim of this chapter is threefold: first, to present some data on household structure in two contrasting areas of rural England between 1851 and 1881; second to provide an analysis of the changing institutions of domestic and agrarian service; and, third, to relate the history of marriage and household formation in late-nineteenth-century rural England to the hypothesis put forward by Hajnal, that in pre-industrial north-west Europe the institution of service acted as 'an essential part of the mechanism by which marriage could be delayed, with the result that population growth was under partial control'.[1]

The research forms part of a more general study of marriage and fertility in nineteenth-century England[2] and uses the CEBs for two small rural areas in the census years 1851–81. The first area is in central Norfolk, in the registration district of Mitford, and the second is in the registration district of Atcham in Shropshire.[3] They were deliberately selected to illustrate the contrast between the predominantly arable eastern counties and the mainly pastoral west. The average population of the Mitford study area over the four census years was 2,900, and that of the Atcham study area, 3,292.

Household structure

The structure of households in the two areas in the census years from 1851 to 1881 is presented in Table 26.1 below, which also includes a set of figures taken from a sample of CEBs for the whole of rural England in 1851 for comparison. Several features of this table call for comment. First, households were larger in Atcham than in Mitford. This was the

1 Hajnal, 'Two kinds of preindustrial household', 481.

2 See Woods and Hinde, 'Nuptiality and age at marriage'; Hinde and Woods, 'Variations in historical natural fertility patterns'.

3 The Mitford study area includes the parishes of Beeston with Bittering, Kempstone, East and West Lexham, Litcham, Mileham, Weasenham All Saints and Wellingham. The Atcham study area includes the parishes of Acton Burnell, Church Preen, Cound, Cressage, Eaton Constantine, Harley, Hughley, Kenley, Leighton, Pitchford, Ruckley and Langley, Sheinton and Wroxeter. PRO HO 107/1825, 1990–1; RG 9/1243, 1861, 1868; RG 10/1848, 2760–2, 2768; RG 11/1981, 2641–2, 2648.

Table 26.1 Mean number of persons per 100 households: Mitford and Atcham study areas, 1851–1881

Relationship to household head[a]	Mitford				Atcham				Rural England
	1851	1861	1871	1881	1851	1861	1871	1881	1851
Head and spouse	175	177	175	171	166	164	170	169	171
Offspring	215	202	187	183	184	167	184	183	210
Relatives	35	24	32	27	47	48	38	36	33
Servants[b]	29	23	21	19	76	74	60	50	33
sub-total	454	426	415	400	473	453	452	438	447
Attached lodgers	14	14	15	11	12	22	13	12	24
Others[c]	7	7	5	7	6	11	5	3	–
Total population	475	447	435	418	491	486	470	453	471
n. of households	631	668	654	630	695	702	668	661	2,467

Notes: *a* = Excluding those stated in the CEBs to be visitors.
b = Including apprentices.
c = 'Others' include those whose relationship to the head of household was not stated in the census, together with those stated in the column headed 'relationship to head of household' to be 'nursechildren', 'adopted children', 'foster children', 'scholars', 'inmates', and a small number whose precise relationship to the head of household was ambiguous or difficult to determine.

Source: The figures for rural England, 1851 are taken from Wall, 'The household', 497.

result of a greater number of relatives and servants in the former area which more than offset a smaller number of members of the nuclear family. Second, the number of attached lodgers and others in the two study areas was small, except in Atcham in 1861, when a railway was being constructed through part of the study area and gangs of 'navigators' were lodging with local people. Finally, the mean size of the household declined over the 30 year period by 12 per cent in Mitford and 8 per cent in Atcham. In both areas there was a punctuated fall in the number of relatives, but this was not the primary cause of the decline in overall household size. In Mitford, a gradual decrease in the number of offspring was largely responsible, but in Atcham a decline in the number of servants was most important.

This contrast can be further illustrated by considering the relative contribution to overall population change in the two areas made by changes in the numbers of offspring, relatives and servants. In Mitford, the total population declined from 3,044 in 1851 to 2,661 in 1881. Offspring accounted for over half of this change (52.7 per cent), whereas relatives contributed only 13.3 per cent and servants 17.0 per cent. In Atcham, where the total population fell from 3,484 to 3,026 over the period, a decrease in the number of servants was the dominant contributor, accounting for 42.3 per cent. Relatives contributed 20.1 per

Table 26.2 Mean number of offspring per 100 households by age: Mitford study area, 1851–1881

Age group	1851	1861	1871	1881
0–4	60	54	54	47
5–9	49	47	46	47
10–14	45	50	40	40
15–19	30	24	24	24
20–24	16	13	15	15
25–29	8	6	4	5
30 and over	6	7	6	4
All ages[a]	215	202	187	183
20 and over	31	26	25	24

Notes: *a* = The figures of all ages may disagree with the sums of the columns as a result of rounding errors.

cent, and offspring only 15.7 per cent. Returning to Table 26.1, the greatest difference between the two areas was in the number of servants, which was more than two and a half times as great in Atcham as in Mitford. In view of this, and the importance of service as an influence on mean household size in Atcham, it is necessary to analyse the structure of the institution more fully. Before considering service, however, it is interesting to look at the decline of the number of offspring in Mitford in a little more detail, in view of its accounting for more than 50 per cent of the total decline in mean household size, and the very close relationship between the latter and the mean number of offspring per 100 households.[4]

Table 26.2 above shows that the decline in numbers was greatest in the age group 0–4 years, but other ages contributed as well. The reason for the reduction seems, therefore, not to be simple. If it were due to a decrease in fertility, we should expect the younger ages to show the greatest proportionate decline, whereas if it were due to offspring leaving the parental home earlier, either to emigrate from the region or to establish new households themselves, we should expect the decrease to be concentrated in older age groups. At first sight, from the evidence in Table 26.2, both processes appear to have been at work, although the decline in fertility was probably the more important of the two. The total marital fertility ratio in Mitford went down from 6.736 in 1851 to

[4] The ratio between the mean number of offspring per 100 households and the mean number of persons per 100 households was between 0.43 and 0.46 in all four census years (Table 26.1).

6.232 in 1881.[5] If, however, we follow cohorts such as those aged 0–4 years in 1851, 10–14 years in 1861 and so on, we find that the exit rates of members of the various cohorts from the household in which they were born do not change much over the period, implying that the age pattern of leaving home amongst offspring did not alter greatly between 1851 and 1881.[6]

Changes in the institution of service, 1851–1881

When considering the history of the institution of service, it is vital to distinguish between domestic, and agrarian or farm service, the former employing mostly females and the latter, males. In the nineteenth century, domestic service was widespread, and would increase in importance nationally for some decades to come.[7] Agrarian service, in contrast, had been in decline for some time, and, according to Kussmaul, had virtually died out, in the south and east of England.[8] In the north and west, however, agrarian service was still an employer of considerable numbers of young men aged between 15 and 29 years.

In order to examine the different patterns of service between the two study areas, we considered those individuals stated to be servants in the column headed 'relationship to head of household' in the CEBs. To distinguish between farm and domestic service, the occupational classification described by Armstrong was applied to the information given in the column headed 'rank, profession or occupation'. In the vast majority of cases, the category of service into which an individual fell was clear from that information.[9]

From Table 26.3 below it can be seen that agrarian service in the Mitford study area was almost extinct, whereas in Atcham it was still firmly established, certainly in the earlier part of the period under

5 The total marital fertility ratio, as calculated here, is a measure of the number of legitimate children a married woman would bear in her life assuming she married when aged 20 and remained in the married state throughout her fertile period. This provides a useful estimate of completed family size, and is derived from a calculation of the numbers of own-children aged 0–4 years living with married women on the night of the census, by 5-year age groups of women from 20–49 years. From these, age-specific child-woman ratios can be obtained, which can be converted into age-specific marital fertility rates by a method described in Grabill and Cho, 'Methodology for measurement', 50–73. The total marital fertility ratio is the sum of the age-specific marital fertility rates over the ages between 20 and 49, multiplied by 5 to take account of the fact that 5-year age-groups are used in the calculation. This method has been applied to CEBs for nineteenth-century England by Haines, *Fertility and occupation*, 155–204, and Woods and Smith, 'Decline of marital fertility', see especially 216–21, with a number of modifications.

6 I am indebted to Richard Wall for pointing this out to me.

7 On domestic service in the nineteenth century, see Horn, *The Victorian servant*.

8 Kussmaul, *Servants in husbandry*, 19–22.

9 There were a number of individuals for whom this was not the case, whether because no description of their occupation was given, or because the description was too imprecise. Such individuals were classified as domestic servants. Only a small proportion of servants fell into this category, except in Atcham in 1851, where the column headed 'rank, profession or occupation' often only contained the unhelpful description 'servant'. For the occupational classification used, see Armstrong, 'Information about occupation'.

Table 26.3 Numbers of domestic and farm servants per 100 households: Mitford and Atcham study areas, 1851–1881

	Mitford						Atcham					
	Domestic servants			Farm servants			Domestic servants			Farm servants		
Year	M	F	Total[a]	M	F	Total[a]	M	F	Total[a]	M	F	Total[a]
1851	4	19	23	2	1	3	11	34	44	28	2	29
1861	2	17	19	1	2	3	6	28	35	30	7	36
1871	1	17	19	1	1	2	6	28	34	22	2	24
1881	1	17	18	1	0	1	5	26	31	18	1	18

Notes: *a* = The totals may disagree with the sums of the individual sexes as a result of rounding errors.
M = Males; F = Females.

Table 26.4 Numbers of servants per 100 households by age and sex of servants. Atcham study area, 1851–1881

Age group	Domestic servants								Farm servants							
	1851		1861		1871		1881		1851		1861		1871		1881	
	M	F	M	F	M	F	M	F	M	F	M	F	M	F	M	F
10–19	5	14	3	12	3	14	2	14	15	1	15	3	13	1	11	0
20–29	4	13	2	10	1	8	1	7	10	1	9	3	6	1	4	0
30–39	1	3	0	3	0	3	1	2	1	0	3	0	2	0	1	0
40+	1	4	1	4	1	3	1	3	2	0	3	0	2	0	1	0
Totals[a]	11	34	6	28	6	28	5	26	28	2	30	7	23	2	18	1

Notes: *a* = The totals may disagree with the sums of the columns as a result of rounding errors.
M = Males; F = Females.

consideration. The figures for Atcham in 1851 are somewhat distorted by the failure of some enumerators to differentiate between the two types of servant, with the result that a proportion of the farm servants have been classified as domestic servants. The figures would probably be almost identical to those for 1861 were this to be taken into account.

To consider the change over time, it is evident that there was a decline in the prevalence of both types of service in both the study areas between 1851 and 1881, the decline being most noticeable for agrarian service in Atcham. It appears that a substantial part of the decrease in mean household size in the Atcham study area over the period can be attributed to the withering of the institution of agrarian service after 1861.

It is interesting to discover which age groups of the population were most affected by this. Table 26.4 above shows that the age group

Table 26.5 Singulate mean age at marriage (SMAM) and percentage of population aged 15–29 years employed in service: Mitford and Atcham study areas, 1851–1881

Year	Mitford				Atcham			
	SMAM		Percentage aged 15–29 in domestic or agrarian service		SMAM		Percentage aged 15–29 in domestic or agrarian service	
	M	F	M	F	M	F	M	F
1851	26.8	25.5	9.1	24.9	30.0	28.4	39.5	40.7
1861	26.9	24.9	5.0	28.9	29.4	28.4	34.3	41.9
1871	25.8	24.3	2.3	26.3	28.9	27.0	33.8	35.6
1881	26.5	24.2	2.5	27.0	30.1	27.9	31.7	36.1

20–29 years bore the brunt of the decline in both types of service, with the younger age group 10–19 also suffering in the case of agrarian service. There is also evidence that agrarian service is becoming more exclusively the domain of males between 1861 and 1881, the number of female agrarian servants per 100 households declining from 7 to 1 (the situation in 1851 is difficult to determine for the reason mentioned earlier).

The relation between service and other demographic indicators

Hajnal has suggested that the institution of service, in particular agrarian service, was a crucial demographic mechanism in pre-industrial north-west Europe.[10] He maintains that it was only because of the widespread nature of service that the age at first marriage was high in these areas, which resulted, first, in what he terms the European marriage pattern of late and non-universal marriage;[11] and, second, in the operation of nuptiality, rather than marital fertility, as the principal demographic component which populations were able to alter in order partially to control population growth.[12]

The institution of service operated to delay first marriage because of the prohibition upon marriage which was a condition of employment as a domestic or farm servant in most cases. It has already been observed that those populations with a high proportion of their females employed as domestic servants, especially in urban areas, had a high mean age at first marriage in nineteenth-century England.[13] Table 26.5

10 Hajnal, 'Two kinds of preindustrial household'.

11 The European marriage pattern is described in detail in Hajnal, 'European marriage patterns'.

12 Hajnal, 'Two kinds of preindustrial household'.

13 See, for example, Anderson, 'Marriage patterns'.

Table 26.6 Servants as a percentage of the total population in each age-group: Atcham study area, 1851–1881

Age group	Males 1851	1861	1871	1881	Females 1851	1861	1871	1881
10–14	22.8	28.7	16.7	8.0	11.7	10.5	15.9	15.7
15–19	50.3	47.0	49.7	47.0	48.8	57.5	50.0	53.1
20–24	34.8	35.2	22.4	25.5	40.6	45.0	38.6	27.6
25–29	30.1	15.8	22.0	11.8	30.1	18.7	16.5	23.1
30–39	8.7	9.1	8.8	6.1	11.3	10.8	11.5	8.0
40+	4.5	5.9	4.5	2.6	5.1	5.6	4.3	4.3
All ages[a]	15.6	14.8	12.1	10.0	14.3	14.8	12.9	12.0

Notes: This table includes a very small number of apprentices in the count of servants.
a = i.e. the percentage of the whole population occupied as servants.

above gives the singulate mean age at marriage (SMAM) for both Mitford and Atcham in the census years from 1851 to 1881 and demonstrates that the prevalence of service is related to the age at marriage as would be expected.[14] Moreover, and although the relationship is by no means exact, the change over time in the SMAM roughly parallels the change in the prevalence of service. The relationship is least exact in Mitford between 1851 and 1861; this may be the result of changes in the age-structure, specifically a decline in the total number of females aged 15–29 years from 406 in 1851 to 357 in 1861.

The age structure of the servant population, and in particular the proportions of the population at various ages which were servants, are important demographic indicators. This is because domestic and agrarian service tended to be a stage in the life-cycle for most people, rather than a form of long-term employment. It is likely that even when the percentage which those occupied as servants formed of the total population was fairly low, a much greater percentage spent some years of their lives in service. Table 26.6 provides an insight into the nature and development of life-cycle service in the Atcham study area between 1851 and 1881.

Two points arising out of this table deserve mention. First, it reinforces the statement made earlier, in that the decline of service was felt mainly, for males, in the age groups 10–14 and 20–29 years, and for females in the age group 20–29 years. Second, despite the decline of the institution in terms of total numbers, even in 1881 around 50 per cent of the population aged between 15 and 19 years was employed in

14 The method of calculating the singulate mean age at marriage (SMAM) is discussed chapter 23, but see also Hajnal, 'Age at marriage', 111–36. The SMAM is defined in Shryock and Siegel, *Methods and materials*, 278, as 'an estimate of the mean number of years lived by a cohort of women before their first marriage'.

Table 26.7 Headship rates amongst males aged 20–29 years: Mitford and Atcham study areas, 1851–1881

	% of males aged 20–29 given in CEBs as heads of households	
Year	Mitford	Atcham
1851	34.2	15.6
1861	39.1	13.4
1871	42.4	21.1
1881	36.3	25.0

either agrarian service (mainly males) or domestic service (mainly females). Rates of participation in service, therefore, declined substantially amongst those aged 20 or over, whilst they did not fall amongst those aged 15–19. This may have been because young people left service earlier in life in 1881 than in 1851; this, however, is difficult to determine from census evidence.

Discussion

The evidence from these two small but contrasting areas of rural England in the latter part of the nineteenth century appears to support Hajnal's hypothesis in principle. It does seem that domestic and, in particular, agrarian service acted as controls upon the mean age at first marriage and consequently upon the formation of new households. This control operated partly because of the prohibition upon marriage whilst in service, and partly because service provided a means by which to acquire the wherewithal necessary to establish a new household. Further evidence to lend weight to this claim can be provided by considering the percentages of males aged 20–29 years which were heading households. Table 26.7 above shows that, in the Atcham study area, this percentage nearly doubled between 1861 and 1881. This was concomitant with a decline in the percentage of males in the same age group in service from 27.4 per cent to 19.1 per cent.

The low headship rates amongst males in their twenties in Atcham, together with the figures presented earlier, also show that an extreme form of the European marriage pattern lingered in the west of England for a considerable time after it had disappeared in the eastern areas.

The figures in Table 26.7 can also be used when considering the question: what happened to those servants (and, perhaps older offspring in Mitford) who disappeared between 1851 and 1881? It appears that in Atcham, and to a lesser extent in Mitford up to 1871, a considerable proportion could have formed new households in those areas. Nevertheless, the fall in the headship rate amongst males aged 20–29 years in Mitford between 1871 and 1881 suggests that a number of these young people in their twenties may have left the countryside in favour of the attractions of urban employment. Emigration from the rural areas was proceeding apace in the late-nineteenth century: according to Lawton, between 1851 and 1911 the sum of the percentage net migrational change for each decade was a loss of between 75 and 100 per cent for the Mitford registration district, and of between 25 and 50 per cent for the Atcham registration district.[15] The total population of the Mitford study area declined from 3,044 in 1851 to 2,661 in 1881, and that of Atcham from 3,486 to 3,026.

Important though emigration was, it should not be allowed to obscure the social and demographic changes which were taking place within the residual population in the countryside. Those who left agrarian service in the east of England prior to 1851 did not all move to the cities; most of them remained as day labourers on the land, augmenting the number of offspring in the average household. Despite the fall in total population in the study areas over the period, there was not a great decline in the number of agricultural labourers employed. In the Mitford study area, the number of household heads and male offspring aged 10 and over stated in the census to be agricultural labourers rose from 420 in 1851 to 471 in 1861, and only fell to 430 in 1881. In Atcham, the corresponding figures were 367, 329 and 337 respectively.[16]

This chapter has tried to show how an analysis of household structure can pose questions, the answers to which lead the researcher into a consideration of complex social changes which have yet to be unravelled. Moreover, the final collapse of the old pre-industrial demographic regime could not occur until the great secular decline in marital fertility of the late-nineteenth and early-twentieth centuries permitted the age at first marriage to fall. Marital fertility then took over from nuptiality as the principal mode of demographic control.

What has been observed, therefore, are two contrasting rural populations at a time of fairly rapid social, economic and demographic change. The decline of the institution of service in Mitford before 1851 had weakened the links between household structure, marriage and service there, whilst in Atcham those links appear to have remained until at least 1881.

15 Lawton, 'Population changes', 59. On rural depopulation in general, see Saville, *Rural depopulation*.

16 In the enumeration district of Litcham, in the Mitford study area, in 1881, all agricultural labourers were described in the CEBs merely as 'labourers'. The figure of 430 agricultural labourers in the Mitford study area in 1881 is calculated assuming that all these individuals were, in fact, agricultural labourers. It is appreciated that this may result in the figure of 430 being something of an overestimate of the true figure. It is unlikely, however, that it is so much of an over-estimate to affect the general observation that the number of agricultural labourers in the Mitford study area did not decline substantially between 1851 and 1881. A similar problem was encountered in the enumeration districts of East and West Lexham in 1881, and in the enumeration district of Cressage in the Atcham study area in 1851.

27

Depopulation and changing household structure in the mining communities of west Cornwall, 1851–1871

MARK BRAYSHAY

Introduction

In recent years much attention has been paid to the study of past household size and structure in this country.[1] Few attempts have been made, however, to explore the relationship between the characteristics of the average nineteenth-century household and short-term changes in economic and social conditions at the local level. While most historical demographers would accept that, in general, household characteristics alter only very slowly, there will undoubtedly have been instances when major economic and social upheaval produced locally more rapid, measurable responses in the size and structure of the average domestic group.

By the second half of the nineteenth century, the process of rural depopulation was well established in England and Wales, and the gradual creaming-off of the younger and more enterprising elements in the population inevitably led, in the longer term, to important social and demographic changes in the countryside.[2] In some parts of the country particular economic circumstances occasionally prompted a more cataclysmic exodus. Areas which depended heavily upon one form of employment, such as the tin and copper districts of west Cornwall, the lead mining areas of Devon and the slate quarry region in north Wales, were especially vulnerable to the vagaries of the market. Often, when a slump came, there was little alternative but to move away. Some workers might try to obtain similar work elsewhere in the country; rather more drifted towards the growing towns and cities. Many left the country altogether and joined the growing tide of emigration to the Colonies and the United States.

Collectively the casualties of local economic slumps represent a significant component in the demographic and social history of the country; yet surprisingly little is known about them. How did ordinary

1 See, for example, the chapters of Wall *et al. Family forms in historic Europe*, and Hareven, 'Recent research on the history of the family' (reprinted in Drake, *Time, family and community*).

2 Saville, *Rural depopulation*; Lawton, 'Rural depopulation'; Lawton, 'Population and society', 311–5.

Figure 27.1

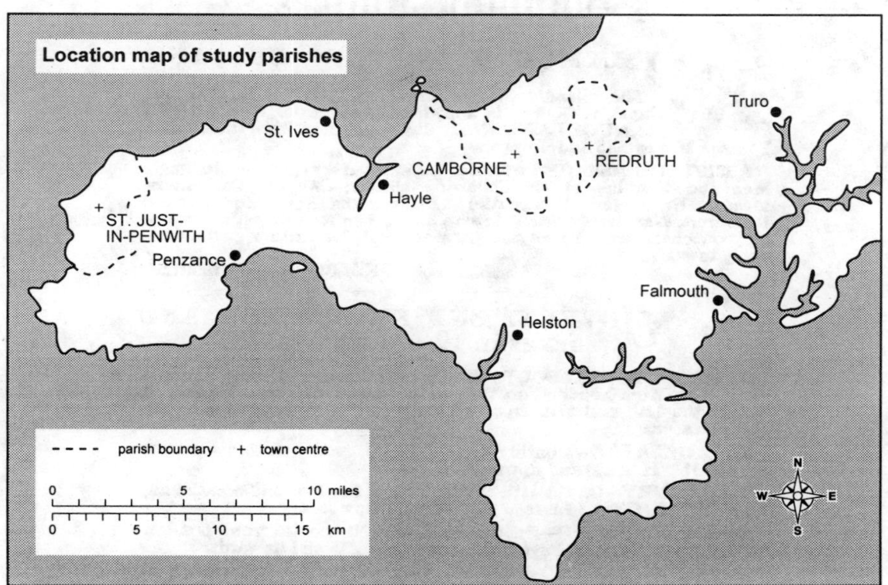

families react to a crisis? Did the average household shrink in size, as for example, husbands and sons boarded the emigrant ship? Was there a measurable reduction in the propensity to marry and establish new households? Were there any changes in the internal structure of households such as the incidence of co-residing relatives or servants? These questions, which concern the responses of ordinary households to localised, short-term problems in the nineteenth century, are not easy to answer; we cannot interview the men and women of history. Nevertheless, because it is often argued that the household is a sensitive barometer of social and economic change, some insight into the changes taking place in domestic arrangements is crucial if the process of depopulation is to be understood fully.[3]

The object of this chapter is to present the findings of a study of changing household structure in the three important Cornish mining parishes of Camborne, Redruth and St Just (see Figure 27.1 above).[4] In the middle of the nineteenth century these parishes were at the heart of one of the most intensively mined areas in the world. More than 45 per cent of the mining population of Cornwall could be found there. Locally, the economy was completely dominated by the mines which

3 For a full discussion of the importance of the study of the history of the household see Laslett, 'Introduction'.

4 This study is part of a wider research project reported in Brayshay, 'Cornwall mining communities'.

Figure 27.2 Advertisements for assisted passages

Shipping Notices.

PLYMOUTH TO NEW ZEALAND.

The splendid Clipper Ship WINTERTHUR, 1500 tons, Capt. W. Goudie, is appointed to sail from PLYMOUTH for AUCKLAND, N.Z., direct on the 25th January inst. Passage Money £15 and upwards.

ASSISTED PASSAGES will also be granted by this ship to Single Men and Families of the following classes:—Miners, Carpenters, Masons, Bricklayers, Stonecutters, Blacksmiths, Farm and General Labourers, Navvies, &c., &c. Also to Single Female Domestic Servants of good character.—To engage passages and for further particulars, apply to

Mr. JAS. B. WILCOCKS, Barbican, Plymouth.

GOVERNMENT EMIGRATION AND GENERAL PASSENGER SERVICE.

TO MELBOURNE—On the 7th and 21st of each month from London on the 5th, 15th, and 20th from Liverpool; and on the 11th and 27th from PLYMOUTH. Passage Money, £14 and upwards.

TO ADELAIDE—Monthly from London, and occasionally from PLYMOUTH. £20 and upwards.

TO SYDNEY—On the 11th and 25th from London, and occasionally from PLYMOUTH. Sixteen Guineas and upwards.

TO QUEENSLAND—On the 25th of each month from London calling at PLYMOUTH every third month. £15 and upwards.

TO NEW ZEALAND PORTS—Weekly from London, calling a PLYMOUTH occasionally, £15 and upwards.

TO CANADA and American Ports—By the "Plymouth Line of Packets," or steam-ships from other ports. he Canada Government Pamphlet sent free on receipt of wo postage stamp

TO NEW YORK—By regular weekly steamers from Liverpoo Passages varying from Four Guineas upwards.

ASSISTED EMIGRATION.

TO SOUTH AUSTRALIA—Families, single men, and single women, on payment of very small sums.

TO QUEENSLAND—Families and single men at £8 per adult single female domestic servants, £4.

To Canterbury, Nelson, Wellington, Otago, and Auckland, New Zealand—Families and single women of suitable classes

FREE EMIGRATION.

TO SOUTH AUSTRALIA.—For families, single men, and women of the required classes.

TO QUEENSLAND -To young married couples without children over 12 months old, and single female domestic servants.

TO MELBOURNE, VICTORIA—For single female domestic servants of good character.

TO AUCKLAND, N.Z. Families and single women of suitabl classes, with a free grant of land in addition.—Apply to

Mr. JAMES B. WILCOCKS, Barbican, Plymouth,

Or to his duly authorised Agents in all the principal towns.

When the mining recession in west Cornwall deepened, many men emigrated. Advertisements such as these for assisted passages were common in the local newspapers. Cornish miners were often specifically mentioned and, in the late 1860s, subsidised passages were available to 'single' men. Many emigrated with the hope, once well-established overseas, of later sending for their family. *Western Morning News*, 19 January 1865.

employed well over 9,000 workers. But the industry was based upon a notoriously fragile financial system and, although some mines could be spectacularly profitable, even a small shortfall in demand or drop in price could have a rapid and serious effect.[5]

A peak of prosperity in copper mining was reached in the late 1850s, but the boom period was short and a searing recession hit the Cornish mining industry soon after. Although the closure of mines and widespread unemployment were not new experiences, a recession had never before lasted so long. Indeed, from this crisis, which began with the collapse of the copper-mining industry in 1866, there was to be no recovery. This change in fortunes took place in a remarkably short period: a few critical months during the summer of 1865 saw a relatively prosperous situation deteriorate to become one of deep recession. Although there was no absolute decline in the total population until after 1871, newspaper reports were suggesting as early as 1866 that emigration had increased to a massive and unprecedented scale, emptying the area of young adults.[6] To make matters worse, the price of some essential foodstuffs was rising and the stark choice thus facing many ordinary mining families was to emigrate or to remain and starve (see Figure 27.2 above).

With the slump, the effects of unemployment were inevitably felt more severely in the communities most dependent upon the mines. Thus Camborne, Redruth and St Just are an obvious choice for a study of the decline of the mining industry in west Cornwall.

Depopulation and the household

In Redruth and St Just, the population had already registered a combined decline of more than 1,000 between 1861 and 1871 (Table 27.1 below). The reduction was largest in Redruth which had always been much more heavily dependent upon copper mining. In St Just there were tin as well as copper mines and some of the former remained in operation. The possibility of exploiting the reserves of tin, which lay deep beneath the exhausted copper lodes, staved off an absolute reduction in the population of Camborne until the 1870s. Indeed the population had actually increased by 1871, albeit at a markedly reduced rate. By 1881, however, neither deep-tin nor indeed the small manufacturing industries of the parish could prevent a reduction in the population of Camborne of 1,868 people or 12.5 per cent.

5 Rowe, *Cornwall in the age of the Industrial Revolution*, 305–26; Payton, 'Cornish emigration'; Rowse, *The Cornish in America*, 161–3.

6 The *West Briton* newspaper reported on 15 June, 1866 'the unprecedented exodus of the bone and sinew of the working population of our county'. For more detail on Cornish emigration in the nineteenth century see: Burke, 'The Cornish diaspora'; Rowse, *The Cornish in America*; Payton, *The Cornish miner in Australia*. For information on the process of emigration from the south-west see Brayshay, 'Using American records' and 'Government emigration from Plymouth'.

Table 27.1 Population totals, 1841–1881

		1841	1851	1861	1871	1881
Camborne	Total	10,061	12,887	14,056	14,929	13,601
	Males	4,827	6,169	6,568	6,735	6,004
	Females	5,234	6,718	7,488	8,194	7,597
Redruth	Total	9,305	10,571	11,504	10,683	9,335
	Males	4,343	4,965	5,228	4,646	3,998
	Females	4,962	5,606	6,276	6,037	5,337
St Just	Total	7,147	8,759	9,290	9,011	6,409
	Males	3,820	4,466	4,587	4,426	3,000
	Females	3,327	4,293	4,703	4,585	3,409

Figure 27.3 Growth rates: St Just and national trend, 1801–1911

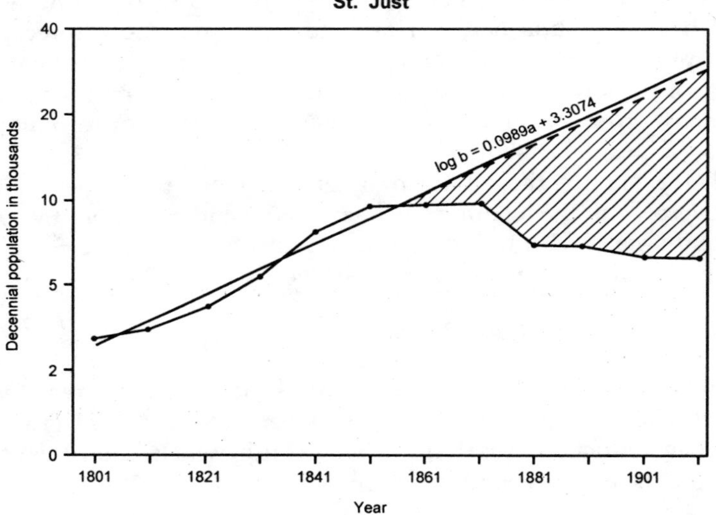

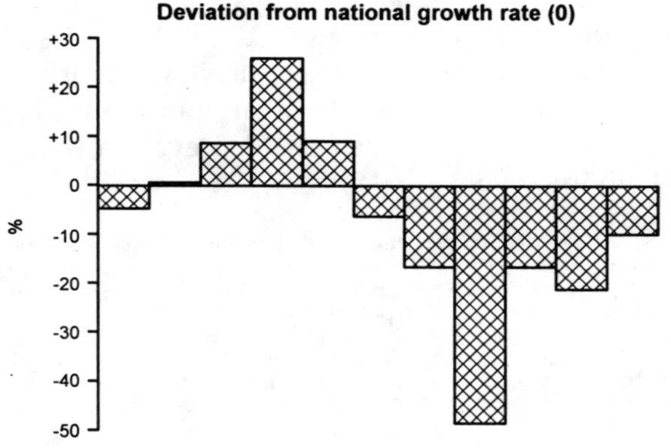

Figure 27.4 Unemployment in the CEBs

Page 78]

The undermentioned Houses are situate within the Boundaries of the

Civil Parish [or Township] of	City or Municipal Borough of	Municipal Ward of	Parliamentary Borough of	Town of	Village or Hamlet, &c., of	Local Board, or [Improvement Commissioners District] of
Redruth					Vogue	

No. of Schedule	ROAD, STREET, &c., and No. or NAME of HOUSE	HOUSES Inhabited	HOUSES Uninhabited (U.), or Building (B.)	NAME and Surname of each Person	RELATION to Head of Family	CONDITION	AGE of Males	AGE of Females	Rank, Profession, or OCCUPATION	WHERE BORN
86	Vogue	1		Nicholas Rogers	Head	Mar	[illegible]		Mine Agent (Unemployed)	Cornwall Gwennap
				Mary A. Do	Wife	Mar		[illegible]		Do Do
				Do Do Do	Daur	Unm		22	Scholar	Do Do
				Sophia Do	Daur	Unm		20	Do	At Sea on board Crane
				Elizabeth Do	Daur	Unm		17	Do	Brazil British Subject
				Charlotte J. Do	Daur			14	Do	Do Do
				Nicholas J. Do	Son		12		Do	Do Do
				Nanny Do	Daur			10	Do	Do Do
				James W. Do	Son		6		Do	Do Do
				Emily Do	Daur			8	Do	Do Do
				Charles Do	Son		5		Do	Do Do
				Amelia Do	Daur			2		Do Do

By 1871 the Cornish CEBs sometimes specifically recorded unemployment. An example is the mine agent Nicholas Rogers, who lived with his wife and nine children in the hamlet of Vogue, on Trefula Moor, near Redruth. The family had clearly tried their luck in Brazil, and had returned within two years preceding the census, a fact revealed by the South American birthplace of their youngest daughter, Amelia, who was only two years old in 1871. It is also possible to pinpoint that 1851 was the year of their departure as their second child, Sophia, 20 in 1871, was listed as born 'at sea on board *Crane*'. PRO RG 10/2317.

Far more important than any fall in absolute population size was the sharp change in the rate of increase, which is clearly shown for the case of St Just in Figure 27.3 above. The difference between the actual census totals of population and those which might have been expected, if the vigorous growth during the period 1801–61 had been maintained, indicate the considerable loss of potential as the recession deepened. A similar pattern occurred in the other two parishes. Figure 27.3 also shows a comparison between the intercensal growth rates of St Just in the nineteenth century and those occurring in England and Wales as a whole. Before 1851, local growth rates consistently exceeded those of the country as whole, but thereafter the position was very obviously reversed.

The recession had its most direct and damaging effect on miners and their families, and the census gives a clear indication of this. In 1851 there were 9,459 people employed at the mines in Camborne, Redruth and St Just. Despite a 10 per cent increase in total population and a related increase in the number of households, by 1871, the census reveals that the mine workforce had actually been reduced by some 12 per cent, or roughly 1,100 jobs. Moreover, this latter figure may underestimate the decline of mining since the census does not accurately record instances of unemployment. There were certainly cases when the enumerators' books specified that an individual was out of work. Thus, for example, the 1871 census of Redruth reveals that Nicholas Rogers of Trefula Moor was a 'Mine agent (Unemployed)', and that Thomas Verran of Vogue was a 'Miner – Copper – Unemployed' (Figure 27.4 above). Such cases represent an exception in the records rather than the rule. In fact, it is highly likely that a large number of people who stated an occupation in 1871, may not have had a job. Moreover, there is a possibility that former miners may have stated that they were labourers (the size of this category of workers in the study area had increased by almost 70 per cent between 1861 and 1871) whereas in reality they were attempting to earn their living by taking on any temporary manual work whenever it was available.

It is against this background of severe economic disruption that this chapter will attempt to explore changes in the average household in Camborne, Redruth and St Just. Most of the information is derived from a 10 per cent sample of households drawn from the CEBs of 1851–71. Every tenth household was included in the sample; its details were coded and the data were analysed by computer.[7]

The census can, of course, only partially answer our questions about Cornish households during the crisis. Although the CEBs contain sophisticated information about every member of the population, they are nevertheless a simple decennial 'snap-shot' and not a continuous record. However, in spite of their limitations, an analysis of the CEBs can shed important light on the processes of change which were taking place in areas of decline during this critical period. The CEBs enable us to gauge the initial impact of an economic recession on ordinary men and women, and on the social units to which they belonged. Indeed, historians increasingly recognise that only through a microscale analysis of this kind is it possible to glimpse the inner mechanics of important social changes which occurred in the past.[8]

Household size and structure in 1851

In 1851, when the mining economy in west Cornwall was still relatively prosperous, the average household encountered in Camborne, Redruth and St Just was not very different from those described by other writers in different parts of nineteenth-century England. However, in as much

7 The conventions established by social historians for analysing CEBs were employed in this study. See Wrigley, *Nineteenth-century society*. Given that occupation types were unevenly distributed over the parishes, it could be argued that a 10 per cent sample might underestimate the extent of the mining crisis. In fact the mining population was fairly well represented throughout the study area. However, specific jobs within the mining industry, as well as jobs in other employment sectors, were rather more concentrated in certain areas and, in these cases, larger samples were drawn for some parts of the analysis. See Brayshay, 'Cornwall mining communities'.

8 Laslett, 'Introduction'.

Table 27.2 Household size in 1851: comparative data

Community	Number of persons per household as a percentage of the total										Mean h'hold size
	1	2	3	4	5	6	7	8	9	10+	
Camborne	2	9	18	14	16	12	14	8	3	5	5.3
Redruth	3	12	16	14	11	16	11	7	5	5	5.2
St Just	1	9	9	20	15	16	11	7	6	6	5.5
York[a]	5	15	16	18	14	13	7	5	3	5	4.8
Preston[b]	1	10	16	17	14	12	10	8	5	8	5.4
Rural Lancashire[b]	3	12	13	12	14	13	11	9	6	9	5.5

Notes: *a* = taken from Armstrong, *Stability and change*;
b = taken from Anderson, *Family structure*.

Table 27.3 Household composition in 1851: comparative data

Community	Residents		Lodgers		Servants	
	n.	%	n.	%	n.	%
Camborne	44	18	20	8	18	7
Redruth	42	21	16	8	23	11
St Just	38	20	14	7	19	10
Combined Cornish data	124	19	50	8	60	9
York[a]		22		21		20
Preston[b]		23		23		10
Rural Lancashire[b]		27		10		28
Nottingham[c]		17		22		12
Ashford[d]		21		18		17

Notes: *a* = taken from Armstrong, *Stability and change*;
b = taken from Anderson, *Family structure*;
c = taken from Smith, *Early Victorian household structure*;
d = based on unpublished work by Drake and Pearce, cited in Armstrong, 'A note on the household structure'.

as the Cornish mining communities were industrial, but in a predominantly rural setting, it is significant that the household size characteristics revealed by this study so closely paralleled those of rural Lancashire and the industrial town of Preston described by Anderson.[9]

Ranging from 5.2 and 5.5 persons in 1851, average household size in Camborne, Redruth and St Just was fairly large, particularly in comparison to pre-industrial households (Table 27.2 above). The

[9] There have been a number of similar studies of nineteenth-century household size and structure. For example see: Anderson, *Family structure*; Armstrong, *Stability and change*; Smith, 'Social structure of Nottingham'. Other useful studies include Constable, *Household structure in three English market towns*; Trevor-Bell, 'Family structure in nineteenth-century Oakham'; Janssens, *Family and social change*. For a detailed bibliography providing details of studies by other authors (working on other areas) who examine mean household size see Mills and Pearce, *People and places*.

incidence of 'extended families' (those containing co-resident kin and servants or lodgers) was, moreover, slightly lower than in other areas (Table 27.3 above). Indeed by far the largest proportion of households in west Cornwall contained no servants or kin and consisted of only a 'primary family group' (man, wife and children) and the large mean size of households, therefore, directly reflected the high level of fertility in this population.

The birth rate in Camborne and Redruth exceeded 37 per thousand in 1851, while in St Just it was more than 42 per thousand. With death rates of around 24–23 per thousand, there was clearly a considerable margin of natural increase.[10] High levels of population growth were, of course, both a cause and an effect of the markedly youthful age structure of the population of 1851.

The fact that the co-residence of kin and the incidence of lodgers was slightly less common in west Cornwall than appears to have been the case in other areas, may be attributed to a number of local characteristics. First, the average cottage in the mining districts was a very modest affair. Most measured only 12 feet by 10 and often comprised only 1 or 2 rooms. Unless there was some exceptional crisis, accommodation may simply have been too cramped for many families to be willing to share their homes with co-residents.[11] Certainly, most of the households which did contain lodgers were concentrated in the towns of Redruth and Camborne where larger, two-storey dwellings were more common and some small lodging houses existed.[12]

In 1851 there was no shortage of cottages in the mining districts, and new households could be established in a separate dwelling more easily than appears to have been the case in many Victorian towns where housing was difficult to find. The 'three-life lease' system whereby landowners permitted the enclosure of marginal land and the building of cottages continued to operate and, in some districts, working miners could even obtain building materials at reduced cost.[13]

Some 9 per cent of households contained servants in the west Cornwall study area. While this comparatively low percentage in part reflects the absence of any middle class in these parishes, it may also reflect the availability of employment at the mines for females who, in other areas, would have worked in service. In fact, many of the servants enumerated in the Cornish returns were very young children. This indicates the common practice in nineteenth-century England whereby surplus children were often lodged in other households where spare room could be found. Many of them were actually related to the

10 Registrar General, *Annual Reports* and *Quarterly Returns*, 1851–71.

11 Weaver, 'Industrial housing in Cornwall'; Rowe, *Cornwall in the age of the Industrial Revolution*, 152–4; Hamilton-Jenkin, *Cornwall and its people*, 318–61.

12 CEBs Redruth 1871, PRO RG 10/2315–8.

13 Weaver, 'Industrial housing in Cornwall', 29.

Table 27.4 Changing household size: combined Cornish sample, 1851–1871

Size	1851 Total	1851 %	1861 Total	1861 %	1871 Total	1871 %
1	9	1.40	22	3.02	23	2.98
2	65	10.16	90	12.35	108	13.99
3	95	14.84	108	14.81	125	16.99
4	100	15.63	101	13.85	134	17.36
5	91	14.22	106	14.54	121	15.67
6	91	14.22	113	15.50	86	11.14
7	78	12.19	70	9.60	67	8.68
8	48	7.50	45	6.17	51	6.61
9	29	4.53	38	5.21	26	3.37
10	15	2.34	20	2.74	13	1.68
11+	19	2.97	16	2.19	18	2.33
Totals	640		729		772	
Mean size	5.31		5.12		4.88	

Figure 27.5 Household size: combined Cornish sample, 1851 and 1871

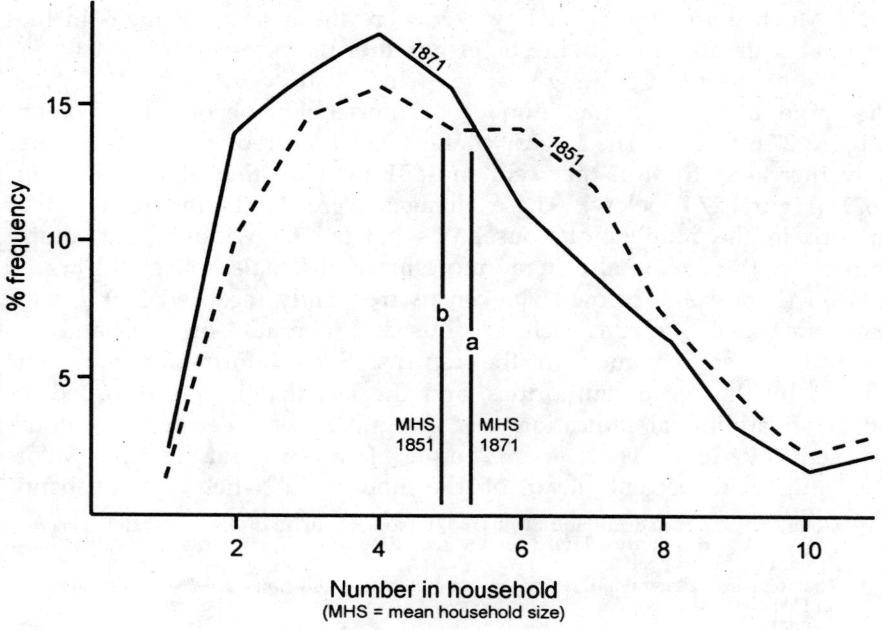

head of the household in which they served and often they were employed as 'child-minders' for the children of parents who had jobs at the mines.[14]

Changing household size and structure, 1851–1871

Thus at the beginning of the study period, households in Camborne, Redruth and St Just were fairly large and most consisted of only a primary family group. The population was youthful and natural increase was at a prodigiously high level. Indeed, household characteristics in this area were not unlike those of other primarily industrial areas of England. However, between 1851 and 1871, the situation began to change. Mean household size fell from 5.31 to only 4.88 persons (Table 27.4 above). There was, of course, a national trend towards smaller households, but the decline in Camborne, Redruth and St Just was larger. Indeed the reduction in St Just was twice that occurring in the country as a whole.[15] However, it may be more important to note that there was a shift in emphasis towards smaller groupings and, by 1871, more than half the households in the sample contained less than four people (Figure 27.5 above). The factors which produced these small changes in household size as well as the distribution of households across the range of sizes in so short a period of time were undoubtedly linked to the decline in the mining industry. Thus, even as early as 1871, it is possible to point to a small but measurable change in the household size characteristics of the study area. Much more significant however were the marked changes in the internal structure of the domestic group after the recession.

One of the most striking changes which had occurred by 1871 was the large increase in the number of households headed by women (Figure 27.6 below). The largest change had occurred in St Just, where they increased from 15 per cent in 1851 to more than 26 per cent in 1871 (Figure 27.7 below). These changes were partly the result of a growth in the number of households headed by widows, but, more important, there were also many more married female household heads in 1871 (Figure 27.8 below). The census frequently recorded that a man had emigrated. Entries such as 'husband abroad', or 'husband in Australia' were common in the returns. Such information was not elicited by the census authorities, and the fact that it was recorded at all is an additional indication that emigration had become a serious problem by 1871. Thus, for example, Jane Bray of Trefula Moor (Redruth) had become head of the household when her husband

14 CEBs Camborne, Redruth and St Just, 1871 PRO RG 10/2315–45. The coding scheme employed in this study allowed for the recording of domestic servants' relationships to the household head.

15 The Registrar General published an estimated average household size for England and Wales as a whole. It is, however, difficult to assess the reliability of this estimate.

Figure 27.6 Absent husbands in the CEBs

Town of Redruth

Redruth

No. of Schedule	Name and Surname of each Person	Relation to Head of Family	Condition	Age of Males	Age of Females	Rank, Profession, or Occupation	Where Born	
4	Jane Body	Head	Mar		47	Husband (abroad)	Cornwall	St Neot
	Jane Body	Daur	Unm		[illegible]	Brick maker	do	Liskeard
	Richard Body	Son		10		Scholar	do	do
	Mary Grace Body	Daur			7	do	do	Redruth
	John Bryant	Head	Widr			Tinplate worker	do	Falmouth
	William Rundle	Head	Mar	[illegible]		Miner	do	Liskeard
	Eliza Rundle	Wife	Mar		42		do	Redruth
	Rebecca Jenkin	Head	W		55	House keeper	do	St Agnes
	John Jenkin	Son	Unm	[illegible]		Tin miner	do	Redruth
1	Thomas Riddle	Head	Mar	[illegible]		Tin miner	do	do
	Eliza Riddle	Wife	Mar		38		do	St Agnes
	Elizabeth Ann Riddle	Daur			9	Scholar	do	Redruth
	Eliza Jane Riddle	Daur			6	do	do	do

The 1871 census reveals many cases of households headed by a married female whose husband is reported to be abroad. The entry for Jane Body of Redruth is an example. The occupation of her eldest daughter is recorded as brick-maker. PRO RG 10/2315.

Figure 27.7 Changes in the percentage of households headed by women and in the percentage of multiple family households

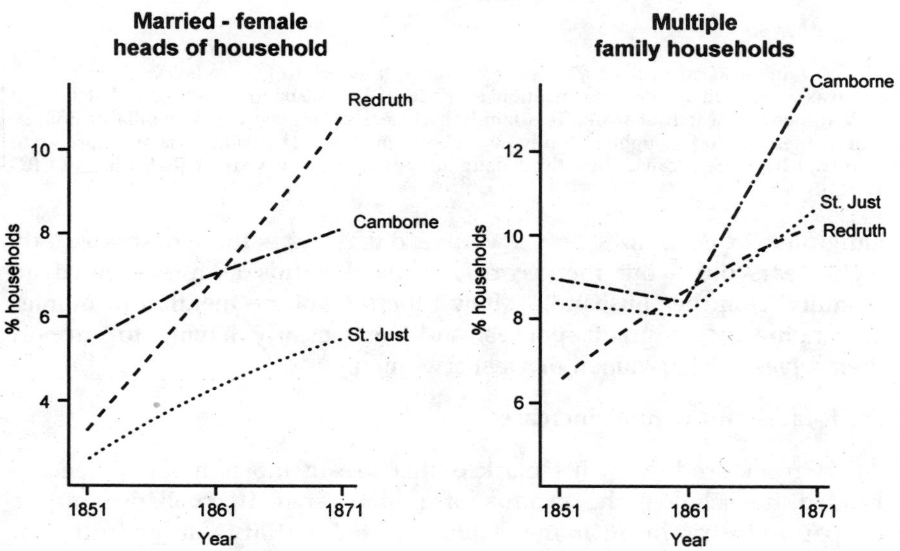

Notes: Multiple family households is used to signify households where two or more nuclear families shared the same dwelling.

Figure 27.8 Female heads of household in the CEBs

The undermentioned Houses are situate within the Boundaries of the [Page 21

Civil Parish (or Township) of	City or Municipal Borough of	Municipal Ward of	Parliamentary Borough of	Town of	Village or Hamlet, &c., of	Local Board, or [Improvement Commissioners District] of	Ecclesiastical District of
Redruth				Redruth		Redruth	

No. of Schedule	ROAD, STREET, &c., and No. or NAME of HOUSE	HOUSES In-habited	HOUSES Unin-habited (U.), or Building (B.)	NAME and Surname of each Person	RELATION to Head of Family	CON-DITION	AGE of Males	AGE of Females	Rank, Profession, or OCCUPATION	WHERE BORN	Whether 1. Deaf-and-Dumb 2. Blind 3. Imbecile or Idiot 4. Lunatic
102	Rosewarne Row	1		James Dunstan	Head	Mar	[illegible]		Engine Man at Mine	Cornwall Redruth	"
				Mary Dunstan	Wife	Mar		71	Eng man Wife	Do Do	"
103	Do	1		Richard Jenkin	Head	Mar	38		Printer, Compositor [illegible]	Do Crowan	"
				Elizabeth Do	Wife	Mar		38	Printer Wife	Do Kea	"
				Jane Do	Daur	Unm		8	Scholar	Do Redruth	"
				Mary Anna Do	Do	Do		6	Do	Do Do	"
				James Do	Son	Do	4		Do	Do Do	"
				Edith Do	Daur	—		1yr	"	Do Do	"
104	Do	1		Eliza Jenkin	Head	Mar		47	House Keep[r]	Do Gwennap	"
				Rosanna Do	Daur	Unm		20	Milliner	Do Redruth	"
				Emily Do	Do	Do		11	Scholar	Tocopillia Bolivia	Britain ufa[illegible]
				Phillipa Do	Do	Do		8	Do	Cornwall Redruth	"
				Catherine Do	Do	—		8	Do	Do Do	"
				Samuel Robert Do	Son	—	4		Do	Do Do	"
105	Do	1		John Loemin	Head	Mar	[illegible]		Ag Lab	Do Do	"
				Catherine Loemin	Wife	Mar		65		Do Do	"
				Mary Hicks	Gran Daur	Unm		14	Servant Domestic	Do Do	"
				Rebecca Hicks	Do	Do		12	" "	Do Do	"
				Agnes Loemin	Daur	Do		6	Scholar	Do Do	"
				Richard Loemin	Son	Do	2	2	—	Do Do	"
106	Do	1		Walter Bennett	Head	Mar	[illegible]		Engine Fitter	Do Ponsanooth	"
				Mary Ann Do	Wife	Mar		30	Eng Fitr Wife	Do Kea	"
				Fredericks Do	Son	—	2		"	Do Redruth	"
				Robert Do	Do	—	1 mon			Do Do	"
5	Total of Houses..	5			Total of Males and Females..		9	15			

* Draw the pen through such of the words as are inappropriate.

Eng- Sheet E.

Eliza Jenkins is listed in the 1871 census of Redruth as head of household, and, although she was a married woman, no mention is made of her husband. It is likely that he had moved away in search of work. This family had clearly emigrated to Tocopilla in Bolivia, where their second daughter, Emily, was born in 1860. They must have returned to Cornwall by 1865, because their third daughter was born that year in Redruth. PRO RG 12/2315.

emigrated to Peru. Mrs Bray had five daughters – the eldest was only eight years old – but the record reveals that this family received an 'annuity' from her husband.[16] Many others made no mention of monies sent home by emigrant spouses, and were clearly having to support themselves as charwomen or washerwomen.

Birth-rates and natural increase

Apart from producing this marked increase in the number of female-headed households, the exodus of miners after the collapse of the copper industry in 1866 inevitably affected fertility. In Redruth, for example, the birth-rate fell from 38 per thousand in 1851 to only 29 per thousand in 1871. There was a similar downward trend in St Just where the reduction was from 42 to 37 per thousand.[17] The propensity to have

16 CEBs Redruth 1871, PRO RG 10/2316.

17 Registrar General, *Annual Reports*, 1851 and 1871.

children seems to have declined even among those couples who managed to remain together in Cornwall during the recession years. The evidence suggests that the 'census family' declined from an average of four children to less than three.[18]

An awareness that an extra child would, at least during the early years of its life, add another burden to an already stretched family budget must have deterred many couples from having more children. There was certainly growing concern about the increase in abortions and infanticide in the district by the 1870s. The trial and conviction of a Redruth woman, charged with murdering her infant, aroused considerable local interest. In reporting a sentence of 10 years penal servitude a contemporary newspaper noted that this punishment had been 'calculated to exercise a very decided influence upon crimes of this nature', Redruth having become 'somewhat notorious for the destruction of newly-born infants'.[19] Catherine Bray, aged 20 years, was tried in April 1867, and sentenced to 7 years hard labour for 'concealing the birth of a male child'.[20]

One of the most startling cases was that of a servant girl, Jane May, who had apparently become pregnant early in 1866, but, although challenged by her employer and others, she constantly denied the fact. In October that year, while driving home from market with a fellow servant she asked him to stop the cart. Getting out and going behind a roadside hedge, Jane May delivered her baby, abandoned it, returned to the cart and thence home to resume her duties without betraying her secret to anyone. The child, however, did not immediately die, its cries were heard and Jane May's crime was discovered.[21]

It is clearly impossible to say with certainty whether family limitation of one kind or another was practised more frequently in west Cornwall during the recession years. Certainly abortions and infanticide occurred in Camborne, Redruth and St Just at this time, and it is probable that the mining collapse created additional problems to which such drastic action was seen as the only solution. It is hard to imagine the degree of destitution which then prevailed. The local newspapers reported 'unprecedented numbers seeking alms' at Redruth Christmas market in 1867. Widows, both young and old, as well as other needy persons, were said to have 'gone about in troops' literally begging for

18 The marriage rate indicated by the returns of marriages to the Registrar General was also falling. This reflects in part a growing imbalance in the sex ratio as adult males moved away. It is also likely that the propensity to marry was in any case diminished during the uncertainties of the economic recession. This trend was noted in the local press where it was reported that in the St Just district large 'numbers of able-bodied men' had emigrated 'leaving wives and families; the labouring classes in some localities consisting chiefly of old men, women and children'. *West Briton*, 23 January 1868.

19 *West Briton*, 3 August 1871.

20 *Royal Cornwall Gazette*, 2 May 1867.

21 *Royal Cornwall Gazette*, 9 May 1867.

Table 27.5 Changing household composition: combined Cornish sample, 1851–1871

	1851			1861			1871		
	[1]	[2]	[3]	[1]	[2]	[3]	[1]	[2]	[3]
Lodgers	50	724	7.81	89	1139	12.21	51	745	6.61
Relatives	124	1022	19.38	136	948	18.66	160	1246	20.73
Servants[a]	60	1619	9.38	71	2193	9.74	70	2790	9.07

Notes: [1] = the number of households containing at least one lodger, relative or servant; [2] = total number of lodgers, relatives and servants in the study area; [3] = percentage of households containing lodgers, relatives or servants.
a = These totals include all those people recorded as 'servants' in the census. Because some were related to the head of the household in which they were enumerated as servants, and were regarded as 'extra' domestic servants, they were not recorded in the percentages of households with servants shown in the upper table.

Figure 27.9 Co-resident households

Person	Relation to Family	Condition	Males	Females	Rank, Profession, or Occupation	Where Born
Richd Moses Hore	Boarder	Unm	20		Gardener	Cornwall Redruth
Mary Rowe	Niece	Unm		[illegible]	Shop Assistant	do Redruth
Catherine Thomas	Head	Widow		70	Greengrocer	do do
Anne Marie Hocking	daught.	Mar		33		do do
Elizabeth do	Grand Daur.			13	Dress Maker	do do
Ann Maria do	do			12	Scholar	do do
Mary Ellen do	do			8	do	do do
Grace Axford	Head	Mar		36	Housekeeper	do Gwennap
Emma do	daught	Unm		13	Scholar	do Lanner
John do	Son		12		do	do do
Mary Ann do	Daught			9	do	do do
Mary Eliz: do	do			7		do Redruth
Jennifer Johns	Head	Mar		[illegible]	Sempstress	do do
Eliz Jane do	daught	Unm		[illegible]	[illegible]	do Cuba British Subject
Zachariah do	Son	Unm	[illegible]		Tailor	Cornwall Redruth
Thomas Benton	Head	Mar	[illegible]		Tailor	Cornwall Egloshayle
Eliz^th do	Wife	do		[illegible]		do Redruth
Julia do	Daugh	Unm		[illegible]	Dressmaker	do do
Eliz do	do	do		19		do do
Charlotte do	do	do		[illegible]	Milliner	do do
Eliza do	do			11	Scholar	do do
Sally do	do			9	do	do do
Ann Bartle	Head	Mar		[illegible]	House Cleaner	do Illogan
Eliz^th do	Daugh	Unm		19	Servt	do do
Mary do	do			10	Scholar	do do
Total of Males and Females..			4	21		

…ds as are inappropriate,

Eng– Sheet R.

Married women whose husbands had, by 1871, left the area in search of work often moved in with their relatives. In this example, Anne-Marie Hocking (who had lived in a separate household with her husband, Thomas, at the census of 1861) had, by 1871, moved with her three daughters to live with her widowed mother, who was a greengrocer in Redruth. On the same page, two further households headed by lone married women are listed – Grace Axford and Jennifer Johns. Sometime between 1850 (when Eliza Jane was born) and 1855 (when Zachariah was born in Redruth) the family had been to Cuba. PRO RG 10/2316.

assistance.[22] Many victims of the recession had no alternative but to seek accommodation in the workhouse. In one afternoon alone, in August 1867, some 15 women were seen on the road from St Just making their way to Penzance Workhouse.[23] The poor law and indeed other relief organisations set up to meet the crisis were simply not able to cope with the sheer scale of the problem.[24]

Household collapse

In the past, the assistance of kin was of much greater importance than it is today. During the nineteenth century there was no state pension scheme, no family allowance and no unemployment benefit. Most of those in real need would – wherever possible – turn to their relatives for help. It is therefore significant to note that the census evidence suggests that the number of households containing co-resident kin had increased by 1871 (Table 27.5 above). Increases in co-residence of kin took place in all three parishes but were most marked in Camborne and Redruth, where, it could be argued, the opportunity, albeit strictly limited, to work in other industries when mines closed, tended to encourage this process (Figure 27.9 above).

Relatives aged less than 25 years – especially females – accounted for the largest share of these increases. The majority were grandchildren of household heads. In fact, grandchildren represented more than one third of the co-resident relative group in 1871. Growing numbers of 'parentless' children were left behind in Cornwall as victims of the recession emigrated to escape its effects.

The importance of this growth in the co-residence of relatives becomes clear when it is noted that there had been an increase in the number of cases which qualified as 'multiple family households'[25] (Figure 27.7). This 'huddling' or 'collapsing' of households has been recognised by other writers as a common response to economic difficulties.[26] It had certainly become fairly widespread in west Cornwall by 1871, and it is suggested that collapsed households represented a significant and recognisable response to the mining recession of the 1860s and 1870s.

Most of the collapsed households contained women whose husbands had emigrated. Unable to afford their own accommodation

22 *Royal Cornwall Gazette*, 28 December 1867.

23 *West Briton*, 23 August 1867. By the beginning of 1868, Penzance Union Workhouse was offering indoor relief to 312 people, said to be the largest number for many years; *West Briton*, 2 January 1868.

24 Coal, Bread and Soap Funds were established all over the county, but it was acknowledged that their resources could not meet the level of need generated by the recession; those in Redruth and Camborne were operating by the end of January 1867. See *West Briton*, 25 January and 1 February, 1867. A Cornwall-wide 'Distress Fund' was formed by 1868. *West Briton*, 23 January 1868.

25 Containing two or more separate nuclear families, see chapter 23.

26 Anderson, *Family structure*, 131–61.

without his support, they had moved to live with their parents or other close relatives. Thus, for example, the census of St Just hints at the difficulties experienced by Mary Wall and her four children. Living in the cottage of her husband's parents, Mary was not described as a widow in the returns, but as a married woman. The record does not tell us her husband's whereabouts, but we do know that the whole family had spent some time in Australia where three of the four children were born. It could be that their father had been forced to emigrate a second time during this latest mining recession.[27]

Co-resident lodgers and servants

While the incidence of co-resident kin had increased by 1871, the number of lodgers in Camborne, Redruth and St Just had decreased by almost 30 per cent. Lodgers represented a highly fluid element in the population. Turnover was rapid, as those unsuccessful in obtaining work moved away, and the more fortunate ones established separate households. A report in the *West Briton* in 1862 gives an indication of the reasons behind the earlier growth in the lodging element and its subsequent decline:

> it was formerly the practice of great numbers of our miners who came from other districts in search of employment to reside here (Redruth) as lodgers, leaving their families at their own houses in other parishes.[28]

Indeed, the majority of lodgers were employed in mining, and there was a tendency for them to reside with the families of fellow miners. In 1861, well over 60 per cent of the lodgers employed in the mining industry in Camborne and Redruth were accommodated in the houses of fellow miners.[29]

When the recession began, the in-flow of lodgers, who had been arriving in a steady stream while the mines remained prosperous, quickly dried up, and those already in the study area were amongst the first to leave. The result was that the number of lodgers in Camborne, Redruth and St Just fell quite sharply from a peak of 1,139 in 1861 to only 745 in 1871: a reduction of more than 34 per cent (Table 27.5). Moreover the percentage of households sharing accommodation with a lodger had fallen from 12.2 per cent in 1861 to only 6.6 per cent.

27 CEBs St Just 1871, PRO RG 10/2343. See also Todd and Laws, *Industrial archaeology of Cornwall*, 60. In the late 1860s and 1870s a 'through ticket' to Adelaide, Johannesburg or Michigan could be purchased from the Post Office in Bank Square at the centre of St Just in Penwith; Payton, 'Cornish emigration', 72–3.

28 *West Briton*, 15 July 1862.

29 When this work was originally carried out, very few standard data processing computer packages existed, and a computer program was therefore specially written to examine the extent to which the occupations of various types of co-residents were the same as those of the household head. The assistance of Dr John Buckett, University of Exeter, is gratefully acknowledged.

Changes after 1861 in the proportion of households which contained domestic servants represent a rather more complicated process. On the face of it there seems to have been very little change in the number of households with servants (Table 27.5). Furthermore, the absolute number of people engaged in domestic service actually increased between 1861 and 1871 by more than 27 per cent (Table 27.5). However, these figures mask a shift away from residential servants to unspecified, non-residential servants. Indeed the number of co-resident servants had fallen by 30 per cent by 1871 and this may reflect the fact that households were no longer able to afford the luxury of a 'living-in' staff.[30] Many traders and businessmen, who had hitherto employed servants, had been hit by the decline of mining. Some even faced bankruptcy.[31] It was inevitable that savings would be sought by reducing expenditure on domestic servants, and this is clearly reflected in the census evidence.

By 1871 more servants were enumerated in their own families than had been the case at the two previous censuses. It may be that rather than living-in with the household which they served, they attended there for work on a daily basis. It could, of course, be argued that such people worked for their own family in a servant capacity, and there were a handful of cases where the record was specific: Elizabeth Trevethan of St Just, for example, was described as 'servant to her aunt'.[32] In the majority of cases, however, it is suggested that the term 'servant' implied a formal relationship with an outside household. The problem of imperfect information on unemployment is also involved here in as much as many jobless female mine workers may have stated their occupation as 'servant' in the returns rather than unemployed. This remains an unknowable in a study of this type.

Added to the larger number of non-residential servants was an increase in 'extra' domestic servants. This category included a large number of deserted female household heads whose occupation was recorded as 'charwoman', 'washerwoman' or 'laundress'. This group had become overwhelmingly dominant in the domestic service sector as a whole by 1871, and it seems reasonable to infer that its growth reflects the attempts of hard-pressed parents to earn an income to keep the family together in the face of the mining crisis.

Conclusion

Although the most obvious demographic effect of the recession in the mining industry of west Cornwall, which had begun in 1866, was growing emigration and an associated decline in total population

30 Brayshay, 'Cornwall mining communities', 315–19 and 362.

31 See, for example, *Royal Cornwall Gazette*, 16 November 1865 and 20 January 1866; *West Briton*, 23 December 1867.

32 CEBs St Just 1851, PRO HO/107.

(apparent in some cases as early as the census of 1871) more hidden and probably more significant were the changes which seem to have taken place in the detailed structure of households. As a response to the process of emigration, particularly of young adults and household heads, mean household size registered a slight decline. An even larger reduction may well be masked by a significant structural change in households produced by the tendency for deserted wives and their families to move to share the accommodation of parents, grandparents or other close relatives. This process of household collapse or huddling as a means of deriving mutual benefit has been observed in other areas of nineteenth-century England, but in the Cornish case it is not easy to see the advantages which might be afforded to the welcoming household.[33] The willingness of the Cornish to take in their needy relatives during this crisis is certainly remarkable, but it may have been seen as only a temporary expedient which, because the slump persisted, unexpectedly became permanent.

In time, the trend towards a declining population must have become self-sustaining. The absence of husbands depressed the birth rate, and so fewer children were introduced into the population. This in turn further reduced the potential for growth in the population.[34] Moreover, the inflow of lodgers quickly dried up as job opportunities declined. The sex ratio decreased as young males left the area in increasing numbers. Depopulation was highly selective. Indeed, this selectivity, above all else, produced the changes in the structure of the household which this study has attempted to define.

The effects of an economic upheaval at local level in the nineteenth century were therefore probably more complicated than a cursory glance at population totals might suggest. Although a good deal more work on this subject needs to be done before final conclusions can be drawn, the Cornish example does appear to indicate that marked changes in the pattern of households could arise which had implications for population change in the future. Laslett has suggested that, over the long term, the household operated as an intricate adaptive mechanism, but the evidence of this study seems to show that under certain circumstances, the domestic group failed to adapt and registered marked structural change.[35]

Many tantalising questions, of course, require further investigation. For instance, this chapter has said nothing about the important differences between the changes observed amongst households in various occupation groups. There were also some differences between

33 See Anderson, *Family structure*, 144–61.

34 The local press declared that the 'real men' had emigrated, leaving 'half men' behind to 'perpetuate the race of the weak, the sickly, the mentally and physically good for little'; *West Briton*, 23 January 1879.

35 Laslett, 'Size and structure of household', 201–2.

the responses of households in remote, rural parts of the parish compared with those located in the towns of Camborne and Redruth. Above all, it remains to be seen whether the changes which have been observed over the relatively short period 1851–71 were still in evidence at the censuses of 1881 and 1891.

Part VI

Residential patterns

28

Residential patterns

K. SCHÜRER AND D. R. MILLS

Locating households

The analysis of families and households provided a focus for each of the chapters presented in the previous section. Clearly, given that one aspect of investigation common across these chapters was the examination of family composition – who lived with whom – they could be seen as examples of residential structures or patterns. So why the distinction between the previous section and this? The key difference is quite simple: geographical space. In the previous section the residential experience of individuals was compared and contrasted both within and across enumeration districts in an aggregate form. Thus, chapter 25 by Dyer, for example, points to the fact that, in Edgbaston in 1851, 59.1 per cent of all children lived with parents who retained servants, while, in Ladywood, only 6.5 per cent did so. The actual location of the households containing these families and servants within the respective enumeration districts is, however, not revealed. This is not to detract from the key findings of Dyer's chapter, the thrust of which is to contrast the overall experience of the two districts. Rather, the point is to illustrate the main distinguishing feature between the contributions of Parts V and VI of this volume. For the research presented in this Part, it is the actual geographic location of households within enumeration districts that is of central importance. In this respect a *spatial* dimension is added to the analysis of residential structure.

If one is intending to locate the households recorded in the CEBs physically, obviously the information provided in the address column takes on a critical dimension.[1] This information, as was mentioned in the introduction to this volume, can, however, be of widely-varying quality. In basic terms there is seen to be a dichotomy between urban and rural enumeration districts, with the quality of the former being rather better than that of the latter. The simple explanation for this is because 'formal' addresses were, out of necessity, more commonly used in town than country. The census authorities were not the only ones who required the establishment of clear and ambiguous addresses. In

1 For a useful introduction to the technique of so-called house repopulation see Mills, 'House repopulation', as well as chapter 29 below, by Henstock.

particular, the public health lobby in the form of the urban sanitary district officers stressed the desirability of regularised address systems in order to facilitate the inspection and monitoring of housing conditions. As such, the Public Health Acts of 1848 and 1875 both included clauses requiring town authorities to maintain an adequate system of numbering houses. Although Liverpool undertook a major numbering of its housing stock in 1856, with large numbers being painted on the outside of houses,[2] it is clear that other towns and cities were not so diligent or enthusiastic. Commenting on the problem of census enumerators locating specific houses within urban areas, in 1871 *The Times* reported that:

> There are many towns containing long lines of cottage streets, formed by the gradual coalescence of buildings erected by several small proprietors; and in such streets it is not uncommon for each proprietor to give his little road a distinctive name and to number the houses it contains from one upwards, without the smallest regard to the numbers in the vicinity! In Nottingham there was formerly a long street which was said to repeat its numbers up to 3 no less than 30 times, and which was the despair of relieving officers and parish doctors. A resident there would give his address as 'the fifth number 3 on the right hand side as you go up', for such names as 'Matilda Place' or 'Eliza Cottages' had long been swept away'.[3]

This quote not only illustrates the problems caused by the rapid rates of urban growth experienced during the nineteenth century, but also indicates the extent to which building was rather piecemeal, with 'infill' within streets being commonly practised. Thus, even the most earnest of civic authorities will have experienced significant problems in their attempts to produce a standard numbering system for the houses under their jurisdiction. A further point raised by the quote is one sometimes too readily overlooked by the historian of urban communities: street names and the numbers within them can change, and may do so more than once. As a consequence it is also possible for two naming and numbering conventions to have been in operation simultaneously.

In rural communities there appears to have been less need and requirement for a formal address system. The smaller populations and lower densities of village settlements have provided one explanation for this in as much that 'who was who' mattered far more than 'which house was which'. Both the larger farms and the principal properties of the village – the vicarage, the school house and so on – will invariably have had formal names associated with them, but these may not have been constant over time. Even in the mid-nineteenth century, farm

2 Lawton, 'Census data for urban areas', 129.

3 *The Times*, 8 February 1871, 12. Quoted in Drake, 'The census', 23.

names can be seen to disappear and change as smaller farms were amalgamated into larger ones. As with urban areas, there seems to have been a general improvement in the recording of 'formal' addresses as the century progressed, in part a result of the wider use and provision of postal services. Thus, in studying a community over time, it is common to witness addresses being recorded more fully in the CEBs for the latter part of the century. However, this said, it must be realised that, irrespective of general trends, the most important factor is the enumerator. Some enumerators clearly took quite a pride in their work, recording address information in a fairly detailed form; others were altogether rather less diligent, providing nothing but the vaguest description. When it comes to identifying the actual location of houses within a CEB the community historian is unfortunately very much reliant on the efforts of the enumerator in question, probably more so that in most areas of study using the CEBs.

Of course, accurate and full addresses in the CEBs is only one side of the coin with regard to identifying actual properties, especially since enumerators may not have recorded the householders' schedules in any strict geographical order. Although it might be possible to walk around the streets of a town or the lanes of a village, copies of a selected CEB in hand, identifying specific houses, a much surer starting point is with a map. Given the degree of change in the physical housing stock between the age of the Victorian censuses and now, it is clearly essential to try and obtain a map with a survey date as close to the point of enumeration as possible. Not only is timing important, but so also is scale: generally the larger the scale the better. Ideally, a map with a scale which allows the identification of individual properties is needed. The most ubiquitous source for the nineteenth-century community historian is the maps produced by the Ordnance Survey.[4] Maps at the scale of 1-inch to the mile (1:63,360) were published virtually throughout the century, with the whole country being mapped and surveyed between 1805 and 1873, the majority of places having maps published at this scale by mid-century. Although more readily available, the 1–inch maps are not of much use for identifying the location of specific properties other than isolated farmhouses and other such prominent buildings. Of much greater use are the 6-inch and 25-inch to the mile series (1:10,560 and 1:2,500 respectively). In the case of the former, buildings can be identified, although not always effectively (especially since the division between adjacent terraced properties might not always be clear). In the case of the latter, property boundaries are clearer and field boundaries and most landmarks are shown with great

4 Excellent guides to the work of the Ordnance Survey are provided by Harley, *Maps for the local historian* and Harley and Phillips, *The historian's guide*. The later is based extensively on the authors' series to articles published in *The Amateur Historian* between 1961–3.

accuracy. The coverage and survivorship of these larger-scale maps is, however, unfortunately, rather poorer than the less useful 1-inch series, the first edition of which has been subsequently republished. Six-inch surveys are available from 1840 onwards and 25-inch from 1853, yet sheets for some rural areas, especially the more remote upland areas of the country, were not published until the latter part of the century. While the British Library holds a complete collection of these in their Map Room, their availability cannot, unfortunately, be taken for granted in local record offices and libraries. Finally, in relation to the publications of the Ordnance Survey, it is worth mentioning that during the latter part of the century especially detailed maps were produced at a variety of scales between 5-feet to the mile and just over 10-feet to the mile[5] for towns with a population larger than 4,000. These can be particularly helpful to those undertaking research on Victorian urban communities, especially if they can be used in conjunction with nineteenth-century town and city directories.[6] In urban areas, an alternative to the large-scale OS maps may also exist in the various privately published town plans, some of which were produced at a scale of 25-inches to the mile. Similar maps were sometimes produced in conjunction with the urban trade directories.

Given the availability and the problems of using Ordnance Survey maps, especially in the case of rural areas, an alternative is to use the normally parish-based maps produced as a result of the Tithe Commutation Act of 1836.[7] At the local level, both the date of the survey and the scale of the resulting map is variable, but the vast majority of surveys were completed between the passing of the act and the 1851 census, while most maps were drawn at scales between 3- and 6-chains to the mile (1:2,400 and 1:4,800), thereby invariably enabling the identification of individual properties.[8] Since three copies of each map were required to be produced – one for the tithe office, one for the parish and the other for the diocese – the survivorship is generally good, with the tithe office maps now being housed in the PRO and one or other of the remaining copies usually being housed in the county record office. The fact that these maps were part of a general survey of property ownership, usage and value makes them particularly useful since they are linked to accompanying apportionment lists which normally provide the names of the owners and occupiers of each

5 There were three series: 5-feet to the mile (1:1,056), 10-feet to the mile (1:528) and 10.56 feet to the mile (1:500).

6 A full list of the towns covered by the surveys is given in Harley and Phillips, *The historian's guide*, 29–30. For trade directories see, Shaw, *British directories* and Shaw and Tipper, *British directories*.

7 For details of this act and the sources resulting from it see Evans, *Tithes* and Kain and Prince, *The tithe surveys*. For a useful county-based analysis of the information contained with the tithe reports see Kain, Fry and Holt, *An atlas and index of the tithe files*.

8 Harley, 'Enclosure and tithe maps'.

identified property. Thus, in addition to the physical location provided by the map, names can also be linked to the information given in the CEBs. Indeed, this has been done for the Derbyshire town of Ashbourne by Henstock, who, in chapter 29 below, details some of the difficulties associated with linking the 1851 census and the 1848 tithe appointment of the town. In the absence of suitable tithe surveys the community historian may instead need to rely on contemporary estate surveys which are normally housed in the local county record office.

Segregation in cities

Many of those who have studied residential patterns using the CEBs have concentrated on the examination of towns and cities. A basic underlying theme to such studies has been the evolution of the so-called 'modern' city of the late twentieth century. In terms of residential structure, medieval and early modern towns and cities were fundamentally different from those of today. For example, traditionally the 'better-off' classes would be located in the central areas of cities while the lower classes would live further out.[9] Today the reverse is more generally true. Despite this basic model, it is also the case that in comparison to the current urban landscape, early modern towns would have experienced relatively more social mixing, not only with rich and poor living in close proximity to one another, but also with residential and business properties, in as much as one can separate the two, often being combined, one in front and/or below the other.[10]

So when and how did this transformation take place?[11] Given that the nineteenth century was one that experienced rapid and large-scale urban growth, unsurprisingly the finger has been pointed quite firmly at the Victorian city. In order to explain the development of the city during this period, geographers, in particular, have utilised the CEBs to map and interpret the residential structures of various urban areas. Virtually all types of the information available from the CEBs has been mapped and analysed. Chapter 30 by Vickers focuses on the experience of one particular occupational group – the jet workers of Whitby – and, by tracing the group's residential pattern within the town, shows that, while workers in the jet industry could be found throughout the town, they were particularly concentrated to the east of the harbour, in and around Church Street. Other researchers have looked at groups or combinations of different occupations in order to try and identify what has been termed 'social zoning' within Victorian cities, in other words the extent to which individuals of the same social class tend to reside in

9 The classic work is Sjoberg, *The pre-industrial city*.
10 See, for example, Boulton, *Neighbourhood and society*.
11 For a useful introduction to this debate see Ward, 'Victorian cities'. Discussion on this point is also provided by Pooley, 'Choice and constraint'; Cannadine, 'Residential differentiation' and Dennis, 'Stability and change'.

delineated areas or 'neighbourhoods' of the city.[12]

Obviously, in trying to identify social areas within cities, it is important to look not only at the occupations of the CEB populations, but also at elements of household composition such as the distribution of households employing servants or letting out rooms to boarders and lodgers, each of which could also be plotted onto the outline maps. The age of the household head and size of household might be other important features of social zoning. One item of information to which particular attention has been given is the place of birth recorded in the CEBs with the aim of identifying and mapping the residential patterns of migrant groups within the city. Attention has been focused on what might be seen as long-distance migrants – the Irish in particular,[13] to a lesser extent the Welsh,[14] yet curiously very little on Scots[15] – living within English nineteenth-century cities in order to assess the extent to which nationally orientated 'ghettos' were formed, yet still relatively little work has been undertaken on other immigrant groups.[16]

In some cases it may prove desirable to supplement the CEB information with other source material which can be linked to the addresses of properties. A key candidate will be the various commercial and trade directories which are available for the second half of the nineteenth century.[17] Combining the information from CEBs and directories has been fundamental to the study of retail geographies of nineteenth-century cities.[18] Alternatively, while studying social stratification in the Victorian city it may be useful to map information from rates books, for example, giving details on the rateable values of properties.[19] Poll and election data may provide another interesting avenue for research.[20]

Because of the combined problem of being able to locate a detailed enough map contemporaneous in date with a census, together with the

12 For example, see Shaw, 'The ecology of social change' for Wolverhampton; Carter and Wheatley, *Merthyr Tydfil*; Warnes 'Residential patterns' for Chorley; Cowlard, 'The identification of social (class) areas' for Wakefield; Dennis, *English industrial cities* for Huddersfield. A detailed analysis of mid-nineteenth-century Liverpool is also provided by Lawton and Pooley, *The social geography of Merseyside* yet unfortunately copies of this classic study are hard to obtain.

13 See, for example, Lees, *Exiles of Erin*; Dillon, 'The Irish in Leeds'; Richardson, 'Irish settlement'; Werly, 'The Irish in Manchester'; Swift and Gilley, *The Irish in the Victorian City*.

14 Jones, 'The Welsh in London'; Jones, 'Welsh immigrants'; Pooley and Doherty, 'The longitudinal study of migration'.

15 See, Drake *et al*, *Getting into community history*, 29–33, for an exception.

16 A notable exception to this is Pooley, 'Residential segregation'. See also Williams, *Making of Manchester Jewry*.

17 See, Shaw, *British directories* and Shaw and Tipper, *British directories*.

18 Examples include Wild and Shaw, 'Locational behaviour or urban retailing'; Shaw and Wild, 'Retail patterns'; Scola, 'Food markets and shops in Manchester'. Information on the availability of directories is given in Shaw and Tipper, *British directories*.

19 Holmes, 'Identifying nineteenth-century properties'. See also Lewis and Lloyd-Jones, 'Rate books'.

20 See Pritchard's *Housing and spatial structure* for an example based on Leicester.

vagaries of household addresses in many CEBs, knowing what unit of analysis to use is often not straightforward. A house repopulation, such as that undertaken by Henstock may not always be possible due to inadequacies of the available source materials. Certainly, a detailed reconstruction of a parish or enumeration district in which each property is identified, house by house, can reveal much about the residential structure of an area, however, it need not be the only method to explore residential patterns. Depending on the nature and scale of the investigation, as well as the sources, it may be desirable in an urban area to use individual streets rather than separate houses as units of study. Indeed this was a technique that was used to great effect as early as the 1890s when Charles Booth conducted his classic survey of London life and labour. The maps which accompany the multi-volume text are particularly useful and immediately striking, with separate streets or groups of streets being highlighted in a different colour in order to illustrate the concentration of a particular occupational group, or the extent of poverty, for example.[21] A similar effect is gained in chapter 30 below, by Vickers, on the structure of the jet industry in Whitby, mentioned previously. Figure 30.2 shows the concentration of jet workers throughout the town, however, in this case the map is constructed by enumeration district, displaying the proportion of jet workers resident across 17 enumeration districts of Whitby. Given that this is a study of the entire town, and that the focus is very specific, the ED-based approach is entirely justified.

Segregation in the countryside?

An approach such as that taken by Vickers, in which whole enumeration districts are mapped, may also prove a useful way in which to investigate geographical patterns of residence type across groups of contiguous parishes, especially in rural areas where ED boundaries are often coterminous with those of the parish. With the notable exception of Mills' study of kinship in the Cambridgeshire village of Melbourn, measuring the extent to which individuals lived in close proximity to their relatives,[22] very little work has been undertaken on residential structures within rural communities. This is largely because, as mentioned previously, the location of houses and cottages within villages is often ill-described by the CEBs, combined with the fact that appropriate maps are not always as available as they are for urban areas. For these reasons, investigating geographical patterns parish by parish may be the only effective solution. An illustration of what can be achieved by this approach is provided in chapter 32 by

21 Booth, *Life and labour of the people in London*. See also O'Day and Englander, *Mr Charles Booth's inquiry*. A reproduction of one of the maps is also available in Drake and Finnegan, *Sources and methods*, 92.

22 Mills, 'Residential propinquity of kin'.

Rawding. In exploring the 'open' versus 'close' village model, Rawding draws a number of comparisons across the parishes of his Lincolnshire selection in which residential structure is an important feature. Much of the analysis concentrates on the occupational mix of the chosen parishes, since this is fundamental to the open–close model of village structure and organisation. However, such parish-level analysis could equally be employed for other attributes of residential structure such as household size, proportion of households with kin or servants and so on.

Choice of scales and units

It must be remembered that the larger the geographical unit being used as a base, the more general and less detailed the analysis becomes. Yet this is not to say that the more detailed the better. To take an extreme example: if one had the time, patience and sources available, it might be possible, in principle, to track down the exact location of every single person in the country on a particular census night. But, having done this, how would one begin to comprehend, explain and interpret the information that had been amassed? In any local study a balance needs to be struck between lack of clarity and over-generalisation. When it comes to the presentation of material for spatial areas one must be careful not to arrive at false conclusions simply as a result of the geographical units employed. In viewing maps which group individual households, whether by street, blocks of streets, or by enumeration district, it is important to realise that the impression given is of homogenous tracts of space, each with *x* per cent of servants, or *y* per cent of lodgers. Although this may be a useful tool to explain the key issues, one must not forget that, in reality, each household is different and does not necessarily conform to the general pattern. This point is particularly important if there are significant differences of experience within the geographical areas being studied. For example, if in Whitby in 1871 one enumeration district had a particularly high concentration of jet workers in the north of the district, yet hardly any in the south, this pattern would be lost in the map presented by Vickers, mentioned earlier, which instead would merge the two halves and depict the district as having an 'average' experience. Thankfully, this is not the case! Figures 28.1 and 28.2 below, which display the location of Irish-born in Huddersfield in 1851 separately by enumeration district and by street address provides a real example of this.

Figure 28.2 showing the enumeration districts suggests two main concentrations of Irish, one to the west and the other to the east of the city centre, with these being joined by a lesser band of concentration running in a northern loop around the city centre. When viewing the

Figure 28.1 Irish-born in Huddersfield, 1851: by street address

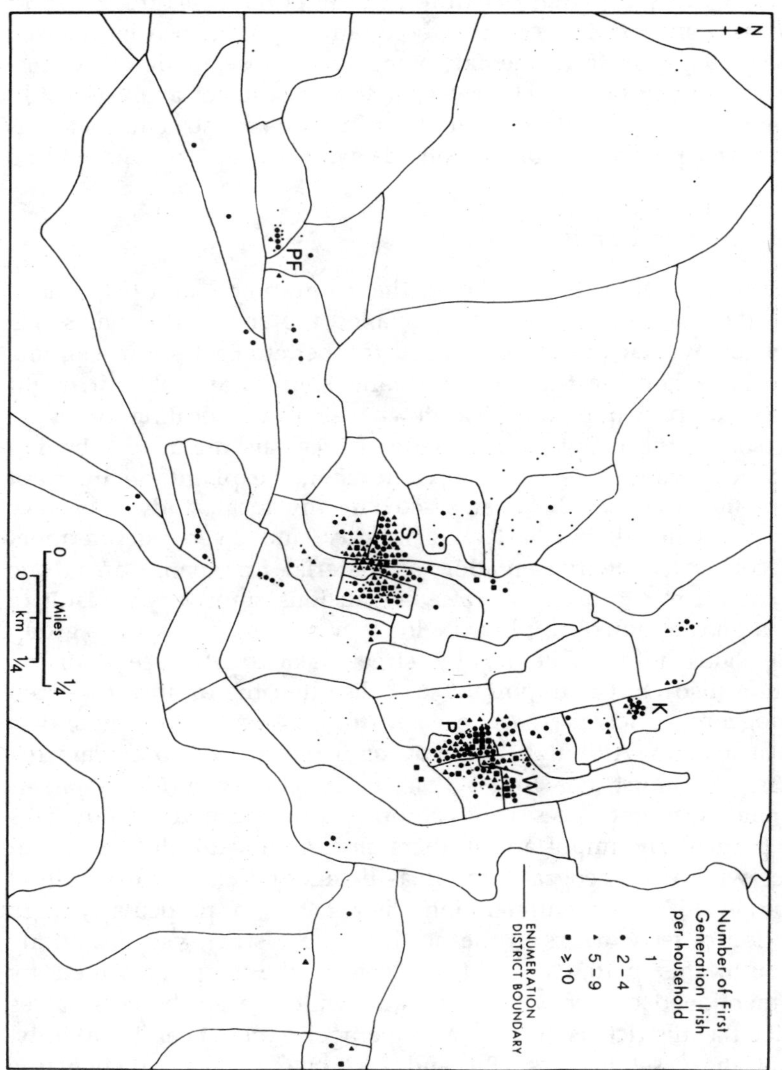

Source: Reproduced from Dennis, *English industrial cities*, 227.

Figure 28.2 Irish-born in Huddersfield, 1851: by enumeration district

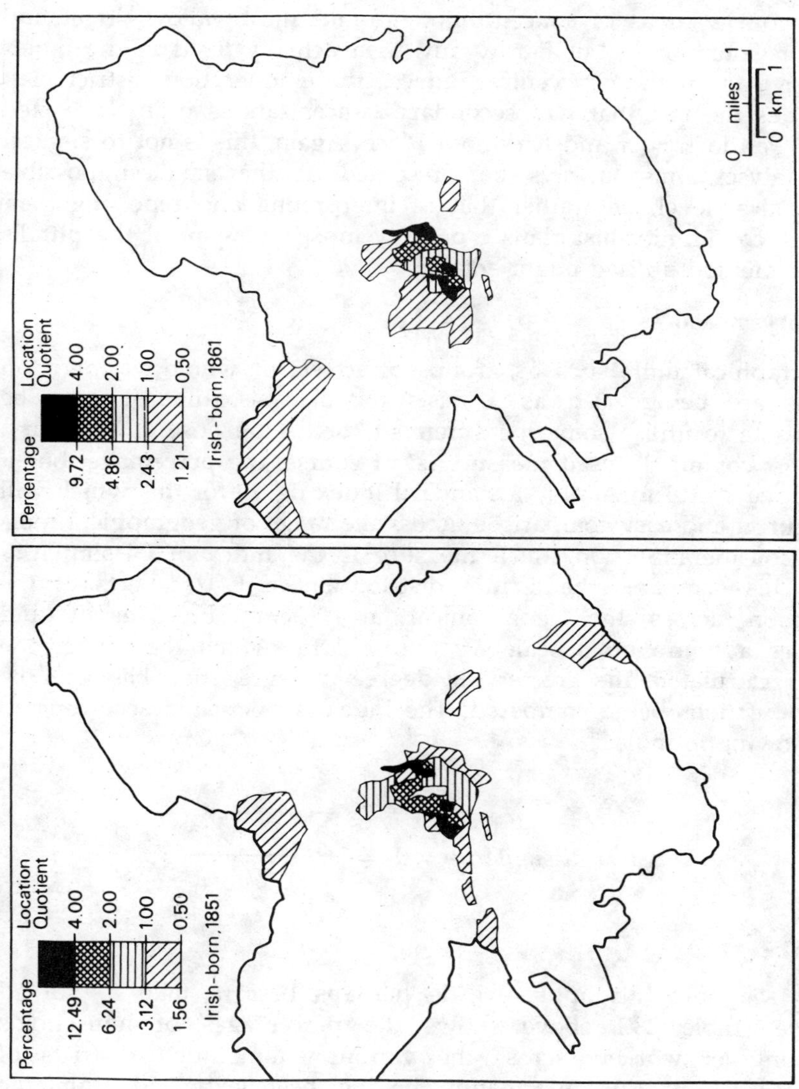

Source: Reproduced from Dennis, *English industrial cities*, 226.

street-based map (Figure 28.1), however, this general picture can be seen to be slightly spurious due the fact that the distribution of Irish-born was uneven within the key enumeration districts. Certainly, there were two key areas of concentration around the Swallow Street and Windsor Court areas, but hardly any Irish actually lived in the inner-northern part of the city centre. Indeed, the enumeration district map also hides the fact that two secondary concentrations of Irish existed around Paddock Foot and Kirkmoor Place. Again, this is not to suggest that analyses must always be presented at the smallest possible geographical level, but rather that in interpreting and reporting their findings, community historians especially must be aware of the pitfalls that the method utilised might entail.

Summary measures

If geographical units such as groups of streets or whole enumeration districts are being used as a basis for analysis, then it may be appropriate to utilise some measurement for the purpose of summary. The most commonly used measure is, of course, the percentage, but it may prove useful to employ a standard index figure for this which will allow direct and easy comparison across the range of geographical units under consideration. One such measure is the Index of Dissimilarity (I_D).[23] This compares the spatial distribution of two aspects of the population across the geographical area being investigated and produces a figure on a scale of 0 to 100 for which the higher the number calculated, the greater the degree of segregation between the two populations being compared. The index is calculated according to the following formula:

$$\textit{Index of dissimilarity} = I_D = \frac{\sum (Xi - Yi)}{2}$$

To see how this applies, it is perhaps best to take a worked example. Table 28.1 above shows the percentages of households containing jet workers across the various enumeration districts of Whitby in 1871, this information having been extracted from the chapter by Vickers. For the purpose of comparison, the hypothetical numbers of households containing professional workers have been placed alongside these. To calculate I_D first the percentage distribution

23 Details of the measures discussed here can also be found in Lewis, 'Measures of residential segregation', on which the next two paragraphs are drawn.

Table 28.1 Calculation of I_D I_S and LQ indices, an example based on Whitby, 1871

ED	[1]	[2]	[3]	[4]	[5]	[6]	[7]	[8]	[9]	[10]	[11]
1	156	5.2	47	6.3	2	2.4	3.9	1.1	2.8	1.212	0.472
2	188	6.2	74	9.9	1	1.2	8.7	3.7	5.0	1.583	0.196
3	225	7.5	51	6.8	1	1.2	5.6	0.7	6.3	0.912	0.163
4	195	6.5	74	9.9	0	0.0	9.9	3.4	6.5	1.526	0.000
5	169	5.6	47	6.3	1	1.2	5.1	0.7	4.4	1.118	0.218
6	168	5.6	61	8.1	0	0.0	8.1	2.5	5.6	1.460	0.000
7	173	5.7	44	5.9	2	2.4	3.5	0.2	3.3	1.023	0.425
8	191	6.3	63	8.4	0	0.0	8.4	2.1	6.3	1.326	0.000
9	155	5.1	42	5.6	3	3.7	1.9	0.5	1.4	1.090	0.712
10	179	5.9	52	6.9	2	2.4	4.5	1.0	3.5	1.168	0.411
11	153	5.1	46	6.1	1	1.2	4.9	1.0	3.9	1.209	0.240
12	266	8.8	31	4.1	5	6.1	2.0	4.7	2.7	0.469	0.691
13	192	6.4	27	3.6	9	11.0	7.4	2.8	4.6	0.566	1.724
14	114	3.8	15	2.0	11	13.4	11.4	1.8	9.6	0.529	3.549
15	157	5.2	36	4.8	7	8.5	3.7	0.4	3.3	0.922	1.640
16	177	5.9	22	2.9	12	14.6	11.7	3.0	8.7	0.500	2.494
20	79	2.6	1	0.1	15	18.3	18.2	2.5	15.7	0.051	6.984
21	79	2.6	17	2.3	10	12.2	9.9	0.3	9.6	0.865	4.656
All	3,016	100.0	750	100.0	82	100.0	128.8	32.4	103.2		

Notes:
[1] = total number of households;
[2] = % of all households;
[3] = number of households containing jet workers;
[4] = % of jet worker households;
[5] = number of households containing professionals;
[6] = % of professional households;
[7] = difference between columns [4] and [6];
[8] = difference between columns [2] and [4];
[9] = difference between columns [2] and [6];
[10] = Location Quotient for jet worker households;
[11] = Location Quotient for professional households.

of jet workers and professions is calculated, as shown in columns 4 and 6 of Table 28.1. For each geographical unit being considered, the absolute difference (i.e. always positive) between these two figures is then calculated (column 7). The sum of these differences is then calculated and the result divided by two. Thus, the I_D between jet workers and professionals is:

$$I_D = 128.8 \text{ divided by } 2$$

$$I_D = 64.4$$

Given that this figure is relatively high, it indicates that it was fairly unlikely for jet workers and our hypothetical professionals to be found living together in the same enumeration district, but it does not tell us anything about how concentrated the residential patterns of each group were. For this we need another measure, the Index of Segregation (I_S), which, as before, ranges between 0 and 100 with higher values indicating a greater degree of residential segregation. The formula for this is:

$$\textit{Index of segregation} = I_S = \frac{I_D}{1 - \frac{\sum Yi}{\sum Xi}}$$

As can be seen, this requires I_D to be calculated initially, but this time contrasting each sub-section being analysed against the whole population. Returning to our example in Table 28.1, this gives us an I_D between all households and households containing jet workers of 16.2 (sum of column 8 divided by 2) and an I_D between all households and households containing professionals of 51.6 (sum of column 9 divided by 2). These figures respectively provide the top half of our I_S equation. In the case of jet workers, the bottom half of the equation is made up as follows:

= 1 – total jet worker households divided by total number of households

= 1 – 750 / 3,016

= 0.751

Finally, dividing the respective I_D figures accordingly produces an I_S of 21.6 for households containing jet workers and an I_S of 53.0 for households containing professionals. Thus we can now see that the hypothetical professionals were rather more concentrated (or segregated) in terms of residence. If by some strange quirk we had a value of 100 for I_S this would mean that all of the particular group under investigation lived within the same enumeration district. But it would not tell us which area was the one in question. To test the extent of concentration of the particular sub-group being investigated in the individual geographical areas one can use the Location Quotient (*LQ*). In formula terms this is written:

$$\textit{Location Quotient} = LQ = \frac{Yi}{Xi}$$

It quite simply means the percentage of the sub-group in a particular area divided by the percentage of the total population resident in that area. Referring to Table 28.1 the *LQ*s for jet workers and professionals are given in columns 10 and 11, having been calculated by dividing columns 4 and 6, respectively, by column 2. A figure higher than 1 represents an over concentration, while less than 1 suggests the opposite. Thus, for jet workers, enumeration district 2 displays the highest concentration, while for professionals it is district 20.

One last point needs to be made. In the example provided by Table 28.1, percentages of households containing various occupations were being analysed for enumeration districts. In this context it is important to realise that none of these features is fixed. Instead of EDs we could have used parishes, or groups of streets, for example, and rather than using households as the denominator we could have used population. Equally, one could use the Indices to contrast any number of different phenomena. Figure 28.2 above, for example, shows the *LQ* scores for Irish-born in Huddersfield, while the distribution of servants, large families and working women could be similarly examined.

Contents of Part VI

This final part of the volume opens with chapter 29 by Henstock which combines the CEB information for 1841 (one of the few studies in this volume to use the initial CEBs) and 1851 with the tithe survey apportionment and plan for the Derbyshire market town of Ashbourne. Using the two sources in conjunction enables the census households to be 'relocated' within the town with a high measure of accuracy, and in turn allows an examination of the residential structure of the town, which would be impossible from the CEBs alone. This is demonstrated most clearly by the various maps reproduced in this chapter. The spatial dimension is also important in chapter 30 by Vickers, which focuses on the jet industry in Whitby. In this study, however, the emphasis is on 'whole' enumeration districts rather than individual properties, highlighting differences in residence and employment patterns across the town. The study by Redfern (chapter 31) introduces another dimension to residential patterns in Victorian towns by analysing the rateable value of properties alongside the CEB household information. This shows quite large disparities in wealth (as measured by property values) in the chosen example suburb of Edgbaston, Birmingham. However, the author places emphasis on stressing the similarities amongst the suburban residents, especially in terms of their middle-class values and ideals.

Chapter 32 by Rawding is the only chapter in Part VI which takes a rural area as a case study, rather than an urban population. As has already been mentioned, the vast majority of work on residential structures has focused on towns and cities. Yet this is not to say that issues such as residential segregation or differentiation are not also important in a rural context. Using the 'open' and 'close' parish model as an investigative tool, Rawding's chapter suggests some ways in which such themes could be usefully explored.

29

House repopulation from the CEBs of 1841 and 1851

ADRIAN HENSTOCK

Introduction

The CEBs of 1841 and 1851 are a well-known source of population statistics, but their greatly enhanced potential when used in conjunction with another well-known basic historical source – the tithe apportionments and maps of the 1830s, 1840s and 1850s – is often overlooked. A new dimension can be given to census studies by correlating the details of each census household in a given community with the house in which it lived as shown on the tithe map, in fact to 'repopulate' the houses with the families who lived in them. Such projects have been carried out by a number of individual local historians for different purposes, but, given the survival of the necessary records, they are theoretically capable of wide application throughout England and Wales. This chapter will deal with the value, feasibility, and methods of carrying out such projects, for which the name 'house repopulation' is suggested, and which lends itself particularly well to group work. The author's experience has been with an adult education class, but any similar group, including classes in secondary schools, could master the technique involved.[1] For work in classes and groups, the visual appeal of a house repopulation project is immediate, and can provide an effective antidote to the tedium of compiling statistical data from the CEBs alone. Even at its lowest level, merely to identify the family who lived in a particular house some 150 years ago will satisfy the basic antiquarian curiosity of many less-advanced students and perhaps prompt them into further enquiry.

The sources and their limitations

The tithe apportionments (often known as 'awards') and their accompanying maps, for which nearly 12,000 were drawn up for townships in England and Wales in the 50 years following the Tithe Commutation Act of 1836, were created as a means of apportioning

1 This chapter is adapted from the author's earlier 'Group projects in local history'. Grateful thanks are due to Mr Christopher Charlton for several helpful suggestions during the revision of the paper.

money payments in lieu of tithes on each unit of property within a township. The apportionments consist of written surveys or 'schedules' describing each unit either by its field-name or by its function, for example, 'house and garden', 'public house, stables and offices', 'malthouse and outbuildings', etc., and these features are identified on the detailed map attached to each apportionment by a series of numbers. In addition, the names of the owners and occupants of each property unit, the area, the land use if agricultural, and the tithe rent-charge are also stated. Most tithe apportionments were drawn in the 20 years following the 1836 Act, but, as pointed out below, a great many parishes and townships did not need to adopt the Act and consequently apportionments were never made.[2]

The CEBs provide a comprehensive coverage of the whole country and are arranged in a standard format, but variation can be found in the details of the addresses of each household, which can crucially affect the success of a house repopulation project. The CEBs may provide street numbers in cities or large towns, but for smaller towns and rural areas it is rare to find such details. Occasionally an enumerator would describe the address of everyone in Weston simply as 'Weston'. The names of outlying farms or prominent residences will almost certainly be stated, but difficulties begin when trying to identify the houses of families living along the main village street or the populous but unnumbered street in a small town or suburb. Consequently, house repopulation unfortunately cannot be carried out for all communities, as much depends on the availability of the two key sources and the amount of detail they reveal.

The viability of the whole project depends on the arrangement of the households in the CEBs, i.e., whether the order accurately reflects the route taken by the enumerator on the night of the census as he walked from house-to-house collecting the individual forms completed by the head of each household. In towns or village streets it is highly probable that he walked up one side of a street and then down the other, or possibly up one side only, turning the corner and down one side of the next street, leaving the other sides to other enumerators. Each enumeration district of the census is preceded by a detailed description of the area covered, usually indicating which sides of streets are included. But if the enumerator has not followed his instructions and has arranged his households in some other fashion, then the project will probably be difficult, though it is unlikely to be totally impossible.

The tithe records present more serious problems. To begin with, there will be no tithe award or map for many parishes, especially the ones which had in ancient times formed part of monastic estates and

2 West, *Village records*, 144–57; Anon, 'The records of the Tithe Redemption Commission', 132–9; Kain and Prince, *Tithe surveys*, 250–1.

were consequently tithe-free, or those where tithes were converted into real estate under the provisions of one of the innumerable local parliamentary enclosure acts of the late-eighteenth and early-nineteenth centuries. It is a useful rule that if an enclosure award exists there will usually be no tithe apportionment, and vice versa, although there are exceptions. In counties where the common field system either did not exist or was subjected to early enclosure, such as Cornwall, Devon, Kent, or Shropshire, something like 100 per cent coverage by tithe apportionment may be possible, but in the East Midland counties where parliamentary enclosure was the rule, tithe apportionments are somewhat rarer. Northamptonshire has only a 23 and a half per cent coverage by tithe apportionments, together with a 52 per cent coverage by enclosure awards. In Leicestershire the equivalent figures are 31 per cent and 38 per cent.[3] Some parishes may have tithe apportionments which for various reasons do not cover the whole parish, sometimes only relating to one or two fields; perhaps the most infuriating are those which are almost complete but leave a number of neat blank shapes scattered over the map indicating small pockets of tithe-free property not subject to the apportionment. However, even where a tithe apportionment is deficient, any similarly detailed survey and map from estate, parish, or other sources would be of use.

The second major factor to be taken into consideration is the date of the apportionment, i.e. how close it is to census years of 1841 and 1851. The essential details of the tithe survey necessary for correlation are the names of the occupants of each property, and consequently the nearer are the dates of the two records the higher is the chance of close correlation. Generally, however, in villages and small towns, probably few changes in occupancy will have taken place between say, 1846 and 1841 or 1851.

A third possible limitation of the tithe documents is the scale and accuracy of the maps. Only where the details of each property are clearly distinguishable is a house repopulation project viable. In the main, however, the standard of accuracy of such maps is very high, (although only those sealed by the Tithe Commissioners are certified as being accurate) and the scale is large enough to define the exact extent of each occupancy unit and the outline of each building. In the cases of market towns or the large villages, a second map of the built-up centre was sometimes compiled on a larger scale in addition to the one of the whole township. An examination of the tithe maps available for Nottinghamshire, for example, has revealed that the detail of nearly all the maps relating to townships with a population in 1841 of under 2,000 is sufficient for house repopulation, as well as those of the market towns, and urban villages of Newark (*c.* 10,200 population), Mansfield

3 Hoskins, *Fieldwork in local history*, 113.

(*c.* 9,800), Southwell (*c.* 3,500), East Retford (*c.* 3,100), Bingham (*c.* 2,000), Arnold (*c.* 4,500), Bulwell (*c.* 3,100), and Selston (*c.* 2,000). This leaves only nine Nottinghamshire settlements with populations of over 2,000 where the tithe records are either non-existent or deficient; and these include the Borough of Nottingham and four of its most populous suburbs. Even in these areas, however, house repopulation may be possible using the evidence of street numbers if given in the census returns.

In some instances it may be found that the urban parts of a town may spill over into adjacent townships, in which case one may have to use two or more different tithe maps, as was necessary with the research based on Ashbourne, Derbyshire described in this chapter. Ashbourne in 1851 was a market town with an urban population of approximately 3,500 people, but the urban area covered no less than four different townships, each with tithe apportionments and maps dated between 1846 and 1849. The township of Ashbourne itself, which included about two-thirds of the urban area, had a detailed large-scale tithe map, and house repopulation was carried out with something like 80 per cent success. The figure was lower for the urban portions of the remaining townships which had less detailed maps.[4]

Method

Assuming that both census and tithe records are adequate, what methods should be adopted for making the actual correlation? The first stage is usually to rearrange the details of the tithe apportionment into an order roughly comparable with the order of the census households. Most tithe schedules list properties by alphabetical order of owners, so that the names of the occupants of adjacent properties together with their map numbers may be scattered over all the pages of the schedule. On the other hand, the tithe maps number their property units in a systematic (if occasionally somewhat irregular) pattern, and adjacent properties along a main street, for example, may or may not bear consecutive numbers. Therefore, it is necessary to re-sort the names of the occupants in the tithe schedule into numerical order of the tithe map number in order to avoid tedious searching each time the name of a particular occupant or the number of a property needs to be retrieved.

This is best achieved by recording each property unit on separate forms, index cards, or as a record in a database. It is then necessary to work through the tithe schedule entering the information for each property unit in this order – tithe number; name(s) of occupant(s); name(s) of owner(s); and description of property. For example:

4 Sections of the Ashbourne tithe map and schedule together with pages from the census and a commercial directory relating to Ashbourne are reproduced in Rogers, *This was their world*, 73.

Tithe Map No: 180	*Occupant*:	Smith, Frances and others
	Owner:	Dawson, John
	Description:	9 Houses and Gardens

The details of each property unit can then be sorted into the order of the tithe map number so that the occupants can be matched to the properties which they occupied. (As an alternative the names of occupants can be sorted into alphabetical order, in which case it will be necessary to reverse the procedure, i.e. one must work from the census households to the tithe occupants and then to the tithe map).

It now remains to link the census households with these property units, and this is achieved by working systematically through the properties on one side of a street or road on the map, checking the name of the occupant from the property unit list by reference to the tithe number, and identifying, where possible, a household head of that name in an appropriate place in the CEBs. The relevant property unit should then be marked with the census page reference and enumerator's schedule number of that particular household, and, conversely the census household should be marked (on the copy of the CEBs) with the tithe number of the relevant property. Depending on circumstance it may be found that initially no more than one in every four or even six households can be placed with certainty (for example, the occupants of a row of terraced houses may be described as 'John Smith and 3 others'), but, having once established these 'hooks', the remainder can be pinned up in between. A pattern should emerge in the order of the census households reflecting the enumerator's original route; once this has been ascertained, the number of uncorrelated households in the census between each identified one should be divided into the available number of houses as shown on the map, and the households marked with a 'possible' tithe number on the property forms. Exact attribution to one of two properties may be impossible in some cases, but to have narrowed the choice down to two is sufficient for many purposes. Also, the number of households may not agree with the number of available dwellings, and here the correlation will have to be interpolated. Certain or highly probable correlations may be marked just with the number, e.g. '95'; likely possibilities with one query, e.g. '96?', and dubious ones with two queries e.g. '97??'. Where two adjacent households or properties cannot be distinguished, then the number of both could be written as, e.g. '96/97?'. Where an enumerator for the 1851 census has followed his instructions carefully, he should have distinguished each house from the next by a longer line drawn across the page than the line used to divide each household, but in the author's experience this convention was widely ignored.

External evidence and information from other sources can often be an invaluable aid to correct identification and should be used wherever possible. Features such as named houses, yards, terraces, or public houses which existed within living memory are an obvious example. The names and addresses given in contemporary commercial directories can be a useful link between the date of the tithe apportionment and the CEBs; electoral registers, rate books, or any contemporary estate surveys or rentals will also fill the same role. It is necessary to bear in mind that the outline of a building shown on the map represents a unit of ownership, and that the block may be subdivided in practice into two or more separate dwellings. The first editions of the Ordnance Survey 25-inch to the mile maps (usually surveyed in the 1870s or 1880s) may indicate these sub-divisions, and old engravings or photographs can be invaluable for showing the appearance of now-demolished properties. If the buildings still exist, field-work may establish how many families could have been accommodated in them in 1841 or 1851. Bundles of title deeds for individual houses which name the occupants in the 1840s and 1850s will also be of obvious value. Parish and probate records can also provide information on property transfers as a result of marriage or death respectively.

However, perhaps the greatest aids to identification are a mixture of intuition and common sense. The latter will suggest that the unidentifiable census family of a butler or gardener named immediately after an identifiable gentry family is probably occupying part of the latter's large house. Similarly, the trades or occupations of unidentifiable household heads may link up with property similarly described in the tithe schedules; the victualler should be occupying the public house, the schoolmaster the school, the alms person the almshouses, and the maltster the 'house and malthouse'. Even if the occupants' names do not agree, then a person in the right place with the same surname, or, if the property is a commercial one, the same trade, will also be highly suggestive of continuity. Status can also be a guide – one would not expect the gentleman to live in the terraced house or the labourer in the mansion – although one must guard against becoming involved in a circular argument if the results are to be used as evidence of social status.

In house repopulation work it is always necessary to be aware of the possibility of misinterpretation arising out of coincidence, circumstantial evidence, or out of the deficiencies or even mistakes in the sources themselves. The census schedules that have been preserved were compiled by the enumerators from the individual returns made by each household head, and there is always the possibility that the enumerators did not copy them exactly in the order in which they were collected; two adjacent households may be transposed or a missed one may appear at the end of the list.[5]

Because of these possibilities, the final result of a house repopulation project must be regarded as no more than an approximation to the true position that existed on the census night. However, it is reasonable to assume that, if all the available evidence has been carefully assessed, the majority of the other correlations will be strong possibilities and that the overall picture will have sufficient validity on which to base broad conclusions.

Once the correlation is completed, the census details should be added to the relevant property unit description, which can then be used as the basis for compiling distribution maps, etc. Copies of the tithe map can be marked with a variety of different symbols, as necessary.

Example

As an example of the method, compare the following extracts of records relating to Ashbourne, Derbyshire. These are: detail from the tithe map of 1846 relating to St John Street (Figure 29.1 below); details of property units extracted from the tithe apportionment schedule of 1846 relating to tithe map numbers 178–84 (Table 29.1 below); extracts from the CEBs for St John Street, 1851 (Table 29.2 below).[6]

1 The property unit details have been arranged in reverse numerical order of the tithe map number, i.e. describing each property on the map from east to west, so as to reflect the probable route of the census enumerator.
2 The column of Table 29.2 headed 'Number of householder's schedule' is simply the enumerator's reference number of each household, which may not equate with a single physically separate house. These numbers are not house numbers nor are they identifiable with the tithe map numbers
3 The names of each property unit's occupiers in Table 29.1 should be compared with the names of the heads of the households listed in Table 29.2. ('In hand' signifies that the owner is also the occupier).
4 The first three households on Table 29.2 (Parker, Toogood and Le Hunt) are readily identified with property units 184, 183 and 182. They are evidently well-off people living in large houses with gardens and employing servants.
5 Property unit 179 – a public house – is identifiable with the household of George Etches, innkeeper. Freebody's commercial

5 For a fuller discussion of the deficiencies of the CEBs, see Tillott, 'The analysis of census returns' and Higgs, *Making sense* and *Clearer sense*.
6 Ashbourne 1851 census, PRO HO 107/2146.

Table 29.1 Abstract from the Ashbourne Tithe Apportionment Schedule, 1846

Landowners	Occupiers	n.	Name and description of lands and premises
Mary Parker	In hand	184	House, Garden, etc.
Fanny Bradley	William Toogood	183	House, Garden, etc.
Peter Bainbrigge Le Hunt	In hand	182	House, Buildings, Garden, Pleasure Ground, etc.
Thomas John Mountfort	James Hood & others	181	8 Houses, Stable & Gardens
John Dawson	Frances Smith & others	180	9 Houses and Gardens
John Albrighton	George Etches	179	Public House, Buildings, Yard, etc.
John Whitman	In hand	178	House, Shop, Warehouses, etc.

Source: Derbyshire Record Office, 662 A/P1 590.

Figure 29.1 Detail from Ashbourne Tithe map, 1846

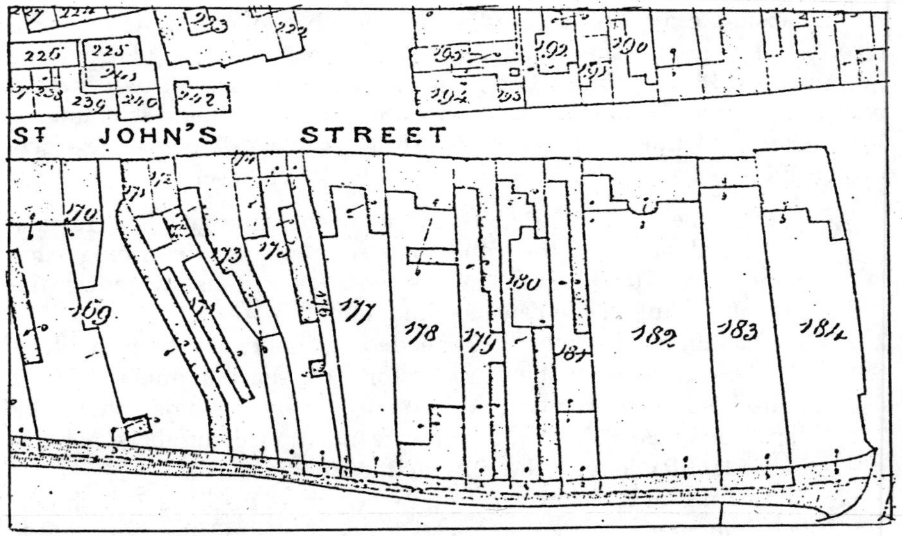

Source: Derbyshire Record Office, 662 A/P1 590.

Directory of Derbyshire for 1850 confirms that Etches occupied the Duke of Wellington public house in St John Street (the public house still exists at the time of writing).

6 Property unit 178 is a commercial property facing the Market Place and with warehouses at the rear. It can be linked with the large household of John Whitham, a druggist. This property is occupied (at the time of writing) by Boots the Chemist.

7 Frances Smith (property unit 180) is identifiable with

Table 29.2 Abbreviated extracts from the CEBs for St John Street, Asbourne, 1851

No. of Householder's Schedule	Name of Street, Place, or Road, and Name or No. of House	Name and Surname of each Person who abode in the house on the night of 30th March, 1851	Relation to Head of Family	Condition	Rank, Profession, or Occupation	Where Born	Allocated Tithe No.
23	St John Street	Mary Parker (+ 2 servants + 1 other)	Head	U	Propritor of Houses	London. Midd.	*184*
24	St John Street	William Toogood (+ 1 servant + 2 others)	Head	U	Surgeon. MLCL	Ashbourne	*183*
25	St John Street	Peter B. LeHunt (+ 3 servants)	Head	U	Magistrate	Staffs, Rocester	*182*
26	St John Street	Ann Dale (+ 1 servant)	Head	W	Annuitant	Derby	*182/181??*
27	St John Street	Francis Hood (+ 3 others)	Head	M	Tailor employing 2 men	Derby	*181?*
28	St John Street	Ann Howard (+ 3 others)	Head	W	Lace Runner	Ashbourne	*181?*
29	St John Street	Charles Blood (+ 3 others)	Head	M	Joiner	Derby	*181?*
30	St John Street	Thomas Lord (+ 2 others)	Head	M	Blacksmith	Derby	*181?*
31	St John Street	Mary Bridden (+2 others)	Head	W	Dressmaker	Staffs, Ilam	*181?*
32	St John Street	Elizabeth Gennis (+ 3 others)	Head	W	Annuitant	Staffs, Musden	*181?*

Table 29.2 Continued.

No. of House-holder's Schedule	Name of Street, Place, or Road, and Name or No. of House	Name and Surname of each Person	Relation to Head of Family	Condition	Rank, Profession, or Occupation	Where Born	Allocated Tithe No.
33	St John Street	William Burgess (+3 others)	Head	W	Plumber	Lancs, Manchester	*181?*
34	St John Street	Fanny Smith (+ 3 others)	Head	U	Annuitant	Ashbourne	*180*
35	St John Street	Jane Brownson (+ 1 servant + 3 others)	Head	M	Dressmaker	Leics, Castle Donnington	*180?*
36	St John Street	John Frost (+ 2 others)	Head	M	Cordwainer	Ashbourne	*180?*
37	St John Street	James Holmes (+ 3 others)	Head	M	Labourer	Derbys, Kniveton	*180?*
38	St John Street	Thomas Elleby (+ 3 others)	Head	M	Blacksmith	Derbys, Clifton	*180?*
39	St John Street	Lucy Thacker (+ 2 others)	Head	W	Laundress	Derbys, Roston	*180?*
40	St John Street	William Pearson (+ 2 others	Head	M	Gardener	Ashbourne	*180?*
41	St John Street	William Allen (+ 3 others)	Head	M	Tanner	Staffs, Tamworth	*180?*
42	St John Street	Thomas Wibberley (+ 6 others)	Head	M	Tailor	Derbys, Stursden	*180?*
43	St John Street	George Etches (+ 2 servants + 4 others)	Head	M	Innkeeper	Staffs, Musden	*179*
44	St John Street	John Whitham (+ 2 servants + 12 others)	Head	M	Druggist	Asbourne	*178*

'Fanny Smith' and James Hood (property unit 181) was probably succeeded by Francis Hood during the intervening four/five years between the dates of the two documents.

8 Property units 180 and 181 each contain nine and eight houses respectively. The tithe map suggests – and this is confirmed by the later Ordnance Survey map, by field work, and by Victorian photographs – that each unit comprised a street frontage house and rows of terraced cottages in long 'yards' behind, each yard approached by a 'tunnel' entrance. It was normal practice in the town for such yards to be named after either the owner or the resident of the front property (if different). The parish registers of the period mention both a Dawson's Yard and a Hood's Yard in St John Street. It therefore seems reasonable to suppose that the former equates with property unit 180, owned by John Dawson, and the latter with property unit 181 owned by T. J. Mountfield but with Francis Hood occupying the front property. As a cautionary tale, however, it should be noted that a later member of the Hood family moved to another property some distance away on the same side of the street, also with a residential yard at the rear. By the 1890s this second yard had also became known as Hood's Yard. The cottages in all the yards were demolished in the early twentieth century.

9 It can reasonably be deduced that the six households in Table 29.2 with the enumerator's reference 28–33 lived in Hood's Yard (property unit 181) and the seven households (references 34–6) lived in Dawson's Yard (180). Nearly all the occupations suggest 'artisan' status and none of the householders employed servants.

10 This leaves only two households on Table 29.2 – Dale (reference 26 and Brownson (35) – not allocated to a specific property unit. Dale must therefore be assigned to property units 181/2? and Brownson probably to 180.

11 The figures in italics in the far right hand column of Table 29.2 do not appear on the original CEBs, but are the property unit numbers allocated to each household as a result of the exercise described above.

Research conclusions

Providing a high degree of correlation can be achieved between the two sources, a house repopulation project can shed significant new light on a particular community. Any census study achieves a new perspective when the households can be linked with buildings on a map, especially in small towns and rural areas where many of the actual buildings may exist; this can be of value to local and social historians, geographers, demographers, and architectural historians alike. The value of the project to the historical demographer or community historian attempting a social analysis of the 1841 or 1851 census returns will be discussed here.[7]

The most important attribute of a house repopulation project is that it gives a geographical and spatial basis to census analysis. Once each household is linked with a particular building, distribution maps can be drawn to illustrate a wide variety of different topics, plotted onto copies of the tithe map. Much significant demographic information can be mapped in this fashion, such as the distribution of households of any given size, related to the types of buildings in which they lived, or the distribution and density of population. Comparisons can be made, between the numbers of persons living on the main streets, the side streets, and in terraced yards behind the main streets of towns; also the numbers living in tenement blocks or in overcrowded courts can often be ascertained, though this may be more difficult.

The results of such exercises can perhaps best be illustrated by examples from the research on the small market town of Ashbourne in 1851, on which this chapter is substantially based.[8] One map was compiled to demonstrate population distribution (Figure 29.2 below), indicating five persons by a single dot. Although this cannot be exact (as the numbers of people in households of less than five have to be added to the figures for the next household), the overall distribution clearly shows the contrast between the large Georgian town houses of the east end of Church Street and the heavy concentrations of population in areas such as Mutton Lane and in the numerous 'yards' situated behind the main streets. Such yards are a common feature of small towns, and in Ashbourne they housed in total some 750 people, i.e. around a quarter of the population. The contrast is particularly marked in Church Street; here the houses on the north side housed 184 people, but a further 104 lived in yards behind the houses in the middle of the street. Similarly, the west side of Dig Street housed 91 people but with a further 94 crammed into four other yards behind. Caution must be exercised in interpreting the maps on their own, however; what appears to be an overcrowded house on the north side of east St John Street is in fact a private school housing 9 resident staff and 36 girl boarders.

The broad pattern of social zoning in the town is illustrated by Figure 29.3 below, which maps all properties by one of three categories – those occupied by professional people or persons of private means; by tradesmen and craftsmen; and by other residents (mainly working-class). This indicates that commercial properties, including something like 80 per cent of the 36 public houses in the town, were concentrated

7 See generally, Wrigley, *English historical demography* and Tillott, 'The analysis of census returns'.

8 For the wider study see Henstock, *Ashbourne.*

Figure 29.2 Ashbourne in 1851: population distribution

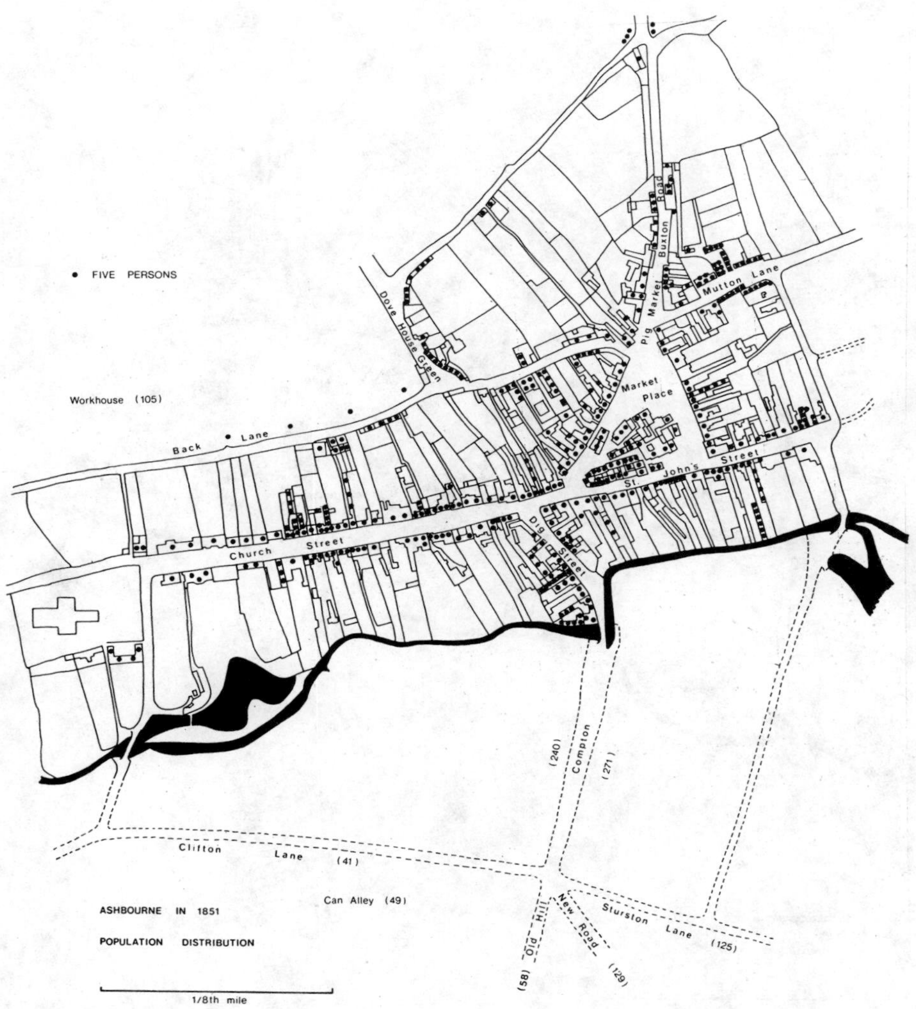

Figure 29.3 Ashbourne in 1851: building occupancy

Figure 29.4 Ashbourne in 1851: resident servants

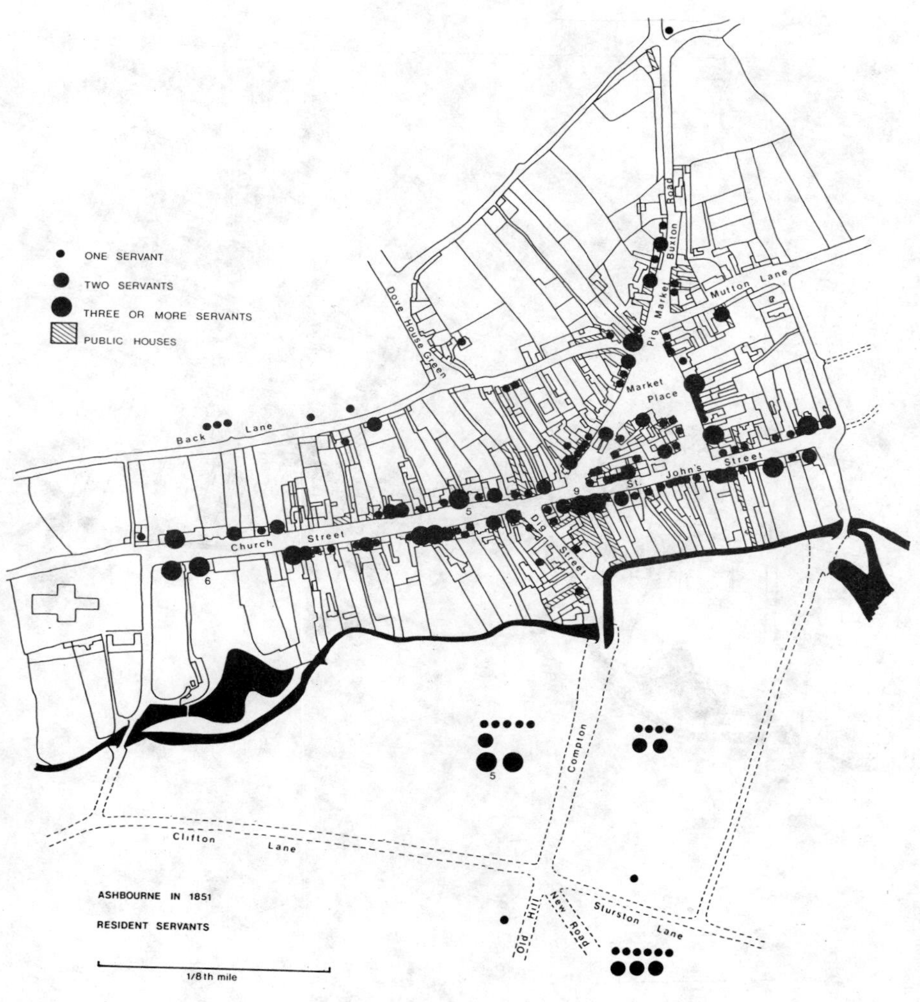

Figure 29.5 Ashbourne in 1851: distribution of poorer classes

in or around the Market Place. The major private residences were mostly in fashionable Church Street and east St John Street, with a marked polarisation towards the western and eastern extremities of the town, attracted by the existence of the parish church at the west end and Ashbourne Hall at the east end. There were only two public houses in Church Street, one serving the cluster of populous yards mentioned above.

The relative distribution of rich and poor is further demonstrated by Figures 29.4 and 29.5, both above. The first of these shows those households employing one, three or more female domestic servants. Although most of the tradesmen kept servants and the largest inn had nine, the greatest numbers were usually retained by professional people or those with private means, again especially in Church Street and east St John Street. The distribution of the poorer classes is even more graphically illustrated by Figure 29.5 which plots the residences of labourers, charwomen and washerwomen, paupers and female domestic lace outworkers. The very marked concentrations in a few locations, especially in Mutton Lane and in the yards north of Church Street and west of Dig Street, are noteworthy. This picture could be further emphasised by including other categories synonymous with poverty, such as households with lodgers, hawkers and other identifiable itinerants, and persons born in Ireland.

The Ashbourne group's project was probably the first such study to use the house repopulation technique to illuminate the demographic and general history of a substantial community in the period *c.* 1840–60, based on the nucleus of the 1851 CEBs and extended by use of other sources as mentioned below. Subsequently, Mills has published details of his study of a Cambridgeshire village based on the 1841 census, and since then numerous individual projects have been carried out for other communities.[9]

Further studies

Another use of a house repopulation project is that it can provide supplementary information on those elusive qualities, the personal wealth and social status of the persons described in the census returns. The problems of classifying persons into functional or social groups are well-known[10] and arise partly from inadequacies in the occupational descriptions given by the enumerators. For example, is a 'maltster' or a 'cotton-spinner' a master or a workman? – but, once households are linked with the houses in which they lived, another yardstick for measuring their wealth and social status becomes available. The

9 Mills, 'House repopulation'. Other studies are listed in Kain and Prince, *Tithe surveys*, 250–1.

10 For a discussion of the problems see Rogers, *This was their world*, chapter 5, especially 105–8.

Figure 29.6 Ashbourne Shrovetide football group portrait, c. 1862

This scene depicts a crowd gathered in the Market Place to play the customary annual Shrovetide football game through the streets of the town. Each individual is identified by name and most can be traced in the CEBs of 1851 and 1861. For example, the figure on the far left with the top hat is John Miers, landlord of the Wheatsheaf Inn, and the figure on the far right is Betty Blove, a well-known street vendor of nuts and oranges.

'maltster' in his substantial house on the main-street becomes immediately distinguishable from the 'maltster' living in the terraced cottage in the yard behind. Even if the houses do not survive to the present day, often their size and position as shown on the map will provide a clue as to the type of property it would have been.

A further indication of wealth is provided by the ownership columns of the tithe apportionments, as it becomes possible to discover whether the head of the census household is the owner or the occupier of the house in which (s)he lives, and also whether (s)he owns any other property in the township or parish.

This can also provide a basis for extended studies, supplementing the CEBs and tithe data by information from other sources. One of the most valuable projects is to use contemporary newspapers to provide yet a further viewpoint of the society whose members fill the pages of the CEBs. Detailed though the CEBs are, no amount of statistical analysis will reveal exactly who were the influential personalities in a community – the social élite and the leaders of local society. The Ashbourne group referred to above inaugurated a project designed to elicit this information accumulating biographical details of the most prominent personalities in a card-catalogue. A card was allotted to each figure, and on each was noted details of the subject and his family, household, birthplace etc., from the CEBs, of his or her place of residence and property ownership from the tithe records, and references to his appearances in public life from the local newspaper, which was examined in detail for the two years either side of the census day. This information was subsequently enlarged by references from other sources such as commercial directories, Guardians' minutes, gas company minutes, membership lists of various local societies, etc., and even a group portrait of named local 'characters' of *c.* 1862 (Figure 29.6 above). As a result, a small group of personalities emerged who were prominent in public life in the town, and about whom brief biographies could be written: in some cases it was possible to glean information as to their character and opinions from the newspaper reports of their public speeches. Admittedly, such detail was available principally for certain members of the upper and middle classes, although, at the other end of the scale, the newspapers also reported the names of misdoers and their crimes. In these cases it was sometimes possible to write 'probation reports' on the miscreants by gleaning details of their social background and physical home environment from the census and tithe records.[11]

Again, given the survival of suitable records, it is possible with some communities to project the repopulation exercise back in time, i.e. by constructing a link between the repopulated community data of 1841

11 Henstock, *Ashbourne*, 21–5.

or 1851 and the land tax assessments of 1780–1832, which record the owners and occupiers of each property on an annual basis. This involves making a leap back to 1832 and identifying, where possible, each property unit, and then tracing changes of ownership and occupancy annually back to 1780. This can be very time-consuming, but it was achieved successfully by the author's group for the main street frontage properties in Ashbourne, for example. The results revealed significant information about ownership patterns and property turnover, social zoning and property development over a 50-year period.[12]

12 Henstock, 'House repopulation'.

30

The structure of the Whitby jet industry in 1871

NOREEN VICKERS

The jet industry in Whitby

In the early years of the nineteenth century a certain Captain Tremlett believed that jet could be worked by machine to produce ornaments and jewellery, and so persuaded two local jet-carvers to turn the jet on a lathe. The method was successful but it was not until the 1850s that the trade was firmly established in Whitby.

According to the *New Whitby Treasury* of April 1854, there were 1,000 persons employed in mining and working jet, including their dependants. Jet goods manufactured in 1853 were valued at £20,000 but the writer freely admits that no accounts were kept and so these figures are only estimates. The trade had been boosted by pieces being shown at the Great Exhibition of 1851 and in 1856 Gillbank's *Directory of Scarborough and Whitby* stated that jet working was the principal occupation of the town.[1] By 1873 the annual value of goods produced was reputed to have reached over £90,000 when the industry was at its peak.[2] In his history of the jet industry published in 1930, Kendall claims that, between 1870 and 1872, 1,400 men and boys worked in the trade.[3] However, Kendall does not detail how he arrived at this figure. It certainly does not tally with the figures obtained from the 1871 CEBs for the town, upon which the analysis that follows is substantially based. These suggest a figure nearer to 1,000. Whatever the exact figure it is the case that the mid to late 1860s marked the zenith of the jet industry in Whitby. In 1875 the *Whitby Gazette* reported that the jet trade was in a very depressed state and could not possibly get any worse and still exist as one of the industries of the town. Yet even before this date the trade fluctuated, for example, as the *Gazette* reported, in 1858 rough jet was bringing two shillings and nine pence per pound, but a year or two earlier it would have brought six shillings.

Woodwark explains the decline in terms of new materials coming onto the market after 1870, such as Spanish jet which was friable and

1 Gillbank, *Scarborough and Whitby*, 32.
2 Raistrick, 'Industrial history', 56.
3 Kendall, *Whitby jet*, 4.

brittle, vulcanite, French jet, glass and celluloid. Soft jet from Whitby itself was also used and this produced inferior articles giving the industry a bad reputation. The fashion in jewellery changed but the Whitby workers did not follow the trend for lighter, smaller pieces, and perhaps the most important factor, the structure of the industry itself was unable to cope with the falling demand. It was a very fragmented trade with many workers sharing a workshop but selling the finished objects individually to dealers at the end of the week. There was no check on quality and no co-operation between men which could have resulted in a joint venture to save the industry.

In 1885 a move was made to form a limited company to enable small workmen and wholesale dealers to combine together to sell the goods for a low but fair price. Nothing came of the agreement. Again, in 1890, it was suggested that the jet ornaments should be marked to show whether they were made from hard, soft or imported jet, but no action was taken.

According to Woodwark there were 600 men employed in the trade in 1883 with average earnings of £1 per week, whereas previous earnings about 1870 had been £3–4. The figures dropped to 300 the following year, but Woodwark does not give any source for this. By 1921 the numbers were down to 40.[4]

The jet articles were sold in the town to residents and visitors alike (the holiday trade was steadily increasing from the 1850s onwards), and there was a strong London market. Queen Victoria encouraged the use of jet as suitable mourning wear after the death of Prince Albert in 1861, giving the industry a great boost. Many pieces were exported to France and jet jewellery was displayed at Paris exhibitions. In 1854 Isaac Greenbury received a commission for a jet chain, four feet six inches long, from the Queen of Bavaria.[5]

Working conditions

For his history of the jet industry Kendall interviewed Matthew Snowdon, an ex-jet worker who had worked in the industry towards the end of the nineteenth century. Snowdon provides a first-hand account of the workshop system at that time. Workshops, he recalls, were to be found in many tenements and houses, especially near the harbour in the old part of the town.[6] They were usually small and cramped and shared by a number of workmen who were probably self-employed. There were no factories in the modern sense of the word, the rooms used being cellars or any room in a house which could be utilised (see Figure 30.1 below). Some masters did have a workshop in

4 Woodwark, *Whitby jet trade*, 10–1.
5 Kendall, *Whitby jet*, 4.
6 Kendall, *Whitby jet*, 6–7.

Figure 30.1 A jet workshop in the 1890s

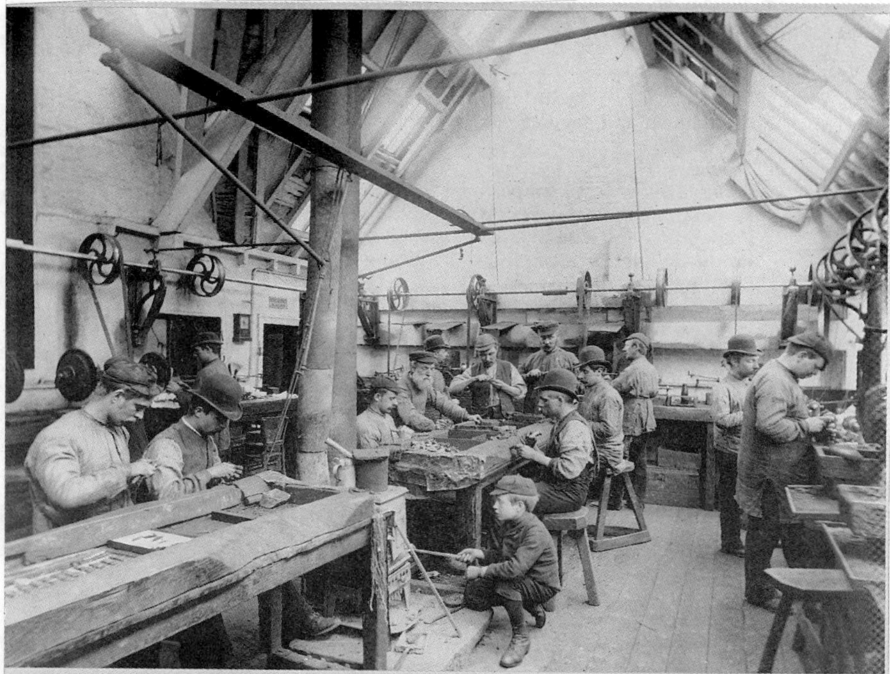

A photograph from the work of Frank Meadow Sutcliffe, Hon. FRPS (1853–1941). Copyright the Sutcliffe Gallery, Whitby. Taken in the 1890s, the picture depicts a large workshop at the time Matthew Snowdon was employed in the jet industry. A similar workshop would have been in operation at the time of the 1871 census.

Table 30.1 Jet workshops in Whitby, 1871

n. in workshops	n. of shops	Total n. of men
1	3	3
2	2	4
3	6	18
4	7	28
5	1	5
6	5	30
7	3	21
8	3	24
12	1	12
13	1	13
14	1	14
17	1	17
26	1	26
29	1	29
38	1	38

Notes: Figures denote workmen only and do not include employers.

Table 30.2 Occupations in Whitby 1871

Category Number	Designation of work	Number of persons
1	Professional men including doctors, lawyers, police, surveyors, bankers	119
2	Churchmen and ancillary workers	25
3	Taxmen	5
4	Teachers	74
5	Booksellers and newspaper men	32
6	Preparation and sale of food, including fishing	302
7	Preparation and sale of drink	83
8	Production and sale of clothes including dressmakers	533
9	Building and allied trades	171
10	Ship building including owners and ships' chandlers	412
11	Workers with minerals including jet	1,123
12	Workers with other natural products such as leather, wood	42
13	Agriculture	119
14	Miscellaneous trades	65
15	Sailors and the harbour	214
16	Postal service	15
17	Transport – horse and rail	127
18	Artistic occupations e.g. painting, music	18
19	Recreational activities including lodging-house keepers	89
20	Shopkeepers	62
21	Office workers	12
22	Servants	985
23	Labourers, scavengers, prostitutes	200
Total		4,827

which they employed their own workforce, but there were 1,006 jet workers according to the 1871 census and only 282 were employees, leaving 724 apparently self-employed. These figures are misleading as many of the latter were youngsters who were not likely to be self-supporting. Probably a number of the men would have a boy to help, but did not state this to the enumerator (Table 30.1 above).

A grand total of 4,827 people were employed in Whitby in 1871. Of these, jet workers constituted the largest group being made up of 1,006 men and boys. There was an unknown number of sailors away at sea, but for the purpose of this chapter only those at home have been counted. The range of occupations is given in Table 30.2 above. This table illustrates the dependence of the town on the jet trade and the ship-building industry. Both of these were to crumble by the end of the nineteenth century. The former for reasons already discussed and the latter because steam ships replaced sailing ships and the harbour at Whitby was too small to cope. The number of servants and workers in the production and sale of clothes, including dressmakers, is very large, but the majority of these were young girls who probably worked for pitiful wages until marriage and in economic terms, would not constitute a vital part of the trade of Whitby.

The division of labour in the jet shops can be broken down to a certain extent, but a vast number of men simply stated that they were jet workers or jet ornament manufacturers. The latter term carries overtones of ownership of a jet workshop, but is applied indiscriminately to youngsters as well as older men. An industry which employs 20.8 per cent of the working population could be thought to have a complicated labour structure, but in actual fact it was a simple cottage industry and this was one of the reasons why it could not cope with the recession of the 1880s and later, being largely fragmented into single units.

Snowdon has some interesting points to make about the apprenticeship system. Apparently it was not usual for boys to be formally apprenticed. Some were, but the majority simply agreed to work for one man for a stated number of years. Thirty-three lads described themselves as such, but there were 303 youngsters aged between 8 and 16 who would be learning the trade. Only six men described themselves as journeymen and three as masters, but many more men would consider themselves capable of carrying out all the processes involved in making ornaments and jewellery. Only one man stated that he mined jet, and he probably worked close to Whitby along the cliffs or shore.

The rough jet was bought by merchants or dealers who would travel to the mines to buy direct, but some miners would come to the town to sell to the small man, or indeed in large quantities to the workshop manager. There were 16 rough jet merchants in Whitby who would grade the jet according to quality and size, storing it in a warehouse divided into various rooms so that the customer could select pieces more easily. These warehouses need not be specially built but could be houses which had been converted. Two warehousemen are listed in the census and two female assistants in jet stock rooms which could have been warehouses, or perhaps they were working with the finished articles.

In the workshop itself the following processes were carried out. First came the chopping out, next the cutting and turning, after that the grinding and milling, then the brushing and polishing and finally the finishing touches were added.[7]

Not all these processes appear in the job descriptions. One finds 14 jet-turners, 4 carvers and 1 medallion carver. It was the foreman who handed out the rough jet to the workmen and was responsible for the smooth running of the workshop. He had to watch very carefully for fire, which destroyed a number of premises, as the jet shavings were very inflammable. Two men described themselves as foremen in these returns.

7 Taylor, *Mourning dress*, 235.

Table 30.3 Ages of jet workers, fishermen and shipwrights

Age	Fishermen	Shipwrights	Jet workers
8			1
9			3
10			12
11			15
12		1	34
13		3	48
14		6	57
15		9	58
16	1	8	75
17	1	7	56
18	2	7	56
19	1	12	54
20	2	11	39
21–30	18	62	269
31–40	23	81	149
41–50	23	80	49
51–60	12	59	19
61–70	4	30	11
71–80	3	12	1
81–86	2	3	–
Total	92	391	1,006

Only four ornament dealers are listed but there must have been many more outlets for the finished articles than this. One of the shops employed a clerk and there were also three clerks working for the manufacturers. There appears one jet mount dealer who would supply the metal mounts for ear-rings and probably fasteners for the necklaces and pins for broaches.

Nine females worked in the jet trade according to the returns and two have already been mentioned. The others were shop women, assistants to the jet workshops, stringers and carders. The former strung beads together whilst the latter fixed the jewellery onto cards. The jet trade did not provide many jobs for women, unlike the fishing industry where the majority of wives and daughters would help with the line baiting and collecting shellfish to sell. No women stated that they worked in the ship-building trade.

Age structure and occupation succession

In studying Table 30.3 above, one is immediately aware of the large percentage of young men working with jet. A total of 492 young men and boys between the ages of 8 and 20 were employed in the trade in 1871, the vast majority of the workforce being below the age of 40. In the case of the fishermen and shipwrights, the pattern is quite

Table 30.4 Number of families in which father and son work at same trade

Trade	Number of families	Number having father/son in trade	%
Fishermen[a]	86	5	5.8
Shipwrights	307	20	6.5
Jet workers	760	42	5.5

Notes: a = There were also 2 mother/daughter relationships among the fishing group.

different. Numbers are small in the younger age groups, gradually building up to the main body of workmen between the ages of 31 and 50. After this there is a gradual decline amongst the older men.

Why should the jet workers be so different? One cause could be financial. Little is obtainable about comparative incomes in the Whitby of 1871 apart from Woodwark's statement that jet men earned between £3–4 per week at the height of the trade.[8] The boys, too, probably earned a good wage which compared well with other trades. Working conditions would be much easier in the jet shops than in the shipyards or at sea. The work was not so physically demanding, the shops were warm in winter and there was less risk of injury.

This does not really explain why there are so few older men in jet work. If the conditions were so good for the youngsters, would not this induce the men to stay in the trade? Compared with the fishing and shipbuilding, jet was a comparative newcomer, but had been in existence since the 1830s. So some young men entering between 1830 and 1850 should still have been working in 1871. Matthew Snowdon claimed that jet workers were healthy, but great quantities of dust were produced and jet does include sulphur which cannot have resulted in favourable working conditions over a long period. Older Whitby people remember jet workers who died young having contracted silicosis, but it is difficult to substantiate these claims.

The CEBs were checked to see whether there was any tradition of sons following fathers into the jet trade (Table 30.4 above). A comparison was made with fishermen and shipwrights, but in all cases very few followed their father's trade. It should be remembered that married sons could have left home and be engaged in the same trade as their father. Judging from the number of young men working in jet, the vast majority of youngsters in Whitby must have been trying their hand at carving jet ornaments regardless of the trade their fathers followed. This is borne out by Table 30.5 below, which illustrates the popularity of jet work amongst young males. Thirty per cent of families

8 Kendall, *Whitby jet*, 7–8.

Table 30.5 Number of sons of jet workers, shipwrights and fishermen

Trade	n. of families with son	1 son empl'd	%	2 sons empl'd	%	3 sons empl'd	%	4 sons empl'd	%
Jet workers	283	170	60.1	85	30.0	23	8.1	5	1.8
Shipwrights	47	38	80.9	9	19.1	–	–	–	–
Fishermen	7	5	71.4	2	28.6	–	–	–	–

having sons working in the jet trade had two brothers working and a few had three or four boys in the trade. Young shipwrights did not appear to follow each other into the trade to the same extent, and the numbers involved in fishing are too small to produce viable results. Again one must remember that there were older, married brothers who had left home.

Examining the birthplace of jet workers given in the CEBs, it appears that there was no great surge of people to Whitby to engage in the trade. Table 30.6 below shows that the greatest number came from Yorkshire itself and most of these were within 15 miles of Whitby. So, although the local young men found the work enticing in 1871, there was little sign of families being attracted from other industrial areas such as London, the Midlands or Merseyside.

Geographical location

Jet workers would appear to have congregated in the older parts of the town, and it is possible to illustrate, by means of a map, that certain streets and yards near the harbour must have held a jet worker and possibly a workshop in every other house (Table 30.7 and Figure 30.2, both below).

Table 30.7 shows that the percentage of workers range from 39.4 per cent to 11.7 per cent. Enumeration Districts (EDs) 20 and 21 are not true percentages as not all households were counted, many being outside Whitby town.

EDs 1 to 6 inclusive covered Church Street, Henrietta Street, Grape Lane, Sandgate and all the yards on the east side of the Esk. Crossing the river, EDs 7 and 8 cover Baxtergate and its yards which run close to the harbour. Moving up the cliff-side Flower Gate falls within ED 9 and Cliff Street and Haggersgate in ED 10. The Cragg in ED 11 is another area thickly populated with jet workers, but ED 12 covers the West Cliff Estate started by George Hudson in 1849 and continued by Sir George Elliot. It catered for the holiday trade and not for local tradesmen. Still on the West Cliff, the houses in Skinner Street, Well Close Square and Clarence Place showed slightly more workers in ED 13, but Bagdale in ED 14, which had some fine Georgian houses, only

Table 30.6 Immigration of jet workers into Whitby

Birthplace	Number of men
Yorkshire North Riding	
within 5 miles	49
within 10 miles	21
within 15 miles	18
within 15+ miles	41
Yorkshire West Riding	17
Yorkshire East Riding	14
Durham Co.	18
Northumberland	3
Derbyshire	1
Lincolnshire	3
Staffordshire	1
Cheshire	1
Cambridgeshire	1
Norfolk	1
Suffolk	1
Kent	4
Hampshire	1
Gloucestershire	2
Devon	1
Cornwall	1
Ireland	5
Scotland	5
Canada	1
USA	1
Greece	1
Total	212

Notes: Total number of jet workers born in Whitby is 1,006 minus 212 = 794.

Table 30.7 Concentration of jet workers' housing in Whitby

Enumeration district	No. of households	No. containing jet workers	%
1	156	47	30.1
2	188	74	39.4
3	225	51	22.7
4	195	74	37.9
5	169	47	27.8
6	168	61	36.3
7	173	44	25.4
8	191	63	33.0
9	155	42	27.1
10	179	52	29.1
11	153	46	30.1
12	266	31	11.7
13	192	27	14.1
14	114	15	13.2
15	157	36	22.9
16	177	22	12.4
20	79	1	1.3
21	79	17	21.5

Figure 30.2 Concentration of jet workers' houses in Whitby

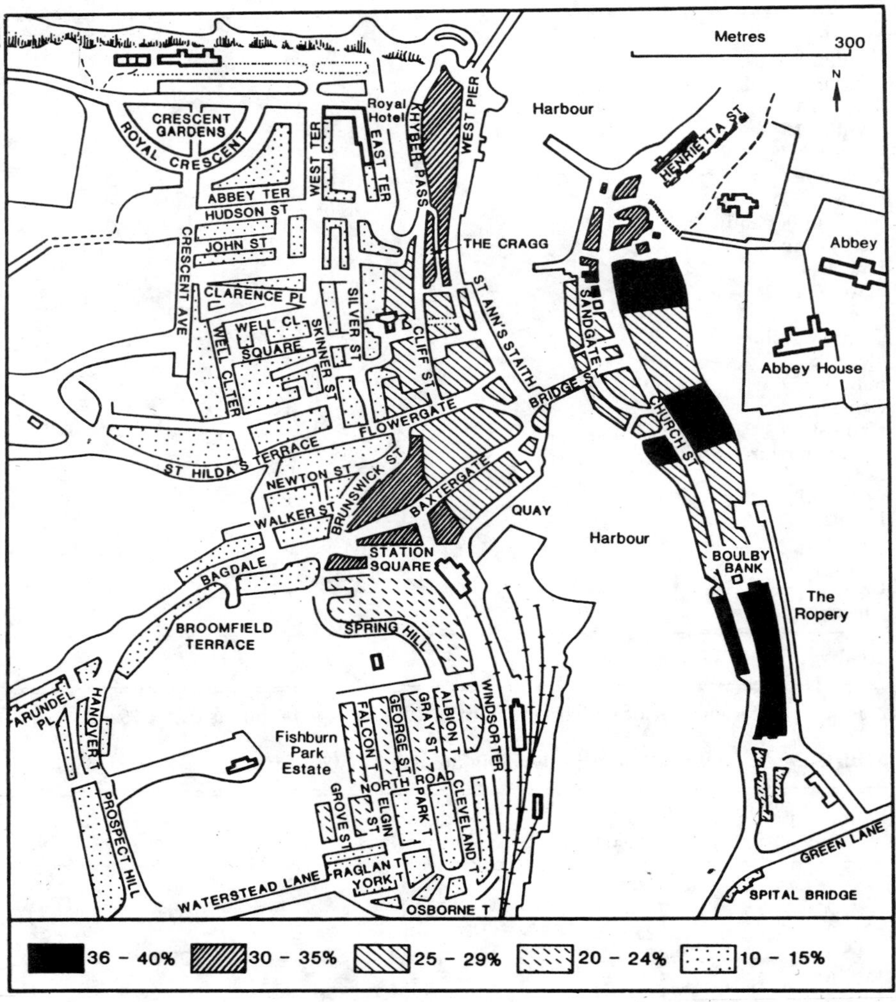

supported jet men in its yards. The other outstanding Georgian terrace, St Hilda's Terrace, contributed nothing to the percentage of workers in ED 13. The Fishburn Park Estate behind the railway station began to rise about 1860, and these houses were not as large as those on the West Cliff Estate nor quite as commodious for visitors. Part of the estate recorded a rate of 22.9 per cent in ED 15, but ED 17 in the same area dropped to 12.4 per cent. ED 21 covers the area of the shipyards at the upper end of Church Street and many of the houses held shipwrights, but the percentage of jet workers was 21.5 per cent. This does not include all the households so the figure is artificially increased.

In it heyday the jet industry was the life-blood of Whitby, but perhaps the town was too dependent on one outlet for work-men and so when the trade eventually dwindled in the 1920s and 1930s a gap was created which has never been successfully filled.

The CEBs are a very rich source for local history research. They provide much more than the number of people in a town and their geographical location. As shown in this chapter, the complete infrastructure of an industry can be recorded and further studies of other groups could produce a picture of all the occupations in the town at one particular point in time.

31

An early Victorian suburban élite: heads of household at home

JOHN B. REDFERN

Introduction

The community on which this study is based is mid-nineteenth-century Edgbaston where the then Lord Calthorpe had developed a planned residential suburb on his estate. Begun before the end of the Napoleonic War, this development was to be slowly but consistently extended by the family throughout the century.[1] By 1851, select suburban streets were wholly or partly lined with smart villas, all built on the basis of the building lease and the image of a superior suburb was well established.

The once truly rural parish of Edgbaston lay close by, to the south-west of Birmingham, of which, since 1838, it had been a ward. It was intersected by two main highways, the Bristol road and that to Hagley going due west. For centuries a rural backwater, suspected by the town for Catholic sympathies, its natural topography had two features vital for an élite suburb. First, it lay on picturesque uplands, providing drainage and supplies of clean water. Second, the prevailing wind blew away the smog of industrial Birmingham on whose prosperity its development was going to depend. The town of a thousand trades and of the small master would always have some currently successful businessmen whose rising expectations were fixed on a modern house in the country.

Edgbaston owed much of its successful development to its élite image already recorded in 1831 in the first edition of Samuel Lewis' well-known and reliable *Topographical dictionary of England*. Interestingly, a few Edgbastonians were subscribers to the 1848 edition.[2] A similar picture is painted in the *Edgbaston directory and guide for 1853*, illustrated by the following extracts.

> The chief portion of the Parish is now in the hands of Lord Calthorpe, whose ancestor, Sir Richard Gough, purchased the Lordship for, it is said, £25,000 [in 1717]. His Lordship has paid much attention to its improvement as to render it,

1 Birmingham Reference Library: Edgbaston Estate Office deeds; Calthorpe Estate Office, Edgbaston: Calthorpe Office papers.

2 Lewis, *Topographical dictionary*.

> independent of other advantages, the most eligible spot for building in the neighbourhood of Birmingham. . .[the ground is] intersected by road laid out with such skill and ingenuity, as to present the most tempting sites for Villa residences, and to afford the most delightful promenades. The result of such care and arrangement has, no doubt, confirmed his Lordship's fullest expectations. The roads are excellent, and for the most part are bordered with trees of luxuriant growth, behind which are ensconced extremely handsome houses, in every variety of style and dimension. There are certainly few points in England, which exhibit such an assemblage of architectural beauty amidst a landscape of so strictly moral a character.[3]

Lewis' 1848 edition mentions in addition the value of the land for building from its proximity to Birmingham, the handsome houses coated with Roman cement, the detached mansions occupied by the principal merchants and manufacturers of the town, the small part of the parish lighted by gas and the ample supplies of water.[4]

The estate had been deliberately developed slowly in marked contrast to mushroom suburbs built by speculators. This was the policy decided initially and consistently carried out by George, 3rd Baron Calthorpe (1787–1851) and his first full-time agent, John Harris, formerly a local businessman. In 1811, there had been nearly two hundred mainly rural dwellings and in the 1851 CEBs there were 1,665, many of them the homes of the new suburbanites.[5] However, the character of the change is better illustrated by the changing sex-ratio for the whole parish. In 1811, there had been 537 males to 643 females, giving a sex ratio of 83.5 (males to 100 females): in 1851, the 3,676 males to 5,593 females gave a sex ratio of 65.7. This was in part due to the greater longevity of women, but more particularly to the influx of female domestic servants, most of them in the suburban households here under consideration.

The Calthorpe Estate covered about four-fifths of this 2,545 acre parish. With careful consideration for its long-term interests, the slow change of land use from agriculture to superior housing was planned, building plots being leased generally for 99 years in the new streets the estate cut, gravelled and drained as well as on older roads. The building lease method was vital for a settled estate, which could not normally sell land to raise capital, and helpful to tenants who were thus saved the expense of buying it; though the houses they built would be a valuable investment in bricks and mortar. Owing to the steady demand for superior villas from Birmingham, they were able to select the right type of tenant; to prohibit industry, trade and other

3 *Edgbaston Directory and Guide for 1853*. Original punctuation preserved.
4 Lewis, *Topographical dictionary*.
5 1851 Census Great Britain, *Population Tables. Part I, vol. I*, BPP 1852–3 LXXXV, tables for Warwickshire and Worcestershire.

'nuisances'; and to control the density and quality of the houses the tenants erected within suitably sized gardens. This was accomplished through the clauses of the building lease and by the firm hand of the Estate office. Eventually, the estate suburb, which had more than fulfilled the expectations of the pioneer suburbanites, must have begun to shape their successors in the same mould.

By the mid-century, the parish contained three well-defined though slowly changing residential zones. The 'town fringe' was to the south-east on non-Calthorpe land, with working-class dwellings, pubs, small food shops and workshops. The 'rural remnant' to the south, west and north of the parish contained farms of the order of 100 acres, small holdings and agricultural labourers' cottages. In between had arisen the estate suburb on new streets and on old roads radiating from Five Ways and along the Bristol and Pershore highways. Overall, the density of the parish was 3.6 persons per acre which contrasts with the 65 of Birmingham parish and the 0.4 of the neighbourhood rural parish of Northfield.[6]

The study population

What kind of people were these new suburbanites who had been impelled to Edgbaston by 'urban push' and 'suburban pull'? This chapter studies 698 heads of household for whom full CEB details are available.[7] The chief criterion for selection was a residence with a rateable value (hereafter RV) of £20 or more, in a street which was chiefly suburban.[8] In the event, this mainly fulfilled the second criterion, that there should be at least one domestic servant living in.[9] Over 50 'working households' where work was not separated from home are excluded, with the exception of professional men. The heads excluded were mainly engaged in rural trades (farmer, blacksmith), or running inns (such as the 'Plough and Harrow') or private schools. Also excluded are over 30 suburban households where the head of the family was absent on census night, thus making classification difficult or not possible at all.

Given its emphasis on occupation, the study concentrates, necessarily, on male heads of household. Neither the wives nor the female heads were given any occupation in the CEBs, all were mistress of the household. The great majority of the children under 16 appear to

6 1851 Census Great Britain, *Population Tables. Part I, vol. I*, BPP 1852–3 LXXXV, tables for Warwickshire and Worcestershire.

7 1851 CEBs, King's Norton: Edgbaston, PRO HO 107/2049.

8 Birmingham Reference Library. Edgbaston poor rate book (28 March 1851).

9 In the 450 houses valued for rating at £30 or more, there are seven in the 1851 census with no domestic servants listed; almost certainly one being absent on the night for various possible domestic or personal reasons. In the other 248 houses (RV £20–29), there are 17 cases. From an inspection of the composition of these households, it is highly probable that there was usually at least one co-resident domestic servant in most and possibly all cases.

be 'scholars', if not always listed as such.[10] There were 26 boarders in 22 households, usually young professional men, and the 13 houses which contained the 14 lodger households have been excluded from the analysis. The nearly 700 or so élite heads have been sorted into six residential groups based on RV in an attempt to create a reliable indicator of relative socio-economic status. They range from group I with a rateable value of at least £80 (the highest is £178.25) to group VI with a RV of £20–29 (see Table 31.2, below).

Group I contains the 'crème de la crème'. Its median RV was £95 and there were no less than 22 mansions where RV exceeded £100. Mean household size (MHS) was 8.3 (see Table 31.3, below), ranging from three to 18 persons.[11] There was an average of nearly four domestic servants living in, the range being one (on census night) to eight. Nearly all the 51 heads here had grounds of at least one acre, even the 3 exceptions averaging half an acre. The median age was 54 years; that of the male heads being 52 and the 4 female heads, 66. To illustrate the cream of the Edgbaston élite, five examples are provided, in descending order of RV (from £145 to £115), each selected as a result of his being highest rated householder in his particular suburban street.

Charles Geach, Esq., JP, was a banker and ironmaster born in Cornwall, with a bank and house also in Union Street, Birmingham.[12] Aged 42 in 1851, he had one of the first mansions in what was to be the exclusive Frances (now Augustus) Road. His two lodges each contained a servant married couple with their children; and five servants, including a housekeeper, lived in. He had a wife Eliza, and three sons and a daughter, aged from 11 to 17.

Charles Shaw, Esq., of 'Greenfields' with its 9 acres (to give its name to the Crescent later erected there) was a 58-year-old nailmaker and merchant. Born in Birmingham, he had married Phoebe, a Londoner, and they lived with a spinster daughter and a married daughter and her army officer husband. The five servants included a footman, and a gardener and his wife who had three small boys. He had a warehouse and (work) shops in Great Charles Street, Birmingham.

Thomas Welchman Whateley was a 57-year-old Birmingham-born solicitor who lived at 'The Laurels' in 3 acres of ground on the Hagley Road. He had a 62-year-old (presumably second) wife Lucy and 7

10 In accordance with the theory developed later in the chapter, all issue of the head of household and/or spouse are termed 'children' if they are under 16, and 'offspring' if 16 or older.

11 Married servants and their families recorded in 5 separate lodges (10 adults and 10 children) have not been included in the figures for mean household size (MHS) or mean number of domestic servants (MDS). Nor does the latter include the children of servants living in the household (8 children in 6 households).

12 The *Birmingham parliamentary register, 1852,* (Birmingham Reference Library), gives not only the suburbanites' residential qualifications in Edgbaston, but also the town premises occupied by them which entitles them to another parliamentary vote.

children aged from 5 to 15.[13] The six servants living in included a lady's maid and a groom. He occupied a house and offices at 41 Waterloo Street, Birmingham, and he and his brother acted for the Calthorpe Estate locally.

William Wills, Esq., JP, of 'Park Mount', of Bristol Road, was described in the CEBs as a proprietor of land, presumably the 14.5 acres here. Birmingham-born and 59, he lived with his wife Sarah and a younger unmarried sister, employing one man and two women house servants. He also had Waterloo Street premises, a house and offices at number eleven where he may have lived before moving to Edgbaston, as Charles Geach and the Whateley brothers may also have done in their town premises.

George Attwood was the elder brother of Thomas Attwood, the Warwickshire-born banker, former leader of the political reformers, and Birmingham's first MP in 1831. By 1851 a widower of 73, he lived with his 29-year-old spinster daughter in a Priory Road mansion with grounds of 9.5 acres. He had three men and three women servants living in, and two warehouses etc. in Birmingham, one at Attwood's passage.

In spite of his relatively modest residence valued for rating at slightly less than the median RV for all these élite heads, one householder must have been as influential as any in the parish. He was George Smart, Birmingham-born merchant with a Great Charles street warehouse. Aged 59 in 1851, he was churchwarden for Edgbaston at least from 1845–53, 'people's' and 'vicar's' in turn. He lived with his Sunderland-born wife, Anne, and two house servants at 15 Calthorpe Street; though later he was to move to Church Road nearer to the 'Old Church' for which he was responsible. The ('select') vestry minutes 1844–53 which recorded his terms of office also give glimpses of how traditional farmers and new suburbanites combined to run the parish – until the 1851 take-over of the town.

While the bottom group VI (RV £20–29) has considerably more modest residences and domestic staffs, they appear to be the same kind of people socially as the top group, apparently sharing the same values and with quantitative rather than qualitative differences in households. This group of 248 heads was nearly five times the size of the top group, just over 20 per cent of them were women and they had a median RV of £24, about a quarter that of group I. The MHS of group VI was 5.4 persons, with a range from 2 to 11. The mean number of domestic servants living-in was 1.2, about two-thirds having one only. The smallest houses would be semi-detached villas and most of the group had gardens from one-tenth to a half acre in extent.

13 In suggesting possible remarried, the respective census age of the (presumed second) wife and of the children of the (presumed first) marriage are used as a guide.

Figure 31.1 Élite heads by sex, marital status and age

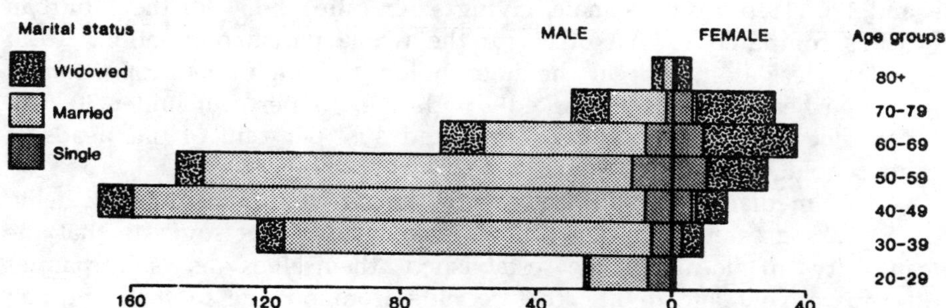

Table 31.1 Élite heads by sex, marital status and age group

Sex	Marital status	Young adults (20–29) %	Mature adults (30–59) %	Elderly (60+) %	All ages (20+) %
		Age group			
Male	unmarried	25.9	5.3	5.6	6.2
	married	66.7	78.5	38.4	67.9
	widowed	3.7	5.5	15.3	7.9
Sub-total		96.3	89.3	59.3	82.0
Female	unmarried	–	3.8	9.0	5.0
	married	–	0.2	0.6	0.3
	widowed	3.7	6.7	31.1	12.8
Sub-total		3.7	10.7	40.7	18.0
All	unmarried	25.9	9.1	14.7	11.2
	married	66.7	78.7	39.0	68.2
	widowed	7.4	12.2	46.3	20.6
Total		100.0	100.0	100.0	100.0
n.		27	494	177	698
% of all ages		3.9	70.7	25.4	100.0

The median age of this group was 57, the male heads slightly younger and the female heads much older with a median age of 61 years.

Age and sex structure

Figure 31.1 above, a population pyramid of the 698 suburban heads, shows their distinction by sex and marital condition in seven age groups, from 20 to 80 and over. Table 31.1 above supplements this by supplying the percentages for single, married and widowed men and women heads; but this time in more meaningful age groups; young adults in their 20s; mature or middle-aged adults from 30 to 59; old persons, 60 or more years of age.

Five hundred and seventy two (82 per cent) of the heads were male and 126 (18 per cent) female, giving a sex ratio of 454 for the suburban heads compared to that of 66 for the whole parish population. Adult males were dominant in the households, although the proportion of women heads increased markedly with age: 3.7 per cent under 30, 10.7 per cent amongst the middle-aged, and 40.7 per cent of old heads of household.

The median age of all heads is 49, that of women heads at 62 being 15 years greater than that of the male heads. This suggests that the majority of local people established themselves as suburbanites comparatively late in life; that recruits from outside to the suburban population were mainly heads with families already formed; and that male heads probably had a considerably higher death rate than female ones. Out of every 100 heads, 4 were in their twenties and no less than 25 were 60 or over (15 men and 10 women). The actual range is from a young man of 21 to an old woman of 89. If wives were on average about the same age as their husbands, the majority of not only female heads but also of their spouses would be well-past childbearing age.

Nuptiality appears to have followed a 'western' marriage pattern of late marriage and many unmarried adults. Out of every hundred heads, 11 were single (6 bachelors and 5 spinsters); 68 were married (nearly 68 men and less than one woman); 21 were widowed (8 widowers and 13 widows). However, of the 11 per cent single, less than 1 in 10 were under 50, leading to the inference that most bachelors remained single by choice. Certainly, the age at which these early Victorian middle classes married appears late by today's standards, as only 20 heads under age 30 (less than 3 per cent of all heads) were, or had been, married. No doubt the proportion would be lower still amongst those of their siblings who were not yet householders. Amongst this social grouping. setting up one's own household was almost certainly a normal adjunct to getting married. There were only 13 households (under 2 per cent) with 14 sets of married offspring at home – in most cases probably temporarily.

To conclude this analysis by sex, age group and marital condition, the principal proportions follow for each major age group. Of young adults, over a quarter of the male heads were bachelors and two-thirds married, while there was only one female, a widow. Of mature adults, over three-quarters were married men and there was only one middle aged married woman head. Of old persons, less than two-fifths were married and not far off a half, widowed, the proportion of widows among female heads being twice as high as that of widowers among male ones. The mode for male heads (388 cases) is middle aged and married; for female heads (55 cases) old and widowed.

Figure 31.2 Élite heads by sex, age and rateable value of residence

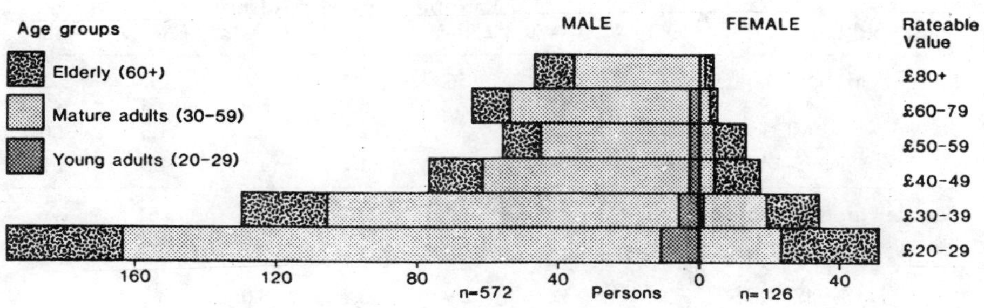

Table 31.2 Élite heads by sex, marital status and rateable value

Sex	Marital status	£80+ %	£60–79 %	£50–59 %	£40–49 %	£30–39 %	£20–29 %	all %	% heads of own sex
		Rateable value of residence							
Male	unmar.	11.8	11.4	1.4	5.3	7.2	4.4	6.2	7.5
	mar.	74.5	75.7	69.6	67.0	63.9	66.9	67.9	82.9
	wid.	5.9	5.7	10.1	9.6	7.2	8.1	7.9	9.6
Sub-total		92.2	92.9	81.2	81.9	78.3	79.4	82.0	100.0
Female	unmar.	2.0	4.3	5.8	2.1	6.6	5.6	5.0	27.8
	mar.	–	–	–	–	-	0.8	0.3	1.6
	wid.	5.9	2.9	13.0	15.9	15.1	14.1	12.8	70.6
Sub-total		7.8	7.1	18.8	18.1	21.7	20.6	18.0	100.0
All	unmar.	13.7	15.7	7.2	7.4	13.9	10.0	11.2	
	mar.	74.5	75.7	69.6	67.0	63.9	67.7	68.2	
	wid.	11.8	8.6	23.2	25.6	22.3	22.2	20.6	
Total		100.0	100.0	100.0	100.0	100.0	100.0	100.0	
n.		51	70	69	94	166	248	698	
% of all values			7.3	10.0	9.9	13.5	23.8	35.5	100.0

Social class as indicated by rateable values

Figure 31.2 and the related Table 31.2, both above, show the distribution of household heads by personal attributes in the six rateable value of residence (RV) groups. In most cases RV can be considered a reliable indicator of socio-economic ranking, especially as it seems by inspection to correlate with the mean size of domestic staff (Table 31.3 below). However, it is a major hypothesis of this study that the 698 heads form a homogeneous social group, at least as far

Table 31.3 Household size, number of domestic servants by sex of household and rateable value

Sex of household head		Rateable value of residence £80+	£60–79	£50–59	£40–49	£30–39	£20–29	all
Male	n. households	47	65	56	77	130	197	572
	MHS	8.5	7.5	7.2	6.2	5.9	5.6	6.4
	MDS	3.9	2.9	2.5	2.1	1.6	1.3	2.0
	MHS–MDS	4.6	4.6	4.7	4.1	4.3	4.3	4.4
Female	n. households	4	5	13	17	36	51	126
	MHS	6.3	6.0	5.2	4.6	4.4	4.3	4.6
	MDS	3.8	2.4	2.3	1.7	1.4	1.1	1.6
	MHS–MDS	2.5	3.6	2.9	2.9	3.0	3.2	3.0
All	n. households	51	70	69	94	166	248	698
	MHS	8.3	7.4	6.8	5.9	5.5	5.4	6.0
	MDS	3.9	2.8	2.4	2.0	1.6	1.2	1.9
	MHS–MDS	4.4	4.6	4.4	3.9	3.9	4.2	4.1
			£50+			£20–49		
	MHS–MDS		4.5			4.0		

Notes: MHS = Mean household size; MDS = Mean number of domestic servants.

as their distribution by personal attributes and kind of household is concerned. This latter implies that the difference between the imposing households of group I and the much more modest ones which become more common as RV decreases will be explained not only by socially conspicuous consumption on residence and on specialised domestic staff, but also by the size, stage and needs of the nuclear family (if any), and to a lesser extent by the presence or not of co-resident kin.

Over a third of all households are in the lowest category (RV £20–29) and only 7.3 per cent fall in the highest category (RV £80 and above). The median RV is £35, with an upper quartile of £50 and a lower one of £25. The median RV of households headed by females is lower at £32. They were therefore only slightly less well housed than men, although much older and more likely to be widowed.

The extent to which the nearly 700 hundred heads formed a homogeneous social group can be further examined by dividing them into an upper composite 'group A' of 190 heads rated at £50 and above (RV groups I to III) and a lower 'group B', of 508 heads with RVs between £20 and £49 (RV groups IV to VI). That is, over 27 per cent of household heads lived in a mansion or large villa with a gross estimated rental of more than £60 per annum, at a time when one gold sovereign would have been a satisfactory week's pay for many artisans.[14]

The sex ratio of heads in group A is 764 (168 males and 22 females), while that of group B is just over half that at 388 (404 males to 104 females). Households which had lost a father, husband or brother were more likely to be in the lower group. As it does not seem likely that the male death rate in the lower group was so much higher, bereavement may have forced many families to less expensive homes. In group A there are 129 middle-aged male heads and 312 in group B, a proportion of 77 per cent in both cases. While the proportions of old and young male heads were also similar for the two groups being approximately 18 and 4 per cent respectively for both composite groups. The proportions of the different age groups in A and B do vary more for female heads, partly due to the smaller sub-group; but there are significantly more old women than middle-aged ones in both. Thus, especially for the men, there is no indication that increasing age on average might have brought a shift to a higher rating bracket.

Eighty-three per cent of the male heads (Table 31.2) were married, 10 per cent widowed and 8 per cent bachelors. The corresponding proportions for female heads are 2 per cent married, 71 per cent widowed and 28 per cent spinsters. The proportion of male heads married was almost exactly the same in groups A and B. It seems a reasonable inference that practically all the male householders could have afforded marriage if they had wished it. Of all heads, there is a higher proportion widowed in group B than in group A (23 and 15 per cent), suggesting that the loss of either partner may have led to retrenchment. While there is a slightly higher proportion of bachelors in group B than in group A the proportion is reversed for spinsters (26 and 36 per cent). The latter proportions are a little surprising when one considers how financially well-endowed these maiden ladies must have seemed; but none were under 30 and nearly half were 60 or older.

Household structure

Household composition and size is probably a useful test of social homogeneity of the 698 heads. Table 31.3 gives a preliminary analysis by sex and RV group of mean household size (MHS) and the mean number of domestic servants (MDS). MHS for all these heads is 6.0, ranging from 1 (one example) to 18 persons. The MHS for each RV of residence groups shows a consistent fall from 8.3 (group I) to 5.4 (group VI). This falling trend appears in households headed by both men and women; though MHS for male heads is 6.4 and that of women heads 4.6, and the households of the latter include only one with more than eight persons in it.

14 Gross estimated rental is usually 25 per cent higher than the rateable value used in this study; Edgbaston poor rate book, March 1851.

For all élite households, the mean number of domestic servants (MDS) is 1.9. It varies from 9.3 in group I to 1.2 in group VI, the range being one to eight. Of the 674 households which recorded at least one house servant on census night, over three-quarters have one or two and less than one quarter, three or more; but the latter comprise 27 per cent of the households headed by men compared to 10 per cent of those with women heads. However, if mean household size 'net' of domestic servants is calculated by subtracting MDS from MHS, it is 4.1 for all heads, but with a much narrower range across RV groups than was the case with the gross MHS figure. Composite group A has a 'net' mean of 4.5 compared to 4.0 for group B, and the figures for the three RV groups comprising each composite group are very similar. This stability is mainly due to the fairly similar distribution of male headed households (overall 'net' mean 4.4) as the figures for households headed by females tend to fluctuate more widely round the mean 'net' value of 3.0 for all RV groups. Moreover, the difference in gross MHS between male and female heads (6.4 and 4.6) is greater than that between the bottom RV groups in A and B (III and VI) for heads of both or either sex.

Conclusions

In summarising this account of a mid-nineteenth-century Midland suburban élite in their domestic environment it must be mentioned that the factors which shaped this particular suburb seem to be the economic structure of the town, the policy of the main ground landlord, the aspirations of the tenants for a fuller life, the local topography and the extent to which the suburban part of Edgbaston became a close-knit community. These factors probably helped to shape the suburbanites too. Just as man made the suburb, so the suburb made the man.

The distribution of heads by RV of residence groups seemingly reflects relative socio-economic circumstances and displays a population of nearly 700 households in very easy circumstances for the time. The upper quartile was valued for rating at £50 and more and included 22 mansions with RV £100 to £174.25; the lower one with RV between £20 and £25; and the rest grouped round the median of £35. This was at a time when the '£10 householder' with the vote could be estimated as a small 'man of property'.

There are obvious economic differences between a middle-aged man with a thriving business, a 'quiverfull' of children, and an imposing mansion, and an old widow in a small semi-detached villa. The domestic staff of one could include a housekeeper, a governess, a footman, or a coachman; the other might consist of a cook and housemaid or, more likely, one maid of all work. However, when household composition and size is considered, it is evident that there were not only considerable variations between the RV groups, but also within them. The apparent economic differences are partly due to heads being of different sexes, of different material status and at different stages in the life-cycle of the family, with consequently different housing and staffing needs. They are also at different phases of fortune, though this appears to be much more due to bereavement than to variations in the age of the head. To a lesser extent, the presence or not of co-resident kin and whether or not, if present, they are age-dependent (young or old) or mature siblings etc., is expected to have some influence on household structure and size.

From the point of view of social status, all the élite households seem to have much in common. If a male, the head's occupation was usually that of merchant, manufacturer, provider of services or rentier. The woman of the house, whether head or wife, was occupied solely as mistress of the household. Most of the children were probably being educated to about 15 only. Afterwards, the boys would be started – at the bottom, of course – on a job with prospects, while the girls made themselves useful at home and waited for a suitable marriage. The house was devoted solely to residential purposes and situated in its own garden on a wide, well-kept and tree-lined street. Normally, there would be one or two servant girls at least living in, and three or more in nearly a quarter of the households. If necessary, the heads seem to have been able to offer shelter to orphaned kin and spinster sisters. None appeared to need to take in borders for financial reasons, the few doing so probably obliging a friend or business acquaintance. Most had probably made money in an industrial town and all appear to be getting as far away from it as they could conveniently do.

Given the focus of this analysis, it is not possible to say if there were other heads with houses valued for rating at less that £20 who might also qualify as 'suburban'. Certainly, there were in Edgbaston 'working households' rated at a much higher sum than those of the farmers. Below the £20 mark there were also working-class dwellings both in the 'urban fringe' and in the 'rural remnant', some with RVs of less than £5 and including the 400 households poor enough to accept vestry-organised charity each Christmas.

The distribution of the heads in the six RV groups by sex, age and marital category does nothing to negate the hypothesis that this is a socially homogeneous group. They seem to be only marginally influenced by economic circumstance, at least the male householders. Certainly, taking all households, there is a marked difference between top and bottom RV groups in MHS (2.9) and MDS (2.7); but the latter practically accounts for the former. Consequently, the figures for mean household size 'net' of the domestic staff reveal much less disparity between the RV groups. Indeed, the difference in mean 'net' households size between male and female heads (1.4) is twice that between the most extreme RV groups for heads of both sexes or for male heads.

The contrasts between male and female householders in personal attributes and in household size seem to reinforce the social homogeneity hypothesis. A new family life-cycle stage would be expected to bring change, and most female heads would have inherited the household from a father, husband or brother. The loss of the latter must more often than not have led to some fall in living standards.

Less than one head in five was a female, a higher proportion in the lower RV groups and a lower one in the top RV groups. She was on average 15 years older than her male peers. Compared to the over four-fifths of men who were married, she was usually single, or, much more often, widowed. She lived in a lower-rated house and mean household size was only just over two-thirds that of the men; though there was much less disparity between them in mean size of domestic staff. The modes summarise the differences concisely; over two-thirds of men householders were middle-aged and married; over two-fifths of female heads old and widowed.

It could be argued that 'improvement' of the family's standard of living and future prospects was this suburban élite's main motivation, and that this had already raised them to the desirable level of a modern home with a good Edgbaston address. Urban push had probably propelled many from the noisy, crowded, smoky and unhealthy town, while suburban pull had drawn them to a new villa with modern conveniences in an environment ideally between town and country. The bright new colour-washed residence with its well-kept garden and a young maid to be seen doing the dirty work in the morning, and answering the bell smartly dressed after noon, must have been a sure symbol of success in the West Midlands. To the family inside, and probably to the servant girls also, once the front gate was closed it surely was a real sanctuary from the evils and discomforts of mid-nineteenth-century town and country life.

For father, work was far enough away to be out of sight sometimes, yet near enough for a short drive in his own carriage, with other businessmen on the horse omnibus, or even on foot. Here, in his own walled garden, he could indulge a romantic love of nature – far from the realities of rural life. The Victorian wife would surely find fulfilment as mistress of the household, mother of her children and on a daily social round. Most of those children could be educated within the parish; the boys trained for a secure occupation, preferably involving brain-work; the girls given social graces and domestic accomplishments. Indeed, the rising generation would start life from an enviable plateau, though youngsters would be introduced at a relatively early age to the doctrine of hard work which had raised the family so far. The suburban household also provided shelter and a niche in life for co-resident kin and to girls in service from a raw country home or urban street to a training in household management which they passed on when married.

The Edgbaston home of this suburban élite answered the rising expectations of those heads who had in most cases made their money in an industrial town such as Birmingham. Most had probably reached a stage in their lives of wanting something better out of life than they could obtain by living close to their work place in the city centre. Once in residence on the Calthorpe Estate, they must have found themselves being moulded in its select image. They in turn would help to make the 40 year old suburb what, by 1851, it surely had become – a self-perpetuating institution.

32

Village type and employment structure: an analysis in the nineteenth-century Lincolnshire Wolds

CHARLES RAWDING

Introduction

The most comprehensive attempt at constructing a nineteenth-century historical geography of rural Britain is to be found in the writing of Mills.[1] Mills based his work on the 'open–close' debate of the mid-nineteenth century, the terms 'open' and 'close' originating from the type of vestry in a given parish. A 'close' vestry was self-appointed, whilst an 'open' vestry was one on which all ratepayers of the parish were allowed to sit,[2] although, of course, many ratepayers were not involved.[3]

Mills, following the line of nineteenth-century commentators, developed the 'open–close' dichotomy beyond its original use by constructing an overall model of nineteenth-century rural society. His initial premise was that social and economic power was a direct consequence of landownership, and that it is therefore possible to ascertain whether a village was 'open' or 'close' by an analysis of the structure of landownership.

To summarise Mills' argument briefly: concentrated landownership enabled the landowners to control the amount of housing provided, thus keeping the poor rates as low as possible, since any resident population that was unemployed or underemployed would undoubtedly rely upon the parish at some point in the year. This, in turn, would result in an increase in the poor rate, the burden of which fell on the occupiers of property in the parish.[4] High poor rates would squeeze profit margins for farmers which in turn put pressure on rent

1 Mills, *Lord and peasant*; Mills, *English rural communities*; Mills, 'The poor laws'; Mills, 'Francis Howell's report'; Mills, 'Spatial implications of the settlement laws'; Mills and Short, 'Social change and social conflict'. For an alternative view see Banks, '"Open" and "close" parishes'.

2 Mills, *Lord and peasant*, 24–5; Banks, '"Open" and "close" parishes', 83.

3 Not surprisingly, the degree of involvement of the parishioners tended to fluctuate according to the issues under discussion.

4 Horn, *The rural world*, 79–129.

levels.[5] Thus, only necessary housing was built. This housing was usually sufficient for the tenant farmer himself and his senior men, the bailiff, the shepherd and his waggoners and was frequently of better quality than that found elsewhere.

As a result of this control on housing, 'close' parishes had smaller populations, and usually required both services and labourers from nearby 'open' parishes.[6] The 'open' parishes, on the other hand, did not have the same concentrated landownership and as a result there was plenty of cottage accommodation. The 'close' parishes were almost entirely agricultural, whilst 'open' parishes had a wider range of trades and services.

In addition to relative population size, there are of course comparative quantitative data of interest to local population students in the context of this 'open–close' dichotomy. One of these, the sex ratio of males to females, is discussed in relation to the prevailing employment structures. Others might be differences in the size of the household, in age, family structures and dependency ratios. Given a wider time perspective, relative population change and the stability or mobility of inhabitants might be included, as might differential fertility and the levels of endogamous marriage, given the use of additional sources.

Landownership

This chapter intends to look at the impact that varying landownership structures had on employment structures and work opportunities within the nineteenth-century countryside with reference to the north Lincolnshire Wolds.[7] The Lincolnshire Wolds are essentially an upland area comprising a chalk plateau with a steep escarpment to the west, rising to heights of 140–50 metres from which a dip slope extends eastwards ranging between 50 and 120m. As such, the Wolds are a distinctive physical region, a distinction which was even more marked during the nineteenth century as patterns of landownership and agriculture were in many ways quite different from the marshes to the east and the glacial sands to the west.

The main sources of information concerning landownership in the nineteenth century are the land tax assessments.[8] For the study area, the

5 Landowners undoubtedly had to respond to falling profits in farming. Rent reductions were particularly common from the 1870s, but even before then, faced with the choice of reducing the rent and keeping the tenant or having to take the farm in hand, many owners opted for the latter.

6 Holderness, '"Open" and "close" parishes'.

7 These arguments are developed more fully in Rawding, 'A study of place'.

8 The values given in the land tax assessments do not directly correspond to levels of land ownership. However, Fuller, in a comparison of the Yarborough estate survey of 1832 and the 1831/2 land tax assessments, concludes that the value given is broadly representative of the acreage owned within a parish. Fuller, 'Landownership in Lindsey', 23–4. For a more general discussion of the land tax, see Turner and Mills, *Land and property*.

Figure 32.1 **Landownership on the Lincolnshire Wolds**

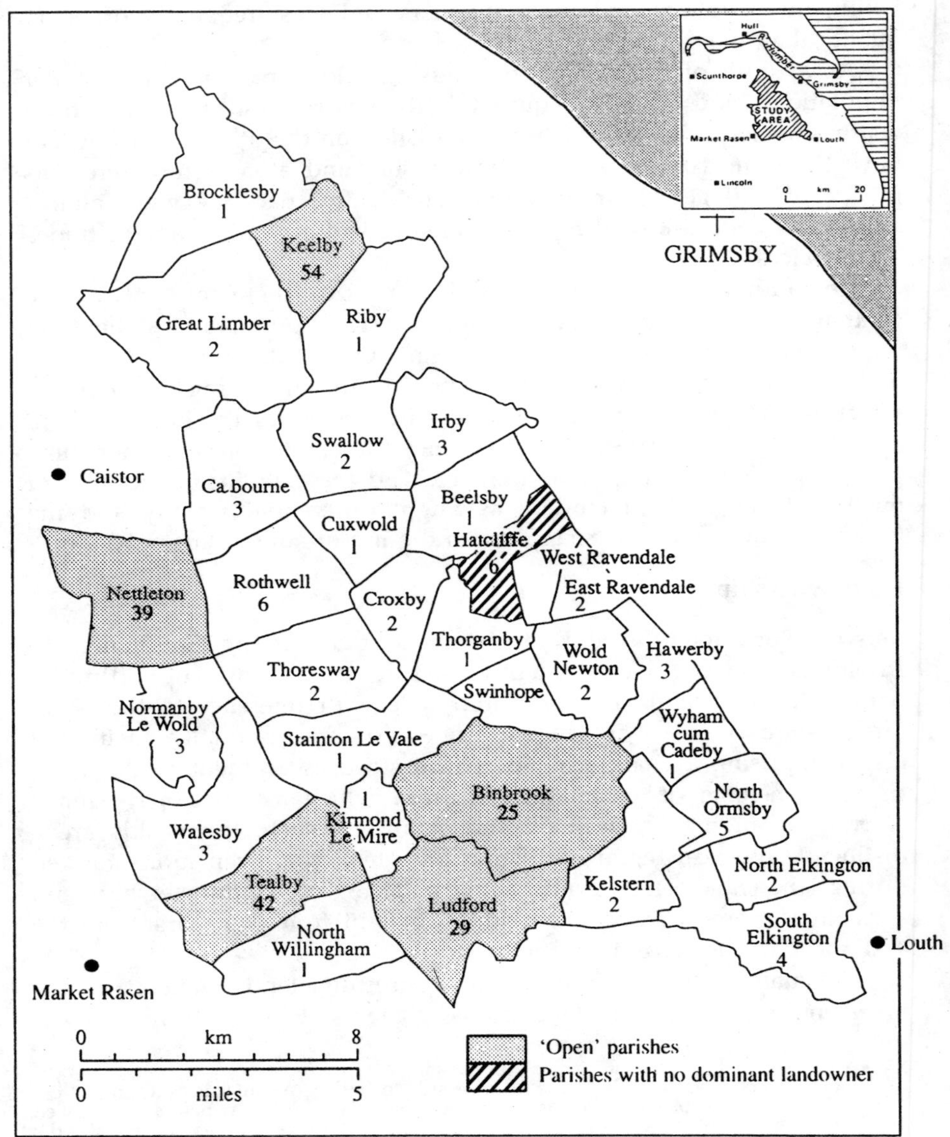

Notes: Numbers indicate number of landowners recorded in the 1831/2 land tax assessment.

last such assessments were in either 1831 or 1832. However, there were few major changes in landholdings during the period, so it is possible to use the assessments with some confidence for a later period.[9] A detailed analysis of the study area shows both the usefulness and limitations of the 'open–close' model. Figure 32.1 above shows the numbers of landowners in each parish of the study area. As 21 parishes out of 32 (78 per cent) might be considered 'close', the study had a very high concentration compared to other parts of the country.[10] The five 'open' parishes were Tealby, Keelby, Nettleton, Binbrook and Ludford. Only Hatcliffe fits uneasily into the idea of an 'open–close' dichotomy.

There were seven parishes which might be categorised as 'close' parishes with a resident landowner: Brocklesby, the home of Lord Yarborough; North Willingham, the residence of the Bouchereits; South Elkington, home of the Smyths; Swinhope, the residence of the Alingtons; Hawerby, owned by Theophilius Harneis; Cuxwold, owned by the Thorolds; and Riby, owned by George Tomline. At first glance these parishes might appear similar. However, a closer inspection of the seven parishes shows marked differences. Yarborough, Alington, Smyth, Boucherett and Harneis were primarily resident in their parishes. Tomline had other houses which were at least equally important, whilst the Thorolds were not always resident at Cuxwold,[11] (Brocklesby was Yarborough's principal residence, although he did have properties elsewhere.)[12] Whilst Yarborough and Tomline can be considered as landed magnates,[13] Boucherett and Smyth both belonged to the middling ranks of the gentry, whilst Alington (1,200 acres),[14] Thorold (1,543 acres) and Harneis (450 acres) had relatively small estates. Thus the influence of these men was bound to vary, due both to their place of residence and their relative wealth and social position.

However, these differences should not be exaggerated, communality of interest and action was greater than any differences between the

9 Major changes in landownership do occur towards the end of the period under study, when landlords, finding themselves in financial difficulties in the 1870s, sold farms principally to their tenants. One exception was the parish of Wyham cum Cadeby which was bought by the Nelson family of Great Limber around 1850 and then sold again in 1864–65. Olney, *Rural society*, 59; Brocklesby Archive, Brocklesby House, Lincolnshire; Sale documents.

10 Holderness, '"Open" and "close" parishes', 129–39 suggested that nationally the average number of 'close' townships was about 20 per cent, rising to 40 per cent in some areas.

11 Apart from Riby Hall, Tomline also owned 1 Carlton House Terrace in London and Orwell Park, Ipswich; Stenton, *Who's who*. The Thorolds illustrate well the dangers of a static classification such as the one used here. The extent to which the family were resident is unclear. They built Cuxwold Hall in 1861 and certainly lived there for some time, but in the 1870s their tenant farmer, John Sowerby, was resident, and indeed bought the whole parish from them in 1877. I am grateful to Mr Michael Sleight for this information.

12 Yarborough also owned Manby Hall, Brigg and 17 Arlington Street, London; Walford, *County families*.

13 Apart from 8,439 acres in Lincolnshire, Tomline also had 18,473 acres in Suffolk; Bateman, *The acre-ocracy of England*.

14 For a brief background of the Alington family see Smith, *Claribel*, chapter 1.

gentry. This would appear the case particularly when viewed from below. It is unlikely that the labourer would perceive any great difference in attitude and behaviour between the owners of 1,000 and 5,000 acres.

In addition to the 'close' parishes with a resident landowner, there were 20 'close' parishes with a non-resident landowner, 10 belonging to Lord Yarborough, 4 owned by other Lincolnshire landowners and 6 owned by landlords from further afield. Quite clearly, even from this somewhat crude categorisation, there must have been considerable differences between these parishes in the role of the landowner.

Apart from these 'open' parishes, there was one other parish with no dominant landowner: Hatcliffe with six landowners, the largest of whom, Francis Sowerby, only owned a quarter of the parish (or at least paid one quarter of the whole tax assessment).[15] This is in sharp contrast to Rothwell, which also had six landowners, but in this instance Lord Yarborough owned over half the parish. We might therefore expect different socio-economic characteristics in Hatcliffe from the 'close' parishes where there was a dominant landowner.

Finally, there were five settlements comprising seven 'open' parishes, Keelby , Nettleton, Tealby, Ludford (Magna and Parva), and Binbrook (St Mary and St Gabriel).[16] These parishes were characterised by a much more fragmented landownership. However, a word of caution is necessary. For instance, Binbrook was effectively a 'close' parish surrounding an 'open' village. Although Binbrook had 25 owners of land, over 5,000 acres of the parish were owned by only four landowners.[17] Similarly the Tennyson d'Eyncourts were resident at Bayons Manor in Tealby, and Sir Culling Eardley Smith had a seat at Nettleton, although he was seldom resident, preferring to live at Belvedere House in Kent.[18]

Having established the nature of landownership across the area, it is now necessary to turn our attention to the occupational structure of the various parishes. In general terms, there were three principal forms of work available in the area; work in agriculture, employment in domestic service or employment in trades and crafts. There were no

15 Lincolnshire Archives Office (hereafter given as LAO), Lindsey Quarter Sessions, 1831 land tax assessments.

16 The parishes of Binbrook St Mary and St Gabriel were formally merged with the building of the church of St Mary and St Gabriel in 1869. St Gabriel had been a ruin since at least the 1820s, LAO COR 85/4/64/4. Grant to Kaye, August 1827. The two Ludford parishes remained separate, although the two livings were consolidated in 1846; White, *Directory of Lincolnshire.*

17 Olney, 'Labouring life', 12. For a more detailed study of Binbrook, see Rawding, *Binbrook.*

18 Burke, *A visitation of the seats,* 137. Smith made sporadic contributions to the life of Nettleton, such as providing the village with allotments in 1833 and building a school in 1835. He died in May 1863 and his landholding was subsequently broken up and sold to several buyers. Nettleton WEA, *Aspects of life and work,* 7–8, 16–7. Sir Culling Eardley Smith changed his name by Royal Licence to Sir Culling Eardley Eardley in 1847. Russell, *A history of elementary schools,* 21.

real opportunities in industry or mining (although there was a small iron mine at Nettleton from the 1860s) and there were very few employed in the professions.

Agriculture

Farming was the main activity underpinning the economic life of the Lincolnshire Wolds. Farms were generally large on the Wolds,[19] and had been so since as early as the sixteenth century.[20] This was initially out of necessity, the poor chalk soils being insufficiently productive to support the smaller farmer. Major changes in agriculture at the end of the eighteenth century led to massive improvements in the productivity of the land. This was made possible by chalking and boning, the planting of turnips, and the use of oil cake for sheep feeding which enriched the land further still.[21] For this land to be cultivated, however, it required large-scale investment.[22] This pattern of large farmers continued throughout the century. In 1832–33, 26,384 acres of the Brocklesby estate were farmed by 46 tenants in holdings of over 300 acres. Of this acreage, 15,244 acres were held by only 20 tenants in farms of 600 acres or more.[23] Moreover, in the 1870s, at the height of the 'Revolt of the Field', a meeting of farmers held in Binbrook was attended by 57 farmers, who between them held over 38,000 acres of land.[24]

At the other end of the farming spectrum, there were few smallholders and little evidence of any 'peasant' tradition.[25] The smallholder, or cottager[26] as he was known locally, was a relatively insignificant element, in terms of acreage, in the agrarian economy of the Wolds. However, he was of greater importance numerically. In 1851, 133 farmers out of 296 (45 per cent) were listed as employing no labour.[27] Although their acreage was insignificant when compared to their larger neighbours, the smallholders were concentrated in specific parishes. The spatial distribution of large and small farms suggests that the physical geography of the area played an important role in

19 Fuller, 'Landownership in Lindsey', 89.

20 Thirsk, *English peasant farming*, 84.

21 Beastall, *Agricultural revolution in Lincolnshire*, 117; Thirsk, *English peasant farming*, 257. On sheep farming see Perkins, 'Sheep farming in Lincolnshire'. For a useful discussion on the importance of the turnip see Timmer, 'The turnip and the agricultural revolution'.

22 Clarke, *Farming of Lincolnshire*, 76–7; Young, *Agriculture of Lincoln*, 21.

23 Olney, *Lincolnshire politics*, 26–7; LAO, YARB 5 Surveys. Farm size does not necessarily correlate with acreage occupied by a single farmer. Many of the wealthier tenant farmers seem to have held several farms at a time.

24 *Lincolnshire Rutland and Stamford Mercury*, 13 March 1874.

25 Reed, 'The peasantry of nineteenth century England'; 'Nineteenth century rural England'.

26 There seems to be no hard-and-fast definition of the term 'cottagers', however, in Lincolnshire at least it is never used for holdings of more than about ten acres.

27 These figures are derived from the CEBs and should be regarded as approximate.

Figure 32.2 Farm size in the study area, 1851

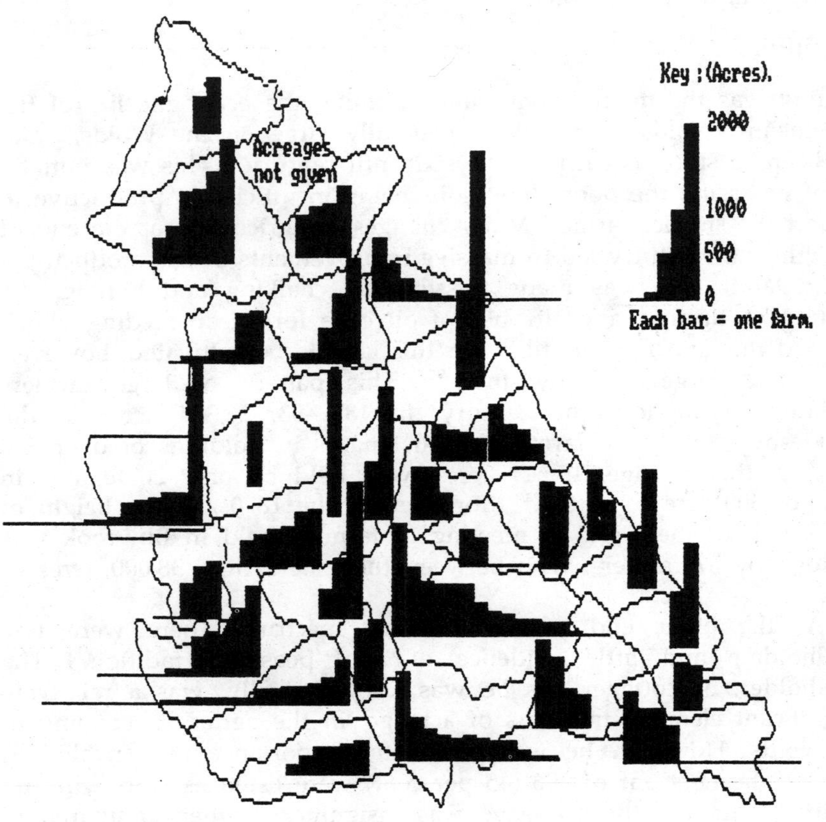

Notes: There are limitations to this data in as much as farm and parish boundaries did not always coincide and acreage information may be incomplete. Nevertheless, the material is useful at the general level to provide an indication of differences between areas.

influencing farm size. Figure 32.2 above shows farm size by parish in 1851. The areas on the higher Wolds, with their lighter, more marginal soils were dominated by larger farms, whilst the few smallholdings were found in the scarp slope parishes, such as Tealby, and to a lesser extent in the large 'open' villages such as Binbrook.

Agricultural work was the principal employment in all parishes on the Wolds, except Brocklesby. However, as might be expected, there were considerable differences between parishes. The 'open' parishes had lower percentages of agricultural workers than the averages (see

Table 32.1 The occupation structure of the labour force in the study area, 1851

	Population 1851	Agriculture		Domestic servants		Trades & crafts	
		n.	%	n.	%	n.	%
'Open' parishes							
Binbrook	1,313	267	50	97	18	152	28
Tealby	861	146	50	48	16	87	30
Keelby	859	151	49	43	14	108	35
Ludford	764	178	65	43	16	51	19
Nettleton	524	141	70	38	19	17	9
Total	4,321	883	54	269	17	415	26
'Close' parishes							
1. *Resident landowner*							
South Elkington	281	70	52	48	36	13	10
Brocklesby	269	31	26	69	58	13	10
Riby	247	65	60	22	20	12	12
North Willingham	234	58	57	27	27	13	13
Swinhope	128	30	58	16	31	4	8
Hawerby cum Beelsby	85	23	62	14	38	0	0
Cuxwold	68	21	61	7	23	3	10
Total	1,312	298	53	203	36	61	11
2. *Absentee landowner*							
Great Limber	531	127	54	64	27	41	17
Walesby	331	96	70	25	18	16	12
Rothwell	265	67	67	17	17	13	13
Irby	253	72	70	15	14	14	14
Swallow	215	59	66	19	22	10	11
Kelstern	195	67	74	13	14	10	11
Thoresway	175	75	77	17	17	3	3
Beelsby	175	57	70	9	11	16	19
Wold Newton	175	52	78	8	12	6	9
Cabourne	165	42	60	15	21	10	14
Normanby Le Wold	149	57	77	16	22	1	1
Stainton Le Vale	144	50	83	10	17	0	0
East Ravendale	135	36	63	21	37	0	0
North Ormsby	131	41	76	7	13	6	11
Wyham cum Cadeby	128	30	60	16	33	1	2
Thorganby	120	37	63	15	25	0	0
Croxby	114	42	70	17	28	0	0
North Elkington	104	33	80	6	15	2	5
Kirmond Le Mire	62	20	80	5	20	0	0
Total	3,567	1,060	69	315	21	156	10
No dominant landowner							
Hatcliffe	147	40	63	13	21	9	14
Overall average	9,347	2,281	62	800	21	641	17

Notes: The classification of the workforce used follows that of Tillott, 'Analysis of census returns'.

Table 32.1 above), as did those parishes with resident landowners, whilst the remaining 'close' parishes had very high percentages employed in agriculture, reflecting the dominance of agricultural work in these parishes when compared with the more diverse employment base of the 'open' parishes and the greater importance of domestic service in those parishes with resident landowners.

The agricultural labour force was highly stratified. This stratification had considerable consequences for the spatial division of labour with the higher-paid socially superior, 'confined' men being abnormally concentrated in the 'close' parishes. Perhaps, to be more accurate, it should be said that these men lived 'on the farms'. The standard of living of these confined men was higher, their employment more secure and their housing of better quality than those below them in the labouring hierarchy.

The day men, with their wives and children, lived in the 'open' villages. Their employment was much less reliable, and the 'open' villages offered the only form of housing that was available. Of labourers, Caird noted in 1851:

> In some localities they pay very high rents for their cottages, being swept out of close parishes . . . and obliged to compete with each other for the possession of the limited number of cottages run up by speculators in open parishes. They are compelled to live at great distances from work. It is quite common for them to ride on donkeys a distance of six or seven miles.[28]

It was also quite common for them to walk.

Agricultural gangs were concentrated in the 'open' villages and surrounding market towns. On the Wolds, Binbrook was the centre of the gangs, supplying labour to many of the surrounding 'close' parishes. In November 1865, there were 6 or 7 gangmasters employing 203 people.[29] These numbers increased in the summer. The rector of Binbrook, John Thomas Huntley, commented:

> The parish of Binbrooke furnishes, perhaps, as extensive an exhibit of the mischief emanating from [what] is called 'ganging' as may be found elsewhere upon the Wolds of Lincolnshire. Binbrooke is encircled by other lordships and hamlets of comparatively sparse population, where the habitations of the poor have been purposely few to avoid settlements under former poor laws; consequently these outlying districts draw largely upon the inhabitants of Binbrooke for agricultural labour, which explains the fact of having so many gangs issuing from my parish.[30]

These spatial variations in the composition of the agricultural labour

28 Caird, *English agriculture*, 197. For a similar situation in Nottinghamshire see Mills, *English rural communities*.

29 *Children's Employment Commission*, BPP 1867, report of Mr F. D. Lange, 5.

30 *First Report of the Commissioners on the Employment of Children, Young Persons and Women in Agriculture*, Appendix Part 1, BPP 1867, Mr Stanhope's report, 6.

force reinforced and heightened socio-economic differences between the 'open' and 'close' villages.

Domestic service

A second major occupational category open to the labouring classes was domestic service. Generally, numbers employed in domestic service reached unprecedented heights during the Victorian period.[31] An analysis of the structure of domestic service on the Wolds provides some insights into the variations in the social structure of 'open' and 'close' villages (see Table 32.1).

The presence of a large landowner in a parish was bound to have a massive impact on the cultural, social and economic life of the parish and its parishioners. At the most basic level, the landowner was likely to be the principal employer, and the occupational structure of the parish would be moulded around his requirements for labour. For instance, in the 1830s, the Yarboroughs employed about 20 men full-time in the kitchen garden and flower garden at Brocklesby,[32] and throughout the century employed a small army of retainers. Domestic life in these large establishments was carefully structured, with a clear-cut division of labour, and distinct segregation between servants, although in more modest establishments this division of labour was less rigid.[33]

In 1851, 58 per cent of the labour force in Brocklesby was in service, reflecting the importance of the Earl of Yarborough's household. Apart from the landowners, the second group which employed large numbers of servants was the larger farmers. An analysis of farm households in the 1851 census indicates this clearly. There were only 12 domestic servants resident on the 60 farms of less than 100 acres (0.2 servants/farm), whilst the 126 farms of more than 100 acres had 285 domestic servants resident (2.3 servants/farm). The larger farms (over 500 acres) had a disproportionate number of domestic servants living-in (59 farms with 186 domestic servants – 3.2 servants/farm). The parishes with the smallest proportions of domestic servants were the 'open' parishes which had less than 18 per cent of their workforce employed in domestic service. The concentration of this form of master–servant relationship within certain types of 'close' parish and its relative absence from the 'open' villages certainly would have increased the social differences between the village types.

31 Horn, *The Victorian servant*. Every self-respecting middle-class household was expected to have a certain number of servants, the number employed reflecting one's social station. The whole system was sufficiently formalised for Mrs Beeton to publish precise guidelines as to how many servants a household should have, and what the various grades of servant should be paid. See Goldby, *Culture and society*, 190–1.

32 LAO, YARB 7/8.

33 Horn, *The changing countryside*, 58.

Table 32.2 Service provision in the study area, 1851

		Occupations																															
	Pop.	1	2	3	4	5	6	7	8	9	a	b	c	d	e	f	g	h	i	j	k	l	m	n	o	p	q	r	s	t	u	v	w
Binbrook	1,313	x	x	x	x	x	x	x	x	x	x	x	x	x	x	x	x	x	x		x	x	x	x	x	x							
Tealby	861	x	x		x	x	x	x	x	x	x	x	x	x	x	x	x	x	x	x													
Keelby	859	x	x	x	x	x		x		x	x	x		x	x	x				x						x	x	x	x				
Ludford	764	x	x	x	x	x		x	x	x	x	x		x						x											x		
Great Limber	531	x	x		x	x	x	x	x	x																						x	
Nettleton	524	x	x		x	x	x		x			x																					
Walesby	331	x		x	x	x		x		x																							
South Elkington	281	x				x					x		x																				
Brockelsby	269	x																x															x
Rothwell	265	x	x	x	x	x		x	x																								
Irby	253	x	x	x			x																										
Riby	247	x		x			x																										
North Willingham	234	x	x	x	x		x						x																				
Swallow	215	x	x	x	x			x					x																				
Kelstern	195	x	x	x	x		x	x																									
Wold Newton	175	x		x			x		x																								
Beelsby	175	x	x	x							x																						
Thoresway	175																																
Cabourne	165	x	x								x																						
Normanby Le Wold	149																																
Hatcliffe	147			x		x			x				x																				
Stainton Le Vale	144																																
East Ravendale	135																																
North Ormsby	131																																
Swinhope	128																																
Wyham/Cadeby	128																																
Thorganby	120	x	x	x																													
Croxby	114																																
North Elkington	104																																
Hawerby/Beesby	85																																
Cuxwold	68																																
Kirmond Le Mire	62																																

Key:
1 = Blacksmith
2 = Wheelwright
3 = Shopkeeper
4 = Publican
5 = Shoemaker
6 = Teacher
7 = Grocer
8 = Miller
9 = Butcher
a = Tailor
b = Carrier
c = Bricklayer/builder
d = Carpenter
e = Land surveyor
f = Doctor
g = Saddler
h = Plumber/glazier
i = Bonnet maker
j = Baker
k = Barber
l = Machine maker
m = Rope and twine maker
n = Agricult. implement maker
o = Tinner/brazier
p = Hairdresser
q = Hawker
r = Mole catcher
s = Painter
t = Seed merchant
u = Druggist
v = Brickmaker
w = Station master

Trades and services

On the Wolds, broadly speaking, the larger the village, the greater the percentage of the working population involved in trades and services (see Table 32.1), and the wider the range of services available. This can be equated with the degree of 'openness' of a parish. The 'open' villages were larger and had a wider range of service provision (see Table 32.2 above). There is a clear distinction between the 'open' parishes where, on average, 26 per cent of the workforce was employed in trades and crafts and the 'close' parishes where only 10 per cent was employed in trades and crafts.[34] The larger villages fulfilled a role as service centres for the smaller villages surrounding them, a factor which further distinguished 'open' villages from their 'close' neighbours.

The spatial variations in the number of tradesmen as a proportion of the workforce has important implications for the study of place. Whilst agriculture was undoubtedly the dominant economic activity and the larger farmers were considered to be the leaders of society, tradesmen, particularly those less dependent on the large landowner or farmer for work, did provide an alternative leadership which might be seen in the chapels and societies of their villages. They were, in many cases, the more politically aware members of the village and where they were concentrated in larger numbers, as in the 'open' villages, society might be very different, and a good deal less deferential, than in the 'close' village where all employment was dependent upon the farmer or landowner. Figure 32.3 below summarises the variations in occupation structure between the parishes on the Wolds. It shows the three principal occupation groupings mapped against each other. From this it can be seen clearly that there were significant differences between the village types. The 'open' villages concentrated in the portion of the graph indicating high trades and crafts, low service and agriculture; whilst those parishes with resident gentry had their occupational structure skewed towards employment in service. For the vast majority of parishes on the Wolds, however, agricultural employment was, without question, the dominant feature of their occupational structure.[35]

Gender balance and culture

Alongside these variations in the occupational structure of the villages, there were also marked differences in the sex ratio of parishes within the area (see Table 32.3 below). There were far more females resident in the 'open' parishes than in the 'close' parishes. As an overall ratio, there were 118 males to every 100 females in the 'close' parishes,

34 PRO IR18 5338. In Tealby, there was also evidence of rural industry during the first half of the nineteenth century when three corn mills and two paper mills were working in the village. However, by 1850: 'only 2 paper mills were now worked – 1 of the 5 had ceased to be used 10 years ago – another 15 years and the other had been divested of all its machinery'.

35 There are also obvious dangers in reading too much into this type of analysis. There were limitations with regard to the occupation descriptions contained in the census returns. A second factor, particularly relevant to those parishes with a resident landowner, concerned whether the landowner was resident at the time of the census or not (see Table 32.3).

Figure 32.3 Occupational structure on the Lincolnshire Wolds: 1851

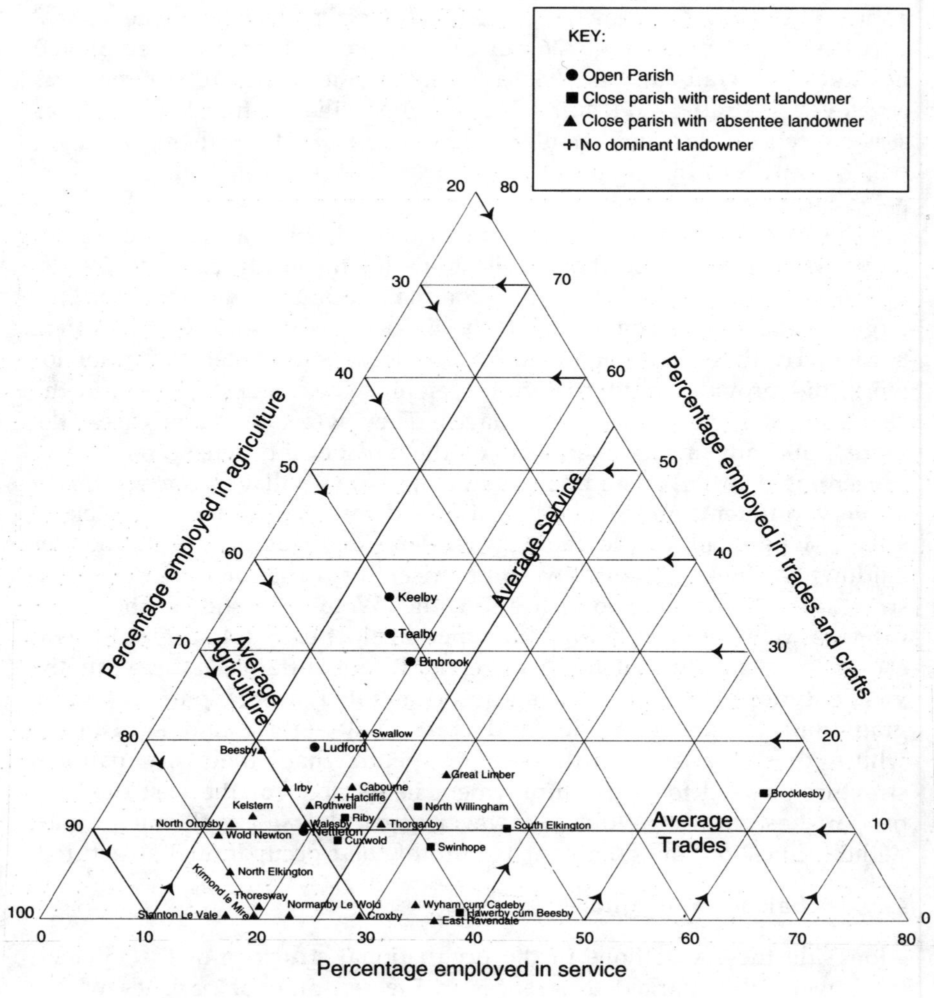

Notes: The figure only shows the principal occupational groupings. In only one instance does any other category involve more than 5 per cent of the total population of a parish, namely Riby with 8 per cent.

compared with 106:100 in the 'open' parishes. This reflects the demands of the labour market. In rural society generally, there were only limited employment opportunities for females. The vast majority of the work available was in agriculture and was considered to be men's work.[36] In

[36] There are dangers in taking the census at face value since it certainly underestimated the amount of female work, particularly in agriculture, see Higgs, 'Women, occupation and work' and Higgs, 'Occupational censuses'.

Table 32.3 The population structure of the Lincolnshire Wolds: sex ratios

	Pop. 1851	Male	Female	Sex ratio m/f
'Open' parishes				
Binbrook	1,313	667	646	103/100
Tealby	861	438	423	103/100
Keelby	859	439	420	104/100
Ludford	764	394	370	106/100
Nettleton	524	281	243	116/100
Total	4,321	2,222	2,105	105/100
'Close' parishes				
Great Limber	531	285	246	113/100
Walesby	331	178	153	116/100
South Elkington	281	146	135	108/100
Brocklesby	269	134	135	99/100
Rothwell	265	144	121	119/100
Irby	253	150	103	146/100
Riby	247	131	116	112/100
North Willingham	234	126	108	117/100
Swallow	215	117	98	119/100
Kelstern	195	106	89	119/100
Thoresway	175	100	75	133/100
Wold Newton	175	97	78	124/100
Beelsby	175	94	81	116/100
Cabourne	165	87	78	111/100
Normancy Le Wold	149	83	66	126/100
Stainton Le Vale	144	76	68	112/100
East Ravendale	135	70	65	108/100
North Ormsby	131	70	61	115/100
Swinhope	128	61	67	89/100
Wyham cum Cadeby	128	60	68	88/100
Thorganby	120	68	52	131/100
Croxby	114	64	50	128/100
North Elkington	104	53	51	104/100
Hawerby cum Beesby	85	43	42	102/100
Cuxwold	62	35	27	130/100
Kirmond Le Mire	62	35	27	130/100
Total	4,879	2,615	2,264	115/100
No dominant landowner				
Hatcliffe	147	80	67	119/100
Surrounding market towns				
Louth	10,467	49,236	5,541	89/100
Grimsby	8,660	4,721	4,139	114/100
Caistor	2,166	1,051	1,115	94/100
Market Rasen	2,100	1,016	1,094	93/100
Total	23,603	11,714	11,889	98/100

the smaller parishes, work was restricted effectively to domestic service only (86 per cent of all female employment), whilst in the larger parishes there were more opportunities for work in trades such as

Table 32.4 Female employment on the Lincolnshire Wolds, 1851

	Occupation category														
	Farmer		Agricult. labourer		Trades/ crafts		Domestic service		Profess-ionel		Other		Total		% of labour force
	n.	%	n.	%	n.	%	n.	%	n.	%	n.	%	n.	%	
'Open'	3	1.1	8	2.8	51	18.0	203	71.7	15	5.3	2	0.7	283	100	17.5
'Close'	3	0.7	10	2.3	40	9.2	376	86.0	7	1.6	1	0.2	437	100	19.8
Overall	6	0.8	18	2.5	91	12.6	579	80.4	22	3.1	3	0.4	720	100	18.8

dressmaking (18 per cent). As can be seen from Table 32.4 above, there was little other difference between the sexual division of labour in 'open' and 'close' parishes. Overall, however, employment opportunities for women were greater in the surrounding market towns where females were in the majority.

The preceding sections have shown that there were clear differences between the populations of 'open' and 'close' villages. The greater diversity of occupation in the larger villages led to a much wider range of interests and reduced the likelihood of dominance – economic, social or otherwise – by one particular group. At the same time, larger villages had better communications and contacts with the outside world. This in turn led to a more cosmopolitan culture with greater access to external influences when compared to the more isolated, and therefore more insular, smaller villages. This is reflected to some extent in the provision of Post Offices, and in the number of carriers present in these villages.[37] These potential effects of size would heavily influence the ways in which people within the different types of village behaved and reacted to given social situations. However, this generalisation is mitigated by the greater stability of the population in larger villages when compared with smaller villages.

A general description of 'close' parishes as landlord-dependent and controlled can be contrasted with the independence of the 'open' villages. However, it is difficult to determine the extent to which independence was a consequence of landownership and to what extent it was determined by the size of the village and also the effect any given theoretical level of independence might have on the actual life of any place, or for that matter whether size influenced landownership.

Differences between life in 'open' and 'close' parishes can be highlighted. Housing provision, the composition of the labour force and spatial variations in the distribution of charity and social provision make it clear that the occupants of 'close' parishes were more privileged materially, enjoying a significantly higher quality of life than their counterparts in the 'open' parishes. Labourers in the 'close'

37 For a more general discussion see Gregory, 'The friction of distance?'.

villages were considered of a higher class than those of the 'open' villages.

The 'open' village contained a greater proportion of tradesmen than the 'close' parishes, whilst its agricultural labour force was dominated by the poorer-paid day-labourers rather than the better-off confined men. The two groups co-existed, but in many ways their activities were diametrically opposed. By articulating this contradiction, we can build up a picture of social life in the 'open' village.

The casual labourer was largely responsible for the less 'acceptable' aspects of the culture of the 'open' villages. The more traditional aspects of 'popular culture' appear to have lingered longer in the 'open' parishes than elsewhere,[38] with reports of 'Rough Music' occurring regularly throughout the century,[39] along with events such as wife-selling.[40]

A second, and very distinct, strand of independence can be traced through the 'respectable and sober' labouring classes who attended chapel and literary institutes, and formed friendly societies, clothing clubs, pig clubs, and cow clubs.[41] This group was found throughout the study area and, although the physical evidence of Temperance Halls, Literary Institutes and Friendly Society Courts and Lodges is concentrated in the 'open' villages, this was almost certainly a consequence of their size and function as central places, rather than a reflection of the exclusivity of this type of activity to the 'open' villages.

The role of the leading members of village society, even in the 'open' villages needs to be emphasised, since many of the cultural and improving activities of the villages were either fostered or encouraged from above. It was a combination of this patronage and the self-improving ethic of the independent labouring man which contributed so much to the respectable ethos within the larger villages.

Summary

We have seen that different villages developed varied socio-economic characteristics as a result of a number of disperate economic and political features. These interacted to create a distinctive and contrasting *genre de vie* for the Wolds.

These findings are clearly of importance to an understanding of the operation of society on the Wolds. The overall differences in population structure can be largely attributed to the operations of the labour

38 See Yeo and Yeo, *Popular culture and class conflict*; Malcolmson, *Popular recreations in English society*, for a fuller discussion of notions of popular culture.

39 As late as 1872, the 'tin-pot band' was used against a promiscuous coal-dealer in Market Rasen, *Lincolnshire Rutland and Stamford Mercury*, 19 January 1872.

40 These were reported with surprising regularity in the first half of the century, although not specifically in the Wolds area – for Barton-on-Humber see *Lincolnshire Rutland and Stamford Mercury*, 2 February 1821, 12 March 1847 and 22 August 1856. I am grateful to Rex Russell for this information.

41 See Russell, *Friendly societies* and Rawding, *Keelby*, 99–102.

market and the somewhat specialised spatial division of labour that developed as a result of the contrasting employment structures between the large 'open' parishes, with their more diverse employment structure and greater concentration of lower-paid agricultural labourers, and the smaller 'close' parishes, where employment was almost entirely agricultural and the resident labourers were the élite of the agricultural workforce. Clearly, the differences in availability and quality of cottage accommodation and the population structure were a salient feature of the socio-economic characteristics of all the villages.

Accumulated Bibliography

Anon, 'The records of the Tithe Redemption Commission', *Journal of the Society of Archivists*, **1** 5 (1957), 132–39.

Anon, 'The Isle of Thanet', in *The land we live in*, (n.d. *c.* 1840s).

Acland, A. D. H. ed. 'Memoir and letters of Sir Thomas Dyke Acland', (London, 1902).

Adburgham, A. *Shops and shopping, 1800–1914: where and in what manner the well-dressed Englishwoman bought her clothes*, (London, 1964).

Akerman, S. 'Internal migration, industrialisation and urbanisation, 1895–1930', *Scandinavian Economic History Review*, **23** (1975), 149–53.

Alexander, D. *Retailing in England during the Industrial Revolution*, (London, 1970).

Anderson, M. *Family structure in nineteenth-century Lancashire*, (Cambridge, 1971).

Anderson, M. 'Urban migration in nineteenth-century Lancashire: some insights into two competing hypotheses', *Annales de Démographie Historique*, (1971), 13–26. Reprinted as an article in Unit 8, D301 *Historical data and the social sciences*, Open University, (Milton Keynes, 1974), 131–43.

Anderson, M. 'The study of family structure', in Wrigley ed. *Nineteenth-century society*, 47–81.

Anderson, M. 'Standard tabulation procedures for the census enumerators' books, 1851–1891', in Wrigley ed. *Nineteenth-century society*, 134–45.

Anderson, M. 'Marriage patterns in Victorian Britain: an analysis based on registration district data for England and Wales, 1861', *Journal of Family History*, **1** (1976), 55–79.

Anderson, M. 'Urban migration in Victorian Britain: problems of assimilation?', in E. François ed. *Immigration et société urbaine en Europe Occidentale, XVI–XX siècles*, (Paris, 1985), 79–91.

Anderson, M. 'Households, families and individuals in 1851', *Continuity and Change*, **3** (1988), 421–38.

Anderson, M. 'What is new about the modern family? An historical perspective', Office of Population Censuses and Surveys, *Occasional Papers* **31** (1983), 2–16. Reprinted in Drake, *Time, family and community*, 67–90.

Anderson Graham, P. *The rural exodus*, (London, 1892).

Ariès, P. *Centuries of Childhood*, (London, 1962).

Arkell, T. 'Multiplying factors for estimating population totals from the hearth tax', *Local Population Studies*, **28** (1987), 51–7.

Arkell, T. 'A method for estimating population totals from the Compton census return', in K. Schürer and T. Arkell eds *Surveying the people. The interpretation and use of document sources for the study of population in the later seventeenth century*, (Oxford, 1992), 97–116.

Armstrong, M. E. ed. *An industrial island: a history of Scunthorpe*, (Scunthorpe, 1981).

Armstrong, W. A. 'Social structure from the early census returns', in Wrigley *et al.* eds *An introduction to English historical demography*, 209–37.

Armstrong, W. A. 'The use of information about occupation', in Wrigley ed.

Nineteenth-century society, 191–310.
Armstrong, W. A. 'A note on the household structure of mid-nineteenth-century York in comparative perspective', in Laslett and Wall eds *Family and household in past time*, 205–14.
Armstrong, W. A. *Stability and change in an English country town: a social study of York, 1801–51*, (Cambridge, 1974).
Armstrong, W. A. 'The census enumerators' books: a commentary', in Lawton ed. *The census and social structure*, 28–81.
Aslett, P. *et al. Victorians on the move: research in the census enumerator's books 1851–1881*, (Thornborough, 1984).
Baines, E. *History, Directory and Gazetteer of the County of York*, Vol. II, (Leeds, 1823).
Baker, D. ed. *The inhabitants of Cardington in 1782*, The Publications of the Bedfordshire Historical Record Society **52**, (1973).
Banks, J. A. 'The social structure of nineteenth century England as seen through the census, in Lawton ed. *The census*, 179–223.
Banks, S. J. '"Open" and "close" parishes in nineteenth century England', (unpublished PhD thesis, University of Reading, 1982).
Bateman, J. *The acre-ocracy of England*, (London, 1876).
Beastall, T. W. *The agricultural revolution in Lincolnshire*, (Lincoln, 1978).
Bell, F. E. E. *At the works*, (London, 1907).
Benjamin, E. A. 'Human afflictions: a study of the north Ceregigion census returns, 1851–1871', *Ceredigion*, **10** (1985), 155–60.
Bennett, W. 'The farming of Bedfordshire', *Journal of the Royal Agricultural Society of England*, **18** (1857), 1–29.
Benwell, R. M. and Benwell, G. A. 'The Llandyrnog householders' schedules for the 1851 census', *Local Population Studies*, **28** (1982), 89–90.
Berry, B. M. and Schofield, R. S. 'Age at baptism in pre-industrial England', *Population Studies*, **25** 3 (1971), 453–63.
Birch, A. *Economic history of the British iron and steel industry, 1784–1879*, (London, 1967).
Body, G. A. 'The administration of the poor laws in Dorset 1760–1834, with special reference to agrarian distress', (unpublished PhD thesis, University of Southampton, 1965).
Booth, C. ed. *Life and labour of the people in London*, 17 vols, (London, 1889–1902).
Boulton, J. *Neighbourhood and society: a London suburb in the nineteenth century*, (Cambridge, 1987).
Bradley, L. *A glossary for local population studies*, 2nd edition, (Matlock, 1978).
Brand, K. *The Park Estate, Nottingham*, (Nottingham Civic Society, n. d.).
Bryant, D. 'Demographic trends in South Devon in the mid-nineteenth century', in K J. Gregory and W. D. Ravenhill eds *Exeter essays in geography in honour of Arthur Davies*, (Exeter, 1971), 125–42.
Brayshay, M. 'Using American records to study nineteenth-century emigration from Britain', *Area*, **11** (1979), 156–60.
Brayshay, M. 'Government emigration from Plymouth in the nineteenth century', *Transactions of the Devonshire Association*, **112** (1980), 185–213.
Brayshay, W. M. 'The demography of three West Cornwall mining communities: a society in decline', (unpublished PhD thesis, University of Exeter, 1977).
Brunner, E. *Holiday making and the holiday trades*, (Oxford, 1945).

Budd and T. Guinnane, J. W. 'Intentional age-misreporting, age-heaping, and the 1908 Old Age Pensions Act in Ireland', *Population Studies*, **45** (1991), 497–518.

Burke, G. 'The Cornish diaspora of the nineteenth century', in S. Marks and P. Richardson eds *International labour migration: historical perspectives*, (London, 1984), 57–75.

Burke, J. B. *A visitation of the seats and arms of the noblemen and gentlemen of Great Britain and Ireland*, (London, 1855).

Burton, A. 'Looking forward from Ariès? Pictorial and material evidence for the history of childhood and family life', *Continuity and Change*, **4** (1989), 203–29.

Burton, V. C. 'Counting seafarers: the published records of the registry of merchant seamen', *The Mariner's Mirror*, **71** 3 (1985), 305–20.

Butler, D. J. *Durham City: the 1851 census*, (Durham, 1992).

Butler, R. M. 'The common lands of the Borough of Nottingham', *Transactions of the Thoroton Society*, **54** (1950).

Caird, J. *English agriculture in 1850–51*, (London, 1968).

Cairncross, A. K. 'Internal migration in Victorian England', *Manchester School*, **17** (1949), 67–87. Reprinted in A. K. Cairncross, *Home and foreign investment, 1870–1913*, (Cambridge, 1953).

Cannadine, D. 'Residential differentiation in nineteenth-century towns: from shapes on the ground to shapes in society' in Johnson and Pooley eds *The structure of nineteenth century cities*, 235–51.

Carter, H. *The study of urban geography*, (London, 1981).

Carter, H. and Wheatley, S. *Merthyr Tydfil in 1851*, (Cardiff, 1982).

Chambers, J. D. *The making of modern Nottingham* (Nottingham, 1945).

Chapman, S. D. 'Working class housing in Nottingham during the industrial revolution', *Transactions of the Thoroton Society*, **67** (1963), 67–92.

Charlton, C. '"Bag in hand, and with a provision of papers for an emergency" – An impression of the 1891 census from the pages of some contemporary newspapers', *Local Population Studies*, **47** (1991), 81–8.

Chartres, J. A. 'Country trades, crafts and professions, 1750–1850', in G. E. Mingay ed. *Agrarian history of England and Wales, 1750–1850*, Vol. VI, (Oxford, 1989), 416–66.

Chartres, J. A. and Turnbull, G. L. 'Country craftsmen', in G. E. Mingay ed. *The Victorian countryside*, Vol. I, (London, 1981), 314–28.

Church, R. A. *Economic and social change in a Midland town*, (London, 1966).

Church, R. A. 'Labour supply and innovation 1800–1860: the boot and shoe industry', *Business History*, **12** (1970), 25–45.

Clark, P. 'The migrant in Kentish towns, 1580–1640', in P. Clark and P. Slack eds *Crisis and order in English towns 1500–1700*, (London, 1972), 117–63.

Clark, P. 'Occupations and the English Small Towns project at Leicester University', in Schürer and Diederiks eds *The use of occupations*, 23–7.

Clarke, J. A. *On the farming of Lincolnshire, Prize Essay*, (London, 1852).

Clifford, F. 'The Labour Bill in Farming', *Journal of the Royal Agricultural Society*, 2nd series **11** (1875), 67–127.

Coale, A. J. and Trussell, T. J. 'Model fertility schedules: variations in the age structure of childbearing human populations', *Population Index*, **40** (1974), 175–258.

Coale, A. J. and Trussell, T. J. 'Technical note: finding the two parameters that specify a model schedule of marital fertility', *Population Index*, **44** (1978), 203–13.

Collins, B. 'Irish migration to Dundee and Paisley', in J. M. Goldstrom and L. Clarkson eds *Irish population, economy and society: essays in honour of the late K. C. Connell*, (Oxford, 1981), 195–212.

Collins, B. 'The analysis of census returns: the 1901 census of Ireland', *Ulster Local Studies*, **15** 1 (1993), 38–46.

Collins, B. and Pryce, W. T. R. 'Census returns in England, Ireland, Scotland and Wales', audio-cassette 2A in P. Braham ed. *Using the past: audio-cassettes on sources and methods for family and community historians*, (The Open University, Milton Keynes, 1993).

Conrad, C. 'The emergence of modern retirement: Germany in international comparison (1850- 1960)', *Population* (English selection), **3** (1991), 171-200.

Constable, D. *Household structure in three English market towns, 1851–1871*, Geographical Papers no. 55, (Department of Geography, University of Reading, 1977).

Cowlard, K. C. 'The identification of social (class) areas and their place in nineteenth-century urban development', *Transactions of the Institute of British Geographers*, new series **4** 2 (1979), 239–57.

Crompton, C. A. 'Changes in rural service occupations during the nineteenth century: an evaluation of two sources for Hertfordshire, England', *Rural History*, **6** (1995), 193–203.

Cumbria Family History Society, *Transcript and Index for the 1851 Census of Wetheral, Warwick, Scotby, Crosby and Walby*, (Manchester, 1989).

Daff, T. 'The establishment of iron making at Scunthorpe, 1853–77', *Bulletin of Economic Research*, **25** (1973), 104–21.

Dainton, C. *The story of England's hospitals; with a foreword by Lord Amulree*, (London, 1961).

Darroch, A. C. 'Migrants in the nineteenth century; fugitives or families in motion?', *Journal of Family History*, **6** (1981), 257–77.

Davidoff L. and Hall, C. *Family fortunes: men and women of the English middle-class 1780–1850*, (London, 1977).

Davin, A. 'Working or helping? London working-class children in the domestic economy', in J. Smith, I. Wallerstein and H. Evers eds *Households and the world economy*, (London, 1984), 215–32.

Davis, D. *A History of shopping*, (London, 1966).

Dennis, R. J. 'Stability and change in urban communities: a geographical perspective', in Johnson and Pooley, *The structure of nineteenth century cities*, 253–81.

Dennis, R. J. *English industrial cities of the nineteenth century. A social geography*, (Cambridge, 1984).

Dillon, R. 'The Irish in Leeds, 1851–1861', *Thoresby Society Publications Miscellany*, **16** (1974), 1–28.

Drake, M. 'The census, 1801–1891', in Wrigley ed. *Nineteenth-century Society*, 7–46.

Drake, M. 'Ashford 1840–1870: a socio-demography study', unpublished Final Report, Centre for Research in the Social Sciences in the University of Kent at Canterbury, (1970).

Drake, M. 'A note on the enumerators', *Local Population Studies Society Newsletter*, **14** (1994), 12–15.

Drake, M. *Time, family and community,* (Oxford, 1994).
Drake, M. and Finnegan, R. eds *Studying family and community history, 19th and 20th centuries, IV, Sources and methods: a handbook,* (Cambridge, 1994).
Drake, M. and Mills, D. R. 'The census enumerators: an LPSS research project', *Local Population Studies Society Newsletter,* **14** (1994), 1–3.
Drake, M., Mills, D. R., Hodges, M. and Rau, D. *Getting into community history,* (Local Population Studies Society, 1995). Copies available from Dr D. A. Gatley, 114 Thornton Rd, Stoke-on-Trent, ST4 2BD.
Dupree, M. W. *Family structure in the Staffordshire Potteries 1840-1880,* (Oxford, 1995)
Ebery, M. and Preston, B. *Domestic service in late Victorian and Edwardian England, 1871–1914,* (Reading, 1976).
Elliott, B. *Wigston in 1891,* (published by the author, Oadby, 1994).
Etherington, J. E. 'The community origin of the Lewes Guy Fawkes night celebrations', *Sussex Archaeological Collections,* **128** (1990), 195–224.
Etherington, J. E. *The Bonfire Boys of Lewes, 1800–1913: a study in nominal record linkage,* (Local Population Studies Society, 1996). Copies available from Dr D. A. Gatley, 114 Thornton Rd, Stoke-on-Trent, ST4 2BD.
Evans, E. J. *Tithes and the Tithe Commutation Act 1836,* (London, 1978).
Everitt, A. 'Country carriers in the nineteenth century', *The Journal of Transport History,* new series **3** (1976), 179–203.
Flandrin, J-L. *Families in former times: kinship, household and sexuality,* (Cambridge, 1979).
Flinn, M. ed., *Scottish population history from the seventeenth century to the 1930s,* (Cambridge, 1977).
Fuller, H. A. 'Landownership in Lindsey circa 1800–1860, with particular reference to the role of the "large" landowner as an agent of agricultural improvement and landscape change', (unpublished MA thesis, University of Hull, 1974).
Fussell, G. 'Four centuries of farming systems in Devon 1500–1900', *Transactions of the Devonshire Association,* **83** (1951), 179–204.
Gales, K. E. and Marks, P. H. 'Twentieth-century trends in the work of women in England and Wales', *Journal of the Royal Statistical Society,* series A, **137** 1 (1974), 60–74.
Garrett, E. M. 'The trials of labour: motherhood versus employment in a nineteenth-century textile centre', *Continuity and Change,* 5 1 (1990), 121–54.
Garrett, E. M. 'The dawning of a new era? Women's work in England and Wales at the turn of the twentieth century', *Social History/Histoire Sociale,* (forthcoming, 1996).
Garrett, E. M., Reid, A., Schürer, K. and Szreter, S. R. S. *As others do around us: place, class and demography in England and Wales, 1891–1911,* (Cambridge, forthcoming).
Gibson, J. *Census returns 1841–81 on microfilm: a directory of local holdings in Great Britain, Channel Islands, Isle of Man,* fifth edition, (Federation of Family History Societies, Birmingham, 1990).
Gibson, J. 'Canal boat families in the Banbury and Neithrop census returns, 1841–91', *Cake and Cockhorse,* **12** (1993), 172–3.
Gibson, J. and Medlycott, M. *Local census listings,* 2nd edition, (Federation of Family History Societies, Birmingham, 1994).
Gillbank, B. H. *Visitors' and residents' directory and gazetteer of Scarborough and*

Whitby, (1855).

Gillis, J. R. Tilly, L. A. and Levine, D. eds *The European experience of declining fertility: a quiet revolution, 1859–1970*, (Oxford, 1992).

Glass, D. V. *Numbering the people. The eighteenth century population controversy and the development of census and vital statistics in Britain*, (Farnborough, 1973).

Glass, D. V. and Eversley, D. E. C. eds, *Population in history: essays in historical demography*, (London, 1965).

Goldby, J. M. ed. *Culture and society in Britain, 1850–1900: a source book of contemporary writings*, (Oxford, 1986).

Goodger, B. C. 'Social science models and historical data: the application of models of industrial structure to census material', *Journal of Regional and Local Studies*, **6** (1986), 45–57.

Goose, N. *Population, economy and family structure in Hertfordshire in 1851. Volume 1, The Berkhamsted Region*, (Hatfield, 1996).

Grabill, W. H. and Cho, L-J. 'Methodology for the measurement of current fertility from population data on young children', *Demography*, **2** (1965), 50–73.

Graham, J. *A history of the print works in the Manchester area*, (first published 1850, reprinted as a series of articles in *The Manchester Guardian*, 1894).

Greenhill, B. and Giffard, A. *Westcountrymen in Prince Edward's Isle*, (Newton Abbot, 1967).

Gregory, D. 'The friction of distance? Information circulation and the mails in early nineteenth century England', *Journal of Historical Geography*, **13** (1987), 130–54.

Grey, P. 'The pauper problem in Bedfordshire from 1795 to 1834', (unpublished MPhil thesis, University of Leicester, 1975).

Grigg, D. B. 'E. G. Ravenstein and the "laws of migration"', *Journal of Historical Geography*, **3** (1977), 41–54.

Gwynne, T. and Sill, M. 'Census enumeration books: a study of mid-century immigration', *Local Historian*, **12** (1976), 74–9.

Haines, M. R. *Fertility and occupation: population patterns in industrialisation*, (New York, 1979).

Hajnal, J. 'Age at marriage and proportions marrying', *Population Studies*, **7** (1953), 111–36.

Hajnal, J. 'European marriage patterns in perspective', in Glass and Eversley eds *Population in history*, 101–43.

Hajnal, J. 'Two kinds of preindustrial household formation system', *Population and Development Review*, **8** (1982), 449–94. Reprinted in Wall *et al.* eds, *Family Forms in Historic Europe*, 65–104.

Hall, R. 'Occupation and population structure in the Derbyshire Peak District in the mid-nineteenth century', *East Midland Geographer*, **6** (1974), 66–78.

Hallas, C. S. 'Economic and social change in Wensleydale and Swaledale in the nineteenth century', (unpublished PhD thesis, Open University, 1987).

Hallas, C. S. 'The social and economic impact of a rural railway: the Wensleydale line', *Agricultural History Review*, **34** (1986), 29–44.

Hallas, C. S. *The Wensleydale railway*, 2nd edition, (Hawes, 1991).

Hammel, E. A. and Laslett, P. 'Comparing household structure over time and between cultures', *Comparative Studies in Society and History*, **16** (1974), 73–103.

Hamilton-Jenkin, A. K. *Cornwall and its people*, (Newton Abbot, 1970).

Hareven, T. K. 'Cycles, courses and cohorts: reflections on theoretical and methodological approaches to the historical study of family development', *Journal of Social History,* **12** (1978), 97–109.

Hareven, T. K. *Family time and industrial time,* (Cambridge, 1982).

Hareven, T. K. 'Family history at the crossroads', *Journal of Family History,* **12** 1–3 (1987), ix–xxiii.

Hareven, T. K. 'Recent research on the history of the family', *American Historical Review,* **19** 1 (1991), 95–124. Abridged version reprinted in Drake, *Time, family and community,* 13–45.

Hareven, T. K. and Vinovskis, M. A. 'Patterns of childrearing in late nineteenth-century America: the determinants of marital fertility in five Massachusetts towns in 1880', in T. K. Hareven and M. A. Vinovskis eds *Family and population in nineteenth-century America* (Cambridge, 1978), 85–125.

Hargreaves, B. *Recollections of Broad Oak,* (1882).

Harrison, B. J. D. 'Iron masters and iron workers', in C. A. Hempstead ed. *Cleveland iron and steel: background and 19th century history,* (Redcar, 1979), 231–53.

Hartley, J. B. 'Maps for the local historian: enclosure and tithe maps', *Amateur Historian,* **7** (1966–7), 265–74. Reprinted in Hartley, *Maps for the local historian.*

Hartley, J. B. *Maps for the local historian: a guide to British sources,* (London, 1972).

Hartley, J. B. and Phillips, C. W. *The historian's guide to Ordnance Survey maps,* (London, 1964)

Harwood, W. *Chaps and maps: St Ives and the census,* (Stockton-on-Tees, 1996).

Haydon, E. 'Recording history for the future: Widworthy's occupations in 1992', *Devon and Cornwall Notes and Queries,* **37** (1993), 87–90.

Hendrick, H. 'The history of childhood and youth: a guide to the literature', *Faculty of Modern Studies Occasional Papers,* **1**, Oxford Polytechnic, (1981).

Henstock, A. ed. *Early Victorian Country Town: a portrait of Ashbourne in the mid-nineteenth century,* (Ashbourne, 1968).

Henstock, A. 'Group projects in local history: house repopulation in the mid-nineteenth century', *Bulletin of Local History: East Midland Region,* **6** (1971), 11–20.

Henstock, A. 'House repopulation from the land tax assessments in a Derbyshire market town', in Turner and Mills eds *Land and property,* 118–35.

Higgs, E. 'Domestic servants and households in Victorian England', *Social History,* **8** (1983), 203–10.

Higgs, E. 'Domestic service and household production', in A. V. John ed. *Unequal opportunities: women's employment in England 1800–1918,* (Oxford, 1986), 124–50.

Higgs, E. *Domestic servants and households in Rochdale, 1851–1871,* (New York, 1986).

Higgs, E. 'Women, occupations and work in the nineteenth-century censuses', *History Workshop Journal,* **23** (1987), 59–80.

Higgs, E. 'Structuring the past: the occupational, social and household classification of census data', *Computing and History Today,* **4** (1988), 24–30.

Higgs, E. *Making sense of the census: the manuscript returns of the census 1801–1901,* (London, 1989).

Higgs, E. 'The Public Record Office, the Historian, and Information

Technology', in G. H. Martin and P. Spufford eds *The records of the nation. The Public Record Office 1838–1988, the British Record Society 1888–1988*, (Woodbridge, 1990), 101–9.

Higgs, E. 'Occupational censuses and the agricultural workforce in Victorian England and Wales', *Economic History Review*, **48** 4 (1995), 700–16.

Higgs, E. *A clearer sense of the census. The Victorian censuses and historical research*, (London, 1996).

Hinde, P. R. A. and Woods, R. I. 'Variations in historical natural fertility patterns and the measurement of fertility control', *Journal of Biosocial Science*, **16** (1984), 309–21.

Holderness, B. A. '"Open" and "close" parishes in England in the eighteenth and nineteenth centuries', *Agricultural History Review*, **20** (1972), 126–39.

Holmes, R. S. 'Identifying nineteenth century properties', *Area*, **6** (1974), 273–7.

Holmes, R. S. and Armstrong, W. A. 'Social stratification', *Area*, **10** (1978), 126–8.

Honeybone, M. *The book of Grantham: the history of a market and manufacturing town*, (Buckingham, 1980).

Horn, C. A. and Horn, P. The social structure of an "industrial" community: Ivinghoe in Buckinghamshire in 1871', *Local Population Studies*, **31** (1983), 9–20.

Horn, P. 'Child workers in the pillow lace and straw plait trades of Victorian Buckinghamshire and Bedfordshire', *Historical Journal*, **17** 4 (1974), 779–96.

Horn, P. *The rural world, 1750–1850: social change in the English countryside*, (London, 1980).

Horn, P. *The changing countryside in Victorian and Edwardian England and Wales*, (London, 1984).

Horn, P. *The rise and fall of the Victorian servant*, (Gloucester, 1986).

Horrell, S. and Humphries, J. 'Women's labour force participation and the transition to the male-breadwinner family, 1790–1865', *Economic History Review*, **48** 1 (1995), 89–117.

Hoskins, W. G. *Fieldwork in local history*, (London, 1967).

Hutchins, J. *The history and antiquities of the County of Dorset*, 2nd edition, (1796).

Jackson, J. T. 'Long-distance migrant workers in nineteenth-century Britain: a case study of the St Helens' glassmakers', *Transactions of the Lancashire and Cheshire. Historical Society*, **131** (1982), 113–37.

Janssens, A. *Family and social change: the household as a process in an industrialising community*, (Cambridge, 1993).

Johnson, J. H. and Pooley, C. G. eds *The structure of nineteenth century cities*, (London, 1982).

Jones, E. 'The Welsh in London in the nineteenth century', *Cambria*, **12** (1985), 149–69.

Jones, E. L. 'The agricultural labour market in England, 1793–1872', *Economic History Review*, 2nd series **15** 1 (1962), 322–38.

Jones, R. E. 'Infant mortality in rural north Shropshire, 1561–1810', *Population Studies*, **30** 2 (1976), 305–17.

Jones, R. M. 'Welsh immigrants in the cities of north west England 1890–1930: some oral testimony', *Oral History*, **9** (1981), 33–41.

Kain, R. J. P. Fry, R. and Holt, H. *An atlas and index of the tithe files of mid-nineteenth-century England and Wales*, (Cambridge, 1986).

Kain, R. J. P. and Prince, H. C. *The tithe surveys of England and Wales*, (Cambridge, 1985).

Katz, M. M. *The people of Hamilton, Canada West: family and class in a mid-nineteenth-century city,* (London, 1975).

Kelly, E. R. ed. *Post Office directory of Yorkshire: North and East Ridings,* (London, 1857).

Kelly, E. R. ed. *Directory of the North and East Ridings, Yorkshire, with the City of York,* (London, 1893).

Kendall, H. P. *The story of Whitby jet,* (Whitby, 1936).

Knodel, J. 'An exercise in household composition for the use in courses in historical demography', *Local Population Studies,* **23** (1979), 10–23.

Krause, J. T. 'The changing adequacy of English registration, 1690–1837', in Glass and Eversley eds *Population history,* 379–93.

Kussmaul, A. *Servants in husbandry in early modern England,* (Cambridge, 1981).

Laslett, P. *The world we have lost,* (London, 1965).

Laslett, P. 'The size and structure of the household in England over three centuries', *Population Studies,* **23** 2 (1969), 199–223.

Laslett, P. 'Introduction: the history of the family', in Laslett and Wall eds *Household and family in past time,* 1–89.

Laslett, P. 'Mean household size in England since the sixteenth century', in Laslett and Wall eds, *Household and family in past time,* 125–58.

Laslett, P. *Family life and illicit love in earlier generations,* (Cambridge, 1977).

Laslett, P. 'The character of familial history, its limitations and the conditions for its proper pursuit', *Journal of Family History,* **12** (1987), 263–84.

Laslett, P. 'The institution of service', *Local Population Studies,* **40** (1987), 55–60.

Laslett, P. *A fresh map of life. The emergence of the third age,* (London, 1989).

Laslett, P. and Harrison, R. 'Clayworth and Cogenhoe', in H. E. Bell and R. L. Ollard eds *Historical essays 1600–1750 presented to David Ogg,* (London, 1963), 157–84.

Laslett, P. and Wall, R. eds *Household and family in past time,* (Cambridge, 1972).

Law, C. M. 'The growth of urban population in England and Wales, 1801–1911', *Transactions of the Institute of British Geographers,* **41** (1967), 125–43.

Lawton, R. 'The economic geography of Craven in the early nineteenth century', *Transactions of the Institute of British Geographers,* **20** (1954), 93–111. Reprinted in Mills ed. *English rural communities,* 155–81.

Lawton, R. 'The population of Liverpool in the mid-nineteenth century', *Transactions of the Historic Society of Lancashire and Cheshire,* **107** (1955), 89–120.

Lawton, R. 'Rural depopulation in nineteenth-century Britain', in R. W. Steel and R. Lawton eds, *Liverpool essays in geography, a Jubilee collection,* (London, 1967), 227–56. Reprinted in Mills ed. *English rural communities,* 195–219.

Lawton, R. 'Population changes in England and Wales in the later nineteenth century: an analysis of trends by registration districts', *Transactions of the Institute of British Geographers,* **44** (1968), 55–74.

Lawton, R. 'Census data for urban areas' in Lawton ed. *Census and social structure,* 82–145.

Lawton, R. ed. *The census and social structure: an interpretative guide to the nineteenth century censuses for England and Wales,* (London, 1978).

Lawton, R. 'Population and society 1730–1900', in R. A. Dodgshon and R. A. Butlin eds *An historical geography of England and Wales,* (London, 1978), 313–66.

Lawton, R. 'Population', in J. Langton and R. J. Morris eds *An atlas of industrializing Britain*, (London, 1986), 10–29.

Lawton, R. 'Peopling the past', *Transactions of the Institute of British Geographers*, new series **12** (1987), 259–83.

Lawton, R. and Pooley, C. G. *The social geography of Merseyside in the nineteenth century*, (Department of Geography, Liverpool University, 1976).

Lee, J. and Gjerde, J. 'Comparative household morphology of stem, joint and nuclear household systems: Norway, China and the United States', *Continuity and Change*, **1** 1 (1986), 89–111.

Lee, R. D. and Lam, D. 'Age distribution adjustments for English censuses, 1821 to 1931', *Population Studies*, **37** (1983), 445–64.

Lees, L. 'Mid-Victorian migration and the Irish family economy', *Victorian Studies*, **20** 1 (1976), 25–43.

Lees, L. *Exiles of Erin: Irish migrants in Victorian London*, (Manchester, 1979).

Levine, D. 'The reliability of parochial registration and the representativeness of family reconstitution', *Population Studies* **30** 1 (1976), 107–22.

Levine, D. *Family formation in an age of nascent capitalism*, (London, 1977).

Levine, D. 'Industrialisation and the proletarian family in England', *Past and Present*, **107** (1985), 168–203.

Lewis, M. J. and Lloyd-Jones, R. 'Rate books: a technique of reconstructing the local economy', *Local Historian*, **17** (1987), 277–80.

Lewis, R. 'Measures of residential segregation', in Drake and Finnegan, *Sources and methods*, 199–201.

Lewis, S. *Topographical dictionary of England*, 7th edition, (London, 1848).

Longstaff, G. B. 'Rural depopulation', *Journal of the Royal Statistical Society*, **56** (1893), 380–433.

Lumas, S. *Making use of the census*, Public Record Office Readers' Guide No. 1, (London, 1992).

Lumas, S. 'Women enumerators', *Local Population Studies Society Newsletter*, **14** (1994), 3–5.

Lumb, G. D. ed. *The registers of the parish church of Methley in the county of York, from 1560 to 1812*, (Thoresby Society, 1903).

Mause, L. de *The history of childhood*, (New York, 1977).

McKendrick, N. 'Home demand and economic growth: a new view of the role of women and children in the industrial revolution', in N. McKendrick ed. *Historical Perspectives. Studies in English Thought and Society*, (London, 1974), 152–210.

McLeod, M. *Class and religion in the late Victorian city*, (London, 1974).

Mageean, D. and Pryce, W. T. R. *Patterns and processes of internal migration*, D301 Historical Sources and the Social Scientist, (Open University, Milton Keynes, 1982).

Malcolmson, R. W. *Popular recreations in English society, 1700–1850*, (Cambridge, 1973).

Marshall, W. *The review and abstract of the county reports to the Board of Agriculture*, Vol. IV (York, 1818). Reprinted by David and Charles publishers (Newton Abbot, 1968)

Mills, D. R. 'The poor laws and the distribution of population, *c.* 1600–1860, with special reference to Lincolnshire', *Transactions of the Institute of British Geographers*, **26** (1959), 185–95.

Mills, D. R. 'Francis Howell's report on the operation of the laws of settlement in Nottinghamshire, 1848', *Transactions of the Thoroton Society*, **76** (1972), 46–52.

Mills, D. R. ed. *English rural communities: the impact of a specialized economy*, (London, 1973).

Mills, D. R. 'Spatial implications of the settlement laws in rural England', in Open University, *Poverty and social policy, 1740–1870, A401 Block IV*, (Milton Keynes, 1974), 18–23.

Mills, D. R. 'The residential propinquity of kin in a Cambridgeshire village, 1841', *Journal of Historical Geography*, **4** (1978), 265–76.

Mills, D. R. 'The technique of house repopulation: experience from a Cambridgeshire village, 1841', *The Local Historian*, **13** 2 (1978), 86–97.

Mills, D. R. *Lord and peasant in nineteenth century Britain*, (London, 1980).

Mills, D. R. *A guide to nineteenth-century census enumerators' books*, D301 Historical Sources and the Social Scientist, (Open University, Milton Keynes, 1982).

Mills, D. R. and Drake, M. 'The census, 1801–1991', in Drake and Finnegan eds *Sources and methods*, 25–56.

Mills, D. R. and Mills, J. 'Rural mobility in the Victorian censuses: experience with a micro-computer program', *Local Historian*, **18** (1988), 69–75.

Mills, D. R and Mills, J. 'Occupation and social stratification revisited: the census enumerators' books in Victorian Britain', *Urban History Yearbook*, (1989), 63–77.

Mills, D. R. and Pearce, C. *People and places in the Victorian census. A review and bibliography of publications based substantially on the manuscript census enumerators' books, 1841–1911*, Institute of British Geographers, Historical Geography Research Series, No 23, (Cheltenham, 1989).

Mills, D. R. and Short, B. M. 'Social change and social conflict in nineteenth century England: the use of the open-closed village model', *Journal of Peasant Studies*, **10** (1983), 253–62.

Minchin, G. S. 'Table of population', in P. H. Ditchfield and W. Page eds, *Victoria History of the County of Berkshire*, volume 2, (London, 1907).

Mingay, G. E. ed. *Rural life in Victorian England*, (London, 1976).

Mitchell, B. R. *British historical statistics*, (Cambridge, 1988).

Mitchell, B. R. and Deane, P. *Abstract of British historical statistics*, (Cambridge, 1962).

Morel, M-F. 'Reflections on some recent French literature on the history of childhood', *Continuity and Change*, 4 (1989), 323–37.

Morgan, W. T. W. 'The development of settlement on the Isle of Thanet, in its geographical setting, with special reference to the growth of the holiday industry', (unpublished MSc (Econ) thesis, University of London, 1950).

Morris, R. J. *Class, sect and party: the making of the British middle class, Leeds 1820–1850*, (Manchester, 1990).

Morris, R. J. 'Fuller values, questions and contexts: occupational coding and the historian', in Schürer and Diederiks, *The use of occupations*, 5–21.

Mumford, L. *The city in history*, (London, 1961).

Nettleton WEA *Aspects of life and work in Nettleton in the nineteenth century*, (Nettleton, Lincolnshire, 1980).

O'Day, R. and Englander, D. *Mr Charles Booth's inquiry: life and labour of the people in London reconsidered*, (London, 1993).

Ohngren, B. *Folk i rorelse . . . (People on the move: social development, migration patterns and popular movements in Eskilstuna, 1870–1900,* (Stockholm, 1974).

Olney, R. J. *Lincolnshire politics, 1832–1865,* (Oxford, 1973).

Olney, R. J. ed. 'Labouring life on the Lincolnshire Wolds: a study of Binbrook in the nineteenth century', *Occasional Papers in Lincolnshire History and Archaeology,* **2** (1975).

Olney, R. J. *Rural society and county government in nineteenth century Lincolnshire,* (Lincoln, 1979).

Orme, N. 'The culture of children in medieval England', *Past and Present,* **148** (1995), 48–88.

Orwin, C. S. and Sellick, R. J. *The reclamation of Exmoor Forest,* (Newton Abbot, 1970).

Oulton, W. C. *Picture of Margate and its vicinity,* (1820).

Pacione, M. *Rural geography,* (London, 1984).

Page, D. 'Commercial directories and market towns', *Local Historian,* **11** (1974), 85–8.

Payton, P. *The Cornish miner in Australia,* (Redruth, 1984).

Payton, P. 'Cornish emigration in response to changes in the international copper market in the 1860s', *Cornish Studies,* **3** (1995), 60–82.

Perkin, H. *The origins of modern English society, 1780–1880,* (London, 1969).

Perkins, J. A. 'Sheep farming in eighteenth and nineteenth century Lincolnshire', *Occasional Papers in Lincolnshire History and Archaeology,* **4** (1977).

Phillips, W. 'Record linkage for a chronic disease register', in E. D. Acheson ed. linkage in medicine, (Edinburgh and London, 1968), 120–53.

Pimlott, J. A. R. *The Englishman's holiday: a social history,* (London, 1947).

Plakans, A. 'Stepping down in former times. A comparative assessment of retirement in traditional Europe', in D. I. Kertzer and D. W. Schaie eds *Age structuring in comparative perspective,* (Hillsdale, New Jersey, 1989), 175–95.

Pollard, S. 'Labour in Great Britain' in P. Mathias and M. M. Postan eds *The Cambridge Economic History of Europe,* Vol. VII, Pt I, (Cambridge, 1979), 97–179.

Pollock, L. *Forgotten children,* (Cambridge, 1983).

Pooley, C. G. 'Choice and constraint in the nineteenth-century city: a basis for residential differentiation', in Johnson and Pooley, *The structure of nineteenth century cities,* 199–233.

Pooley, C. G. 'The residential segregation of migrant communities in mid-Victorian Liverpool', *Transactions of the Institute of British Geographers,* new series **2** (1977), 364–82.

Pooley, C. G. 'Residential mobility in the Victorian city', *Transactions of the Institute of British Geographers,* new series **4** (1979), 258–77.

Pooley, C. G. and Doherty, J. C. 'The longitudinal study of migration. Welsh migration to English towns in the nineteenth century', in Pooley and Whyte eds *Migrants, emigrants and immigrants,* 143–73.

Pooley, C. G. and Turnbull, J. 'Migration and mobility in Britain from the eighteenth to the twentieth centuries', *Local Population Studies,* **57** (1996), 52–73.

Pooley, C. G. and Whyte, I. D. eds *Migrants, emigrants and immigrants. A social history of migration,* (London, 1991).

Pritchard, R. M. *Housing and the spatial structure of the city,* (Cambridge, 1976).

Raistrick, A. *Quakers in science and industry: being an account of the Quaker contribution to science and industry during the seventeenth and eighteenth*

centuries, (York, 1950).
Raistrick, A. 'Industrial history', in A. Raistrick ed. *North York Moors, National Park guide no. 4*, (1969).
Rau, D. 'Who chose Chalcots? Aspects of family and social structure in 1851', *Camden History Review*, **11** (1984), 27–33.
Ravenstein, E. G. 'The laws of migration', *Journal of the Statistical Society*, **48** (1885), 167–227.
Ravenstein, E. G. 'The laws of migration', *Journal of the Royal Statistical Society*, **52** (1889), 214–301.
Rawding, C. K. *Keelby: parish and people: part two 1831–1881*, (Keelby, Lincs., 1987).
Rawding, C. K. 'A study of place: the north Lincolnshire Wolds, 1831–1881', (unpublished DPhil thesis, University of Sussex, 1989).
Rawding, C. K. ed. *Binbrook in the nineteenth century*, (Binbrook, 1989).
Razi, Z. *Life, marriage and death in a medieval parish: economy, society and demography in Halesowen, 1270–1400*, (Cambridge, 1980).
Razzell, P. E. 'The evaluation of baptism as a form of birth registration through cross-matching census and parish register data', *Population Studies* **26** 1 (1972), 121–46.
Reay, B. 'Before the transition: fertility in English villages, 1800–1880', *Continuity and Change*, **9** 1 (1994), 91–120.
Redford, A. *Labour migration in England 1800–1850*, (Manchester, 1926).
Reed, M. 'Nineteenth century rural England: a case for peasant studies?', *Journal of Peasant Studies*, **14** (1986), 78–98.
Reed, M. 'The peasantry of nineteenth century England, a neglected class?', *History Workshop*, **18** (1984), 53–74.
Richards, A. and Robin, J. *Some Elmdon families*, (Elmdon, 1975).
Richards, E. 'Women in the British economy since about 1700: an interpretation', *History*, **59** (1974), 337–57.
Richardson, C. 'Irish settlement in mid-nineteenth-century Bradford', *Yorkshire Bulletin of Economic and Social Research* **20** (1968), 40–57.
Robin, J. *Elmdon: continuity and change in a north-west Essex village 1861–1964*, (Cambridge, 1980).
Rogers, A. *This was their world: approaches to local history*, (London, 1972). Reprinted as *Approaches to Local History*, (London, 1977).
Rothwell, M. *Industrial heritage: a guide to the archaeology of Accrington*, (Accrington, 1979).
Rowe, J. *Cornwall in the age of the Industrial Revolution*, (Liverpool, 1953).
Rowse, A. L. *The Cornish in America*, (Redruth, 1991).
Royle, S. A. 'Social stratification from the early census returns: a new approach', *Area*, **9** (1977), 215–9.
Royle, S. A. 'Reply to Holmes and Armstrong', *Area*, **10** (1978), 128–9.
Royle, S. A. 'Irish manuscript census records: a neglected source of information', *Irish Geography*, **2** (1978), 110–25.
Royle, S. A. 'Aspects of 19th century small town society: a comparative study from Leicestershire', *Midland History*, **5** (1979–80), 50–61.
Royle, S. A. 'Irish manuscript ecclesiastical census returns: a survey with an example from Clogherny parish, Co. Tyrone 1851–52', *Local Population Studies*, **29** (1982), 35–49.
Ruggles, S. *Prolonged connections. The rise of the extended family in nineteenth-*

century England and America, (Madison, 1987).

Russell, R. C. *A history of elementary schools and adult education in Nettleton and Caistor,* (Nettleton, Lincolnshire, 1960).

Russell, R. C. *Friendly societies in the Caistor, Binbrook and Brigg area in the nineteenth century,* (Nettleton, Lincolnshire, 1975).

Saville, J. *Rural depopulation in England and Wales, 1851–1951,* (London, 1957).

Schama, S. *The embarrassment of riches. An interpretation of Dutch culture in the Golden Age,* (London, 1987).

Schofield, R. S. 'Age-specific mobility in an eighteenth century English parish', *Annales de Démographie Historique,* (1970), 261–74.

Schürer, K. 'A note concerning the calculation of the singulate mean age at marriage', *Local Population Studies,* **43** (1989), 67–9.

Schürer, K. 'The future for local history: boom or recession?', *Local Historian,* **21** (1991), 99–108.

Schürer, K. 'The role of the family in the process of migration', in Pooley and Whyte eds, *Migrants, emigrants and immigrants,* 106–42.

Schürer, K. 'The 1891 census and local population studies', *Local Population Studies,* **47** (1991), 16–29.

Schürer, K. 'Understanding and coding the occupations of the past: the experience of analyzing the censuses of 1891–1921', in Schürer and Diederiks, *The use of occupations,* 101–62.

Schürer, K. and Diederiks, H. eds *The use of occupations in historical analysis,* (St Katharinen, 1993).

Schürer, K. and Pryce, W. T. R. 'Nominal lists and nominal record linkage', audio-cassette 2B in P. Braham ed. *Using the past: audio cassettes on sources and methods for family and community historians,* (The Open University, Milton Keynes, 1993).

Scola, R. 'Food markets and shops in Manchester, 1770–1870', *Journal of Historical Geography,* **1** (1975), 153–68.

Shannon, H. A. 'Migration and the growth of London', *Economic History Review,* **5** (1935), 79–86.

Shaw, G. 'The content and reliability of nineteenth century trade directories', *Local Historian,* **13** (1978), 205–9.

Shaw, G. *British directories as sources in historical geography,* (Geo Abstracts, Norwich, 1982).

Shaw, G. and Tipper, A. *British directories: a bibliography and guide to directories published in England and Wales, 1850–1950; and Scotland, 1773–1950,* (Leicester, 1989).

Shaw, G. and Wild, M. T. 'Retail patterns in the Victorian city', *Transactions of the Institute of British Geographers,* new series, **4** (1979), 278–91.

Shaw, M. 'The ecology of social change: Wolverhampton, 1851–71', *Transactions of the Institute of British Geographers,* new series, **2** (1977), 332–48.

Shorter, E. *The making of the modern family,* (London, 1975).

Shryock, H. S. and Siegel, J. S. *The methods and materials of demography,* (New York, 1976), condensed edition by E. G. Stockwell.

Sigsworth, E. M. 'The City of York' in P. M. Tillott ed. *Victoria County History of the County of York,* (London, 1961).

Sjoberg, G. *The pre-industrial city, past and present,* (Glencoe, 1960).

Smith, C. T. 'Population', in W. G. Hoskins and R. A. McKinley eds *Victoria History of the County of Leicester,* volume III, (London, 1955), 129–175.

Smith, P. *The story of Claribel (Charlotte Alington Barnard)*, (Lincoln, 1965).
Smith, R. *The process of inner city housing regeneration: a micro study*, Trent Papers in Environmental Studies No. 1, (Nottingham, n.d.).
Smith, R. J. 'Social structure of Nottingham and adjacent districts in the mid-nineteenth century', (unpublished PhD thesis, University of Nottingham, 1968).
Smith, R. J. 'Early Victorian household structure: a case study of Nottinghamshire', *International Review of Social History*, **15** (1970), 69–84.
Smith, R. M. 'Fertility, economy and household formation in England over three centuries', *Population and Development Review*, **7** 4 (1981), 595–622.
Snell, K. D. M. 'Agricultural seasonal unemployment, the standard of living and women's work in the south and east 1690–1860', *Economic History Review*, 2nd series **24** 3 (1981), 407–37.
Steedman, C., Urwin, C. and Walkerdine, V. eds *Language, gender and childhood*, (London, 1985).
Steel, D. I. A. *Lincolnshire village: the parish of Corby Glen in its historical context*, (London, 1979).
Stenton, M. ed. *Who's who of British Members of Parliament*, Vol. I 1832–1885, (Hassocks, 1976).
Strathern, M. *Kinship at the core: an anthropology of Elmdon, a village in north-west Essex in the nineteen-sixties*, (Cambridge, 1981).
Strange, F. G. S. *The history of the Royal Sea Bathing Hospital, Margate, 1791–1991*, (Rainham, 1991).
Swift, R. and Gilley, S. eds *The Irish in the Victorian city*, (London, 1985).
Szreter, S. R. S. *Fertility, class and gender in Britain, 1860–1914*, (Cambridge, 1996).
Taylor, A. J. 'The taking of the census, 1801–1951', *British Medical Journal*, **1** (1951), 715–20.
Taylor, L. *Mourning dress: a costume and social history*, (London, 1983).
Tetielbaum, M. S. *The British fertility decline*, (Princeton, 1984).
Thirsk, J. *English peasant farming: the agrarian history of Lincolnshire from Tudor to recent times*, (London, 1957).
Thomas, K. 'Age and authority in early modern England, *Proceedings of the British Academy*, **62** (1976), 205–48.
Thompson, F. M. L. *English landed society in the nineteenth century*, (London, 1963).
Tillott, P. M. 'The analysis of census returns,' *The Local Historian*, **8** 1 (1968), 2–10.
Tillott, P. M. 'Sources of inaccuracy in the 1851 and 1861 censuses', in Wrigley ed. *Nineteenth-century society*, 82–133.
Tillott, P. M. and Stevenson, G. S. *North-west Lindsey in 1851*, (University of Sheffield, Department of Extramural Studies, 1970).
Timmer, C. P. 'The turnip, the new husbandry and the English agricultural revolution', *Quarterly Journal of Economics*, **24** (1969), 375–95.
Todd, A. C. and Laws, P. *The Industrial Archaeology of Cornwall*, (Newton Abbot, 1972).
Trevor-Bell, E. 'Family structure in nineteenth-century Oakham: a study of the 1851 census', *Rutland Records*, **13** (1993), 108–17.
Turnbull, G. *A history of the calico printing industry in Great Britain*, (Altrincham, 1951).

Turner, M. 'Two census songs', *Local Population Studies,* **23** (1979) 45–7.
Turner, M. and Mills, D. R. eds *Land and property: the English Land Tax, 1692–1832,* (Gloucester, 1986).
Vince, S. W. E. 'The rural population of England and Wales, 1801–1951', (unpublished PhD thesis, University of London, 1955).
Wardley, P. 'The Lincolnshire iron industry, 1859-1914', (unpublished PhD thesis, University College, Swansea, 1983).
Walford, M. *The county families of the United Kingdom,* (London, 1877).
Wall, R. 'Mean household size in England from printed sources', in Laslett and Wall eds *Household and family in past time,* 159–203.
Wall, R. 'Reconstitution and census: Colytonians in parish register and enumerators' book', *Exeter Papers in Economic History,* **11** (1976), 73–90.
Wall, R. 'The age at leaving home', *Journal of Family History,* **3** 2 (1978), 181–202.
Wall, R. 'Work, welfare and the family', in L. Bonfield, R. M. Smith and K. Wrightson eds *The world we have gained: histories of population and social structure, essays presented to Peter Laslett on his seventieth birthday,* (Oxford, 1986), 261–94.
Wall, R. 'Leaving home and the process of household formation in pre-industrial England', *Continuity and Change,* **2** 1 (1987), 77–101.
Wall, R. 'Introduction', in Wall *et al.* eds *Family forms in historic Europe,* 1–64.
Wall, R. Robin, J. and Laslett, P. eds *Family forms in historic Europe,* (Cambridge, 1983).
Wallenberg, J. K. *The place-names of Kent,* (Uppsala, 1934).
Ward, D. 'Victorian cities: how modern?', *Journal of Historical Geography,* **1** (1975), 135–51.
Warnes, A. M. 'Residential patterns in an emerging industrial town', in *Social patterns in cities,* Institute of British Geographers, Special Publication no. 5, (1973), 169–88.
Weaver, M. 'Industrial housing in West Cornwall', *Industrial Archaeology,* **3** 1 (1966), 23–45.
Werly, J. 'The Irish in Manchester', *Irish Historical Studies,* **18** (1973), 345–58.
West, J. *Village records,* (London, 1962).
Whellan, T. (& co.) *History and topography of the City of York: and the North Riding of Yorkshire,* Vol. II, (Beverley, 1859).
White, W. *History, gazetteer and directory of the East and North Ridings of Yorkshire,* (Sheffield, 1840).
White, W. *Directory of Lincolnshire,* (Sheffield, 1872).
Whyman, J. *Aspects of holidaymaking and resort development within the Isle of Thanet, with particular reference to Margate, circa 1736 to circa 1840,* 2 volumes, (New York, 1981).
Wild, M. T. and Shaw, G. 'Locational behaviour of urban retailing during the nineteenth century: the example of Kingston upon Hull', *Transactions of the Institute of British Geographers,* **61** (1974), 101–18.
Williams, B. *The making of Manchester Jewry 1740–1875,* (Manchester, 1976).
Williamson, J. A. *The English channel: a history,* (London, 1959).
Willigan, K. A. and Lynch, J. D. *Sources and methods of historical demography,* (New York, 1982).
Wojciechowska-Kibble, B. 'Migration and the rural labour market: Kent 1841–71', (unpublished PhD thesis, University of Kent at Canterbury, 1984).
Woods, R. I. 'Approaches to the fertility transition in Victorian England',

Population Studies, **41** (1987), 283–311.

Woods, R. I. *The population of Britain in the nineteenth century*, (London, 1992).

Woods, R. I and Hinde, P. R. A. 'Nuptiality and age at marriage in nineteenth century England', *Journal of Family History*, **10** 2 (1985), 119–44.

Woods, R. I. and Smith, C. W. 'The decline of marital fertility in the late-nineteenth century: the case of England and Wales', *Population Studies*, **37** (1983), 207–35.

Woodwark, T. H. *Rise and fall of the Whitby jet trade*, (Whitby, 1922).

Woollings, B. 'An Orsett census enumerator', *Local Population Studies*, **56** (1996), 54–9.

Wright, N. R. *Lincolnshire towns and industry, 1700–1914*, (Lincoln, 1982).

Wrigley, E. A. *et al.* eds *Introduction to English historical demography*, (London, 1966).

Wrigley, E. A. ed. *Nineteenth-century society: essays in the use of quantitative methods for the study of social history*, (Cambridge, 1972).

Wrigley, E. A. *Identifying people in the past*, (London, 1973).

Wrigley, E. A. 'Baptism coverage in early nineteenth-century England: the Colyton area', *Population Studies*, **29** (1975), 299–316.

Wrigley, E. A. 'A note on the life time mobility of married women in a parish population in the later eighteenth century', *Local Population Studies*, **18** (1977), 20–9.

Wrigley, E. A. 'Births and baptisms: the use of Anglican baptism registers as a source of information about the numbers of births in England before the beginning of civil registration', *Population Studies*, **31** 2 (1977), 281–312.

Wrigley, E. A. 'Men on the land and men in the countryside: employment in agriculture in early-nineteenth-century England', in L. Bonfield, R. M. Smith and K. Wrightson eds *The world we have gained: histories of population and social structure, essays presented to Peter Laslett on his seventieth birthday*, (Oxford, 1986), 295–336.

Wrigley, E. A and Schofield, R. S. *The population history of England, 1541–1871: a reconstruction*, (London, 1981).

Yasumoto, M. *Industrialisation, urbanisation and demographic change in England*, (Nagoya, 1994).

Yeo, E. and Yeo, S. eds *Popular culture and class conflict 1590–1914: explorations in the history of labour and leisure*, (Brighton, 1981).

Young, A. *General view of the agriculture of the County of Lincoln*, (Newton Abbot, 1813).

Supplementary Bibliography

The supplementary bibliography contains material relating to the use of the CEBs which has been published in *Local Population Studies*. This listing of additional articles is provided in order to assist those undertaking research work of their own on the CEBs.

Bristow, B. R. 'Population and housing in nineteenth century urban Lancashire: a framework for investigation', **34** (1985), 12–26.

Collins, B. and Anderson, M. 'The administration of the 1851 census in the county of East Lothian', **20** (1978), 32–7.

Davey, C. 'A note on mobility in an Essex parish in the early nineteenth century', **41** (1988), 61–6.

Edgar, M. J. D. 'Occupational diversity in seven rural parishes in Dorset, 1851', **52** (1994), 48–54.

Foster, D. 'Mobility and economy in new towns: the case of Fleetwood', **14** (1975), 42–3.

Garner, A. 'The use of census enumerators' returns in local history studies: an extra curricular schoolroom project', **30** (1983), 35–41.

Gerrish, M. 'Following the fish to Grimsby', **50** (1993), 39–50.

Glyn-Jones, A. 'The repopulation of the countryside in Devon and Cornwall', **46** (1991) 20–31.

Jarvis, C. 'The reconstitution of nineteenth century rural communities', **51** (1993), 46–53.

McCallum, D. M. 'Enumeration practice in 1871', **26** (1981), 63.

Peek, R. 'Farm labour in mid-nineteenth century Warwickshire', **31** (1983), 42–51.

Rau, D. 'The 1891 census in Spitalfields', **52** (1994), 55–6.

Ross, A. L. 'Local population studies in schools. Understanding local populations in a primary school: the role of the microcomputer', **35** (1984), 25–37.

Schürer, K. 'Servant groups and household structures', **36** (1985), 58–9.

Sill, M. 'Mid-nineteenth century labour mobility: the case of the coal-miners of Hetton-le-hole, Co. Durham', **22** (1979), 44–50.

Steel, D. I. A. 'The enumerator of Corby, Lincs.', **19** (1977), 35.

Stevens, L. 'History in the primary school', **29** (1982), 10–6.

Tillott, P. M. 'Comment on correspondence on finding nineteenth-century census returns', **1** (1968), 41–3.

Tillott, P. M. 'An approach to census returns', **2** (1968), 25–8.

Turner, M. 'A census enumerator's experience (by one of them) from : *The Eccles Journal*, Friday April 10, 1891' **27** (1981), 79–82.

Warwicks, M. and Warwick, D. 'Burley-in-Wharfedale in the nineteenth century: a study of social stratification and social mobility', **54** (1995), 40–55.

Williams, J. A. 'A local population study at a college of education', **11** (1973), 23–39.

Index